W9-BGR-052

NEW PRINCIPLES OF POLITICAL ECONOMY

NEW PRINCIPLES OF POLITICAL ECONOMY

Of Wealth in Its Relation to Population

J.-C.-L. Simonde de Sismondi

Translated and annotated by
Richard Hyse

With a Foreword by
Robert L. Heilbroner

Transaction Publishers
New Brunswick (U.S.A.) and London (U.K.)

Library of Congress Catalog Number: 90-10824
ISBN: 0-88738-336-X
Printed in the United States of America

Library of Congress Cataloging-in-Publication Data

Sismondi, J.-C.-L. Simonde de (Jean-Charles-Léonard Simonde), 1773–1842.
[Nouveaux principes d'économie politique. English]
New principles of political economy, or, Of wealth in its relation to population / J.-C.-L. Simonde de Sismondi : translated and annotated by Richard Hyse ; with a foreword by Robert Heilbroner.
p. cm.
Translation of: Nouveaux principes d'économie politique.
Includes bibliographical references.
ISBN 0-88738-336-X
1. Economics. I. Title. II. Title: Of wealth in its relation to population.
HB163.S613 1990 90-10824

To JO

Contents

THIRD BOOK
Of Territorial Wealth

FOURTH BOOK
Of Commercial Wealth

Appendix

Foreword

Robert L. Heilbroner

Jean-Charles-Léonard Simonde de Sismondi—the name is irresistible—belongs in that group of obscure economists whose names we encounter in prestigious places, but whose texts we rarely or never get to read. The reason for both is very simple: Sismondi was read and taken seriously by Marx and Mill and Schumpeter, but until now there has been no adequate translation of his major work into English. Would-be students were therefore able to catch something of the analytic originality and imagination of Sismondi by thumbing through Marx's *Capital* or Schumpeter's *History of Economic Analysis,* but they had no way of absorbing the full flavor and quality of his thought.

This difficulty has now been removed with the publication of Richard Hyse's excellent translation of *New Principles*. Perhaps even more useful is the commentary that precedes and accompanies the text. Here Professor Hyse takes the reader on a conducted tour as he points out Sismondi's differences from and criticisms of Smith and Ricardo and Say, on the one hand, and Marx on the other. It is a dialogue that enriches our understanding of both classical and modern political economy.

Why has Sismondi for so long been overlooked? Partly, as the reader will discover, because he is discursive to a fault, so that large sections must be skimmed rapidly, lest one bog down before coming to the remarkable parts. But, then, this is true also of Mill, not to mention Marx. Or, it is possible to account for the neglect of Sismondi's work by the fact that he wrote in French, not the mother tongue of economic discourse. But as Thomas Sowell points out in his article on Sismondi in *The New Palgrave,* so did Jean-Baptiste Say, whose work enjoyed a degree of renown as notable (and as underserved) as Sismondi's obscurity.

It is more likely that Sismondi's thought was neglected because it was too much in advance of its time. A half-century before Walras, Sismondi was speaking of aggregate "equilibrium" (his term). An equally lengthy time before Marx, he devised the first crude but revealing algebraic model of economic growth. In this list of premature insights, we can include an early analytical criticism of Say's Law (ten years before Mill's essay "On the Influence of Consumption upon Production"), and one of the earliest uses of marginal utility analysis to explain value. To complete the account, in Schumpeter's estimation, Sismondi is the father of dynamic analysis in the modern sense, and everyone agrees that he is the first serious student of business cycles.

This sampling of Sismondi's accomplishments is enough to suggest the need that this volume fills. But I would be remiss if I failed to mention two other reasons that Sismondi appeals to me. The first is his passion for social reform—a passion very different from Marx's huge historical project of social revolution or the Utopian Socialists' fanciful schemes of instant betterment. Sismondi has a deep affection for the bourgeois way of life that rules out revolutionary projects, and a stubborn feeling for the frictions and particularities of social structures that prevents him from constructing Utopian designs. He therefore embodies a combination of far-reaching intentions with conservative reservations—a position that ill accorded with the dramatic hopes and expectations of earlier times, but that has its appeal to our own. Sismondi's reformist social policy is based on a capitalist economy, encouraged to develop its potential energies, combined with an intervention-minded state, standing by as a guarantor of social decencies. This points in the direction of change that has led from nineteenth-century England to twentieth-century Sweden, and that may well be the main avenue of advance into the twenty-first century.

Second, I must record my pleasure in Sismondi's rejection of Ricardian economics (of which he insisted he was a sincere admirer) wherever it elevated the elegance of abstract argument over the untidiness of real-world considerations. As Schumpeter has said, Sismondi's approach, although "oversimplified and otherwise unrealistic," nevertheless sufficed to "show that the economic process . . . harbors a world of problems that simply do not exist for Ricardian analysis" (1954, 495).

I will not spoil Dr. Hyse's pleasure by pointing out the many instances of Sismondian realism that will be found in the *New Principles,* but I am sure he will not begrudge me one example. In his chapter "on Gross and Net Revenue" in his famous *Principles,* Ricardo reasoned that it was only the "net produce"—rents and profits—that constituted the real wealth of a nation. The "gross produce" included, in addition to rents and profits, the revenues that replenished the employer's wage fund, and thereby made it possible for him to employ his workers. But to Ricardo gross produce was of no importance. What mattered was the net produce, because only rents and profits, never wages, provided the funds for accumulation needed by capitalists, and only rents and profits, never wages, provided the tax revenue needed by the sovereign. Hence, in Ricardian analysis it was a matter of national as well as private indifference whether a given gross product gave employment to a larger or a smaller workforce, as long as the surplus over wages was the same.

Sismondi's reply was devastating. "Indeed? Wealth is everything, men are absolutely nothing? What? Wealth itself is only something in relation to taxes? In truth, then there is nothing more to wish for than that the king, remaining alone on the island, by constantly turning a crank, might produce, through automata, all the output of England" (p. 563, footnote in the manuscript text).

I commend to the reader a further acquaintance with the interesting and surprising Monsieur Sismondi and his percipient docent, Dr. Hyse.

Preface

A translation of a scholarly work such as this is a mark of respect for the author. It always assumes that the original has an important message for the audience for which it is translated. It is also a labor of love because there can be only minimal expectations of recognition or pecuniary reward, although there always lingers in the background the possibility of a runaway best seller as a pleasant surprise. It is doubly a labor of love if the author is long deceased and his work, in his own time, never excited enough enthusiasm to encourage a translation for a wider audience.

This translation had its genesis in a graduate seminar on economic thought at New York University with Professor Arthur Z. Arnold. Like all courses with Professor Arnold, this was a scholarly debate, enlightened by the encyclopedic knowledge of the instructor. A term paper was required on an economic thinker of our own choice, and Sismondi attracted my attention because his early rebellion against the certainties of Say's Law and Ricardian dogma paralleled my dissatisfaction with received microeconomic theory. Sismondi's business viewpoint appealed to the evening student who, after a long day at an exporter's office, could not reconcile everyday trade practices with abstractions that were supposed to represent and explain such practices, but that signally failed to do so.

Eventually, I made my peace with microeconomics, but the memory of Sismondi lingered. For one thing, the term paper was still around; more important, the spiritual descendants of Ricardo—the followers of Marx—showed signs that all was not well with the theory they proclaimed to be the salvation of mankind. My research for the term paper had clearly indicated that there existed an unacknowledged intellectual debt to Sismondi on the part of Marxist theory, as well as the possibility of a different course of action, of evolution rather than revolution. And I discovered, to my surprise, that the centerpiece of Sismondian writing, *Nouveaux Prin-*

cipes, had never been translated into English. The time had come to remedy this glaring omission.

Time is not always a plentiful commodity in a busy academic career, and a labor of love often has to take a backseat to more pressing concerns. It was not easy to enter into the style and thinking processes of a Genevese republican of the eighteenth century, but as the work progressed there were growing satisfactions with discoveries of economic insights that had been ascribed to later authors. There were purely literary pleasures in reconstructing the involved genesis of the work, following the mind of a vigorous pamphleteer dealing with the turbulent world of the French Revolution and its lasting aftermath.

A ten-year odyssey has many helpers and companions. There were, first, many work-study students who patiently typed and retyped many manuscript pages, shaping what was to become the first draft. I never noted their names down—some of their faces are still in my memory—but I want to thank them here collectively for their patience as well as for their perseverance.

The departmental secretaries assigned the work to the students—I owe them thanks not only for parceling out the work, but also for copying an increasing volume of paper. Three ladies—Kim Skelly, Norma Tyler, and Becky Truax—have my thanks for providing the logistic support to the project.

There were other supporters of the project: my colleague Tom Marshall for helping me over linguistic hurdles, which he did with great insight into the changes that had taken place over 150 years; Nan Cole and Paul Morman for support at crucial junctures; an unknown reviewer who pointed to the shortcomings of the first draft and turned a mere translation into a scholarly enterprise; and last, but not least, my wife, who gave the unwavering moral support that was needed along the way, and to whom this book is dedicated. Thanks to all of them; I owe them a debt of gratitude.

A special acknowledgment, and thank you, must go to Professor Heilbroner who, despite a busy schedule, graciously agreed to write a foreword for this translation. His willingness to do so testifies to his continuing interest in the development of economic reasoning, even if it should lead into little-explored side streets of the discipline.

At the moment of publication of this work, major ideological changes have either already taken place, or are still in a process of evolution. It is my hope that this translation will add another important voice to a debate that has been, so far, carried on in a more or less polarized fashion, not recognizing other alternatives.

Richard Hyse

Translator's Introduction

A Cosmopolitan Life

It is a commonplace of literary analysis that works of fiction usually have some autobiographical content. Treatises in political economy, for example, Adam Smith's *Wealth of Nations,* or this work, *New Principles*, are not thought of as autobiographical in the same sense as Dickens's *David Copperfield.* They nevertheless reflect the lives of their authors, although in a more subtle way. Analysis of social phenomena must take its themes from real problems; past experience shapes perception, selects the problems that will receive attention, and will also suggest some of the answers. Therefore, before reading this translation, a look at the life of the author of *New Principles* will help explain his, for the times, often unorthodox viewpoint.

Sismondi's *New Principles* mirrors the formative years of his life from 1786, when he was thirteen, to 1801, when he was twenty-eight and published his first work of social analysis, the *Tableau de l'agriculture Toscane*. *New Principles* projects the insecurity of a young exile whose family lost its wealth and its station in life, and who finally, by his own efforts, succeeded in building a distinguished career as a writer and historian, but who never again knew complete financial ease. The book also reflects the independence of mind that was necessary to achieve this transition in one of the most turbulent periods of European history. The major propositions of *New Principles,* such as Sismondi's opposition to paper money, his opposition to revolutionary changes in social structures, his championing of private property and advocacy of de-centralization of economic and political power, can all be connected to his experiences during these years. On the other hand, they also show the mental struggle of a writer who felt that prevailing political-economic doctrine did not supply the answers to important social problems, and who therefore proposed alternative solutions. To understand fully the ideas of *New Principles,* it is necessary to know some details of the author's life.[1]

Sismondi was born Jean Charles Leonard Simonde on 9 May 1773 in the then-independent city-republic of Geneva, and he died there on 25 June 1842. He would add *de Sismondi* to his name much later in his life to emphasize what he believed was his descent from a family of Pisan patricians. The adoption of this name was an act of personal reinvention, connecting the born Genevese to the country that would engage his life and his historical research for many years.

The simple juxtaposition of dates shows that Sismondi's life spanned one of the most revolutionary periods in European history, when the economic, social, and political institutions of the modern national-industrial state were formed. Three years after Sismondi's birth, Adam Smith published the *Wealth of Nations*, and the American Revolution began. His death occurred just six years before the revolutions of 1848 and the publication of the *Communist Manifesto*. At his birth, the fastest speed of locomotion was the gallop of a horse, as it had been for thousands of years; at his death, railroads had begun to span the European and American continents, transporting goods and persons at ever-faster speeds. He died in his native city after a residency of about forty years, but this fact merely underscores that he was a member of a cosmopolitan class that shaped European opinion, and that he had been involved in some of these developments directly as a writer, historian, political economist, and pamphleteer.

Sismondi was the oldest child of the Huguenot minister Gédéon François Simonde and his wife Henriette Girodz, daughter of an old and well-to-do Genevese family. The Simondes were members of the Genevese establishment, a part of the patrician class that used to rule independent city-republics in Europe. Gédéon Simonde became a member of the Council of Twohundred, the governing body of Geneva, in 1782.

The Simondes were in comfortable circumstances, with a town house that was part of Mrs. Simonde's dowry, and a small country estate, Châtelaine, in the Rhône valley. Young Jean-Charles played at Châtelaine with the neighbors' children, the Constants and the Gallatins; the former were the family of Benjamin Constant, the author of Napoleon's Hundred Days constitution, and the latter were the family of Albert Gallatin, secretary of the treasury under Jefferson and Madison. Tutored at home, Jean-Charles was eventually sent to the *Collège*, a school founded by Calvin to provide education for the sons of Genevese citizens. In 1786, at age thirteen, he entered the *Académie de Genève*, essentially a *gymnasium* for advanced studies. The academy was dedicated to the Calvinistic idea of theological democracy, but at least two of the teachers, A. Pictet and P. Prévost, were eighteenth-century rationalists who most likely gave Sismondi's mind the rationalistic bent he was to retain for the rest of his life. However, he was not destined to complete his education. The collapse of the *ancien régime* in France would also claim the Simonde family as one of its victims.

France had incurred great debts as a consequence of its involvement in the American War of Independence, and of the lavish expenditures of the court of Louis XVI. Since the aristocracy and the clergy were exempt from most taxes, borrowing had served to raise the money needed by the court and government. The famous physiocrat Turgot had attempted to reform the system but had been unsuccessful, and he was forced to resign. Louis XVI recalled his former director-general of finances, the Genevese banker Jacques Necker, to deal with the crisis. Necker tried to stem the tide, partly by more borrowing, partly by again trying to reform the system. It was at his suggestion that the Estates-General were called to approve new taxes, which in turn led directly to the Revolution.

Necker had used his reputation and connections in Geneva to sell French state obligations, and Gédéon Simonde, relying, mistakenly as it turned out, on Necker's reputation as a successful banker and his Genevese background, had invested the bulk of his capital in these obligations. With the collapse of the French monarchy, the obligations became worthless, and the Simonde family lost most of its wealth, as did many other citizens of Geneva.

Gédéon Simonde decided to take his son out of the academy to be educated as a business man, and apprenticed him with the Genevese silk dealers Eynard in Lyon, France. Jean-Charles, whose one outstanding characteristic was obedience to paternal wishes, went to Lyon in 1792 to learn bookkeeping and any other skills merchants of that time were supposed to know. The stay in Lyon was destined to be short. The Revolution broke out in the city, and Salis mentions (1973, 20) that forty-one years later Sismondi still remembered vividly, and with a sense of aversion, the events of that time. Sismondi returned at the end of 1792 to Geneva, after a nine-month stay. However, the skills he learned during this time, by his own admission, stood him in good stead for the rest of his life. According to Salis, the orderliness of office routine contributed greatly to the success of his historical studies. *New Principles* shows that his short apprenticeship in Lyon also gave him a business viewpoint with respect to political economy.

He arrived in Geneva just in time to witness the outbreak of the Revolution in his native city. On 28 December 1792, revolutionary committees took over the city government. Even though there was as yet no terror in the city, the Simonde family quickly decided to leave the city and go to England to avoid any possible accusations against Gédéon Simonde who, as a prominent member of the governing body of Geneva, was considered an aristocrat. They left in February 1793 for England. At age nineteen Sismondi was an exile and the oldest son of a family that had lost its social position and most of its wealth.

The stay in England transformed Sismondi into a cosmopolitan. He visited London from the family lodgings in Kent; since English had been spoken habitually at home in Geneva, he had no language problem and could observe the life of the metropolis without hindrance. As Salis puts it: "he learned to look farther than the walls of a venerable, but constrained city" (1973, 24). He also showed the first signs of his ability to observe social phenomena: he took extensive notes on the English constitution that were eventually incorporated in his *Études* more than thirty years later.

The Simondes returned to Geneva in 1794 because Madame Simonde had taken ill and wanted to return to her native city. They returned to a city in the grip of revolutionary terror. Father and son Simonde were immediately imprisoned, and released after a short time; their remaining assets, except their real estate, were sequestered, and most valuables were stolen during a house search. Revolutionary courts were imposing death sentences on aristocrats in great numbers. A friend of the family who had sought refuge at Châtelaine was dragged from the house and shot in the immediate neighborhood by revolutionary guards.

The frightened family decided to flee again, this time to Tuscany and the city of Pisa, which family tradition said was the original home of the Simondes. To raise money, Châtelaine was sold, and the family crossed the Alps in the fall of 1794. Sismondi was charged with finding a suitable home, a small farm, while the family stayed in Florence. The twenty-one-year-old scoured on foot the valleys of Tuscany and finally found a small *metayerie* ("half-shares farm") in the Val de Nievole, in the neighborhood of Pescia, that was affordable. He installed his family there and the farm was renamed *Vaucluse* as a reminder of the country the family had left. The farm itself was cultivated by a farmer who paid one-half of the crop as rent to the owners, the Simondes, who exercised some managerial function and had to supply the farm implements and make any repairs on capital structures, such as barns.

The Simonde family had found a haven, as yet not touched by the general warfare that had engulfed the rest of Europe. Tuscany in 1794 was an independent neutral Grand Duchy under Ferdinand III of Lorraine, son of Leopold II, emperor of Austria. Both father and son had followed an enlightened policy with respect to local administration and laws protecting small landholders, and the small territory was, as a result, one of the few prosperous states in Italy.

Gédéon Simonde eventually returned to Geneva to conduct a small business, which his fellow aristocrats considered to be déclassé. Sismondi, his mother, and his younger sister Sara stayed on the farm, just barely adequate to support the family in modest comfort; the Simonde family had found a new home, but it would never regain the comfortable circumstances of Geneva.

Sismondi studied the agriculture of the region, its legal institutions, and its commerce, and identified more and more with his adopted country. His sister married a notable's son in Pescia; the farm would stay in the possession of the family, and Sismondi would return to it from time to time in later life.

Tuscany was invaded by Napoleon in 1796 and became a hostage in the war between the anti-French coalition and Napoleon as the commanding general of the Directorate. Sismondi was thrown into prison three times—by the French because he was considered pro-Austrian, and by the Austrians because he was considered pro-revolutionary and pro-French, a telling sign of his future problems as a writer on political economy.

Sismondi returned to Geneva in 1800 and in 1801, published his first work, the *Tableau de l'agriculture Toscane,* which made him instantly famous. It was a work of a type much in vogue then, a descriptive analysis of a region that combined travelogue, technical information, and social observation into an informative and readable whole. It was a scholarly work, the fruit of personal experience and astute observation of conditions, colored by romantic descriptions of the beauty of the countryside. It made Sismondi an expert on agriculture and secured for him a position as secretary to the Council of Commerce of Geneva. The Tuscan experiences would later influence the third book, "Of Territorial Wealth," of *New Principles*.

Soon after again settling in Geneva (he lived with his grandmother Madame Girodz), Sismondi was introduced to the salon of Madame de Staël, the daughter of Jacques Necker. Madame de Staël lived in Coppet, outside of Geneva, and was one of the most outspoken critics of Napoleon; she was a literary celebrity and her salon attracted a galaxy of thinkers; Sismondi was awkward and, at first, felt ill at ease because he had not received the same formal education as the other guests, but he soon gained the friendship of Madame de Staël and the esteem of people like Benjamin Constant and Bonstetten, the famous Swiss historian who would decisively shape Sismondi's historical views.

Undoubtedly influenced by his associations with the circle around Madame de Staël, and sharing their aversion to Napoleon, by 1803 Sismondi had completed his first major work in political economy, *De la richesse commerciale*. It was published within a few months of Say's *Traité d'économie politique*, and both works had an ulterior political motive beyond the stated, ostensibly nonpolitical one of expounding and popularizing Adam Smith's *Wealth of Nations*. They were treatises advocating free trade, and by inference condemning Napoleon's system of protection and severe regulation. The two works reflect two different approaches to social analysis that have persisted to the present day, and in a way have proven to be incompatible with each other: Say's *Traité* is theoretical, highly analytical, and abstract, amending the labor theory of value by introducing utility reasoning, and advancing what has since been known as *Say's Law*, the *loi des débouches* ("law of Markets"). The *Traité* became a standard text in many countries, with translations into English and other languages. Sismondi's opus, essentially institutional-historical, was directed to policy, and did not deviate in any way in its theoretical assumptions from the *Wealth*. It was for this latter reason better received than the *Traité,* and was considered a true French presentation of Adam Smith's doctrine. However, already here Sismondi introduced ideas that pointed toward his later concern with macroeconomic magnitudes and the role of the state in economic affairs.

Sismondi became famous beyond the borders of Geneva, so much so that he even received an invitation in 1804 from Czar Alexander to go to the University of Vilna to take the chair of political economy, an offer he declined.

During the next decade, Sismondi published the first three volumes of the *Histoire des républiques Italiennes du moyen âge,* a tract on Austrian paper money, a result of his travels with Madame de Staël in Germany and Austria, and a four-volume history of the literature of southern Europe. He was a path breaker in the history of the Middle Ages, being the first writer to treat this subject with attention to historical detail and original sources. The history of the Italian republics had the same hidden agenda as *Richesse*, namely the desirability of local self-government and individual freedom as most conducive to human happiness. As Salis points out (1973, 74–75) Geneva was a part of France, but it also was a center of pro-English sentiment, and Sismondi advanced the English viewpoint against Napoleonic domination whenever possible.

By the end of the Napoleonic wars, Sismondi was established as a historian, a writer, and a member in good standing of the European intelligentsia; he was recognized as a political economist, even though his analytical powers may not have met the standards of his contemporaries or later economists.

The abdication of Napoleon was greeted with joy by Sismondi and the circle around Madame de Staël, but their joy turned to dismay when the returning aristocrats began to turn the political clock back, installing reactionary governments everywhere. Sismondi became a partisan of Napoleon, whom he now regarded as a democratic reformer, as did his friend Benjamin Constant, greatly distressing some members of the Staël circle; he was received by Napoleon in audience and was offered the Legion of Honor, but declined, characteristically because he wanted to preserve his independence.

Sismondi was approached in 1818 by the editors of the *Edinburgh Encyclopedia* to write an exposition on political economy (he was most likely recommended by one of his friends in Geneva), which was to be a generally understandable version of classical doctrine. He did so, in English, producing a seven-chapter piece that is, on the whole, a conventional outline of Adam Smith's system, with some institutional touches added here and there.

Shortly after 1815, Europe had experienced a severe economic depression, caused by English manufacturers' attempts to reduce their swollen inventories, mostly textiles, by distress sales on the Continent. European governments had tried to protect their infant industries, a result of the Continental Blockade, by prohibitive tariffs. This led to a general depression. The depression had returned, after a short upswing, in 1818, followed by another in 1824. These cycles were the first general, worldwide business fluctuations that clearly originated in the economic system itself, and they seemed to Sismondi to be connected to the ever-increasing use of new machinery and greatly expanded outputs.

Agriculture had also suffered for a long time from depressed markets, resulting from concentration of landholdings and the application of new farming methods. Increased yields, especially in England, and cheaper grain coming from Russia and Poland lowered prices. As a consequence, the agricultural population began to migrate in great numbers to the cities in search of jobs, creating frightful conditions in communities that were in no way prepared for the massive influx of new populations. Urban crime spawned an extended literature on population, of which Malthus's *Essay on the Principle of Population* is the most famous example.

The owners of new factories found in these masses cheap labor for their mills. The movement was most advanced in England, which had a head start as the originator of the Industrial Revolution, but in Belgium, northern France, and the Rhineland similar conditions began to appear as well. In addition, Continental producers were threatened with extinction by the competition from the greatly superior products from England, thereby increasing cutthroat competition among manufacturers everywhere.

Sismondi, according to his own words in the introduction to *New*

Principles, had seen these conditions of distress in Italy, France, and Switzerland, although they would not have been nearly as severe as in England or Belgium because the transformation of industry had not yet advanced as far. To the inductive-minded historian Sismondi, the abstractions of contemporary (Ricardian) political economy did not explain the observed conditions, much less suggest a remedy. He also saw that a major part of the problem lay in the transformation of social conditions, which was driven by technological change but which was not addressed by contemporary writers in political economy. Nor could he fully analyze the problem in the article.

Sismondi reworked his *Encyclopedia* article into a treatise, expanding the seven chapters of the article into seven books, and adding whatever he felt was needed to transform the basic tenets of Smithian doctrine into a new, more comprehensive theory that would fill the gap he perceived.

New Principles appeared in 1819, the year Sismondi was to marry Jessie Allen, and thus become a member of a family that included Sir James Mackintosh and Josiah Wedgwood, and that would later include Charles Darwin. While there is no direct connection between this marriage and the publication of *New Principles*, together they clearly show that Sismondi was a respected intellectual who was accepted as an in-law by a family that represented a liberal intellectual tradition in England.

Salis assesses the impact of *New Principles* after its publication and concludes (1973, 419) that Sismondi was an *outsider* who failed to shake what would be called today *the conventional wisdom*. There may be valid theoretical reasons for this failure, such as Sismondi's analytical diffuseness—the multivariate, complex character of his model—but it is also appropriate to mention that Sismondi was a French-Swiss writer, working in a different intellectual climate from English thought, seeing different economic structures (even though he was quite familiar with English thought and conditions), and responding to different economic needs. In this respect, Sismondi's thought, and impact on economic theory, bears a close resemblance to that of another non-English economist, Friedrich List, whose essentially German (and American) perspective on economic development remained outside the mainstream of nineteenth-century political economy.

After his marriage to Jessie Allen, Sismondi settled in Chêne (at that time a village outside Geneva and now an integral part of metropolitan Geneva), in a house that has recently been restored, and devoted his time to writing. Jessie Allen Sismondi created a salon that attracted a great number of the intellectual elite of Europe and that became a successor to the salon of Madame de Staël—Ricasoli, Cavour, and Louis Napoleon (later Napoleon III) met there, and there is some evidence that Cavour secured the support of Louis Napoleon for the Italian unification movement at the Sismondi residence.

Sismondi died, apparently, of stomach cancer. One of his last acts was an appearance before the Constituent Assembly of Geneva to speak against the adoption of a democratic (that is, general franchise) constitution on the grounds that such a constitution would lead to excesses by the least-responsible elements of the community. This was another echo of his long-past experiences in the French Revolution and his patrician inheritance. He did not live to see the disturbances of 1848, and it is doubtful that he would have approved of them, although the aims of these revolutions were also his aims, being essentially uprisings of the lower middle class against the police states of the Holy Alliance. However, Sismondi believed that revolutions cost more in destruction than they gained in benefits from new social structures, and as he makes clear in *New Principles*, he was asking only for *indirect and gentle means* to improve the lot of all classes of humanity, thereby to achieve his main goal, the enjoyment of happiness for every citizen of a nation.

A Summary of Sismondi's Critique of Ricardian Political Economy

Sismondi was the first non-Utopian, nonsocialist critic of classical political economy who analyzed the first business cycles the Industrial Revolution had produced, and who was *not* dedicated to the proposition that only a new communal order could save society. He was also the first to diagnose cycles as inherent in the economic structure itself, thus running counter to what was then (and for more than a century afterwards) the dominant theory of economic equilibrium, Say's Law: Production costs are incomes to resource holders and therefore provide the means to purchase the goods produced; partial market disequilibria and *gluts* (satiated markets) could occur, but the action of the market would prevent a general depression by adjusting costs and prices. All costs are accounted for by market prices, and the income shares of resource holders exhaust the product during the production period.

New Principles is an attack on this theory in two ways: first, an appeal to facts that falsified Ricardian analysis; second, an examination, mainly by implication, of the dominant methodology of political economy.

Adam Smith, in his critique of mercantilism, changed the focus of economic discourse by changing its underlying assumptions and methodology. Starting from the Cartesian framework of physiocracy, he took political economy away from the administrative tasks he had still expounded in his *Lectures* at the University of Glasgow, and firmly placed it into a causative context—he assimilated what had heretofore been a collection of administrative rules and regulations, based on experience, to the great engine of a mechanical, Newtonian universe.

Smith had laid the groundwork for this transformation in *The Theory of Moral Sentiments,* where he postulated an innate human propensity, sympathy, as a mover of human behavior. Similarly, he ascribes the existence of the division of labor to the *human propensity to truck, barter, and exchange*. Just as celestial orbits obey physical laws, human actions are guided by social laws that could be scientifically discovered, objectively tested, and represented in a scientific notation. In addition, he postulated social harmony in the *Invisible Hand,* which ran counter to mercantilistic assumptions of individual and social opposition of interests needing government intervention to be resolved. As has been pointed out in innumerable anthologies of the history of economic thought, the very title chosen by Smith for his work was intended to set it apart from the last major work in the mercantilistic mode, Sir James Steuart's *Political Economy,* for precisely these reasons.

It took Smith twelve years to realize his goal, and the result is a clear indication that the author, for all his theoretical advances, struggled to escape prior frameworks of analysis. His Newtonian structure is everywhere tempered by long disquisitions of a historical nature, institutional modifications, and long asides. As has been stated many times, *The Wealth of Nations* is not an orderly treatise—it fell to Say to, in the words of Ricardo, *''place the science in a more logical and more instructive order,''* and to Ricardo *''to determine the laws which regulate this distribution . . . respecting the natural course of rent, profit, and wages''* (Italics added).[2]

The methodological mold these three writers imprinted on political economy has not materially changed to the present day—economics is still firmly in the orbit of linear Newtonian mechanics, despite its apparent transformation since Smith's time. It was the work of Ricardo and Say that gave a reductionist cast to political economy and turned analysis away from institutional considerations. To most writers after Ricardo, the institutional framework was given and, mainly, invariant. Alfred Marshall's *Principles of Economics* is a major example of this viewpoint.

In economics, value plays a role equivalent to the law of gravitation in Newtonian mechanics: it determines the movements of the investigated units. However, gravitation is a measurable natural independent force, while value is a concept without independent existence apart from the definitions given to it by the investigators. It is circular, ''just a word,'' as Joan Robinson put it in her *Economic Philosophy* (1962). And it is immaterial that we now use *utility* and mathematical formulae, following Walras and Marshall; of necessity, a social science must find its *basic* defining criteria in human ideas, which, existing only in men's minds and therefore not directly testable, depend for their very existence on human consensus and definition—they are beyond independent proof, *metaphysical.* Since human perceptions change over time under the influence of experience, the assumption, silent in classical analysis, that laws of human behavior (as determined by introspective deduction) are valid for all times is for this reason alone false.

The sudden and unpredictable changes in social position that Sismondi experienced as a very young man must have given him a lifelong appreciation of the precariousness of the human condition and an insight into the connection between social structure and individual fortune. His studies of the English constitution in 1792–1794 and his subsequent historical researches would strengthen such ideas. He would therefore be led quite logically to an institutional view of social progress (and process), and away from any reductionist social analysis. The additional changes in social structure, caused by industrial technology, that he witnessed during the next twenty years must have reinforced his views. Sismondi had received a rationalistic education at the academy, but in many respects he was an autodidact who broadened his curtailed formal training by extensive reading and, as he himself states, by observation. Combined with his business experience, this would predispose him to factual inquiry and to distrust of abstract philosophical systems. Sismondi had worked as a *merchant*, Ricardo as a *banker,* Say as an *industrialist;* Sismondi would be more inclined to give greater weight to discretionary consumer behavior than either of the other two authors, and less to abstract monetary or utility considerations.

Assuming the existence of human propensities as leading man to certain actions, Sismondi would take the position that only those propensities that were shown by historical analysis to be relatively invariant over time would be admissible as explanatory factors of human behavior. Hence, *New Principles* reverts time and time again to historical example to substantiate its deductions. However, it is the essence of the classical approach to postulate invariance first and to then use this assumed invariance to explain human actions.

The Wealth of Nations is eclectic enough to support claims of legitimacy, and serve as a starting point, for inductive and deductive political economy; hence, the historian Sismondi *and* the deductive analysts Say and Ricardo could claim the mantle of the master. Sismondi's first work in political economy, *De la richesse commerciale,* is still a fairly straightforward exposition of Adam Smith; then, and to some extent afterwards, he was in agreement with Adam Smith. As stated many times in *New Principles*, his disagreement was with the abstractions of Ricardo and Say.

New Principles starts from the rationalistic assumptions of Smith's

Wealth, but, as Sismondi makes clear in the last chapter of the first book, " it is the aim of this book to develop and complete" the doctrine of Adam Smith, "because it is to him that we owe the discovery of truths he himself had not known." Experience in the intervening half-century showed that the *practical* results of the doctrine were different from the conclusions Smith had arrived at, and it was therefore necessary to "draw . . . quite different conclusions." On the other hand, the English disciples of Adam Smith, according to Sismondi, had changed political economy from an experiential science to an abstract, speculative system that lost sight of the human beings to whom wealth ought to bring happiness. It is the latter method he wants to oppose in *New Principles.*

Sismondi raises important questions about the goals of political economy and its method. His critique of the Ricardo-Say model is diffuse, spread over seven books, with repetitions and inconsistencies. It is evident that he tries, as did his model Adam Smith before, to free himself from the conventional wisdom of contemporary writers and still remain within what he sees as the legitimate realm of political economy. Yet, the main outlines of his critique and what he wants political economy to be are clear. Starting from the proposition that the major problem, and ultimate goal, of political economy is the diffusion of enjoyment or happiness to the highest degree among the greatest possible number of individuals, he concludes: "That nation is but half civilized where no individual suffers, but where no one enjoys sufficient leisure or comforts to feel intensely, or to think deeply," and "wealth and population are not, indeed, absolute signs of prosperity in a state; they are only so in relation to each other." The existence of business cycles and widespread unemployment, sixteen-hour workdays, child labor, and widespread poverty among the working class are seen as proof that contemporary political economy, that is, Ricardian distributive analysis and Say's law of markets, did not present a theory that offered an understanding of economic behavior, or solutions to these problems. Sismondi wants to bring political economy back to its policy-oriented origins, from which it had been diverted by the work of Ricardo and Say.

Smith had stated that consumption is the end of all production, but the methodological bias of a labor theory of value is in favor of production; its main focus is economic development. Even Say, using utility and erasing the distinction between productive and unproductive labor, displays this bias in the Law of Markets—consumption is seen as infinitely elastic, ever replenished by the distribution of the incomes/cost shares of the factors of production. Sismondi, on the other hand, advances the idea that "it is a great mistake . . . to represent consumption as a force without limits, always ready to absorb an infinite production."

Sismondi claimed that aggregate production of goods *can* exceed aggregate consumption, in particular that the consumption of *necessities* has a satiation point. Consequently, the end of production is not only consumption in the Smithian sense of consumption of material goods, but *leisure;* "the Solitary worked above all to have leisure; he accumulated wealth in order to enjoy it without work; leisure is a natural inclination for man, it is the goal and reward of work. . . . Man does not tire himself, except to rest thereafter; he does not save except to spend; he does not aspire to wealth except for enjoyment." And, in a footnote added as an afterthought, "if all members of a nation labor, if they labor incessantly, the goal of wealth would not be reached at all, there would be no rest nor enjoyment, neither to make man more perfect; the nation, by multiplying its wealth, would sacrifice the end to the means." In the same way, leisure is also the key to the exploitation argument—a worker would not work more than necessary to produce the equivalent of his own livelihood, devoting the remainder of his life to leisure and enjoyment. It is the separation of capital and labor that allows the owner of machines to demand from the worker effort beyond this necessary minimum; that is, he exploits the worker to produce a surplus (*mieux value*) for himself, or, in other words, he pays less than subsistence.

Sismondi's lagged, nonlinear, short-run period model is presented in book 2, chapter 6, developed in book 3 on agriculture, further elaborated in book 4 on commercial wealth, and then again in the last chapter of book 7 on population. A look at the plan of the book in book 1, chapter 7, shows why he distributed the discussion over so many different parts of the work. *New Principles* is derived from the *Encyclopedia*—the chapter headings there become books here. But the article only had a historical introduction to general economic thought, as then existing, and hence had no room for any explicit analytical discussion of alternative systems. Further, as a historian, Sismondi sought to adduce historical data to analytical argument; therefore, analysis became imbedded in historical narrative. His approach is more complex than the linear microeconomic model of classical analysis. It shares with Keynesian analysis a multivariate approach, which allows asymmetrical nonequilibrium economic states.

In *New Principles* Sismondi divides population into two main parts: the poor, or workers, and the rich, further divided into capital owners and capital users. Three classes are postulated: workers, capitalists (divided into landlords and rentiers), and entrepreneurs. Surprisingly, four income shares in the national product are also assumed: wages, rent, interest, and profit, an unusual view for the time. Rent and interest are seen as analogous, payment for scarce resources, and the landlord and the contract farmer of book 3 (agriculture), and the factory owner and the rentier of book 4 (commerce or industry), are all members of the wealthy, or capitalist class.

The wealthy hold capital, from which they derive an income; part of the capital is used to employ the poor (a wages fund), who have no other means of subsistence. The poor offer their labor in the market; they can realize their income (labor) only if they are employed, and the income will be spent only *after* the labor is sold; the size of the income is determined by the demand for it—if demand is lacking no income will be realized by the poor. The consumption expenditures of the poor are determined by the income received, and are for wage goods only.

The income of the rich is derived from the labor of the poor, in the sense that the rich advance the wages of the poor (only labor can produce wealth, according to Sismondi; in this one respect he remains a faithful disciple of Adam Smith, as indeed he always emphasizes). Production of wealth is dependent on consumption—if produced goods are not removed from the market by consumption (becoming part of the consumption fund), then reproduction, that is, the replacement of depleted inventories, will not take place. The income of the rich is received only *after* the produced goods are sold in the market, analogous to the income of the poor. If goods remain unsold because of declining consumption, the capitalist will not receive his customary income; if goods are sold at less than customary prices because of overproduction or declining demand, the income of the rich will also be reduced. If the income of the rich is reduced, their consumption will decline *and* the wages fund for the next period will be reduced; fewer workers will be employed in the next period; that is, unemployment will result or, alternatively, wages will be lowered by competition among workers. Unemployment and/or lower wages in turn will reduce the demand for wages goods again, lowering total consumption. Lower aggregate consumption will lead to lower production and, under the influence of competition, to cost reductions and battles for market share among producers. Producers will use new machines to reduce the use of the main cost item in production, labor, to lower their costs and offer lower prices in the market to regain their share of the market. The displaced labor will add to the competitive struggle in the labor market, lowering wages even more. On the other hand, the struggle between producers will lead to concentration of production, forcing some producers out of business, and causing more unemployment.

The descending spiral, as outlined in the previous paragraph, can also become an ascending spiral, in a general reversal of the descending scenario. If consumption increases autonomously, the rich will add to their consumption and their capital (save) because of higher incomes from increased sales. They will increase the wages fund (or invest), the poor then will have more to spend, and more output will be produced. If this additional output does *not exceed* the existing demand, the rich will realize in the next period a higher income because of sustained sales, which again will increase both the wages fund and market demand. "This process, executed with prudence and moderation, can then perpetuate itself." Based on the idea that production must be converted into money, a process that takes some time, Sismondi postulates that the income of the *present* year purchases the production of the *next* year, and it is *not* necessarily true that these two entities will match exactly. In the case of an ascending spiral, the income of the last year is smaller than the production of next year, hence causing losses. If these losses are on the aggregate small, that is, if next year's production does not exceed by much this year's income, and if the losses are well distributed over a large number of producers, the increases in production will not be interrupted and the economy will expand.

The requirement that losses in the ascending phase be small and well distributed over a large number of producers can be most easily met by moderate inflation, although Sismondi would have rejected this solution. Nevertheless, the Keynesian prescription for the death of the rentier and Sismondi's proposal agree quite well if it is assumed that one of the requirements for a progressing economy is a constant reduction in fixed debt load by a slow advance in prices.

Monetary and fiscal analysis should have been part of the general discussion of economic cycles, but they are treated separately in books 5 and 6, respectively. The analysis adds little to the basic model and can be summarized quickly.

Sismondi is a determined opponent of *any* type of paper currency, reflecting his own experiences with the schemes of Jacques Necker, the revolutionary assignats (paper money issued during the French Revolution), and the general financial instability of the postrevolutionary period. His view of business credit as a potential overstimulator of real capital expansion and, consequently, unwanted production is the one connection this book makes to his macroeconomic views. His hard-currency, specie-only as currency views can also be seen as proof of a belief that price stability is a direct result of specie circulation and a necessary condition of limiting business cycles. Here he diverged greatly from his master Adam Smith.

Book 6 on taxation reflects the *technical* limitations direct taxation of incomes faced at the time. The discussion shows that Sismondi was greatly influenced by utility considerations. His tax schemes are based on the benefit principle and the ability-to-pay principle. Unlike Smith, he recognizes the growing scope of government involvement in economic affairs, and the need to finance this involvement from taxes, rather than from borrowing. There is no hint here on how to influence the economy by fiscal policy; rather, the opposite position is taken that governments cannot be trusted to guide the economy. However, government expenditure and consumption are seen as substitutes for each other.

Schumpeter called the Sismondian analysis the first *dynamic model* of the economic process, for which Sismondi need not share any credit with anybody else, and despite his low opinion of Sismondi as an analyst, regarded this model as his major original contribution to business-cycle analysis. The following quote summarizes the model:

> In short, income is born from reproduction; but it is not production by itself which is the income; it does not take that name, it does not act as such till it is changed to money, till after each produced commodity has found its consumer who has the need or desire for it and who, withdrawing it from circulation to add to his consumption stocks, has given its price in exchange. This is how the producer makes his calculation; from the sales he will be able to make, he will first recoup his capital in its entirety; he realizes then the profits that remain; they will then in turn be devoted to his pleasures and to the resumption of his business.

The model is based on the business experience of the merchant's counting house. The example used to illustrate the model uses Lyon hatters, showing that indeed Sismondi's apprenticeship in Lyon influenced his analysis of the business cycle. It resembles Marx's C-M-C (Commodity-Money-Commodity) process, but it is closest to Keynesian analysis in its short-run outlook. The lagged character of the model and the requirement that the money income of the previous period pay for the production of the present period introduce a variable akin to liquidity preference, which in turn may increase or decrease consumption, determining total output. The initial distribution of income between consumption and additions to the wages fund (investing) by the rich in the ascending phase is apparently discretionary, although it is assumed that if income increases because of increased sales, the wealthy will add to the wages fund in order to increase production and ultimately their income. In the descending phase, reduced income will *always* lead to a decline of production, because Sismondi assumes that the rich will decrease their own consumption *and their contribution to the wages fund.* The model is therefore asymmetrical and resembles the Keynesian analysis in the implied assumption that the existing economic system has a bias toward recessions.

Changing technology will aggravate all of these effects by accelerating the ability of large aggregates of capital to introduce labor-saving devices that will make factory workers redundant (this also applies in a lesser degree to agriculture), adding to downward pressure on wages and reducing overall costs. The economy will become more unstable, since the imbalance between consumption and production will increase with each improvement in productivity. This argument is coupled with the assertion that modern market-oriented producers have no *direct* knowledge of actual demand and will therefore base decisions for the introduction of new technology and/or production methods on the availability (cost) of *financial* capital, and thus *tend to overshoot* aggregate demand whenever financial capital is cheap, that is, in the beginning phase of the business cycle or because of subsidies by an expansion-oriented government. There is a hint here that abundant financial capital will lead to speculation, but the argument is mainly concerned with unwarranted increases in production. Sismondi postulates that the individual factory owner has no alternative in this regard, because competition will force him to use new technology or be ruined. Since in the ascending phase of the business cycle profits are usually higher, the producer has an additional incentive to produce more with the same labor force, or the same output with a smaller number of workers.

The argument apparently disregards the standard economic analysis that lower prices make it possible to buy more of the product, leaving the worker better off and increasing demand; however, aggregate consumption of wages goods is assumed to be inelastic and the effects of price declines are therefore necessarily limited. Book 7, chapter 7, deals with this question by pointing out that the labor displaced by more productive machinery, and the income thus lost, is usually larger than the corresponding price decline; that is, the effects of machine production on aggregate purchasing power are again asymmetrical: "The same observation may be extended to all improved manufactures; they have never diminished the price of their produce, except in arithmetical progression, while they have suspended workmanship in geometrical progression."

The nature of wages goods is left open, in the same way that Ricardian analysis is vague about what constitutes subsistence. There is the intimation that *necessities* are all goods that are basic to consumption (food, clothing, housing) of both the poor and the rich. However, Sismondi's introduction of leisure as an alternative to increased consumption would argue that he saw wages goods as essentially socially defined, subject to institutional change—his view of the distribution of the national dividend as the result of a *struggle* between capitalist and worker (book 2, chapter 5) clearly implies that if a power shift between capitalist and worker occurs, income distribution will be altered. There is nothing here of the inevitability of the Ricardian economic laws of distribution—distribution is a social problem. It should be noted that Robert L. Heilbroner ascribes this insight to John Stuart Mill (1986, 129–30), and although this is the Marxian exploitation argument in its entirety, no teleological implications as to the possible future shape of society are drawn, and indeed the conclusion of *New Principles* states that "he feels powerless to sketch the means of its implementation [that is, of economic justice] . . . it seems to me to be almost beyond human capability to imagine an arrangement of ownership entirely different from the one we know from experience."

Sismondi disagreed strongly with the Ricardian argument, (cited in a footnote) that it is immaterial to an investor whether his capital employs a hundred or a thousand men, provided that the realized profit remain the same, and that *the interest of the nation is the same, provided that its net real income, its rents and profits remained the same.* This led him to the often-quoted observation that nothing more needed to be wished for than that the king of England, alone on the island, ought to produce all output by turning a crank. Essentially, he took the position that what is true of the individual in the economic process need not be true for society as an aggregate of individuals—in other words, he advanced the fallacy of composition as a compelling argument against Say's Law.

Technological change is an area where economists are careful to tread even today, except insofar as any technological change can be assimilated to observable changes in interest rates, that is, the cost of financial capital, or rates of return. Institutional-societal changes due to technological advances (for example, the forced changing of incorporated skills in a labor force, the restructuring of demand patterns, and, in Sismondi's day, as today, the migration of populations from country to city) are generally disregarded. They are often hard to quantify and difficult to causally connect to any particular technological change, and they are usually long-term and insidious in the sense that the costs they impose on society are initially dispersed over a large number of individuals and not directly perceived by everyone. In addition, economics has a theoretical bias in favor of increasing efficiency, postulating that increasing efficiency increases utilization of scarce resources in production, and therefore tends to disregard any of these problems in favor of the argument that the resulting lower prices for goods will compensate for such dislocational costs.

To Sismondi, technological change was a major factor in the progress of the business cycle, coupled, as he saw it, to the Ricardian insistence on increasing the *net product*, that is, profits. It increased antagonism between the classes, while their interest lay in cooperation because the production process is a cooperative one in which the capitalist needs the worker and the worker needs the capitalist.

As the third book of *New Principles*, "Of Territorial Wealth," makes clear, the postulate basic to the model, the separation of capital ownership from labor, is based on Sismondi's extensive acquaintance with Italian agriculture and its processes, legal structures, and general institutional arrangements. To a present-day reader, the discussion of agricultural practices would seem to be mainly of antiquarian interest, agriculture being, in all developed countries, a vital activity that occupies only a small fraction of the total population. However, it was then the dominant industry, engaging powerful political forces—as the English debate on the Corn Laws shows—and therefore Sismondi's ideas deserve attention. In addition, there are some observations on concentration of landholdings and what is today called *agrobusiness* that have evident contemporary applications. In the next (fourth) book, "Of Commercial Wealth," many of the conclusions derived from the agricultural sector are transferred to the commercial-industrial sector, and some of the main dissents from classical economy originate here.

The most remarkable feature of Sismondi's view is his insistence that property rights in land are not derived from the physiocratic original work on the land (*avances foncières*), nor are they simply assumed as existing, as they are in Ricardo; rather, they are a social convenience that can be modified, abolished, or changed in any way to suit the purposes of society. It deserves to be quoted at length:

> The ownership of land is, indeed, not based on a principle of justice, but on a principle of public utility. . . . It is for society's advantage, for the poor as well as the wealthy, that it has taken landlords under its protection; *but it can attach conditions to a concession it grants, and it ought to do so in the spirit of that very concession; it must submit property of land to legislation which will indeed bring about the general good, because it is the general good which alone justifies such ownership*. The appropriation of land has been recognized as advantageous for all society, because it gave to him who worked it the certainty that, to remotest time, he would enjoy fully the fruits of his labor. . . . Every contract, every division of fruits which separates ownership interest from interest in cultivation tends to destroy, or at least diminish, the good effect which society had expected from the appropriation of land. . . . But the division of rights to property is born from special circumstances, from chance schemes, often from passions or vanity. The distinction between the proprietor, the farmer, and the day worker has neither contributed more zeal to the first, nor more intelligence to the second, nor more vigor to the third. It has in no way been a reason that a task was done always by the same person, and therefore was made better or quicker. The division has often been replaced by others, entirely different; it must be judged, as all the rest of social institutions, by the good or bad that has flowed from them for humanity; by the quantity of happiness they produce, and the number of individuals who participate therein. However, it is a gift of society, and in no way a natural right which preexisted.

> History proves this, since numerous nations exist which have not at all recognized private possession of land; this argument proves it also, because property in land is not in any way completely created through industry, like a work of man. (Italics added.)

This entire argument can be applied, with minor modifications, to *all* property rights.

To Sismondi, that nation is the happiest that has, first, an agricultural sector composed of many independent farmers, and second, laws that prevent the land from being immobilized (entailed) in large estates. This undoubtedly combined observations of Tuscan (and Swiss) conditions, physiocratic ideas, and Smithian aversion to monopoly in a general view of agriculture decidedly at variance with Ricardian rent theory. Sismondi has an essentially historical-institutional view of land ownership; however, it should be noted that he strongly defends small landholding, what he calls patriarchal cultivation, on utility grounds, as best suited to improving agriculture and to securing long-term interest in the maintenance of sound cultivation. The owner-cultivator is a better guardian of the soil, of the cultivation of crops, than the large estate; Sismondi contrasts the family farms of Switzerland, France, Italy (Tuscany), and Germany with the large estates in the Romagna that had gone to weeds and the vast holdings of English magnates that had sent great numbers of destitute cottagers into the slums of the English cities.

The main political conclusion of the work is summarized in these observations:

> The strongest safeguard of an established order may lie in the existence of a numerous class of peasant proprietors. However advantageous it may be for society to safeguard property, it is an abstract idea difficult to grasp by those to whom it seems only to guarantee privation. When land ownership is taken from the cultivator, and *the ownership of factories from workers,* all those who create wealth and who see it passing through their hands without end, are strangers to all its benefits. *They form by far the most numerous part of the nation; they see themselves as the most useful part, and they feel disinherited.* Constant envy stirs them up against the rich; one can hardly dare to discuss civil rights before them, because one must always be afraid they will go from this discussion to that of property rights, and they will demand the distribution of possessions and land. (Italics added.)

This is followed up with a description that vividly reflects Sismondi's experience: "A revolution in such a country is frightful; the whole order of society is subverted; power passes into the hands of the multitude, which holds physical force, and this crowd, having suffered much, kept in ignorance by need, is hostile to all types of law, all degrees of distinction, all types of property."

Individual ownership of what Marx would later call *the means of production,* widely dispersed among smallholders in agriculture, and among workers as part owners of factories, is therefore the solution to violent changes in society and to social distress. As the chapter on slave cultivation in book 3 makes quite clear, absentee ownership removes the owner from the direct consequences of his actions and thus lowers the care he has for his property. The slave, or more generally, nonholder of property, including the hired manager, has no concern for the property either; hence economic conditions deteriorate under such a regime.

The argument is made in defense of patriarchal agriculture, but it applies equally to industry. Property holding, by engaging the self-interest of the worker, will improve production, whether on the land, or in the factory. It will also have the effect of breaking, or at least mitigating, monopoly power by large economic aggregates. The argument is different from that of Adam Smith, inasmuch as it acknowledges the changed shape of industry since 1776—Sismondi prefers the small producer as closer to the buyer, but given the reality of factory production, he desires a *share* in the ownership of industry for the worker, preferring, however, the family farm to any other form of agriculture.

Reasoning by analogy from the family farm as the basic unit that provides the individual *lifelong* support, Sismondi proposes that day laborers on large farms and factory workers have a *right* to be secure from poverty due to old age, sickness, or unemployment; he sees the skills of the worker, whether agricultural or industrial, as a form of fixed capital that is acquired by expenditure of funds and effort, and that cannot be changed quickly to respond to changes in production. Consequently, a daily wage that does not compensate the worker for the depreciation of this investment is in effect a shifting of costs from the capitalist to the worker. The capitalist is able to lower his costs of production because he does not pay fully for the costs of his labor. He is able to do this shifting because of the *power* he has in the marketplace, given to him by his possession of real capital. Indeed, he puts these costs on *the shoulders of society* by leaving the workers to public charity (in England, the poor laws); in other words, the contemporary practice of paying daily *market* wages determined by short-term demand and supply conditions, with immediate discharge of workers at an economic downturn, is seen as an *externality:* "The advantage of an employer of labor is often nothing else than the despoliation of the worker . . . he does not profit because his enterprise produced more than its costs, but because he does not pay all the costs."

Hence, large-scale employers should provide for these conditions, either in the form of higher wages or by direct support of the worker. Large agricultural employers should be charged with the support of their day laborers, and large-scale employers of factory hands should be charged with their support, leaving small producers, either in agriculture or industry, free from any contributions. However, the best safeguard for the worker is participatory ownership of the factory and continued sharing in its profits.

Sismondi applies this idea only to labor, but the argument can be easily generalized to *all* factors. It then raises the question whether the success of capitalism was not based on extensive externalities, that is, costs that were passed off to society at large (for example, smoke), thus making lower prices for commodities possible. Ricardian distributive analysis and Say's Law do not recognize externalities; all costs are assumed to be covered by the market price, mainly because they assume that factors are flexible and infinitely transferable between applications. This argument is also different from the previously cited exploitation argument, inasmuch as Sismondi here does not assume that the workers *produce* a surplus incorporated in the product the capitalist appropriates, but rather that the capitalist does not pay the full *cost* of the work force.

Similar reasoning is used to show that the inability to transfer real capital in a depression, or from an industry in a decline, will result in bankruptcies and factory closings, creating unemployment and lower consumption. Specialization (that is, the advancing division of labor and mechanization of the production process) will make any transfer of capital, whether circulating (labor), or fixed (machines) ever more difficult, thus increasing losses. This argument leads him to the conclusion that smaller, weaker factory owners will be driven out by larger producers, resulting in industrial (and agricultural) concentration, because larger economic aggregates have more market power, hence more control over *costs,* and thus can pursue price wars against their weaker competitors. The small artisan and shop owner is forced to descend to a class called *proletarians,* a class without property but with many children who will swell the ranks of the unemployed. Therefore, Sismondi believes that a more equal property distribution will eventually reduce the total incidence of childbearing among the poorer classes, arguing that property holding will make men inclined to postpone marriage.

Sismondi disclaims any ability to offer a solution to what he sees as the basic cause of economic distress: a faulty property distribution that leads to large income inequalities. He believes that all remedies have to be applied by government in an indirect and gradual way, but his proposals to change the distribution of income shares and property rights were farsighted, indeed greatly ahead of his time, and much superior to Utopian, Marxian, and other socialist solutions. They are in fact proposals that have become, 150 years later, the accepted institutions of *democratic capitalism:* wide distribution of share ownership in large corporations, unions and industry-wide bargaining, unemployment insurance, pensions and social security, and equalization of incomes by government-decreed minimum wages and the progressive income tax. Essentially, all of these developments are a recognition that the market does not account for all costs of production—the sharing of profits by workers through indirect stockholding in pension plans, for example, is clearly a device to equalize distribution of income shares over all producers.

On the other hand, some of the proposed solutions have a much less progressive tenor, and his proposed remedies for excessive childbearing by the poor, such as governmental restrictions on marriages, were taken out of the first edition because they aroused protests as being too reactionary.

Sismondi also advocated governmental restrictions on the introduction of new, labor-saving inventions, unless it could be shown that their introduction is justified by preexisting demand, a difficult criterion to satisfy. He advocated the abolition of patent protection as a means of slowing the pace of technological change, reasoning that inventors, deprived of their governmentally protected monopoly, would be reluctant to rush into the market with their inventions.

Taken together with such remedies as his call for a revival of guild protections for the worker, Sismondi projected an alternative picture of a conservative who wanted to reverse the direction of the surging Industrial Revolution, and he was excoriated as such by writers like McCulloch and, of course, Marx. Yet the impression would be false. Clearly, the remedies he advocates are monopolistic, trying to give existing producers a command over technological change. But they are attempts to find a solution, however imperfect such a solution would be, to the problem of externalities, based on redistribution of economic power in the marketplace. It is in this context that his professed inability to visualize other social institutions with greater economic justice for all should be understood. He sees the danger of renewed guild controls over the production process and wants no part of it. He rejects government subsidies for new industries and agriculture as usually counterproductive, which is somewhat at variance but not inconsistent with his call for government regulation of new technology. Certainly, the rise of unions and their growing control over the supply of labor would argue that he indeed foresaw future developments, including the deleterious effects of too much union control over the production process.

Adam Smith solved the problem of economic power in the marketplace by postulating what is today called *perfect competition,* economic units so small that they could not influence the market, and further by postulating the *invisible hand,* the unsupported assumption of economic harmony at the macroeconomic level. Even in his day, this was utopian and became less realistic as the Industrial Revolution progressed. The exclusion of government from the economic sphere except for narrowly defined tasks was never fully a reality, and would become much less so as the scope of production increased, necessitating an expansion of the administrative and legal responsibilities of government *at all levels*. By the time Sismondi wrote *Richesse,* industrial production began to penetrate continental Europe; by the time he wrote *New Principles,* production in some sectors, for example, textiles, had been transformed into the factory mode he identified as giving the owners of capital power over their resource markets. The social consequences of such expansion could not be ignored.

Sismondi was a rationalist who believed in moderation, balance in all social concerns, and equal rights for all human beings to share in the bounty of this earth. He was a romantic in his belief in the ameliorative effects of property rights. His characterization of landed property as a social convenience and his insistence that it be made divisible and marketable are as revolutionary as anything that was advocated by his socialist contemporaries. His demands that workers have a day of rest, shorter working hours, and a share in the ownership of factories were for his time, and many years thereafter, revolutionary proposals. His analysis of the business cycle was a result of his humane concern with the sufferings of the workers because of technological change, and his model, so reminiscent of Keynesian ideas, was an attempt to remedy the dysfunction of the developing capitalistic system by showing the analytical mistakes of its main theoreticians.

Sismondi was unsuccessful in this endeavor, as he himself admits in the two forewords to this work. A later writer, Marx, who clearly used most of Sismondi's ideas, was much more successful in influencing his and later times. There remains, therefore, the questions why he did not make a greater impact on his contemporaries, and why and how Marx succeeded where Sismondi had failed.

The New Principles and Marxian Ideology: Evolution Versus Revolution

The English publication record of economic treatises has an evident gap: Sismondi's *New Principles* was never fully translated. Only a very abbreviated, partial translation of selected passages exists, dedicated to Jessie Allen, even though other, linguistically much more difficult books of the same general type, for example *Das Kapital*, and a later work of Sismondi's, the *Etudes*, was translated. There are translations of *New Principles* into German and Russian, as well as long references to it in anthologies of economic doctrine, both English and American. It is also a well-known work in Marxist literature, at least by reference—Sismondi is the only author mentioned in *The Communist Manifesto*, and *New Principles* is the most cited work on political economy in the first volume of *Das Kapital*, the only volume fully authored by Marx. Lenin attacked Sismondi's ideas in a pamphlet, characterizing him as an economic romantic, showing his familiarity with Sismondi's work.

To explain this peculiar omission is an exercise in both theoretical and historical speculation, an undertaking fraught with the danger of looking at an early nineteenth-century author through the glasses of the post-Keynesian twentieth century. However, modern economics has seen theoretical cycles, swinging from inductive to deductive analysis and back, since its major codification by Alfred Marshall, and to explain the neglect of an early, and clearly seminal, critique of mainstream theory may illuminate some of the reasons for such swings of opinion in what is usually billed, and accepted, as a science.

Gide and Rist call Sismondi the forerunner of the German movement known as *Socialism of the Chair* as well as *Christian Democracy* or *Christian Socialism*; as noted above, Marx cited Sismondi extensively, and many of the economic concepts advanced for the first time in *New Principles*, for example, *surplus value, class struggle, exploitation, proletarian*, reappear in Marx. He accuses Malthus, in *Theorien über den Mehrwert*, of having copied most of his ideas in the *Principles* (1820) from Sismondi. This is possible because some arguments from *New Principles* were known from the *Encyclopedia*, and the first edition of *New Principles* appeared in 1818. However, it is much more likely that Marx himself was guilty of the sin he ascribed to Malthus and would therefore be inclined to accuse him of such behavior. German historicism and its American offspring, institutionalism, are traceable to Sismondi. Yet, Sismondi did *not* found a *school* of economic thought, there are no recorded Sismondian English authors, and there exists only one major analysis of his work in English (Mao-Lan Tuan's *Simonde de Sismondi as an Economist*, 1927). What explains this neglect, in the English literature, of a work that was undoubtedly seminal in its day, and that even today has something important to say about industrial capitalism, technological change, and the business cycle?

Sismondi accepted Smith's proposition that labor created value and was therefore in the mainstream of accepted theory. As the previous section shows, his ideas on a lifelong wage and security for the worker are derived directly from the labor theory of value. Therefore, an explanation for

Sismondi's failure to attract a following in England must be sought elsewhere.

Political economy as a scientific method of social analysis was seen by Sismondi as a historical-institutional endeavor that relied on observation and postulated a minimum of human *natural* tendencies. He was the first writer to use the method, and at the time of the first publication of *New Principles* the only one in Europe. For instance, his main postulate, that consumption is limited, is based on the observation that sales fluctuate due to discretionary spending of income earners and to fluctuations in their incomes. His lagged-cycle model incorporates the observation that spending is not instantaneous, as assumed in classical theory, but dependent on the mode of income disbursement. However, although reasoning from historical analogy and institutional analysis provides process models and adds to their realism, these models have a major drawback—they are analytically diffuse and do not lend themselves easily to determinate, clear-cut solutions, and they are usually nonlinear. They therefore do not give what is most sought from the social scientist, as it is from the physical scientist: certainty. They also require constant reevaluation. Social systems are in a constant state of change, adding to a sense of predictive unreliability.

Therefore, the most likely reason for Sismondi's failure would appear to be his rejection of Say's Law, which implied the rejection of the Newtonian mold of political economy, and the substitution for it of a complex macroeconomic model that had no determinate solution. This theoretical change had political dimensions: first, it ran counter to the interests of the rising entrepreneurial class, particularly to their views on the use and remuneration of labor; second, it put into question policies—free labor markets, free trade, minimum government intervention—that were deduced from the labor theory of value and classical microeconomic market analysis.

Sismondi's quarrel was not with Smithian doctrine, but with Ricardian distribution theory and *method*. He accused Ricardo of abstracting away all of the actually observed economic behavior of businessmen and farmers-landlords, misrepresenting the causes that determined distributive shares, in particular rent on land. The result was a model that could only have the most misleading influence on governmental policy and business decisions. Since Sismondi did not see the social world of labor as a mechanistic, Newtonian universe, guided by unchanging laws, but as a succession of continuously changing structures of social relationships, the changes had to affect the very structures from which they emanated.

This macroeconomic feedback mechanism and the wage externality argument had to lead Sismondi to the conclusion that the individual profit motive may have socially negative consequences, which needed to be compensated by governmental action. He therefore opposed, as a matter of theory and policy, the main conclusions of the classical school—an opposition that was greatly at variance with the spirit of a free-trading, individualistic entrepreneurial class that had embraced wholeheartedly Adam Smith's gospel of economic freedom.

As the subsequent theoretical development of political economy shows, the analysis of economic distribution has no need of a labor theory of value—Ricardo's analysis of distribution of income shares is really based on relative market prices and implied market power. The first chapter of Ricardo's *Principles* on value can be excised without affecting the main argument. Similarly, the derivative Marxian assertion that labor creates a surplus is no more than that, since according to Marx, neither the worker nor the capitalist are aware of the existence of the surplus product, except as it manifests itself as profit, which, however, is different from surplus, although it is derived from it. The existence of a surplus is inferred from the existence of a surplus called profit—if a loss occurs, then, presumably, it could be inferred that no surplus value has been created. Similarly, the Marxian exploitation argument needs no analysis of labor value, since it is based on Sismondi's model of relative market strength of worker and employer.

Sismondi gave a conventional Smithian exposition of the labor theory in *Richesse*, and in *New Principles* he is content to repeat, in book 2, the same ideas; but it is apparent already by the third chapter of the book that he is more interested to take up what he perceives as real economic problems—the poverty of those who are the theoretical value producers, the instability of the system, the role of machines in contributing to these problems—and considers any deeper analysis of value as of limited usefulness.

The original aim of the labor theory of value advanced by Locke (and based on Aristotle) was the defense of private property: man, having mixed his effort with inanimate matter, thereby possesses it, and transforms it for his use. It is therefore beneficial, it contributes to the happiness of man, and the *natural* right to *individual private property* derived from effort is the mainstay of civilized society. The U.S. Declaration of Independence and Constitution are prominent expressions of this idea.

Adam Smith used the labor theory to provide a broader methodological base than land, the physiocratic origin of value, for his arguments. Trade, the mercantilistic value creator, was even more unacceptable to him. Labor is a concept associated with production in a much more pervasive manner, because it enters *all* production. His choice reflected possibly existing structural differences between the French and English economies—the former was still mainly agricultural with a rudimentary industrial sector, mostly court-directed and subsidized, with land as the basis of the economy; the latter, by 1776, was already well on the way to an industrialized society, especially where Smith had occasion to observe it, in Glasgow and northern England. The new source of value also served as a convenient theoretical basis for rejecting both physiocracy and mercantilism as viable foundations for *political* action.

The labor theory of value supplied to entrepreneurs and inventors, like Smith's friend James Watt, the perfect justification for their successes and supported fully their claims to absolute rights in property—their machines were not only the fruit of their efforts, they were so in an extended sense, because they had been acquired with savings, with labor spent in value creation that was denied its ultimate fulfillment, consumption.

True, Smith had stated that the landlord and the master took away from the worker the shares of rent and profit, strongly hinting that the actual value creator, the worker, was being robbed of his rightful portion, but this was a minor blemish—in the Smithian world of small businesses the master was also a worker and therefore entitled to the value created by him and with his machines. Competition and the invisible hand guaranteed that nobody would become powerful enough to alter the rules by which the shares of production were distributed.

It needed only an additional scheme showing the distribution of income shares to be determined by natural forces, analogous to gravity, to supply a justification for the existence of profit and rent (even though rent was considered a pure return to monopoly). Ricardo supplied this scheme, showing that wages will tend to a subsistence minimum, not because capitalists withhold part of the workers' production, but because of workers' unfortunate insistence on squandering their excess earnings on having more children, who depress wages by oversupplying the labor market. Even more calamitous, the unchecked rise in population increases the need for food, and thereby supports the landlords' monopoly, siphoning profits into rents over the long run and bringing the economy finally to stagnation.

This was called the *dismal theorem*, but there was one message of hope in it: before total future stagnation would be reached, the intervening period of increasing production would lift living standards for *all* classes, even though the stipulated distribution *between* classes would remain unchanged. In 1848 John Stuart Mill would call the end of progress the *stationary state* and suggest that it would end competitive strife in the marketplace, leaving all classes to lead a more tranquil and happier life. But in this Mill did not reflect the prevailing mood of English producers—

his was the sentiment of a philosopher and bureaucrat, and not of a practical businessman.

Moreover, the model showed, based on Say's Law, that economic progress would be steady before the stationary state was reached, with only occasional, partial market disequilibria, *gluts*, that were merely due to temporary misallocations of resources. On balance, therefore, economic progress was certain as long as the natural working of the economy was not disturbed—the profit incentive of the capitalist was the reliable engine of progress.

A logical flaw remained, however: if labor alone produces value, then the laborer is entitled to the possession of the *entire* product, and the shares of the owner of real capital, and those of the owner of land (profit and rent respectively) were unjustified deductions from the workers' share. The defect was not remedied by the Ricardian postulate that machines were accumulated, embodied, past labor and contributed therefore a share of that labor to the value-creating process—it left open the question whether the labor was that of the owner or of the workers he had employed.

The Ricardian socialists had stated the problem shortly after the publication of Ricardo's *Principles*, and demanded the obvious solution—the entire product belonged to the worker. This clearly called for a change in social organization—the abolition of private property in the means of production. Sismondi refers to Owen and Thompson as representative of that view, strongly disassociating himself from them. Marx, as a trained philosopher and logician, would take up the question and draw the theoretical consequences always present in the labor theory of value and its Ricardian distributive version—private property in the means of production is *always* exploitation, or as Proudhon put it: *Property is theft*.

Except for Sismondi, all of these authors offered a coherent model of society—determinate and appearing to conform to experience at the individual level. They have clear explanations of, or solutions to, an obviously complicated problem—the creation of wealth and the simultaneous existence of inequality and poverty among those who produce the wealth in the first place. Their systems are in the Newtonian mold—just like gravity, the process of production and value creation determines the shape of society like a natural force. Again, John Stuart Mill would state a version of this view in 1848 when he declared that the theory of value was complete, and its only difficulty was to formulate it in such a way as to anticipate its remaining problems.

The rise of natural science, especially its rapid growth from the seventeenth century onward, was always associated with the ability to provide determinate solutions to difficult problems—a better understanding of the natural world was not only a goal in itself, but it led, inevitably, to a better life, to *progress*. The assimilation of political economy to the Newtonian system implied that the new *social science* would do likewise—it would provide the insights that would improve social relations, eliminate injustices by improving everyone's living standard through rising production, or, alternatively, it would show that the existing social system was determined by forces transcending human volition, which, if properly understood, could be harnessed like steam to drive the engine of social progress. Say's Law is the perfect paradigm for this view—there is no hint of social discretion or volition in the statement that production will create its own consumption. At the macroeconomic level, individual discretion disappears in the actions of the market—the mercantilistic and cameralistic concerns with group action and governmental responsibility for a social whole were sublimated in the invisible hand.

There was a minor caveat: the forces of human action are understandable only to the initiated. As Sismondi repeated over and over again, Ricardian analysis had become so abstract that only a few understood his system. The application of Ricardian principles of political economy had to fall to the initiated, for example, McCulloch, who would guide mankind through progress to the stationary state. On the socialist side, only the practitioners of Marxian *scientific socialism,* (Platonian guardians, or socialist priests) would be able to determine from their arcane knowledge of social development just what state of perfection humanity had achieved.

Marx, as an economic autodidact, took his theoretical equipment from Ricardo—he is the last major labor economist before the advent of utility analysis. His system is as Newtonian as Ricardo's. Marx's classes have no discretion to exploit or not—the system is constituted the way it is as a natural consequence of forces that are beyond the reach of individual decision, and the system denies the existence of free will in the economic sphere. It supplies a perfect excuse for economic failure—poverty is not the result of laziness, ineptitude, or any other human, individual shortcoming, but of the faulty organization of society, and, therefore, society had to be changed. This certainly suited Marx—it supplied the perfect explanation for his lifelong inability to provide a living for himself and his numerous family.

It is often said that Marx brought the idea of social change to the social invariance of the Ricardian system. But this view is not supported by fact. As Aftalion has shown in his analysis of Sismondi's work (1970), Marx used Sismondi's ideas on the dynamics of the business cycle, as transmitted by Rodbertus—the major concepts usually associated with the core of Marxian scientific socialism are, as this translation clearly shows, taken from Sismondi, and fitted into the mold of a rigorous ideology—a closed philosophical and political system which has no room for social change.

The Marxian canon is an amalgam of three social viewpoints: the Ricardian labor theory of value, the Hegelian dialectic, and Sismondi's macroeconomic critique of classical political economy. Marx superimposed, by his own admission, a philosophical mechanism, the Hegelian dialectic, acquired directly from the master at the University of Berlin, on the Newtonian model of Ricardo's *Principles*. He then added to it Sismondi's strongly descriptive categories of class, exploitation, and technological displacement, all joined to the Sismondian underconsumptionist dynamics of macroeconomic cycle theory. With a deterministic political-economic model, he gave to the world a utopian vision of a Newtonian millennium, to come once the forces of economic progress had worked their way to their teleological end. A new religion was born, paralleling closely, as Bertrand Russell has shown, the major categories of Christianity, but promising the heavenly city already on this earth. The model, of necessity, also emphasized the classical preoccupation with production (as against consumption)—latter-day supply-siders and Marxians share the deterministic outlook of the mechanistic Ricardian world, which explains why Marxist regimes dote on heavy industry, and modern supply-siders on trickle-down schemes.

Ricardo and Marx are ideological brothers, perhaps more appropriately spiritual father and son—they share not only value theory, but both believe in innate, irresistible natural forces of human behavior. They really only differ in their interpretation of a logical problem in the labor theory of value—and it is quite clear why they differ there: their fundamental and preexisting *political* agenda is concerned with the opposing interests of what are seen as competitive, even hostile, participants in production.

New Principles, then, measured against classical and Marxian writings, fails in this single, but crucial respect: it does not provide a clear-cut, determinate policy prescription buttressed by rigorous deductive analysis. Indeed, it could not, being built on inductive method and historical example. It is *ameliorative* because it is the work of a man whose ideas were as much in transition as the social landscape he observed around him, who had a much less dispassionate view of social change and its accompanying suffering than did Ricardo, and who would have abhorred the equally cold-blooded revolutionary zeal of Marx.

As has been argued much later in the case of Veblen, members of an outside group tend to see their enveloping social landscape in a much more detached way than does the dominant majority, even though they may become members of the majority. Ricardo and Marx, both Jewish by birth, and therefore members of an outside group, left their faith, the former because of a marriage to a Christian, the latter because of the conversion of his father. Both married women outside their station of life, Marx the daughter of a Rhenish aristocrat, Ricardo the daughter of a Quaker. Ricardo broke with his family and eventually became a member of the establishment, but his economic analysis is a detached view of the contemporary scene, abstract not only because as a banker he dealt with abstractions of real production, money, and credit, but probably also as a consequence of his former outsider status. Marx broke, not with his family, but with his whole society. He was for the greater part of his life an exile and poor, the proverbial alienated outsider.

The Marxian canon seems to present an engaged and compassionate view of society, but it only *seems* so, because Marx, unlike Ricardo, the successful banker, and Sismondi, the successful pamphleteer, was never in his lifetime a success at anything he ever tried. Therefore he was resentful, bitter, and frustrated. The permanent outsider looking in on the amenities other people gained from the system hated it for this very reason; his work is the detached view of an implacable enemy of the contemporary scene—the abstractions of Ricardian analysis showed to the Hegelian philosopher that the system was rotten and ready to be discarded. For all the displayed concerns with the miseries of the working class, the worker as an individual is abstracted into living labor, only a shade different from the undifferentiated labor Ricardo sees as the recipient of wages. The Hegelian dialectic of scientific socialism propels the classes to their destiny without much concern for individual choice, free will, or happiness. The old adage that a revolutionary is most likely a person who cares for mankind in general, but is little concerned with individual happiness clearly applies here. The contemporary experience of Marxist-led countries is living testimony to this view.

Sismondi's insistence on individual property holding and the petit-bourgeois concern with dignified self-sufficiency he displays in his discussion of agricultural systems, and then transfers to the industrial realm, represent the opposing view. His concern with individual happiness and social proportion reflect the humanitarian component of Calvinism, enjoined on, and practiced by, the congregations in Geneva as well as in, for example, Calvinistic Amsterdam. From *Tableau* through *Richesse* and his historical works, he strongly identifies with his social environment and his policy prescriptions are based, not only on introspection, but on observation and knowledge of population habits. Indeed, even his prescriptions for limiting marriages among the poor, condemned as reactionary and deleted from the second edition of *New Principles*, are another proof that Sismondi was very much a part of his society—they are the suggestions of a patriarchal landowner who just knows how irresponsible his charges may be in the springtime.

Sismondi, like Keynes, wanted to make the system work by evolutionary changes because he could not conceive of a better alternative to the existing social organization. He failed to command an audience and a following because he saw and described dysfunctions of the new capitalistic systems that were, in the Ricardian analysis, consequences of a natural order. Conveniently and advantageously for property holders, they appeared to be unalterable. The English Industrial Revolution was a force of nature—the wounds it inflicted on the less fortunate could be, perhaps, bound up by charity, but its course was ordained. Ebenezer Scrooge expressed it well: "Are there no prisons . . . And the union workhouses? . . . Are they still in operation? . . . The treadmill and the Poor Law are still in full vigour then?" To argue that social organization is a matter of community convenience and therefore alterable was to deny the *scientific* character of the phenomenon.

The appropriation of Sismondi's analysis of the business cycle by Marx in effect submerged the ameliorative spirit of *New Principles* in another determinate system, opposed in its conclusions to classical political economy, but claiming with even greater authority its scientific mantle.

Sismondi's groping suggestions for a full sharing of production costs through redistributive social arrangements fell squarely between the two chairs of scientific classical theory and scientific socialism. When *New Principles* appeared for the first time in 1819, it did not serve the political agenda of capitalists, nor did it support the revolutionary agenda of the rising socialist movement. More important, perhaps, *because* these suggestions seem so plausible from the perspective of 170 years later, they now can be seen to have been far ahead of their time.

About sixty-five years after the first publication of *New Principles,* the first old-age-insurance scheme was put into operation by a conservative Prussian prime minister. His efforts, and others along the same lines at other times, were denounced by laissez-faire advocates on the propertied Right as pampering of the poor, *and* by revolutionaries of the communist Left as window dressing, yet such schemes are now the standard of enlightened government. So are profit-sharing plans and pension rights. Even unions, those latter-day guilds, have followed the course predicted by Sismondi—they have turned from a protective blessing of the working population into monopolistic bastions of privilege.

New Principles found no English resonance because the dominant economic spirit of nineteenth-century England, and its twentieth-century American successor, was *progress*, incorporated in scientific development and quantifiable material achievement. Economics, the Marshallian successor to political economy, and utility economics, the mathematical version of deductive certainty, plus many of their theoretical descendants, are still dedicated to this idea because it seems to provide certain answers to an uncertain future. Marxism, for its part, has now lost its claim to infallibility, but both offspring of Adam Smith have in the past shrugged off and forgotten, not only the critique of Sismondi, but, equally, the many failures that are part of their predictive record. It would seem that Sismondi's work was forgotten because he offered, not the security of dogmatic certainty and clear-cut solutions, but only the tentative prescriptions of historical analogy and pragmatic experiment.

Notes to Translator's Introduction

1. The biographical details given here follow closely Jean R. De Salis's *Sismondi 1773–1842 La vie et l 'ouevre d' un cosmopolite philosophe,* Slatkine Reprints, Geneve, 1973. The biography profited also greatly from additional details from the article *La place du "Tableau de l'agriculture Toscane" dans l'oeuvre du jeune Sismondi,* by Paul Waeber, Conservateur at the Library of the University of Geneva, published in Musées de Geneve, no. 211, January 1981. During my visit to Geneva in 1987, Mr. Waeber was most helpful in commenting on this translation.
2. David Ricardo, *Principles of Political Economy and Taxation,* ed. E. C. K. Gonner. (London: George Bell, 1895), foreword.

Foreword to the First Edition

This work which I submit today to the judgment of the public, can in many respects be regarded as an extension of the article *Political Economy* which I published in the *Edinburgh Encyclopedia*.[1]

When the editors of that great collection, where so much knowledge joined to lofty sentiments can be found, honored me by asking for an article on that science, I accepted in the belief that I would have to do no more than to expound universally accepted principles, to show the status the theory had attained, and which I believed to be settled. I was truly convinced that nothing further needed to be done in political economy than to spread among statesmen, and the mass of the people, a doctrine on which all theorists, it seemed to me, were in universal agreement. I had done the same in various writings I had published at different times, either on the whole body of political economy, or on several of its branches.[2] I flattered myself that I had expounded Adam Smith's system more clearly, but without adding anything to his ideas, and it did not appear to me that contemporary authors were bolder than I, or were more fortunate therein.[3]

The piece I undertook for the *Encyclopedia* had to be clear and short. An author cannot expect to possess these two attributes unless he follows the train of his ideas, instead of following someone else's. I retraced basic assumptions, I drew conclusions in my way, and I began to build the theory as if nothing had been settled as yet. I did not go back to any book on a subject that for a long time was the object of my thoughts; I walked alone, hardly distinguishing what I found in my memory from what was the consequence of a new analysis. In this way, without having such intent, I remained unconstrained by any settled authority.

It seems to me that by this method I achieved greater accuracy in the presentation of principles I regarded for a long time as settled; but above all, and this impressed me even more, they led me to quite novel conclusions. In the more than fifteen years since I had written about *Commercial Wealth,* I had read very few works on political economy; but I had never ceased to study facts. To me some of these seemed to contradict the principles I had held. Suddenly they seemed to fall into place, to clarify each other, because of the new development I gave to my theory. The more I progressed, the more I became convinced of the importance and the truth of the modifications I brought to the system of Adam Smith. When considered from this new viewpoint all that had heretofore remained obscure in this science, became clear, and my assumptions gave me solutions to difficulties I had never dreamed of before.

I completed my short piece for the *Encyclopedia*; but I limited myself to hint but lightly therein at what appeared to me to be new viewpoints. Works of this kind ought to be repositories to which only those facts and principles are admitted on which there exists universal agreement. It is a great monument erected to science in its present state, and not a scaffold for raising it higher; all controversy would be misplaced, and everything in current vogue would be lost therein.

It seemed to me therefore proper to rework the same article, to bring out what I had merely touched upon, and to establish as firmly as I knew how, those ideas I had advanced with timidity.[4] I was deeply moved by the business crisis Europe had experienced in the last few years; the cruel suffering of the factory workers I witnessed in Italy, Switzerland, and France, and which all public accounts showed to be equally severe in England, Germany, and Belgium. I became convinced that governments and nations were on the wrong track, that they aggravated the distress they were seeking so much to remedy. I had noted with equal sadness the combined efforts of landowners, legislators, and writers, to change cultivation systems which spread so much happiness in the countryside, and to destroy the comfort of the peasants in the hope of increasing the net product.[5] The politicians as well as the writers seemed to me to stray in their quest, sometimes for what could most increase wealth, sometimes for what could most increase population; whereas one or the other, considered by themselves, are only abstractions, and the real problem for statesmen is to find that combination and proportion of population and wealth that would safeguard the greatest happiness to humanity in a given space. It seemed to me that I saw on all sides well-intentioned people who created evil, patriots who ruined their countries, charitable souls who multiplied poverty. Perhaps I shall be accused of conceit for attacking the opinions of so many men whose knowledge and character I hold in such high esteem. But, since we are concerned here with the science of public welfare, an honest man cannot let himself be deterred by any personal considerations.

Everything that was barely outlined in my article in the *Encyclopedia* appears to me here in a bright light, and I pride myself that I will be understood without weariness. Perhaps the most knowledgeable readers will at first believe that they are going over all too familiar ground again since the principles of Adam Smith served as my guides at all times; however, by combining these principles with the new ideas I believe to be needed, these readers will see quite different conclusions emerge. Hence, I beg them not to lay me aside after reading what seems to them a presentation of well-known truths; I beg them again, when they will come to these unexpected conclusions, not to reject them without examination. I have pursued for a long time the road they are on today, and the public has apparently formed an opinion, since I published *Commercial Wealth*, that if I have made no discoveries, at least I have known my way. The motives which made me forsake opinions I had developed with great dedication, appear to me to merit some attention.

I have not had any reservations about including in this work verbatim the greater part of my article in the *Encyclopedia*; it constitutes almost one-third thereof.[6] Every time I believed I had expressed my thoughts clearly, it would have been tedious to seek a new formulation to retell the same things, and they would have doubtlessly lost in precision. Moreover, since that work was only published in English, I would have less the feeling of repeating myself by changing the language.[7] But whereas that little work contained the germ of my ideas on the creation of income, on the manner in which it can limit consumption, and then production; on the development which suits agricultural wealth, on the effects of unlimited competition, on the effects of the progress of machinery, and finally, on the natural limits of population which, it seems to me, Mr. Malthus has misjudged; it is only now that I have dared to give these ideas the development to which they seemed to me to be susceptible, and to have shown the important uses for the science that concerns itself with guarding the happiness of the human species.

J.-C.-L Simonde de Sismondi

Translator's Notes to the Foreword to the First Edition

The first edition of *New Principles* was published in 1819 by Delaunay and Treuttel et Wurtz, in Paris. The work was the result of Sismondi's writing of an exposition of principles of political economy for the *Edinburgh Encyclopedia*, as indicated in the first paragraph, combined with his observations of the effects of the first major European business cycle in 1818–1819 after the end of the Napoleonic period.

1. "Political Economy" was written at the request of the editors. It is unclear why

they chose Sismondi; other, more eminent English writers were available for this task, for example, McCulloch, James Mill, or even Ricardo. However, Sismondi was well known for his *De la richesse commerciale*, published fifteen years earlier, which had had a very favorable reception as a readable and not-too-theoretical popularization of *The Wealth of Nations*. He was therefore seen as well suited to write a generally understandable exposition of what was regarded then, as today, as a difficult subject. There is also some indication that someone in Geneva recommended Sismondi to the editors.

2. Sismondi probably has in mind *Tableau de l'agriculture Toscane* (1801), *De la richesse commerciale* (1803), and one article on Austrian paper currency, written and published in 1810, while traveling with Madame de Staël in Germany. *Tableau* is not strictly a work in political economy, but a type of descriptive economic analysis much in vogue at the time.
3. The reference is to J. B. Say, who published his *Traité* the same year (1803) as Sismondi published *Richesse*. Both works were advertised as popularizations of *The Wealth of Nations*. Say's book became a major theoretical work in political economy, and is noted for the first use of utility reasoning in classical economic analysis. It also contains the famous law of markets, otherwise known as Say's Law, which Sismondi will make his main target in this work.
4. Sismondi is not quite candid here. Already in *Richesse* he had done more than just popularize Smith. There are passages there, as well as in the *Encyclopedia*, that foreshadow the arguments of this work, in particular the view that political economy ought to be concerned with human happiness rather than wealth, and an emphasis on observation as opposed to abstract theorizing. However, Sismondi insists throughout *New Principles* that he is a faithful follower of Adam Smith; the reason seems to be a need to legitimize what he must have seen as a clear departure from established theory. He stresses everywhere that his disagreement is with Ricardo and his followers, not with Smith.
5. The term *net product* should be taken in its physiocratic sense. Sismondi hints here at his Tuscan experience, which was *not* typical of share farming in the rest of Italy, or indeed elsewhere. The third book of *New Principles*, on agriculture, reflects these experiences, and is colored by the romantic view advanced in the *Tableau*. Sismondi, by 1819, had traveled a great deal in France, Italy, and Germany, often as a companion to Madame de Staël. The Industrial Revolution entered the Continent from England mainly through Belgium, and spread into the Rhineland, following the availability of coal for steam production. Sismondi had occasion to fully observe the effects of industrialization in England only after his marriage to Jessie Allen in 1819, when he began visiting his English relatives. The remark also reflects Sismondi's opposition to governmental policies of industrial development, which were greatly spurred by the Napoleonic wars and the Continental Blockade.
6. A comparison of the table of contents of *Political Economy* with those of *New Principles* shows that the chapter headings of the former have become the titles of the seven books in the latter. No exact assessment of the actual proportion has been made for this translation—the ratio varies from chapter to chapter, and in any case the most important material is in the additions. In this translation, passages, sentences, and paragraphs that could be clearly identified as having been directly included in *New Principles* are taken from *Political Economy* and enclosed in brackets. In some cases several paragraphs, or the better part of an entire chapter, may be so identified. The bracketed material follows the British

spelling used by Sismondi, for example labour-defence-endeavour, as well as some of the grammatical peculiarities of his time.

7. Sismondi was fluent in English, which was spoken habitually at his parents' house, French, and Italian.

Foreword to the Second Edition

Seven years have passed since I published the work of which I offer today a second edition. I cannot conceal that it has never found the approval of those who are today properly considered to have made the greatest advancements in the science; I must even attribute to their personal goodwill the delicacy with which they have opposed my book. I am not in the least astonished that I have not made a deeper impression—I cast doubt on principles considered settled—I disturbed a science which, by its simplicity, by the clear and methodical deduction of its laws, appeared as one of the most noble creations of the human mind; finally, I attacked an orthodoxy, a dangerous undertaking in philosophy as well as in religion. At the same time, I had another disadvantage—I separated myself from friends with whom I shared political opinions—I pointed to the dangers of innovations they recommended—I showed that many institutions they had attacked for a long time as evil, had beneficial consequences—and finally, on more than one occasion, I called for the intervention of the state to regulate the progress of wealth, instead of reducing political economy to the simplest, and apparently most liberal motto of *laisser faire et laisser passer*.[1]

I had no reason to complain—I waited since truth is stronger than the spirit of the system. If I had erred, the course of events could not fail to so show—if, on the other hand, I had discovered new principles which, however, in my own eyes, began to attain importance only now, then facts would not wait long to support them, and I could say, with all due respect to the pontiffs of the science, like Galileo: *Eppur si muove!*

Seven years have passed, and it seems to me that the facts have victoriously fought on my side. They have proven, much better than I could have ever done, that the wise men with whom I parted ways have pursued a false prosperity; their theories, where they were put into operation, could well increase material wealth, but they diminished the sum of enjoyments destined for each individual; if these theories tended to make the rich even richer, they also made the poor poorer, more dependent and deprived. Entirely unforeseen crises have followed each other in the business world; industrial progress and opulence have not saved those producers[2] who created this wealth from unheard-of suffering. The facts have neither conformed to common expectations, nor to the predictions of the pundits, and despite the implicit trust the disciples of political economy have in the teachings of their masters, they are now forced to seek elsewhere new explanations for events which diverge so much from laws they have believed settled.

Among these explanations, those which I had given in advance have totally agreed with the events. Perhaps one should ascribe to such coincidence the quick sale of my book, and the demand which has brought me to prepare a new edition. I have done so in England. England has brought forth the most celebrated economists; their science is practiced there even today with redoubled ardor. Government ministers, already well versed in the doctrines of public welfare, have been seen to pursue studies with one of the most qualified professors of political economy; they have been heard to invoke his reasonings in Parliament.[3] Universal competition, or the effort to always produce more, and always at a lower price, has been for a long time the English system, a system I have attacked as dangerous. That system has enabled English industry to make giant strides, but it also has, twice, thrown producers into frightful distress. It is in the face of such economic upheavals that I have seen it as my duty to review my arguments and compare them with the facts.

The study I have made of England has proven to me the validity of my *New Principles*. I have seen in that amazing country, which seems to go through a great trial for the instruction of the rest of the world, production increased while happiness decreased. The greater part of the nation, as well as the philosophers, seems to forget that increased wealth is not the goal of political economy, but the means it has to procure happiness for everyone. I have looked for such happiness among all classes, and I do not know where to find it. The upper English aristocracy has actually achieved a measure of wealth and luxury which surpasses everything one could see in all other nations. Nevertheless, it does not at all enjoy the opulence which it seems to have acquired at the expense of other classes; it lacks security, and in every family privation is felt more keenly than abundance. When I visit houses whose splendor is altogether regal, I hear their owners assert that if the corn monopoly they practice against their fellow citizens is abolished, their fortunes will be destroyed, because their estates, which extend over whole provinces,* will not pay anymore the cost of production. Around these men I see numerous children, unequaled in any other aristocratic class; often one counts ten, twelve, sometimes more, but all the younger sons, and the daughters, are sacrificed to the glory of the eldest son; their share of the inheritance is not even equal to a year's income their brother receives. They must grow old as bachelors, and their dependence, at the end of their lives, is the high price they must pay for the luxury of their early years.

Below this titled and untitled aristocracy I see business occupy a distinguished position; its enterprises embrace the whole world; its agents brave the icy regions of the poles, and the heat of the equator, whilst everyone of its leaders, meeting at the Exchange, can dispose of millions. At the same time, in all the streets of London and of other large English cities, the shops display goods sufficient for the consumption of the entire universe. But has this wealth secured to the English merchant that kind of happiness one would expect? Not at all—in no other country are bankruptcies as frequent. Nowhere are such colossal fortunes, sufficient in themselves to finance a public loan, to support an empire or a republic, destroyed more quickly. Everyone complains that business is scarce, difficult, hardly profitable. Within a span of a few years two terrible crises have ruined part of the bankers and spread desolation among all English manufacturers;[4] at the same time another crisis has ruined the farmers, and its repercussions have been felt in the retail trade. On the other hand, business, despite its immense extent, has ceased to call for the young men who seek a career; all positions are taken, and in the upper, as well as the lower ranks of society most offer their labor in vain, without being able to obtain remuneration.

Finally, has this national opulence, whose material progress strikes every eye, benefited the poor? Not at all! The working classes in England are without comfort now, and without security for the future. There are no more freeholders on the land; they had to yield to day laborers; there are hardly any craftsmen left in the villages, or independent owners of small businesses, but only manufacturers. The factory hand, to use a word the system itself has coined, does not know what it is to have a station in

*[ALL STARRED FOOTNOTES APPEARING ON THE SAME PAGE AS OTHER RELATED TEXT ARE SISMONDI'S OWN FOR THE ENTIRE TRANSLATION—ED.] I have talked elsewhere about the estate of the Countess of Sutherland, which extends over 400,000 hectares. Generally, one can assume that for every thousand pounds sterling income of an English lord he owns two square miles of surface; but in Scotland, in Ireland, and in Wales, the same income presupposes estates that are more than double in extent. The huge increase in landed wealth in recent times is sufficient to explain the decline in the number of proprietors.

life; he only gains wages, and since these wages cannot suffice equally for all seasons, he is almost every year reduced to ask alms from the poor-house.

This opulent nation has found it more economical to sell all the gold and silver she possesses, to give up good coinage, and to accomplish its circulation with paper. She has thus voluntarily deprived herself of the most valuable of all the advantages of specie, price stability. The holders of provincial bank notes risk ruin every day from frequent, sometimes epidemic bank failures, and the entire state is exposed to a convulsion in all fortunes if an invasion, or revolution, should shake the credit of the national bank. The English nation has found it more economical to give up crops which demand much manual labor, and she has discharged half the cultivators who lived on the land; she has found it more economical to replace workers with steam engines, and she has dismissed, then rehired, then dismissed again, the workers in the villages; weavers have yielded to power looms, and now succumb to famine; she has found it more economical to reduce all workers to the lowest possible wages on which they can still subsist, and the workers, being no more than *proletarians,*[5] have no fear of plunging themselves into even greater misery by raising ever larger families. She has found it more economical to feed the Irish with nothing but potatoes, and clothe them in rags, and now every packet boat brings legions of Irish who, working for less than the English, drive them from all employments. What are then the fruits of the immense accumulation of wealth? Has it had any other effect than to make all classes share sorrow, privation, and the specter of total ruin? Has England, by forgetting men over things, sacrificed the end for the means?

The English example is so much more striking because it is a free nation, enlightened, well governed; all her sufferings proceed alone from having followed a false economic guidance. No doubt foreigners are struck in England by the arrogant pretensions of the aristocracy, and the accumulation of wealth in the same hands tends to continually increase it. However, in no other country is the independence of all classes of the nation better secured, and nowhere does the poor man, despite a deference which astonishes us, preserve better in his very soul a sense of his dignity. In no other country does a feeling of confidence in the law, and respect for its authority, pervade more deeply all classes; in no other country is pity more widespread, or the wealthy more eager to come to the aid of the distressed; in no other country is public opinion more powerful, in no country is government more enlightened, more determined to seek the common good, and better equipped to find it. Would then so many means, so many virtues be useless to human societies? Yes, if they have the misfortune to be misdirected! England, more enlightened, freer, more powerful than other nations, has merely come earlier to an end that an error led her to pursue. Her vitality, and the talents of her statesmen will help her, if she has the firm will to do so, to return more easily than any other nation to the right track; but the science[6] has its prejudices, nations have their habits, and even today the English, in their distress, do not take any measures which do not aggravate that distress.[7]

In this book, which I present anew to the public, I have sought to establish that if wealth is to contribute to general happiness, being, as it is, the mark of all material enjoyments of man, its increase must be in proportion to the increase in population, and its distribution among that population must be in a proportion that cannot be disturbed without extreme danger. I intend to show that it is necessary for general happiness that income should increase with capital, that the population should not outrun the income on which it must subsist, that consumption should increase with population, and that reproduction should be proportioned to the capital which produces it as well as to the population which consumes it.[8] At the same time I have shown that each of these relations may be disturbed independently of the others; that income often does not increase proportionately to capital, that population may increase without income being increased, so that a population more numerous, but more miserable, may have a diminished consumption; that reproduction, in short, may be proportional to the capital that spurs it on, and not to the population that demands it; but every time one or the other of these relations is disturbed, there will be suffering for society.

It is on that proportionality that my *New Principles* are founded; it is in the importance that I attach to it that I differ essentially from philosophers, who, in our time, have expounded in such a brilliant manner the economic science of Messrs. Say, Ricardo, Malthus, and McCulloch. They appear to me to have constantly abstracted from obstacles which have impeded the train of thought of their theories, and to have arrived at wrong conclusions because they never separated what was difficult for them to isolate.

All the modern economists have in fact recognized that public wealth, being but the sum of private fortunes, is born, increased, distributed, and destroyed by the same means as the wealth of each individual. They all know perfectly well that in private fortunes the most important item of consideration is income; that consumption and expenditure must be determined by that income, or else capital will be destroyed. But, since in the commonwealth the capital of one becomes the income of the other,[9] these economists have been hard put to decide what was capital, and what was income, and they have found it easier to leave the latter entirely out of their considerations.

By neglecting to define such an essential variable, Messrs. Say and Ricardo have come to the conclusion that consumption was an unlimited power, or at least having no other limits than those of production, whereas it is in fact limited by income. They have declared that whatever wealth is produced, it would always find consumers, and they have encouraged the producers to cause that glut in the markets which today occasions the distress of the civilized world; whereas they should have warned the producers that they could count only on those consumers who disposed of an income. Through the same omission, Mr. Malthus, in pointing out the danger of an unchecked increase in population, gives it no other limit than the quantity of subsistence the earth can produce, a quantity which will be long susceptible of increasing with extreme rapidity;[10] whereas if he had taken into account income, he would soon have seen that it is the disproportion between the working population and their income which causes all their sufferings. Mr. McCulloch, in a little essay intended to enlighten the people on the question of wages, affirms that the wages of the poor are of necessity regulated by the relation of population to capital; whereas wages, being a consequence of labor demanded, must also be in proportion to consumption, which proportions itself to income. In the same pamphlet he exhorts the poor man to tailor the increase of his family to the increase of the nation's capital, a quantity of which he is unable to form even the most confused idea, whereas he might have observed that every man, when marrying and starting a family, is always bound to be guided by his own income, from which it is easy to conclude that it would be sufficient for the nation that all men guide themselves by the income of the whole.

Hence, I republish with greater confidence today my *New Principles of Political Economy*. This somewhat vague title might lead to the supposition that this book is merely a new manual of the basic propositions of the science. I carry my pretensions much farther; I believe that I have placed political economy on a new foundation, be it by the determination of national income, be it by an inquiry into the distribution of that income which extends the most the happiness of the nation, and which therefore best attains the goal of the science.

Other principles, equally new, but of less general application, again flow from the former. I have shown that territorial wealth is so much more productive as the cultivator has a greater share in the ownership of the soil; that the laws intended to preserve to old families their patrimonies caused the ruin of these very families; that the equilibrium between gains of rival industries, on which modern economists have founded their reasonings, has never been attained except by the destruction of fixed capital and the mortality of workmen laboring in a declining industry; that although the invention of machines which increase the powers of man may be a benefit to mankind, the unjust distribution we make of these benefits turn them into a scourge for the poor; that the metallic currency of a nation is, of all its public expenditure, the most useful, of all its luxuries the most reasonable; that the public funds are nothing but an imaginary capital, a mortgage on income which may be born from labor and industry; that the natural limits of population are always respected by men of property, and are always exceeded by men who possess nothing. Therefore, let me not be accused of having wanted to take backward steps in this science; on the contrary, I have carried it forward to new ground. I earnestly entreat that I may be followed there, in the name of the calamities that afflict today such a large number of our brethren, and which the old science neither teaches us to understand, nor to prevent.[11]

The critiques to which the first edition of *New Principles* was subjected have not been lost on me—I have almost totally recast the work. Most often I have sought to clarify what might have been left obscure. By fixing the attention of my readers on England,[12] I wanted to show, in the crisis she is now experiencing, and the cause of our present sufferings, and by the connection that exists among the various industries of the world, the history of our own future, if we continue to act according to the principles she has followed. But I also sometimes show my deference to criticisms that appeared to me to be just, by eliminations or alterations. However, I believe I should protest against the manner, so often superficial, so often false, in which a work on the social sciences is judged in the world. The problem which they offer to resolve is tangled in quite another way than those that arise from the natural sciences; at the same time it appeals to the heart as well as to reason. The observer is called upon to recognize unjust sufferings that come from man, and of which man is the victim. We cannot consider them coldly and pass them over, without seeking some remedy. Sometimes these remedies will shock either the sentiments or the prejudices of the readers; sometimes they are superfluous or inapplicable.[13] Undoubtedly, these are errors, but they are errors of application rather than of political economy. The author or the reader may be mistaken as to application, because all the circumstances on which such application is founded are not met with in the book. Still, the deduction of principles should not be disturbed by some conclusions given over either to controversy, or mocking ill-will. If the principles are true, if they are new, if they are fruitful, they will, in spite of some errors, real or supposed, have advanced social science, the most important among the sciences because it is that of the happines of man.

There is in political economy a polemical side necessarily tied to the present and supported by recent circumstance, which must change to the extent by which circumstances change or develop. Each new edition of a work of this kind must necessarily in some way become a new work; likewise, it is impossible for us to furnish buyers of older editions supplements containing those changes, as it can be done easily, and should be done, for historical works of long standing.

I believed that I should reprint, at the end of this work, so to speak making it a part thereof, two articles which appeared in periodicals, and were destined to deal in more detail with some of the important questions in political economy on which I differ from my predecessors.

J.-C.-L. SIMONDE DE SISMONDI

Translator's Notes to the Foreword to the Second Edition

This foreword, together with other selected writings of Sismondi, was translated and published in 1847 in England by an anonymous friend of Sismondi's wife Jessie, after Sismondi's death in 1842. The occasion for the publication was apparently a gathering of friends of Jessie Allen-Sismondi and her late husband, to honor the ideas of the latter, and the pieces so published are somewhat in the nature of a festschrift. That translation of the foreword is the only translation of any part of the entire *New Principles*. It has not been used here because the underlying text for this early translation was taken from the September 1826 *Revue Encyclopedique*, and not from the actual work, according to a footnote to the translation. While *Nouveaux Principes* have been translated into Russian and German, the apparent failure of the work to shake the dominance of English political economy must be considered responsible for this interesting omission. The ideas of Sismondi entered English political economy only in their more radical transformation of Marxist ideology.

1. The reference here most likely to Sismondi's friends in the earlier circle around Madame de Staël, who were all ardent free-traders and Smithians, and to his English in-Laws and friends, like Josiah Wedgwood, who equally were committed to Smithian and Ricardian free-trade ideas. Geneva, during the Napoleonic period and after, remained a focus of Anglophilia and liberal free-trade ideas.
2. The term *industriels* used here is now translated as 'manufacturer,' but most likely meant factory hand in Sismondi's times. *Producers* has been used here, and elsewhere, as better fitting the context. Since Sismondi was mainly concerned with the well-being of workers, the reference is most likely to them as the creators of material wealth. His attitude, it should be noted, is entirely in conformity with Adam Smith's distinct bias against masters.
3. The reference is probably to Ricardo, but could also be to McCulloch because Ricardo died in 1823, and the statement is not clear as to the circumstances. It is known that Ricardo was consulted by Robert Peel and William Huskisson.
4. Sismondi refers to the two crises of 1818 and 1825. The former must be classified as a primary postwar contraction; the latter was caused by overspeculation in Latin America. It would most likely be classified today as a secondary postwar depression.

5. The first use of this word in this context. Sismondi explains its use in the last book. Marx most likely appropriated it from Sismondi.
6. *Science* stands for classical, "Ricardian" economics.
7. The institutional view Sismondi brought to his work is first indicated here. A part of the analysis in this book is based on the assumption of societal inertia.
8. This paragraph points forward to the business-cycle theories Sismondi will advance in this work. Already, in this very condensed version, it is apparent that he rejects Say's Law, and its implied automatic adjustment in the marketplace, and with it the whole notion of Smith's invisible hand. Malthus advances a similar idea in *Principles,* published after the first edition of *Nouveaux Principes*. Marx accuses Malthus of plagiarizing Sismondi, probably a self-serving claim since Marx cited Sismondi extensively and utilized most of his categories, all the time denouncing him as a petit bourgeois scribbler. There is no question that Sismondi was the first writer to take up business-cycle analysis, and most later writers on the subject were influenced by him.
9. Sismondi had a straight wages-fund model: employers set aside a part of their income as circulating capital, which in turn becomes wage expenditure.
10. Time proved Sismondi right here, although he has not disproven the Malthusian theorem. Both authors would probably be astonished, and appalled, to see the present population of this planet.
11. This paragraph is an almost complete summary of the major points of the work. It also expresses graphically Sismondi's chagrin about the rejection of his ideas by writers like McCulloch. Here and in the next paragraph Sismondi shows the strain of the intellectual struggle that must have accompanied his leaving the established church of Smithian certainties.
12. A good part of the new material that was introduced into the second edition refers to English conditions Sismondi had occasion to observe on his trips to England after his marriage to Jessie Allen. The second post-Napoleonic depression was worldwide and severely affected England, the major manufacturing nation of the time. There are echoes of these conditions in Charles Dickens's *Hard Times*.

    As the next sentence shows, Sismondi was probably also one of the first writers to see clearly the beginning intertwining of national markets into a large global market. Unlike Ricardo, who concentrated on the benefits of a global division of labor, Sismondi in effect shows that a global market is not different from a national market as to saturation of demand; that is, he had already advanced then a fallacy-of-composition argument for international trade.
13. This is a direct reference to the excision of a proposal in the first edition that poor people not be allowed to marry until such time as they have an adequate income, which had drawn heavy criticism.

First Book

Object of Political Economy and Origin of the Science

Introduction

New Principles starts with the heading of chapter 1 of the *Encyclopedia* article, and the first chapter with the second introductory sentence. However, Sismondi defers to the next chapter extensive quotations from the article and inserts here an essentially programmatic statement that will serve as a kind of leitmotif for the rest of the work. Despite repeated assurances throughout the work that he is a faithful disciple of Adam Smith, his divergence from classical political economy becomes immediately apparent in choosing, for the title of the chapter, the term *Science of Government* as a synonym for political economy. By 1819, political economy was mainly seen as the science of wealth creation and only secondarily as concerned with government—undoubtedly a result of the thrust of Smith's argument that government should not interfere in the market. Yet, Sismondi will place great emphasis on governmental regulation of technology and business practices in this work, and is therefore ideologically much closer to Sir James Steuart, the mercantilistic predecessor of Smith, than to Smith.

1

Double Goal of the Science of Government

[The object of government is, or ought to be, the happiness of men united in society. It seeks the means of securing to them the highest degree of felicity compatible with their nature, and at the same time of allowing the greatest possible number of individuals to partake in that felicity.] In none of the political sciences should one lose sight of this double goal of the legislator. He has to care at one and the same time for the degree of happiness that mankind may attain through social organization, and the equitable participation of everyone in that happiness. He has in no way accomplished this task if, in order to assure equal enjoyment of happiness to all, he makes it impossible for outstanding individuals to develop fully, if he permits no one to rise above his peers, and if he does not offer anyone as a model to mankind, and as a guide to discoveries which will benefit everyone. He has not achieved it any better if, having no other goal than the improvement of these gifted individuals, he raises a small number above their fellow citizens at the price of suffering and degradation of all others. That nation is but half-civilized in which no individual suffers, but where no one enjoys sufficient leisure or comforts to feel intensely, or to think deeply, even if that nation should offer to its lower classes an adequate opportunity for happiness. That nation is enslaved where the great mass of people is exposed to constant privation, to painful anxiety about its existence, to anything which will suppress its will, corrupt its morals, stain its character, even though it may count among its upper classes newly successful men who have achieved the highest degree of happiness, whose every ability has been developed, whose every right is guaranteed, whose every enjoyment is assured.[1]

When, on the other hand, the legislator does not lose sight of the development of the few as well as the happiness of everyone, when he succeeds in organizing a society in which individuals can achieve the highest perfection of spirit and soul, as well as the most sensitive enjoyments, but in which at the same time all members are assured to find protection, education, moral development, and physical comforts, then he has fulfilled his task; and without a doubt, this is the noblest task a man may set as his goal on this earth. In pursuing this sublime end the science of government represents the loftiest theory of welfare. It cares for individuals collectively as well as individually. It protects all those whom the imperfections of our institutions have rendered unable to protect themselves, and the inequalities it defends cease to be an injustice because, if it favors some men, it is to prepare in them new benefactors for humanity.[2]

Yet, nothing is more common in all of the political sciences than to lose sight of one or the other aspect of this double goal. On one side the passionate lovers of equality rise against any type of distinction: in evaluating the prosperity of a nation they compare at all times its total wealth, the sum of its rights, its total knowledge, with the share of each, and the gap they find between the powerful and the powerless, the well-to-do and the poor, the idler and the worker, the educated and the ignorant, brings them to the conclusion that the sufferings of the latter are monstrous faults in the social order. If those on the other side, who always look merely in the abstract at the goal of human effort, find guarantees for various rights and means of resistance, as in the republics of classical antiquity, they call that order liberty, even though it is founded on the slavery of the lower classes. If they find an inventive spirit, deep thoughts, an inquiring philosophy, and a brilliant literature, among the distinguished men of the nation, as in France before the Revolution, they see in that social system a high degree of civilization, even though four-fifths of the nation cannot read, and all provinces are immersed in deep ignorance. If they find a tremendous accumulation of riches, an improved agriculture, a prosperous business community, manufactures which multiply without end all products of human industry, and a government that disposes of almost inexhaustible coffers, as in England, they call the nation opulent that has all of these things, without stopping to inquire whether all those who work with their hands, all those who create this wealth, are not reduced to mere subsistence; whether every tenth member among them must not apply each year to the public welfare; and whether three-fifths of all individuals, in a nation that is called rich, are not exposed to more privation than an equal proportion of individuals in a nation called poor.

The association of men in a political body could not take place formerly, and cannot be sustained even today, for any other reason than the common advantage they derive from it. No law can be established among them if it is not founded on that trust which they have reciprocally extended to each other, contributing to the same end. The system continues to exist because the overwhelming majority of those who belong to the body politic see in the system their security; and the government exists only to provide, in the name of all, the common benefit everyone expects of it. Thus, the many benefits, unequally divided in society, are safeguarded by society because from that very inequality flows advantage to all. The means to bring some individuals to the highest possible excellence, the means to turn such individual excellence to the greatest common benefit, the means to save all citizens from suffering, and to prevent that anyone should be hurt by the play of passions and the pursuit of self-interest by his fellow-men, all of these varied objectives make equality a part of the science of government, since all of them are equally necessary in the development of the national happiness.[3]

Translator's Notes to Chapter 1, First Book

1. Sismondi has been called the father of Christian Socialism, mainly because of his ameliorative, humanistic approach to social organization. As this first paragraph of his work makes clear, his view of an ideal social organization is derived from the concepts of Calvinistic, republican Geneva. No radical democrat, he sees a class stratification of society as inevitable, but he also desires no excessive extremes in the distribution of wealth and its concomitant, power. These are the ideals, and practice, of Calvin. The thrust of the argument in this work is consistently in this direction—his most cherished idea of ownership participation by workers, in factories and on the land, is a device to diffuse economic power at the same time that the benefits from growing production are equitably distributed. Already here, Sismondi abandons, perhaps more by implication than openly, the notion of the invisible hand, substituting for it the legislator. Probably because of this attitude, Marx dismisses Sismondi contemptuously as a petit bourgeois, implying a small-minded, small-town rentier, unsuited to an understanding of the new forces of capitalism. As *New Principles* quite clearly shows, nothing could be further from the truth. Sismondi understood the thrust of the developing Industrial Revolution, half a century before Karl Marx, quite well, and indeed supplied the latter with most of his major analytical categories. However, his approach leads to conceptual problems because at every step of his analysis he must weigh incremental benefits against incremental costs without having an analytical tool for doing so. Eventually this inability leads Sismondi to confess at the end of his work that he cannot see how his goals could be implemented. Thus, in the eyes of the radical Marx he was seen as a stand-patter, an ineffective critic of the existing order. However, the problem does not lie in the economic analysis—Sismondi, unlike Marx and his classical contemporaries, was not prepared to accept the inequities of social organization as a consequence of immutable economic laws, which decreed one social organization or the other; he saw them as faults of human perception, which could be corrected by the application of common sense and good will. As Schumpeter points out, Sismondi was not a master of economic analysis; as this

first, programmatic, statement clearly shows, he is first a humanist, and only second a political economist.

2. The reference to the imperfection of our institutions is a reminder that the author was mainly a historian, a describer and analyzer of human interaction. *New Principles* is an institutional work in the sense of *institutionalism* as a method of economic analysis. Sismondi was the first to recognize that the advancing Industrial Revolution changed the ways in which a nation conducted its business and that technology caused economic displacement and destroyed established social categories, an insight that was quintessentially institutionalist. Therefore, to Sismondi, the classical analysis was inadequate—neither Smith's invisible hand, nor Say's Law of Markets could explain the future course of society. And he explicitly rejected the communal solutions of his radical and utopian contemporaries, Owen especially, as even more destructive of an equitable social order.
3. There is undoubtedly a strong taste of utilitarianism in the concluding paragraphs of this chapter, but it is not evident that this was due to the influence of Jeremy Bentham. Given Sismondi's physiocratic views, voiced in the third book on agriculture, as well as his close association with Italy and Italian literature, it is more likely that his models were the Italian forerunners of Bentham, mainly Beccaria. However, it is very likely that Sismondi knew Bentham's work, if only because of his association with the liberal economic establishment in England. Since in the fashion of the times Sismondi did not acknowledge his sources, there is no proof, but we can infer as much because we know that he was a voracious reader.

2

Division of the Science of Government. Public Policy and Political Economy

The science of government is divided into two large branches, in accordance with the means they use to achieve their goal of general happiness. [Man is a complex being; he experiences moral and physical wants; therefore his happiness consists in his moral and physical condition. The moral happiness of man, so far as it depends on his government, is intimately connected with the improvement of that government; it forms the object of civil policy, which ought to diffuse the happy influence of liberty, knowledge, virtue, and hope, over all classes of the community. Civil policy should point out the means of giving to nations a constitution, the liberty of which may elevate the souls of the citizens;[1] an education which may form their hearts to virtue and open their minds to knowledge; a religion which may present to them the hopes of another life, to compensate for the sufferings of this. It should seek not what suits one man or one class of men, but what may impart most happiness by imparting most worth to all the men living under its laws.

The physical well-being of man, so far as it can be produced by his government, is the object of Political Economy. All the physical wants of man, for which he depends on his equals, are satisfied by means of wealth. It is this which commands labour, which purchases respectful service, which procures all that man has accumulated for use and pleasure. By means of it health is preserved, and life maintained; the wants of infancy and old age are supplied; food, and clothing, and shelter, are placed within the reach of all. Wealth may therefore be considered as representing all that men can do for the physical well-being of each other; and the science which shows to the government the true system of administering national wealth is an important branch of the science of national happiness.[2]

Government is instituted for the advantage of all persons subject to it;

hence it ought to keep the advantages of them all perpetually in view. And as in respect of civil policy it should extend to every citizen the benefits of liberty, virtue, and knowledge, so it ought likewise, in respect of political economy, to watch over all the advantages of the national fortune;] it ought to seek the order which will assure to the poor as well as to the rich a share in the comforts, sweetness, and leisure of life; an order which will not leave even one person in the nation in suffering, in uncertainty about the future, unable to procure for himself by his own work food, clothing, and shelter which are necessities to him and his family, so that life may be a joy and not a burden. [Abstractly considered, the end of government is not to accumulate wealth in the state, but to make every citizen participate in those enjoyments of physical life which wealth represents.][3] The repository of power[4] [is called upon to second the work of providence, to augment the mass of felicity on earth, and not to multiply the beings who live under its laws, faster than it can multiply their chances of happiness.

Wealth and population are not, indeed, absolute signs of prosperity to a state; they are only so in relation to each other.[5] Wealth is a blessing when it spreads comfort over all classes; population is an advantage when every man is sure of gaining an honest subsistence by his labour. But a country may be wretched, though some individuals in it are amassing fortunes; and if its population, like that of China, is always superior to its means; if it is contented with living on the refuse of animals; if it is incessantly threatened with famine, this numerous population, far from being an object of envy, is a calamity.

The improvement of social order is generally advantageous to the poor as well as to the rich; and political economy points out the means of preserving this order by correction, but not of overturning it. It was a beneficent decree of Providence, which gave wants and sufferings to human nature, because out of these it has formed the incitements, which are to awaken our activity, and to push us forward to develop our whole being. If we could succeed in excluding pain from the world, we must also exclude virtue; if we could banish want, we must also banish industry.[6] Hence it is not equality of ranks, but happiness in all ranks, which the legislator ought to have in view. It is not from the division of property that he will procure his happiness,] since he would destroy thus the will to work which alone creates all property, and which finds its incentive in that very inequality which labor constantly renews;[7] on the contrary, it is created by always guaranteeing to every labor its reward. [It is by maintaining the activity and hopes of the mind; by securing to the poor man as well as to the rich, a regular subsistence and the sweets of life, in the performance of his task.

The title given by Adam Smith to his immortal work, on the science we are now engaged with, *The Nature and Causes of the Wealth of Nations,* forms at the same time the most precise definition of that science. It presents a much more exact idea than the term political economy, afterwards adopted.] This term, at least, should be understood according to the modern usage of the word *economy* which we have made synonymous with *saving*, and not in its etymological sense of *Rule of the Household.* [In its present sense economy denotes the preservative, administrative, and the management of property; and it is because we use the somewhat tautological phrase *domestic economy* for the management of a private fortune, that we have come to use the phrase *political economy* for the management of the national fortune.]

Translator's Notes to Chapter 2, First Book

This chapter is almost entirely a quote from chapter 1 of the *Encyclopedia* article. As noted, the quoted material is set in brackets here and in all subsequent material and may include several paragraphs, as well as single sentences. Since Sismondi used the English spelling, for example, of *labour,* throughout, the quoted material can be easily identified by this characteristic, because all other material uses the American spelling, for example, *labor*.

A comparison of the French text of this work with the English text of the *Encyclopedia* shows that Sismondi often rendered the English rather freely, trusting more to the sense than producing a precise translation. However, all text included here and later, and marked as coming from the *Encyclopedia,* is clearly identifiable. Where such text could not be reconciled with the French text, a new translation was made.

Chapters 2 to 7 of this book are a loose compilation of economic theory and historical narrative of past economic practices. They show the influence of Adam Smith, and chapter 7 gives a plan of the book similar to the Introduction in *The Wealth of Nations*, in addition to an outline of the Smithian canon.

1. Salis, Sismondi's biographer, relates that Sismondi as a youngster played with neighboring children at governing the republic Con-(Constant) Si-(Simonde) Gal(Gallatin), and that he drew up a constitution for the republic.
2. Sismondi uses national happiness as a synonym for political economy, a notion that may have struck his contemporaries as romantic. While on the surface, his contemporaries, and later economists, may disagree with this notion, the idea that a steady increase of national wealth, distributed by efficient markets, will make everyone better off is a welfare notion not substantially different from the one expressed here.
3. The sentence clearly shows that Sismondi shared Smith's goal of moving away from mercantilism and its avowed goal of enriching the state, as opposed to enriching the individual. But the thrust of the preceding argument also rejects the goal of wealth creation for its own sake, and therefore by implication the argument that increases in wealth, even if concentrated in a few hands, will be shared eventually through market activity.
4. The *Encyclopedia* has "government."

5. This is an important point to Sismondi, hence the subtitle of the work *Of Wealth in Its Relation to Population*.
6. Another instance of Sismondi's Calvinistic spiritual inheritance, although the argument he makes here can also be traced to utilitarian notions.
7. The observation undoubtedly has its origin in Locke's *Second Treatise*, and his argument that property is derived from labor.

3

Management of the National Product, before Its Theory Became an Objective of Scientific Inquiry

[From the time when men first entered into social union, they must have occupied themselves with the common interests originating in their wealth. From the beginning of societies, a portion of the public wealth was set apart to provide for public wants. The levying and management of this national revenue, which no longer pertained to each, became an essential part in the science of statesmen. It is what we call *finance*.

Private fortunes, on the other hand, made the interests of each citizen more complex; being exposed to the attacks of cupidity and fraud, their wealth required to be defended by the public authority, according to the fundamental article of the social contract, which had combined the strength of individuals to protect each with the power of all.[1] The rights over property, the divisions of it, the means of transmitting it, became one of the most important branches of civil jurisprudence, and the application of justice to the distribution of national property, formed the essential function of the legislator.][2]

Need had stimulated industry, and industry had created different kinds of wealth with the help of experience and habit. As men acquired gradually more knowledge, they reflected further on the tasks by which they provided for their wants; they reduced them to a body of knowledge, and they clarified their theory by observations on the general laws of nature.[3] Agriculture had provided for the first needs of mankind long before the development of any science; but during the times when it lavished its treasures on the inhabitants of Greece and Italy, clever men had reduced the means to multiply that part of the national wealth to a body of doctrines.[4] Trades and manufactures were born in the family, but soon industrious men borrowed from scientists, doctors, and mathematicians, the knowledge of many substances, and the means to imitate those that nature produces; of those inanimate forces man can direct, and finally of the arithmetic of dynamics, and the industry of the cities, like that of the farms, had its science. Trade, which compared the needs and wealth of many people and makes the latter profitable to everyone through exchange, had also its own science; it was founded on many-sided knowledge, and it presumed altogether the study of goods, of numbers, of men and laws.

But while every part of public wealth had its own theory, wealth itself had none. The ancients had considered public wealth as a fact whose nature or causes they were never concerned to investigate. They had entirely abandoned it to the individual efforts of those engaged in creating it; and since the legislator was called upon to limit these in some way, he believed again that he needed to attend to individual interests only, and never directed his attention to the financial interests of the entire society.[5] The disciplines which had as their object each of the branches of national wealth did not relate to any common body of knowledge; they were in no way corollaries of a general science; they were isolated treatises, and as such they had contained within themselves their own principles. Thus, in establishing taxes, the collector only considered the greater or lesser resistance he would find among the taxed, the equality of assessment, the certainty of collection, whereas he never examined the influence each kind of tax would have on the increase or decrease of the public wealth. The lawyer concerned himself with care with all the safeguards to property, with all means to perpetuate it in families, with all the dormant rights he sought to preserve in their entirety, or to revive; but he never dreamt, in contriving his mortgages, substitutions, his ingenious distinctions between the real, and the world of credit, of asking himself whether he contributed thus to the increase or decrease of the value of the national wealth, and whether it led to an increase if the interests of those who created it would be divided or abrogated. The cultivator considered the cruel question of slavery only in relation to the master's interest, and not that of the public interest; thus, rural, industrial, and commercial legislation was never based on inquiries into what would produce the greatest increase in public wealth. In the vast body of Roman law, where one finds at every turn so much righteousness, and so much subtle reasoning, and where the motives for the laws are given to us with as much care as their rules, one does not find one sanction which could be based on a principle of political economy, and this lack is perpetuated in our laws to the present day. As to [the philosophers of antiquity] they [were engaged in proving to their disciples that riches are useless for happiness; not in pointing out to government the laws by which the increase of those riches may be favored or retarded.]*

However, the speculative genius of the Greeks had set the goal of attaining all the human sciences.[6] A small number of works of their philosophers relative to economic inquiry have come down to us; it is proper to devote a moment of attention to them, if only to assess when the principles of the production of wealth were unknown to peoples which nevertheless achieved the highest known form of social development, and who accumulated for a numerous population all that could make life easy, all that could develop the human faculties, all that could form the human spirit.

Xenophon, in his *Economics*, after having defined economics as the art of household improvement, and declaring that he understood by household everything we possess, and everything we can turn to our use,** considered economics from the viewpoint of the philosopher rather than the legislator. He insists on the importance of order in the distribution of goods, as well as in the distribution of work; he concerns himself with the molding of the character of the woman who will preside over this domestic order; he continues with the conduct of slaves, and remembering that in educating them they resemble animals more than human beings, he recommends leading them by gentleness, example, and rewards. He then compares the two careers which could lead to fortune, those of the mechanical arts, and those of agriculture: he justifies his contempt for the former, then universal on the grounds that they weaken the body, undermine health, deaden the soul, and debilitate gallantry, all the while painting a charming picture of agriculture, the source of happiness for the families engaged in it, and he shows its close connection with body strength, courage, hospitality, generosity, and all the virtues. The work breathes the spirit of love for the beautiful, of honesty, a sweet philosophy, a sincere and tender piety, which makes most attractive reading, but this is emphatically not the political economy we seek.

Aristotle, in the first book of his *Treatise on the Republic,* has devoted four or five chapters (8 to 13) to the science with which we are concerned; he even gives it a more suitable description than the one we have chosen (*Chrematistics,*[7] *The Science of Wealth*. His definition of wealth, *abundance of produced private and public goods,* is most appropriate.*** The explanation of the invention of money is not any less so. His mind, rich in definitions and distinctions, classifies with great precision the different

*Socrates, in *Xenophont. Oeconom.*, Vol. VI, p. 442.
***Xenophon*, edit. de Gail. in 4°, Vol. VI, p. 486.
***Edit. Paris, fol. Vol. II, p. 304, *de Republica*.

modes of gain, that is, by agriculture, through the mechanical arts, and by interest on capital. Like all ancient thinkers, he gives first preference to agriculture; moreover, he excludes all of *Chrematistics* from pure politics; that is the matter, he says, on which the laws act, and not their objective.

After this judgment, one would expect to find a more precise approach in his two books *On Economics*. But the greatest part of the Greek text has been destroyed, and the work rests on nothing more firm than a Latin translation by Leonardo Aretino. The first book is devoted to persons who comprise the family, the second to goods. The latter begins with a division of the economic administration of kings, satraps, cities, and individuals, which seems to promise interesting observations on public wealth; however, he merely brings together an odd listing of all the expedients used by tyrants, rulers, or free cities to raise money in times of need. The modern invention of the tax collector probably did not exist then, since one does not find one example thereof in the book, but what is strange is that Aristotle, or the pseudonymous author, enumerates them in no particular order, good and bad, to the most violent, to the most extravagant, without criticism, or even indicating their dangers.

Finally, Plato, in the second book of *The Republic,* in trying to trace the origins of the city, or of human society, develops his economic system with a clarity and precision which could not be surpassed by a disciple of Adam Smith. According to Plato, the common interest brings people together and forces them to pool their efforts. He shows how this single principle must lead to the division of labor,[8] how everyone makes better what he produces alone, and how everyone thus produces more. Trade is to him a consequence of the progress of manufacturing and agriculture; the main encouragement he demands for trade is liberty. From this active and enterprising trade he distinguishes the sedentary routine of the small shopkeeper who contents himself with retailing the goods the merchant collects. Alone to the progress of society he attributes the opulence of some of its members who have chosen leisure, pleasure, or study, precisely because the others work. The unequal distribution of wealth, the corruption of health and justice, and the conflicting needs of rival cities leads him finally to the conclusion that there should be guardians, supported by the rest of the people through their work.*

It is not without some astonishment that one sees the philosopher who, in his republic, establishes communal rights to goods and women, at least for his guardians, analyze with so much accuracy the origins of pecuniary concerns and the formation of society. The ancients sometimes let themselves be carried away by the liveliness of their imagination, and they were

***Divi Platonis de Rep.*, lib. II, p. 369, et.seq., edit. fol. 1578, Henrici Stephani.

much inclined to substitute speculative theories for the lessons of experience they lacked. But at least they never lost from view that wealth had value only as long as it contributed to national happiness, and precisely because they never considered it only in the abstract, their point of view is sometimes more correct than ours.

The Romans have left us some books on rural economy, but nothing on the science with which we are concerned.

Besides, self-interest does not wait for philosophers to outline to it a theory of wealth before seeking it; and the ruins of the ancient civilizations of the Greeks and Romans which we see still standing, bear witness that the wealth of nations can be brought almost to the highest state without the science having been practiced which teaches how to hasten its development.

Translator's Notes to Chapter 3, First Book

Most chapters in this book, reviewing historically the development and current state of political economy, are taken from the *Encyclopedia*. However, there Sismondi devoted only a half paragraph to ancient thought, with mostly negative comments. In rewriting, he must have felt that he had unduly slighted the ancients; he expanded the material so that most of this chapter is indeed new.

The historical review of prior doctrine was of course an acknowledgment of Smith, but also both a legitimizing device and the preliminary establishment of the author's theoretical position. It is noteworthy that Marx, prior to and while writing *Das Kapital,* engaged in a similar exercise. He wrote a massive survey and criticism of prior theories, collected and published as *Theorien über den Mehrwert*, essentially the fourth volume of the main work. Curiously enough, Sismondi, the most frequently cited author in *Das Kapital*, is *not* mentioned separately in *Theorien*.

1. Sismondi echoes here the great debate of the eighteenth century, and of course the ideas of his fellow Genevese J. J. Rousseau. However, Sismondi takes the position that the right to property, especially real property, exists only as a grant of convenience and usefulness from society, a trust which, if violated in any way, can be rescinded. This is a fundamentally different conception than the one underlying Ricardo's differential rent theory and undoubtedly reflects the differences in real estate law on the Continent after the French Revolution, as compared to England.
2. It should be kept in mind that economics at French universities is a subdivision of jurisprudence. A degree in political economy is a law degree.
3. This should be compared with Adam Smith's postulate of the division of labor. Sismondi does not posit a natural law tendency based on a human propensity to *barter, truck, and exchange,* but a historical process that clearly took a long time to attain its present development. The difference is fundamental to *New Principles*—Sismondi from the very first rejects, consciously and subconsciously, the Newtonian mold of political economy. Already here a clear argument is made that human actions are not fully predictable and are chained in time, thus negating some of the most cherished assumptions of classical analysis.

4. The choice of the word *doctrine* is Sismondi's. He uses it deliberately to distinguish these ideas from what he considers the scientific approach of political economy proper.
5. A clear echo of Adam Smith, but it also points in the direction of Sismondi's belief that there exists a difference between the sum of all individual interests and the interest of the whole.
6. Here the text is ambiguous: the term *les sciences humaines* can also be translated as the 'social sciences.'
7. The term appears also in Greek spelling.
8. Sismondi uses the term *division des métiers*.

4

A First Revolution in Political Economy, Brought About by the Ministers of Charles V in the Sixteenth Century

If the Romans and Greeks, standing at the summit of civilization, had never dreamt that political economy could be a scientific discipline, they who had applied their inventive intelligence to such a great variety of subjects, who sought to understand the causes of everything they observed and who, enjoying great liberty, made use of it for the study of governmental science, and had carried it in many different ways to great perfection, then one should not expect that this science would be born in the Middle Ages, since exploration away from the road the ancients had delineated was scarcely permitted, and the power to spread ideas seemed to have left mankind. Indeed, it is during a time quite close to our own that [the attention of thinking men was at length directed to national wealth by the requisitions of the state, and the poverty of the people.

An important change which occurred in the general politics of Europe, during the sixteenth century, almost everywhere overturned public liberty; oppressed the smaller states; destroyed the privileges of the towns and provinces, and conferred the right to dispose of national fortunes on a small number of sovereigns, absolutely unacquainted with the industry by which wealth is accumulated or preserved. Before the reign of Charles V, one half of Europe, lying under the feudal system, had no liberty or knowledge, and no finance. But the other half, which had already reached a high degree of prosperity, which was daily increasing its agricultural riches, its manufactories, and its trade, was governed by men who, in private life, had attended to the study of economy, who, in acquiring their own property, had learned what is suitable in that of states; and who, governing free communities to which they were responsible, guided their administrations, not according to their own ambition, but according to the interest of all. Till the fifteenth century wealth and credit were no where to be found but in the republics of Italy, and of the Hanseatic league; the imperial towns of Germany; the free towns of Belgium and Spain, and perhaps also in some towns of France and England, which happened to enjoy great municipal privileges. The magistrates of all those towns were men constantly brought up in business, and without having brought political economy to the form of a science, they had yet the feeling as well as the experience of what would serve or injure the interests of their fellow citizens.[1]

The dreadful wars which began with the sixteenth century, and altogether overturned the balance of Europe, transferred a nearly absolute monarchy to three or four all-powerful monarchs, who shared among them the government of the civilized world.[2] Charles V united, under his dominion, all the countries which had hitherto been celebrated for their industry and wealth—Spain, nearly all Italy, Flanders, and Germany; but he united after having ruined them; and his administration, by suppressing all their privileges, prevented the recovery of former opulence.

The most absolute kings can no more govern by themselves, than kings whose authority is limited by laws. The former transmit their power to ministers whom they themselves select, in place of taking such as would be nominated by the popular confidence. But they find them among a class of persons different from that in which free governments find them. In the eyes of an absolute king, the first quality of a statesman is his being in possession of a rank so high that he may have lived in noble indolence, or at least in absolute ignorance of domestic economy. The ministers of Charles V, whatever talents they showed for negotiation and intrigue, were all equally ignorant of pecuniary affairs. They ruined the public finances, agriculture, trade, and every kind of industry from one end] of the immense Austrian monarchy [to the other; they made the people feel the difference, which might indeed have been anticipated, between their ignorance, and the practical knowledge of republican magistrates.

Charles V, his rival Francis I, and Henry VIII, who wished to hold the balance between them, had engaged in expenses beyond their incomes; the ambition of their successors, and the obstinacy of the house of Austria, which continued to maintain a destructive system of warfare during more than a hundred years, caused those expenses, in spite of the public poverty, to go on increasing. But as the suffering became more general, the friends of humanity felt more deeply the obligation laid on them to undertake the defence[3] of the poor. By an order of sequence opposite to the natural progress of ideas, the science of political economy sprang from that of finance.

Philosophers wished to shield the people from the spoliations[4] of absolute power. They felt that, to obtain a hearing from kings, they must speak to them of royal interests, not of justice or duty.[5] They investigated the nature and causes of national wealth, to show governments how it might be shared without being destroyed.]

Translator's Notes to Chapter 4, First Book

This chapter is almost entirely taken from the *Encyclopedia* article. Its general tone is strongly influenced by Sismondi's Genevese republicanism and, most likely as a consequence of this viewpoint, by his historical studies of the Italian republics in the Middle Ages. Sismondi deplores the passing of the independent city-state before the rise of national empires and royal absolutism, in particular the overwhelming power of the Hapsburg dominions.

1. The narrative is clearly inspired by a romantic view of life in the city-republics of the Middle Ages. Sismondi's *History of the Italian Republics* is a detailed description of the political struggles of the towns against the Holy Roman Empire and the pope, but it gives scant attention to the conditions of the lower classes in those city-republics. They often lived in squalid conditions, hardly sharing in the immense wealth accumulated by the merchants. The repeated uprisings of the *ciompi* ('wool workers') in Florence attests to the underlying discontent, which was not confined to Florence. On the other hand, even the workers in towns were much better off than the serfs in the countryside. "City air makes free" was a saying that indicated where the common people believed the better life was to be found.
2. Sismondi obviously has a European viewpoint and ignored the vast civilizations of the East. However, references to China and India in *New Principles* indicate that by his time they were seen as decayed and semi-barbaric.
3. As with *labour,* Sismondi uses the English spelling: defence. See note 6, Foreword, First Edition.
4. The reprint text of the *Encyclopedia* article has here *speculation;* the original French text, in both editions, has *spoliation*. Since the French term fits the sense, and the English does not, it must be assumed that a misprint occurred in the *Encyclopedia*.
5. This wording is a paraphrase of Adam Smith's "We adress ourselves, not to their humanity, but to their self-love, and never talk to them of our own necessities but of their advantages." Sismondi refers to the writings of the cameralists and mercantilists, while Smith of course refers to the operation of the free market, but the similarity is not accidental. Belief in self-interest as a main driving force of human behavior is common to mercantilism, physiocracy, the forerunner of classical economics, and classical political economy. However, mercantilists and cameralists believed that self-interest had to be limited by governmental intervention, while Smith postulated the invisible hand as a limiting factor of self-interest. Sismondi tried to steer a middle course between these two extremes in *New Principles*.

5

The Mercantile System

During the sixteenth and seventeenth century [too little liberty existed in Europe to allow] the first philosophers [who occupied themselves with political economy to present their speculations to the world; and finances were enveloped in too profound a secrecy to admit of men, not engaged in public business, knowing facts enough to form the basis of general rules. Hence the study of political economy began with ministers, when once it had fortunately happened that kings put men at the head of their finances who combined talents with justice and love of the public weal.

Two great French ministers, Sully under Henry IV, and Colbert under Louis XIV, were the first who threw any light on a subject till then regarded as a secret of state in which mystery had engendered and concealed the greatest absurdities. Yet, in spite of all their genius and authority, it was a task beyond their power to introduce anything like order, precision, or uniformity into this branch of government. Both of them, however, not only repressed the frightful spoliations of the revenue farmers,[1] and by their protection communicated some degree of security to private fortunes; but likewise dimly perceived the true sources of national prosperity, and busied themselves with efforts to make them flow more abundantly. Sully gave his chief protection to agriculture. He used to say that *pasturage and husbandry were the two breasts of the state*. Colbert, descended] as far as is known [from a family engaged in the cloth trade], an origin which the vanity of the court of Louis XIV obliged him to hide, [studied above all to encourage manufactures and commerce. He furnished himself with the opinion of merchants, and asked their advice on all emergencies.[2] Both statesmen opened roads and canals to facilitate the exchange of commodities;[3] both protected the spirit of enterprise and honoured the industrious activity which diffused plenty over their country.

Colbert, the latter of the two, was greatly prior to any of the writers who have treated political economy as a science, and reduced it to a body of doctrines. He had a system, however, in regard to national wealth; he required one to give uniformity to his plans, and delineate clearly before his view the object he wished to attain. His system was probably suggested by the merchants whom he consulted. It is now generally known by the epithet *mercantile,* sometimes also by the name of *Colbertism.* Not that Colbert was its author, or unfolded it in any publication; but because he was beyond comparison the most illustrious of its professors because, notwithstanding the errors of his theory, the applications he deduced from it were highly advantageous; and because, among the numerous writers who have maintained the same opinion, there is not one who has shown enough of talent even to fix his name in the reader's memory.*

It is but just however, to separate the mercantile system altogether from the name of Colbert. It was a system invented by trading subjects, not by citizens,] who were kept away from public business while asked for advice, and who were forced to know only their own interests while they had to judge that of others. [It was a system adopted by all the ministers of absolute governments when they happened to take the trouble of thinking on finance, and Colbert had no other share in the matter than that of having followed it without reforming it.

After long treating commerce with haughty contempt, governments had at length discovered in it one of the most abundant sources of national wealth. All the great fortunes in their states did not indeed belong exclusively to merchants; but when, overtaken by sudden necessity, they wished to levy large sums at once, merchants alone could supply them. Proprietors of land might possess immense revenues, manufacturers might cause immense labours to be executed; but neither of them could dispose of any more than their income or annual produce. In a case of need merchants alone offered their whole fortune to the government. As their capital was entirely represented by commodities already prepared for consumption, by merchandise destined for the immediate use of the market to which it had been carried, they could sell it at an hour's warning, and realise the required sum with smaller loss than any other class of citizens. Merchants therefore found means to make themselves be listened to, because they had in some sort the command of all the money in the state, and were at the same time nearly independent of authority—being

*The mercantile system can be seen developed in various works of Charles Davenant, 1699, 1700; in Melon, *Essai sur le Commerce*, 1734; in James Steuart, *Inquiry into the Principles of Political Oeconomy*, 4 vol. Lond. 1763; and in Anton. Genovesi, *Lezzioni di Commercio ossia d'Economia civile*, Milano, 2 vol. 1768.

able, in general, to hide from the attacks of despotism a property of unknown amount, and transport it, with their persons, to a foreign country, at a moment's notice.

Governments would gladly have increased the merchant's profit, on condition of obtaining a share of it. Imagining that nothing more was necessary than to second each other's views, they offered him force to support industry; and since the advantage of the merchant consists in selling dear and buying cheap, they thought it would be an effectual protection to commerce, if the means were afforded of selling still dearer and buying still cheaper. The merchants whom they consulted eagerly grasped at this proposal; and thus was founded the mercantile system. Antonio de Leyva, Fernando de Gonzaga, and the Duke of Alva, viceroys of Charles V and his descendants—the rapacious inventors of so many monopolies—had no other notion of political economy. But when it was attempted to reduce this methodical robbery of consumers into a system; when deliberative assemblies were occupied with it; when Colbert consulted corporations; and when the people at last began to perceive the true state of the case, it became necessary to find out a more honourable basis for such transactions; it became necessary not only to study the advantage of financiers and merchants, but also that of the nation: for the calculations of self-interest cannot show themselves in open day, and the first benefit of publicity is to impose silence on base sentiments.[4]

Under these circumstances the mercantile system was moulded into a plausible form; and doubtless it must have been plausible, since, even till our own times, it continued to seduce the greater part of practical men employed in trade and finance.[5] Wealth, said those earliest economists, is money; the two words were received into universal use as almost entirely synonymous; no one dreamed of questioning the identity of money and wealth. Money, they said, disposes of men's labour and all its fruits. It is money which produces those fruits] because it offers to pay for them; [it is by means of money that industry continues in a nation; to its influence each individual owes his subsistence and the continuation of his life. Money is especially necessary in the relation of one state to another. It supports war and forms the strength of armies. The nation which has it, rules over that which has it not.[6] The whole science of political economy ought, therefore, to have for its highest object the increase of money in a nation. But the money possessed by a nation cannot be augmented in quantity,] except that it be extracted anew from the earth, or that it is imported from the outside.[7] Therefore, silver mines must be worked with zeal, if the nation has any, or it must try to supply itself by foreign trade with what other nations have extracted from their mines.[8]

Indeed, add the authors of this system, [all the exchanges carried on within a country, all the purchases and sales which take place among Englishmen, for instance, do not increase the specie contained within the shores of England by a single penny. Hence,] all profits which are realized by domestic trade or industry are illusory. Individuals gain indeed, but at the expense of others who lose; and what the one gains, the other has lost, and the nation has, after all these exchanges, precisely the same number of pounds as before, it is neither richer or poorer; what was the industry of some, was the laziness or prodigality of others.

But foreign trade has entirely different results; because all its transactions are effected in specie, its natural result is the import or export of specie to or from the nation. In order that the nation become richer, that it add to the number of its pounds,[9] it ought to regulate its foreign trade in such a way that it sells much to other nations, and that it buy little from them. Pushing this system to its logical conclusion, one would have to say that a nation ought to always sell and never buy; but since it is well known that such a prohibition to buy would destroy all trade, the authors of this theory have contended themselves with the demand that a nation make no other exchanges than those which would have the final result of a payment in specie; for, they say, [in the same way as each merchant in settling with his correspondent, sees at the year's end whether he has sold more than he has bought, and finds himself accordingly creditor or debtor by a balance account which must be paid in money; so likewise a nation, by summing up all its purchases and all its sales with each nation, or with all together, would find itself every year creditor or debtor by a commercial balance which must be paid in money. If the country pay this balance, it will constantly grow poorer; if it receive the balance, it will constantly grow richer.][10]

The necessary consequence of this system was to confer, through the government, a constant preference to export trade; to ask it at the same time to constantly look after industry, so that it would take the one direction that would make it profitable to the state without being more so to individuals. It was understood that the merchant who profited from domestic trade did not make his country wealthier, that he ruined it by forcing it to buy foreign goods, and that, should he to the contrary ruin himself by selling domestic goods to foreigners, he profited the nation by bringing in specie. Everyone was therefore subjected to regulation to take the place of private interest which, it was believed, one could not trust; industry was regimented to force it to export constantly, and the borders were watched by guards to prevent imports, or to impound specie, if one wanted to carry it out.

The authors of the system had also told the government that in order to draw much specie from foreigners, it was important to sell to them, not the raw materials of the country, but those goods national industry had raised in value; that the manufactures of the cities had doubled and often increased tenfold the price of rural products; that it was therefore needful to encourage manufactures; and that the authorities must intervene in order to prevent that a raw material, which could receive a higher value through national industry, from going to foreigners in its unworked state, because it was worth but little in specie. Hence, the regulations born from the mercantile system took on a second character; they prohibited the export of raw materials, and encouraged that of manufactures and, entirely preoccupied with the profits of export merchants, they used every device to give to them the opportunity to buy cheaply and to sell dearly, even though that should result in a clear loss to the other classes of the nation.[11]

Today the mercantile system is not advocated openly by any writer, but it has left deep marks in the mind of all those who are concerned with government. It still influences by force of prejudice, and by confusion of language, those who shy away from abstract theories. The majority of all regulations to which people are subjected, even today, are only applications of this system, and the balance of trade exists only for those who espouse it, although many still persist in calculating it. There is no more important task than to inquire into the origins of universally accepted ideas, and to show to those who believe that they uphold a principle, that it is no more than the consequence of another opinion that has not yet been examined.

Translator's Notes to Chapter 5, First Book

Most of this chapter is also taken from the *Encyclopedia,* and its general tenor reflects Adam Smith's opinions of the business-interest-driven governmental regulatory system to which he had given the name *Mercantilism*. However, it should be noted that Sismondi refers to French and Spanish instances of such practices, and only incidentally to English writers, reflecting his greater familiarity with Continental history.

1. Up to the French Revolution, France was divided into so-called *fermes*, tax districts in which the crown sold to the highest bidder the right to collect taxes from the population. The tax farmer, usually a wealthy financier, was at liberty to devise any taxes that would reimburse him (with a profit, of course) for the payment made into the royal coffers. The taxes were collected with the help of royal soldiers. Abuses were endemic, and the system is considered to have been a major contributor to the impoverished condition of France, which eventually led to the Revolution.
2. The French sentence reads here: "Il s'entoura des conseils des negociants, et il sollicita de partout leurs avis." The discrepancy between the English text of the *Encyclopedia* and the French text of *Nouveaux Principes* was considered to be small enough to justify the use of the former.
3. Here the French text reads "les divers genres de richesses."

4. This paragraph is in many ways remarkable. First, to blame the ministers of Charles V for inventing mercantilistic practices is unfair and historically inaccurate. The cited practices were commonly employed by all European governments, including the nonabsolutist English. The only major exception were the United Provinces of the Low Countries, which were free-traders because they dominated European trade. Sismondi seems to have had in mind the gold monopoly that assured to the Spanish crown the entire benefits of the gold shipments from the Spanish colonies in the New World. Second, the sentiment in the last sentence on the benefits of publicity is firmly in the Smithian tradition. It should not be forgotten that the *Encyclopedia* article was addressed to the educated English public, many of them business people and generally in agreement with the idea that royal expenditure should be controlled by Parliament.
5. The sentence recalls vividly the famous dictum of Keynes: "the ideas of economists and political philosophers, both when they are right and when they are wrong, are more powerful than is commonly understood, indeed the world is ruled by little else. Practical men, who believe themselves to be quite exempt from any intellectual influences, are actually the slaves of some defunct economist." Considering that we see the world ruled by capitalism à la Smith, Keynesian mixed economy, and Marxism, the sentiment seems to have some validity. It is a fact that mercantilistic practices are even now seen as advantageous to a country, despite all the theoretical arguments advanced by believers in classical free trade.
6. This sentence reads in French: "le peuple qui en a, commande celui qui n'en a pas."
7. The sentence indicates clearly that Sismondi is a determined specie-in-circulation supporter. As he will make abundantly clear in the fifth book, "Of Money," he condemned paper currency as leading to inflation.
8. It should be noted that Sismondi refers exclusively to *silver mines*. The monetary standard of the Latin Monetary Union was the French *silver* five-franc piece, and until 1871 most countries, with the notable exception of England, were on silver standards, or practiced bimetallism.
9. Sismondi uses the French term *écu;* in the translation, pounds and shillings will be substituted for French monetary units in examples where the sense is not affected.
10. As the case of present-day Japan shows conclusively, free trade cannot compete against determined mercantilistic trade policies intended to maximize the return to a nation. It is remarkable that the free-trade doctrine has retained the status of an unassailable truth, when in fact it is true only under special *political* and theoretical assumptions. In a free-trading world, a mercantilistic competitor can take advantage of the system by violating it; in the same way a cartel member can take advantage of the cartel by violating its rules.
11. Sismondi is the first writer to use the term *classes* in a consistent manner to identify group interests, a usage that is always attributed to Marx.

6

The Agricultural System, or of the Economists

[For a century, the mercantile system was universally adopted by cabinets;[1] universally favoured by traders and chambers of commerce; universally expounded by writers, as if it had been proved by the most unexceptionable demonstration, no one deeming it worth while to establish it by new proofs; when after the middle of the eighteenth century, Quesnay[2] opposed to it his *Tableau Economique*, afterwards expounded by Mirabeau and the Abbé de Riviere, enlarged by Dupont de Nemours,] analyzed by Turgot, [and adopted by a numerous sect which arose in France, under the name of Economists. In Italy too this sect gained some distinguished[3] partisans. Its followers have written more about the science[4] than those of any other sect, yet they admitted Quesnay's principles with such blind confidence, and maintained them with such implicit fidelity, that one is at a loss to discover any difference of principle, or any progress of ideas in their several productions.*[5]

Thus Quesnay founded a second system in political economy, still named the *territorial system*,[6] or more precisely the system of the economists.[7]] He sought above all to determine what constituted wealth, since gold and silver appeared to him to be only a token, only a means of exchange among men, and merely the price of all commodities; their mere abundance did not appear to him in any way to constitute the prosperity of a nation. Therefore, he focused his attention on the different classes of men in whose hands wealth can be seen accumulating. He sought among them those men to whom he could attribute a creative power, the men with whom he would see wealth originate, to be then transmitted to others.

**Tableau économique et Maximes générales du gouvernement économique*, par François Quesnay, Versailles 1758.—*L'ami des hommes*, par Mirabeau, Paris 1759.—*L'ordre naturel et essentiel des sociétés politiques*, par Mercier de la Rivière, 1767.—*Physiocratie*, par Dupont de Nemours, Paris, 1768.

The first ones he looked at appeared to him only to be occupied with exchanges, who circulated wealth, but who did not create it.

[The merchant who carries the productions of both hemispheres from one continent to the other, and on returning to the ports of his own country, obtains, at the sale of his cargo, a sum double of that with which he began his voyage, does not, after all, appear, in the eyes of Quesnay,[8] to have performed any thing but an exchange. If, in the colonies, he has sold the manufactures[9] of Europe, at a higher price than they cost him, the reason is, they were in fact worth more. Together with their prime cost he must also be reimbursed for the value of his time, his cares, his subsistence, and of that of his sailors and agents during the voyage. He has a like reimbursement to claim on the cotton or sugar which he brings back to Europe. If, at the end of his voyage, any profit remains, it is the fruit of his economy and good management. The wages allowed him by consumers, for the trouble he has undergone, are greater than the sum he had expended. It is the nature of wages however, to be entirely expended by him who earns them; and had this merchant done so, he would have added nothing to the national wealth, by the labour of his whole life; because the produce which he brings back does nothing more than exactly replace the value of the produce given for it, added to his own wages, and the wages of all that were engaged with him in the business.

Agreeably to this reasoning, the French philosopher gave to transport trade the name of economical trade,[10] which it still retains. This species of commerce, he asserts, is not destined to provide for the wants of the nation that engages in it, but merely to serve the convenience of two foreign nations. The carrying nation acquires from it no other profit than wages, and cannot grow rich except by the saving which economy enables it to make on them.

Quesnay,[11] next adverting to manufactures, considers them an exchange, just the same as commerce; but instead of having in view two present values, their primitive contract is, in his opinion, an exchange of the present against the future.] According to him, the goods produced by the artisan were only the equivalent of his accumulated wages. While he worked he had consumed the fruits of the soil in order to live; another product of the earth was the object of his work. The weaver must recover in the price of the cloth taken from his loom, first, the price of the linen or hemp from which it was made, then the price of the wheat and the meat he had consumed while he was spinning and weaving it. The work produced by him represented nothing but these different economic values.

[The economist[12] next directs his attention to agriculture. The labourer appears to him to be in the same condition as the merchant and the artisan. Like the latter, he makes with the earth an exchange of the present against the future. The crops produced by him represent the accumulated value of his labour; they pay his hire, to which he has the same right as the artisan,][13] and the merchant, since, in the same way, it is compensation for all the fruits of the earth he has consumed while making them come forth anew. [But when his hire has been deducted, there remains a net revenue, which was not to be found in manufactures and commerce; it is what the labourer pays to the proprietor for the use of his land.]

This income of the landowners seemed to Quesnay to be of an entirely different nature from all the others. These were not at all *reprises* after the expression he had adopted to designate the recovery of the advances made to the workers; this was not at all a wage, this was not at all the result of an exchange, but the price of earth's spontaneous labor, the fruit of the benevolence of nature; [and since it alone does not represent pre-existent wealth, it alone must be the source of every kind of wealth. Tracing the value of all other commodities, under all its transformations, Quesnay still discovers its first origin in the fruits of the earth. The labours of the husbandman, of the artisan, of the merchant, consume those fruits in the shape of wages, and produce them under new forms. The proprietor alone receives them at their source from the hands of nature herself, and by means of them is enabled to pay the wages of all his countrymen, who labour only for him.

This ingenious system] inverted, by its fundamental assumptions, that of the mercantilists. [The economists denied the existence of that commercial balance to which their antagonists attached so much importance.] They believed it to be impossible to attract from abroad, into one country, an uninterrupted stream of specie; and could they have succeeded at it, they saw no profit in it; finally, they denied to artisans and merchants, the favorites of the mercantile system, the ability to produce anything; thus dividing the nation into three major classes; [they could see only proprietors of land, the sole dispensers of the national fortune; productive workmen, or labourers producing the revenue of the former; and a hired class, in which they ranked merchants also], and artisans, as well as all the officials of the state, intended to maintain law and order therein.

[The plans, which these two sects recommended to governments,[14] differed not less than their principles. While the mercantilists wished authority to interfere in every thing, the economists incessantly repeated *laissez faire et laissez passer,* for as the public interest consists in the union of all individual interests, individual interest will guide each man more surely to the public interest than any government can do.][15]

In politics, the economists, seeing the landlords as the hosts who received the entire nation in their anterooms, the dispensers of all wealth, and the masters of the subsistence of all their fellow citizens, also saw them as the sole sovereign of the state. Their principles led them to the establishment of an absolute aristocracy, although they would have to accommodate to the monarchical government under which they were born. The duties they imposed on the landed owners and public authority were the same, and the use of public authority was to rest in the hands of such owners.

In finance,[16] the economists, confounding all revenues with that which the earth gives annually to its owners, did not doubt at all that all taxes, under whatever form collected, had to be paid in the last analysis from that revenue; hence they considered that the exchequer ought to ask for a single tax from him, who, in the last instance, always had to pay it, that this tax always ought to be levied on the revenue of the land, and that any other manner of collecting it would have the result of costing much more to the same landlord who reimbursed it, and to irritate unnecessarily all those who advanced it.

In administration, the economists asserted that the art of government should tend to guarantee to the subjects of the first class, that is, the landed proprietors, the entire command over the land, and the peaceful enjoyment of its fruits; to the second class, that is, the cultivators,[17] their wages and repayment of their annual outlays; to the third class, that is, the subordinate class which comprises manufacturers, merchants, those who engage in the fine arts, and those who engage in trades and professions, all the rights which they expressed by the three words *liberty, immunity,* and *competition*.[18]

In foreign trade, the economists asserted the principle that no export of any production or any domestic merchandise should ever be forbidden;

that the importation of any foreign production or merchandise should ever be prohibited;

that no tax should ever be levied on the exportation of products and commodities of the nation;

that no tax ever be levied on the importation of products and commodities coming from abroad;

that no distinction be made between foreigners and nationals in ports and markets.[19]

[An excessive ferment was exited in France by the system of the economists. The government of that nation allowed the people to talk about public affairs, but not to understand them. The discussion of Quesnay's[20] theory was sufficiently unshackled; but none of the facts or documents in the hands of the administration, were presented to the public eye. In the system of the French economists, it is easy to discern the effects produced by this mixture of ingenious theory and involuntary ignorance.[21] It seduced the people, because they were now for the first time occupied with their own public affairs. But during these discussions, a free nation, possessed of the right to examine its own public affairs, was producing a system not less ingenious, and much better supported by fact and observation; a system which, after a short struggle, at length cast its predecessors into the shade; for truth always triumphs in the end, over dreams,[22] however brilliant.]

Translator's Notes to Chapter 6, First Book

This chapter was heavily rewritten for the second edition, although the reason for it is not quite clear. The *Encyclopedia* version was used wherever the French text was close to it, and the notes will reflect the changes made for the second edition.

The French writers discussed here are usually referred to today as the physiocrats, after a term given to them by one of them, Dupont de Nemours. It should be noted that Thomas Jefferson and Benjamin Franklin subscribed to physiocratic doctrines, and Jefferson's ideal of a republic of yeomen farmers is a physiocratic concept. Quite generally, the idea of competition among many small producers, advanced by Adam Smith, and advocated by economists to this day, is based on this physiocratic idea.

1. The first edition and the *Encyclopedia* read "cabinet." The second edition reads "government."
2. Both the the first and the second edition read "le docteur Quesnay," the *Encyclopedia* reads "Quesnay."
3. "Distinguished" was omitted in both editions of *New Principles*.
4. Both editions have here added "qui nous occupe."
5. Both editions read here "ou quelques progrès entre ses écrivains."
6. Both editions read "le système des physiocrates."
7. Both editions read "mais plus communement le système agricole ou économiste."

   The following part of the paragraph was rewritten sufficiently to justify discarding the *Encyclopedia* text for a new translation.
8. See note 2 above.
9. Both editions of *New Principles* read "les étoffes." In Sismondi's time, textiles were the main manufactures to be exported; hence the substitution is a natural one.
10. The term is italicized in *New Principles*, but not in the *Encyclopedia*.
11. See note 2.
12. The French text reads "l'économiste *français*."
13. The *Encyclopedia* reads from here: "to his wages, or the merchant to his profits."
14. The French text reads: "Les conseils que les deux sectes donnaient au gouvernement . . ."
15. The paragraph from the *Encyclopedia* corresponds to the first edition, except that in the *Encyclopedia* Sismondi supplies the English translation after *laissez passer*. In the second edition of *New Principles*, he changed the sentence after

laissez passer to: "car par cela même que l'intérêt public se compose de la reunion de tous les intérêts personnels, ils estimaient que l'intérêt personnel de chaque individu le guiderait plus sûrement que le gouvernement vers l'intérêt public dont le sien faisait partie."

16. As stated above, finance to Sismondi means government finance.
17. Sismondi assumed throughout this work, openly in the case of share cultivation, tacitly in all other cases, that the landlord is not the cultivator, but rents the estates to either sharecroppers or capitalistic farmers. This reflects a widespread practice of his times—Ricardo makes the same institutional assumption in his theory of rent.
18. The terms imply freedom from state regulation, immunity from taxation, and freedom from guild regulation. Since the sterile class in physiocratic theory was assumed not to produce any values, but merely to transform them, any of these mercantilistic policies could only hinder the functioning of the economy. It should be noted that Adam Smith took this idea over in its entirety and broadened it by applying it to value creation by labor in general, rather than only by land.
19. The allusion here is to staple rights and market privileges, which effectively reserved the home market to local producers and were therefore vigorously defended by the guilds.
20. *New Principles* omits Quesnay.
21. The *Encyclopedia* version used here corresponds to the first edition. In the second edition, Sismondi changed this to read: "On peut reconnaître, dans le système des économistes français, les conséquences de leur ignorance involontaires des faits sur lequels ils auraient dû fonder leurs théories ingénieuses, mais mal assurées. Toutefois ce système séduisit la nation."
22. The French text uses here erreurs.

7

Adam Smith's System; Division of The Rest of This Work

Adam Smith, the author of the third *System of Political Economy,*[1] instead of seeking, like his predecessors, to invent *a priori* a theory[2] to which he would then endeavor to connect all the facts, recognized that the science of government was experimental; that it had to be based on the history of many people, and that principles could be deduced only from a discerning observation of facts. His immortal work *An Inquiry into the Nature and Causes of the Wealth of Nations*, which he published in 1776, and which was preceded in 1752 by *Lectures on Political Economy*,[3] are actually the result of a philosophical study of the history of mankind. It was only after the author had analytically clarified past economic changes that he progressed to general laws of wealth accumulation and presented them for the first time.

Rejecting two equally exclusive systems, one of which wanted to attribute wealth creation only to commerce, the other only to agriculture, Adam Smith sought its source in labor. All work which results in an exchangeable value appeared to him productive, whether it belonged to the land or the city, whether it created an exchangeable object that became part of wealth, or whether it increased the value of a thing already existing.

In the same way that labor was the only creator of wealth, parsimony[4] was to him the only means to accumulate it. Parsimony created capital, a term in which he included not only gold and silver, as the mercantilists did, but wealth of all kinds, accumulated by human labor, and used by their owners to yield a gain, to perform a new task.

In his eyes, national wealth consisted of land which, made productive by human labor, not only repays this labor with profit, but also produces, to the gain of its owner, a net revenue which he called rent;[5] capitals which, employed to quicken industry, make it lucrative, such that their circulation produces for their owners a second revenue he called profit; finally, labor which produces for those who perform it a third revenue he called wages.

Adam Smith not only recognized that each type of labor contributed in its own way to the advantage of everyone and the growth of wealth; he asserted in principle that society demanded in turn that labor of which it had the greatest need, through the agency of those who offered to pay for it; that these demands and offers were the sole expression of social harmony that could be trusted, and that government could, with entire safety, be based on individual interest insofar as the progress of industry is concerned.

He also asserted that the labor which would be in greatest demand would be at all times the most suitable to the general interest; for that reason it would be the best paid; and it would also be the best performed. To the extent that wealth increased, and the nation could dispose of more capital and more hands, it would, in his opinion, direct its activities in turn to agriculture, domestic trade, manufacturing for domestic consumption, foreign trade, manufacturing for foreign consumption, and finally the carrying trade;[6] he asserted that market demand would determine at all times the flow of capital and of hands from a declining industry to a more profitable one; he asked from government no other favors for agriculture and industry than entire freedom, and he rested all hopes for the development of national wealth on *competition*.*

It would be redundant to expound here with greater detail a system which it is the aim of this book to develop and complete. Adam Smith's doctrine is ours; the torch his genius carried to the subject of this science, having shown his followers the true road, all the advances we have made therein since, are owed to him, and it would be childish vanity to strive to expose all points on which his ideas were not yet clarified, because it is to him that we owe the discovery of truths he himself had not known.

After this profession of our deep admiration of this creative genius, of our keen gratitude for the enlightenment we owe to him alone, one will no doubt be astonished to learn that the practical results of the doctrine we take[7] from him, appeared to us often diametrically opposed to those he drew from it, and that, by combining his very principles with the experi-

*The doctrine of Adam Smith is explained in his own work *An Inquiry into the Nature and Causes of the Wealth of Nations,* 3 vol. in 8o. See also *Traité d'économie politique,* by J. B. Say, 2 vol. in 8o, Paris. *Cours d'économie politique,* or *Exposition des principes qui déterminent la prospérité des nations,* by Henri Storch, 6 vol. in 8o, Petersburg, 1815. Finally, a work which I have published fifteen years ago, *De la Richesse commerciale,* 2 vol. in 8o, Geneva, 1803.

ence of a half century during which his theory was more or less put into practice,[8] we believe we can show that it was necessary, in more than one instance, to draw from it quite different conclusions.

We declare, with Adam Smith, that labor is the sole source of wealth; that parsimony is the sole means of accumulating it; but we also add that enjoyment is the only end of such accumulation, and that there is no increase in national wealth unless there is also an increase in national enjoyments.

Adam Smith, considering wealth only, and seeing that all those who possess it have an interest in increasing it, has concluded that such increase could never be better aided than by giving society over to the free exercise of all individual interests. He has said to government: "The sum of individual private fortunes makes up the wealth of the nation; there is no wealthy person who does not strive to become even richer; let him do as he pleases; he will enrich the nation by enriching himself."

We have examined wealth in its relation to the population which it must support or make happy; a nation does not seem to us in any way grown richer by the sole increase in its capital, but only if its capital, in increasing, is spreading more comforts among the population it must support; because, without a doubt, twenty million people are poorer with six hundred million of income, than ten million people with four hundred million. We have seen that the rich could increase their fortunes, be it by a new manufacture, be it by taking for themselves a greater part of what was previously reserved for the poor;[9] and in order to regularize that division, to make it equitable, we invoke almost constantly that intervention of the government which Adam Smith rejects. We see the government above all as the protector of the weak against the strong, the defender of him who cannot defend himself, and the representative of the long-term, if quiet, interest of all, against the temporary, if vociferous interest, of each.

Experience seems to us to justify this new viewpoint of an old system. Although the authority of Adam Smith has not by far reformed all parts of economic legislation, the fundamental thesis of free and universal competition has made very great advances in all civilized societies; this has resulted in prodigious development of the powers of industry, but also very often it has led to frightful suffering for many classes of the population. It is through experience that we have felt the need for that protective authority we call for; it is necessary to prevent men from being sacrificed to the progress of wealth from which they derive no benefit.[10] Only such authority can rise above the material calculus of increases in commodities which is enough to motivate individuals, and compare it with the calculus of increases in enjoyments and comforts for all, which should be the goal towards which all nations should aspire.*

We believe that we must warn our readers in advance of this important difference in conclusions, while at the same time we refuse to make them an object of controversy. We will not stop in any way to fight against the opinions of Adam Smith we do not share, nor will we mark the occasions where we part with him and the many writers who have commented on his work. The principles of the science of politics ought to form a single whole and flow from each other. We have presented them in what appears to us their natural succession, without trying to distinguish our contributions from those of our predecessors. If these principles really support each other, and if they really form a well-connected whole, we will have arrived at our goal, since we do not pretend in any way to erect a new system in opposition to that of our master, but merely show such modifications as experience would force to bring to his.

We shall arrange this system under six main divisions which appear to us to encompass all of the science of government, as related to the physical welfare of its subjects, as follows: (1) Formation and progress of wealth; (2) Agricultural wealth; (3) Commercial wealth; (4) Money; (5) Taxes; and (6) Population. Each shall be the subject of one book. Agricultural wealth and population were not in any way the object of special inquiries for Adam Smith.[11]

By moving totally in the opposite direction to this very day, the disciples of Adam Smith in England have departed from his doctrine, and moreover, it seems to us, from his method of searching for the truth. Adam Smith considered political economy as an experiential science; he strove to examine each fact in the social context to which it belonged, and never to lose sight of the many different circumstances to which it was tied, the different consequences through which it could impinge on national happiness. In criticizing him today we take the liberty of saying that he was not always true to this synthetic manner of reasoning; that he did not always have in view the main goal he set himself, the relationship of wealth to population, or with national happiness. His new disciples, in England[12] have thrown themselves even more into abstractions which make us lose

*Others, before us, have remarked that experience has not fully comfirmed the doctrines of Adam Smith. One of the most illustrious among his followers, M. Ganilh, has completely abandoned the system he had supported before. Generally, Adam Smith had considered the science as exclusively subordinated to the material calculus, while it is, in many of its relations, in the domain of feeling and imagination, which cannot be measured. It is true that M. Ganilh, in pursuing other considerations, of which the foundations seem to be quite uncertain, appears to us to have moved away from the goals of the science even more.

from view entirely the human being to whom the wealth belongs, and who ought to enjoy it. In their hands the science has become so speculative that it seems to separate itself from all practice. One would believe at first sight that in freeing the theory from all surrounding circumstances, one would make it clearer and easier to comprehend; the opposite has happened; the new English economists are extremely obscure and can only be understood with much effort, while our mind is loath to accept the abstractions they require of us. But this very aversion is a warning that we move away from the truth, because, in the social sciences[13] where everything is linked, we have to make great efforts to isolate a principle and see nothing but it alone.

The ingenious work of Mr. D. Ricardo, which appeared in 1817[14] and was quickly translated into French and enlarged by M. Say with comments that sparkle with lucid criticism, seems to us a noteworthy example of this new direction followed by the economists in England. These *Principles of Political Economy and Taxation* have had a tremendous effect on the English. A journal whose authority in the science is commanding,* advertises them as having made the greatest step forward in political economy which it has ever made since Adam Smith. Still, we are so aware that we walk another road that we would have hardly had the occasion to refer to this work, or to rely on its speculations, or to fight them, if its fame would not have made this sometimes a duty for us.

A French minister, whose name is no secret, although he has not attached it to his book, has also published in the same year *Elements d'Economie politique* which he intended, he says, for those who work in government. I am astonished that, given his goal, he has considered the science from such an abstract viewpoint. In his so-called *Elements* there is much of the spirit of political economy; but it seems to me that practice, so essential to a statesman, has remained far from his thoughts.

End of First Book

Translator's Notes to Chapter 7, Book 1

This chapter is a greatly expanded version of the last paragraph of the first chapter of the *Encyclopedia* article without any literal incorporation of text. While the preceding chapters are a straightforward history of economic thought as Sismondi knew it from his historical studies, this chapter was used by him to establish a theoretical position in the contemporary mainstream of political economy. Fully aware of his opposition to Ricardian analysis, Sismondi wanted to secure his legitimacy as a faithful follower of Adam Smith, as opposed to Smith's epigones, particularly Ricardo. However, already here he makes it clear that he also differs with Smith, not on theory, but on the conclusions and practical policies Smith had derived from his analysis. It is noteworthy that Sismondi imitates Smith in giving an outline of the rest of his work, just as Smith did at the beginning of *The*

**Edinburgh Review,* No. 29, June 1818.

Wealth. *New Principles* has otherwise little in common with Smith's work; the subject headings of the *Encyclopedia* article, which become the books of *New Principles*, resemble more the division of cameralistic writings and show some affinity to Italian works.

1. These three words are italicized in *New Principles*, although why is not quite clear.
2. Sismondi, intentionally or not, inverts Adam Smith here. *The Wealth of Nations* is clearly a presentation of an a priori deductive theory, selectively supported by historical examples. However, by presenting Adam Smith in this light, Sismondi allies him with his own approach and thereby further strengthens his own legitimacy as a faithful follower of Smith.
3. This is a puzzling reference. According to Edwin Cannan's "Editor's Introduction" to Smith's *Lectures on Justice, Police, Revenue, and Arms*, the manuscript of the *Lectures* had not survived when Smith's manuscripts were destroyed shortly before his death, and was rediscovered in 1895 by Cannan in a manuscript made by a student who had attended Smith's lectures in Glasgow. There is no other reference to such a publication anywhere. However, Smith lectured at Glasgow in 1752.
4. Sismondi uses the term "économie." 'Parsimony' was used to make a clear connection to Smithian terminology.
5. The text was changed from the first edition to "un revenue *net, le fermage*, qu'il nomma la rente." The words in italics are the addition. Since *le fermage* is equivalent to the meaning of rent, it has not been separately rendered.
6. The text was changed from the first edition: "Il jugea qu'elle exploiterait agriculture . . ." to "Il jugea qu'elle tournerait son activité vers l'agriculture . . ."
7. Sismondi uses the word "empruntons." He clearly wanted to convey the fact that all followers of Smith, himself included, had not made actual, new contributions to the theory. However, the word 'borrowed' as a literal translation seemed to be misplaced.
8. The first edition reads for this clause: "sur lequel ses écrits ont prodigieusement influé."
9. The first of many references (oblique, as this one, or quite open) to an exploitation theory. As Aftalion points out in his critical evaluation of Sismondi's work, socialism, and in particular so-called scientific socialism, owes a great spiritual debt to Sismondi.
10. The last sentence in the paragraph was changed from: "Elle doit toujours intervenir, pour comparer le calcul égoiste de l'augmentation des produits, avec le seul calcul national de l'augmentation des jouissances et de l'aisance de tout."
11. Sismondi's term "richesse territoriale" was translated interchangeably as 'agricultural wealth' or 'landed wealth.' The presence of a special book on this subject early in the work is indicative, first, of Sismondi's personal experience and interest in the subject; second, of the important part agriculture played in the economic affairs of Europe, as is also evidenced by Ricardo's rent theory; and third, of Sismondi's sympathy for some physiocratic ideas, as expressed in various parts of the work, and noted in the chapter comments.
12. The first edition reads: "Ses nouveaux disciples, en Angleterre, se sont au contraire jetés."
13. "Les sciences morales."
14. The first edition reads: "qui vient paraître, traduit en français et enrichi."

Second Book

Formation and Progress of Wealth

Introduction

This book is an exposition of Sismondi's theoretical framework. Like Marx, Sismondi has no own value theory, but accepts Smith's labor theory of value. But, again like Marx, Sismondi is not really interested in propounding a new value theory—his interest lies in the social relationships that surround and sustain value, and in particular in what he sees as economic instability flowing from unequal economic power. His theoretical structure rests on a division of society into classes that are obviously related to the categories of labor, capital, and land of classical analysis, but that anticipate the Marxian ideas of shared interests and interclass antagonism. The division of the national income between these classes leads Sismondi to a dynamic model of income, consumption, and production that departs in essential ways from the linear Newtonian mold of classical economics and anticipates some features of Keynesian analysis. The entire book has both a strong Marxian and Keynesian flavor—not very surprisingly since, in the case of Marx, many of his main analytical categories were taken from Sismondi, as evidenced by the citations in the first volume of *Das Kapital*. Sismondi can lay claim to being the first economist to construct a business cycle model that rejects Say's Law and tries to replace it with a realistic macroeconomic view of the economy. The similarities to Keynes are explained by Sismondi's macroeconomic business view of economic behavior, flowing from his acquaintance with business thinking and practice, in the same way that Keynes brings to his analysis business categories. In particular, it is consumption, that is, the ability of a merchant to sell in a market, which is the governing variable in this book, much as aggregate consumption is the main variable in the Keynesian model. Compared to Ricardo, this book has a distinctly modern tone, even though the examples are contemporary to Sismondi's experience. It may be that Sismondi's work was forgotten because his macroeconomic view of society was too far ahead of the concerns of his time.

1

Formation of Wealth for Solitary Man

[Man brings into the world with him certain wants, which he must satisfy in order to live; certain desires which lead him to expect happiness from particular enjoyments; and a certain industry or aptitude for labour which enables him to satisfy the requisitions of both.[1] His wealth originates in this industry; all that he creates is destined to be consumed in satisfying his wants and desires. But, between the moment of its production by labour, and its consumption by enjoyment, the thing destined for man's use may have an existence more or less durable. It is this thing, this accumulated and still unconsumed fruit of labour, which is called wealth.

Wealth may exist not only without any sign of exchange, or without money, but even without any possibility of exchange, or without trade.] On the other hand, it cannot exist without labor, any more than without the desires and wants this labor must satisfy.[2] [Suppose a man to be left on a desert island; the undisputed property of this whole island is not wealth, whatever be the natural fertility of its soil, the abundance of the game straying in its forests, of the fish sporting on its shores, or the mines concealed in its bosom. On the contrary, amid all these benefits presented to him by nature, the man may sink to the lowest degree of penury, and die perhaps of hunger. But, if his industry enables him to catch some of the animals that wander in his woods; and if, instead of consuming them immediately, he reserves them for his future wants; if, in this interval, he gets them tamed and multiplied, so that he can live on their milk, or associate them to his labour, he is then beginning to acquire wealth, because labour has gained him the possession of these animals, and a fresh labour has rendered them domestic. The measure of his wealth will not be the price, which he might obtain for his property in exchange, but the length of time during which no farther labour will be requisite to satisfy his wants, compared with the extent of those wants.[3]

By subduing those animals, the man has made them his property and wealth; by subduing the ground, he will in like manner, convert it into property and wealth. His island is destitute of value as long as no labour has been bestowed on it; but if, instead of consuming its fruits the moment they come to his hand, he reserves them for future want; if he commits them again to the earth, again to be multiplied; if he tills his fields to augment their productive power, or defends them by inclosures from wild beasts; if he plants them with trees, the fruit of which he does not look for till many years have elapsed;[4] he is then creating the value, not only of annual produce raised by his labour from the ground, but also of the ground itself, which he had tamed, as he tamed the wild beasts, and rendered fit to second his exertions. In that case he is rich, and the more so the longer he can suspend his labours without suffering new wants.

Our Solitary, being now liberated from the most pressing of all demands, that of hunger, may devote his exertions to provide lodging and clothes, or to improve those already provided. He will build himself a hut, and fit it out with such furniture as his unaided labour may suffice to construct; he will change the skin and fleeces of his sheep into shoes and coats;[5] and the more convenient his dwelling shall be rendered, the better his storehouse shall be filled with provisions for his future food and clothing, the more rich may he call himself.

The history of this man is the history of the human race.] It is most important that one thinks first of showing step by step all the actions by which he can move from penury to opulence;[6] the mind can follow them for an individual; it loses them soon from view in a society. However, the wealth of the whole is only the sum of the wealth of each one; it begins for the whole as it has begun for everyone, with labor; it accumulates for the whole as for everyone, by the excess of the products of daily labor over daily needs; it is destined, for the whole, as for each one, to procure enjoyments which must destroy and consume it; if it ceases to provide such enjoyments, if there is no one who can use it for his needs, it would have lost its value, it would not be wealth any more.[7] All that is true of the individual, is true of society, and vice versa. But while nothing is as easy to imagine as the opulence or penury of a solitary man, exchanges, forever shifting such wealth around, blur our vision and make a positive thing into an almost metaphysical one.

[However great the beneficence of nature, she gives nothing gratuitously to man; though, when addressed by him, she is ready to lend her assistance in multiplying his powers to an indefinite extent.[8] The history of wealth is, in all cases, comprised within the limits now specified—the labour which creates, the economy which accumulates, the consumption which destroys. An article which has not been wrought, or has not mediately or immediately received its value from labour, is not wealth, however useful, however necessary, it may be for life. An article, which is not useful to man, which does not satisfy any of his desires, and cannot mediately or immediately be employed in his service, is not more entitled to the name of wealth, whatever labour may have been bestowed on producing it. And finally, an article which cannot be accumulated or kept for future consumption is not wealth, though created by labour and consumed by enjoyment.]

We have said that the labor which creates wealth can be mediate or immediate. Indeed, man, in appropriating natural objects, often bestows value on them merely because he thus saves them for future labor, to which he will join them, although not changing their substance at all. The solitary, having enclosed a meadow, has given value to the grass he has never touched, but which he has merely sheltered from the predations of wild beasts; when he has multiplied his cattle, he has given value to the pastures which are most at his command; and when he has taken advantage of a waterfall for turning his mill, he has given value to the stream itself. That which is true of the isolated individual is even truer of society; past labor gives value to things which will help future labor.

We have also said that use may be mediate or immediate; thus the hay the solitary reaps has value, not for himself, but for the cattle it feeds. Finally, we have said that everything which combines only two of the three conditions we have enumerated, and lacks the third, can never be wealth. Air, water, fire are not only useful, they are necessary to life; they can be saved for future enjoyment; but, in general, there is no need for labor to procure them and they are not at all wealth.[9] All labor which has failed to attain its end is in no way wealth since no enjoyment can be drawn from it, even though the worked object may remain.[10] Exercise, music, dance, are all labor and enjoyment, but they constitute no part of wealth, because the enjoyment cannot be saved for another time.

[Before possessing any medium of exchange, before discovering the precious metals which render it so easy to us, our Solitary] whom we have assumed on his island, [would ere long learn to distinguish the different kinds of labour in their relation to wealth. Labour producing no enjoyment is useless; labour, whose fruits are naturally incapable of being stored up for future consumption, is unproductive; whilst the only productive kinds of labour—the only kinds producing wealth—are such as leave behind them, in the estimation even of our Solitary, a pledge[11] equal in value to the trouble they have cost. Thus the man, misled by analogy, may have imagined that he could multiply his olive-trees by planting the olives; he may not have known but that the stones would germinate as in other such vegetables; till, after preparing the ground by a complete and fatiguing tillage, experience would teach him that his toil had been useless, for no olive tree was produced by it. On the other hand, he may have secured his dwelling from wolves and bears; and the labour would be useful but unproductive; for its fruits cannot accumulate. If previously accustomed to civilized life, he may have passed many hours in playing on a flute, saved, we shall suppose, at his shipwreck; the labour would still be useful, and probably regarded as his own pleasure; but it would be as unproductive, and for the like reason, as before. He may have bestowed on the care of his person and health much time, very usefully employed; this will also be quite unproductive of wealth. The Solitary will clearly perceive what difference there is between productive labour and the labour of honors in which he amasses nothing for the future; and, without excluding himself from such occupations, he will call them a loss of time.][12]

Translator's Notes to Chapter 1, Second Book

A large part of this introductory chapter was taken directly from the *Encyclopedia*, somewhat similar to the second chapter of the first book. There is no set pattern to the use of *Encyclopedia* material in *New Principles*, clearly implying that far from mechanically using the article as a departure for the book, Sismondi very carefully analyzed his material and expanded it to conform to the new viewpoint he had gained on classical theory. From the way the original material was interwoven into the overall text it must be concluded that Sismondi must have used extensive notes on, and annotations to, the original text.

1. The French text reads "qui le met en état de satisfaire les uns et les autres."
2. Here and below Sismondi combines utility concepts with the labor theory of value. The sentence clearly implies that supply is provided by labor, and is met by demand generated by want for the utilities labor provides. The argument comes close to Marshall's scissor argument, but of course lacks its refinement. Say advanced utility arguments in the *Traité*, but in general the time was not ripe for them. It is likely that both Sismondi and Say were influenced by Italian authors. It already becomes apparent here that Sismondi sees wants as an important limiting factor on production, thus leaving the classical idea of production generating demand behind. The idea will be elaborated gradually throughout the work and become the main concept in his analysis of the business cycle. The Marxian analysis of the business cycle is essentially Sismondi's macroeconomic model coupled to Ricardo's value theory.
3. This paragraph is an echo of Defoe's *Robinson Crusoe*, but also of Locke's idea that property is acquired by labor, as expressed in the second book "Of Civil Government." It should be noted that the physiocrats traced the right of property in land to the original work done to clear the land.

   While starting with a Robinson economy is still a favorite device to introduce basic economic concepts in a simple and evident manner, the use by Sismondi was also part of a larger fashion of the times, namely to extol the simple pleasures of rural life, to return to nature. Paintings by Boucher, Watteau, and Fragonard in the eighteenth century of prettily clad shepherdesses and amorous shepherds, with fleecy little white lambs in attendance, gambolling on green pastures, are the more frivolous expression of this trend. Jean-Jacques Rousseau's work is its philosophical, serious equivalent.

4. Although this appears self-evident, the sentiment illustrates an important distinction between Sismondi's approach to economic development, and that of classical economics. While Ricardian analysis stresses "the long run" in which market forces will work themselves out, the actual viewpoint of the analysis is short-term, or at least is seen in that way by business people. Sismondi, on the other hand, has a deliberate long-term view of business investment, both as far as real capital is concerned, and especially with respect to *incorporated capital* residing in the labor force, a neglected category in classical analysis. It is the mismatch between this so-to-speak hidden resource and the short-term changes in demand and technological development, plus the great difficulty of making short-run adjustments that create business cycles, which will be discussed especially in the last book of this work.
5. The French text reads "étoffes" instead of "coats."
6. 'Penury' was used for *misère* to conform to Sismondi's previous usage.
7. As the paragraph referred to in note 2 above, this short sentence also clearly combines labor-theory-of-value concepts with utility concepts in a manner that anticipates Marshall: production (labor) on the supply side, consumption (utility) on the demand side.
8. This is an echo of physiocratic doctrine—nature labors alongside man to produce the only surplus for the economy, the net revenue. Sismondi exhibits also the quite common uncritical view of the early technological revolution by assuming that nature can multiply man's powers to an infinite extent. He will later use this idea to explain the underconsumption, overproduction causes of the business cycle.
9. Sismondi includes fire in what must be taken as his list of so-called *free goods*. It is doubtful that fire should be listed in this way—labor is needed to make fire, and it cannot be saved for future use, as Sismondi assumes. The enumeration is reminiscent of the original Greek classification of the elements that were supposed to make up the universe.
10. This concept should be compared to Marx's idea of "socially necessary labor," which postulates that labor not representing the accepted standard of efficiency must be excluded from surplus value creation, that is, "it does not attain its end," as Sismondi puts it.
11. Sismondi will use the term *pledge* later in his book on money in conjunction with the substitution of gold by paper. It is evident that he had a very precise idea here—namely that for anything ephemeral, such as expended labor, or credit, there must come into existence a concrete equivalent that validates and stands for the former, either as a commodity, or as specie money.
12. The flute is again not only an echo of Robinson, but also of classical Greek shepherds tending their flock, playing panpipes. From the present standpoint one would take issue with Sismondi on personal care being a waste of time, but this remark should be seen in the context of his time and the standards of personal care that were possible then. If Sismondi would have used fully the utility ideas of the Italian writers, and his own, he might have come to a different conclusion.

2

Development of Wealth in Society through Exchange

We have seen what constituted the creation, the preservation, and the use of wealth by isolated man. The same transactions occur in precisely the same manner and with the same goal among men united in society, with the single difference that the former needed only to consider himself, and that in the creation of his wealth he never lost view of its use, that is, his own enjoyment and his own rest; whereas the latter, living among a great number of fellow citizens with whom he has a continual exchange of services, works so that others may enjoy and rest, and he counts on the work of others for his own enjoyment and rest. Thenceforth, man being a part of society, an abstract being, whose wealth and needs are hypothetical, cannot anymore follow his work to the moment where its fruits are consumed, nor can he judge the needs for which he ought to provide, or the time when he ought to rest; he works without pause to fill the common coffers, leaving to society the worry of finding a use for the things he has made.

Exchange between two men, both working, and producing like our Solitary, the wealth they wanted to consume, [first arose from superabundance: "Give me that article which is of no service to you, and would be useful to me," said one of the contracting parties, "and I will give you this in return, which is of no service to me, and would be useful to you." Present utility was not, however, the sole measure of things exchanged. Each estimated for himself the selling price, or the trouble and time bestowed in the production of his own commodity, and compared it with the buying price, or the trouble and time necessary for procuring the required commodity by his own efforts; and no exchange could take place till the two contracting parties, on calculating the matter, had each discovered that it was better thus to procure the commodity wanted than to make it for himself.][1]

However, exchange had not in the least altered the nature of wealth; it was always a thing created by labor, saved for future need, and having no value except for that need. The relation between production and consumption was the same, in spite of the fact that somebody had taken the place of the producer to consume. One can, with respect to the produced thing, abstract from all the exchanges of which it was the object; one man has worked it, a man has saved it, because a man had need of it and consumed it; it does not matter that this man be the same, many successive exchanges have made of the last only a stand-in for the first.

Exchange had not only things as its objects; it extended also to labor, the means through which all things are produced. He who possessed stores of food, offered to feed him whose granaries were empty, on condition that the latter would work for him. This undertaking given for labor was called a *wage*.

Exchange no more alters the nature of labor, than it does that of produced things. [For the society, as well as for the Solitary, there may be a useless as well as an unproductive kind of labour; and, though both of them be paid, they still preserve their distinct character, since the first corresponds not to the desires or wants of the labourer's employer, and the second admits no accumulation of its fruits. The wage paid to the workmen in either case must not mislead us; it puts the payer of it in the workman's place. The part which we formerly supposed to be performed by the single individual, is now shared among two or more persons; but the result is not altered in the least. The day-labourer who plants olives performs a task which is useless to his employer,[2] though if he receives his hire, it may be advantageous to himself. The man who defends his master or society against bears or hostile enterprises; who takes charge of the health or the person of others; who provides the enjoyment of music, or dramatic exhibition, or dancing, performs, just like the Solitary, a work which is useful because it is agreeable, which is lucrative to him because he receives a hire for his labour, whilst he abandons the enjoyment of it to his employers; but which is unproductive notwithstanding, because it cannot be the object of saving and accumulation. He who paid the wage, no longer has either the wage itself in his possession, or the thing for which he gave it.

Thus labour and economy—the true sources of wealth—exist for the Solitary as well as for the social man, and produce the same kind of advantage to both. The formation of society, however, and with it the introduction of commerce and exchange,] have changed the creation of wealth, be it by increasing the productive powers of labor through its division, be it by providing a clearer aim to the economy, and thus multiplying the enjoyments wealth provides. [Thus men, combined in society, produced more than if each had laboured separately; and they preserve better what they have produced, because they feel the value of it better.

This accidental advantage] that two men of equal ability for work and accumulation found in exchanging products for which they had no immediate need, [soon pointed out to both a constant source of advantage in trading, whenever the one offered an article which he excelled in making, for an article which the other excelled in making; for each excelled in what he made often, each was unskillful and slow at what he made but seldom. Now, the more exclusively they devoted themselves to one kind of work, the more dexterity did they acquire in it, the more effectually did they succeed in rendering it easy and expeditious. This observation produced the division of trades; the husbandman quickly perceived, that he could not make as many agricultural tools by himself, in a month, as the blacksmith would make for him in a day.

The same principle which at first separated the trades of the husbandman, shepherd, smith, and weaver, continued to separate those trades into an indefinite number of departments. Each felt that, by simplifying the operation committed to him, he would perform it in a manner still more speedy and perfect. The weaver renounced the business of spinning and dyeing; the spinning of hemp, cotton, wool, and silk, became each a separate employment; weavers were still farther subdivided, according to the fabric and the destination of their stuffs; and at every subdivision, each workman, directing his attention to a single object, experienced an increase in his productive powers. In the interior of each manufactory, this division was again repeated, and still with the same success. Twenty workmen all laboured at the same thing, but each made it undergo a different operation; and the twenty workmen found that they had accomplished twenty times as much work as when each had laboured separately.]

Machines were born from the division of labor. Nature offers us blind forces, infinitely superior to those of man, but which are not in any way intended to serve him. It was a triumph of human ingenuity to tame them and make them obedient; once they could be made to perform human tasks, they did them with a rapidity, a scope which infinitely surpassed the power of man using only his own strength.[3] Water, wind, and fire cannot perform complicated tasks, but the division of labor has made all tasks simpler. When, in a factory, each worker was assigned to a single operation, he soon found the one motion by which he could carry it out; shortly after he found the command he could give to the natural agent to accomplish the task without his help. The waters were burdened with the milling of wheat, with pushing saws, and lifting hammers; and undertakings for which thousands of workers would not have sufficed, were completed by unfeeling workers which had no needs.

The division of labor increased in another way the productive faculty man possesses. Many members of society, abandoning manual tasks, devoted themselves to those of knowledge. They studied nature and its properties, dynamics and its laws, mechanics and its applications, and they deduced from their inquiries almost infinite means to increase man's productive powers. These are means of production which in our day are called *scientific forces*, which can accomplish through more powerful agents than we are, works humanity never could have undertaken with its own unaided strength.

Translator's Notes to Chapter 2, Second Book

The heading of this chapter really hides the intent of the author, rather than clarifying it. The main body of the chapter is taken from the *Encyclopedia*, but Sismondi adds the new concept of the *unknowability* of the market in an extended exchange economy; that is, that a producer does not work directly for the consumer, as in guild days, but for an impersonal abstract institution whose collective intentions are veiled in secrecy. Implicitly, Sismondi rejects here the informational function of market prices—an advanced division of labor in which the producer makes only a fraction of the entire product, or is involved in only one phase of the production cycle, appears to Sismondi as an invitation to overproduction because the producer looks at his costs first, rather than responding to overt demand. The theme will recur again and again. It entered the Marxian canon as the general law of capitalist accumulation, and is the main engine of overproduction, both relative and absolute. Sismondi's reference to the detachment of the worker from the end product is likewise the precursor of the Marxian concept of *alienation*—although it should be noted that Smith mentions that the advancing division of labor will force workers to perform repetitive tedious tasks. However, Smith's invisible hand was assumed to balance effort and reward, an assumption that is essentially lacking from Sismondi's and Marx's view of the economic process. However, Sismondi gives a fairly optimistic account of the benefits of the advanced division of labor and the concomitant increase in productivity. Here there is already a strong hint that each development by itself has beneficial effects, but that the enjoyment of such beneficial effects depends on the careful, deliberate balancing of the social forces that are involved. In effect, Sismondi goes back to late mercantilistic views, especially those of Sir James Steuart.

1. This paragraph blends very skilfully utility reasoning with Smithian labor concepts, although the former clearly predominate. It should be noted first, that exchange arises out of *superabundance*, not from a propensity to *truck, barter, and exchange*, and secondly, that the paragraph comes from the *Encyclopedia*. Sismondi discards the hypothetical Smithian natural propensity for the much more plausible assumption that what is available in abundance is of lower value than what is scarce. However, Sismondi, in his mental struggle to free himself from classical doctrine, proves unable to do so entirely throughout *New Princi-*

ples, thus introducing into his analysis the fuzziness Schumpeter deplores in his *History of Economic Analysis*.

2. In the French version, Sismondi uses ''semer,'' 'seeding' instead of 'planting,' a clear reference to the example in the previous chapter illustrating useless labor. Actually, the *Encyclopedia* text, here used, is ambiguous because planting may mean planting trees, as well as planting seeds.
3. The first edition reads: ''dont l'homme seul n'aurait pu approcher.'' Although below Sismondi refers to watermills et cetera, his account implies that the taming of natural forces is a very recent one, with a view to the use of steam and the developing Industrial Revolution. Historically, man has always tried to harness the forces of nature, with sails and watermills, forges and windmills. The distinction of the Industrial Revolution lies in the broad scientific advance that was made in the many ways of using these forces, and using them in more efficient ways. Whether this is as direct a consequence of the division of labor as Sismondi claims in the last paragraph is debatable.

3

Increase of Needs of Social Man and Limits of Production

Since mankind formed a society and practiced division of labor, more work was performed on earth. Everyone, limiting himself to only one task, had acquired an extraordinary skill in performing it; everyone had gained by increasing his output through the blind forces of nature he had succeeded in taming; everyone had multiplied his own powers by the scientific forces the engineers had shown him to use. While in the barbarous state, a man could barely provide for his most pressing needs; it would be enough, in this most perfected society, that one man in a hundred, perhaps in a thousand, would work in its factories with the same application, to produce a quantity of goods equal to what could have been produced by a hundred, or a thousand, before, while all others could remain idle. Agricultural tasks, it is true, are not amenable to a similar saving of labor.

[Much more work was executed in the world by the division of labour; but, at the same time, much more was required to supply the consumption. The wants and enjoyments of the Solitary, who laboured for himself, were both very limited. Food, clothing, and lodging he indeed required; but he did not so much as think of the delicacies, by which the satisfaction of those wants might be converted into pleasure; and still less of the artificial desires, induced by society, which in their gratification become new sources of enjoyment. The Solitary's aim was merely to amass, that he might afterwards repose. Before him, at no great distance, was a point in the accumulation of wealth, beyond which it would have been foolishness to accumulate more, because his consumption could not be increased proportionately. But the wants of the social man were infinite, because the society's labour offered him enjoyment infinitely varied. Whatever wealth he might amass, he could never have occasion to say *it is enough*; he still found means to convert it into pleasure, and to imagine at least that he applied it to his service.]

However, it is a great mistake, into which the greater number of modern economists have fallen, to represent consumption as a force without limits, always ready to absorb[1] an infinite production. These eonomists do not cease to encourage nations to produce, to invent new machines, to improve their industry, in order that the output for the year always be larger than that of the previous year; they are distressed to see the number of unproductive workers increasing; they expose the idle to public indignation, and, in a nation where workers' capacities have increased a hundredfold, they would wish that everyone be a worker, that everyone work for a living.[2]

Yet, the Solitary worked above all to have leisure; he accumulated riches in order to enjoy them without work; leisure is a natural inclination for man, it is the goal and reward of work; men would likely give up all the perfection of the arts, all enjoyments which we receive from the manufactures, if we had to purchase them by constant labor, such as that of the factory hand. The division of trades and ranks,[3] while dividing tasks, has not changed the end of human effort. Man does not tire himself, except to rest thereafter; he does not save except to spend; he does not aspire to wealth except for enjoyment. Today, effort is separated from reward: it is not the same man who works and then rests; but it is because one man labors that the other can rest.*[4]

After all, the needs of the working man are necessarily very limited. After the prodigious multiplication of the productive forces of labor, he would soon be provided with food, shelter, and clothing, given the capabilities of the whole society. Could one assume that the life of everyone would be better, if the whole nation would work like the single worker; if as a consequence it would produce ten times the food that each of them could consume? Quite the contrary! Every worker would have for sale like

*The rest we discuss here is the termination of labor destined to create wealth; it must not be confused with idleness. Almost all bodily exercises we find most agreeable, cease to be so if they are in the service of gain. Exercise which does not have gain for its object, is therefore part of the leisure of the wealthy; but above all, all exercises of the mind are part of such leisure, and are compatible with it only. While man accumulates in order to be able to exercise his mind and purify his soul, he consumes the fruits he has gathered. The nation accumulates in order that each person have the necessary leisure to develop the faculties of the mind, and so that some, among their number, ennoble human nature by approaching perfection. If all members of a nation labor, if they labor incessantly, the goal of wealth would not be reached at all; there would be neither rest nor enjoyment, to make man more perfect: the nation, by multiplying its wealth, would sacrifice the end to the means.

ten, and could buy only like one; every worker would sell so much less that he would find himself even less able to buy; and the transformation of the nation into a vast manufacture of constantly employed productive workers, far from creating wealth, would cause universal misery.*[5]

From the moment that there is a superabundance of goods, superfluous labor must be devoted to luxury objects. The consumption of necessities is limited, that of luxury goods is without limits.[6] All the clothes, shoes, all the grain, all the meats which workers will consume, are soon produced, given the station in life to which they are reduced today. Even if, through a more equitable organization of society, we would succeed in reserving for them a larger part of the wealth they create, we would still quickly provide the enjoyments that could agree with work. Undoubtedly, the time will never come that we send them to their workplaces in carriages,[7] or let them work at their trade in velvets and gold brocades; if that would be the result of the zeal to produce that animates all the writers, and which all governments encourage, the workers would quickly renounce the luxury they would have to buy with odious labor.[8] If all the fringe benefits[9] of wealth were offered to the factory hand, as payment for unremitting labor of twelve to fourteen hours of work a day, such as he does today, there would not be one who would hesitate to chose less luxury and more leisure, less frivolous adornments and more freedom. This choice would be that of the entire society, if conditions were kept more or less the same; no producer, if he profited from all his industry, and compared the almost invisible enjoyment he derived from the most beautiful clothing with the additional labor it would cost him, would want to buy them at that price.[10] Luxury is only possible if it is bought with the labor of others; unremitting labor, without rest, is possible only because it can provide, not the luxuries, but the necessities of life.[11]

The indefinite multiplication of the productive powers of labor can then have only the result of increasing luxuries, or the enjoyments of the idle rich. The Solitary worked to rest, social man works so that someone may rest; the Solitary gathered to enjoy thereafter, social man accumulates the fruits of his sweat for him who can enjoy them; but from the moment that he and his peers produce more, and infinitely more than they can consume, then what they produce must be destined for the consumption of people who will live in no manner like him, and will not produce at all.[12]

Thus the progress of industry, the progress of production compared to

*I have, for this argument, abstracted from external trade. If one wishes to take this into account, one nation could in effect be the provider of its neighbors; but the argument would hold again for mankind, or for all that part of mankind which trades with each other, and which, in some form, comprises today a single market.

population, tends to increase inequality among men. The more a nation has progressed in the arts, in the manufactures, the greater is the disproportion between the status of those who labor and those who enjoy; the more the one live in misery, the more the others display luxury, at least until government corrects the distribution and assures to those who create all the means of enjoyment a greater share of such enjoyment through such institutions that seem to be opposed to the purely economic end of increasing wealth. The establishment of a weekly day of rest, by diminishing the productive powers of the poor, has reserved to them a share in the enjoyments they create for society. By suppressing such a day of rest, produced wealth would be increased by a seventh; the wealthy would be summoned to more luxury, and the poor would be more miserable.[13]

The legislator can, in the same spirit, give to the poor some other safeguards against universal competition. Just as the establishment of a rest day, these safeguards will be condemned by those who esteem only the increase of wealth, whereas they would have the approval of those who value such increase only if it spreads more happiness among all the ranks of the nation.

But the rich who consume the product of the labors of others, can only obtain it by exchange. Yet, if they give their acquired and accumulated wealth in return for these new products that are the objects of their desires, they seem to be liable to dissipate quickly their reserves; we have said that they do not work at all, and they even cannot work; one would then believe that each day must see their old wealth shrink, and that, nothing being left to them, nothing will be offered in exchange to the workers who labor for them exclusively. The workers, as we have seen, will never make use of either carriages, or velvet suits; if the wealthy cease to be wealthy, precisely because they have used their wealth for some time, the carriage makers and velvet manufacturers will have to perish in misery.

But, in the social order, wealth has acquired the quality to reproduce itself by the labor of others, and without its owner participating therein. Wealth, like work, and by work, gives an annual return which may be destroyed each year without making the rich any poorer. This return is the *income* which is born from *capital*; the distinction between one and the other became the foundation of social prosperity. Production comes to a halt from the moment it cannot be exchanged against income. If all of a sudden the wealthy classes resolved to live off their work, just like the poorest, and to add all their income to their capital, the workers, who counted on the exchange of that income for their livelihood, would be reduced to despair and would die of hunger; if, on the other hand, the wealthy class would not content itself to live off its income, but expended also its capital, it would soon find itself without income, and the same exchange, so necessary to the poorer class, would also cease. We will see hereafter that this would not be the only disastrous result that would follow from the destruction of capital. Hence, production must find its measure from the social dividend, and those who encourage an infinite production, without bothering to understand this income, push a nation to its ruin, while believing that they open to it a road to wealth.

Translator's Notes to Chapter 3, Second Book

This chapter is a greatly expanded and revised version of about three paragraphs towards the end of the second chapter of the *Encyclopedia* article. Just one whole paragraph is included here, the remainder rephrased. Sismondi comments on the maldistribution of wealth, but the main thrust of the chapter is against Say's Law—the assumption that increasing production will generate an inexhaustible pool of consumption. As a former merchant, Sismondi knew that consumption is not inexhaustible, at least in the short run, particularly if the distribution of income is highly skewed away from the majority of the population. These two main themes will be elaborated in the rest of the work—here they appear as part of what must be taken as the theoretical core of Sismondi's political economy.

1. The French word used is "devorer."
2. The basis is laid here for Sismondi's argument of the expansion of *unproductive labor*, that is, services, an argument that Malthus would take up in his *Principles*.
3. Sismondi uses "condition," which can mean status or special employment (such as a household domestic). Since Sismondi's analytical unit was class, the status of class members with respect to wealth receiving and spending becomes crucial to an understanding of the concept *satiation of demand*.
4. The note was added to the second edition, apparently as an afterthought. Sismondi differs from all his contemporaries in his emphasis on leisure, his understanding that work is subject to diminishing utility. This assumption allows him to postulate that, with increasing production, a part of the income must be converted to leisure because of the satiation factor for goods. Marx takes this idea, and the later idea of a surplus, from Sismondi to develop his exploitation theory.
5. This paragraph illustrates the time-bound nature of all social science, and of economics in particular. Nobody would assume today that the needs of the working man are necessarily limited—indeed, the mass-consumption economy assumes the very opposite. However, the argument can be generalized and then comes close to Keynesian concepts. If consumption is assumed to be limited, that is, if we assume a relatively declining consumption function, then ever-widening production will indeed meet a deficiency of demand, which Sismondi wants to correct by diminishing production through increased leisure. Sismondi obviously could not see the unsatisfied demand slumbering in the greater part of the European population, an unsatisfied demand that fueled the expansion of the nineteenth century. But on the other hand, his approach rightly points to the crucial need for a dynamic balance between increasing production and lagging consumption. Keynes fills the gap preferentially by investment, but Sismondi would point out that such action would quickly

aggravate the situation, because every investment must lead to increased production. In retrospect Sismondi was proven right, after a long struggle, in his plea to shorten the workweek.

6. The assumption is questionable, but could be argued to be dependent on the definition of luxury goods.
7. How would the author react to a normal rush-hour traffic jam on a freeway in Los Angeles, or any other major industrialized city anywhere in the world, given the sentiments expressed here?
8. Here Sismondi assumes, from his viewpoint as an intellectual, with some justification, that the working class *wants* only a limited amount of luxury, and more importantly, that they *wish to stay at that level of consumption*. The same tacit assumption underlies all socialist reasoning to the extent that class consciousness is assumed to make the worker wish for *social luxuries*, not *individual* ones. Marx, as an intellectual and writer like Sismondi, has the same outlook and therefore assumes that the working class will respond to social incentives, not individual ones. The assumption misreads, of course, the nature of the so-called working class as essentially and fundamentally different from the higher orders.
9. The French term is "pompons."
10. Again, it should be noted that this argument is based on *marginal* utility considerations.
11. For Sismondi this was a statement that obviously had not taken stock of his own lifestyle. According to his biographer de Salis, Sismondi was a workaholic who spent eight and more hours a day at his desk, writing, even though, by his own standards enunciated here, he did not need to do so.
12. This idea is at the heart of an underconsumption cum exploitation theory. The Marxian version, decked out with the engines of Hegelian philosophy, is not more advanced than this view.
13. Here again, the overproduction-exploitation argument points to Marx. However, the call for governmental intervention to *correct* distribution, and the call for a weekly day of rest for the producing poor are, by today's standards, nonsocialist, ameliorative measures which assume, like Keynes later, that the framework of private property is optimal for economic progress. They were radical for Sismondi's time. This paragraph also assumes that the market is not efficacious in allocating income shares in any fair scheme of distribution. This and the next paragraph were inserted into the second edition. There can be little doubt that they were inspired by English conditions and were directed against English contemporary thought. Dickens immortalized this type of entrepreneurial thinking in Mr. Gradgrind in *Hard Times*.

4

How Income Is Created from Capital

[Trade, the generic name given to the total mass of exchange, complicated the relation required to subsist between production and consumption; yet far from diminishing, it increased its importance. At first, everyone procured what he himself intended to consume;] knowing his needs, he regulated his work accordingly. [But when each had come to work for all, the production of all must be consumed by all; and each, in what he produced, must have an eye to the final demand of society, for which he destined the fruit of his labour. This demand, though not well ascertained by him, was limited in quantity; for, in order to continue his expenditure, every one must confine it by certain restrictions, and the sum of those private expenditures constituted that of society.

The distinction between capital and income, which in the Solitary's case was still confused, became essential in society. The social man was under the necessity of adjusting his consumption to his income, and the society, of which he formed part, were compelled to observe the same rule; without incurring ruin] they dare not, [they could not annually consume more than their annual income.] If society encroached once on their capitals, they destroyed at one and the same time their means of reproduction, and means of future consumption. [All that they produced, however, was destined for consumption; and if their annual products, when carried to the destined market, found no purchaser, reproduction was arrested, and the nation ruined] in the midst of abundance.[1] We touch here on the most abstract and difficult question in political economy. The nature of capital and income are continuously confused with each other in our imagination; we see that what is income to one, becomes capital to another, and the same object, passing from hand to hand, receives successively different names; while its value, which separates itself from the consumed object, appears to be a metaphysical entity which one spends, and another exchanges, which perishes for one with the object itself, and which renews itself and persists for another as long as circulation lasts.[2] However, although it is difficult to distinguish the capital from the income of a society, nevertheless the distinction is important. More than one ruinous system has been built on their confusion. Sometimes prodigality was spurred as a means to encourage industry; sometimes capitals instead of incomes were afflicted with taxes, and those who invoked the parable of the goose that lays the golden eggs, to conserve the national capital, were rebuffed as visionaries.[3] We have said above that all wealth is the product of labor. Income, being a part of wealth, must spring from this common origin; it is however usual to recognize three types of income under the name of rent, profit, and wages, as coming from the three different sources, the earth, accumulated capital, and labor.[4] On closer inspection one realizes that these three divisions are three different ways in which to share in the fruits of the work of man.

Because of the advances in industry and the sciences which have subordinated to mankind all forces of nature, every worker can produce every day more and ever more than he has need to consume. But at the same time that his labor produces wealth, that wealth, if he were to enjoy it, would make him less fit to work; also wealth almost never remains in the possession of him who uses his hands for a living. Wealth, however, cooperates with labor, and he who possesses it, withholds from the worker, as compensation for the help he has given him, a part of what the laborer has produced over and above his consumption.[5]

In general, the husbandman has never been able to keep the ownership of land; yet, the earth has productive powers which human labor has been able to direct to the uses of mankind. The owner of the land to which labor is applied, reserves for himself, as compensation for the advantages obtained from the help of these productive powers, a share of the fruits of that labor with which his land has cooperated. This is the income of the landowner, which is deducted from the work of the cultivator, and which can be consumed without reproduction. The economists call it *rent*.[6]

In our state of civilization, the cultivator could no longer maintain possession of an adequate store of goods suitable for his consumption, in order to live while he finished the work he had undertaken, till such time as he found a purchaser. Neither has he any longer in his possession the raw materials, often brought from far away, which he needs for his work. He owns even less the complicated and costly machines by which his labor is made easier and infinitely more productive. The rich man, who owns the consumption goods, the raw materials, and the machines, can forego working himself, since he is in some way the master of the laborer's work, to whom he has provided them. As a compensation for the advantages he has placed into the laborer's hands, he withholds the most important share of the fruits of the laborer's work. That is the profit of the capital he has advanced, or the income of the capitalist.

Though the laborer, by his daily work, has produced much more than his daily cost of living,[7] it is rare that, after having shared with the landlord and the capitalist, he retains much over and above his daily needs. However, what remains with him is his income, and is called *wages*; he can consume it without reproduction.

Let us follow, from their origin, and during their progress, the various incomes in a domestic economy.

To the eyes of the Solitary, through which we have studied first the creation of wealth, [every kind of wealth was a provision made beforehand against the moment of necessity; yet still in this provision he distinguished two things—the part which it suited his economy to keep in reserve for immediate, or nearly immediate use, and the part which he would not need before the time when he might obtain it by a new production. One portion of his corn was to support him till the next harvest; another portion, set apart for seed, was to bring forth its fruit the following year.[8]

The formation of society, the introduction of exchange, allowed him almost indefinitely to multiply this seed—this fruit-bearing portion of accumulated wealth. It is what we name *capital*.

The ground and his animals were all that the isolated man could force to work in concert with him; but in society, the rich man could force the poor to work in concert with him.][9] The cultivator [after having set apart what corn was necessary till the next harvest, it suited him to employ the remaining surplus of corn in feeding other men, that they might cultivate the ground and make fresh corn for him; that they might spin and weave his hemps and wools;] that they would work his mines; [that, in a word, they might take out of his hands the commodity ready for being consumed, and at the expiration of a certain period, return him another commodity, of a greater value, likewise destined for consumption.]

In performing this operation, the cultivator changed a part of his income to capital; and actually this is how new capital is always created. The corn which he had harvested over and above what he will eat during his own work, and over and above what he needs to sow to maintain his cultivation at the same level, was a wealth he could give away, dissipate, consume in idleness, without becoming any poorer; it was income. But once he had employed it to feed his productive workers, once he had exchanged it against labor, or the future fruits of the work of his laborers, his weavers, and his miners, this was a permanent multiplying value which did not perish anymore—it was capital. Now then, this value separated itself from that of the provisions which had created it; it remained like a metaphysical and nonsubstantial quantity, always in the possession of the same cultivator, for whom it took merely different guises. First, it had been corn, then an equal value of labor; then an equal value of the fruits of that labor; later a credit to him to whom these fruits were sold for later payment; then money, then again corn or labor. All of these successive exchanges did not in any way alter the capital; and they did not make it leave the hands of him who saved it in the first place.[10]

During that same time, each of the exchanges this capital accomplished, had furnished to others consumption goods, most often spent as income, without causing a loss. An exchange always assumes two values; each can have a different fate, but the attribute of capital or income dos not follow the object exchanged; it attaches itself to the person who is its owner. Thus, the workers have only their labor as income; they have given it in exchange for corn, which then became for them their income, and they could consume it without there being a diminution of substance, while their labor has become capital to their employer; the latter then exchanged the fruits—they were the wool cloths he has sent to a merchant; the exchange between them was capital against capital; each one kept his own, but in a different form. The merchant has finally sold the wool cloth to a consumer who wanted to make a suit out of it. The latter has purchased it with his income; therefore he could consume it without diminishing his substance; but the part of the income he had given to the merchant, has become for the latter a part of his capital.

Since labor alone has the property of creating wealth by shaping objects such that they can satisfy the needs of humanity, all capital must at first be employed to set labor in motion; all wealth which one does not wish to destroy, must be exchanged against a future wealth that labor must produce. [Wages were the price at which the rich man obtained the poor man's labour in exchange. The division of labour had produced the distinction of ranks.] With each new generation, many individuals came into the world without any other income than their labor; as a consequence they were obliged to take the kind of work which was offered to them. [The person who had limited his efforts to perform only one simple operation in a manufacture, had made himself dependent on whoever chose to employ him. He no longer produced a complete work, but merely a part of a work; in which he required not only the cooperation of other workmen, but also raw materials, proper implements, and a trader to undertake the exchange of the article which he had contributed to finish. Whenever he bargained with a master-workman for the exchange of labour against subsistence, the condition he stood in was always disadvantageous, since his need of subsistence and his inability to procure it of himself were far greater than the master's need of labour;] he demanded subsistence to live, the master demanded labor to profit; [and therefore he constantly narrowed his demand to bare necessaries, without which the stipulated labour could not have proceeded; whilst the master alone profited from the increase in productive power, brought about by the division of labour.][11]

The dependence of the workers, and the miserable condition of those who create the national wealth did not cease to grow with the increase in population; the number of those who have no other income but that of their hands, and who want to work, being always greater, they will be always more pressed to accept work of whatever kind offered, to submit to conditions that are imposed on them, and to reduce their wages to the bare minimum. The advantage of an employer of labor is often nothing else than the plunder[12] of the worker he hired; he does not profit because his enterprise produced much more than its costs, but because he does not pay all the costs, because he does not grant to the worker sufficient compensation for his work. Such an industry is a social evil since it reduces to ultimate penury those who perform the work, while it secures only an ordinary profit of capital to him who manages it.

However, every time the rich man obtained a gain from using labor, he [was situated, in all points, exactly as the husbandman who sows the ground. The wages paid to his workmen were a kind of seed which he entrusted to them, and expected in a given time to bring forth fruit. Like the husbandman] he knew that this sowing would bring him a harvest, namely, the work completed by his workmen, and that from the product of that harvest he would recover, first of all a value equal to his sowing, or in total the capital he had employed to perform the work, and which remained for him an inalienable quantity; further, any surplus of goods he called his profit and which constituted his income. The latter, reborn each year from an equal wealth, could be consumed or destroyed without reproduction, and without thereby making its owner poorer.[13]

The master-workman [like the husbandman, does not sow all his productive wealth; a part of it had been devoted to such buildings, or machines, or implements, as make labour more easy and productive; just in the way that a part of the husbandman's wealth was devoted to permanent works, destined to render the ground more fertile. It is thus that we see the different kinds of wealth springing up and separating.] A part of these which society has accumulated, is destined by each of its holders to make labor more profitable by being used slowly, and to execute through the blind forces of nature a human task; they are called *fixed capital,* and they comprise the cleared land, the irrigation canals, the machines, the workers' implements, and structures of every kind. A second part of this wealth is destined to be consumed quickly in order to be reproduced in the work which it helps to complete, to change its form without end and keep its value; this part, called *circulating capital*, includes seed, raw materials to be worked up, and wages. Finally, a third part of wealth separates itself from the second one; this is the value by which the realized output surpasses the advances that had been made; this value, called the *income* from capital, is destined to be consumed without reproduction; it is exchanged a last time before being consumed, against the things everyone has need for his own use. The sum of all the things which everyone destines to satisfy his needs, things which for him do not reproduce themselves anymore, and which were bought at the sacrifice of one's income, are designated by the name of *consumption fund*.

[It is essentially important to remark, that those three kinds of wealth are all equally advancing towards consumption;] because all that has been produced has a value for man only if it satisfies his needs, and his needs are only satisfied by consumption. But fixed capital is used only in an indirect manner; it is consumed slowly to help reproduce what man designates for his use; circulating capital, on the contrary, does not cease to be used directly for man's use. It enters the worker's consumption fund, of which it represents wages that were received in exchange for the labor which is his income; when the operation is completed, and there has been reproduction, it passes into the consumption funds of another class of men, to those of the buyers who have obtained it with whatever other income. Every time a good is consumed, there is someone for whom this is final; at the same time there may be someone for whom it is consumed with reproduction.[14]

This movement of wealth is so abstract, and it demands such great concentration to understand it well, that we believe it useful to follow it in the simplest of transactions, by fixing our attention on a single family. [A solitary farmer], in a distant settlement, on the edge of a desert, [has reaped a hundred bags of corn, and is destitute of any market to which he can carry it. At all events, this corn must be consumed within the year, otherwise it will be worth nothing to the farmer.[15] But he and his family may require only thirty bags of it; this is his expense,] the exchange for his income, they are not reproduced for anybody. He will then call in workers; he will make them fell trees, drain the neighboring swamp, and cultivate a part of the desert. These workers will eat another thirty bags of corn; for them this will be an expenditure; they will be in a position to do so, at the price of their income, by practicing their trade; for the farmer this will be an exchange; he will have converted these thirty bags into fixed capital. Finally, he is left with forty bags; he will sow them this year, instead of the twenty he had sowed the preceding year; this will be his circulating capital which he will have doubled. [The hundred bags are thus consumed; but seventy of them are put out to profit, they will re-appear] with a great increase, [partly at the next harvest, partly at those which follow.][16]

The very isolation of the farmer we had postulated, makes it easier for us to see the limits of such an operation. [If this year, out of the hundred bags which he reaped, he could get no more than sixty eaten, who will eat the two hundred bags produced next year by the augmentation of his seed? *His family, which will multiply*, it may be said in answer. Doubtless; but human generations do not grow as fast as food.][17] If our farmer had the hands to repeat each year the postulated operation, his corn harvest will double every year, and his family can at most double every twenty-five years.[18]

[Resuming these three sorts of wealth, which, as we have seen, become distinct in a private family, let us now consider each sort with regard to the whole nation, and see how the national revenue may arise from this division.

As the farmer required a primitive quantity of labour to be expended in cutting down the forests, and draining the marshes which he meant to cultivate; so for every kind of enterprise, there is required a primitive quantity of labour to facilitate and augment the circulating capital.[19] The ore cannot be obtained before the mine is opened; canals must be dug, machinery and mills must be constructed, before they can be used; manufactories must be built, and looms set up, before the wool, the hemp, or the silk can be weaved. This first advance is always accomplished by labour; this labour is always represented by wages; and these wages are always exchanged for necessaries of life, which the workmen consume in executing their tasks. Hence what we have called fixed capital, is a part of the annual consumption, transformed into durable establishments, calculated to increase the productive power of future labour. Such establishments themselves grow old, decay, and are slowly consumed in their turn, after having long contributed to augment the annual production.

As the farmer required seed, which, after being committed to the earth, was returned five-fold in harvest; so likewise, every undertaker of useful labour requires raw materials to work upon, and wages for his workmen, equivalent to the necessaries of life consumed by them in their labour. His operations thus begin with a consumption; and this is followed by a reproduction which should be more abundant, since it must be equivalent to the raw materials worked upon, to the necessaries of life consumed by his workmen in their labour, to the sum by which his machinery and all his fixed capitals have been deteriorated during the production, and lastly to the profit of all concerned in the labour, who have supported its fatigues solely in the hope of gaining by it.[20] The farmer sowed twenty bags of corn to reap a hundred; the manufacturer will make a calculation nearly similar. And as the farmer at harvest must recover not only compensation for his seed, but likewise for all his labours, so the manufacturer must find in his production, not the raw materials only, but all the wages of his workmen, all the interest and profits of his fixed capital, with all the interests and profit of his circulating capital.

In the last place, the farmer may augment his seed every year; but he will not fail to recollect that, since his crops increase in the same proportion, he is not sure of always finding men to eat them. The manufacturer, in a like manner, devoting the savings of each year to increase his reproduction, must recollect the necessity of finding purchasers and consumers for the increasing products of his establishment.

Since the fund destined for consumption no longer produces anything, and since each man strives incessantly to preserve and augment his fortune, each will also restrict his consumable fund, and instead of accumulating in his house a quantity of necessaries greatly superior to what he can consume, he will augment his fixed and circulating capital,] at least momentarily, [by all that he does not expend. In the present condition of society, a part of the fund destined for consumption remains in the retail-dealer's hand, awaiting the buyer's convenience; another part destined to be consumed very slowly, as houses, furniture, carriages, horses, continues in the hands of persons whose business it is to sell the use of it, without abandoning the property. A considerable portion of the wealth of opulent nations is constantly thrown back into the funds destined for consumption; but although it still gives profits to its holders, it has ceased to augment the national re-production.]

Translator's Notes to Chapter 4, Second Book

This chapter was greatly expanded from the *Encyclopedia* article. Sismondi amplified his views on the relations between production, demand, and consumption by introducing the idea of unequal market power of employer and employee, the consequent ability of the employer to appropriate a larger share of the product than the employee, and postulating as a result permanent underconsumption by the working class. Sismondi's reasoning is heavily influenced by utility ideas, despite his claim to be a disciple of Adam Smith and an adherent of the labor theory of value. He is, first and foremost, a macrotheorist preoccupied with the emerging imbalances of the new capitalist-industrialist system. To him, unfair income distribution and misery in the midst of plenty are unacceptable results of that new order. He discards the very notion of economic equilibrium and tries to take a dynamic view of economic processes, with a concomitant rejection of Say's law. His analytic ability is severely taxed in this attempt to free himself from classical categories, resulting in weak economic reasoning.

1. The term *reproduction* is used by Sismondi throughout in its physiocratic

sense. He understands by it the replacement of what has been used in the production process, including the subsistence of the worker, that is, consumption goods. In making a clear connection between the *variable* demand and the production process by postulating that the former may be insufficient to absorb the total supply of goods, Sismondi rejects Say's law. The reference to *ruin in the midst of abundance* is clearly intended to show that it is not *nonproduction* which will lead to distress. It should be noted that this idea is already in the *Encyclopedia* article.

2. The meaning is obscure, but it seems that Sismondi refers here to the dichotomy between monetary value and real (use) value, a separation that, later, also gave Marx difficulties in his inability to derive a theory of price from his labor theory of value.
3. The next four paragraphs were changed from the first edition. In the first edition, Sismondi enumerates and discusses separately the three sources of wealth: land, labor, and *the lives of the working population*. Capital does *not* appear as a separate source of wealth. What changed his approach is not known, but it is possible that Sismondi was influenced by the writings of Robert Owen. The absence of capital as a separate factor in the first edition is peculiar because it was generally recognized as such by classical writers, and certainly by Adam Smith.
4. It should be noted that Sismondi omits interest, or rather substitutes profit for interest.
5. Here, in a nutshell, is a statement of Marxian exploitation theory. Sismondi bases his statement on the assumption of a wages fund, that is, a postulate of a productive exchange between the employer-provider of subsistence, and its recipient, the worker. Marx regards the wage of the worker in the Ricardian sense as a market-determined measure of subsistence. Exploitation for Sismondi is a decision of the employer, using his power; for Marx, a result of an indifferent market. As a consequence Sismondi can postulate later an ameliorative change in property, while Marx must call for a total revolution to abolish the capitalistic market system.
6. It is not clear whether Sismondi meant here the physiocrats, or *les économistes,* or economists in general. Probably the first, since this paragraph and others before and after have strong affinities to physiocratic reasoning.
7. The French term is *dépense journalière.*
8. In *New Principles* these two paragraphs are joined.
9. Again, it is important that this statement of unequal economic power flowing clearly from property holding already appears in the *Encyclopedia* article.
10. Clearly, Sismondi tries to explain with economic arguments what is actually a legal arrangement that could be changed at any time. The original saver retains title to the property he uses for further production after he has made the choice between consumption and investment. Later, in discussing agricultural property in the third book, Sismondi explains that rights in land are granted as a convenience to society and can therefore be revoked. He could have done the same here, explaining that property rights are incentives to savers for the sake of increased production. Economics does not deal explicitly with property relations—most economic theory takes social institutions for granted and fails thereby to consider dynamic changes that may affect economic variables.
11. This paragraph shows clearly how much of Sismondi's exploitation theory was already incorporated into the *Encyclopedia* article. Sismondi stands the bene-

fits of the division of labor on their head, after extolling them in the previous chapter, and turns them into the main engine of exploitation and class distinction. The theme of unequal market power will run throughout *New Principles,* and the solutions advanced are all directed to equalizing this power in the market place by equalizing *property rights.*

12. This statement is a combined recapitulation of classical wage subsistence theory and Marxian *reserve army* analysis. Sismondi turns the classical approach around and makes the greater market power of the capitalist the determining factor in the distribution of the national income. The French term *spoliation* can be translated as 'extortion', 'robbery', or 'ruination', which would come close to Marxian usage. It should be noted that Sismondi raises in the next sentence the problem of externalities, unaccounted costs of doing business, by charging that labor is not paid full compensation for its efforts. The Marxian exploitation argument is an amended version of Sismondi's analysis.
13. The paragraph is a straightforward exposition of the physiocratic model. Sismondi frequently oscillates between Smithian concepts and physiocratic analysis. As a general matter he favors, naturally so, physiocratic ideas whenever he refers to agricultural problems, and labor theory categories whenever he deals with industrial problems.
14. Schumpeter and Aftalion have accused Sismondi of analytical ineptitude and general fuzziness. This paragraph is a case in point, and it also demonstrates why Sismondi was analytically weak. It is evident that the preceding statement was based on physiocratic notions, including the idea of reproduction. On the other hand, Sismondi had a perfectly workable model of the circular flow of the economy in mind, which was based on the concepts of Adam Smith, as is evidenced by the analytical use of the two kinds of capital. The theoretical groundwork for his analysis of business fluctuations depended, as will be seen later in this book, on the uninterrupted flow of capital and income. The notion of reproduction was crucial to the model—production and employment would decline if the consumption fund would not ask for the *reproduction* of what was used up in the preceding stage of production. If Sismondi would have discarded the notion of reproduction and would have made a simple division between consumption and investment, as already existing in classical political economy, and would have linked investment with consumption, rather than reproduction (or interest, as Ricardo did), he would have come very close to a Keynesian model. As the statement stands, it has to be interpreted as an intermediate sector model, in which consumption changes impinge on the use of capital indirectly.
15. Why Sismondi believes that the corn should be valueless at the end of the year is not explained. Obviously, the value of last year's corn depends on the amount of the new crop and the state of demand for food. Even assuming an isolated farmer does not argue for worthlessness—the total farm population may want to increase their food consumption, or they may want to increase their provision for failed harvests. It may be that Sismondi argued from his own experience as a farmer—conditions at that time in Italy being such that corn could not in fact be stored beyond a year without spoiling.
16. One of the main tacit assumptions is that each production cycle *adds* to existing stocks. Sismondi eventually takes into account the possibility of losses in all industries, but even in his cycle model the *normal state* is one of increasing

income in all sectors of the economy. Particularly in agriculture, there is no warrant to assume this as a normal state of affairs. There may be some justification for assuming this for industry, especially under the assumptions of market power that Sismondi makes for the industrial employer, but even there losses are not unknown.

17. These two sentences, starting with the italicized *His family*, were incorporated into both editions from a footnote in the *Encyclopedia*. There they are followed up with this additional remark: "This is the reverse of what Mr. Malthus has advanced. We shall afterwards examine this discrepancy." Sismondi returns in the seventh book to his disagreement with Malthusian population theory.
18. The assumption of twenty-five years is also used by Malthus. It is possible that Sismondi simply took it from there, but it is more likely that this figure was a generally accepted one as representative of population and generational change.
19. The term *primitive labour* recalls the physiocratic term *avances primitives*. Sismondi also uses this idea to justify ownership of land, although he modifies the concept. Today all of these ideas would be subsumed under the general heading of *infrastructure investment*.
20. The reference here is apparently to any creditors-investors who have financed the entrepreneur.

5

Division of the National Income between Different Classes of Citizens

We have said that labor had created three permanent sources of wealth in society, and that they gave rise to three incomes. The first of these sources is land, whose spontaneous power, always ready to produce, needs merely to be directed to the advantage of mankind;[1] it receives this direction through labor. The capital used to pay wages to labor is the second of these sources. Life, which gives the power to work, is the third. Hence, all three have a direct relation to labor, and without labor there is no wealth.[2]

Land, as a source of income, has products easy to acquire with fixed capital, with machines, mills, forges, mines, whose ownership also gives an income which, in order to be born, waits only to be developed by human labor. Land, like the machine, helps this labor and makes it more productive; the fruits of this labor comprise, together with the hire of the workman, in one case the hire of the land, in the other the hire of the machine which has worked like a human.

But the power of the machine to produce is owed entirely to previous human labor, which has created it in its entirety. The productive power of land is owed only partly to such previous labor, which has enclosed it, cleared it, and has made it capable of producing as soon as annual labor fertilizes it. There exists also in the earth, in nature, a productive force which does not in any way come from man, and to which he claims ownership, solely in return for the effort he makes to direct it.[3] The economists have therefrom concluded that labor devoted to fertilizing land was much more productive than any other, because it was helped by a spontaneous force, which needed only to be awakened.[4] However, machines on their part bring into play forces infinitely superior to those of man, the movement of air, that of water and steam, and their products, at least everywhere where land has become property, are more profitable than those of agriculture. In the colonies, where land belongs to those who wish to take it, agricultural pursuits[5] are the most profitable, since they are the first for which society feels a need.

In contrast to land, the other two sources of wealth could be combined: life, which gives the ability to work, and capital which pays for it. When these two powers are united, they together possess an expansive force, and the labor the worker will perform during the year, will always be worth more than the labor during the preceding year, with which he will maintain himself.[6] Industry provides a constant increase in wealth as a consequence of this surplus value,[7] which is so much larger when the arts, or the sciences in their application to the arts, have made much progress. This increase may either become the income of the industrial classes, or be added to their capital. But, generally, the capital which pays the wages of labor and makes work possible, never remains in the hands of those who work. It is a consequence of a more or less unequal division between the capitalist and the worker, a division in which the capitalist is determined not to leave to the worker more than what is just necessary to maintain life, and keeps for himself all that the worker has produced over and above the value of that life. The worker, on his part, battles to keep a somewhat larger part of the labor he has performed.[8]

To examine this battle, whose outcome is important, it will be easier to abstract from all those workers who are at the same time capitalists, and of all capitalists who are at the same time workers; according to whether the income they expect comes more from their work or their capital, they will tend towards one or the other class.[9] We must also abstract from the basic difference between incomes which come from land, and those which come from capital, to which we will revert later. It is equally by capital and labor that the former spring from the soil; the farmers, the rural entrepreneurs, are capitalists. They are, to their workers, in an analogous position to the city capitalists; after having made advances for the workers' upkeep, they strive to keep for themselves all the gains of their work, and leave to the worker only that share necessary for his subsistence, and to preserve to him the strength he needs to perform his work.

From this second point of view, national income consists of only two parts, one included in the annual product, the other outside of it: the first is the profit which springs from wealth, the second is labor power which springs from life. Under the heading of wealth we include in this instance landed property as well as capital; and under the title of profit, we include the net income which will be given to the landlords, as well as the gain of the capitalists. The former take no part in the battle; it is only after its conclusion that their rent, less the profits of capital, will be handed over to them.[10]

Similarly, the annual product, or the result of all the work performed during the year by the nation, consists of two parts: one is the same we are going to discuss, the gains which spring from wealth; the other is labor power, which is assumed to be equal to that part of wealth for which it is given in exchange, or the subsistence of those who work.

Thus, the national income and the yearly product are in mutual balance and seem to be equal quantities.[11] All of the annual product is consumed, partly by workers who, in exchanging it for their work, convert it into capital and reproduce it; and partly by capitalists who destroy it by giving their income in return. Moreover, one should never forget that labor power is incommensurable with wealth. Wages do not represent an absolute quantity of labor, but only a quantity of goods which has sufficed to maintain the workers of the previous year. The same quantity of provisions will set in motion, in the following year, a larger or smaller amount of labor; from that change in the proportion between these two values stems the increase or diminution of national wealth, the well-being or misery of the productive class, the expansion or destruction of the population.[12]

It must also be pointed out that the national income consists of two quantities, one of which is from the past, and the other from the present; or, if one wishes, one from the present and the other in the future. One, the gains from wealth, is at present in the hands of those who demand to consume it; and it is the result of work done in the preceding year; the other, the will and ability to work, will not become real wealth except as the opportunity to work presents itself, and as that ability exchanges itself simultaneously against consumption goods.[13]

The entire annual income is destined to be exchanged for the total annual product; through this exchange, everyone provides for his consumption, everyone replaces a productive capital, and everyone makes room and causes a demand, for a new production. If the annual income did not buy the total annual product, a part of that product would remain unsold, it would glut the warehouses of the producers, immobilize their capital, and production would stop.[14]

If those whose income consists of profit from wealth, experience such losses that the profit does not cover their living expenses; or if they abandon themselves to luxury and prodigality that cause them to increase their expenses without their incomes being increased; and finally, if for whatever reason, they devote to their consumption more than their income, they can take this extra expense only from their capital; but in this case, after having increased for one year the incomes of the working class, they diminish it as much for all subsequent years, because all they call capital ought to be given in exchange for labor, which is the income of that class. The wealthy gives the law to the poor; if he eats his capital, he ruins himself, certainly, and his self-interest alone ought to deter him; but if he closes his eyes to that interest, if he eats his capital, the remainder of that capital is all that the poor will receive as the price for the labor of the following year. The income of the poor is still the same, because he has still the same ability to work, but the value is not anymore the same. As long as the wastrel eats his capital like income, he gives to the working class, in return for all the product it can turn out, a greater share in the national product. When the wastrel has no more income, having used up his capital, that part of the annual product which is offered to the working class in exchange for all the work they can perform, is diminished by as much; for its work it obtains less subsistence.

If, on the contrary, the rich man saves from his income to add to his capital, he takes for himself a smaller part of the annual output of industry, and he leaves a larger part to be given in exchange for labor; as much as he has cut back on his income, so much is the income of the poor increased; not only because he receives a larger share of subsistence in exchange for his work, but also because the work he gives is larger. If the population is not adequate to accomplish an increase in work, it increases soon because of the increase in wages, since there is nothing like penury to stop the expansion of the human species. From the moment that such penury ends, the children, which would die at a tender age, live to enjoy this new abundance; the bachelors, who would have no children at all, marry to have them, and have them profit from the demand for labor.

The wealthy therefore benefits the poor when he saves from his income to add to his capital, because in making the division of the annual product, all that he calls income he keeps for his own consumption; all that he calls capital he hands over to the poor, so that he can make it his income. But the wealthy man, in making this division, ought to have another consideration in mind, namely never to encourage labor which is not demanded; because the product of labor which will have been ordered without justification, either will not sell, or sell badly; hence the profits he expected in the following year will either be diminished, or will have been changed to a loss; and after having caused the birth of an active population that has no other income than their hands, he deprives it of subsistence he had made them expect in exchange for their work.[15]

By his prodigality the rich man has been able to produce a very similar result. As long as he has eaten his capital together with his income, he has demanded a larger quantity of work, and he has offered for it an ampler wage; but, after having encouraged in this way an increase in the population of the working class, he suddenly withdraws his revenue because he has dissipated even his capital. One has few occasions to observe these fluctuations, after the downfall of the spendthrift, because in general the saving of one compensates for the prodigality of the other; but if the government itself eats its capital, which happens above all during a war, where heavy loans are intended to meet annual expenses, it begins to create an artificial prosperity, because it spends the principal of the loans, and then soon reduces to a most cruel penury the population it has called into being, it has fed with that capital, at the very moment it begins to pay its debts, instead of borrowing anew.[16] After these general reflections on the first division of income it will be appropriate to follow its distribution through all branches of society.

[The farmer, after deducting from his crop a quantity equal to the seed of the foregoing year, finds remaining the part which is to support his family;] and he takes it and consumes it in exchange for his income which consisted of his annual labor; [the part which is to support his workmen, who have acquired right to it by the same title; the part with which he is to satisfy the landlord, who has acquired right to this revenue by the original improvement of the soil, now no longer repeated], or simply by occupation of vacant land. [Lastly, the part with which he is to pay the interest of his debts, or indemnify himself for the employment of his own capital—a revenue to which he has acquired right by the primitive labours which produced his capital.] One can even add a fifth part which was also born from the annual production of his fields, namely the hire he will pay to all the guardians of his rights, of his person, and of society. These guardians, magistrates, soldiers, lawyers, physicians, acquired a right thereto by nonproductive labor, one which leaves nothing behind.

[So, likewise, the manufacturer finds, in the annual produce of his manufactory, first the raw material employed; secondly, the equivalent of his own wages, and those of his workmen, to which their labour alone gives them right;] the equivalent of the interest of the annual depreciation of his fixed capital, an income to which he, or its owner, has acquired a right by primitive labor; finally, the interest and profit [of his circulating capital, which has been produced by another primitive labour.]

One sees that, despite the opposition we have postulated between the incomes that spring from wealth, and those which are only labor power, there exists nevertheless between them a necessary connection: their source is the same, but from a different time period. [Among those who share the national revenue, some acquire a new right in it every year by a new labour, others have previously acquired a permanent right by a primitive labour, which has rendered the annual labour more advantageous. No one obtains a share of the national revenue, except in virtue of what he himself or his representatives have accomplished to produce it;

unless, as we shall soon see, he receives it at second hand,] as compensation for services he has given to others. [Now, whoever consumes without fulfilling the condition which alone gives him a right to the revenue; whoever consumes without having a revenue, or beyond what he has; whoever consumes his capital in place of revenue, is advancing to ruin; and a nation composed of such consumers is advancing to ruin likewise. Revenue, indeed, is that quantity by which the national wealth is increased every year, and which accordingly may be destroyed, without the nation becoming poorer; but the nation which, without re-production, destroys a quantity of wealth, superior to this annual increase, destroys the very means by which it would have acquired an equal re-production in subsequent years.][17]

Translator's Notes to Chapter 5, Second Book

This chapter is new material, except for a small paragraph at the end. Sismondi expands here the idea advanced in the previous chapter—unequal market power of capitalist and worker. Sismondi introduces the concept of *mieux value,* that is, surplus value, defined as the value the worker creates over and above what he would produce if he would provide only for his necessities. Crises in the production process, periodic overproduction of commodities with resultant business failures, are created because the surplus value is appropriated by the capitalist, leading to a deficiency of demand because the capitalist cannot spend all of the appropriated surplus, and the workers as a class are unable to buy what was produced because they do not receive the full value equivalent of their production. All the concepts advanced here by Sismondi reappear in Marx, either with direct citation, or without. While there may be some question whether Marx appropriated Sismondi's model deliberately, there can be no question that Sismondi was first to develop the nomenclature as well as the concepts. All of the arguments advanced in this chapter and in the rest of the work essentially question the realism, and by extension, the validity, of Say's law. Since Say's law is a generalized version of Smith's invisible hand, Sismondi's attack is also directed at *The Wealth,* despite his professions that he is a faithful disciple of the master. Keynes remarked, in his *Essays in Biography,* how Malthus's approach to economics was obliterated by Ricardian analysis, and how much this had proven to be a disaster for the progress of economics. Since Sismondi preceded Malthus by a couple of years, leaving aside Marx's accusation that Malthus had plagiarized *New Principles,* Keynes's remark applies even more to the forgotten work of Sismondi.

1. As noted in the previous chapter, physiocratic ideas are quite influential in Sismondi's thinking, including his use of the *Tableau* as a model for the circular flow of incomes in society. Eventually in the next chapter he will develop, from the physiocratic circular, but static, flow, his dynamic spiral model of business fluctuations, which Schumpeter sees as the first such model in economics.
2. This sentence relates directly to the four paragraphs in chapter 4 of the first edition, which were changed for the second edition. Apparently Sismondi did not notice that the reference did not fully apply anymore. See note 3, chapter 4.

3. Again, as the very next sentence clearly indicates, this statement has physiocratic origins. Sismondi substituted in the second edition "The economists have therefrom concluded . . ." for "Il en resulte."
4. The remainder of this paragraph was changed from the first edition, possibly with reference to English conditions. In the first edition there is no reference to machines and natural powers, merely to the division of the product between labor, farmer, and landlord.
5. The French term is *l'industrie territoriale*.
6. Sismondi obviously believes that machine production, just spreading to the Continent, will increase output incrementally every year. Since the worker's wage is paid from a wages fund based on last year's output, the wage bill must always be smaller than the product for this year. On the one hand, this assumption leads to Sismondi's idea of the *surplus value,* first advanced in the next sentence; on the other hand, it leads to his dynamic model of spiral expansion and contraction, expounded in the next chapter.
7. The French term used is *mieux value*. Aftalion, in his detailed evalution of Sismondi's theoretical work, discusses at length the use of Sismondi's concepts in Marx's writings, mainly the *Manifesto* and *Das Kapital*. While there can be no conclusive proof that Marx appropriated Sismondi's ideas, the evidence is strong that that was indeed the case. It is psychologically significant that Marx cites Sismondi more than any other writer, and supports key sections of *Das Kapital* with these citations, but does *not* discuss his theories separately in his critique of political economy, the *Theorien über den Mehrwert,* often called the fourth book of *Das Kapital*. This supports the presumption that Marx did not want to expose fully the main source of his central criticism of capitalism. While the germ of the idea is already contained in Smith's assumption that the landlord and the capitalist appropriate part of the product of labor, the connection between what the worker would produce for his own subsistence, and what he produces for his employer over and above this subsistence, central to Sismondi's later insistence on leisure for the worker, is original to Sismondi. The term occurs nowhere else before. Even if Aftalion absolves Marx (and his forerunner Rodbertus) of outright plagiarism, the very use of the term and its crucial importance to the Marxian system raise questions of priority that shed a curious light on the integrity of Marxian scholarship, especially if seen against Marx's accusation that Malthus had cribbed his *Principles* from Sismondi.
8. Antagonism, or opposed interest, between employer and employee, master and worker, is, in political economy, logically inherent in the labor theory of value (being also a fact of life), as long as it is accepted that *ownership* of capital or land entitles the owner to a share of the product, leaving to the worker less than the value of what he produced. The classical writers thought they had solved the problem by shunting the issue to an impersonal market mechanism that supported a subsistence theory of wages. However, this overlooked that the distribution of the national product is not a natural consequence of God-given laws, but the result of social arrangements that have changed over time. This clearly implies that the division of the product is a *political matter*, in the sense that distribution is a matter of market power and therefore subject to negotiation and the application of such power. It further implies that the state, as a representative of all interests, has the right, and the duty, to intervene in this battle to bring about an equitable distribution of the product. Sismondi, as a historian, had to be aware of this view, and was the first writer to state this

issue bluntly. By positing distribution as a battle between opposing interests, Sismondi denies the possibility of a theoretical equilibrium and the validity of the subsistence theory of wages, the mainstay of Ricardian economics. If the idea of a continuous battle between employer and employee is accepted as a realistic description of social economic action, the concept of a stable equilibrium must be discarded, except perhaps as a heuristic device of limited use for theoretical analysis. Marx obviously drew this conclusion and manufactured a new Edenic equilibrium in the postrevolutionary classless state, in which the product theoretically belongs to the workers. As later experience shows, the Marxian utopia overlooks (which Sismondi did not!) that *control* over the means of production, that is, economic, de facto ownership, not legal title, is the determining factor in the distribution of the product. Both Say's Law and Smith's invisible hand are devices to eliminate the issue entirely from analysis.

9. Sismondi's main claim of opposition to Ricardian economics was his realism. Even though he postulates a class struggle, he recognizes that class divisions are not as clear-cut as theory, and especially socialist theory, would have it. Sismondi's qualifications also mirror a reality that Ricardo should have been aware of, and that had changed somewhat by the time Marx composed his major opus, but again not to the extent that he postulated in his theory of class war. During the first half of the nineteenth century, small entrepreneurs were a hallmark of the Industrial Revolution, men who used their own and often their families' savings to start a business, and who often worked, at least in the beginning of their careers, alongside their workers. Sismondi foresaw concentration of industry and advocated dispersion of ownership by participatory sharing, an idea that may have returned in employee stock options, pension plans, and similar arrangments. In Sismondi's analysis, an employee with such rights might indeed favor one or the other class, depending just how much his income is dependent on one or the other source. Sismondi may have had in mind the many new entrepreneurs of the new Industrial Revolution when he analyzed the new industrial age in *New Principles*.
10. This is a mainly physiocratic view of the landlord; Ricardian economics saw the rent receiver in the same light, but it should be kept in mind that this view was in turn derived from the physiocrats via Adam Smith. It is also likely that it is an accurate description of reality. Sismondi, for instance, as an owner of a Tuscan *métayage,* was in fact the passive receiver of a rent; the farmers who cultivated landed estates in England paid the noble lords their rents after deducting their profits on invested capital.
11. The next sentence was inserted into the second edition.
12. A clear reference to price changes in basic subsistence goods and in wage rates. Sismondi uses variability in factor and commodities prices, determined by final demand, to evolve a dynamic model of business cycles. Sismondi here assumes downward flexible prices, and hence immediate results on labor supply.
13. For the first time in political economy, Sismondi spells out an assumption that is reasoned away with Say's Law—remunerative work is *not* at all times available! The opportunity to work is chained to the need for reproduction, Sismondi's concept of replacing consumption goods used up in the normal course of economic activity. If reproduction declines, because consumption declines, available employment will decrease together with profits and the size of the wages fund.

14. Sismondi clearly describes an inventory accumulation with subsequent recession, triggered by declining consumption. The classical answer to this assumption was of course that prices would adjust to clear the accumulated inventories. Why did Sismondi omit this possibility here when he implied it just two paragraphs before? Subsequent argument will show that he assumed that capitalists would not be prepared to abandon their businesses, and that they would also attempt to cover their losses by a reduction of costs (labor) rather than by writing down their inventories. The model is a forerunner of Keynesian analysis, as well as of Marx's depression theory. The inconsistency is most likely a result of the difficulties Sismondi had with pure analysis, as well as with liberating himself from established theory.
15. The preceding three paragraphs constitute a rudimentary business cycle model. Sismondi assumes a wages fund that is tied to the preceding year's income of the capitalist *and* to his consumption. If the capitalist increases consumption by reducing his capital/investment, he will stimulate consumption expenditure beyond the society's capacity to produce; that is, he will induce inflationary expansion beyond the full-employment point. If the capitalist increases savings to add to the wages fund he will raise the wages of the workers, leading also to an expansion of both population and production. But since his own consumption has been decreased, the expansion is apparently assumed to be noninflationary. The caveat that no production should be called forth that is not demanded is a recurring theme in this work; while analytically vague, to Sismondi it meant that in response to larger available capital (increased saving), production would increase in the hope that the market would absorb the new goods, even though satiation may have already set in.

    The entire model is close to Keynesian analysis—aggregate spending increases by either increased consumption or increased investment. In the first case, no off-setting increases in saving/investment will increase capacity, leading to an inflationary gap. If saving increases *and* is transformed into investment (Sismondi assumes later that such is not always the case), aggregate expenditure will also increase, but increased capacity will bring about full employment. If the increased capacity leads to an expansion in the production of unwanted goods (overexpansion at the top of the cycle), losses will force cuts in production because of inventory accumulation, and declines in aggregate spending, with serious consequences for the working population. It must be remembered that Sismondi assumed that children would work from a tender age—the expanded wages fund would indeed lead to an oversupply of labor in a very short time.
16. One wonders what Sismondi would have said about pump-priming and governmental deficits to cure unemployment. However, it should be noted that he opposes *extraordinary* expenditure financed by borrowing. The implication is clear that he would have regarded regular government expenditure financed by taxes as a legitimate exercise of business-cycle control.
17. These last few excerpts from the *Encyclopedia* reflect strongly Sismondi's own experience with deficit financing to sustain a prodigal French court. More generally, Sismondi really raises the legitimate question whether a large expansion of credit must not ultimately lead to a repudiation of such borrowing, either by inflation, or by default. The distinction between capital and income was apparently clear enough to Sismondi, but as an analytical device it lacks precision.

6

Reciprocal Determination of Production by Consumption, and of Expenditure by Income

The progress of national wealth follows a circular course; [every effect becomes a cause in its turn], each step is determined by the preceding one, and determines the one that follows, and the last one brings back the first in the same order.[1] The national income ought to regulate national expenditure which, in turn, ought to absorb, in the consumption fund, total production; the entire consumption causes an equal or larger reproduction, and from reproduction springs income. [The national wealth continues to augment, and the state to prosper], if a speedy and total consumption always causes a larger reproduction, and if the other parts of wealth, [which are proportional to each other], follow this progress at the same pace, [and continue to augment in a gradual manner; but when ever the proportion among them is broken, the state decays.]

The national income ought to regulate the national expenditure. We have seen that this income is of two kinds: a material gain for the wealthy, the power to work for the poor. The former need only to ask themselves to exchange this gain from wealth, which constitutes their income, for the many consumption goods that will satisfy their needs or desires; but if they spend beyond their income, they are necessarily forced to take from the very principal of their wealth which creates their gains, they diminish their future gains, and ruin themselves.[2]

The poor who have only their labor as income are, before spending it, dependent on the upper class. They must convert this labor into money,[3] they must sell it before they can obtain the enjoyment of its fruits; and they can sell it only to those wealth holders who, after having spent their income for themselves, exchange their remaining capital with the poor.[4] Labor power is an income from the instant it is employed; it is nothing if it finds no buyer; and, even if employed in its entirety, it increases or diminishes in value according to whether it is more or less sought after. Hence, the poor will spend his income, work, only after having sold it, and he will regulate his expenditure by the price for which he will have sold it. All expenditures he makes beyond this price, whether he provides them from his small savings, or from loans, are ruinous for him and society;[5] on the other hand, every hardship he takes upon himself resulting from the smallness or termination of that price, is equally ruinous for society as soon as it assaults his life, his health, or his strength, because it diminishes, or destroys, his future ability to work that forms such an essential part of the social revenue.[6]

Thus the poor, as well as the rich, must not exceed their realized income by their expenditures, and total social expenditure is regulated by social income.

On the other hand, national expenditure must absorb, through the consumption fund, total national production. In order to follow this reasoning with greater certainty, and to simplify the problems, we have, till now, completely abstracted from foreign trade, and we assume an isolated nation; humanity is that isolated nation, and all that would be true of a nation without trade, is equally true of the human race.

We have seen that providing for his needs is the sole goal of man's labor, and that only those goods have value which can be turned to his use; that such use always involves destruction, sometimes quickly, sometimes with extreme slowness; but ultimately, from the moment he either begins to enjoy wealth, or withdraw it from circulation, he begins to consume it. It does not matter, in order for wealth to have achieved its goal, that it be already dissipated for the use of man; it suffices that it be withdrawn from the market and converted to enjoyment, or that it have passed into the consumption funds.

As long as wealth has not reached that end, it halts the reproduction of an equal quantity which should replace it. The Solitary, once he has more food, more clothing, more lodging than he can use, stops working. He will not sow, in order not to reap, weave in order not to dress, build in order not to dwell; he will, without doubt, find enjoyment in a certain excess and, if he can, will create for himself, not necessities, but luxury. Such abundance is a pleasure of the imagination; it has nevertheless its limits. If the excess will not beguile anymore his imagination that it will be essential to his wants, the Solitary will stop working; he will find that he is paying too dearly for such an insignificant pleasure by buying it with fatigue. Society is exactly like this man; by dividing the tasks, it has in no way changed the reasons which motivate it. It does not want more food if there is nobody to eat it, and if no one believes that it will be eaten; it does not want more clothes if no one wants to hang them in their closets any longer, nor houses if no one wants to keep them for living quarters.[7]

But the limits which consumption imposes upon reproduction are felt even more in society than with the isolated individual: even though society includes a great number of individuals poorly fed, poorly clothed, and poorly housed,[8] it only wants those who can buy; and as we have seen, one can buy only with one's income. If there are too many luxury goods produced which only the wealthy can obtain from the income of their capital, then perhaps these wealthy people will have a desire to have them, and they will fancy how they could get new pleasures from them; however, they will not buy them if, at the risk of ruin, they would have to mortgage their capital; that is, they would take away from the present income of the poor, and from their own future incomes. On the other hand, he who will have produced the luxury goods, being unable to exchange them against the income of the wealthy, never recovers his capital, and will be unable to restart his operation, and his business will be interrupted.[9]

If many more subsistence goods were produced for the poor, not only could they consume them, but since they would also receive income in exchange for their labor, there can be no doubt that they would be much inclined to be better fed, better clad, and better housed; however, they will not remain so because the envy of the rich will dispose them not to offer a higher wage, but to demand more labor from them; they, who either have nothing to give in exchange beyond such labor, or, if they have a small fund, expend it, become more penurious. Corn[10] can then remain unsold in the midst of a multitude who will suffer hunger, and the producer, not recovering his capital, cannot renew his advances, so that his operation will end.[11]

An oversupply of goods leads always to greater consumption through a decline in prices; but this result is not that much more advantageous. If the producers bring to market twice the amount of luxury goods than the total income of the wealthy, and if they are determined to sell them, they will be forced to give all goods for the total amount of that income, that is, at a 50 percent loss. The rich will believe to have gained as consumers, by obtaining cheaper what they scarcely desire; but it is among the wealthy that producers are also found, and in that capacity they will lose more than they will have gained because they will lose what is essential. Their loss of 50 percent on the sale of the annual production will be divided between their capital and their income. By diminishing their income it will reduce their consumption in the following year; by diminishing their capital it will reduce the demand for the labor of the poor, and it will reduce their income in all of the following years.

If producers bring to market subsistence goods of twice the value of the wages of the poor, they will be equally obliged to give these goods for the value of these wages, and with a loss of 50 percent. The poor will profit as consumers for that year; but the loss of 50 percent from the capital or revenue of the producer will make itself grimly felt the following year. All that the rich will have lost from income, he will cut back from his consumption, and there will be less demand for the fruits of labor of the poor; all that the rich will have lost from his capital, he will subtract from the wages he pays, and labor, which is the income of the poor, will be worth less.[12]

This is how the national expenditure, limited by income, must absorb, in the consumption fund, the entire production.

Aggregate consumption determines an equal or greater reproduction. It is here that the circle can enlarge itself and change into a spiral: last year has produced and consumed as ten; one can fancy that next year, by producing at eleven, will also consume at eleven. The greater or lesser ease with which consumption is achieved indicates the more or less happy result of a similar operation which took place the previous year. Already the wealthy had subtracted something from their revenue to add to their capital, or the wages they offer to the poor. As a consequence more output has been produced. If more output is sold, and at a good price, this new capital has thus given birth to a proportionate income, and that income demands new consumption. The savings of the past year will be divided the next year: one part, as income, will increase the pleasures of the rich, one part, as wages, will increase the pleasures of the poor. This process, executed with prudence and moderation, can then perpetuate itself. But it would be made harmful by hastening it. It is the income of the past year which must pay for the output of this year; it is a predetermined quantity which serves as a standard for the undefined quantity of labor to come. The error of those who urge an unlimited production comes from their mistaking this past income with future income. They have said that to increase labor means increasing wealth, with that, income, and by reason of the latter, consumption. But wealth is only increased by increasing demanded labor, labor that will be paid its hire; and that hire, fixed in advance, is the preexisting income. After all, the total yearly production can only be exchanged for the entire production of the previous year. Hence, if production increases gradually, the exchange of each year ought to cause a small loss at the same time that it improves future circumstances. If that loss is small and well distributed, everyone bears it without complaining about his income; this very process makes up the national economy, and the chain of these small sacrifices adds to capital and public prosperity. But, if there is a great disproportion between the new and the previous production, capitals are reduced, there will be suffering, and the nation regresses instead of advancing.[13]

In short, income is born from reproduction; but it is not production by itself which is the income; it does not take that name, it does not act as such till it is changed to money, till after each produced commodity has found the consumer who has the need or desire for it and who, withdrawing it from circulation to add to his consumption stocks, has given its price in exchange. This is how the producer makes his calculation; from the sales he will be able to make he will first recoup his capital in its entirety; he realizes then the profits that remain; they will then in turn be devoted to his pleasures and to the resumption of his business.[14]

By everything we have just said it can be seen that [a derangement of the mutual proportion subsisting among production, revenue, and consumption, becomes equally prejudicial to the nation, whether the production give a revenue smaller than usual, in which case a part of the capital must pass to the fund of consumption; or whether, on the contrary, this consumption diminish, and no longer call for a fresh production. To cause distress in the state, it is enough that the equilibrium be broken.[15] Production may diminish when habits of idleness gain footing among the labouring classes; capital may diminish when prodigality and luxury become fashionable; and lastly, consumption may diminish from causes of poverty, unconnected with the diminution of labour, and yet, as it will not offer employment for future re-production, it must diminish labour in its turn.

Thus nations incur dangers that seem incompatible; they fall into ruin equally by spending too much, and by spending too little. A nation spends too much whenever it exceeds its revenue, because it cannot do so except by encroaching on its capital, and thus diminishing future production; it then does what the solitary cultivator would do if he should eat the corn which ought to be secured for seed. A nation spends too little, whenever, being destitute of foreign commerce, it does not consume the excess of its production above its exportation; for, if so, it soon comes into the condition of the solitary cultivator, who having filled all his granaries far beyond the probability of consumption, would be obliged, that he might not work in vain, partly to abandon his cultivation of the ground.]

Luckily, as long as a nation does not adopt a wrong system, as long as its government does not give it an impetus that diverts it from its natural interests, the increases of capital, income, and consumption most often advance in step by themselves, without any need for guidance; and if one of the three component parts of wealth happen to exceed, for the time being, the others, then foreign trade is almost always ready to reestablish equilibrium.

One could believe that, when I accuse the most famous economists to have devoted too little attention to consumption, or to sales, there being no merchant who does not know their decisive importance, I fight an error which exists only in my imagination. But I find this opinion reproduced in the latest work of Mr. Ricardo, from a viewpoint which lays itself open to criticism; and Monsieur Say has in no way fought in his writings against an opinion which does not differ from his, which, up to a point, can even be attributed to Adam Smith.

"When the annual productions of a country," says Mr. Ricardo,*[16] "more than replace its annual consumption, it is said to increase its capital; when its annual consumption is not at least replaced by its annual production, it is said to diminish its capital. Capital may therefore be increased by an increased production, or by a diminished consumption. If the consumption of the government, when increased by the levy of additional taxes, be met either by an increased production, or by a diminished consumption on the part of the people, the taxes will fall upon revenue, and the national capital will remain unimpaired."

How now? It is equally a sign of prosperity for the Lyon hat industry to have made 100,000 hats in 1817, and then 110,000 in 1818, or else having made 100,000 last year, but not having sold more than ninety thousand; because, in either case, 10,000 hats are left over? Without any doubt one would not find a hatter who, without taking himself to be a great economist, would not hesitate to answer that, if in 1818 110,000 hats were made instead of 100,000, there is a profit, provided that all of them were sold at their price; that there is a loss if the extra ten thousand could not be sold; but that, if in 1818 only 100,000 hats were produced as in 1817, and if moreover 10,000 hats were left over unsold, there is most certainly a loss.

In order to see some truth in Mr. Ricardo's proposition, foreign trade must be brought into the equation; and it soon becomes apparent how many modifications it needs.

If the Lyon hatters have produced, in 1817, 100,000 hats which they sold at twenty francs apiece to the consumers of that city alone, this will amount to two million received by one class of Lyon citizens, and paid by another; and if in 1818 they manufacture an equal quantity of hats which sell equally quickly at the same price, however in such a way that 10,000 were bought by the inhabitants of the countryside, while 10,000 Lyon citizens did not buy hats, one can say that the latter have saved two hundred thousand francs while the hatters have not lost anything. If, on the contrary, in 1818 the hatters sell at the same price and equally quickly 100,000 hats to the inhabitants of Lyon, and another 10,000 to the farmers, one can say that the manufacture of hats has increased its capital by two

*_Principles,_ Chapter VII, p. 239.

hundred thousand francs, without any cost to the Lyon consumer, and the two outcomes, from a certain point of view, can be considered the same for the city of Lyon. But there is no increase in production in the first case; there is no decrease of consumption in the second, which will increase or maintain the national capital; it is the new demand coming from consumers who can pay, and pay the same price. As far as the sale to the farmers is concerned, as opposed to the inhabitants of Lyon, it results in a difference in the trade balance of Lyon, and none for France; similarly, with respect to the difference between sales to Frenchmen and to foreigners, it exists only in the trade balance of France and not in that of human society at large. If one examines the latter, which governs world trade, one always sees that a consumption increase may alone determine an increase in reproduction, and that on its part consumption can only be determined by the income of the consumers.[17]

Translator's Notes to Chapter 6, Second Book

The chapter summarizes and completes the various ideas on consumption and production advanced in the preceding chapters. It is the heart of Sismondi's case against Ricardian classical political economy, and the assumptions of Say's Law. It presents for the first time what Schumpeter has called "a method of dynamics that is called period analysis." Sismondi will amplify this basic model in several ways in later parts of the work. The model is based on an assumption similar to Keynesian concepts—the discretionary nature of the savings-investment cycle—expressed here as contributions to a wages fund which encompasses all labor, both for consumption and capital production. Increases in the wages fund are dependent on sales and the realization of profit, that is, on an early version of an implied consumption function. Sismondi makes spending a function of income in the previous period, actually a year, which leads him to several awkward conclusions. In addition, he assumes that production in the present period to replace what has been consumed is a separate variable that he calls *reproduction*. If he had combined the two ideas and dropped the reproduction idea, he would have advanced a macromodel of the economic process much superior to anything that was developed in the nineteenth century. Whether the model would have been accepted is nevertheless questionable because it departed from the discussion of value theory and the Newtonian mold of classical analysis.

1. Another echo of Quesnay's *Tableau,* especially in its insistence that the last step in the chain brings back the first one *in the same order*. However, Sismondi uses the chaining concept in a different manner—to show that expenditure, as a variable, has effects on production and investment that are not fully predictable, and that are not fully explainable by natural law assumptions. As Schumpeter expressed it: "He [Sismondi] realized that the most important of the reasons why transitional phenomena are of the essence of the economic process—and hence not only relevant to its practical problems but also to its fundamental theory—is that the economic process is chained to certain sequences that will exclude certain forms of adaptation and enforce others" (1954, 495).

2. Sismondi uses here the *produit net* concept—the net surplus from production is the only amount available for consumption. This repeats the argument of the previous chapter.
3. The French term used is: "Il faut qu'ils réalisent ce travail . . ."
4. It should be noted that, while Sismondi assumes a wages fund as capital, the implication is clearly that the owners of investible funds have the option *not* to invest. This assumption is contrary to classical reasoning—the interest rate will indicate to the rational wealth holder what the trade-off between present and future consumption is, and the wealth-holder will accordingly divide his funds between the two without any hoarding.
5. Sismondi clearly disliked credit, especially under circumstances of low income, but the paragraph makes an important point about consumer credit—consumer credit is based on the assumption that income to pay principal and interest is continuous, an assumption that Sismondi regards at least as nonproven. In his day, as his call for worker security makes quite clear, workers' income was not an assured amount over long periods of time. Clearly, his personal experiences with credit in his youth shaped his opinion.
6. Sismondi is quite clear about his assumption of variable consumption—the income of the worker is variable in accordance with the size of the wages fund; hence consumption of subsistence goods is also variable. This formulation abandons the subsistence equilibrium of classical analysis and substitutes a demand theory for labor, which is governed by the spending decisions of wealth-holders.
7. The main assumption of Say's Law, namely that any production will be absorbed by the equivalent income is explicitly rejected with this statement. By postulating an *attainable* level of satiety, Sismondi splits income into a necessary and a *discretionary* part—the latter will not be spent if satiety has been reached. The subsistence theory of labor assumed that for the largest part of the population spending was automatic, since by assumption labor received only what was necessary, that is, subsistence. Sismondi modifies this assumption in two ways: first, the size of the wages fund is a discretionary variable, and, second, even with a subsistence wages fund, it is possible for society to be at the satiation stage, in which case spending will cease. Sismondi, like his contemporaries and later writers, silently excludes spending for social monuments of no economic value, such as cathedrals and arenas, which in effect would, and did, absorb the otherwise unspent wealth.
8. The language recalls a later orator, and not without reason. Sismondi's prescriptions for the taming of the business cycle, expounded mainly in book 7, resemble in many ways what the New Deal put into effect.
9. Sismondi returns consistently to an inventory accumulation model, that is, unintended investment, to come to the pessimistic conclusion that there will be a decline in the wages fund and suffering among the working poor. It would seem that this reflects the merchant's fear of unsold goods in warehouses, a fear he may have shared when he apprenticed in Lyon and the approaching Revolution threatened the sales of his employers.
10. Sismondi uses *blé*, 'wheat,' here, which he translates in the *Encyclopedia* as 'corn.'
11. A clear descripton of class war in which the governing class, here read *capitalists*, use their economic power to get a larger share of the social product, as opposed to the classical theory, which assumes that the laboring classes will

come to subsistence because of more children. Exploitation will, however, carry its own retribution—the inability of the workers to spend an adequate income will curtail *reproduction* and thus lower the social product. In Keynesian terms, an unequal income distribution due to unequal market power will lower the consumption function and the marginal propensity to consume, lowering aggregate expenditure and aggregate supply. The description of conditions used here again evokes pictures from the Great Depression more than a hundred years later.

12. This takes up the classical argument that price changes will restore full-employment equilibrium. By postulating the same mechanism as in the previous paragraph for luxury goods, that is, introducing an income effect, Sismondi shows that such price changes will not restore a stable equilibrium, even if it is assumed that market prices are in temporary equilibrium.
13. Here is the heart of Sismondi's macroeconomic model. As would be expected from an author who struggles to free himself from the domination of a popular and logically seamless theory, concepts are not clear and apparent mistakes occur. But the general import is unmistakeable—the size of the national product is a dependent variable determined by the decisions of wealth-holders to add, or not to add, to the wages fund, read *investment*.

    Sismondi starts with the basic assumption that the ease of consumption this year—whether the output was sold at expected prices—is the basis for production decisions for the next year in the same way that ease of consumption last year determined the production decisions of this year. If there were adequate sales, the wealthy, (savers), have added to their capital, which means in Sismondi's model additions to the wages fund. Hence production has increased. *If* this enlarged output is sold at a *good price*, that is, with the expected profit, the process will continue in what Sismondi called a *spiral*, an ever-widening circle of increased consumption-saving-investment. But it will do so only if the increases are moderate. Why? Sismondi postulates that since the income of the previous year buys this year's product, any large difference between the two must lead to a reversal of the process.

    Let us assume that the income of last period (year) is much smaller than the product of the new period (year) because a small production in the last period (year) led to a total sale of all available goods. Savers will have increased sales expectations and add the largest possible amount to the wages fund. This will lead to a much larger output. However, the income of the last period is then inadequate to purchase the new output, sales will decline, inventories will accumulate, and the next period will see a decline in investment and income. On the other hand, as the next paragraph implies, the assumption of a large income in the first period does not necessarily mean that expectations for the next period will induce investors to add to the wages fund—this will depend on how well products were sold in the first period. A near-equality of the income of the last period with the production of the next period will ensure prompt sales with only small, distributed losses, which will not negatively affect expectations, and therefore the process of allocation of savings to the wages fund in a manner that will sustain prosperity.

    Sismondi's suggestion that small, well-distributed sacrifices will add to capital seems paradoxical, but if his argument is framed in expectational terms, as done here, it is entirely plausible. Alternatively, the idea can be taken to imply a moderate amount of inflation, which will let the real product lag just a little bit behind the monetary income. In this case, real losses will be incurred that will be distributed over the whole population, but the inflationary bias of the monetary veil would increase expectations, sustaining an expansion. However, if the inflation rate increases, fueling speculation, the cycle will reverse itself because of the mismatch between production and subsequent consumption.

Measured against the classical model, this sketchy one-paragraph outline is awkward and appears self-contradictory. But, again, it must be taken as a determined attempt to disprove Say's Law, to oppose the merchant's knowledge of the changeability of consumption decisions to the certainties of the producer who assumes that all the income shares of the product will be spent to buy the product immediately. Sismondi implicitly assumes the same disjointedness that Keynes built into his model in the spending of income by *lagging* his spending-production cycle *in parallel* with his consumption-investment cycle, creating in effect an overlap with two independent variables, additions to the wages fund and consumption by income receivers.

14. This should be compared to Keynes's discussion of effective demand in chapter 3 of *The General Theory of Employment*, footnote 2, p. 24. It is interesting that a writer with limited business experience, and an academic economist (who was, however, a successful financier) should give major importance to changing business expectations in the determination of aggregate economic activity, while businessmen like Ricardo, a banker, and Say, a successful factory owner, would set aside such considerations in favor of a deterministic model of economic activity that eventually found its way into Marxist ideology. The assumption of uncertainty and expectational variability of aggregate spending in effect divides the work of Sismondi and Keynes from the classical school and its socialist offspring, Marxism.
15. Sismondi chose *equilibrium* here, but *proportionality* would have been a better choice. It is obvious that he uses the term not in its accepted static meaning, but as an expression of a dynamic balance.
16. The citation is from p. 131 of the Gonner edition, third and fourth paragraph from the beginning of chapter 8. Sismondi does not quote the entire second paragraph, probably because Ricardo comes to a conclusion that partially agrees with Sismondi.
17. This paragraph should be compared to Keynes's discussion of the propensity to consume, chapter 8 of *The General Theory of Employment,* and the following remarks on page 89: "The aggregate demand function relates any given level of employment to the "proceeds" which that level of employment is expected to realise. The "proceeds" are made up of the sum of two quantities—the sum which will be spent on consumption when employment is at a given level and the sum which will be devoted to investment"; also on page 104: "Opportunities for employment are necessarily limited by the extent of aggregate demand. Aggregate demand can be derived only from present consumption or from present provision for future consumption."

7

How the Circulating Medium Simplifies the Exchange of Wealth

[We have designedly carried on our history of the formation and progress of wealth thus far, without mentioning a circulating medium[1] to show, that, in fact, such an instrument is not necessary for its development. A circulating medium did not create wealth; but it simplified all the relations, and facilitated all the transactions of commerce; it gave to each the means of finding sooner what suited him best; and thus presenting an advantage to every one, it still further increased the wealth, which was already increasing without it.

The precious metals are one of the numerous values produced by the labour of man, and applicable to his use. It was soon discovered that they, more than any other species of riches, possessed the property of being preserved without alteration for any length of time, and the no less valuable one of uniting easily into a single whole, after being divided almost infinitely. The two halves of a piece of cloth, of a fleece, and still less of an ox,—though these are supposed to have once been employed as money,—were not worth the whole; but the two halves, the four quarters of a pound of gold are always, and will be, a pound of gold, however long they may be kept.[2]

As the first exchange of which men feel the need, is that which enables them to preserve the fruit of their labour for a future season, every one became eager to get precious metals in exchange for his commodity,[3] whatever it might be; not because he at all intended to use those metals himself; but because he was sure of being able to exchange them at any time afterwards, in the same manner, and for the same reason, against whatever article he might then need.[4] From that time the precious metals began to be sought after, not that they might be employed in the use of man, as ornaments or utensils, but that they might be accumulated, at first, as representing every species of wealth, and then that they might be used in commerce, as the means of facilitating all kinds of exchange.

Gold dust, in its primitive state, continues, even now, to be the medium of exchange among the African nations. But when once the value of gold comes to be universally admitted, there remains but a single step, much easier and far less important, till it be converted into coin, which warrants, by a legal stamp, the weight and fineness of every particle of the precious metals employed in circulation.

The invention of money gave quite a new activity to exchange.] It divided in some manner each contract into two parts. Before, it was always necessary to consider at the same time what one wanted to get, and what one wanted to give; with the help of the circulating medium each of these actions was made separately: the acquisition of what one wanted to get was called *purchase*; the surrender of any surplus one wanted to dispose of was called *sale;* and the two exchanges were made independent of each other. The farmer, to dispose of his corn, needed no longer to meet the clothier[5] who would furnish him with the article he needed; it was enough for him to obtain money, certain that, against this money, he would always get the desired article later. [The buyer, too, on his side, needed not to study what would suit the seller; money was always sure to satisfy all his demands. Before the invention of a circulating medium, a fortunate concurrence of conveniencies was requisite for an exchange; whereas after this invention, there could scarcely be a buyer that did not find a seller, or a seller who did not find a buyer.]

All the processes which we have noted in the preceding chapters, and which form the progress of wealth in a nation, were simplified by the introduction of a medium of exchange; but as it on the other hand doubled the number of all contracts, they became less easy to understand for the observer. We have seen that the creative action of wealth is the exchange of one part of the yearly consumable production that makes up the capital of the rich, against the labor that makes up the income of the poor. But this process is divided into a great number of contracts, and is expressed by entirely different sums of money. The producers sold the annual output, and from its total they will calculate, in money, on the one hand their income, on the other their capital. With the income they bought the goods they needed or desired for their consumption; this was their expenditure; and through these two contracts the exchange was completed. With their capital they bought as labor the income the poor had to sell; this labor was estimated in money; the poor, in turn, bought with this money the goods they needed for their subsistence; this made up their expenditure; and the second part of the exchange of the annual output was completed.[6]

Not only was capital thus measured by money, but it appeared in actuality to be only money; language helped to confuse the two ideas, and it requires always a special effort of concentration to remember that capital is not money, or at least it is such only at a given moment; that it is really that part of consumable wealth which is given to the workers in exchange for their annual labor.

The income of the wealthy was equally measured by money, and it also needed a social effort of attention to remember at all that money is but momentarily its measure; whereas the income comprises in reality that part of consumable wealth the rich exchange against another part of the same wealth, of the same value, destined to provide for their needs.

Finally, the wages of the poor are always counted in money, and it needs a similar attention to recognize that they are identical with the capital of the wealthy; that is to say that they are that part of consumable wealth given to the workers in exchange for their annual labor.

Thus, the circulating medium simplified all commercial transactions and complicated all the philosophical observations which have these transactions as their object. As much as this invention showed everyone clearly the goal to be pursued in every transaction, by that much it made the totality of these transactions intricate and unclear, and the general direction of commerce difficult to grasp.

Translator's Notes to Chapter 7, Second Book.

The chapter is a basic, short, and mostly pseudohistorical introduction to money. Major parts of it are taken from the *Encyclopedia*. It is mainly a literary device to connect the foregoing theoretical discussion with the following arguments about foreign trade, and the main argument that modern production and market organization prevent the producer from knowing his market, that is, actual demand, thus creating economic instability because of mismatched actual production to expected demand.

1. This is of course not true, because in the previous chapters he used money in several ways, but Sismondi had not made an explicit analysis of the concept. The connection here is awkward because he reverts back to the *Encyclopedia* text and the lead paragraph comes from a slightly different context. However, since the translation tries to use the *Encyclopedia* material wherever there is a close fit to the French text, the *Encyclopedia* version was used here.
2. Sismondi separates here by a paragraph what was one paragraph in the *Encyclopedia*. In this statement he disregards the fact that melting and remelting of the precious metals also result in losses.
3. In *New Principles* this was changed to "*superflu*," 'surplus'.
4. An early indication of the author's uncompromising hard-currency position in the later book on money. Historically, the description of the rise of money is not very accurate, since many commodities preceded the widespread use of metals, and particularly gold. The implied assumption, spelled out later, that the precious metals imply stable prices is, of course, also historically incorrect.

5. The French term is ''marchand d'habits.''
6. The argument is similar to Marx's C-M-C discussion. Marx quotes Sismondi as to the definition of capital: ''Capital . . . a permanent multiplying value'' (1957, chapt 4, 2nd book, p. 162).

8

How Commerce Helps Production and Replaces the Producer's Capital

First trades, and then sales and purchases which took their place later, were usually voluntary acts in which each person did not commit himself till after he had determined that the commodity given to him in exchange was worth as much as what he gave up. Hence, [it might be inferred that all values were given for value completely equal,] and that the mass of yearly exchanges added nothing to the nation's wealth. However, these transactions could also be considered from another viewpoint; and trade is indeed based on a more precise understanding of their ends. [Bargains were never made without advantages to both parties. The seller found a profit in selling, the buyer in buying. The one drew more advantage from the money he received, than he would have done from his merchandise; the other more advantage from the merchandise he acquired, than he would have done from his money. Both parties had gained, and hence the nation gained doubly by their bargain.[1]

On the same principle, when a master set any workman to labour, and gave him in exchange for the work expected to be done, a wage which corresponded to the workman's maintenance during his labour;—both those contractors gained; the workman, because he had received in advance the fruit of his labour, before it was accomplished;—the master, because this workman's labour was worth more than his wages.[2] The nation gained with both; for as the national wealth must, at the long run, be realized in enjoyment,[3] whatever augments the enjoyment of individuals, must be considered a gain for all.[4]

The produce of the soil and of manufactories belonged often to climates very distant from those inhabited by their consumers. A class of men undertook to facilitate all kinds of exchange, on condition of sharing in the profits which it yields. These men gave money to the producer, at the time when his work was finished and ready for sale; after which, having transported the merchandize to the place where it was wanted, they waited the consumer's convenience, and retailed to him in parcels what he could not purchase all at once. They did service to everyone, and repaid themselves for it by the share which is named profits of trade. The advantage arising from a judicious management of the exchanges was the origin of those profits. In the north, a producer reckoned two measures of his merchandize equivalent to one of southern merchandize. In the south, on the other hand, a producer reckoned two measures of his merchandize equivalent to one of northern merchandize. Between two equations so different there was room to cover all the expenses of transport, all the profits of trade, and interest for all the money advanced to carry it on. In fact, at the sale of such commodities transported by commerce, there must be realized, first the capital repaid to the manufacturer; then the wages of the sailors, carriers, clerks, and all the persons employed by the trader; next the interest of all those funds to which he gives movement; and lastly, the mercantile profit.]

The trader places himself between the producer and the consumer, to render a service to both, letting himself be paid for this service by both. In the same way that there existed a division of productive labor among the workers, there was a division of this second type of labor that involved managing capitals, and its effect was the same; after such a division more output was more advantageously produced with the same resources. The care to supervise the workers, to direct their efforts, to distribute to them raw materials, to inspect the output, demanded an entirely different use of intelligence, and an entirely different training than the attention to compare the diverse goods and needs of distant climates and people set apart by law and language. The transactions were more secure, the service more regular when these two occupations were no longer united. The wholesaler made it his business to buy from the producer the merchandise at the moment it was finished; and after having compared the demand in various markets, sending it to the one where the consumer seemed the most eager to buy it.[5] In this operation, the merchant was again, in some fashion, a director of labor, and he had workmen following his orders, to wit: his clerks on the one hand, his sailors, truckers, porters on the other. All cooperated indirectly with production; because production, having as its object consumption, cannot be considered as achieved unless it has placed the produced article at the doorstep of the consumer.[6]

The comparison of different markets of distant people created an opportunity to also pay attention to different moneys and different ways of payment; and trade subdivided itself to give to bankers the function of balancing the exchanges of the producers of one country with the producers of another, the consumers of one country with the consumers of another, in such a way that it sufficed to ship commodities to effect reciprocal payment without the need to also ship specie. The bankers, who thus separated themselves from the merchants to serve them, contribute no less, although indirectly, to the great exchange of production against the income of the consumer, and of the latter against reproduction.[7]

The study of world markets could divert the business man from another study not any less essential and much closer to him, that of the needs of the consumer who lived at his doorstep; the retailer took over and relieved the merchant, and he agreed, for a share of the profits, to keep in his store what the consumer would have added to his consumption stocks, if he had already had the disposition of his income with which he would have had to acquire it. The retailer waited for his convenience, and made him pay for it.

Trade employs a considerable capital which appears, at first glance, to be no part of the capital whose circulation we have described in detail. The value of cloth stored in the warehouse of the draper seems at first indeed alien to that part of the annual production the wealthy gives to the poor as wages to enable him to work. However, this capital has done nothing but replace the capital of which we have spoken. In order to grasp clearly the progress of wealth, we have caught it at its creation, and we have followed it to its consumption. Now, the capital employed in the manufacture of cloth, for instance, has always seemed to us the same; exchanged against the income of the consumer, it divided itself into only two parts: one has served as income of the producer as profit, the other has served as income to the workers as wages, while they produced new cloth.[8]

But one soon discovers that, to the advantage of everyone, it were better that the various parts of this capital substitute for each other, and that, if one hundred thousand écus sufficed to accomplish the entire circulation between the producer and the consumer, these hundred thousand écus would divide themselves equally between the manufacturer, the wholesaler, and the retailer. The first, with only a third, produced the same output he would have made with the whole, because at the moment when his production was finished, he found the merchant as a buyer much earlier than he would have found the consumer. The capital of the wholesaler on his part found itself quickly replaced by that of the retailer. Thus the workmen who work on a building pass from hand to hand the heaviest materials they move; the exertion is much shorter and rest more frequent, but the work is the same. The difference between the sum of advanced wages and the buying price to the ultimate consumer must constitute the profits of capital. It divides itself between the manufacturer, the merchant, and the retailer, according to how they had divided their functions between themselves, and the achieved output was the same even though three persons and three fractions of capital were employed instead of one.

Translator's Notes to Chapter 8, Second Book

The chapter, similar to chapter 6, owes a great deal to Sismondi's apprenticeship in Lyon with the Genevese merchant firm Eynard and Cie. According to Sismondi's biographer, Salis, the young Charles became an excellent bookkeeper, and the commercial training he received in Lyon formed his future habits of methodical work and his preference for factual verification of all theoretical speculation. Much of the argument here and elsewhere is formed by business practice and a commercial viewpoint, even though Sismondi was only in Lyon a short time. Ricardo was a very successful banker and stock-market speculator and obviously acquainted with business practice. But the world of finance is in a sense more abstract and operates at one remove from the world of commodities and production that the merchant has to deal with everyday. A financier deals with representations of real wealth, both debt and ownership, and has only an abstract involvement with the underlying processes of production; a merchant deals in a very personal way with goods, buyers, and sellers and is therefore much more aware of individual economic motivations that determine the aggregate action of the marketplace. Ricardo and Cantillon (also a banker) have much in common in their abstract analytic approach. It is perhaps also pertinent that Sismondi administered a small estate for his family and himself as a landholder in Tuscany, certainly an experience of economic motivation at the microlevel. For all that, Sismondi never had a great aptitude for aggressive business ventures. He was never rich, sometimes being only moderately well off. On the other hand, he was never destitute, either, in the manner of Karl Marx, and was always able to provide adequately for himself and his family.

1. This and the following paragraph were part of the same paragraph in the *Encyclopedia*. The argument is clearly based on marginal utility considerations. Say and Sismondi both employed utility concepts, as opposed to the English labor economists, suggesting that Continental thinking had already been heavily influenced by the Italian writers of the eighteenth century, for example, Beccaria. It is unclear how much Jeremy Bentham contributed to these ideas, but in any case *he* derived most of his ideas from the same source.
2. This concept was clearly developed by analogy with the preceding analysis of market exchange, and the utility notion that exchangers in a free contract situation must both gain because each one gives up what is of lesser value, and receives what is of more value to *him*. The analogy obviously does not work with respect to labor, especially if, like Sismondi, one assumes that labor is the only thing that can be offered, and that it would be offered only to the extent of attaining a comfortable subsistence. The formulation leads immediately to the concept of *unearned surplus* received by the capitalist, as indeed Sismondi advances the idea of a *mieux value,* a surplus appropriated by the capitalist.
3. *New Principles* inserts here: "tout ce qui est plus commode."
4. The next paragraph is not a direct successor in the *Encyclopedia,* but two paragraphs further on.
5. Clearly, this entire description is based on utility considerations and personal business experience; the analysis belies the term *unproductive labor* applied to

services that was part of the classical canon, and indeed of Sismondi's own. It should be noted that he recognizes the diversity of skills necessary to sustain the economic cycle, and the common-sense conclusion of a resultant divison of labor. Classical analysis, despite its primacy in the discovery of the division of labor, tends in its post-Smithian disciples, including Marx, to assume homogeneous labor, and factors of production with approved interests, called "classes."

6. The last sentence follows logically from the dynamic model discussed in chapter 6—the entire economic cycle is complete only if the produced goods are withdrawn into the consumption fund—with the implication that the cycle is not necessarily always completed or self-sustaining.
7. The classification of middlemen, including bankers, as indirectly contributing to production saved Sismondi from the error of Marxist analysis, derived from classical (and physiocratic) theory that these classes are unproductive and therefore *can be dispensed with* in a socialist economy. (It is, however, at variance with his definition of unproductive labor.) He rightly sees that the circular flow would be less efficient if these functions did not exist, deriving the conclusion from the simple observation that the rise of specialized trades was due to a need in the marketplace. This is not to say that his pseudohistorical description of the process is in fact an accurate version of what really happened.
8. The analysis is derived from Quesnay's *Tableau*, but it also incorporates the experience of the owner of a *métayage*. In agriculture, the workers must be paid *before* the crop is in—the farmer in effect sustains his workforce before the product is marketed, and in fact produced. Sismondi did not see (at least he gives no indication thereof) that in a manufacture the worker is usually paid *after* he has produced the output. This accounts for the awkward construction of the reproduction concept, that is, the production which replaces in *this period* the goods taken into the consumption fund. If Sismondi would have assumed a continual flow from producer to consumer he could have constructed a dynamic model, which could have worked with arbitrary time periods instead of the confusing year interval.

9

Classes Who Work without the Value of Their Work Being Embodied in an Object Produced by Them

[Society requires something more than wealth; it would not be complete if it contained nothing] but owners or capitalists and [productive labourers.] Society requires administrators who direct its efforts at home to a common goal, and who protect its interests abroad; it requires legislators who determine the respective rights of its members, it requires judges who make it respect these laws, and lawyers who defend it. Finally, it needs an armed force that maintains the internal order the nation has established, and which repels abroad, by land and sea, foreign challenges that could disturb it. This whole protective force[1] from the head of state to the least soldier, produces nothing. [Their labour never assumes a material shape; it is not susceptible of accumulation. Yet without their assistance all the wealth arising from productive labour would be destroyed by violence; and work would cease, if the labourer could not calculate on peaceably enjoying its fruits.][2]

The guardians of the nation perform a necessary labor which deserves reward; they can in other respects belong to the wealthy class, and as such have an income derived from property. But, as guardians, they work, they are workmen, and their income consists of the annual value of their work. However, this income is not paid to them, like that of the other working class, from the national capital. And it should not be. That capital must not in any way be destroyed, it can only be exchanged against material goods which represent it in its totality, and the product of the guardians has no substance, it is not capable of a new exchange which perpetuates it.

Hence, [to support this guardian population,] it became necessary to encroach on the income of society, but not its capital. It became necessary that everyone give up some of his needs to pay for his security because security is also a benefit. The rich reserved the income born from their property to satisfy their needs through the consumption of a part of the annual production. They renounced a proportionate part of what was their share in this output in return for the security that was guaranteed to them; and the guardians consumed that part given up by the wealthy. The poor destined their income, that is, the wages they received for their work, to the procurement of their subsistence; they consented to give the same amount of labor, and to receive less subsistence in return, while the part taken from them was consumed by the guardian population as payment for the established order.

[But as the service done to the community, by the guardian class, how important soever it be, is felt by no one in particular;] it could not have been an object of free exchange.[3] [The community itself was under the necessity of paying it by a forced contribution from the revenue of all.] The authority, brought into being by free choice, soon destroyed all balance between the values of the goods exchanged, all justice between the contracting parties. The contribution was paid to those who commanded the social authority to reward them when they ordered it. Soon they abused it. They laid a heavy hand on the taxpayers whose contributions they themselves determined; [civil and military offices were multiplied far beyond what public weal required; there was too much government, too much defence of men, who were forced to accept these services, and to pay them, superfluous or even burdensome as they might be; and the rulers of nations, established to protect wealth, were often the main authors of its dilapidation.][4]

Even if governments would be considered only from the economic viewpoint, still, one would have to come to principles of representative government. In all dealings between owners and those from whom they demand some product, the wage rate is negotiated between the two parties; but in the work the guardian population performs, the worker fixes his own salary, and forces those he serves to pay him that. This population does not serve individuals, but society; it therefore behooves society to name its representatives to negotiate with it. This is the right and duty of national representatives in free governments; and, despite their intervention, it is a rare nation that is still not expensively defended, because a great deal is required to make the representatives defend the interests of those they represent as they would defend their very own.

[Society needs that kind of labour which produces mental enjoyments; and as mental enjoyments are, nearly all, immaterial, the objects destined to satisfy them cannot be accumulated. Religion, science, the arts, yield happiness to man.] To spread this happiness, those who practice these arts must labor; but this labor does not produce material fruits, because [what belongs only to the soul is not capable of being treasured up.] If one wanted to call all enjoyment wealth, the wealth they create is dissipated at the very moment of its creation; it is put to man's use without having passed, even for an instant, into his reserve fund.[5] Also, the two transactions of bringing it about, and of buying it for use, are made and paid by the same person, who is the consumer. This labor, as the previous one, exchanges itself only once, and against income; because there is not a sufficient interval, between the creation of its fruits and their destruction, for capital to interpose itself to be able to buy and resell them.

Each consumer divides his income as he wishes, between his material and immaterial enjoyments; and it is usually by a free exchange that he replaces with his income alternatively, sometimes the capital of the producer, sometimes the labor of the workers who are called *unproductive*. The latter in turn consume that part of the material output the other consumers have given up to hear them.

Government has decided that among the enjoyments of the soul, there were some of great usefulness to society that were not at all sufficiently demanded; it has feared that if it let everyone pay for his religion and education, according to everyone's desire, religion and instruction would be neglected. Government has abolished their free market, and it has provided for the stipends of their practitioners, similarly to its own upkeep, through a forced contribution. The result of this was, as in its own case, that by making the workers independent from those for whom they performed the work, and who paid for it, the work has been less well performed, with less zeal, and most often with less success. In the countries which have abandoned this practice, where religion and education are left to free competition, this has not happened, because those who had to pay for them were not lacking a taste for either, and those who had to work at them have shown more enterprise and talent.[6]

These serious enjoyments of the spirit, as well as those of a more fleeting nature, such as reading poetry, music, theater, are exchanged against the income of the poor classes as well as the rich; the former give up a part of their subsistence, the latter a part of their material abundance, to indulge in the luxury of the spirit; and that part of the consumption that came to them in the first exchange, goes to the unproductive workers as their substitutes.

It must also be said that if [a nation does not reckon literature and the arts among its wealth, it may reckon literary men and artists; the education they receive, the distinction they acquire, accumulate a high value on their heads; and the labour which they execute being often better paid than that of the most skillful workmen, may thus contribute to the spread of opulence.] In general, the skill acquired by workers, to whatever class they belong, is a kind of fixed capital.[7]

[Society, in the last place, needs those kinds of labour, the object of which is to take care of the persons, not the fortunes of men. Such labour may be of the most elevated, or of the most servile kind; according as it requires either the knowledge of nature, and the command of her secrets, like the physician's labour, or merely complaisance and obedience to the will of the master, like the footman's labour. All of them are species of labour intended for enjoyment, and differing from productive labour, only in so far as their effects are incapable of accumulation. Hence, though they add to the well-being of a state, they do not add to its wealth; and] the income of that class, or the value of their work, is always given in exchange for income, and not against the capital of all the others. The distinction between productive and unproductive workers which we are restoring, has been rejected by the latest authors in political economy.[8] The name of unproductive workers, which was given to them by Adam Smith, because their output was not tangible, has been deemed to be a kind of insult to very respectable classes. It would be difficult to decide, depending on how the two titles of productive and unproductive are understood, whether one would be more honorific than the other; but the distinction between the two classes is real: one always exchanges its labor against the capital of a nation, the other always exchanges it against a share of the national income. This distinction is necessary in order to understand what the capital of a nation is, and how in turn it becomes the income of one, and it replaces the income of the others, or is replaced by it. All the rest is but a quarrel about words and not worth being considered.

End of the Second Book

Translator's Notes to Chapter 9, Second Book

This chapter is a restatement of Smith's division of labor into productive and unproductive workers, which became a vital part of the labor theory of value, and, by extension, the major reason for Marxian exploitation theory. Today's Marxist planning practice, which divides the economy into A and B sectors, or commodity production and services, respectively, is a direct consequence of this classification. Although Sismondi uses utility concepts, he apparently felt that he had to use this particular Smithian analysis to maintain his claim that he was a true disciple of the master. A good part of the chapter is taken from the *Encyclopedia* and it may be assumed that Sismondi, in advancing concepts that in his mind were intended to illustrate the present state of political economy without any additions, may have felt that to rewrite this particular theoretical material was not called for. He also used the distinction to reinforce his previous separation of income and capital, but he is not very successful in giving a clear explanation of his concept.

1. Sismondi uses the term "*population guardienne*," which he renders in the *Encyclopedia* literally as 'guardian population'. In the context, the term used here was more descriptive, even though the echoes of Plato and Quesnay are not immediately obvious.
2. The acceptance of armies, navies, and general state administration as necessary, with the implication that they are not always the best if they are the least, as Adam Smith would have it, reflects Sismondi's personal experience with unsettled times and the perceived desirability of the maintenance of law and order. In justifying taxes to pay for these unproductive workers, Sismondi uses a benefit theory of taxation.
3. The *Encyclopedia* reads "be an object of exchange," and the word "free" was added to the second edition of *New Principles*. Sismondi eliminated the words "like other services" for *New Principles*.
4. This is an expression of the aversion of the Genevese citizen, and of the Swiss in general, to organized armies that, in Sismondi's time, were mostly mercenaries and therefore expensive. It also coincides with Adam Smith's view of government proliferation. Under today's circumstances, this sentiment and the one in the next paragraph takes on a common-sense realism—it seems natural that even elected government officials are concerned to protect their vested interests.
5. Sismondi alludes here to a part of what he called at other places in this book the consumption fund, the accumulation of tangible assets that can be exchanged, or that yields its services slowly over time. His position that science in particular does not produce anything was just understandable for his time, but clearly overlooks what was evident already then: its great contribution to increased productivity.
6. Unfortunately, Sismondi does not specify which countries he has in mind—it may be an allusion to the United States, although basic public education was never entirely in private hands even in the beginning of the Republic. The argument seems to be entirely plausible, but since education, at least, like fire and police protection, is not divisible, and therefore cannot be sold in a market, the basic education of children cannot be left to private enterprise; hence this is a spurious comparison. It is, however, fully in agreement with Adam Smith's views on education.
7. A repetition of Smith's definition. However, Sismondi uses this definition in the last book in unexpected ways (for his time) to explain certain peculiarities of the business cycle.
8. The reference is most likely to Say, who, in the *Traité*, explicitly rejected the distinction (book 1), but it is unclear what other authors Sismondi may have had in mind. He may have referred to Bentham, the older Mill, and the philosophical radicals. See Schumpeter 1954, 629–31.

Third Book

Of Territorial Wealth

Introduction

The third book of *New Principles* expands the third chapter of the *Encyclopedia* article. It reflects the author's familiarity with agriculture and his experience with Tuscan *métayage,* but also the romantic, idyllic vision of small homestead farming he previously expressed in the *Tableau de l'agriculture Toscane*. In many ways his views are very similar to those of Thomas Jefferson, and therefore most likely go back to the common theoretical root of physiocracy. But there is also a flavor of Swiss experience, relating perhaps to Sismondi's happy childhood on the family estate, Châtelaine, outside of Geneva, and the Swiss village which, even today, 150 years later, reflects the sturdy independence of small family farms. Despite his romanticism, Sismondi is very much aware that legal and fiscal arrangements shape the outcome of economic effort. He clearly sees these as a result of historical accident—economic development is therefore not necessarily, or even mainly, the outcome of the working of immutable natural laws, but the end product of legal and fiscal happenstance combined with human propensities. The evolutionary bias Sismondi shows throughout *New Principles*, as opposed to the revolutionary fervor of Marx, is closely connected to this belief. It is first fully expressed in this chapter—social institutions, like property in land, are man-made and can therefore be changed by men for the greater good of society. Whereas Smith uses historical example to support what he calls "the natural cause of things," Sismondi uses historical example to show the changeability of human institutions. A corollary of this approach is Sismondi's often-expressed conviction that social structures change only slowly over time, and that such change is not costless, either to society or the individual. Hence, he wants to minimize such costs through evolution and social compromise, expressed in suitable legislation, rather than the social engineering one would expect from this view of society. This book is closer to cameralistic thinking than to either Quesnay or Smith, a viewpoint to be used again in the last book. On the other hand, agriculture is seen in this book as already greatly influenced by technological change, anticipating Marx again on the bourgeois "destruction of idyllic relations," and sounding much less nostalgic than the latter about this development.

1

Legislation's Object as It Concerns Territorial Wealth

[The riches proceeding from land should be the first to engage the attention of an economist or a legislator. They are the most necessary of all, because it is from the ground that our subsistence is derived; because they furnish the materials for every other kind of labour; and lastly, because, in preparation,[1] they constantly employ the half, often much more than the half, of all the nation.[2] The class of people who cultivate the ground are particularly valuable for bodily qualities fitted to make excellent soldiers, and for mental qualities fitted to make good citizens.[3] The happiness of the rural population is also more easily provided for than that of a city population; the progress of this kind of wealth is more easily followed; and government is more culpable when it allows agriculture to decay, because it almost always lies in the power of government to make it flourish.][4]

In the most advanced state of civilization, where not only labor is divided among men, but where all the various rights to property one can possess are most often found in different hands, because the income created by wealth is customarily separated from the income created by labor, the yearly [revenue of land, or the annual crop, is decomposed,[5] as we observed above, in the following manner: One part of the fruits, produced by labour, is destined to pay the proprietor for the assistance which the earth has given to the labour of men, and also for the interest of all the capital successively employed to improve the soil. This portion alone is called the net revenue. Another part of the fruits replaces what has been consumed in executing the labour to which the crop is due, the seed, and all the cultivator's advances.[6] Economists call this portion *the resumption*. Another part remains for a profit to the person who directed the labours of the ground: it is proportionate to his industry and the capital advanced by him.[7] Government likewise takes a share of all those fruits, and by various imposts diminishes the proprietor's rent, the cultivator's profit, and the day-labourer's wages, in order to form a revenue for another class of persons.[8] Nor do the fruits distributed among the workmen, the superintendant of the labour, and the proprietor, entirely remain with them in kind: after having kept a portion requisite for their subsistence, the whole then equally part with what remains, in exchange for objects produced by the industry of the towns; and it is by means of this exchange, that all other classes of the nation are supplied with food.][9]

As we see every day this division of territorial income take place around us, it is important to understand it well, in order to connect each kind of income to its proper source, and to distinguish those which arise from past labor from those which come from present labor. But, although this division continues to exist in many very civilized societies, it is in no way essential for territorial wealth. The three titles of owner; director of labor, or farmer, and day laborer, can be united in one person, without in the least halting, or interrupting annual production, and without there being any other social disturbance; the division of trades has had a very strong and advantageous influence on the progress of industry, and the increase of its total output. But the division of rights to property is born from special circumstances, from chance schemes, often from passions or vanity.[10] The distinction between proprietor, farmer, and day laborer, has neither contributed more zeal to the first, nor more intelligence to the second, nor more vigor to the third. It has in no way been a reason that a task was always done by the same person, and was therefore made better or quicker. This division has often been replaced by others, entirely different; it must be judged as all the rest of social institutions, by the good or bad that has flowed from them for mankind; by the quantity of happiness they produce, and the number of individuals who participate therein.[11]

[Proprietors frequently imagine that a system of cultivation is the better, the higher] their net revenue,[12] or if that portion of the products from the soil which remains with them, after all the costs of cultivation are paid, is larger. [What concerns the nation, however, what should engage the economist's undivided attention, is the gross produce, or the total amount of the crop; by which subsistence is provided for the whole nation, and the comfort of all classes is secured. The former comprehends but the revenue of the rich and idle; the latter farther comprehends the revenue of all such as labour, or cause their capital to labour] in agricultural industry.[13]

The increase of the net income at the expense of the gross product, can be in reality, and often is, a great national calamity. If the owner of an estate, cultivated in the most scientific and expensive way, has leased the land at one hundred écus, though its gross product be valued at a thousand, and he finds thereafter that he will draw from it 110 écus by leaving it fallow, and leasing it without cost for common pasture, he will dismiss his gardener or vintner, and he will profit ten écus; but the nation will lose thereby 890; it will leave useless, and consequently profitless, all the capitals used to bring forth such an abundant output; it will leave unemployed, and consequently without income, all the day workers whose labor is represented by this output; even the treasury will lose more than the proprietor will gain, because it shared in all the incomes of the day workers and the farmer, as well as those of the proprietor, and the share that accrued to it was perhaps larger than the whole revenue of the latter.[14]

[But a gradual increase of the gross product may itself be a consequence of a state of suffering,] if the nation is not richer, but merely more numerous; it means little if the total sum of the national product be greater, if the pro rata share of each person is smaller. The wealth of a nation is not only demonstrated by the totality of its income, but by the proportion of such income to the number of those who must live from it. Hence, a bad administrative system of territorial wealth can raise an overabundant population, which, by more labor, will succeed to wrest from the soil more abundant crops, but will pay dearly for them.[15] In this case, be it that those who work are themselves proprietors, and let themselves be induced to work for a loss by their love for their property, be it that they are simple day laborers who, fighting against a monopoly of the owners and farmers, content themselves with wretched wages, the class of cultivators will suffer in the midst of abundance. The harvests will have greatly increased while those who have raised them will buy with excessive labor an insufficient subsistence, and will languish in misery. [There is no department of political economy which ought not to be judged in its relation to the happiness of the people in general; and a system of social order is always bad when the greater part of the population suffers under it.[16]

Commercial wealth is augmented and distributed by exchange; and even the produce of the ground, so soon as it is gathered in, belongs likewise to commerce. Territorial wealth, on the other hand, is created by means of permanent contracts. With regard to it, the economist's attention should first be directed to the progress of cultivation; next to the mode in which the produce of the harvest is distributed among those who contribute to its growth; and lastly, to the nature of those rights which belong to the proprietors of land, and to the effects resulting from an alienation of their property.]

Translator's Notes to Chapter 1, Third Book

This introductory discussion of what economic legislation should accomplish can be seen as an overture that states briefly all the themes eventually to be developed in the book. The first chapter strongly reflects physiocratic doctrine—the first paragraph is taken unaltered from the *Encyclopedia*—and emphasizes the importance agriculture indeed had in Sismondi's time. Yet, he rejects natural law as an explanation of existing distribution and thus moves from the mainstream of contemporary economics to a new position.

1. In *New Principles* Sismondi uses "exploitation."
2. There exist no reliable figures on the distribution of employment for Sismondi's time, and it is unlikely that he had good statistical information beyond immediate personal observation. European countries differed greatly in this respect, even as far as their own regions were concerned. England, being the most advanced industrially in 1819, had about one-third of the labor force in agriculture; Germany, on the other hand, had more than one-half of the labor force on the land in its eastern provinces. The paragraph from the *Encyclopedia* seemingly was plausible to the author and his readers, based on personal experience.
3. This repeats a common notion still prevailing—that the free peasant is sturdy, independent, and patriotic, always ready to defend his country. The Swiss citizen army corresponds even today to this ideal; in other countries, for example, Germany, the illiterate country bumpkin was seen by the officer caste as abundant and convenient cannon fodder.
4. *New Principles* has here "le gouvernement est plus coupable lorsqu'il laisse dépérir les campagnes."
5. Sismondi would use "disaggregated" today. He omitted "as we observed above" in *New Principles*.
6. This is a change in *New Principles* to "et toutes les avances de l'agriculture."
7. Smith makes profit explicitly a function of invested capital (see Smith 1937, 48).
8. Sismondi refers here to the guardian class, a reference to the last chapter of the preceding book.
9. The paragraph was clearly derived from Quesnay's *Tableau*. According to Meek, physiocratic doctrine had a strong influence on underconsumptionist theories. (See Meek 1963, 329–32 for Sismondi and 333–39 for Malthus.)
10. Sismondi as a historian rejects the prevailing ideas of natural law as a causative factor in property distribution and incidentally lays the groundwork for his theoretical conclusion that economic equilibrium cannot be achieved, except by accident, because of the distracting influences of noneconomic actions and institutions.
11. This is one of the most radical statements made in *New Principles*. It is obviously based on utility considerations, as expounded by Bentham, but it also incorporates the historical sense of change that made Sismondi look at all human institutions as phases of continuing development, hence subject to human control. He must therefore be considered a forerunner of the German historical school and its rejection of natural law in political economy.
12. Sismondi substituted *net revenue* for *rent*.
13. It should be noted that the last three words to this paragraph were added, showing thereby that he already saw agriculture as an economic sector analogous to other industries.
14. Sismondi will come back to this argument again and again, with special reference to the Roman Campagna and extensive sheepherding there and elsewhere. The argument that, generally, economic responses to net profit are

not always beneficial to the entire economy questions the role of profits as an efficient allocator of resources, an argument that Lord Lauderdale made in his *Inquiry* (1804). It assumes that the act of shifting resources has a cost element that is disregarded in the net profit calculus—a major point in Sismondi's later analysis of the industrial business cycle. As Schumpeter pointed out, he is very much aware that economic outcomes depend on preceding conditions and *not* on long-run tendencies towards equilibrium.

15. This is an anticipation of modern development theory and the related shift from emphasizing production to distribution.
16. This paragraph was changed from the first edition. After "can raise an over-abundant population . . ." the first edition reads: "qui ne trouvera plus dans le salaire du travail une récompense suffisante. Alors ces malheureux, luttent sans protection contre les propriétaires de terre ou leurs fermiers, auxquels la limitation de leur nombre donne la force du monopole, achètent par un travail excessif une trop chétive subsistance, et languissent dans la misère." This reflects Smith's dictum that masters band together to keep wages low, and it conforms to Sismondi's vision of *mieux value*.

2

Influence of Government on the Progress of Agriculture

[The progress of social order, the additional security, the protection which government holds out to the rights of all, together with the increase of population, induce the cultivator to entrust to the ground, for a longer or shorter time, the labour which constitutes his wealth. In the timorous condition of barbarism, he will not, at his own expense, increase the value of an immovable possession, which perhaps he may be forced to abandon at a moment's warning.[1] But in the security of complete civilization, he regards his immovable possessions as more completely safe than any other kind of wealth. In the deserts of Arabia and Tartary; in the savannahs of America, before civilization has begun; in the pastures of the Campagna di Roma, or the Capitanata de la Pouille, after it has ended, men are contented with natural fruits of the ground, with grass for their cattle to browse; and if those vast deserts yet retain any value, they owe it less to the slight labour by which the proprietor has inclosed them, than to the labour by which the herdsman has multiplied the oxen and sheep which feed upon them.

When the population of such deserts has begun to increase, and an agricultural life to succeed that of shepherds, men still abstain from committing to the ground any labour whose fruit they cannot gather till after many years have elapsed. The husbandman tills, to reap in the following season; the course of a twelve-month is sufficient to give back all his advances. The earth which he has sown, far from gaining a durable value by his labour, is, for a time, impoverished by the fruits it has born. Instead of seeking to improve it by more judicious cultivation, he gives it back to the desert for repose, and next year tills another portion. The custom of fallowing, a remnant of this half savage mode of agriculture, continues to our own time, in more than three-fourths of Europe], a monument to a formerly universal practice.[2]

[But when population and wealth have at last increased so as to make every kind of labour easy, and when social order inspires security enough to induce the husbandman to fix his labour in the ground, and transmit it with the soil to his descendants, improvement altogether changes the appearance of the earth. Then are formed those plantations of gardens, orchards, vineyards, the enjoyment of which is destined for a late posterity;[3] then are dug those canals for draining or irrigation, which diffuse fertility; then arise upon the hills those hanging terraces, which characterized the agriculture of ancient Canaan. A quick rotation of crops of a different nature reanimates, instead of exhausting, the strength of the soil; and a numerous population lives on a space, which, according to the primitive system, would hardly have supported a few scores of sheep.]

Thus, total agricultural production increased rapidly because of the security given to property. The multiplication of the products of the soil, to the point of being able to feed, with those who cultivate it, that other class of the nation that lives in cities, is only possible because the earth, otherwise captured by the first occupant, or the most powerful, becomes, under the operation of the law, a property not less sacred than if it were itself the work of man. He who, after having enclosed a field, uttered the first *This is mine,* has summoned him who possesses no field, and who could not live if the fields of the first would not bring forth a surplus product. This is a fortunate usurpation, and society, for the benefit of all, does well to guarantee it. However, it is a gift of society and in no way a natural right which preexisted. History proves this, since numerous nations exist which have not recognized private possession of land at all; this argument proves it also, because property in land is not in any way completely created by industry, like a work of man.

The Arabs, the Tartars, who do not in any way permit land to remain with the person or family who have first enjoyed its free gifts, are not any less scrupulous to safeguard the property of man in all that his industry has produced from the free gifts of the earth. Their flocks are rightly theirs, as are the tents they have woven from their wool, or the furniture they have fashioned from wood they have cut. They do not contest in any way the harvest to him who has sown a field; but they do not see why another, a peer, should not have the right to sow in his turn. The inequality which flows from the asserted right of the first occupant does not appear to them to be founded on any principle of justice; and when territory happens to be divided entirely among a certain number of residents, it results in a monopoly of those against the remainder of the nation, to which they will not submit themselves anymore than to the title which may lay claim to the waters of a river by those who own its shore.

The ownership of land is, indeed, not based on a principle of justice, but on a principle of public utility. The first occupants do not have a higher right, but a right that was given to them by society because of the advantage it finds in thus increasing its means of subsistence, by giving this guarantee to their efforts; society cannot force the earth to grant all its fruits except by increasing the share of those who ask her for them. It is for society's advantage, for the poor as well as the rich, that it has taken the landlords under its protection; but it can attach conditions to a concession it grants, and it ought to do so in the spirit of that very concession; it must submit property in land to legislation which will indeed bring about the general good, because it is the general good that alone justifies such ownership.

[The trade or the manufactures of a country, are not to be called prosperous, because a small number of merchants have amassed immense fortunes in it. On the contrary, their extraordinary profits almost always testify against the general prosperity of the country. So likewise, in countries abandoned to pasturage, the profits realized by some rich proprietors ought not to be regarded as indicating a judicious system of agriculture. Some individuals, it is true, grow rich; but the nation, which the land should maintain, or the food which should support it, are no where to be found.] There is not a Tartar chief who does not have an immense treasure, vast herds, numerous slaves and sumptuous furnishings; but to bring a small number of men to such a degree of opulence, the vast steppes of northern Asia had to be kept untouched, the cities and villages razed in the country where the herder's life was intended to be introduced, in such a way that a horde could, as the Tartars expressed it, run without stumbling in the space which these once occupied; it was necessary to raise with the skulls of the inhabitants those horrible monuments in which Genghis and Tamerlane gloried. It was thus that the three main cities of Khorasan were destroyed by the former, and after the massacre of 4,347,000 residents, some thousands of Tartars can live in ease, with their herds, in a land which had fed a nation.*

We have seen parts of civilized Europe similarly returned to pastoral life, without first, it is true, massacring the inhabitants, but by exposing them to die of hunger. At the return of Ferdinand to his Kingdom of Naples, he learned that the vast province known by the name of *Tavoliere Di Puglia*, which for three centuries was deserted and condemned to pasturage, had been put under cultivation by his predecessor; and that

*Herbelot, *Bibliothèque orientale*, (1697), pp. 380–381.

land ownership which, under the Bourbons, according to old custom, was drawn by lot every year, had been granted in emphyteutic lease under Murat.[4] In his horror of all innovation, he has forbidden the cultivation that was about to be introduced, he has prohibited the use of a plow whose share was sufficiently long to uproot the weeds, and he has forced the owners to devote their lands anew to pasturage, even though it was less profitable to them.*

Not by higher authority, but for the profit of the owners, and by abuse of the right of property, has northern Scotland seen almost all of its inhabitants driven from their ancestral homes, crowded together in the cities to perish there in misery, or onto vessels that transport them to America, because the lords of the land, in tallying their accounts, had discovered that they gained more by making less advances and having less returns; and so they have replaced a faithful, courageous and industrious population, but which needed to be fed with oaten bread, by herds of cattle and sheep that were satisfied with grass.** Numerous villages have been abandoned, the nation has been deprived of a share of its children, and perhaps the most valuable ones;[5] it has lost with them all the incomes on which the peasants lived themselves, and which they created by their labor. The landed lords have, it is true, increased their fortunes considerably, but they have broken the original contract by which society guaranteed their property. Whenever the nation is brought down to a pastoral lfe, land should be in common; society guaranteed the right of the first

*The Neapolitan minister has done me the honor to make his offices write a little tract to challenge what I have said about the *Tavoliere Di Puglia* in the first edition of this work. He reproaches me for not at all mentioning the good intentions the king proclaimed in his edict forbidding cultivation, but he admits the fact as I have reported it.

**The Scottish Highlanders held their land under the obligation to follow their master to war, to give him one day of work a week on his fields, and to pay him one-twentieth part of the oatmeal they harvested themselves. This rent was small and cultivation was very poor; but never have lords also been more loved and better obeyed by their vassals. The profit the Scottish lords find today in raising herds is due to the large market England offers them, where the cattle are afterwards fattened.[7]

In the *Revue Encyclopedique* I have given details about the revolution brought about in Sutherland County by the Marchioness of Stafford to whom this county belongs for the greater part. She has expelled the ancient population from the interior of the country, and has settled the Highlanders on the shores of the sea, ordering them to live henceforth from fishing. In a tract she has had published to justify these *improvements*, she asserts that she had been much more moderate than her neighbors towards her hereditary vassals, which is no doubt true, and which proves once again to what abuses the right of property can lead if only the net product is considered, and no other advantage than that of the owner is sought.

occupant on condition that the owners raise its cultivation to a higher stage, and through it shall spread opulence to all classes.[6]

Translator's Notes to Chapter 2, Third Book

An expansion of the central theme of the previous chapter, that the legal framework influences economic activity, and the associated idea that legal institutions are not determined by some preexisting natural law, but are predominantly the result of historical development, and indeed historical accident. Sismondi shares this position with the German romantic movement. It is likely that he acquired these ideas through his association with Madame de Staël and the tutor of her children, Friedrich von Schlegel, a leading German romantic philosopher, during the Napoleonic period. The right to landed property is based on social utility; absent such utility, any system of property rights should be changed to establish it. Social utility is defined as the achievement of personal security and maximization of social happiness, as represented by a well-fed population owning its homes and deriving its livelihood either from a small business, or participating in a larger one; no one being either overly affluent or poor. Any extreme in income distribution is seen as defeating the goal of maximum happiness for the nation. Landlords who violate the original landholding covenant should lose their estates, either to society for reassignment, or to the tenants who cultivate the land. The discussion shows strong influences of Locke and Rousseau, although a fair amount would have to be classified as cameralistic. As Salis shows in his biography (1973, 13–16), Sismondi's character was decisively shaped by the democratic ideals of Genevese Calvinism and an admiration for J. J. Rousseau, the most famous son of Geneva. On the other hand, some utility reasoning from the Italian writers and Bentham can be identified. Aftalion, in his analysis of Sismondi's work, believes that the eighteenth-century Italian authors were known to Sismondi, but admits that to trace this influence would amount to speculation (1970, 35–37). Despite the apparent revolutionary thrust of the argument, Sismondi sees the process as evolutionary. Land reform would be accomplished by legislation in a gradual manner, presumably with compensation to the dispossessed landlords. The discussion clearly begs the question of how the proper degree of social utility is to be defined, and how its maximization is to be measured. However, to Sismondi the argument seemed understandable enough, and sufficiently self-evident to serve as a legislative guide.

1. This is most likely an echo of the sudden sale of Châtelaine after the Simondes' friend Caila had been shot by revolutionary guards, and they had decided to flee Geneva for the comparative safety of Tuscany.
2. Again, this recalls the upheavals in France during the Revolution and the neglect of the soil that was a companion to the unsettled times of revolutionary and Napoleonic warfare that Sismondi witnessed.
3. Sismondi's romantic description of Tuscan conditions in the *Tableau* echoes here. Despite such romantic views, Sismondi recognizes that the countryside hides a great deal of poverty and ignorance, although he believes that the life of the husbandman is much more favorable to happiness than that of the displaced worker in the factory. Most socialist writing of the time favored deurbanization and land redistribution. Fourier's *phalanges* are a radical example of such thinking. It should be noted that in its revolutionary stage Marxism also favors

land distribution among the peasants, and only later champions the collective. In Europe, wherever socialists came to power, workers' settlements were created in the countryside (for example, England after World War II), which incorporated some of these ideas.

4. Joachim Murat, brother-in-law of Napoleon, was king of Naples from 1808–1815. He was executed by firing squad after failing to persuade the anti-Napoleonic coalition of his usefulness in that position. Ideologically very close to Napoleon, and therefore seen as a dangerous revolutionary, he introduced French reforms into what was, even by the standards of the time, a backward country with a reactionary government. The returning Bourbon king Ferdinand was reinstated by the Congress of Vienna, and proceeded forthwith to undo every reform introduced by Murat. The extreme poverty and backwardness of the *Mezzogiorno* (Italy south of Rome), which has troubled Italy ever since its unification is partly a result of this policy. The term *emphyteutic lease* is explained below in chapter 9 of this book. Its closest English equivalent is the *copyhold*.
5. The following paragraph was added to the second edition. It is an impassioned and clear description of the results of the English enclosure movement. By the time Sismondi wrote this note, the crest of the enclosure movement had passed and a large part of the agricultural population had wandered off to the cities where they lived in the wretched conditions that gave Dickens, parliamentary commissions, and, much later, Marx ample raw material for condemning capitalism. Indeed, much of the anticapitalist rhetoric of the twentieth century, and the accompanying propaganda art, are derived from that period. The addition is another example of Sismondi's responding to English conditions in the second edition of *New Principles*.
6. Sismondi assumes here, in line with his expressed belief that the children of small farmers make better citizens, that the displacement of the rural population to the cities made it impossible to raise such children.
7. Obviously, Sismondi did not consider sheepherding, that is, wool farming, a higher stage of agricultural production, a view that accords with his often expressed preference for intensive agriculture along the lines of Tuscan garden farming. Despite his professed adherence to Smithian doctrine, Sismondi is clearly prepared to disregard market preference if it conflicts with his view of social happiness. However, his view raises the pertinent question whether the transformation of English agriculture by enclosure created social costs which were never fully accounted for as charges against the increased profits of the landlords. The surplus value concept is merely another expression of this idea.

3

Of Patriarchal Cultivation

[The first proprietors of land were doubtless themselves cultivators, and executed all kinds of field labour, with their children and servants.] No other social organization guaranteed more happiness and virtue in the most numerous class of the nation, more opulence for all, more stability to public order. The appropriation of land had been recognized as advantageous for all society, because it gave to him who worked it the certainty that, to remotest time, he would enjoy fully the fruits of his labor.[1] Agriculture is the slowest of industries; some of its products take a century to mature; it is the grandson who will fell the oak whose acorn was planted by the grandfather. The tasks of irrigation and drainage, diking, draining of marshes, render their fruits after many seasons; and the common labors of agriculture, independent of their immediate profit they may bring, produce of and by themselves a lasting improvement which can be passed on from generation to generation. Every contract, every division of fruits which separates ownership interest from interest in cultivation tends to destroy, or at least diminish, the good effects which society had expected from the appropriation of land. It is useless that the laws of nations who have most encouraged agriculture, have recently facilitated long leases for farms; it is sufficient that a lease have a terminal date in order that the interest of the farmer be less intense than that of the owner.

But, independent of interest, the love the owner has for the land he cultivates, is one of the great stimulants to the improvement of agriculture. The love of an ancestor for his unknown descendants, not yet born, would rarely be sufficient for him to sacrifice in their favor his own enjoyments, if the pleasure connected with the creation, the increase, the beautification, had not come to be associated in his mind with a creation of a benefit so far removed. Man has labored for his remotest descendants because he loved his work as well as he loved them. He has saved from his enjoyments to create, through improvement of the land, a perpetual annuity in favor of his descendants, and he has done it without consideration of personal interest, because the pleasure to participate in a time he can never see, and to still act when he does not anymore exist, was his main reward. One sees at every step the signs of love which the cultivator bears for the house in which he lives, and the land for which he cares, in countries where the farmer is owner, and where the fruits belong without sharing to the same men who have done all the work, countries whose cultivation we call patriarchal. He does not ask what the footpath he builds will cost him in days of labor, or the spring he channels, or the thicket and garden he embellishes with flowers; the very work he lavishes on them is a pleasure; he finds the time and the strength to do them, because satisfaction does not fail him; money would not make him do more than what the love for his land makes easy for him.[2]

A third advantage connected with the appropriation of land is the progress which experience and the advancement of knowledge can bring to agricultural science. Both are equally necessary, both are blunted and destroyed in every cultivation whose fruits are divided. In those happy lands where cultivation is patriarchal, the very nature of each field is studied, and that knowledge is transmitted from fathers to children; the proper grain, the right time for sowing, the dangers of hail or frost, all is noted; and whoever has lived with farmers, knows that there is no farm so small in which observation does not recognize differences, from one plot to the other. But it is not enough to recognize these differences, the results must be matured through judgment; and we have hardly any other means to develop this than to give the cultivator comfort and ease of mind. Cultivation in large estates, guided by wealthy individuals, will perhaps rise more over prejudice and routine. But knowledge will not flow down to the laborer, and it will be badly applied.

Consequently, as one crosses almost all of Switzerland, many provinces in France, Italy, and Germany, there is no need to ask, with regard to a piece of land, whether it belongs to an owner-cultivator, or a farmer. The obvious care, the delights readied for the husbandman, the appearance the land has received from his hands, indicate quickly the former. It is true that an oppressive government can destroy comforts and brutalize the intelligence which property should give, that taxes can take away more than the net product of the fields, that the insolence of the agents of authority can disturb the security of peasants, that the impossibility of obtaining justice against a powerful neighbor can throw the soul into despair, and in the beautiful country given over to the rule of the King of Sardinia,[3] an owner carries the uniform of misery just as much as a day laborer. It is all very well to obey one single rule of political economy, but it cannot bring about virtue all by itself; at any rate it lessens the evil.

Patriarchal cultivation improves the mores and character of that most numerous part of the nation who must do all the work in the fields. Property inculcates habits of order and economy, daily abundance destroys the taste for feasting and drinking: privation leads to excess, and cares seek to drown themselves in the brutishness of drink. Quick trades give a necessary stimulus to commerce; in order to profit from their advantages, one must put up with their drawbacks. These are mainly the ones which change the good faith of a people. No one looks for long for a good deal without seeking to overcharge, or to deceive; the more trouble the seller has in finding his livelihood, the more he will be tempted to use deception. The complaint is often made that the country folk do not anymore deserve their reputation of trustworthiness; but it is the owners-cultivators who have created it, and it need not extend itself to other classes of countrymen; those, called upon to sell every day their labor and their provisions, have to scheme to defend their scanty subsistence, to haggle over all their contracts, and thus should have lost the virtues the owner-cultivator preserves, because the latter, making almost only trades with nature, has less occasion than any other industrious worker to mistrust men, and retaliate against them with the weapon of dishonesty.*

In countries where patriarchal cultivation has been maintained, the population increases steadily and rapidly till it has attained its natural limits, that is, inheritances continue to divide and subdivide among many sons, until, with an increase in labor, each family can draw an equal income from a lesser portion of land. The father who owns a vast extent of pasturages, divides them among his sons, in order that they turn them into fields and meadows; these sons divide them again, to exclude the fallow system; each improvement of agricultural science permits a new division of holdings; but it should not be believed that the owner raises his children to turn them into beggars; he knows exactly the inheritance he

*The inhabitants of the United States have been accused of being totally preoccupied with calculations of profit, and of not bringing too much sensitivity to their transactions. However, they know only patriarchal cultivation; but the exception proves the rule: land itself is, in America, the object of constant trading. The farmer does not care to maintain himself in comfort, but to enrich himself; he sells his land in Virginia to go to Kentucky; he then sells it in Kentucky to set up in the territory of Illinois. He speculates at all times like a member of the stock exchange. From so much activity comes more wealth, but less morality; the class which should guard the ancient principles is itself involved in too quick a train of events; this is an extraordinary condition of a small nation inhabiting an immense continent; it cannot be compared to the slow forward march of an old society.

can leave them; he knows that the law will divide it equally between them; he sees the time when this division will bring them down from the station he himself has occupied, and a proper family pride, found in peasant as well as nobleman, stops him before he has brought into the world children for whose future he could not provide. However, if they are born, at least they will not marry, or they might choose themselves among many brothers the one who will continue the family. In the Swiss cantons one never sees peasant inheritances subdivide in such a manner that they will fall below the level of respectable comfort, although the custom of foreign military service sometimes causes an overabundant population by opening to children an unknown and uncertain career.[4]

The strongest safeguard of an established order may lie in the existence of a numerous class of peasant proprietors. However advantageous it may be for society to safeguard property, it is an abstract idea difficult to grasp by those to whom it seems only to guarantee privation. When land ownership is taken from the cultivator, and the ownership of factories from workers, all those who create wealth, and who see it passing through their hands without end, are strangers to all its benefits. They form by far the most numerous part of the nation; they see themselves as the most useful part, and they feel disinherited. Constant envy stirs them up against the rich; one can hardly dare to discuss civil rights before them, because one must always be afraid they will go from this discussion to that of property rights, and that they will demand the distribution of possessions and land.[5]

A revolution in such a country is frightful; the whole order of society is subverted; power passes into the hands of the multitude which commands physical power, and this crowd, having suffered much, kept in ignorance by need, is hostile to all types of law, all degrees of distinction, all kinds of property. France experienced such a revolution at a time when the vast majority of the population was a stranger to ownership, and as a consequence to the blessings of civilization. But this revolution, amid a deluge of evils, has left behind many blessings; one of the greatest, perhaps, is the assurance that a similar calamity will never again return.[6] The revolution has multiplied prodigiously the class of peasant proprietors. Today we count more than three million families in France who are absolute masters of the land they dwell on; this implies more than fifteen million individuals. Thus more than half the nation has, for its own benefit, an interest in upholding all laws. The numbers and physical power are on the same side as the law; and if the government should fail, the masses themselves would hurry to reestablish another which would protect safety and property. This is the major reason for the difference between the revolutions of 1813–1814, and that of 1789.[7]

It is true that the call by the peasants to become owners caused great violence: the confiscation and sale of national property of whatever kind. But the calamities of war, either civil or foreign, are evils tied to our nature, much as floods and earthquakes are part of our living on this planet. Once the calamity has passed one must thank Providence if it has brought some good. Without doubt, nothing could be either more precious or stronger. Every day the division of great inheritances continues, every day great estates are sold with profit to farmers who cultivate them; the nation is still far from having harvested all the fruits it can expect from this breakup of properties, because habits are slow to develop, and the taste for order, economy, neatness, elegance, must be the result of a much longer enjoyment.

In the same manner as Switzerland on the old continent, so has free America on the new not separated land ownership from the cares and benefits of cultivation, and that is one of the causes of its rapid prosperity. This way of farming, the simplest and most natural, must have been that of all people at its beginning, and that is why we have named it the patriarchal one. It is found again and again in the history of all nations of antiquity. Only, at that time, it had been defiled by slavery.

[The continual state of war, which exists among semi-barbarous societies, introduced slavery at the remotest era. The stronger found it more convenient to procure workmen by the abuse of victory than by bargain. Yet so long as the head of each family laboured along with his children and slaves, the condition of the latter was less wretched; the master felt himself to be of the same nature with his servant; he experienced the same wants and the same fatigue; he desired the same pleasures, and knew, by experience, that he would obtain little work from a man whom he fed badly.] The servant of the peasant cultivator, in all of France, eats at the table of his master; the slave of the patriarch was not more abused. This was the agriculture of Judea, [that of the golden days of Italy and Greece,] and it is today that of the interior of Africa, as well as many parts of the American continent, where the slave works alongside the free man.[8]

Among the Romans, before the Second Punic War, farms under cultivation were so small that the number of free men who worked in the fields had to exceed greatly that of slaves. [The former had a full enjoyment of their persons, and the fruits of their labour; the latter, degraded rather than unhappy, like the ox, man's companion, which interest teaches him to spare, seldom experienced suffering, want still more rarely. The head of each family alone receiving the total crop, did not distinguish the rent from the profit or the wages; with the excess of what he wanted for food, he procured the produce of the town in exchange, and this excess supported all other classes of the nation.]

Translator's Notes to Chapter 3, Third Book

This chapter is entirely new, except for the introductory sentence and the transition to the next chapter on slavery. It advances the main argument, later applied analogously to the factory worker, that property ownership, even if small, provides incentives for productive effort and supports the existing order, meaning that ownership of property is both economically advantageous and politically conservative. Hence, a political system should encourage small landholdings, or share participation in a corporation for the factory hand, and discourage large estates, or great accumulations of capital. Part of the argument is rooted in the classical aversion to monopoly power, part in physiocratic views (Jefferson's republic of small farmers), but it seems that a major part is based on observations of the effects of the land reforms introduced by the French Revolution and Napoleonic conquest. Sismondi recognizes that the roots of the Revolution lay in the exclusion of the majority of the population from land ownership. He would have most likely endorsed land distribution schemes as long as they could be implemented without violence and the accompanying destruction of existing beneficial social institutions. His descriptions of the Revolution reflect strongly his Geneva experiences during the terror, and demonstrate and explain his lifelong aversion to violent social action.

The description of the benefits of smallholding seem to be mainly based on Swiss experience. *Patriarchal Cultivation* is best rendered as *family farming,* but it does not capture the full flavor of the argument and was therefore not used.

Sismondi is aware that the attractive picture he painted was not entirely true to reality; he assumes throughout that the small producer will be able to sell his product at the physiocratic *bon prix* covering costs and yielding a net return, an assumption he knows is wrong. In the *Tableau de l'agriculture Toscane* he shows at length that the economic condition of the share farmer in Tuscany was far from prosperous, and that agriculture was not indeed the producer of prosperity as he and some other authors presented it to be (for example, Arthur Young.) He also refers to prejudice and routine, and feels compelled to defend the peasant against sharp dealing by laying the blame on government and unscrupulous merchants who try to exploit the peasant. The chapter serves as a counterpoint to the critique of English enclosures and Italian *latifundia* in the previous chapter by stressing the idyllic nature of the small homestead.

1. The premise that appropriation of land was recognized as beneficial must be classed with Smith's argument that man has an innate propensity to *barter, truck, and exchange,* as an unsupported assertion. However, Sismondi was closer to understanding human nature than Marx, who disdained the petit bourgeois love of property in favor of communal property holding. Not surprisingly, Marx never held any real property, while Sismondi did all his life. In view of later developments, the difference takes on great historical significance.
2. The *métairie* Sismondi bought for his family (near Lucca in Tuscany), when they had to leave Geneva, was to him always a reminder of the family estate Châtelaine where he spent a carefree childhood. He recreated for himself a retreat in Chêne after his marriage, but he was never an active farmer. It is perhaps this combination of rural enjoyment and absence of actual physical involvement in the arduous labor of a real peasant that accounts for his romantic view of agriculture.
3. The reference is to Victor Emmanuel I, who, like Ferdinand of Naples, instituted

an extreme reactionary policy on his return to the throne of Sardinia (Piedmont) after the Congress of Vienna. The rosy picture Sismondi draws, and the blame he lays on higher authority for any shortcomings in the rural economy, leaves out the instances where owner-cultivators were lazy or simply poor managers, or had holdings that were too small for making a decent livelihood, or any number of reasons why farms may not be as well administered as he would have it. As a pamphleteer he was accustomed to state his position in the starkest terms, and this is one of many instances of this habit in the book.

4. Historically, foreign military service was a means of providing for an overabundance of males who had no expectation of cultivating their own land, a fact conveniently overlooked here. Although Sismondi's view makes quite clear that birth control was an accepted contemporary practice among the populations he knew, it is also evident that such control was not always very effective.
5. Sismondi here gave a classic description of what became later known as *alienation*. It should be noted that his argument is quite general, and applies equally to agriculture and industry, as was probably intended. The description of discussions is probably based on personal experience during the Geneva Revolution.
6. The history of the French Republic does not support this optimistic assessment, although the violence of the revolutions of 1830, 1848, and 1871 did not quite match the fury of the original terror. Sismondi was, however, right in assuming that the small landowner would be a conservative force in French politics—the countryside has proven since then to be a bulwark of conservative politics.
7. This may refer to the national uprisings against Napoleon, but it may also refer to the rural uprisings against the Revolution. The Prussian uprising was indeed based on the support of the entire population, which had been brought into the political process through the reforms of the Stein-Hardenberg government. The Vendée uprisings started in 1793 and lasted for several months. There were also uprisings in Lyon that were brutally suppressed. Sismondi was a witness to all of these.
8. Sismondi again romanticizes and prettifies reality to make a point about smallholding as a cure for monopolization. Small landowners who held slaves were not always the benevolent masters he assumed—economic necessity (and plain sadism) often induced them to extract from their slaves the maximum of effort with a minimum of care.

4

Of Slave Cultivation

[But the progress of wealth, of luxury, and idleness, in all the states of antiquity, substituted the servile for the patriarchal mode of cultivation. The population lost much in happiness and number by this change; the earth gained little in productiveness. The Roman proprietors extending their patrimonies by the confiscated territories of vanquished states, the Greeks by wealth acquired from trade,—first abandoned manual labour, and soon afterwards despised it. Fixing their residence in towns, they entrusted the management of their estates to stewards and inspectors of slaves;*[1] and from that period, the condition of most part of the country population became intolerable.[2] Labour, which had once been a point of communion betwixt the two ranks of society, now became a barrier of separation; contempt and severity succeeded to affectionate care; punishments were multiplied as they came to be inflicted by inferiors, and as the death of one or several slaves did not lessen the steward's wealth. Slaves who were ill-fed, ill-treated, ill-recompensed, could not fail to lose all interest in their master's affairs, and almost all understanding. Far from attending to their business with affection, they felt a secret joy every time they saw their oppressor's wealth diminished, or his hopes deceived.]

It is believed that great savings can be made if the man who is made to work is not paid; however, he must be fed, and all the greed of the masters does not prevent that the subsistence of the slave costs almost as much as that of a free man. If some of his needs are not met, he will, on his part, take great pleasure in squandering the possessions of his enemy, instead of saving them. Moreover, he must be bought; and the interest on his purchase price should be compared, not to his hire, but to what could have been saved on the wages. Physiologists have noticed that the cheerfulness

*Those whom Columella calls *villici,* as opposed to *coloni.*

of the working man increases his powers, and makes him feel less fatigue. This one principle gives a great superiority to the work of a free man over that of a slave, even given equal strength. Columella, who wrote around the year A.D. 40, advised landowners to use slaves whenever they could supervise them themselves; but to stay with free cultivators, the colons, if their estates were distant, and they did not want to live in the country, at the head of their workers.*

[The study of science, accompanied with habits of observation, certainly advanced the theory of agriculture; but its practice, at the same time, rapidly declined; a fact which all the agricultural writers of antiquity lament.** The cultivation of land was entirely divested of that intelligence, affection, and zeal, which had once hastened its success. The revenues were smaller, and the expenses greater; and from that period, it became an object to save labour, more than to augment its produce. Slaves, after having driven every free cultivator from the fields, were themselves rapidly decreasing in number. During the decline of the Roman empire, the population of Italy was not less reduced than that of the *Agro Romano*[3] is in our days; while at the same time, it had sunk into the last degree of wretchedness and penury.]

The slave war of the years 73 to 71 B.C. made Rome recognize the danger of letting the subsistence of the state depend on a population that was simultaneously reduced to misery and despair. Pompey defeated Spartacus; but innumerable slaves were killed, and the frightened masters preferred to give up a part of their harvests so as not to increase the number of their enemies on their estates. Wheat growing was almost given up in Italy, and Rome relied on the harvests of Africa and Egypt for its food. Moreover, it was proven in Rome, as in the Gulf of Mexico, that slave farming could not be sustained without the slave trade. One can read in Caesar's *Commentaries* how often the conquerors condemned the vanquished people in their entirety to be sold under the lance of the praetor. At the frontiers of the Rhine and Danube, of Africa, and the Euphrates, where the slave markets were, the farmers of Italy, Gaul, and Greece were recruited, and it was with blood that blood was bought.*** But victory deserted the enslaved Romans. The Roman provinces were as often pillaged by the barbarians, as the barbarian nations had been harassed by the Roman legions. The slaves were removed from all the farms,

*De Re Rustica, lib. I, cap. VII.

**Columella, *De Re rustica*, lib. I, in Prooemio.

***Slaves were divided into those who worked unfettered, and those who worked in chains. The latter, who were incarcerated during the night, were in the majority prisoners taken in wars against the barbarians, whereas the former were born in residence. (Colum., *de Re rustica,* lib. II, cap VII).

resold in distant provinces, or taken to Germany; and while Alaric and Radagais crisscrossed Italy, their armies swelled with the multitude who still spoke the teutonic language, and with every slave who could call himself Goth or German. At about the same time the uprisings of the Bagaudes, in Gaul, in Italy, and in Spain, showed that the oppression of the rural population had not ended with the decrease of their number, and that the danger of slave cultivation was always the same.

The whole nation had slowly disappeared under this odious regime. Romans were only found in Rome, Italians only in the big cities. Some slaves still tended some sheep in the countryside; but the rivers had broken their dikes, the woods had spread to the fields, and wolves and wild pigs had again taken possession of the old realm of civilization.

[The cultivation of the colonies situated on the Mexican Gulf, was founded, in like manner, on the baneful system of slavery; it has, in like manner, consumed the population, debased the human species, and deteriorated the system of agriculture. The Negro trade has of course filled up those voids, which the barbarity of planters annually produced in the agricultural population; and doubtless under a system of culture, such that the man who labours is constantly reduced below the necessaries of life, and the man who does not labour keeps all for himself, the net produce[4] has always been considerable; but the gross produce, with which alone the nation is concerned, has uniformly been inferior to what would have arisen from any other system of agriculture, while the condition of more than seven-eighths of the population has continued to be miserable.][5]

Furthermore, today the net income as well as the gross revenue in the colonies has declined so much that one cannot be enough amazed at the obstinacy of the colonists in maintaining slave cultivation. The land is infinitely more fertile in the West Indies than in France; the stronger sun produces there a much richer vegetation; their products can only grow in a limited space while they are sought after in the whole world; the expense of government, and that of defense, is borne by the mother country; and yet, the colonies are able to save their plantations only because their sugar and their coffee have been given the monopoly of the entire French market; and even with such an advantage, as tremendous as it is unjust, the land is valueless, and the price of a plantation represents only the capital used in its cultivation. Thus, the disadvantages of slave cultivation were sufficient to offset all the advantages of fertility, climate, the absence of taxes, and monopoly.

Power over slaves is not a right, but only robbery which, in certain countries, and under certain circumstances, the law does not punish. The slavemasters, the planters, speak often of their rights, the guarantees the laws of their country owe to their property; but the silence of the laws would not be able to change the morality of deeds; the impunity guaranteed to him who takes away the welfare of another does not abolish the distinction between right and wrong. Land ownership is a grant of the law made for the advantage of all; but the ownership of one's own person, and in the fruits of one's own labor is prior to the law.[6] The slave was not only robbed on the day he was sold into servitude, he is robbed every day, because he is deprived of the fruits of his daily labor without compensation. The punishments and tortures with which the master penalizes his resistance are again new offenses the laws neglect to punish, because it concerns only a slave. The European master can have no illusions about the criminality of his acts; they are as much against natural law as they are against the civil law of his country. The legislator seems only to have refrained from punishing the violations too far from his oversight; if master and his slave return to France and England, the slave comes again under the protection of the common law, and everyone of the injustices the master committed against the slave is punished, as they would be with respect to another citizen. Because in the Antilles civil law has not ratified the clearest provisions of natural law, the master may well claim immunity for the previous crimes against his slave, but he has no right whatever to demand that the law in the future not extend its protection to all men, and not suppress all wrongs. It is his fault that he has acquired knowingly a stolen good, that he has paid for the right to commit an injustice which is repeated every hour, and on whose nature he can have no doubt. If there is anyone in this who should be indemnified by the public, it is the slave, for the long abuse to which the injustice of the law has exposed him.

The question of emancipation, the substitution of another cultivation for slave cultivation, presents without doubt difficulties; but that is above all relative to the vigorous protection owed to a race a long time oppressed, as against the consequences of moral degradation to which we have subjected it. The legislator, after having brutalized the Negroes, then having allowed that these dehumanized beings be introduced into civilized society, has assumed the obligation to raise them again to the rank of human beings before according them rights; he owes them education, he owes them a gradual emancipation, because too quick a transition can only be fatal to them. But he owes nothing to their masters; in law, because their property is only validated by a progression of offenses, it merits no guarantee whatsoever; in reality, because this property has today no value. Indeed, if the monopoly of the colonies were abrogated, if all the ports were opened to the coffee and sugar produced by free labor, in the Indies and on the American continent, the expensive slave cultivation would not be able to meet competition; if the European garrisons were withdrawn from the Antilles, if the Creoles were not anymore protected against the

Negroes by a foreign force they do not pay, then the last Creole would hasten to depart before the last soldier. This very day the Negro is not an asset, he is a cause of loss and danger to the white. It is not the slave at all who creates an income for the planter; the income is taken entirely from the pocket of the European consumer, to whom the colonial products are sold at monopoly prices; and the same consumer pays again to his government taxes to maintain, by armed force, a cultivation method which is not only tainted with injustice and cruelty, but is also more expensive and more ruinous than any other.

Generous people have sought to alleviate the fate of the Negroes, by attacking with determination the hateful traffic by which they are procured. They have succeeded in prohibiting it; and they have thus halted, at least in the English colonies, the continuation of a monstrous crime, and the destruction of new multitudes of unfortunates. As to the relief of the Negroes already enslaved in Jamaica and in the English colonies, the remedy has proven ineffectual. It is said that the owners cannot desire the destruction of their human herds anymore than the destruction of their animal herds. But for the most part, these owners lived in Europe. Self-interest motivates only the farmer who himself watches over his teams; it has no influence on his servant who makes it his business to profit therefrom. Is there a rentier who loaned his horses to a hackney driver, who in doing so, did not expect that they would perish in harness? And here are humans whose work, subsistence, and punishments have been handed over to underlings! The entire span of the earth separates masters from slaves and from the barbarous contractor who feeds them, and has the right to punish them. The latter has no interest whatever in the value of the plantation, in the condition of the slave gangs, and the entire esteem in which he is held by his master is proportional to the annual income he sends him. If the law allows an institution so unjust and cruel as slavery, if it pledges its security, it ought to attach the condition that the slave will always live under the eyes of his master, so that he can appeal to him. It is bad enough that these unfortunates have no other protection than the compassion of those on whom they depend. The latter need not leave their station to feel such compassion. On a European estate, the herds belong to the farmer and not to the owner; and the farmer actually manages his own herds. If the plantations of the absent colonials were rented to farmers, and if the slaves were made a part of the assets of the farmer, their suffering would undoubtedly be less severe. In no other system of cultivation does the owner oblige himself to furnish the machinery of a farm three thousand miles away from his home. However, in no other could such a trust be more deadly. European laws declare that Negro free who debarks in a European port; they would be more just if they would declare that Negro free whose master has gone to Europe.

Translator's Notes to Chapter 4, Third Book

This chapter is a greatly reworked part of the *Encyclopedia* article, and it also incorporates a major change between the first and second edition of *New Principles*. Sismondi uses the chapter to reinforce the foundation of his central idea—individual participation of every citizen in ownership is the basic requirement for a prosperous nation, the foundation of general happiness. To this end he mixes ethical and economic arguments to attack slavery in the Americas. The discussion derives much heat from the contemporary antislavery movement that had led to the 1808 British and U.S. antislavery acts, and that resulted after the Congress of Vienna in further national legislation against the slave trade. But slavery persisted in the colonies and the slave trade continued in the southern hemisphere, mainly in Brazil. Also, the legislation was not really enforced by France, Spain, or Portugal. As a consequence, major tropical products, particularly sugar, were produced with slave labor. Sismondi tries to show, without real proof, that the colonial slave economies were uneconomical, noncompetitive, and sustained only by the monopoly position the goods enjoyed in the mother country. He repeats an argument that was a favorite of the abolitionist movement, showing that slavery was not only immoral, but also wasteful, and therefore doubly evil. While the issue is still debated by historians, and data are scarce and not very reliable, the wide discrepancy between survival rates of slaves in the West Indies and in the United States would support Sismondi's position on slavery in the former. Even in his attack on slavery, Sismondi is careful to call for *evolutionary* measures—he demands that slaves be gradually emancipated, with a transition period for education, before being granted full civil rights. He extends his romantic view of the smallholder to slave owning by assuming that the small slaveholder, while working next to his slaves, would be more sympathetic to slave needs. Hence, he demands as a first step that slaveholders should not be absentee landlords, a conclusion that overlooks many of the other undesirable features of slave owning, and gives too much credit to the humaneness of the small slaveholder.

1. None of Sismondi's notes to this chapter are part of the original *Encyclopedia* article.
2. Sismondi shows that he was an astute observer—most present-day development economists ascribe the poor state of underdeveloped nations to a disdain of manual labor and the excessive status of the so-called professions, like lawyers.
3. The Roman Campagna. Sismondi will have to say a great deal later about the depopulation of that part of Italy because of the extension of *latifundia* agriculture—large-scale farming with emphasis on monoculture of grains.
4. That is, the net profit of the operation, as opposed to the gross income, which would include, according to Sismondi, the subsistence of the slaves.
5. The next three paragraphs were added for the second edition. The reason must be sought in Sismondi's perception that, despite legal abolition of the slave trade, slavery continued in the West Indies and South America. It is possible that he received information about the status of slavery there from his relatives who supported abolition. Sismondi uses impassioned language with appeals to natural law and Lockean property-rights arguments, based on the identification

of incorporated labor as a right of ownership. The argument can be used with very little change to condemn *wage slavery*.

6. Compare this sentence to this citation from Locke, *Of Civil Government, Second Treatise*, chapter 5, paragraph 27: "Though the earth and all inferior creatures be common to all men, yet every man has a property in his own person; this nobody has any right to but himself. The labour of his body and the work of his hands we may say are properly his." And Rousseau, *The Social Contract*, book 1, chapter 9: "Since every owner is regarded as the trustee of a public property, his rights are respected by every other member of the state."

5

Cultivation by Metayage, or for Half-Shares

[The invasions of the Roman Empire, by the barbarians, introduced new manners, and, with them, new systems of cultivation. The conqueror[1] who now became proprietor, being much less allured by the enjoyments of luxury,] and being more warlike than those he had defeated, [had need of men still more than of wealth. He had ceased to dwell in towns, he had established himself in the country; and his castle formed a little principality, which he wished to be able to defend by his own strength, and thus he felt the necessity of acquiring the affection of such as depended on him. A relaxation of the social bond, and the independence of great proprietors, produced the same effects without the limits of the ancient Roman empire as within. From the epoch of its downfall, masters in every part of Europe began to improve the condition of their dependents; and this return to humanity produced its natural effect; it rapidly increased the population, the wealth, and the happiness of rural labourers.

Different expedients were resorted to for giving slaves and cultivators an interest in life, a property, and an affection for] their work, [the place of their nativity, as well as for its lord. Adopted by various states, these expedients produced the most decisive influence on] the subsequent progress of [territorial wealth and population. In Italy, and part of France and Spain, and probably in most part of the former Roman empire, the master shared the land among his vassals, and agreed with them to share the crops in a raw state. This is cultivation for half produce.*[2]

*In Italy today, metayers are still called *coloni,* in the language of the law. This was also the name the Roman laws gave to the free peasants. Thus, it is likely that the same name has remained with the same contract which is known to be based on a custom that is lost in the mists of time.

Cultivation for half-share, according to a report from a knowledgeable traveler, is a universal practice in the kingdom of Algiers and Tripoli; this traveller adds that the peasants have appeared to him happy, and that the land is covered with abundant crops. Tyranny is painfully felt only in the towns.

In Hungary, Poland, Bohemia, and all that portion of Germany occupied by Slavonic tribes, the master much more rarely enfranchised his slaves. Keeping them always under an absolute dependence, as serfs attached to the soil,[3] he gave them, however, one half of his land, reserving the other to himself. He wished to share, not the fruits of their labour, but the labour itself, and therefore he obliged them to work for him two, three, and in Transsylvania, four days of each week. This is cultivation by *corvées*.

In Russia, and several provinces of France and England, masters likewise distributed their land among vassals; but, instead of wishing to participate either] in their time, [in the lands, or the harvests, they imposed a fixed capitation. Such was the abundance of uncultivated land always ready to be cleared, that, in the eyes of those proprietors, the only difference in the condition of agricultural families was the number of workmen included in them. To capitation was always joined the obligation of personal services, and the vassals' continuation in a servile state. Yet, according as the laws watched more or less strictly over the subject's liberty, cultivation upon this principle[4] raised the husbandman to a condition more or less comfortable. In Russia, he never escaped from the servitude of the soil; in England, by an easy transition, he arrived at the rank of farmer.

The system of cultivation by *metayers,* or cultivation at half produce,[5] is perhaps one of the best inventions of the middle ages. It contributes, more than any thing else, to diffuse happiness among the lower classes, to raise land to a high state of culture, and accumulate a great quantity of wealth upon it. It is the most natural, the easiest, and most advantageous step for exalting the slave to the condition of a freeman, for opening his understanding, teaching him economy and temperance, and placing in his hands a property which he will not abuse. According to this system[6] the peasant is supposed to have no capital, or scarcely any, but he receives his land sown and fully stocked; he takes the charge of continuing every operation, of keeping his farm in the same state of culture, of delivering to his master the half of each crop; and, when the lease expires, of returning the land under seed, the folds furnished, the vines propped, and everything, in short, in the same state of completeness as it was when he received it.

A metayer finds himself delivered from all those cares which, in other countries, weigh heavily on the lower class of people. He pays no direct tax, his master alone is charged with it; he pays no money-rent, and therefore is not called to sell or to buy, except for his own domestic purposes. The term, at which the farmer has to pay his taxes or his rent, does not press the metayer; or constrain him to sell before the season, at a low price, the crop which rewards his industry. He needs but little capital. because he is not a dealer in produce; the fundamental advances have been made once for all by his master; and as to the daily labour, he performs it himself with his family; for cultivation upon this principle brings constantly along with it a great division of land, or what is called cultivation on the small scale.

Under this system, the peasant has an interest in the property, as if it were his own; without the anxieties of wealth,[7] he finds in his farm every enjoyment, with which nature's liberality rewards the labour of man] without having so much abundance that he could forego working. Yet, there exists on the fields no one inferior to him, no day laborers, no farmhands, whose condition would be even worse; his own, however, is quite tolerable. [His industry, his economy, the development of his understanding, regularly increase his little stock. In good years, he enjoys a kind of opulence; he is not entirely excluded from the feast of nature which he prepares;[8] his labour is directed according to the dictates of his own prudence, and he plants that his children may gather the fruit.

The high state of culture to be found in the finest parts of Italy, above all of Tuscany, where the lands are generally managed in this way; the accumulation of an immense capital upon the soil; the invention of many judicious rotations, and industrious processes, which an intelligent, observing spirit alone could have deduced from the operations of nature; the collection of a numerous population, upon a space very limited and naturally barren, shows plainly enough that this mode of cultivation is as profitable to the land itself as to the peasant, and that, if it imparts most happiness to the lower class who live by the labour of their hands, it also draws from the ground the most abundant produce, and scatters it with most profusion among men.][9]

Cultivation by metayers was introduced into Santo Domingo after its liberation, and the Haitians have made a wise choice in adopting it. Whereas the English philanthropists looked to gradual liberation of their colonial Negroes, the Haitians have on their part shown the practical means, the infallible means, to habituate the freedman to work, to motivate him, to revive his intelligence, and to make him taste the charms of property acquired by work. All plantations are cultivated at half-share in Haiti, with the exception of the sugar mills which demand a very large capital advance; that advance was made by the owner, the share of the colonist is reduced to one-quarter of the net product in sugar, and it is quite clearly equivalent to one-half of any other product.[10]

Yet, in France, this system was very far from having had equally beneficial effects. On the one hand, it has been changed, because generally the metayer was charged with the payment, or the advance, of taxes, and submitting him to the necessity of finding money on a set day, he was made to suffer all the difficulties and losses of the small farmer. On the other hand, this system was adopted mainly in the provinces south of the Loire, where there are few large towns, few centers of enlightenment, few communications, and where it is obvious that the peasants have remained in deep ignorance, attached to their traditions, to their agricultural routines, and incapable of following the march of civilization in the rest of France. Such is the cultivation system in the Vendée that the peasant is still in total dependence on his lord and his priest, where the Revolution has changed none of his products, has added nothing to his rights, and where no learning can penetrate the countryside, and where no prejudice seems changeable.[11]

Truly, cultivation by metayage is a first advance in the condition of the husbandman, but it alone cannot assure other subsequent advances; the condition of the peasant is happy enough, but it is always the same; the son is exactly in the same station his father occupied; he does not dream of becoming richer, he does not try to change his status at all.[12] One might believe seeing an Indian caste, irrevocably bound by religion to the same trades and the same practices. In a country like France, where there is progress everywhere, and everything hums with activity, a class which comprises nine-tenths of the population in many provinces, and which has remained immobile for four or five centuries, must be much behind the rest of the nation. In Italy, the same class had participated in the progress of universal civilization, because it made up just about half of the nation, which constantly intermingled with the other half in the cities, and which made rapid progress in all knowledge, at least during the time when Italy has experienced its true development, with so many, then prosperous towns, throughout the land.

In France, a liberal constitutional government will be established firmly in the reactionary provinces south of the Loire only when a portion of the land will be owned outright by the cultivators, and when another class of peasants, inspired by greater hope, and enlightened by more education, will be intermixed with the metayers; then the latter will finally see the possibility of progress before them, instead of always looking backward.

In some parts of Italy,[13] where these disadvantages have not been felt, another is experienced through the excessive increase of a population that also lives under the metayage system. Since individual ownership and security are reasonably well guaranteed to this class, the agricultural population has soon reached its natural limits, that is, the sharecropping farms were divided and subdivided to the point where, given the state of agricultural knowledge, a family has been able to maintain itself in moderate comfort, by modest effort, with its share of the harvest, on the amount of land left to it. We have seen that in patriarchal cultivation population increases would have stopped then; if it would be left to the metayers, the population would also remain stationary in this system; but they are not the sole masters of their fate. A family of share farmers has never been known to propose to the owner that the farm be divided, unless the work was really more than they could handle, and they had the certain knowledge that they would retain the same benefits on a smaller plot of land. One never sees in a family many sons marry at the same time and create as many new households; one alone takes a wife and assumes the cares of a new household; not one of his brothers marries, unless the first one has no children, in which case a new share farm is offered to that other brother.

But the estate is hereditary; a share farm depends on the good will of the master. A family of share farmers can be dispossessed either for its failures, or by the whim of the owner; and immediately a second son of a peasant family is on hand, ready to marry and found a new family. The former, reduced to penury by the loss of his livelihood, offers his services to all owners; to induce acceptance he is ready to submit to more onerous conditions. The second sons who wish to marry also offer their hands, and a mad auction results which causes the owners to divide their farms beyond reasonable limits. Each division, by increasing the amount of labor employed on the land, also increases its gross product; but against this product the withdrawals of the cultivators ought to become steadily larger; yet they are always the same. The owner who takes one-half of the gross product, sees his income increase with each division; the peasant, exchanging more work for the same amount, sees his dwindle. The share farmers, thus fighting over the share the owners are willing to leave to them, must finally [content themselves with the most niggardly subsistence, with a portion which is barely sufficient in good years, and which in bad years leaves them prey to famine.

This foolish species of competition[14] has reduced the peasantry, on the coast of Genoa, in the republic of Lucca, in several provinces of the kingdom of Naples, to content themselves with a third of the crop, in place of a half. In a magnificent country, which nature has enriched with all her gifts; which art has adorned with all its luxury; which annually gives forth a most abundant harvest—the numerous class that produce the fruits of the ground never taste the corn which is reaped, or the wine which is pressed, by their labour.] Its share is millet and maize, and its drink inferior wine, or water in which the skins of grapes have been fermented. Hence, [it struggles continually with famine. The same misfortune would probably have happened to the people of Tuscany, if public opinion had not guarded the farmer; but there no proprietor dares to impose terms unusual in the country; and when he changes one metayer for another, he changes no article of the primitive contract.[15] So soon, however, as public opinion becomes necessary for the maintenance of public prosperity, it ought, in strict propriety, to be sanctioned by law.][16]

It is a truth often stressed by the Economists, that each person can take care of his own interest better than a government; from which they have concluded that all those laws which seek to guide everyone in the care of his own fortune, are at all times useless, and often counterproductive. But they have also very quickly asserted that the interest of each to avoid a greater evil ought to be the interest of the whole. It is to the advantage of him who wants to despoil his neighbor, to steal, and in the latter's interest to let him proceed in order not to be assaulted, if the former employs physical force; but it is not in the interest of society that one uses force and the other gives in to it. Now, the entire social system confronts us at every step with a similar constraint, not always with the same degree of violence, but the same danger in resisting it. Society, through its institutions, has almost always given rise to such constraint; it ought not also support it with all its weight. It has most often forced the poor into the need to submit to onerous and ever-more-onerous service, under pain of dying from hunger; by placing him into such a precarious situation, it is obligated to come to his defense. Not to be satisfied with less than one-half of the harvest as the price of their labor is without a doubt in the interest of all the share farmers; but the interest of the share farmer who has lost his farm and cannot find another, is to be satisfied with a third, less than a third, and thus to jeopardize the livelihood of all his peers. The interest of the day laborer lies, no doubt, in wages for ten hours which are sufficient to live on, and raise children to maturity; this is very much the interest of society; but the unemployed worker is interested in finding bread at whatever price; he will work fourteen hours a day, he will bring his children to a factory at the age of six, and he will endanger with his health and life the existence of his whole class, to escape the pinch of dire need.[17]

The English Parliament has recently seen it necessary to intervene in contracts between the poor and the rich to protect the weakest; it has fixed the age below which a child may not work in a factory, as well as the total hours during which they can be made to work. The laws of the Roman Emperors, who certainly were not in favor of the lower classes, had taken under their protection the *colons*, whose condition seemed to have approached that of the Russian *serfs,* being subject to a head tax. A law of emperor Constantine (*Codex Justianini,* lib. XI, tit. 49, lex 1) decrees: "All colons whose master exacts a larger quit-rent than had to be paid before, and which had not been paid before him in prior times, must have recourse to the first judge in whose presence he may find himself, and expose this offense, so that he who will be convicted of having demanded more than it was customary, shall be prohibited to continue, and shall be forced to restore what he had extorted beyond his right." And since the serfs could not sue their masters, a later law by Arcadius and Honorius (ibid. 1. II) gave them the legal right to do so on such occasion.[18]

In general, [whenever vacant lands are no longer to be found, proprietors of the soil come to exercise a kind of monopoly against the rest of the nation;] the law authorizes this monopoly by permitting proprietorship in land; it has deemed it to be useful to society, and has taken it under its protection;[19] but [wherever monopoly exists, the legislature ought to interpose, lest they who enjoy may also abuse it.] Without the permission of the comparatively small class of landowners, no one in the nation would be able either to work himself, or make the soil fertile, or to obtain food. The Economists have deduced therefrom that the landowners alone were supreme, and that they would be able to send the nation home whenever they pleased. Much rather ought it to be concluded that such a great privilege could not have been given except in the interest of society, and that society ought to regulate it. It could also have given ownership to water, and no one would have been able to drink without the consent of the owners of rivers, or their lessees. It has not done so, for the single reason that no social advantage would have flowed therefrom. It has given ownership in land; but, in doing so, it must also guarantee the social advantage it had expected from it. Society must guard the interests of those who claim land, or food, or work.

Translator's Notes to Chapter 5, Third Book

Almost one-half of this chapter comes from the *Encyclopedia*. This presented a special translation problem because Sismondi uses *metayer* and *metayage* in the article. It seemed appropriate to continue this usage to preserve continuity of style, even though the term *sharecropper* would have been technically correct. However, it is associated, at least in the United States, with a different set of social circumstances, and was therefore considered inappropriate. Sismondi occasionally uses the term *cultivation at half-fruit;* its limited use suggests that he found the expression awkward. Therefore, his usage was employed throughout this chapter. As was noted in the prefatory note to the first chapter, the argument in this book follows the general pattern of Smith's discussion, but it is also clear that Sismondi has his own agenda: (1) that individual incentive is a direct function of ownership, taken up later with reference to the factory worker; (2) that increased production need not lead to a higher standard of living for everyone, except when population does not increase faster than production, and provided that the increase is distributed widely over the entire population. The parts of the chapter taken from the *Encyclopedia* dealing with these ideas are optimistic in tone, even romantic; the additions to *New Principles* reflect Sismondi's historical knowledge and personal experience, and are therefore more realistic, and indeed pessimistic. This pattern is repeated throughout the work and probably earned Sismondi the reputation of being indecisive.

1. Sismondi changed "conqueror" in the *Encyclopedia* to "conquerants" in *New Principles.*
2. *"Cultivation for half produce"* is italicized in *New Principles.* The first paragraph of the note appeared in the first edition, the second paragraph was added for the second edition.
3. *Serfs attached to the soil* is also italicized in *New Principles.*
4. This was changed for *New Principles* to "l'exploitation par capitation."
5. See note 2 on italics.
6. The words "According to this system" were dropped for *New Principles.*
7. *New Principles* drop the words "without the anxieties of wealth."
8. Compare this to Malthus's expression in the *Second Essay:* "At nature's mighty feast there is no vacant cover for him."
9. The next paragraph was added for the second edition.
10. This is an optimistic assessment of Haitian development not borne out by later experience.
11. The conclusion of chapter 3 is ignored, namely that ownership, or participation in ownership, as Sismondi describes some forms of metayage, leads to conservative politics. It also contradicts the idealized picture of metayage as a progressive agricultural system he had derived from his experience with Tuscan conditions, and just described in the preceding paragraphs.
12. The first edition reads: "En effet, l'exploitation par metayer n'a rien de progressif en elle." This was modified to read in the second edition: "En effet, l'exploitation par metayer est un premier progrès dans la condition du laboureur."
13. The words "some parts of" were added to the second edition.
14. The characterization of the Italian share farmer leaves out of account the absence of alternative employments for the sons who cannot hope to run another farm. The overpopulation Sismondi describes was eventually responsible for the massive later emigration from Italy to the New World, both north and south.
15. The primitive contract is the original contract on the property. Sismondi uses the term *primitive* here in the same sense as the physiocratic *avances primitives.*
16. *New Principles* reads: "Il vaudrait mieux qu'elle fût sanctionnée . . ."
17. A forerunner of Marx's argument that capitalistic society oppresses the poor, including the idea that the poor do not have the same market power as the capitalists because of competition. The argument goes further than the classical justification of the subsistence wage, because it does not include a so-called market corrective, that is, the dying of the surplus population unable to find work at the subsistence wage.
18. Sismondi clearly implies that such a law would also help the contemporary factory worker, but it is questionable whether the Roman serfs, needing employment, actually took advantage of this Justinian law, any more than a nineteenth-century worker would have taken advantage of such a law in the face of being blackballed by his employer.
19. Marx would have argued that the law protects the landowner because either

he, or the legislator who does his bidding, makes the laws. Sismondi assumes here that legislatures protect the interest of the whole against the individual. This is most likely a reflection of Sismondi's experience as a Genevese citizen, as compared to Marx's status as an alienated intellectual in a foreign country.

6

Cultivation by Corvée

We have designated cultivation by *corvée* the contract by which the owner, or more often the lord of the manor, gives to the peasant, serf, or vassal, a cottage with a certain amount of land attached thereto, a right to the pasturages and firewood of the manor; in return, he demands from his peasant a fixed number of workdays in the week with his team of oxen, to cultivate what land has remained in the hands of the lord.

This system of cultivation was already introduced during the decline of the Roman Empire, because the rapid decrease in the number of slaves, and the impossibility of capturing new ones from enemy nations, led to a search for ways to improve their lot. It seems that among the peasants, who the Justinian code designated by the name of colons, many cultivated the land by corvée. The same system of cultivation has left traces all over Europe, outside as well as inside the frontiers of the old Roman Empire; in the German lands, whence came the feudal system, in the Slavic lands, and in Scotland, where properly speaking fiefs have never existed. The tenure of the Highlanders,[1] or the Mountain Celts of Scotland, whose courage and devotion to their lords is so famous, was of the same nature; it is the general practice in Eastern Europe as far as Turkey, and it was met with again among the fakirs of Eusofzyes at Cabul.*[2]

Cultivation by corvée seemed to be one of the first expedients which occurred to the ingenuity of slaveholders to get from their workers the largest share without having to worry about their subsistence. It seems very probable that the lands of the Gauls were cultivated in this manner in Caesar's time, who describes the inhabitants of the countryside as having a status approaching serfdom, although he never lived in the houses of the knights.** In some colonies of the Gulf of Mexico, instead of feeding the

*M. Elphinstone, *Account of Cabul* (1815) p. 344.
**De Bello Gallico,* lib.IV., cap. XII and XV.

slaves, they are given part of the week to cultivate a plot and thus provide their subsistence; but because of the harshness which characterizes all laws concerning Negroes, they have been limited to two days a week, of which one ought to be a day of rest. In Transylvania, the serfs have only two workdays for themselves other than Sunday.

[Cultivation by corvées was very far from being as happy an invention] as cultivation by half-product. [No doubt it gave to the peasantry a kind of property, an interest in life; but it reduced them to see their domestic economy disturbed every moment, by the vexatious demands of a landlord or his stewards. The peasant could not perform the operations of his husbandry at the day fixed upon; the landlord's work must always be done before his own; the rainy days constantly fell to the share of the weaker party.[3] Under this system, the labourer performs every service for his master with repugnance, without care for its success, without affection, and without reward. In the landlord's fields, he works as badly as he can without incurring punishment. The steward, on the other hand, declares it absolutely necessary that corporal penalties be employed, and the infliction of them is abandoned to his own discretion.

Servitude of the soil has nominally been abolished in several countries, which have adopted the system of cultivation by corvées, but so long as this general system of agriculture is in force, there cannot be any liberty for the peasant. And although the abolition of servitude has given vassals a property and rights] to their persons, and the fruits of their labor, which the law did not recognize before, it gave them almost no means to realize them. [They are as constantly thwarted and disturbed in their own operations as before; they work quite as ill during the landlord's days; they are quite as miserable within their own huts; and the master, who had been flattered with hopes that the abolition of slavery would increase his revenue, has derived no advantage from it. On the contrary,[4] he is ever an object of hatred and distrust to his vassals; and social order, threatened so incessantly, cannot be maintained except by violent means.

The ground of the metayer's contract is every way the same, as that of a contract with a cultivator by corvées. The landlord in Hungary, as in Italy, has given up his land to the peasant, on condition of receiving half of its fruits in return. In both countries, the other half has been reckoned sufficient for supporting the cultivator, and repaying his advances. A single error in political economy has rendered what is highly advantageous for one of these countries, disastrous for the other. The Hungarian has not inspired the labourers with any interest in his own industry; by sharing the land and the days of the week] instead of the fruits, [he has made an enemy of the man, who should have been his coadjutor. The labour is performed without zeal or intelligence; the master's share, inferior to what it would have been according to the other system, is collected with fear; the peasant's share is so reduced, that he lives in constant penury; and some of the most fertile countries in the world have already been for ages doomed to this stage of wretchedness and oppression.]

However, an initial betterment in the status of the poor classes, and without a doubt the substitution of the corvée for total slavery was such an improvement, leads most often to new improvements. The reciprocal interest of the master and the vassal made them both wish for a more precise evaluation of the *services* which the former had a right to demand from the latter. Often they were converted into a tax paid either in kind, or in money. The corvées, and the head tax, which we will discuss in the next chapter, were combined in different ways. A fixed quantity, either in money or in corn, was levied from each villager, and as a sign of his ancient servitude, and the rights of the lord, certain obligations to discharge in person certain tasks, such as working on the moat of the castle, or perform any other services which defined his lower status, were just added to his dues. In France and England. almost all the lands held in *vilenage*,[5] and those which were designated by the name *copyholds* in the latter, had been originally subject to the corvée or head tax; but their people have freed themselves by and by from all that was demeaning in their condition. The quit-rent and the copyhold have become legacies joined almost entirely to others; rent which was arbitrary, has become perpetual and unchangeable; depreciation of the coinage has made them almost everywhere light in relation to the value of the land, and the only disadvantage which remained connected to such property is the payment of the lord's dues for alterations, which take away from the cultivator, for the benefit of the lord, a part of the capital destined to be used for the improvement of the land.

In the kingdom of Poland, where the liberation of the peasants is still quite recent, the corvées are paid in kind; but since they are the result of a free contract, the number of days the peasant owes are generally proportional to the number of acres the lord gives to him. Therefore the condition of the peasant will be truly stable only when he will exchange this quit-rent against an equal value payable in products of his lands.

[But the legislator's interference, which was claimed for the metayer, has, in] almost all [countries cultivated by corvées, actually taken place in favour of the vassal, peasant or serf.] In old France, quit-rents were declared indefeasible and not redeemable, but they also could not be raised by the lord. In England, the copyholder had to pay the quit-rents fixed by the will of the lord; but the law mandated that such will was construed by the customs of the manor, and that those were inalterable.*[6] [In the German provinces of the Austrian monarchy, contracts between the lord and the peasant are, by law, made irrevocable, and most of the corvées have been changed into a fixed and perpetual rent of money, or of the fruits in a raw state. By this means, the peasant has acquired a true property in his house and land; only, it continues to be charged with a rent, and some feudal services. Still farther to protect the peasantry from being afterwards oppressed or gradually expelled from their properties, by the opulent lords living among them, the law does not allow any noble to buy a vassal's land; or, if he does buy any, he is obliged to sell it, on the same condition, to some other family of peasants; so that the property of the nobles can never increase, or the agricultural population diminish.][7]

This population, enjoying abundance and security, has reached soon, in those provinces, the limits which generally suited its ease and proper husbandry, but it has not exceeded them. The heads of families, aware of their resources, have avoided plunging themselves into poverty, or to marry off more children than they could provide with a livelihood. Men can be relied upon to maintain their status if they are able to assess it,[8] and if they rely only on themselves. The class which always overburdens the nation with a poverty-stricken population is the one which, expecting to live only by the strength of its arms, and on the goodwill of others, has no means of estimating the opportunities which will be available to its children.

[These regulations of the Austrian government in behalf of an order, which, if left to itself, must needs be oppressed, are almost sufficient to redeem the errors of its general system, by this increase of happiness to the subject, and the stability to the system itself. In a country deprived of liberty, where the finances have at all times been wretchedly administered, where wars are eternal—and still disastrous, obstinacy there being always joined with incapacity; the great mass of the population, composed almost wholly of peasant proprietors living in easy circumstances, have been rendered happy; and this mass of subjects, feeling their own happiness, and dreading every change, have mocked all the projects of revolution or of conquest directed against their country.][9]

Translator's Notes to Chapter 6, Third Book

Like the previous chapter, chapter 6 presents a special translation problem. The term *corvée,* unlike *metayer,* has no equivalent in English. The best translation would probably be *serf cultivation*—and in the sequence of Sismondi's argument it represented both in the *Encyclopedia* and in *New Principles* the logical next step

*This wise law was not extended to land tenures in vilenage, customary in Scotland and Ireland, or to more recent contracts between lords and their tenants. Hence the gradual expropriations of peasants in the three kingdoms.

up from slavery. But Sismondi uses the term in the *Encyclopedia,* indicating that to him at least there was either a difference in meaning, or that he found the term, not surprisingly, awkward to translate. To avoid a stylistic break his usage was adopted.

Sismondi fleshed out the chapter from the original *Encyclopedia* version, but it is otherwise a part of the historical progression of systems of cultivation that he surveyed and described to support the argument that widely dispersed ownership of land, and, later, of economic resources generally, is the most efficient way to improve the workers' lot, and to attain what he sees as the most important goal of economic activity, general happiness. His preference for property sharing is evidenced by his comparison of Hungarian and Italian agriculture, and the laudatory references to metayage, which he favors over even a very attenuated serf agriculture.

1. The English term is used in the French text.
2. Afghanistan.
3. As elsewhere in the work, especially with reference to factory workers, the argument stresses unequal market power of contracting parties. This view differs from both the classical political economists who, from Adam Smith on, saw the market as a place where individual contracts were made at arm's length, and also from Marx, who ascribed the inferior bargaining power of the proletarian essentially to the increasing organic composition of capital and the resulting increase of the reserve army. To Sismondi, the unequal market strength of the worker and the master is related to social and legal structures, which have a historic developmental basis and are therefore alterable.
4. These three words were dropped for *New Principles*.
5. The spelling is not used anymore; it denotes a serf who is free except to his lord. The word *villain* is derived from this root.
6. The note was added to the second edition of *New Principles*. The term *copyholder* in this sentence was used in the French text.
7. Sismondi presents this arrangement as protective of the peasants, which it was, but it was also designed to maintain a steady supply of recruits for the imperial armies. Despite stringent measures to maintain the peasant population, lords did acquire larger holdings, and peasants left the land for better-paying jobs in the cities.
8. A variation of the argument that the new, market-oriented, economy makes it difficult, if not altogether impossible, for the producer to know precisely the demand he faces, and therefore he must either over-, or under-produce.
9. The paragraph in the *Encyclopedia* ends with ". . . the government of which is so little able to defend itself." This was omitted in *New Principles*. This last critical remark in a very critical paragraph may be related to Sismondi's experiences in Austria while traveling with Madame de Staël.

7

Cultivation by Capitation

Cultivation by a system of head-taxes has existed, most likely, in all countries where slavery has been permitted by law. It is one of those expedients which the greed of the landlord invented to profit from this abominable law without, at the same time, having to care for the upkeep of the slave, and the supervision of his labors. The master who has slaves, and who does not wish to make them work for his account, can elect to hire them out to others who will work them, or he could let them hire their own time, drawing from them the value of the rent he would have been able to receive from another renter. This annual rental of a person, which the Russians call *obroc*, is what we have called a head-tax.[1] It is not at all unknown in the Antilles; the small owners permit the Negroes quite frequently to practice for their own account a craft, or a small trade, while paying a head-tax. It is commonly adopted in Turkey, where the rajahs are subject to a head-tax, to ransom annually their life, which is considered forfeited and saved only by the leniency of the Sultan. It has been imposed in all countries where feudalism flourishes, and it is for this reason that head-taxes were considered everywhere a mark of slavery.

But this rent levied on the person, as compensation for the right of the master to the person's labor, could not become a means to cultivate the soil, except where land is so abundant, and so universally empty, that the labor of the man is everything and the income from the land counts for nothing. Such was most likely the state of Russia because the *obroc* was levied on the peasants of the crown. There existed more fertile land than anybody could cultivate, and none of the lands had yet been improved by any work. As a consequence, the crown abandoned to its peasants the absolute use of the fields where their villages were located, and instead of asking in exchange either for half of the crop, or corvées, or a quit-rent, either in kind or in money, and levied on the land, it exacted from them the *obroc*, which each male slave paid when he reached manhood. The amount of the ransom was not the same everywhere in Russia. The provinces[2] of this empire were divided into four classes, and the *obroc* of each was higher or lower according to the fertility of the soil, or its distance from markets, but it is the same for all men in the same province. We repeat the barbaric word, because the Russian peasant, in addition to the *obroc*, paid a second head-tax which alone is known by this name; this is the general tax levied on all subjects of the empire.

Freedom has made so much progress in the last half century that the peasants who pay *obroc* are today perhaps the most numerous class among the slaves of civilized nations. In 1782, 4,675,000 male individuals were counted among the Russian peasants as belonging to the crown. These are by far the most fortunate among the serfs of that empire, from whom it is not at all exceptional to hear them extolling their good fortune to those who deplore the old ways, and who would want to see with anxiety man regain his rights. In truth, their tax is moderate, their property is guaranteed by law, and each village, with authorization of its own magistrates, distributes the lands which were allotted to it, to the individuals who make up the village.[3] They have recently acquired the right to purchase land outright; they may, for a money payment, acquire the right to travel for up to three years inside the empire; for a cash payment they can also obtain the permission to register as citizens of towns. With these privileges, they enjoy in reality some comfort in their houses, and some have made large fortunes. However, even this privileged class can all at once lose all these advantages—they can be assigned to factories, hired out for lease, or sold, or transferred to private owners who place these unfortunates back into total slavery. Finally, this class was recently subjected to a special levy imposed in accordance with a general plan to establish military colonies, whose consequences are difficult to foresee today.

The encouragement of manufacture and mining has been the policy of this century in Russia, as in the rest of Europe. The crown itself has mines and factories to which it assigns peasants of the class who stop paying *obroc*, instead being subject to the corvées, and who cannot leave their trade at which they work from that moment on, anymore than those sentenced to forced labor in prisons can. The crown parcels out villages in the same manner to those who introduce into the state some new industry, and the conditions of the unfortunate peasants whose grantee changes them into factory workers becomes even more miserable.

The crown holdings in the provinces previously under Swedish or Polish rule are often given on quit-rents to civil or military service members whom the sovereign wishes to reward, and the farming contractor, or the subcontractors, can hardly fail to make the conditions of the peasants more miserable. Finally, new territories have often been created by Catherine and her predecessors, to reward some favorite; the peasants of the crown lands, so given over, lose all their privileges and become slaves. Emperor Alexander has refrained from ever handing any over, but there exists no law in this respect which ties his hands, or those of his successors.

In 1782, the slaves who belonged to the Russian nobility made up a population of 6,678,000 male individuals. Among these, the greatest number were forced to do agricultural work, and to pay the *obroc*; these were the least unfortunates, although the *obroc* is variable at the will of the lords; and the remainder of their possessions, any more than their persons, does not enjoy any security, so that all they have saved by long industriousness could be taken away at once quite legally. Others perform corvées for their master; finally, others are rented out to farm contractors. Moreover, all slaves of the nobility may be removed from agricultural work to be sent to the mines, to factories, and to trades, or be employed as domestics, either by their lords, or by those to whom they are leased.

It is true[4] [the disinterestedness of some noble families, who for several generations have not changed the capitation,[5] has inspired the peasantry with confidence sufficient to reanimate their industry, to infuse a taste for labour and economy, and sometimes even to permit their realizing very large fortunes which, however, always depend on the master's good pleasure.] Russia is thus the only country where the slave population can be seen to maintain not only its numbers, but to increase them without importation.[6] Nevertheless, slavery has not in any way changed its nature; the slave [was always liable to be ejected, carried off, sold, stript of all the property amassed by his industry; and thus the kind of authority to which he was subject incessantly reminded him, that, whatever he saved, he took from himself to give it to his master; that every effort on his part was useless, every invention dangerous, every improvement contrary to his interest, and finally, that every sort of study but aggravated his wretchedness by more clearly informing him of his condition.][7]

We have said that in Western Europe capitation was also one of the first steps by which the peasants emerged from servitude. It was at first a means to redeem the corvées, and it was afterwards joined to the value of the land given by the lord, and thus gave rise to *farm leases*. We will not repeat the history of these improvements in the status of the peasants which we have outlined at the end of the previous chapter.

Translator's Notes to Chapter 7, Third Book

The term *capitation* is taken from the *Encyclopedia*—the tax is now usually called a poll tax. Although this chapter is almost entirely new material, the use of the original term employed there was thought to be appropriate for the translation. The specific discussion of the *obroc* goes beyond the *Encyclopedia* and most likely can be explained by Sismondi's preference for concrete historical examples. His justification for the existence of the tax, in the second paragraph, is farfetched; the availability of free land ought to lead to migration away from feudal impositions, as it did earlier in Europe, or the establishment of free farms, as it did later in the United States. The detailed discussion of Russian village organization in the third paragraph is interesting because it demonstrates the relative invariance of social institutions over time. The modern Soviet cooperative has many parallels to the old *mir*, including its semi-serf status under the Communist party and the assignment of tasks by the leaders of the commune.

1. There is no reference by name to this tax in the *Encyclopedia*.
2. The French term used is ''gouvernements,'' which was the name used by the Russian government for its adminstrative subdivisions. ''Provinces'' was used in the translation as a shorthand for ''provincial governments.''
3. Sismondi consistently equates freedom and population increases. Here he associates more lenient conditions of feudal servitude with larger families, although he fails to show, as he did with metayage, whether the additional population was in fact able to cultivate more land.
4. In the *Encyclopedia,* Sismondi uses ''Even in Russia . . .''
5. The unchanged poll tax is equated with a general easing of servitude, although one condition is not necessarily related to the other. However, it must be assumed that Sismondi had in mind the same devaluation of the currency that occurred elsewhere in Europe and was responsible for the decreased weight of feudal obligation earlier referred to. The rest of the paragraph modifies the initial optimistic tone of this sentence.
6. Sismondi was apparently not aware that this was true also of the United States, as opposed to the Caribbean.
7. The sequence of paragraphs in the *Encyclopedia* is reversed here—this quotation precedes the sentence beginning with ''the disinterestedness.'' There is a consistent and continuing argument here and throughout the work that only free property owning induces individuals to improve themselves and their lot.

8

Cultivation by Farm Lease

In the wealthiest countries, the farm lease has replaced every other kind of contract[1] resulting from former servitude; it has more than any other attracted the attention of the Economists, and it is generally considered as being everywhere the consequence of the advance of civilization.

[By a farm lease, the proprietor yields his land, and nothing more, to the cultivator; and demands an invariable rent for it; whilst the farmer undertakes to direct and execute all the labour by himself; to furnish the cattle, the implements, and the funds of agriculture; to sell their produce, and to pay his taxes. The farmer takes upon him all the cares and all the gains of agriculture; he treats it as a commercial speculation, from which he expects a profit proportionate to the capital employed in it.

At the time when slavery was abolished, the system of farms could not be immediately established; freedmen could not yet undertake such important engagements, nor were they able to advance the labour of a year, much less than that of several years, for putting the farm in a proper condition. The master, on giving them their liberty, would have been obliged to give them also an establishment; to furnish them with cattle, instruments of tillage, seed and food for a year; and after all these advances, the farm would still have been a burdensome concern for the owner, because by his contract he had renounced the profit of good years on condition that his farmer should warrant him against bad years; but the farmer who had nothing could warrant nothing, and the master would have given up his good crops without any return.

The first farmers were mere labourers; they executed most of the agricultural operations with their own hands; they adjusted their enterprises to the strength of their families; and as the proprietor reposed little confidence in their management, he used to regulate their procedure by numerous obligatory clauses; he limited their leases to a few years, and kept them in a continual state of dependence.] This is still quite generally the status of farmers, wherever this type of cultivation is adopted, except in Rome and in England. It is true, however, that the obligatory clauses were gradually dropped from the lease, or disregarded in its execution; the farmers dispose of their land much more freely than they did even fifty years ago, and they obtain longer terms. Nevertheless, they have not ceased to be peasants; they man their own plows; they look after their cattle, in the fields and the stable; they live outdoors, accustoming themselves to ordinary hard work and plain food, which form robust citizens and courageous soldiers. They hardly ever employ day laborers to work with them, but only household servants, selected from their peers, treated as everybody else, eating at the same table, drinking the same wine, and wearing the same clothes. The farmers and their servants thus form only one class of peasants, moved by the same feelings, sharing the same diversions, exposed to the same hardships, and bound to the fatherland by the same bonds.[2]

In this condition the farmers are doubtless less happy than the smallholders, but they are happier than the metayers; at least, if they have more cares, if the obligation to find at a fixed date the price of the rent and the money for taxes exposes them to cruel distress, to more severe losses, they also have more prospects. Their career is in no way limited, they can better themselves, they can become wealthy and advance to the status of landlord, to which they all aspire. This mixture of hope and fear develops character, it brings home the cost of experience, and it leads to noble feelings; the farmers of France are Frenchmen, the metayers are merely vassals.

But in England the farmers, sharing in the general advance of well-being and the accumulation of capital, are part of a more exalted class of society. In order to invest their savings [they have taken farms of larger size; more extensive knowledge, and a better education have enabled them to treat agriculture as a science. They have applied to it several important discoveries in chemistry and natural history; they have also in some degree united the habits of the merchant with those of the cultivator. The hope of a larger profit has induced them to make larger advances; they have renounced that parsimony which originates in want, and stands in direct opposition to enlightened economy; they have calculated and recorded the results of their operation with greater regularity, and this practice has furnished better opportunities to profit by their own experience.

On the other hand, farmers from this time have ceased to be labourers; and below them has of course been formed a class of men of toil, who, being entrusted with supporting the whole nation by their labour, are the real peasants, the truly essential part of the population. The peasantry, strengthened by the kind of labour most natural to man, are perpetually required for recruiting all the other classes; it is they who must defend the country in case of need; whom it most concerns us to attach to the soil where they were born; and policy itself would invite every government to render their lot happy, even though humanity did not command it.[3]

When the system of small farms is compared, as is often done, with that of great farms,*[4] it has not been sufficiently considered that the latter, by taking the direction of his labour out of the peasant's hands, reduces him to a condition greatly more unhappy than almost any other system of cultivation. In truth, hands performing all the labours of agriculture, under the command of a rich farmer, are not only more dependent than metayers, but even than serfs, who pay their capitation or their service. The latter, whatever vexations they experience, have at least a hope, a property, and a heritage to leave to their children. But the hand has no participation in property, nothing to hope from the fertility of the soil, or the propitiousness of the season; he plants not for his children; he entrusts not to the ground the labour of his young years, to reap the fruit of it, with interest, in his old age. He lives each week on the wages of the last. Ever exposed to the want of work by derangements in his master's fortune; ever ready to feel the extremes of want, from sickness, accident, or even the approaches of old age, he runs all the risks of ruin without enjoying any of the chances of fortune.]

In the condition to which the field hands are reduced, it is scarcely probable that they will practice economy. Every day, privation and suffering habituate them to wish for daily distraction. Besides drink, which most likely becomes a necessity to dull their sorrows, the thought of a man who is likely to lack every day proper nourishment, is constantly preoccupied

*The use of the words "small" or "large" farm, "small" or "large cultivation" may give rise to some confusion. In hot climates, where on the same land three or four crops are harvested annually, wheat, for example, beans, wine, and olive oil, an acre is equal to four in northern climates, whether measured in quantity of production, or in manual labor demanded. Moreover, man must perform all work in the vineyards, the olive groves, and the fruit arbors, and he has done by animals all those of the closes, the fields, and the woods. If large cultivation is considered identical with the use of the plow, which presupposes farms of about fifty acres, and small cultivation with the use of the spade and ditching, which presupposes farms of seven to eight acres, with part in vineyards, then attention must be paid to climate, soil formation, amount of capital accumulated, to make a choice between them. I have intended to compare another aspect, the farms of peasants which I assume to be on flat land with fifty to sixty acres,[5] and which I still designate as small, and the farms of speculators, which can be seen to run from five to six hundred acres up to five and six thousand acres, which are those Arthur Young and the English agronomists and economists classify by the name of *great farms*.[6]

with what he eats or drinks, in the same way in which practice of vigils and fasts stimulates indulgence in good food. The common people must have their pleasures, and it is not the fault of the day worker if social organization has reduced him to knowing only the most vulgar.[7]

Moreover, though the day worker [should succeed in collecting a little capital, the suppression of all intermediate ranks hinders him from putting it to use. The distance between his lot and that of an extensive farmer, is too great for being passed over; whereas in the system of cultivation on the small scale, a labourer may succeed by his little economy, in acquiring a small farm, or a small metairie; from this he may pass to a greater, and from that to everything.[8] The same causes have suppressed all the intermediate stages in other departments of industry.[9] A gulf lies between the day labourer and every enterprise of manufacture or trade, as well as farming; and the lower classes have now lost that help which sustained them in a former period of civilization. Parish aids which are secured to the] English [day labourer, increase his dependence.[10] In such a state of suffering and disquietude, it is not easy to preserve the feeling of human dignity, or the love of freedom; and thus at the highest point of modern civilization, the system of agriculture approximates to that of those corrupt periods of ancient civilization, when the whole labour of the field was performed by slaves.

The state of Ireland, and the convulsions to which that unhappy country is continually exposed, show clearly enough how important it is for the repose and security of the rich themselves, that the agricultural class, which forms the great majority of the nation, should enjoy conveniences, hope, and happiness. The Irish peasants are ready to revolt,[11] and plunge their country into the horrors of civil war; they live each in a miserable hut, on the produce of a few beds of potatoes, and the milk of a cow; more unhappy, at the present day, than the cottagers of England, though possessing a small property, of which the latter are destitute. In return for their allotted portion of ground, they merely engage to work by the day, at a fixed wage, on the farm where they live; but their competition with each other has forced them to be satisfied with a wage of the lowest possible kind.* A similar competition will act likewise against the English cottagers. There is no equality of strength between the day labourer, who is starving, and the farmer, who does not even lose the revenue of his ground, by

*In Ireland, the multiplying of cottagers beyond the needs of agriculture is not due to the division of inheritances in each family, but to the original allotment made by the owners. An overly small piece of land has been attached to each cottage, and the owners, who were still warlords, wanted to have a larger number of them, but the original allotments have rarely been divided by the will of the peasants themselves.[12]

suppressing some of his habitual operations; and hence the result of such a struggle between the two classes, is constantly a sacrifice of the class which is poorer, more numerous, and better entitled to the protection of the law.]

However, once the system of large farm estates begins to be introduced, the family farmers cannot withstand their competition; the smallholders see themselves ruined by rivals who perform their tasks with more economy, and who sell their products at the most propitious moment. Since taxes have greatly multiplied, each owner is no more than some kind of farmer for the tax collector. One notices in England that those who are called small *free-holders* generally exist in a state of misery. Thus the system which makes people more miserable, tends, by its internal dynamic, to prevail over all others.[13]

This advantage is easily explained: the profits of the farmer are the result of three very different battles he must conduct—against the consumer, the landowners, and the workers who work for him. He can increase his profits, either by selling his products at a higher price, or paying less for rent, or inducing his hands to be satisfied with a smaller wage. In each of these situations, the large farmer who commands large capitals is better placed than the small one.[14]

With respect to the consumer, the smaller the number of farmers, the easier it is for them to reach an understanding to price their products at a monopoly price. In the Papal States, more than one town is found that is surrounded by one estate—the citizens of Nepi, or Ronciglione, are quite definitely in a state of absolute dependence on the farmer whose land surrounds them on all sides;[15] they buy only from him all the provisions which cannot be transported over long distances, or spoil easily, such as milk, garden produce, and poultry. As Velletri borders on four estates, and Tivoli on ten, the lot of the consumers there will be less wretched, because they will have more suppliers; and the smaller the farms will be, the less the farmers can exact a monopoly price.

With respect to the day laborers, the farmers hold a similar monopoly. The citizens of Nepi or Ronciglione, when they offer their services for wages, must deal with a single man, who has absolute power to reduce them to the lowest possible terms. Those of Velletri may hope for more competition among four neighbors, and those of Tivoli for an even greater one among ten; however, it is far from certain that they are assured that their work will be paid at market rates.

Moreover, the large farmer achieves an immediate saving through the state of wretchedness to which he has reduced the workers' families. A thousand acres were cultivated under the system of small farms by fifty families living in moderate ease; a large farmer, in order to unite the same land into a single farm, substitutes for them at once fifty day-laborer families who will live in poverty; he will gain as a consequence the entire difference between their consumption, and that of their predecessors. Can such a windfall be deemed advantageous to a nation?

However, that farmer will soon make another of the same kind; he will discharge his hands, put their village to cultivation, and will rely, for the discharge of his work in the busy season, on outside workers called in from elsewhere.

After having sold his crop at a favorable price, and paid less to his hands, the planter of a thousand acres will be surely in a position to pay to the owner a larger rent than the fifty smallholders he will have displaced. He will begin this by tearing down the modest huts that have become superfluous for his system of cultivation; he will plow through the garden, through the orchard from which every small household drew enjoyment; he will level the enclosures which serve no more purpose, and subject his thousand acres to a uniform rotation of crops. But if now the owner would have liked to return to garden farming,[16] he will not anymore have the means. He would need a new advance and large capitals to return everything to its previous state. The large estate suits only the large contractor. Nobody can even dream of one unless he has sufficient capital to cultivate a thousand acres. The number of such entrepreneurs is much more limited than that of the working farmers they have replaced. They come easily to an understanding, they avoid making each other dangerous competition; soon they find themselves in a position to lay down the law to the owner, and the large farmer who has profited more than the small one from the sale of his crops, who gets more than the small one from the livelihood of his workers, again profits more than the small one on his contract with the owner.[17]

Thus, when the system of large estate farming collides with that of small farms, without the latter being protected either by law or public opinion, the former must prevail although society derives no benefits therefrom. The small farmers, the small landowners, may find themselves unable to compete with their rich neighbor, but this fact, quite frequently observed, should not lead to a verdict in favor of the victorious system, if considered from the viewpoint of national prosperity.[18]

The advantages we just mentioned are all associated with the conditions the large farmers are able to impose on those with whom they deal. Some others flow from an increase in real wealth. The small owner rarely employs a capital sufficient even for his little cultivation; he is always under pressure to sell, and he is seldom in a position to buy at the right time. Moreover, the large farmer saves much time that is lost to the small one. The management of the workforce demands about the same degree of attention and effort regardless at what level it is performed, and forty workers are as easily directed as four.[19] But ten farmers performed before within the same time the same task as one does now; all that would be allocated to wages for nine of these ten, can now be saved. In combining ten fields into one, several enclosures and access roads can be eliminated; the very village with all the land that was taken up by its houses and alleys, can be put to the plow.

[Cultivation, on the great scale, spares much time which is lost in the other way;[20] it causes a greater mass of work to be performed in the same time by a given number of men; it tends, above all, to procure from the employment of great capitals the profit procured from the employment of numerous workmen; it introduces the use of expensive instruments, which abridge and facilitate the labour of man. It invents machines, in which the wind, the fall of water, the expansion of steam, are substituted for the power of limbs; it makes animals execute the work formerly executed by men. It hunts the latter from trade to trade, and concludes by rendering their existence useless. Any saving of human strength is a prodigious advantage, in a colony, where the supernumerary population may always be advantageously employed.] In the Antilles, [humanity justly solicits the employment of machines to aid the labour of the negroes, who cannot perform what is required of them, and who used to be incessantly recruited by an infamous commerce.[21] But in a country where population is already too abundant, the dismissal of more than half the field-labourers is a serious misfortune, particularly at a time when a similar improvement in machinery causes the dismissal of more than half of the manufacturing population of the towns.[22] The nation is nothing else but the union of all the individuals who compose it, and the progress of its wealth is illusory, when obtained at the price of general wretchedness and mortality.]

One can gauge the danger which threatens the country that changes over to great farm cultivation by looking at the condition to which the Roman province of Campagna has been reduced. This is the name given to all the territory extending from the mountain of Viterbo to Terracina, and from the sea to the Sabine mountains. In this province, ninety miles long by twenty-five miles wide, or 2,250 square miles, no more than about forty farmers can be counted. It is true that they are not called by that name anymore, which they would consider to be beneath their station. They are called *mercanti di tenute,* traders in lands. They employ in this business immense capitals; and by their extreme wealth make the land untenable for all their competitors. But their way of cultivating the land leaves no doubt that for them the most profitable course is economizing on human labor in every way, to be satisfied with the natural products of the soil, to rely on herding, and to eliminate by degrees what remains of the population. The Roman territories, so prodigiously fertile, where five acres fed a family and provided one soldier, where vines, olives, and figs intermingled in the fields, and allowed three or four crops per year, almost like in the state of Lucca, which is not more favored by nature; this land has seen single houses gradually disappear, villages, the whole population, enclosures, vineyards, olives, and all those crops which demanded continuous attention, work, and above all human care. Then vast fields followed, and the *mercanti di tenute* have found it more economical to have the sowing and the harvesting done by workers who come down out of the Sabine mountains each year; they, accustomed to live on a piece of bread, and to sleep in the open covered with dew, perish by the hundreds of *Maremma* fever[23] every harvest for lack of care, and content themselves nevertheless with the most wretched wages for risking these dangers. A native population in the Roman Campagna would be useless to the farmers, and it has completely disappeared. Some towns remain in the middle of the vast fields which belong to a single master; but Nepi and Ronciglione may quickly see their inhabitants, who were alienated from the soil by which they ought to live, disappear, and one can calculate in advance the expected day when the plow will go over the land where their houses stand, as it has passed already over the ruins of San Lorenzo, Vico, Bracciano, and Rome herself. Moreover, the fields in turn gave way to pasturage, and every day brambles and gorse take the place of grass there; in the center of civilization the steppes of Tartary can be seen reborn.[24]

Without a doubt, the legislator is called upon to halt this banishment of people brought about in the name of property. The right of the first occupant was not guaranteed in order to keep the earth from producing, and man from employing his labor usefully. But the duty of the legislator is made even more compelling because all this evil which flows from this flawed cultivation is his work. Nature has provided a remedy against the misfortunes brought about by the amassing of estates: the multiplication of families, and the equal division of inheritances that must follow. The calamity of great wealth, not any less terrible for society than that of great poverty,[25] would have dissipated of its own accord, if the legislator would not have sought to make it everlasting by primogeniture. Perchance, the law cannot regulate the extent of a farm without making its weight felt too much; but it ought to have constantly in mind the need to divide properties frequently, so as to escape the greatest national misfortune, the expulsion of the nation from its own hearth, illustrated today by the Roman Campagna.

[Whilst, in England, the peasantry are hastening to destruction,] and have already been destroyed in the Roman Campagna, [their condition is improving in France; they are gathering strength, and without abandoning manual labour, they enjoy a kind of affluence; they unfold their minds, and adopt, though slowly, the discoveries of science.] A long war and heavy taxes have not been able to halt the progress the acquisition of property rights has brought to the rural population. The most industrious provinces have been led thereby to an unexpected modification of the farm lease, the *subdivisional lease*. [A large proprietor now rarely gives his farm to be cultivated by a single person; he finds it infinitely more advantageous, at present, to share his domain among a number of neighbouring peasants, each of whom takes as much land as is requisite to occupy him all year. No doubt, the peasant will generally sacrifice the land which he farms, to that which is his property; but both these portions are cultivated with the ardour which a direct interest excites in the labourer, and with the intelligence which is developed in him, now that his lord can no longer oppress him. The agricultural classes] in France [are as happy as the political circumstances of the country, loved with enthusiasm, permit them to be.][26]

In looking for an understanding of what grave defects may come from the vastness of farms, and the disavowal of all manual labor by the farmers, we have not yet fully addressed the question of large versus small agriculture; we could not do so because it falls more properly into the realm of agronomy than political science. Climate, location, and markets determine the kind of crops grown on the land, and the nature of these crops determines the size of the farms or metairies. The system which suits wheat fields and grasslands is disastrous for vineyards, olives, and orchards. Large-scale farming is proper for crops that are raised especially with the help of animals, small-scale farming is proper for crops that require the diligent and sometimes intensive care of man. Most often we have no choice among them; also the size of farms does not determine at all the preference given to one or the other. In Tuscany, land of small farms, a large estate, *una fattoria*, is divided into twenty or thirty metairies; in the patrimony of St. Peter, a land of large farms, seven or eight farms are often combined under the same farmer.

But without giving preference to either system, we only wanted to recall how each could be pushed to excess; and how society is in no way safeguarded against such excess by the interest of the owner. We have seen, in chapter 5, that, in Italy, it was the owner who often prompted the excessive division of metairies and thereby made the condition of the metayers miserable. We did believe that we had to show how, in England, the excessive consolidation of farms is often caused by the owner against the interest of the nation. England has increased its prosperity so much, carried the application of the natural sciences to agriculture so far, perfected domestic animal breeds, used manuring crops and clever machines, that at first glance the drawbacks of its large estates are not obvious. After having admired the well-tended fields, one has to take account of the population which works them; it is less than half of what it would be in France on the same amount of land. In the eyes of some economists[27] this is a gain, in mine it is a loss. But this smaller population is at the same time much poorer. The cottager is below the peasant of almost all the other countries of Europe in happiness, hope, and security; from which I conclude that the goal of wealth creation has been missed.

And looking at it more closely, I am troubled to see that all the small joys nature has in store for us disappear with the people who ought to enjoy them. No more orchards, no more fruit trees brighten the countryside; it is not the climate that keeps them out—it is equal to that of a part of France, and better than that of Germany; but the diligent care of fruit trees is beyond the attention of a farmer of five hundred acres; similarly he does not make an effort to raise poultry—boats loaded with eggs come from Normandy to supply English markets. He has great herds of cows, and his milk sheds are managed with an elegance and cleanliness that makes us envious, but he sells no butter, cream, or milk products. Finally, he scorns even more the art of gardening, such that one finds vegetables in abundance only in the vicinity of large cities, or in the kitchen gardens of lords. The rich farmer concerns himself only with the wheat and cattle markets; all the small aspects of agriculture which bring little money, but much happiness to the poor households of the Continent appear to him as beneath his dignity.

All is thus sacrificed to the task of producing wheat; but by what quirk of fate is the English farmer unable to stand up to the competition from Continental producers, and why has he a need for a monopoly, so that his fields repay his advances? The import of wheat is prohibited, and this very year (1826) it needed all the persuasiveness of the government to get from Parliament permission to bring in a limited quantity, paying an import duty of about 20 percent, because the harvest was insufficient.

It cannot be denied that agricultural science has made tremendous progress in England, thanks to, if you wish, the great farms. But one asks with astonishment who profits therefrom? Are there more peasants? No; the main advantage that has been kept in view was the saving of manual labor, and the rural population has been reduced by more than half. Are the peasants happier? No; they are not better fed, nor better clothed, nor better housed than those of France, and they have none of the safeguards of the French peasants; the cottager is never assured of yearly employment, or even for the coming week; he is ever obliged to return to the workhouse, and to the assistance of his parish. Are the farmers getting rich? No; almost all were ruined a few years ago by sudden changes in the prices of provisions; the landowners extract from them the highest rent they can pay, *rack rent,* and with all their industriousness they have much trouble to keep their heads above water. Then the landlord reaps all the fruits of agricultural progress? No; the rent of twenty-five francs per acre,[25] which can be considered average for England, is below the average for France; moreover, it is gained only with the assistance of a monopoly which today antagonizes the nation, and which cannot be upheld. The consumer, finally, gains at the expense of the producer? No; he cannot get either fruit or poultry, nor milk products or vegetables; he pays for meat as much as on the Continent, and he fights a losing battle to allow him to buy wheat on the Continent even with an import duty of 20 percent. Surely, a system that leads to such results cannot be held out as a model to copy.

Translator's Notes to Chapter 8, Third Book

Chapter 8 represents the centerpiece of Sismondi's review of different systems of landowning and cultivation. Throughout the discussion in this book the emphasis has been on the relationship between ownership and the distribution of the product between the actual cultivator—slave, serf, *métayer,* smallholder farmer, as the case may be—and the owner of the land or product, either the lord, or the contract farmer, respectively. The intent of the argument is quite clear: given the separation of ownership and productive effort, the main proposition of *New Principles*—that system which maximizes happiness for the largest number of individuals is the preferable one—becomes the criterion for the evaluation of such economic systems. This premiss does not preclude inequality of income; however, assuming such inequality, Sismondi prefers the system that minimizes income differences between classes. In his mind, such a goal is best achieved by what is called in the United States *homesteading*, or in general the family farm, as it existed and still exists in Switzerland. The distinction between gross and net product, criticized by reviewers as muddleheaded (see, for example, Gide and Rist, 1948), becomes understandable in this context. In a cultivation system where the actual producer has direct access to, and control over, his own consumption resources, as on a small farm, profit becomes a secondary consideration, and consumption the primary one. In addition, the existence of many small farms is believed to prevent the existence of the large estates, which, to Sismondi, exercised such a bad influence on general happiness in the Roman Campagna. Small farms would thus forestall the exploitation of the economically weak by the economically strong. Both ideas are applied later in *New Principles* to industry and factory work, leading to his advocacy of profit sharing and participatory ownership. Although many of these proposals have been characterized as looking back to guild rule, he is a true disciple of Adam Smith in his aversion to monopoly, and his concern for the working man. Marx deals with the same problem by identifying communal ownership with individual interest, a proposition Sismondi rejects because he sees, accurately, as it turns out in retrospect, that communal ownership, that is, government control, is merely another form of monopoly.

Sismondi's concerns belong properly to welfare economics; by implication he raises again the problem of unaccounted cost, the existence of externalities, which was recognized only much later. His aversion to large-scale cultivation is based on his empirical observation that in the creation of large estates people are displaced from the land without compensation. The deprivation these people suffer because of new methods are a cost to society, and should consequently be borne by the contract farmers who caused the costs to come into existence because they displaced small producers. Again, this analysis will be applied in an analogous manner to the factory worker, but will not result in a clear programmatic statement. However, the analysis leads directly to the idea of exploitation because it assumes *ab initio* that the worker will be underpaid, because the daily market-determined subsistence wage does not reflect the real social cost of the individual worker.

1. The introductory paragraph is a modified version of the concluding observation on capitation in the *Encyclopedia*, which reads as follows: "On the other hand, such contracts helped to produce the notion of farm-leases, which, in the wealthiest countries of Europe, have succeeded every other kind of convention between proprietor and cultivator."
2. It seems to be a common characteristic of writing intellectuals to see workers and peasants in a romantic glow, coupled with a certain superciliousness towards the "lower classes." This paragraph, obviously based on personal observation of his own métayer and his peasant neighbors, is not quite as romantic as Marx's veneration of the proletariat as the font of all wisdom, but it shares essentially the same viewpoint. While motivated by a concern for the welfare of the workers, both overlook some of the less endearing aspects of proletarian and peasant existence.
3. At the present time, all industrialized countries subsidize in varying degrees their agricultural sector, thereby maintaining a larger farm population than would be the case if the market alone were to determine the total number of farms. The enunciated policies of governments closely parallel the opinions expressed by Sismondi in this paragraph. Modern production methods have changed agriculture from a dominant sector to one which typically employs only about 5 percent, or less, of the working population. Therefore, such sentiments represent an anachronism during peacetime. However, the subsidization of agriculture, sometimes at great cost, as in the European Community, Japan, and the United States, is seen as justified by the anticipated demand for food during a future war.
4. The note was added to the second edition of *New Principles*.
5. Sismondi uses the *arpent* as his land measure. One arpent is approximately one-and-one quarter English acre.
6. The reference to Arthur Young is an important indication that Sismondi derived some of his information from the work of the most important agricultural author of the time. The following quotation agrees with Sismondi's language in the next text paragraph: "Nazeing, Essex. The common rights regulated by act of Parliament. The poor were remarkably idle and dissolute; but Mr. Palmer offering to advance money for every poor man who could not afford to buy live stock, many accepted it, and every man of them repaid him in two years, some sooner. They are converted by this property to as sober and regular a people as they were before licentious" (Young, 1801).
7. It is one of Sismondi's main ideas that social conditions shape human behavior. In this he is not a Calvinist, but a child of the Enlightenment and the French Revolution. Marx carried this notion to its extreme in his concept of *alienation*,

in essence freeing the individual from personal responsibility for his actions. As the previous citation from Arthur Young's work shows, the idea was generally held by intellectuals of the period; it has been continued to the present day in all penal schemes that stress rehabilitation over straight punishment for committed crimes.

8. " . . . from that to everything" was changed in *New Principles* to ". . . or to land ownership."
9. "departments of industry" was changed in *New Principles* to "careers."
10. The description parallels recent analyses of the welfare system, and the new concept of a new, permanent underclass always dependent on welfare.
11. This was changed in *New Principles* to "who are always close to revolt." The change reflects the passage of time, and the change in conditions between the publication of the *Encyclopedia* piece and *New Principles*. From the perspective of more than a century-and-a-half later, the paragraph would indicate that not really all that much has indeed changed.
12. Sismondi omits the fact that conditions in Ireland were due to English policies that were directed to the entire subjugation of the Irish population, and the carpetbagging activities of the English lords who received large estates in Ireland. The implied assumption that there is a similarity between English and Irish conditions, expressed in the next text sentence, is not valid. The note was added to the second edition of *New Principles*.
13. The observation appears to have been adressed to present conditions, that is, the competition between family farms and *agrobusiness*. While Sismondi recognizes the economic advantages of large-scale farming, his sympathies are with the small family farm, partly out of sentiment and experience, but partly because he believes that conversion to large farms creates an externality of human displacement, and a loss of desirable crops which would make agriculture more vulnerable to economic distress.
14. An exclusion by omission of the possibility of producing more with the same resources and at the same cost, that is, higher efficiency. The omission is probably intentional—agriculture being one industry that was not, at that time, amenable to great advances in efficiency. It had just experienced great increases in productivity in the eighteenth century, and to Sismondi it must have appeared that further advances were unlikely, particularly with the small peasant farm, short on capital to invest in better machinery and seeds, or cattle. Therefore, increases in profits were a matter of market power—a concept that reappears in Marx in his discussion of the creation of surplus value.
15. The towns referred to in this paragraph are still in existence; Nepi and Ronciglione are to the north of Rome, Tivoli and Velletri to the east and south, respectively. The latter two are larger than the former today.
16. Sismondi uses the term *petit culture*. In the context of his own discussion and the distinctions he made as to the crops most likely to be cultivated under each system, the term *garden farming* seemed to be the most appropriate.
17. The argument indicates that Sismondi had observed the operation of large-scale farmers and knew of their dealings with workers and owners. There is a decided tone of animosity, which most likely can be traced back to his Tuscan experience.
18. A macroview is consciously opposed to the classical market microview. Although the arguments have a strong cameralistic flavor, they are by that reason

not wrong. As the next paragraph shows, Sismondi is aware of the advantages that flow from economies of scale, but seen again in his welfare context, the displacement of many workers is an externality that takes away from the happiness of the nation.

19. This may be true for a simple agricultural operation, such as reaping grain or picking crops, but it is not true of more complicated tasks which demand coordination of specialized skills.
20. The subsidiary clause "spares much time which is lost in the other way" was left out of *New Principles*.
21. Sismondi is referring to slavery.
22. An implied statement of the increasing organic composition of capital and the creation of a reserve army. Sismondi consistently stresses the adverse effects of a too-rapidly advancing division of labor, already recognized by Smith but seen as a necessary cost of increasing total production. During the extended period of technological displacement that Sismondi witnessed everywhere in Europe, misery among workers, both agricultural and industrial, was widespread; neither he, nor his contemporary socialist writers, like Owen, nor Marx, almost a half-century later, were able to see beyond the immediate problem to an eventual resolution by combined market adaptation and government intervention. When Marx published his most pessimistic assessment of the future of the capitalistic system, he addressed a problem that was already evolving toward a solution. However, only Sismondi clearly recognized the nature of the problem—the externalities that lower the cost of production to the entrepreneur. Hence, his proposals for regulation and profit participation are more realistic than the socialization projects because they force an accounting of such externalities. In the light of historic perspective, the Marxian system merely transferred the benefits of unacknowledged costs to the state and a governing elite without any obligation to share such benefits with the workers.
23. Malaria; the marshes around Rome were drained during the Mussolini regime and malaria eradicated. The decline of the region had already started in Roman times with *latifundia* slave cultivation, and it continued for centuries. Sismondi's description was only a reiteration of what was well known at his time.
24. The state of decay of Rome and the surrounding countryside was a favorite subject of romantically inclined painters and other artists during the eighteenth and nineteenth centuries.
25. This is one more unequivocal expression of Sismondi's belief in the evils of unequal property distribution, and, therefore, implicitly in the benefits of a wide dispersal of property and resulting incomes.
26. All of the following discussion was added to the second edition, undoubtedly prompted by his visits to England after his marriage to Jessie Allen.
27. In this instance the term most likely refers to Ricardo and McCulloch, not the physiocrats. This use of terminology is a particularly good example of Sismondi's imprecise handling of words, and his consistent failure to define his terms.
28. The equivalent in British currency could not be computed. Since, according to Sismondi, the rent is below that of France, the equivalent is not of much importance.

9

Cultivation by Emphyteutic Lease

[To conclude our review of the systems, by which territorial wealth is incessantly renewed, we ought yet to bestow a moment of attention on the system of *emphyteuses*, or perpetual farms,] which create for the benefit of the cultivator a quasi-property, and which raise in the state a class of peasants almost as industrious, as happy, and as attached to their country as the small landowners.

[In other systems of cultivation,] where the enjoyment of the fruits is separated from ownership,[1] [the agriculturist acquires all the fruits of his annual advances, but he can never be sure of profiting from those irredeemable advances by which a perpetual value is added to the land, from draining, plantations, and breaking up of the soil. Proprietors, of themselves, are seldom enabled to make such advances.[2] If they sell the land, the purchaser, in order to acquire it, must surrender that very capital with which he might have made those improvements. The lease of *emphyteusis*, or plantation, which is the proper meaning of the word, was a very useful invention, as by it the cultivator engaged to break up a desert, on condition of acquiring the *dominum utile* of it forever, whilst the proprietor reserved for himself an invariable rent to represent the *dominium directum*. No expedient could more happily combine, in the same individual, affection for property, with zeal for cultivation; or more usefully employ, in improving land, the capital destined to cultivate it.

These advantages are undoubtedly partly offset by the fairly serious drawback of giving two persons a permanent right on the same object, and making their respective status dependent on a contract which could have been drawn up long before any of the present parties were born. The troubles the two co-owners can make for each other in maintaining their rights would not be advantageous for the estate; it must lead to lawsuits, which are evils *per se*, and whose judgments must become more uncertain, and often more unjust, the more they refer to a very old law.

The emphyteuses have an evident relation to quit-rents, of which we have already spoken, except that the latter have their origin in feudal law during the era of bondage; the emphyteuses come from Roman law, and a time when the cultivators were still free. Feudal stipulations were often inserted into the leases in modern times; the cession of land, instead of being perpetual, has been made for one, or for many lives; at the expiration of the stipulated generations, the owner has taken back his land with all the advances and improvements made by the cultivator, such as to cause the ruin of the latter's family.[3] In Italy, and above all in Tuscany, where the Grand Duke Peter Leopold[4] leased out by emphyteuse, or *livello*, almost all the property of the crown, and a great part of that of the church, [restored to the most brilliant state of cultivation whole provinces, which had been allowed to run to waste.][5] The ruler decreed at the same time that the emphyteuses for four generations could always be renewed, it merely being necessary to pay five times the value of the annual rent, which was assumed to be 3 percent, or 15 percent of the capital at *laudemio*.[6] The law undoubtedly was a very wise one, it increased the value of emphyteutic leases, and encouraged the cultivator not to relax his care when the term of the lease was about to expire. On the other hand, it is always a bad practice which takes from the cultivator a share of his capital in the place of rent, and which is due in one year, instead of sharing regularly in the fruits of his sweat.

The emphyteutic lease can be an attractive means to induce farmers of large estates to share in the ownership of properties whose lords do not wish to sell; [it cannot, however, become a universal mode of cultivation, because it deprives the direct proprietor of all the enjoyment of property, exposing him to all the inconveniences, with none of the advantages, in the condition of the capitalist; and because the father of a family can never be looked upon as prudent or economical, when he thus alienates his property forever, without at least retaining the disposal of the price to be received in exchange for it.]

English law has sought, on its part, to favor this type of contracts; it considers emphyteutic farmers as freeholders;[7] with this status, it allows them to vote in elections, and it excludes copyholders, as well as the leaseholders. Nevertheless, the numbers of the former decrease markedly with each census.* Almost every time such a lease expires, the owner,

*It is not really the number of freeholders which decrease in England, but the extent of land which is cultivated under this system. The lords, in order to have a large number of voters at their disposal, multiply the number of freeholds when general elections are imminent; but they hardly ever give large estates in this manner to their farmers, but on the contrary reduce them to the lowest legal limit, of an annual value of forty shillings, while they lease to farmers all the lands from which they wish to draw a rent.

instead of renewing it, rents his land for a term of twenty-five years; and he lets no freeholds continue, except those he considers necessary to maintain his influence in the county elections. In Ireland, the smallholdings allotted to the cottagers are given to them for life which makes so many freeholders completely dependent on the lord at each election. If the legislator wanted to encourage this system of cultivation he ought to have called for the enjoyment of an income well above the forty shillings the law sets, for the freeholder to hold the right to vote. The bonus given to parceling by this single system of cultivation, and the declared exclusion of all others, are as opposed to the economic as well as the political goals originally intended. The law has in no way multiplied the class of truly independent farmers, and it is not because of their independence that it gives them the right of representation.

In Scotland, the emphyteuses are perpetual and much subdivided, but only in the neighborhood of towns, and on land suited for house construction. These pieces of land, which can be seen by the hundreds, advertised *to feu*[8] around Edinburgh, are not anymore a system of rural cultivation; it is an encouragement to these imprudent speculators who have constructed many deserted streets and have ruined many contractors around the Scottish capital.

Emphyteutic leases are known in some provinces of France, and in Savoy, by the name of *abergements*; they have not sufficiently multiplied to have a discernible influence on the status of the farmer.

Translator's Notes to Chapter 9, Third Book

This short chapter is an expansion of two paragraphs in the *Encyclopedia*. Sismondi altered the context of the discussion by enlarging on its subject. In the introductory paragraph of the *Encyclopedia*, which supplies the opening sentence here, the concluding clause reads: "the most suitable of all when government has grants of land to make." However, government leases are not discussed at all, except for an approving mention of the policy of the Tuscan Grand Duke. Here, as elsewhere, it is the goal of the discussion to promote the participation of the producer, that is, the worker on the land or at the machine, in the rights of property, both as to management and profits. Not unexpectedly, the emphyteutic lease also fails to gain his unqualified approval on this point, just as others have before. This shows most clearly the major problem of Sismondi's approach: he sees all the drawbacks of social institutions and therefore is unable to fully support any one system as optimal, leading eventually to his statement that he is unable to propose a solution to the problem of equitable allocation of national product shares. This characteristic most likely explains his minimal influence on political economy, both in his time and later. The foremost advantage classical writers and socialists share is the offering of convincing solutions to social problems, based on what appears to be scientific analysis. For example, Sismondi clearly supplies most of the basic Marxian analytical categories, as is evident so far, and will become more obvious in later parts of this work. But it is Marx, the constructor of an internally consistent and abstract philosophical system, who decisively influences policy, even though the system is analytically fatally flawed. This raises the contentious questions of what the proper method of social inquiry should be, and what goals should be achieved by it. As a historian, institutionalist, and welfare economist, Sismondi seeks happiness for everybody—as a critic of existing conditions he sees all the warts of the system, but as a theoretician he was unable to advance acceptable alternatives, a failure that excluded him from the mainstream of economic inquiry.

1. A short insertion introduces Sismondi's favored idea into this chapter; the separation of ownership and work as a consequence of the division of labor, a concept that becomes, in the hands of Marx, *alienation*. It is Sismondi's goal to recombine these two aspects of economic effort in the small family enterprise, or alternatively heal the split by share ownership and/or profit sharing in large enterprises.
2. The statement assumes that landowners have limited means other than their landholdings. This is not a generally true assumption, and Sismondi contradicts it by describing the wealth of the English lords elsewhere. However, it is likely that he draws again on his Tuscan experience—he certainly had very limited means for capital expenditures, and many other landowners in the province may have been in a similar position. The next sentence is revealing—it assumes that in agriculture there is a shortage of liquid capital. The discussion of the various lease arrangements up to this point clearly revolves around this problem and the associated question of product distribution.
3. Apparently the possibility that the lessee could extract his capital from the operation before the lease expired, by, for example, transferring profits elsewhere and ceasing to invest some time before the lease expires, was not considered.
4. The Grand Duke was the son of Leopold II of Austria, who had been Duke of Tuscany before he became emperor. As duke he had introduced so-called enlightened policies into Tuscany, derived from cameralistic, and possibly physiocratic, ideas. Tuscany at the beginning of the nineteenth century was one of the more prosperous Italian states, with a liberal government.
5. The French text reads: "et où il retira ainsi de dessous les eaux les provinces qui sont aujourd'hui les plus florissantes . . ."
6. 'Tribute', that is, the assumed capital represented by the land. Compare this to Petty's discussion of rent in the *Treatise,* (1963, chapter 4, para. 19–27). The subject was a popular one with writers of the time because, first, land taxation was the main source of government income, and, second, because property holding in land began to change as land became a tradeable commodity.
7. Sismondi uses "*franc tenanciers*" and then supplies the English term in brackets.
8. A term in Scottish law denoting the renting of land for money by a vassal.

10

On the Corn Laws

We have reviewed the systems of cultivation by which, in the various countries, agricultural wealth is produced every year; the harvests, once collected, are part of commercial wealth and are already commodities and many of the rules which we shall seek to establish in the following book on commercial wealth, can also be applied to trade in corn[1] and other products of the soil, as well as to the exchange of products of the industries of cities. However, because corn is at one and the same time the basis of sustenance for man, and that product of the soil which employs the largest number of workers, and whose aggregate mass represents the greatest value, it has been the object of special legislation, which it is appropriate to examine here, since it is closely linked to the results of different systems of cultivation.

Ever since legislators have tried to regulate the corn trade, the first goal they wanted to achieve was the maintenance of a low price in the markets; and it cannot be denied that this is a desirable end, although the legislators have almost constantly gone astray whenever they have sought to attain this goal with legislation on food prices, surplus warehouses, engrossers of corn, and by all their attempts to force selling at low prices what was costly to produce.[2] It would be wasting our time to fight errors already abandoned; everyone recognizes today that forcing the farmer to sell at a loss would mean a halt in production, and would entrench in the country dearness and even famine, instead of low prices; the apparent monopolizers of corn are traders who maintain the equality of price among the several provinces, and between the seasons; the public surplus granaries supply the people more expensively and less well than the grain traders would; and finally, all earlier government efforts to lower the price of corn have had constantly the opposite effect.

But it should not be concluded that the low price the legislators intended was of no national benefit. Everyone is a consumer of corn, everyone benefits from plenty and low prices; all that one could wish is that a low price be lasting, that it be *remunerative,*[3] as the English say, meaning that it pay back all the advances of production in such a way that its continuation is encouraged. The price of corn becomes the basis for wages. If corn stays at a high price, all the goods made with human labor must also rise in price, and the dearness of corn must, after a certain time, spell the ruin of all manufactures destined for export.

Yet, the most industrialized nation, the richest, and the most knowledgeable in political economy, England, has laws uniquely destined to raise the price of grain. These laws, whose repeal is now demanded by one half of the English people with great anger against those who uphold them, while the other half wants to keep them, with cries of indignation against those who wish to abolish them; these laws, on which the government is divided, on which Parliament, mainly composed of landowners, hesitates to take a stand which could lead to violent convulsions, and even a civil war, are the only ones which at this present moment well deserve to be examined.

England, as we have seen, is a country of large estates. There cultivation takes place under the management of contract farmers, with day laborers who are paid in cash every week; in order to continue their business, these farmers must recover the money outlays from the sale of their harvests, which enter the market almost in their entirety. These farmers cannot continue a losing business; if the grain they harvest and sell does not repay the wages they advanced,[4] they will withdraw their capital from agriculture, and will return the abandoned land to the owner, who will not anymore receive any income, which is of no concern to the farmers; they will lay off their workers, who will die of hunger, which does not concern them either, and the production of corn will cease. Hence, the farmers and the landowners in England say with one voice that the actual price of fifty to sixty shillings a quarter is barely a *remunerating price*[5] just returning the costs of production, and which, if it should go any lower, would force them to abandon the growing of grain.

On the other hand, the countries which border the Baltic, the Black Sea, and the Mediterranean, and the countries on the great rivers of America, offer quantities of wheat sufficient to feed all of England at a price infinitely lower than that *remunerative price*. Top grade wheat, which is sold for fifty-six shillings the quarter in England, was offered at Danzig, in August of 1826, and even in Lübeck, at seventeen shillings. This spring, the government was alarmed about the state of the harvests in England, and it has asked Parliament for permission to import in case of need a limited quantity of grain, with a duty of ten shillings per quarter; even this temporary measure has met with violent opposition from the aristocracy, and the government has won only by rallying all its forces around it.

However, a business crisis plagues the manufacturers of a nation which sent more than half of its people to the trades in the cities, and which, in consequence, cannot exist without the help of outsiders, to whom it has undertaken to provide them with all manufactured commodities. One half of the craftsmen who must live from wages, received no wages; foreign markets were blocked and did not buy; the poor felt hunger, and they could not hear, without anger, that the bread of which they could afford just enough to be half-starved, was sold to them at exorbitant prices, to ensure a better income to the great lords who enjoyed already one or two millions in rent; that all the grain offered at the ports for less than half price was excluded, and that the famine they experienced was entirely the work of the rich. The leaders of industry added that the glut they found in the markets was the consequence of the same laws; that the rich on the Continent could not buy their goods because they could not sell their wheat, that the factories on the Continent were more prosperous because, food being cheaper, wages could be lower, and the goods cost the producers less. Thus the two halves of the nation are opposed to each other in a controversy which turns around, not merely profit, but life itself; and the government experiences not only great difficulty ascertaining for whom it should decide; it does not yet know how it can get the cooperation of Parliament, made up mainly of landowners and judge in its own cause.

The opening of the market to foreign grain would probably ruin the English landowners, and would bring prices of farm leases down to a very low level. Without a doubt, this is a great misfortune, but it is not an injustice. Landlords have only one right—to receive, by leasing their estates, a compensation equal to the value of their services to society—by making their land available for cultivation. If such service is nil, they have nothing to claim; if all the others have no need for them, and they force these others to accept a service not asked for, and which must be paid at a price the owners set themselves, then they rob the others. Doubtless society will be much poorer if the landlords lose their income, but it cannot help but to impoverish itself, if it takes the income of everyone else to give it to the landlords.[6]

It is true that the landlords are not the only ones interested in agriculture; the farmers and the day laborers as well live from this industry; the farmers will be the first to make a decision, they will withdraw their capital which, at any rate, can in part nourish another industry—they will transfer it to America, where their talent will be rewarded; they are neither tied to their fields, nor to their trade, they will not perish, the nation will merely lose them.

But what will the day laborer do? Despite the unbelievable diminution of manual labor employed in agriculture because of the estate system, there remain in England about 600,000 families of workers, paid from day to day for field work. The work will stop, the fields will be converted to empty pasture; the cultivator will limit himself to raising herds, and for his new needs will not need more than a tenth of the hands he required for the production of wheat. What will become of the 540,000 families to whom he will refuse employment? Supposing that they could work at any type of trade, is there today an industry in any condition to absorb them? In England, agriculture employs fewer hands than all other trades together, whereas in France it employs four times as many as all other trades together; how will a single trade, or all the trades together, take in all the farmhands?

Is there a government that can willingly expose one-half of the nation it rules to such a crisis? If it did, can it then withstand the explosion of its despair? Would those to whom the farmers are thus sacrificed find any advantage therein? These very farmers are the nearest and surest consumers of English manufactures. The end of their consumption would bring to industry a deadlier setback than the closing of one of the largest foreign markets.

I believe that, without a doubt, I shall be accused of carrying matters to extremes, and already I hear an economist telling me that in the countries which supply wheat to England, as well as in England, wheat growing would not continue if it did not bring a remunerative price; if the wheat fields of Poland do not render the profit which can be found in any other industry, the Polish farmers will employ their capitals differently; that the number 4, 5, 6, quality lands will not be farmed in Poland as in England, whereas lands of the first, second, and third quality will continue to be cultivated in England, as they are in Poland.[7]

The economists who argue in this way, and who believe that with their eight numbers they can, not only designate all degrees of fertility, but also all the causes that affect agricultural production, have never thought about the different modes of cultivation; they have no idea that, in corvée farming, the work which will produce the grain has been paid once and for all, that it will continue to be rendered from generation to generation, such that he who sells the wheat will never find it to be too expensive, or that he sells it at too low a price to continue cultivation; the wheat costs him nothing but some hundreds of lashes dealt out among his peasants, and at whatever price he sells, he considers himself always paid for the lashes he has given.

We have seen how, in the immense lands that are cultivated by serfs, and which comprise all of Poland, the most fertile regions of southern

Russia, and also other barbarous regions, the land is divided in two parts, that of the peasant, and that of the lord. The peasant's part feeds the farming nation; the product of the lord is sold in its entirety abroad; it is this which inundates European markets today, and which can be sold at any price, because the grain of Poland and the Ukraine costs nothing to those who sell it. The wheat of Egypt and Barbary, cultivated by metayage, costs no more to the pashas, or beys, who reap one-half. In the countries where farming is done by serfs, the peasant hardly ever cares to know what the market prices of the provisions he produces are; he does not till with the intention to sell his crops; the land that was given to him by his lord in place of wages need only to feed him; he at most exchanges some of his products, but he never buys and sells anything; if he pays, he works, he does not tender any money. He eats his corn, his milk, the meat from his herds, he shods his feet with their hides, he clothes himself with their wool, he spins his hemp—he builds from his woods his house, his furniture and tools; his poverty is more a consequence of the crudity and poor quality of the things at his command, than that he is deprived of them. War and oppression have depopulated his land, and he finds at all times an abundance of untilled soil; he tills it as soon as he enjoys enough security so that his family may grow, and despite lower prices for the fruits of his efforts, which he may not even be aware of, he is today in a comparatively improved situation.

But the other half of these lands belong to the lords; that half, which exceeds in extent France and England taken together, and is a better wheat land than either, is tilled by the peasant at his own expense, whereas its products are sold for the account of the lord without any compensation. Without a doubt, the lord loses if wheat sells poorly, because his income is less; but it is a free income; it has cost him neither work nor capital; however low the price may fall, it will still be advantageous to him that his peasants produce wheat, because in this way he gets something; if he stops them working he would have nothing; on the contrary, the low price will encourage him to farm a larger amount of land to recoup, with a greater number of bushels sold, the income the smaller number gave him before.[8]

A country which cultivates its soil by the estate system cannot possibly match such competition, a competition of sellers who always can sell their products at a lower price than you. If English ports were opened to the grain of the Baltic and the Black Sea, wheat growing will have to stop completely in England;[9] because whatever the perfection of English agriculture, and the fertility of its soil, wheat costs the English farmer a determinable amount; whatever might be, to the contrary, the ignorance of the Polish peasant, and even the sterility of his soil, the wheat he produces costs the lord who sells it nothing. The wheat does not cost any more to the Egyptian pasha, or the bey of Tunis and Tripoli, who collects it as a tax paid in kind.

What then can be done? Must the ports of England be opened or closed? Must either the English manufacturers or the husbandmen be condemned to hunger and death? Surely, the question is appalling; the position in which the English government finds itself is one of the thorniest statesmen may encounter; we believe we had the duty to call their attention to the consequences of serf cultivation that seem to have escaped their notice;[10] but we now await new light from the parliamentary discussions on the subject, rather then pretend to solve them. Another, more general conclusion becomes however clearer, namely the danger of estate cultivation, the danger of leaving agriculture subject to a system of speculation. We cannot cease to reiterate that material wealth is not the goal of society, it is but one of the means to achieve that goal. The system of large farms, of great capitals employed in agriculture, the mating of the natural sciences to this large-scale cultivation has favored, which we do not deny, a certain progress in wealth; tilling is done better, weeds are better controlled, the harvests are more abundant compared to the seed planted, as the care of cattle is better understood; but the industry on which the very subsistence of the nation depends is constantly exposed to the play of the market; grain growing must be taken up, or abandoned, in England according to how the merchants of Danzig, Taganrog, or Kentucky, determine the profit or loss for English wheat, or for Russian or American wheat. This suits a country where wheat is grown only for sale; a farmer of a thousand acres, harvesting each year, either from one part of his fields, or from the other, about twelve hundred quarters of wheat, will not consume more than twenty or thirty for himself and his family; all the rest must be sold, and the market value is the only thing that interests him in his production. But if the farms were fifty acres instead of a thousand; if the twenty families who would replace the large farmer, cultivated their own soil, each would consume twenty to thirty quarters from the sixty they would harvest, each would continue the cultivation of corn for its own use, even though each would experience some loss on the price for which it sells, in accordance with the price to which the foreign grain, grown by serfs, would have fallen.

Today this happens all over continental Europe. The grains of Poland and Russia are quite close to France; those of Bohemia and Hungary are closer to Germany than to England; the grains of the Black Sea and Barbary are even closer to Italy. No doubt, agriculture suffers from the low prices to which foreign grain has fallen. Yet the majority of governments has not dreamt of excluding them, or laying a heavy import duty on them, and the farmers of France, Germany, and Italy, while curtailing slightly their corn growing, on which they make a loss, do not for one moment think of abandoning it, because they must have it to feed themselves.

The more exchanges increase in a nation, the more everyone becomes accustomed to buy what he needs, and to sell what he produces, the more will the circulating medium increase in that nation, and the likelihood of wealth, and even the means to command great capitals. But there are also benefits of security, contentment, tied to the ability to provide for oneself, to feed oneself, to clothe oneself with one's own production, without having recourse to the market. Poets know such pleasures and have often spoken of them. They enjoy picturing the farmer finding abundance in his barns, in his farmyard, in the shearing of his lambs, and the cloths from his linen and his hemp. The Economists have long called such love of everyone for his own products illusion, and they often repeated that if each performs better one operation, there will be at one and the same time perfection and economy in buying and selling, instead of producing for oneself all the things man needs. The example of England shows us that this practice is not without danger.[11]

If it were true that the husbandman who sows his own field in order to eat his corn, produced that corn at a higher cost than he who sells almost all his corn in order to buy the labor with which he will produce new corn, then it would still be better that the great mass of husbandmen belong to the first, rather than the second class. The high cost at which such corn will be produced is in truth a national expense, but no better use could be made of national wealth than to buy security.[12] Now, it would not suit national security if its subsistence were to depend on the fluctuations of the market; if, whether the price of corn is high or low, speculators were to encourage population increases or hunger; if, in spreading plenty in one year, speculators were to give no guarantee against dearness in the following year, and if they were to make a nation go through all kinds of crises for its subsistence, all the alternatives of market gluts and scarcity that are already difficult enough to tolerate in manufactures, and which are often the necessary consequence of speculators noticing, all at the same time, that there was too little of their goods in the market, or that there were too many. In France and Italy, where it is reckoned that four-fifths of the population belong to the agricultural class, these four-fifths are fed by domestic wheat, whatever the price of foreign wheat might be. The fluctuations from speculation will be felt only by the remaining fifth; from the entire crop, four-fifths are fixed and merely one-fifth is variable. In England, not only is less than one-half of the population in agriculture, but there is not one-tenth of the cultivators who eat their own grain. The fluctuations caused by speculation, those that arise from the two errors the English call *over trading and under trading*[13] are felt in the total amount of grain produced and affect the entire nation.

This is not all: the English hold their large farms up as the sole means to perfect agriculture, that is to say for furnishing a greater abundance of agricultural products at lower cost, and here to the contrary they produce them more expensively. Here it happens that these rich farmers, so intelligent, so well assisted by the progress of science, whose harnessed teams are so beautiful, whose hedges are so tight, whose fields are so devoid of weeds, cannot stand up to the competition of the wretched Polish peasant, ignorant, brutalized by serfdom, finding his only refuge in drink, and whose farming is still in the infancy of the art. The grain harvested in the center of Poland, after having paid the freight of hundreds of miles of transport, by rivers, over land and sea, after having paid import duties of 30 and 40 percent, is still cheaper than that from the richest counties of England.

To explain the paradox which confounds them, the English economists, who have never wanted to examine what happens in other countries, blame alternatively the government for the burden of duties that weigh on them, and changes in money. I have never been successful in understanding the arguments of the modern school on debasement of money, nor could I persuade myself that those who employ them understand them themselves.[14] As for duties, it is certain that they are heavy and that they must increase the prices of all goods; but it would be counting British freedom for little not to agree that the absence of all security, of all civil rights,[15] of all justice, is a heavier tax on the Polish peasant, on the Egyptian or Barbary fellah, than all the taxes paid by the British workers.

It is always appropriate to demand from the government economy and tax reductions, but as all these reductions cannot change the interest on the debt, the duties cannot be greatly reduced anymore. It is the farming system that is bad, which rests on a precarious basis, and which must be changed, not violently and suddenly, but at least with determination. It is the same system which has been held up recently for our admiration by all authors, and which on the contrary it behooves us to understand well in order to prevent us from imitating it.

I do not know how, in England, effective, but neverthelss gradual steps could be taken which return to honor the small farms, while half of the nation, employed in manufactures suffers from hunger, and the actions which are taken threaten the other half, employed in agriculture, with famine. I believe that the Corn Laws need to be greatly modified; but I counsel those who demand their total abolition to examine carefully the following questions:

1. If the wheat produced by serf cultivation, costing nothing to its seller,

comes to England without duties, will it be possible for one single English farmer to continue sowing a single wheat field?

2. If the English nation, finding it cheaper to buy foreign wheat, gives up wheat farming, what will be the decrease in the number of hands employed in agriculture? What will be the expense to the manufacturing class to maintain, in work houses, all the families of dismissed farm hands? What will manufacturers lose from the suspension of consumption by a whole class of English workers who make up close to one-half of the nation? What will the manufacturers lose by the suspension of consumption of the wealthy whose rent income will be almost wiped out?[16]
3. On what security can a nation count whose subsistence depends totally on foreigners, and particularly on those who can quite easily become its enemies, the most barbarous and despotic governments of Europe, who will be less deterred by the damage they do to their own subjects while wanting to inflict damage on her? What will become of English honor if the Russian czar, every time he should want some concession from England, can starve her by closing the Baltic ports?[17]

These are the difficulties, and many others, which must be weighed in the shaping of a law which could cast out the husbandry of England; these are the difficulties which will return in another form in ten or twenty years, when the rapid increase of sheep in Australia will bring to British ports such prodigious quantities of wool, at such low prices, that sheep raising in England will become as little profitable as is the tilling of fields today. These are after all the consequences of universal competition, producing everything at the lowest price, whose result ought to be foreseen, now when our progress leads us to see the whole universe only as one huge market.[18]

Translator's Notes to Chapter 10, Third Book

This chapter was added to the second edition of *New Principles,* reflecting Sismondi's involvement in the heated English debate over the Corn Laws after his marriage to Jessie Allen in 1819. Jessie Allen was one of three sisters who were well known in English society. The other sisters were Mrs. Josiah Wedgwood, wife of the industrialist best known for his porcelain, and Lady Mackintosh, wife of Sismondi's friend Sir James Mackintosh M. P., judge and professor of political economy at Haileybury from 1818–1824, that is, a colleague of Thomas R. Malthus. Sismondi was therefore related by marriage to two influential individuals in England. After their wedding in 1819, the Sismondis visited England, with other visits to follow in subsequent years. Taking into account his earlier stay in England as a young man and his Anglophile family background, he must have been quite well informed about, and sensitive to, English conditions, both political and economical. The chapter shows this familiarity, as do later chapters on commercial and industrial conditions. However, this chapter also shows a much wider range of concerns about the Corn Laws than shown either by Ricardo or the other pamphleteers on the subject. It is likely that Sismondi gained this wider viewpoint by his association with a group of very diverse minds who congregated at his new residence in Chêne. There, the Sismondis entertained former friends of the deceased Madame de Staël, and new rising stars, such as Cavour and the future Napoleon III. (The house was slated for demolition, but has been restored by the community of Chêne as part of the *mairie* and now carries a plaque commemorating Sismondi's residence there).

The Corn Law controversy was part of a much larger European debate on protection and the applicability of Adam Smith's free-trade theory. After the end of the Napoleonic wars, most governments had imposed strict protectionist policies, partly as a matter of prior mercantilistic policies, partly because of financial need. The exception was Prussia, which introduced in 1818, as part of a general tariff reform, a revenue tariff that was mostly free-trade oriented, although in parts mildly protectionist. Its adoption had generated a great deal of controversy in the Prussian government, but it proved to be very successful in promoting economic development. In England a similar, but public, debate centered on the protection the landed lords received from tariff legislation. Parliament, before the Reform Bill, overrepresented landed interests because of the rotten borough system. On the other side of the question were the rising manufacturing interests, defended by writers like Ricardo. Parliament, not unexpectedly, favored protection to keep grain prices at "remunerative levels" for the landed interests. The industrial interests wanted to import cheaper grains from Poland and Russia to lower the cost of the most basic foodstuffs of the factory worker in 1819, bread and beer, and thus lower the wages they would have to pay. However, manufacturing was itself well protected from foreign competition. The debate was conducted actually more in a mercantilistic framework than a Smithian free-trade context. Sismondi had most likely read all of the writings published during this time, as a comparison of this chapter with Barnes, *A History of the English Corn Laws from 1660–1846* (Kelley 1965) clearly shows, even though there are no citations in *New Principles* to prove this. Sismondi seems to be most sympathetic to Malthus's *Grounds of an Opinion,* especially the consumption argument: diminished purchasing power among bankrupt farmers, landlords whose rents had drastically declined, and laid-off farm workers would all lead to distress in the manufacturing sector. As previous chapters have shown, Sismondi was concerned mainly with employment, not efficiency; given a particular output, he would have wanted as many individuals involved in its production as possible. He therefore advances again his favorite remedy, the breakup of large estates into family farms. This obviously disregards the principle of economies of scale, which he acknowledged when he discussed large-scale farming in the Roman Campagna, but he anticipates later discussions about optimal production size in all sectors of the economy. Sismondi anticipates later Marxist ideas on "land reform," that is, the distribution of estates to landless peasants. As later chapters on commerce and manufacturing make clear, he believed that small enterprises are superior because they distribute income more widely, thereby stabilizing consumption and the economy in general.

1. Sismondi uses everywhere *blé,* 'wheat'. However, in order to conform to the title, which clearly refers to what was known in England as the Corn Laws, and also to avoid boring repetition, wheat, corn, and grain were used interchangeably in the translation.
2. The reference here is almost certainly to medieval (and perhaps mercantilistic)

practices, as engrossers' laws were enacted in medieval cities to safeguard grain supply and prevent monopoly, that is, corners on the grain market.

3. This word is italicized in the text.
4. This shows convincingly that the concept of the wages fund is derived from agricultural practices first formalized as theories by the physiocrats. Since agricultural production spans a year, advances to workers are the normal way of doing business. With the growth of industrial production the notion becomes less and less applicable, because production, sales, and new production begin to overlap. The wages fund, both in reality and as a theoretical device, proves to be unusable as an analytical tool.
5. Sismondi italicizes *remunerating price* as a translation of the French term *prix remunerateur.*
6. The argument stands in stark contrast to Ricardo's partial equilibrium analysis with its strong conclusion that rent is paid in accordance with generally applicable and immutable natural laws. The revolutionary solution Marx proposes is grounded in Ricardo, and therefore also perpetuates in a socialist guise the notion of the inevitability of economic causality. Sismondi, the German historical school, and the American institutionalists, see human institutions as changeable, convenient arrangements to achieve socially desirable ends which must yield if they fail in their assigned function. Admittedly, defining the function introduces an important element of arbitrariness into the analysis, but as Joan Robinson has pointed out in *Economic Philosophy,* Ricardian-Marxian analysis does the same thing, hiding the desired conclusions in the premisses. At least, Sismondi openly presents the alternatives for understanding human actions.
7. This paragraph and the next one are clearly directed at Ricardo and McCulloch. Sismondi was closer to reality than his two ideological adversaries, and one could apply Keynes's observation on Malthus here that "he had attained to fragments of practical wisdom which the unrealistic abstractions of Ricardo first forgot and then obliterated." (Keynes 1956, 340.)
8. The argument presents the basic assumptions of the Cobweb theorem.
9. Sismondi was proven wrong in this assumption. Britain grew wheat after 1846, the year of the abolition of the Corn Laws. Wheat cultivation ceased almost completely only after 1872 when modern transportation delivered wheat at low cost from America, Australia, and Argentina.
10. This is a pamphleteer's ironic stab—it really does not belong in a work that purports to advance new principles of political economy. *New Principles* advocates a particular position without disguising that fact behind a screen of theoretical niceties that hide the bias of the author, as for instance Ricardo's *Principles* do. Sismondi is in this one respect really a true disciple of Adam Smith.
11. An anticipation of Veblen's *instinct of workmanship,* that is, the argument that man, contrary to utility theory, derives from work pleasure that cannot be measured in the marketplace. Sismondi also calls into question, as Smith did eventually in a halfhearted way, the benefits of the division of labor, if carried to its extreme conclusion. The argument, aside from its practical significance, was mainly directed against the most prominent disciples of Smith, Ricardo and especially McCulloch, who had indeed extended the concept in the name of theoretical logic beyond the qualifications Smith had hedged around his model. In the last analysis, the disagreement is between realism and practical

application on the one hand, and deductive analysis, which wants to derive all practical applications only from the most universal principles, on the other hand.

12. This argument is used now by agriculture ministers in the European Economic Community to justify the high subsidization of that sector by the consumer through higher prices.
13. The two terms and the connective were in English and italicized in *New Principles.*
14. An apparent reference to the bullion dispute between Ricardo and Bosanquet in 1810–1811. It more likely refers to the 1825–1826 banking crisis, in which sixty English country banks failed and the government passed legislation authorizing joint-stock banks of issue outside of London. Since Sismondi was an uncompromising defender of specie he must have viewed this move as dangerous and contrary to sound economic principles.
15. The text reads "de toute garantie."
16. Sismondi is the first writer in political economy who shifted the emphasis of analysis from production to consumption. As Gide and Rist have pointed out, Keynes's theory of underconsumption and oversaving bears a close resemblance to Sismondi's arguments. Keynes may have read Sismondi; however he does not mention him anywhere in his work. It is therefore more likely that the economic conditions of the interwar years in England, paralleling closely English experience of Sismondi's time, led to the same conclusions by an author who also analyzed them from a business viewpoint.
17. Sismondi anticipates here, correctly, as it turned out, the difficulties England experienced in both World Wars in supplying herself with food in the face of a determined enemy. For his time, he typically overstated the case—given the political realities of his time, it was highly unlikely that the closing of Baltic ports would have forced the British into political concessions.
18. Sismondi was undoubtedly more sensitive to all implications of free-trade doctrine than his contemporaries. His prediction that Australian wool will supersede English production came true later in the century. His Genevese citizenship, the small size of that city-state, apparently made him aware that classical analysis had a political corollary most English writers, including Smith, simply ignored: free trade and the international division of labor demand that national interests be subordinated to international requirements. International interdependence, brought about by free trade, and national interests, were not necessarily at all times compatible with each other. Keynes also recognized the problem and addressed it in the *Treatise* (1950, vol. 2, chapt. 34, et.seq.)

11

Sale of Real Estate

[For reproducing territorial wealth, it is sufficient, in general, that the use of the ground be transmitted to the industrious man, who may turn it to advantage, whilst the property of it continues with the rich man, who has no longer the same incitements or the same fitness for labour, and who thinks only of enjoyment. The national interest, however, sometimes also requires that property itself shall pass into hands likely to make better use of it. It is not for themselves that the rich elicit the fruits of the earth; it is for the whole nation; and if, by a derangement in their fortune, they suspend the productive power of the country, it concerns the whole nation to put their property under different managers.

Personal interest is, indeed, sufficient to bring about this transmission, provided the law offers no obstacle.] Suppose that a man, a stranger to manufacturing,[1] [a soldier comes to inherit a machine for making stockings, he does not keep it long; in his hands, the machine is useless for himself and the nation; in the hands of a stocking maker it would be productive, both for the nation and the individual. Both feel this; and a bargain is soon struck. The soldier receives money, which he well knows how to employ; the stocking maker receives possession of his frame, and the production recommences. Most of our European laws respecting immovable property, are like a law made to hinder the soldier from parting with the frame, of whose use he is ignorant.[2]

The value of land cannot be unfolded, except by employing a capital sufficient to procure the accumulation of that labour which improves it. Hence, it is essential to the very existence of a nation, that its lands be always in the hands of those who can devote] labor and [capital to its cultivation. If it were not in any case allowed to sell a workman's implement, it would not, certainly, at least, be forbidden to make new ones for the use of new workmen; but new lands cannot be made,[3] and so often as the law prevents the alienation of an estate by one that cannot use it, so often does it suspend the most essential of all productions.

The systems of cultivation, which we have now glanced over in review, certainly cause the earth to produce, by the hands of temporary cultivators, when the permanent advances have been made; but they absolutely discourage such cultivators from making those permanent advances which, as they give a perpetual value to property, cannot be laid out except by those with whom that property is destined to continue. Legislators in general, altogether occupied with preventing the alienation of immovables, and preserving great fortunes in great families, have dreaded lest such an alienation might clandestinely be brought about by a lease, for a long term, and without return. They have eagerly attempted to defend the rights of proprietors against proprietors themselves; and they have guided that class of people by forfeits and resolutory clauses; they have fixed upon a short term for farm leases; they seem continually repeating to the cultivator: "This land, on which you work, is not yours; acquire not too much affection for it; make no advances which you might run the risk of losing; improve the present moment, if you can, but think not of the future; above all, beware of labouring for posterity."

Besides, independently][4] of obstacles legislators have not ceased to put in the way of perpetual leases, [it belongs to the very nature of a farm lease never to allow a farmer to take as much interest in the land as its proprietor. It is enough that his lease must have an end, to induce the farmer, as this end approaches, to care less about his fields, and to cease laying out money for improving them. The metayer, with smaller power, at least never fears to improve the land committed to him as much as possible; because the conditions of his lease are invariable, and he is never dismissed except for bad behaviour.[5] The farmer, again, is liable to be dismissed directly in consequence of his good management. The more he has improved his farm, the more will his landlord, at renewing the lease, be disposed to require an augmentation of rent; and besides, as part of the advances laid out by the cultivator, on the ground, create a perpetual value, it is neither just nor natural that they should be made by one whose interest is merely temporary. The farmer will carefully attend to the fields and meadows, which, in a few years, are to give him back all his advances; but he will plant few orchards; few high forests in the north, few vineyards] or olive groves [in the south; he will make few canals for navigation, irrigation or drainage; he will transport little soil from one place to another; he will clear little ground; he will execute, in short, few of those works which are most conducive to the public interest, because they found the wealth of posterity.[6]

None of these labours, on which the increase of the whole national subsistence depends, can be undertaken, save by a proprietor, rich in movable capital. It is not the preservation of great fortunes that concerns the nation, but the union of territorial fortunes with circulating ones. The fields do not flourish in the hands of those who have already too much wealth to watch over them, but in the hands of those who have enough of money to bring them into value. Territorial legislation ought, therefore, without ceasing, to strive that mobile capital be united with fixed; property which] the English call personal with property they call real. It ought to facilitate the sale of real estate. [Legislation, over almost all the world, has striven to do quite the contrary.]

The natural consequence of the accumulation of wealth in a society must be always the further separation of work from enjoyment.[7] It ought to be the constant task of the legislator to reunite enjoyment with work. The man who has made his fortune ought to desire rest and comfort; these are the fruits of his work, and it is right that he enjoys them; but it is also one of his expected enjoyments to see his family increase without worry; and if the legislator does not strive to fill him with antisocial prejudices, he will be happy to raise many children, to divide his estate equally among them, and to see them start in life as he himself did.

On the other hand, every time a landowner's fortune is in danger, it is desirable for him, his family, and society, that he sell his property, instead of borrowing on it. Love of ownership, prejudice, and above all vanity, predispose him almost always to do the opposite. He is left saddled with a debt disproportionate to his capital, his physical strength, and the attention he can give to it. He borrows under burdensome conditions, and the payment of interest again diminishes every year the capital with which he should improve his farm; he will finally produce less on his whole property than he would have realized from one half thereof, if he had sold the other half. That other half, however, being in the hands of a buyer who would not be in need, would be cultivated again, and society, instead of having one gross product, would have two.[8]

Legislation ought not deny to the landowner the means to borrow, but it must make it easier for him to use the expedient which suits him best—to sell; it ought to give to the lender, in his proper interest, strong guarantees against the borrower; and the strongest of all ought to be the ease with which the property can be sold if the debtor defaults. Almost all legislators have adopted a contrary rule; in their reverence for landed ownership, they have made dispossession so difficult that the interest of the owner, who was to be favored, is sacrificed, as well as that of his creditor. [The rank of creditors on land has been regulated according to their date, whilst an absolute equality prevails among creditors of all dates, who claim only on movable property.] But the privileges of the former are either completely useless, and consequently dangerous, because more complicated laws lead to litigation; or they must give to the owner the advantage of borrowing at a lower rate of interest, in return for stronger security. However, this is the opposite of what has happened. In France today, commercial interest is often found at 4 percent, while borrowing on land on first mortgages is at 6 percent. In effect, forced dispossessions are so slow, so costly, so difficult to obtain, that the creditor has less safety if he lends on land than when he lends on a draft.[9]

To the same degree that the law has shown itself cautious and timid when it deals with the sale of land, it shows little consideration when it comes to imprison the person. In almost all countries, the arrest of a debtor is easier to accomplish than the attachment of his chattels, and that in turn is easier than the sale of his real estate. However, the legislator, given the respect individual liberty deserves, should have followed the opposite course with the only aim of caring for the national welfare. In arresting the person, the income is destroyed that labor could have created; seizing chattels, they must be sold well below the value they had for the owner; in seizing merchandise, the merchant is often ruined; in seizing land, neither the debtor nor the nation are damaged.[10] Much would have been done already for the prompt settlement of debts, if the law authorized the sale of land every time that it today authorizes putting the debtor into prison. Then the greater part of old debts would be extinguished, and the lands which ought to feed the nation, would be in the hands of those who could bring them, by their capital and efforts, to provide such subsistence. Instead of coming to such a result, one-half of European lands are now in the hands of people who, far from possessing means to cultivate them, are on the contrary debtors for considerable amounts of capital which cannot be mobilized. Hence these impecunious landowners have ever had recourse to ruinous expedients, either to draw money from their lands, or to sell their woods, and to let their land deteriorate, whilst they are unable to employ capital to increase the value of their holdings.

Translator's Notes to Chapter 11, Third Book

The first half of this chapter is taken from the *Encyclopedia*, the second half is new material. The chapter serves as an introduction to the next chapter, a lengthy and impassioned plea against all legal devices to keep land in perpetual ownership within a family. At the beginning of the nineteenth century land was not yet fully marketable; feudal remnants kept large parts of Europe out of the market. The rent discussion of the time reflects this condition—the leasing of land to a farmer/entrepreneur must be classified as a device to accommodate fixed ownership to efficient, profit-oriented management. Sismondi's approach reflects the fact that agricultural yields were still small and uncertain in many parts of Europe because fertilizers and new machinery had not yet come to the average farm. The law of diminishing returns, though of general applicability, arises out of the agricultural condition, as does the Ricardian rent theory—his various degrees of fertility of the soil do not describe an agriculture where fertility of land is an artifact of technological investment.

1. This clause was inserted for the second edition.
2. Sismondi assumes here, as elsewhere in his discussion of classes, immobility of individuals as well as clearly defined habits that distinguish members of one class from another. In the preceding paragraph, landowners are characterized as thinking only of enjoyment; here the soldier is referred to (probably ironically) as someone who knows how to employ money; that is, he will spend it on drink and loose living. The stocking maker on the other hand is obviously a sober citizen who will produce and increase the wealth of the nation. Clearly, the bulk of Marxian analysis rests on the same foundation: capitalists are compulsive accumulators, proletarians drudges and dupes. Neither Sismondi nor Marx assumes that technological change would increase mobility for all classes, even though by Sismondi's time, and certainly by Marx's time, clear evidence of increasing mobility was available.
3. This is correct in the sense that the total surface of the earth is finite, but wrong in the sense that arability is not only a function of existing surface—arable land can be created by diking, drainage, and by fertilization.
4. In the *Encyclopedia* and in the first edition, Sismondi uses "Besides, independently of legislative errors . . ." The change in the second edition was considered too important to be omitted in favor of the *Encyclopedia* text.
5. This should be compared to the ending paragraphs of chapter 6.
6. Sismondi raises here, in a very special context, the general and important problem of short-term versus long-term resource use. *New Principles* is in the main a continuous plea for maximizing long-term resource use. Agricultural property holding, perpetual leases, profit sharing for workers, the duty of the employer to care for his employee over his lifetime, are conceptual devices to accomplish this end. All short-term expedients that may increase profits now at the cost of later decreases in economic benefits are condemned. The reference to landlords increasing rents to farmers who have improved their farm yields is one example of a self-defeating practice for extracting maximum short-term rents, with applicability to present-day store leases in shopping malls whose rents increase with the profitability of the store. Sismondi logically concludes that the only social arrangement which ensures long-term interest is individual ownership. (However, it should be noted that he is in favor of marketability of land, which may, under certain circumstances, not lead to maximal long-term resource use.) Against Marx's communal ownership, Sismondi, in hindsight, wins the argument: centralized social systems separate the worker from direct participation in ownership and control, as well as profits, and thus lead directly to alienation and disinterest in efficiency and rational long-term resource use. The same holds true for large corporate enterprises, in capitalistic countries, that employ thousands of workers who have no share in profits, or participation in the decision process. This question will be raised again in the last book with reference to manufacturing.
7. A deduction derived from his assumption that the ongoing division of labor will increase wealth, as postulated by Smith. However, this postulate of increasing alienation, later adopted by Marx, also has roots in the utilitarian assumption

that work is painful and therefore usually avoided. As Veblen tried to show, this psychology is at least not proven. However, extended division of labor, as on an assembly line, separates work from enjoyment by attaching the monetary reward exclusively to the former, without any consideration of improving the workplace beyond the absolute minimum required by the production process itself.

8. Nineteenth century literature is full of landed aristocrats who fall into the hands of loan sharks because their lifestyle is beyond the income they receive from their mismanaged estates, or because they have mortgaged their lands to start some special task, either industrial or agricultural, of which they have little knowledge. Sismondi's argument would then merely reflect a common condition attributable, as he implies, to the legal impediments of selling land.
9. The paragraph remained unchanged from the first to the second edition, raising the question whether interest rates were then as stable as this would imply.
10. Sismondi advances what would become accepted common-sense economic arguments against debtors' prisons, just as Dickens condemned them on moral grounds in *Pickwick Papers* and *Little Dorritt*.

12

Of Laws Intending to Keep Landed Property within Families

The interest of society demands that property can be dispersed[1] in the same manner as it is accumulated, and that, through quick circulation, all in turn can enjoy a wealth that is produced by all through their labor. Society prospers by everyone's effort to increase his wealth, but it suffers from the moment where this activity ceases, and it is at its expense when a system that should be progressive for the good of all is made stationary.

But this is not at all what legislators have understood. Almost always recruited from the classes who have made their fortunes, they have believed that it is not enough to secure to the rich the enjoyment of their wealth, but that it is moreover necessary to provide that this wealth always belong to them and their children. What had been acquired by effort, they intended to be preserved in idleness, such that the effort of others could not do what they themselves had done; hence, they have elevated to a rule of state that the task of the social order was the preservation of old wealth in old families.

It is a constitutional question, and not one of political economy, to investigate to what extent an aristocracy is necessary to a monarchy, and old landed wealth to that aristocracy. But it is a question of political economy to examine how the development of agriculture and industry was influenced by the guarantees[2] given to family pride through entail, majorats,[3] rights of primogeniture, family redemptions, and all the precautions taken to prevent the wealthy from ruining themselves and selling their estates. It is also a question of political economy, closely tied to the previous one, to investigate to what extent these laws had the expected effect, and have perpetuated without diminution the same patrimonies in the same families.

The laws of monarchies have permitted entails of many types, the creation of fiefs, the foundation of commanderies in religious and military orders, the creation of simple family trusts, majorats, trusts in favor of a second son, or the daughter. By these various devices, a landowner takes away from his heirs command over his estate, he does not leave them the power either to sell it, or to divide it, or to mortgage it in any way, or to dispose of it through letters testamentary. On the contrary, he mandates them to leave that inheritance in its entirety, from male heir to male heir, to the future representatives of the family who, even before their births, are assumed to have a better claim than that of the present generation. This perpetual substitution, which the English know by the name of *entail*, and the Spaniards by that of *majorazgo*, is called in Italy *fedecomesso*, because the actual owner is but considered to be the fiduciary heir for the benefit of yet-unborn generations.

The founder of an entail has always exempted a part of his property, not in any way subjected to the chains of the *fideicommis* or the *majorat*, which he divides equally among his children. His oldest son may still preserve a share of this free property, which serves him to give a competence to his younger sons and to his daughters. As long as the younger sons of rich families could use their efforts and their small capitals, they have advanced in the army, the navy, the arts, the church, as well as in business[4], always through the basic endowment the paternal house has made for setting them up in business, or at least for their education, and one has seen them mending by their parsimony the waste of their elders. Most of them acquire their wealth too late to think of marriage, and the heritage of an old uncle rescues again and again the patrimony of a family on the road to ruin.

But the foreordained end of entail is to take away from the heir in the third generation any free capitals of which he could dispose. Two successive divisions of the unencumbered property have endowed in turn his uncles and aunts, his brothers and sisters; what can remain to endow his sons and daughters?

Should he have acquired wealth on his own? But entail seems to be more intended to hinder him from increasing his own than from diminishing it. Since he is not at all permitted to dispose of the capital, he cannot profit from his wealth by any lucrative enterprise. From income one can only save; profits can be made only from capital. The fiduciary heir of a landed estate can neither put his property into business, nor start, or participate in, a manufacture, nor share in one of those undertakings for the public interest which increase the value of the estates he must leave to his descendants. He is without the means to open a canal, dig a harbor, build a bridge, construct a machine to lift the waters of a stream. Further, he cannot use one part of his wealth to improve the other, undertake extensive land clearings, drain swamps, divert streams, exploit a peat bog, a marl pit, mines, or profit from any of the wealth his own land may conceal. All that ready cash may do for the benefit of a country is made impossible to this perpetual wealth; and this is the main, and most fatal result of the chains placed on estates. Riches call forth labor; they create new wealth; but all those entailed are immobilized, are rendered, if not sterile, then at least incapable of improving themselves.

By taking away the free management of their property from the living, in order to subordinate it to the will of the long deceased, and to the expectations of the as-yet unborn, it was made impossible for them to work for the gradual improvement of their country; they have become detached from a land which has become to them in some way alien; they have been disinherited of the common right of man, the right which in his lifetime he should wield over the goods of this earth in the same untrammeled manner his predecessors had practiced before him, and his successors will practice one day. But this is not all: by this unjust distribution of fortunes, the moral dispositions of those who were to be favored are changed; effort is kept away from their spirits, in the same way as it kept away from the capital entail has chained to their use.

In a country where he inherits the entire estate, and even more where such estate is entailed, the eldest brother sees his younger brothers alone as destined to enter active and profitable careers. As far as he is concerned, he will believe that he has discharged his duty if he cares for the patrimony left to him by his fathers. He learnt early on that it was a virtue to live as a gentleman; he was kept from pursuits, studies, information, that were described to him as fit only for subordinates, and which were called to his face mercantile, mechanical, and servile. He was made to understand that, while his brothers sought by divers means to make their fortunes, to him belonged the honor of maintaining the ancient splendor of his house. The name and reputation of that house are always portrayed to him as the objects of some cult. The servants, the craftsmen who depend on him, the parasites who attach themselves to him, are assiduous to tell him with what luxury his father, his grandfather, in their youth, made themselves worthy of the respect they left to him; what the number of their retainers was, of their coaches, their horses, their hunting dogs; how magnificent their celebrations were, how elegant and tasteful their furniture, their kitchen, and their domestic life. No other type of fame is ever shown to the heir of a great fortune; no other reputation seems to be within his grasp, except what he will attain by his extravagant spending. All those who profit from such prodigality applaud it as long as it lasts; even the public forgets the serious, if distant interest in the preservation of the national wealth, so as to listen only to the daily interest in a pomp which amuses. Also, at all times, and in all places, the public has shown itself more forgiving of spendthrifts than of misers.

At the death of a head of a family, his eldest son, who succeeds him, is called upon to prepare a dowry for each of his sisters, and to pay at least a pension to each of his brothers. The dowry of a daughter is capital for which a means must be found to separate it from the estate; and if the father, on his death, has left nothing but lands and no funds, then either lands must be sold, or mortgaged to borrow on them, or given outright in place of a dowry. Yet, no entailed estate can be sold, or mortgaged, or given in gift;[5] the fiduciary heir profits from the credit his income secures to him, to assume, without security, a debt he expects to repay with his income.

From that moment on he finds himself yoked to his creditors on a course from which it will be almost impossible to escape; his very luxury, which must destroy his credit, contributes for some time to enhance it; and he needs the credit to continue, because he seeks already, in deceiving himself, to deceive his creditors. He has to pay the debts of his youth; he must provide for the expenses of his household, of his marriage; but no one refuses him money on his word, or his simple note; all merchants rush to sell to him, all craftsmen to work for him, all domestics to serve him. They give him easy credit for their supplies, their wages, their hire, and they let him be ensnared in a long profligacy before they refuse him their trust. Everyone knows the amount of his income; everyone counts his debts and remains convinced that with two, four, six years of strict saving, he can discharge all his obligations. Everyone expects that he will be paid when such saving will begin; and, by waiting, everyone contributes with new credit to the postponement of that time. The merchant sets whatever price he wants on the goods he sells on credit; the craftsmen, the servants, pay themselves with the provisions of the house. They benefit from the prodigality of the master and his dissoluteness; consumption increases and the products of labor diminish, without the master daring to complain about people he does not pay, and who would have even more reason to complain about him.

Who does not know that in all of Europe this is the fate of all great fortunes—that they rarely last for three generations without falling into the hands of a spendthrift? Such a one fights, for most of his life, with the difficulties he has created for himself; he cajoles his creditors to obtain delays he does not know how to turn to his advantage; he enters into a succession of agreements, one more ruinous than the other, to obtain a brief respite from his distress; he finally suffers all the miseries of poverty, all its fears, all its cares, all its humiliations, unwilling to give up his carriages, his seeming affluence, the idle pomp with which he surrounds himself, and which gives him no pleasure; and he comes to the end of his life, crushed by debts he has no means to satisfy.[6]

The prodigal finally dies; and the entailed estate passes in its entirety to the new fiduciary heir, without the latter being responsible for the mistakes and faults of his father. This is what the original testator wanted when he created the entail; this is what the legislator wanted when he put it under his protection. However, all the father's creditors are ruined by his default.[7] He had pledged five, ten times the value of his entire income; this was their capital; when they lose it, the nation loses it with them. The merchants, the manufacturers who have sold to him go bankrupt; the tradesmen, the servants see the savings disappear they had made for their old age. The long and burdensome austerity of the saving classes is destroyed in a day by the prodigal class, and entail assures it the privileges of the bankrupt. This is not the way in which great fortunes should be divided and recirculated.

But does the entailed estate really pass in its entirety to the fiduciary heir? One should not believe it. The invention of entail surely hinders wealth from accumulating, but it does not prevent it from dissipating. The landowner who lived in a state of constant penury for twenty or thirty years, could not devote any capital, any saving, to the improvement of his lands, to investments, to great undertakings which maintain their value. After all, the earth owes its productive powers to the work of man; his effort must maintain it.[8] The canals dug for irrigation and drainage silt up; at the end of a shorter or longer period they must be reopened; dikes crumble; enclosures deteriorate; cottages, stables, winepresses decay. New capital is needed to replace them, and it does not exist. Plantings need to be constantly renewed to remain in good condition. One olive tree in a hundred, one mulberry tree in fifty, one vine in twenty, must be replanted every year. The landlord must make these advances from which the farmer or the metayer may harvest the fruits. If he neglects this for many years in succession, everything decays, and finally the moment arrives when the farm becomes almost deserted, when vineyards, mulberries, and olive groves do not repay the labor they need, and yield no more than if they were fields or meadows. These, in turn, need numerous teams of horses, wagons, and an agricultural installation the spendthrift has let waste away; the cattle herds he had sold in a moment of need; some servants and workers he has dismissed because, lacking money, he has economized on all agricultural expenditures. Thus it becomes more profitable to abandon field cultivation, to change them to pasture, and to rent the grazings to some owners of great herds. This is the slow decay by which a land, comparable to the pleasant territory of Lucca, which bears in four years six rich crops, not counting those from olives, vines, figs, mulberries that cover it, can finally come to resemble the vast fields that stretch around Rome, or those of the Capitanate.[9] Thistles and sterile brush encroach every day on the grass destined for a wretched pasturage in the same way in which the latter replaced earlier all the abundance of a rich vegetation. In those deserted provinces land is nevertheless entailed; the same family owns always the same number of acres, but those acres, abandoned by man, represent neither for them, nor for the nation, the same value.

Entailed estates are not only menaced by the chance of being managed by a spendthrift; one must also expect that the family estate does not always pass from the father to the eldest son without interruption, in direct descent. If the fiduciary heir has no children, if he has only daughters, or bastards, he sees himself from then on condemned to leave upon his death his entire estate to a brother, a nephew, a cousin, to the detriment of his widow, his daughters, the objects of his tenderest affections. From that moment on, he has no other goal in life but to save for those he loves, and more often again to hurt those which the opposition of interest makes him hate. In order to create a little hoard, a small capital he can command, he cuts the trees on his lands, he sells the furnishings of his houses, he avoids any expense he would have to make to maintain the value of an estate he will have to dispose of against his will. How often indeed has one not seen that the constant opposition of interest between the actual holder and the presumptive heir, between him who has to make all the advances, and him who stands to reap all the fruits, between him who waits to hand over his property one day, and him who expects to receive it and appoints himself its guardian in advance, creates a hostility where it is least expected, between a father and his oldest son. The father strives without pause to separate some part of the property from the entail; he rejoices over every tree he has cut down, because he can realize therefrom some guineas he can pass on to his younger sons; he resists the planting of any trees, any new vines, because these are guineas he must take away from the purse reserved for his poor sons, to the benefit of the rich son. His jealousy of one of his sons combines with his love for his others. His greed and his fairness, his virtues and his vices together form a union, and their combined force leads to the destruction of the property which is entrusted to him.

General experience seemed to have convinced all legislators of the deleterious consequences entails bring with them. However, family pride or prejudice which support the preservation of an aristocratic interest, often bring forth new defenders. They ride high in Scotland. In England, where the law *de donis conditionalibus* (13 Edw. I, c.1) gave rise to entails, courts have constantly sought to undo them through subtlety; less indeed through the aristocratic principle by which estates could be confiscated for high treason; and in reality, since the reign of Edward IV, and above all since that of Henry VIII, an artificial practice, known to English law by the name *Fines and Recoveries*[10] has given to the holders the means to annul them; but the law has taken under its protection a first entail *(remainder)*, and that, being constantly renewed, had almost the same effect. Entails have long contributed to the ruin of Spain, Portugal, and their colonies; they are common in Germany; and have been anew permitted in France, by Napoleon, who sacrificed the well-recognized interest of the state to the desire to create majorats for his new aristocracy, and they have been confirmed again since the Restoration; finally, the majority of the restored Italian governments have given them their old power, in defiance of the philosophic principles with which they were attacked.

Many circumstances must come together to make the results of entails as disastrous as we have described them. When a country has come, like England, to a high degree of prosperity, when all careers are open to active and industrious men, when the ranks of government, the navy, the army, business, and the Indies, offer numberless opportunities, and when the credit of a father, or an influential brother, suffices to secure and advance a career of young, well-educated gentlemen with names, but few funds, then national prosperity, and that of great families is maintained, not by entails, but in spite of them. If the prosperity of such a country were once disturbed, if numerous bankruptcies would ruin its business, if price increases for its manufactures would close foreign markets, if the disturbance of its finances would force it to reduce its army, its navy, and its numberless governmental offices,[11] if for all of these reasons the only active men of the upper classes of that nation, those who contribute today most to its wealth, the younger sons of great families, were condemned to idleness, this nation would learn, by bitter experience, what the ruinous effects of entail would be, and that to destroy them means that family pride itself must be attacked, and all children must be called to an equal share in the estate.

In reality, in all countries alike, not only entail, but the prevalent custom of leaving all land to the oldest son, and giving him great preference, diverts him from any profitable pursuits, and has condemned him to idleness precisely because of his wealth; whereas, for the good of the country, just this wealth should be put to use; because without it no industrial, commercial, or agricultural enterprise is possible; and it is much less important to push men to work than to fertilize the land with capital and credit.

The inevitable effect of the right of primogeniture, not any less than that of entail, is the separation of ownership of money from the possession of land. The prosperity of families, as that of a nation, depends crucially on the union of fixed with circulating capital. But an entail, or merely the prejudice that attaches the reputation of a family to the conservation of all lands they have once held, renews at each succession the ruinous separation of money from land. On the death of each family head, all circulating capital passes to the daughters, to the younger sons, to the widow; and the lands alone, weighted down with debts to the full extent permissible, go to the heir. The means to cultivate them become every day more difficult; the more his property decays with the passage of time, the more it becomes impossible for him to restore it without the cash advances[12] he is unable to make. How many owners would recover their lost freedom if they sold one half of their inheritance to employ the proceeds to clear the other half; but that is precisely what entail, law, and prejudice forbid them to do.

Finally, entail not only deprives landowners of employment and circulating capital, it denies them also credit. It was in some way a question of mismanagement which prevented the rich from inspiring the confidence that would have put at their disposal the capital of others; entails have resolved that problem. A landowner, on whose prosperity depends the fate of sixty families who work his holdings, could have doubled the value of these holdings by erecting a dike which would have sheltered them from flooding; by digging a canal that would have dried his swamp, or irrigated his fallow, or which, by internal navigation, would have opened new markets for his products; he could profit from a favorable location by covering a now barren hill, producing nothing but a few weeds, with a rich vineyard, change it to an olive grove, a planting of mulberries, and into fields and meadows the fallow the thorny gorse disputes to the heather. But to accomplish such an undertaking, as advantageous to the nation as to himself, not any less profitable to his peasants than his heirs, he would need forty, sixty, a hundred thousand guineas, on which he would gladly pay interest, by mortgaging his lands he wants to improve. Entail forbids him to do so; it does not permit any mortgaging of his lands; it tells his creditors that, if they are sufficiently imprudent to advance him the funds, they will lose at his death the very capital that will have made the fortune of his heirs.

As a result, the legislator has completely missed the end he wanted to achieve by the institution of entail and majorat. He has condemned to idleness all the sons of families whose renown he wanted to preserve; he prohibited to all of them, the eldest because of pride, to the younger because of inability, industry, the sole means of increasing wealth, while it leaves them exposed to all human hazards which do not cease to attack all that is old, and which must always end by destroying all wealth that is not regenerated.[13]

Experience has upheld these important lessons; it shows us, through the history of all nations that, wherever it was intended in the interests of the aristocracy, to maintain the ancient splendor of its families, this was accomplished by the law of equal division among children, because then each father avoided having many children; whereas if the law favored the eldest, it lifted from the father such restraint. Hence, however small the share of the younger children might be, it must of necessity destroy the richest patrimony if they are numerous.

All of the aristocracies that have survived in the world, in Greece, in the Roman Republic, in Florence, in Venice, in all the Italian republics of the Middle Ages, in all those of Switzerland and Germany,[14] were governed by the law of equal distribution among children. Immense fortunes were perpetuated in these families for many centuries, even in those who were engaged in trade, like those of the Strozzi and the Medici in Florence, or the Fuggers in Augsburg. Rarely was a large number of brothers seen in these families, and they did not die out any faster.

All the nobilities that were seen to fall prey to degrading poverty in the kingdoms of Spain, Italy, Germany, or ancient France, have lived under the rule of entail or majorat. One always saw every father have a large number of sons, of which the younger ones were condemned to idleness and misery. Their number did not keep noble families from dying out; it is even common knowledge in such countries that the father who has eight children has seldom grandchildren. But if it happens sometimes that the younger sons marry, they give rise to new branches who live in misery, and thus destroy the esteem that was intended to be attached to historic names.

This truth, which can be regarded as constant in world history, is explained by the principle we have already indicated, and which we will develop in our last book: that population is always regulated by income. In the meantime, we can assert here that rich and noble families, far from multiplying indefinitely, have, on the contrary, always tended to die out [to be convinced, one need only compare, in all countries, the aristocratic registers from century to century][15] that these families die out just as fast if they have many children, or only one, because the more children there are, the less do their parents wish to marry them; that, in the interest of these families and the nobility, it is desirable that these families only be comprised of a small number of individuals, and that they will never exceed this number if the fathers have always before them the thought that the estate will be divided equally among all their children; that the family fortunes are preserved by the means by which they were acquired, and that they will be destroyed if they are made nontransferable; that the great names attract to themselves the great estates, and there is no need for the law to be involved so that a peer of France reestablish, by a rich dowry, the fortune his rank demands, whilst one of the numerous hazards to which all what is human remains exposed, would have unsettled him.

Translator's Notes to Chapter 12, Third Book

The concluding paragraph of the *Encyclopedia*'s third chapter is used at the end of this chapter, but the main theme of this chapter is only tersely outlined there and expanded and commented upon here. It is the second part of Sismondi's three-pronged, basically institutional, attack on Ricardo's rent theory—chapter 11 dealing generally with the problem of ownership and lease farming, chapter 12 dealing with the legal impediments to making land marketable, and chapter 13 being a direct discussion of Ricardo's rent theory. Sismondi's main objection to the Ricardian rent theory is its disregard of the social framework that essentially immobilized the factor land. To Sismondi, such immobility has ramifications on economic development beyond agriculture; that is, the Ricardian assumption of equality of profit across industries is thereby made impossible. Similarly, rent is not seen as a payment for the original powers of the soil, but as a use price paid to a monopolist. The discussion is dated in the sense that these impediments have been removed in the meantime, but it can be argued that it still has relevance in all cases where land is not in fact marketable, for example, in planned socialist economies where it belongs to the state. The worst-scenario approach habitually used then to emphasize the point that immobility of land lowers production may also explain now the generally observed phenomenon of declining agricultural output in such economies. Beyond this immediate goal, the argument here more firmly establishes Sismondi's major objection to classical analysis—the absence of the implied mobility of all factors of production, a point he will reenforce later in his discussion of manufacturing and business fluctuations. He would admit, as a proclaimed disciple of Adam Smith, that classical analysis is correct *if* all factors were freely mobile, but he would forcefully argue that such a blessed state is unattainable and therefore irrelevant to economic analysis, or the formulation of economic policy. As the first institutional critic of classical analysis, Sismondi here opens a dispute that has persisted to the present time—he was joined over time by the German and British historicists and the American institutionalists without making much of a dent in the armor of mainstream analysis. Marx ostensibly uses a *historical* approach, but in reality he reenforced the abstractions of Ricardian analysis by welding Ricardo's version of the labor theory of value to the idealistic philosophical categories of Hegel. The historical phases of Marxian development are as unreal as Ricardian rent theory.

1. The text reads "*divise,*" but the term *dispersed* seemed to be more appropriate when related to *accumulated*. In this chapter, Sismondi supports the inheritance policies introduced by the French Revolution.
2. The last paragraph of chapter 3 of the *Encyclopedia* starts: "But the props lent to family pride . . ."
3. Sismondi everywhere uses *substitutions perpétuelles* for *entail*. In the *Encyclopedia* he uses *fideicommissa* for majorats.
4. This enumeration refers clearly to English conditions—on the Continent the great majority of the aristocracy was in the armed services or governmental administration.

5. The phrase "or given in gift" was added in the second edition.
6. The aristocratic spendthrift was a standard character in the nineteenth-century novel, such as Lord Verisopht in Dickens's *Nicholas Nickleby*—undoubtedly representing an existing reality. But Sismondi's morality tale has the flavor of the bourgeois Calvinist merchant's resentment against nobles who never paid their bills and added insult to injury by treating their suppliers with disdain. For obvious reasons, he does not mention landlords who managed their estates with care and became rich in their own right. As far as English estates were concerned, Sismondi painted a different picture earlier in this book with respect to the huge incomes some members of the aristocracy commanded. Many of them participated in business ventures with funds they had obtained from their rents. On the Continent there are also instances of aristocratic entrepreneurs, like the counts of Donnersmark in Silesia, who operated mines and factories and were millionaires.
7. Under entail, none of the debts of the father pass to the son. Creditors could only protect themselves by charging high interest, and trying to collect the debts before the death of the debtor.
8. This statement stands in clear opposition to Ricardo's postulated "original powers of the soil." It is also a departure from physiocratic doctrine, although less so, inasmuch as Sismondi apparently does not here assume that "the earth labors along with man." As the next few sentences make quite clear, he had a better appreciation as the owner of a metayage of the work needed to keep a farm productive than either the gentleman-farmer Ricardo, or the court intellectuals who created physiocracy.
9. The Capitanate was a province of the Kingdom of Naples comprising what is today known as the Abruzzi, in general the area around Campobasso.
10. This appears in the French text in English and italicized, as does the word "remainder" below.
11. The French text reads "et a porter la reforme." The paragraph has a prescient quality with respect to British difficulties after World Wars I and II, and United States problems in the 1980s, although the circumstances are admittedly quite different.
12. The text reads "sans une advance de fonds."
13. This paragraph is very similar to the concluding two sentences of the third chapter of the *Encyclopedia*, but Sismondi had changed them enough to justify the translation.
14. Clearly, *the world* means to Sismondi Europe. The enumeration shows a bias towards what he favored—mostly republican city-states governed by an aristocracy of wealth, a patriciate.
15. The brackets are Sismondi's.

13

Mr. Ricardo's Theory of the Rent of Land

One could say that we have described the nature and development of agricultural wealth very imperfectly if we pass over in silence the new doctrine being advanced by a new writer who enjoys great fame in England; a doctrine entirely opposed to that of Adam Smith, and so far removed from ours that we have not even had an occasion to argue against it while expounding our own principles. It is that of Mr. Ricardo, as stated in his new work *Principles of Political Economy and Taxation*,[1] which M.Say has partly refuted in his excellent annotations to his translation.*

Mr. Ricardo asserts in principle that a perfect equilibrium is always maintained between the profits of each type of industry, because as soon as any one industry is becoming less profitable than all the others by some accidental circumstance, those who are engaged in it will leave it, whereas they will flock to the one which is more profitable. He believes that by this constant movement of men and capital the level of profits is equalized in the entire nation.[2] He concludes therefrom that farmers will make an equal profit on every type of land, because no one would want to cultivate the worst land if he could not profit from it as much as on the best. In his view this equilibrium among all farmers is restored by the price they pay for their rent. He assumes that those who farm the worst land will not pay any rent, and that the rent of those who are better situated is always calculated on the relation of all others with that one, who to him is a no-rent producer[3]. Hence, if a given capital and labor would produce on the worst land under cultivation 100 bushels[4] of corn, and the same labor and capital would produce on the better lands 110, 120, 130, and 140 bushels of corn, then he judges that the rent of each would be equal to the value of ten, twenty, thirty, and forty bushels of corn, respectively.

***Principles of Political Oeconomy and Taxation*, by David Ricardo, Esq., 1 vol. in 8o, 1817. We have cited the translation because of the annotations.

After reducing rent to the simple estimate of the differences in the productivity of different soils, Mr. Ricardo draws several conclusions on the manner in which taxes on net income, gross product, and provisions, affect the various classes of society. To us, these conclusions do not seem, in any way, to follow from his premisses. However, we will not concur with his arguments, no matter how important the results may be, because we do not accept his fundamental proposition. We shall also remark in passing that Mr. Ricardo, in common with all English economists, considers rent farming as the sole means of taking advantage of agricultural wealth, whereas, in his very own country, possibly superior cultivation systems are also found in use.

We will start by declaring that we do not in any manner accept the basic principle of Mr. Ricardo's argument, that is, the stable[5] equilibrium of profits in all industries. We believe to the contrary that, given the inability of all owners of fixed capitals to liquefy them and to change their use, they continue to work with them long after these capitals will yield no more than an income below that of all others. Their persistence in remaining in the same trades is again much increased by their unwillingness to lose all the skills they have acquired, and their inability to master a new trade. The more numerous a class is, the larger is this obstacle; therefore, while some workers, giving in to discouragement, change trades, new ones come from the new generation and replace them, and equilibrium is never reestablished. Farmers can never of their own free will become weavers; farmers from one district find it difficult to migrate to another; and if there is ever anything proven by experience, it is that their profits are not in any way equal in all provinces, or on all kind of lands.[6]

Similarly, we shall object to the assumption that farmers generally dictate the terms of leases to the owners. It seems to us that more often they receive them from the owner. The quantity of arable land is limited and cannot increase; the quantity of capitals and the number of hands offered increases without limit, and hence one should find in a nation more often people who demand land for cultivation than people who are willing to provide it.

But, without dwelling on these fundamental differences, even though they endanger Mr. Ricardo's entire system, we will dispute his conclusions in his very own way of reasoning. Because population increases, and has an income with which it can buy its subsistence, it requires the cultivation of lands which before were fallow, but at the same time it secures to their owners the means which will pay them for their use. If the uncultivated lands of bad quality do not belong to anybody, and if everyone were alike free to work them whenever anybody believed that an advantage could be had therefrom, then Mr. Ricardo's argument would be valid. But it is well known that in all civilized countries all lands, good and bad, cultivated or fallow, are owned, either by individuals, or by communities; that nobody, as a consequence, can work them without buying the consent of the owner, and the price of this purchase is called rent. Even in America, at the very edge of western civilization, where new lands of immense extent ever call for new cultivation, land can only be obtained by buying it from the government for two dollars an acre. This price is without a doubt minimal, but it does represent a capital of a rent in all respects independent from the comparisons made by Mr. Ricardo. The ownership of land always means something; our author has supposed that it is nothing.[7] The lowest limit of his comparative scale he has called zero; where he put *zero* he should at least have put *one*.

We have called the total of the annual crop the *gross product* because it must be divided between all those who have contributed to its creation, and *net product* that part of the crop which comes to the owner after payment of the costs that were incurred in its creation. The net product serves as a base to determine rent if the land is leased out. In every other system of cultivation it represents always the annual value of the right of ownership.[8]

But incomes of a quite different nature are classified under the name of a net product. Actually, the owner intermingles in the rent he charges (1) the compensation for the contribution of the land, or the quantity that its productive capacity actually added to the value of the produce which labor drew from its depths; (2) the monopoly price he receives when he refuses its use to everyone who wants to work it and has no land; and all those who want to consume and do not find provisions; (3) the surplus value he receives from the comparison of land of a superior quality with land of an inferior quality; finally, (4) the income from the capital he has joined to his land to make it arable, and which he cannot withdraw from it anymore. Of these four parts of income Mr. Ricardo recognizes but the last two, and even that he does not do in a very clear manner.

In political economy one must distinguish at all times, and this observation applies to the entire work of Mr. Ricardo, two types of value, one intrinsic, the other relative; one comes into being by production, the other by competition; one is the relation of the produced good to the labor which created it, the other the relation of the good to the demand of those who need it. The estimation of these two values can be compared in the determination of the net income.

Intrinsic value is absolutely independent of all exchange. The husbandman who has sown five bushels of corn, and who has harvested twenty-five, has no need to investigate market demand to know that his production is intrinsically superior to the value of his advance, because it puts him in the position to not only begin anew the same work, but to produce from it even more. What is due him for cultivating, manuring, seeding, and harvesting these five bushels of corn is perhaps represented by another ten bushels; with fifteen bushels he would find himself in exactly the same position in which he began the previous year. Yet ten bushels remain to him which represent the work of nature.[9]

As agricultural labor is the only one sufficient to sustain life, so also is it the only one which can be evaluated without any exchange. The soil can supply to a man all that he needs to live while he cultivates the land. If he wears the skins of his sheep, if he feeds himself with their meat and the grain he harvests, if he builds his hut from the timber of his woods, he can compare without any intermediary the quantity produced by his work with the quantity consumed during his work, and he can thus establish that the second is inferior to the first. He sees arising before him, and for him, a net product absolutely independent of all competition, any market demand, any value against which he will exchange this product. In all other undertakings, the labor of the worker would not be destined in its entirety to his consumption; he lives therefore not from that product, but what he obtained in exchange for it. Also, the excess of his production over his consumption depends on the conditions of exchange; and the net income of all industrial labor, despite the help it also receives from nature, or from science which engages natural forces, is not at all realized in such a clear and certain way as the income of agriculture.[10]

But when the cultivator has taken care of his own needs, the surplus of corn he has grown has no other value but in exchange. From that moment it is necessary for him to assess its relative value, or the relation between market demand and production. Equilibrium establishes itself through the opposing forces of demanders and suppliers, and the cultivator sells his remaining ten bushels, not for the price of the days labor he had to spend to grow them, but at the price of the days labor of the goods he is offered for purchase. On some occasions, the cultivator employs to his advantage monopoly power, because the quantity of land under cultivation is limited, and the demand of the population exceeds his output. Then he raises his expectations, and he sells his corn at the price which the most remote producer from his market agrees to accept in the same market, because the latter has expended as much on production, and has paid in addition the freight from his fields to the market. In the same case, the distant producer sees the power of monopoly turned against him. He has no buyers sufficiently near, and he is forced to hand over to the buyer a part of his income to dispose of his corn.[11]

When lands are leased, the cultivator, after having haggled over the price of his corn, haggles with his landlord over the price of the farm; and for determining that, he must not only take into account the ease of supply, he is forced to estimate the number of his competitors who offer, like him, labor and agricultural capital, and he dictates the rent to the landlord, or gets it dictated, according to whether the capitals and men offered are more or less numerous than the land.[12]

Thus, the net income of agriculture, or the surplus value of the harvests over the costs of the cultivator, is a positive amount which enriches society, independently of market fluctuations, and it gives an actual basis to the rent of land. But the commercial value of this income may be determined by a double and even threefold battle, such that, according to circumstances, it sometimes accrues in its entirety to the landlord, even commands a monopoly price; sometimes it will remain in the hand of the farmer, or the laborer who grows the crops; finally, the consumer often will profit from it. Thus in the new westernmost settlements of the American continent, in the Illinois territory, where the settler buys land at two dollars an acre, which sets the rent at most to twenty *cents* per year* it is not that agriculture does not render from these fertile soils a much larger net profit; but this net profit is divided between the farmer, the farm hand, and the grain merchant in New Orleans, in such a way that the first makes a much larger gross profit, and the second gets a much larger wage, and the third buys it much cheaper than all three could do so in New York. The high ground rent that must be paid in New York, but is not paid in Illinois, is enough to absorb the profits of these three classes of individuals.[13]

The work of nature, this creative labor, which she would do without man, but which she would not put to his use, is thus the source of the net product of land, considered intrinsically. Market demand, or the relation between the income of consumers and the quantity of the gross product offered for sale, determines the value of the net product, or sets its relative price. The right of ownership, or the monopoly guaranteed by society which the landlord exercises against two classes of individuals—on the one hand, those who demand provisions; on the other hand, those who offer to work to raise them—forbids that, on the one hand, the rent of land, and on the other hand, the price of provisions, should be reduced to their lowest value.[14]

It is only after these three causes have been operative, with infinite variations depending on circumstances, that the other causes recognized by Mr. Ricardo make themselves felt. In the same region a farmer, choosing between two parcels of land, will pay in effect to the owner of the better one a surplus value equal to the greatest return this land yields

*The *cent*, or one-hundredth part of the dollar, equals almost the sol of France.

over the other one with the same labor. To estimate this superiority, he will have to take into account the improvements the owner has made with his own capital, as well as the nature of the land. Among these improvements many are long term; the canals of Lombardy, the terraces of Tuscany, are three or four hundred years old. Similar improvements become part of the very characteristics of the land.

Sometimes the net product nature provides ceases absolutely, while the net product a monopoly secures to the landlord increases in value. The cultivated gardens within the walls of Paris[15] yield a very high rent; this rent represents the power of nature which is quite strong; because this soil, enriched by centuries of manuring, produces many more provisions than can be consumed by working it. But if a highway were to be built across these gardens, the land will cease to produce absolutely; and it will sell at a higher price than if it were covered with rich harvests. The owner makes himself paid for the advantageous location, and moreover for all the crops he has given up to produce. This rent on a land which is prevented from producing is found in all prosperous cities. In Pittsburgh, in Lexington, even in the towns of western America which were founded less than ten years ago, but whose prosperity increases rapidly, building sites in the better parts of town are more expensive than in the best streets of London.*

Therefore, far from concluding with Mr. Ricardo that *the rent always falls on the consumer and never on the farmer,*** we see rent, or rather the net product as being born directly from the soil to the profit of the landlord; he does not take anything from the farmer, nor from the consumer; but we believe that, according to the state of the market, sometimes the farmer or the consumer profit from a part of that rent; sometimes the landlord not only receives the entire rent, but exacts a monopoly price whose loss is unequally divided between the farmer and consumer. One should generally beware in political economy of absolute statements as well as all abstractions. Everyone of the forces destined to equilibrate each other in every market, can by itself and independently of the one with which it is supposed to be in equilibrium, experience variations. Nowhere is an absolute quantity to be found, always-equal forces are never found; and every abstraction is always a deception. Also, political economy is not a mathematical science, but a moral science. It misleads if one wants to be guided by numbers; it only leads to a goal if the feeling, the needs, and the passions of mankind are taken into account.[16]

*H.Fearon, *Sketches of America*, p. 203.
**Ricardo, ch.vi, transl. p. 167.

End of the Third Book

Translator's Notes to Chapter 13, Third Book

Sismondi wrote this chapter for the first edition as a refutation of Ricardo's rent theory, which had found its definitive form in the 1817 *Principles*. No part of this chapter appeared in the *Encyclopedia*. It was used for the second edition of *New Principles* unchanged except for a small addition to one of the last paragraphs (see note 13). The reference to Say's translation of the *Principles* in the very first paragraph shows that the polemic of this chapter is but one voice in the contemporary debate about the nature of rent. (This is the only reference to an annotated translation of the *Principles* by Say that could be found. Sismondi must have had a copy in his possession, but no evidence of the existence of such a work could be obtained.) Schumpeter's discussion of the rent debate in his *History* (1954, 671–79) makes it quite clear that there existed a great deal of theoretical groping and confusion. This chapter shows once again the basic difference between Sismondi's approach and classical analysis. As a historian and therefore an institutionalist, Sismondi rejected all models that disregarded, or abstracted from, legal property arrangements and social structures that influenced market power. He always insisted, as he does at the end of this chapter, that political economy deals with interdependent forces having moral dimensions that cannot be neglected. In one of his last sentences of the chapter he sounds like Alfred Marshall when he states: "One should generally beware in political economy of absolute statements as well as all abstractions." But this view has its negative side—Sismondi can hardly be credited with having promoted a better understanding of rent. He attacks Ricardo with his major argument that the relative immobility of fixed assets invalidates the assumption of a long-term profit equilibrium across industries, and the existence of property rights, such as entail, invalidates the assumption of no-rent land. If we accept Schumpeter's causes for rent, scarcity and requisiteness, then this last objection has validity in the sense that all factors of production are owned by somebody and must be brought to their use by some remuneration. (See also Marshall 1948, book 4, chapt. 2.) However, it is not really Sismondi's intent to advance a new rent theory, but to make existing theory take account of actual practice. He rejects Ricardo's mistaken effort to remove rent from value determination for ignoring the institutional factors that made agricultural practices and payments quite different in different parts of Europe. Here as elsewhere, the final determination of distributive shares for Sismondi is a result of market power possessed by the contracting parties, and not determined by invariant economic laws. As a theoretical contribution to value analysis this approach fails, but it raises important methodological questions about the nature and purpose of economic reasoning. Again, Sismondi's ideas on market power form an important part of Marx's theory of the class struggle and exploitation.

1. Sismondi uses here the French title of the translation *Principes de l'Economie politique et de l'impôt*. The footnote uses the English title.
2. The text reads: "le niveau des bénéfices est maintenu dans toute la nation."
3. The text here is: "est le zéro de son echelle . . ."
4. Sismondi uses *muids*, an obsolete measure equivalent to about fifty-nine gallons. Since the actual size of the measure does not affect the argument, the term *bushel* was used here as the most commonly known in English usage.

5. The text reads "equilibre constant des profits." The term *stable* was considered to be more in consonance with English usage.
6. Sismondi brought to his arguments the historian's respect for facts and a considerable store of personal observations made during his European travels. Immobility of factors in general, and not just of labor, was to him the most evident and major departure from the mostly implied assumption of classical analysis that factors were at all times freely transferable between uses. While it may be true that in the long run all factors, that is, including labor, are indeed mobile, this does not suffice to explain economic fluctuations, nor does it correspond to observed reality with respect to the subsistence theory of labor, which assumes that labor is freely interchangeable in the short run. As Sismondi clearly states here, and he will return to this point over and over again in later chapters of *New Principles,* labor is not a homogeneous mass of unskilled labor, nor are specialized machines a homogeneous mass of capital, and therefore a cost is incurred every time economic change affects industries' resources differentially. The Smithian view that remuneration of special types of labor are adjusted by the market actually begs the question of what the real cost of labor is, not only in wages, but in the cost of incorporated skills acquired by formal study, apprenticeships, and work experience. Ricardo as a long-term theorist could reply to this criticism that he was interested in analyzing the basic forces of economic behavior, and not superficial day to day changes, but this answer is unsatisfactory precisely because the *Principles* are clearly intended to provide guidance, not only for the long run, but for everyday questions. Actually, Sismondi stands alone among his contemporaries and later writers, particularly again Marx, in advancing this argument for all resources, but especially for labor.
7. The argument should be compared with the quotation: "Thus the rate of interest at any time, being the reward for parting with liquidity, is a measure of the unwillingness of those who possess money to part with their liquid control over it" (Keynes 1956, chapt. 13, 2, p. 167). Obviously, Ricardo abstracted from ownership benefits and risk avoidance, Sismondi and Keynes took them explicitly into account and therefore come to the same conclusion, namely that a resource will be withheld from the market if a minimum payment representing these benefits is not made.
8. The troubling question of monopoly is raised, and indeed the classical approach sees the rent question essentially as a monopoly problem. But if it is assumed that (1) a factor is scarce, and (2) in demand, then its ownership cannot be detached from its scarcity. Labor earns a Marshallian *quasi-rent* if it has a high degree of scarcity. Only free goods are so abundant that everyone can have them for the asking, which is really saying that nobody owns them, because by definition everybody has them. This by inference answers also the question why communal landholding makes for bad agriculture—there is no price attached to the use of what is seen as a free resource.
9. The argument and the following discussion are again physiocratic in origin. Sismondi's use of *intrinsic value* to denote the fact that a farmer, as far as his personal provisions are concerned, is independent of the market, is a special use of the term *value in use*. The argument is specious in the sense that Sismondi takes fifteen bushels of corn to stand for all the commodities that the farmer and his family would need to live for a year. Ricardo did not discuss such a possibility because he analyzed rent strictly in a framework of lease

farming, pointing up the then-existing difference between English and continental agriculture.

10. "Realized" is used here to translate *ne se degage,* which can be taken to mean 'disposed of' or 'cleared', meaning the exchange in the previous clause, namely to realize an income by the sale of the production in a market. The distinction between agricultural and industrial labor is related to Sismondi's cycle theory: agricultural labor can sustain itself independently of the market from its product, industrial labor is dependent on the market to convert production into consumption of provisions. Obviously this excludes agricultural labor in a monoculture, for example, a cane harvester on a sugar plantation—Sismondi had expressed his distaste for such cultivation in the preceding chapters.
11. Sismondi is always preoccupied with the possibility of market price fluctuations disadvantageous to the producer, unlike Ricardo who assumed that the exchangeable value of raw produce will inevitably be raised by the greater difficulty of production because of increasing population and limited supply of land (conclusion of the chapter "On Rent.") Consumption and market demand are not chained to the realization of income in Sismondi's analysis, as they are in Ricardo's and Say's model, but are openly, or by implication, always seem as independent variables, hence the possibility of a mismatch between production offered and demand. Loss or profit on sold production will *influence* consumption, but in unpredictable ways. Sismondi always assumes the most pessimistic scenario; hence all mismatches will lead to a decline of economic activity because of realized losses. Keynes resembles Sismondi here in his assumption that there is only one full-employment equilibrium with a given consumption function and technology; that is, the economy has a chronic tendency to deflation.
12. This model of market behavior is much less benevolent than the classical assumption of arms-length transactions believed to be power-neutral and orderly. It proposes, in modern terms, a stochastic model of market behavior where the stochastic term resides in the relative, and changing, market strength of the transactors.
13. The last sentence in this paragraph was added for the second edition. However, Sismondi did not change his reference to "Illinois territory" from the first edition. Illinois was admitted to statehood in 1818, one year before the publication of the first edition.
14. This paragraph sums up the previous argument. Stated this way, Sismondi's reasoning can be seen as a combination of physiocratic ideas and classical demand-supply analysis. Importantly, he relates consumer income to the quantity of the gross product. While the postulated relationship is analytically fuzzy (as so much else of Sismondi's), the idea is part of an overall view of economic fluctuations—spending by consumers on the gross output determines the monetary value of the output, thereby either increasing or decreasing the income available to the factors of production, which in turn determines future spending. (See chapter 6 of book 2.) The market power of landlords invalidates the assumption of perfect competition and makes the attainment of a stable competitive equilibrium difficult, if not outright impossible.
15. The text reads *enceinte* which could mean either walls or city limits. Since *New Principles* was written well before the renovation of Paris under Napoleon III, the term *walls* was considered more appropriate.
16. Compare this to Alfred Marshall's arguments in the first book of the *Principles*.

Addendum to Chapter 10

In all countries where serfdom is established, the peasant is subject to harsh treatment if he does not show the zeal and activity his tormentors demand of him, and which, after all, can hardly be expected of him. But if the lord or grain merchant makes hardly any other advance to cultivation than whip lashes administered in his name, one should not believe that the peasants' condition who grow this grain is the same everywhere, or that they are very unhappy; on the contrary, it is, from a purely material viewpoint, singularly comfortable in those immense regions of Poland and southern Russia that export their grain through the Black Sea, and which offer it today at such a low price that no agriculture of any civilized country can compete with it. Perhaps some facts on these new territories, which affect the business of the entire world, will be read with interest, but which we have left out till now because they would have interrupted the continuity of our argument.

The limitless plains that extend in all directions north of the Black Sea seem, among all the countries of the world, the most suited for the cultivation of grains. A rich loam, partly laid down by the great rivers that flow through them, partly created by the remains of centuries of grasslands which cover them, constitute the soil to a great depth. No stone stops the plow here, no roots hold back the clearing of the land. The steppes of Russia and Tartary are covered with grasses rather than forests. Light work suffices for cultivation, no manure is brought to the fields, and wheat, sown broadcast, renders commonly fifteen to one.

But this rich region which, through the centuries, has been open to the depredations of Cossacks and Tartars, is almost totally deserted. For centuries cultivation will be able to expand here, and the population to increase rapidly. To this day its only industry is the production of grain for export, and of children, so as to produce in the next generation even more grain. There are no cities, no industrial or mercantile populations to consume the fruits of the fields, but only some nobles, each owning thousands of peasant families.

In that part of Poland which borders on Bessarabia,[1] it is common custom that the lord gives to each family, or cottage of peasants, fourteen *morgues* of arable land, equivalent to ten hectares French measure, or twenty-five acres English measure, and rights to common pasturage to raise cattle. In return, as the only quit-rent, each family is obliged to give to the lord forty-eight days of work per year; the day worker supplies his team of oxen for part of these days; all the remainder of his time belongs to him and his family; all the products of his lands and cattle are his, and he lives in great comfort, without fear for the future livelihood of his children because, as they get married and wish to move away from him, the lord takes it upon himself to give them a new piece of land and a new cottage; he calls for emigrants from all the neighboring countries, and he knows quite well that the only way to increase his wealth lies in an increase in the number of his peasants.

The income of the lord consists entirely of the grain his peasants produce for him by their forty-eight days labor on the lands he has reserved for himself. All of this grain is destined for export, because the entire population is adequately fed from what the peasants grow on their lands. This grain costs the lord nothing, except the perpetual lease of a portion of land without value; thus he comes to sell it at whatever price he may get for it. As a result, the *chetwert*, a Russian grain measure* sufficient to sow two morgues of land, or about a hectare and a half, and which sold ordinarily in a normal year for fifteen francs, and which was sold for forty francs in a dear year, is offered today for three francs and fifty centimes to four francs, delivered at Odessa, and even at that low price, the grain of these provinces finds no takers, while, again at that low price, the population, and with it the clearing of land, continues to make rapid progress, so that they can supply with ease all the markets of civilized Europe, which will leave it open to the Russians and the Poles.[2]

*According to Robert Hamilton, *Introduction to Merchandise, Edinburgh,* 1820, the chetwert equals 5.528 bushels Winchester. The chetwert is divided into two osmins, and each one of those is divided into four chetweriks. *Art. Russia, Dry Measures*, page 299.

At this price, the quarter of eight bushels of good wheat is worth less than five shillings at Odessa, and the hectoliter, weighing 160 pounds French, is worth less than two francs ten centimes.

Translator's Notes to Addendum, Chapter 10, Third Book

This addendum appears at the end of the first volume, i.e. after the end of Book Four. As Sismondi observes at the end of the introductory paragraph, this position in the volume was deliberate because he did not want to weigh the chapter with extraneous material. The argument appears contrived because chapter 10 could have accomodated this extra material easily and indeed would have benefitted from a fuller explanation of the comparative advantages enjoyed by Russian grain. It is more likely that it was an afterthought inserted later and left at the end of the first volume so as not to disturb the printing sequence. The addendum has now been moved to the end of the third book from its original position to keep it in logical proximity to the chapter to which it belongs.

1. This is an ambiguous reference because the area "of Poland" bordering on Bessarabia was either Rumania (known in 1826 as Moldavia-Wallachia) or the northern part of the Ukraine which belonged to the Austro-Hungarian Empire and was generally known as Galicia. The context could also suggest that, on the one hand, Sismondi might have thought of that part of Poland that belonged then to Russia north of Bessarabia, or, more likely, of the Ukraine east of Bessarabia which had been, at one time, part of Greater Poland and to which the description given here is quite appropriate.
2. Throughout the nineteenth century the Ukraine was indeed the breadbasket of Europe. Eventually Ukrainian grain had to compete with United States wheat as the railroads opened the prairies.

Fourth Book

Of Commercial Wealth

Introduction

This book corresponds to the fourth chapter of the *Encyclopedia* article. The muted criticism of classical analysis of economic cycles there is fully expressed here. The full employment assumptions of Say's Law are for the first time questioned openly and confronted with assumptions and arguments derived from business experience. The individual chapters of the book show that Sismondi must have taken great pains with his analysis. In addition to greatly expanding material from the *Encyclopedia,* he reworked several chapters and added others for the second edition. The additions show the influence of the depression of 1819, which was a part of the general post-Napoleonic decline of economic activity in Europe and elsewhere. The book also shows clearly the conceptual difficulties Sismondi experienced in freeing himself from the Smithian categories he had fully accepted, and that supported the Ricardian abstractions, in order to construct a model closer to reality. The major part of these difficulties can be traced to the terminology he used to analyze the circular flow of the economy, especially his use of the originally physiocratic concept of reproduction for the replacement of goods sold during the accounting period. It obscures his fundamentally sound idea that consumption spending is not automatic, particularly by high-income recipients—a reduction may bring about a deficiency in demand and consequent contraction of production. This book strongly reinforces the previously expressed idea that great inequalities in income will cause failings in the circular flow of the economy, since investment cannot be depended on to offset the shortfall in consumption caused by deficient demand. Some of the discussion has a distinct Keynesian flavor, and there are clear allusions to later Marxian usages.

1

National Prosperity in a Commercial System

[By labour man drew his first wealth from the earth, but scarcely had he satisfied his primitive wants, when desire made him conceive other enjoyments, not to be obtained without the aid of his fellows. Exchanges began. They extended to whatever had any value, to whatever could produce any; they comprised mutual services and labour, no less than the fruit of labour; and gave room to the formation and increase of a new kind of wealth, which was no longer measured by the wants of him who produced it, but by the wants of all those with whom he might transact exchanges, with whom he might carry on commerce; and hence we have named it *commercial wealth*.]

From then on such wealth was seen as entirely separated from landownership; it consisted of the collection of everything that man's labor had fashioned for his use, and made fit to satisfy all his needs, and to humor all his whims. From the moment that the products of the earth, of whatever kind, had left the hands of the cultivator, to the moment they came into the hands of the consumer, they constituted commercial wealth. During that period of time some are subjected to various transformations which would make them even more valuable to the consumer; if they are the object of any labor, they are called raw materials, because everyone who works on them forgets the workers who preceded him, and regards as raw the materials so used; others, already finished, and ready to be used by the consumer, journey to the place where the consumer wants them, or else await his pleasure in warehouses and retail shops, and then they are called *merchandise;* others again are destined for the consumption of the producers themselves; their value must be added to that of the raw materials the worker uses, and in that case they are deemed to be the circulating capital of the manufactures; finally, others are destined to help human labor and to increase the various products of his industry, and in that case they are called *fixed capital.* All belong equally to commercial wealth, and the several classes of capitalists, manufacturers, factory workers, merchants, retailers, sailors and truckers, employed in the production and transport of commodities, live equally from commerce.

We have seen that agricultural wealth apportions itself more or less unevenly between those who contribute to its creation; but that, for a nation to be truly prosperous, even if it is not important that everyone have an equal share in the fruits of the earth, it is at least essential that everyone be assured that he will obtain from his labor not only mere subsistence, but the amenities of life; and that population is checked before it comes to the point where it would fight over a miserable subsistence. A similar rule should be applied to commercial wealth. In one as in the other, it is not at all the net product, it is not the opulence of some owners or managers which matters to a nation, it is not even the achieved output quantity without proportion to its remuneration: it is the general comfort, everyone's happiness, of which wealth is but the symbol.

As long as commercial wealth increases only in proportion to the needs which determine its formation, it spreads comfort among all those who contribute to its creation; on the other hand, it causes but misery and ruin, at least for the lower classes of the population, as soon as its creation outruns needs. The farmer, the landowner who need clothes, will pay without hesitation to the person who will procure them, a share of the produce of their fields, amply sufficient for his livelihood, because they will find, by comparison, that such a share is much less than what they would need to consume to perform the work themselves. But if the clothier and the tailor have made more clothes than the landlord and the farmer can consume, or want to consume; if many clothiers, many tailors fight over a buyer, and offer their wares at a discount, they will obtain only an insufficient share for their livelihood, and the abundance of commercial wealth will cause the poverty of merchants.

A nation is truly prosperous, in commerce and in agriculture, if the circulating capital it has accumulated is sufficient to set in motion all the labor which is advantageous for it to employ; if any improvement, or any new product which the population actually needs and which it can pay for, will not remain beyond reach for want of adequate accumulated capital sufficient to allow workers to live until such time when they will be able to exchange their products for the income destined for them. This capital, which corresponds to an already existing income, and which this new income will replace, will not fail in any way to find an appropriate remuneration for the essential service it provides;[1] interest will be high, and commercial profits will be substantial, two new shares of income will be born from it next year; they will enable those who will dispose of them to live in ease, and they will contribute to abundant reproduction by rapid consumption.[2]

If capitals are, for a long time, below demand, it is unlikely that this causes distress, because the population they would have sustained does not yet exist; there is merely a lack of pleasure for beings as yet unborn. However, insufficient capitals already in being render a proportionally higher return; they make saving easier, and encourage it by showing the uses to which they can be put; they encourage the raising of children by promising beforehand the increase in funds which will make their employment possible. That is the condition of free America. There capitals are already substantial, but greatly below needs and demand. They leave many useful tasks for the nation yet to be done, much work by which a much more numerous population than now existing could live. The shortfall of happiness in which a population not yet born could have shared is the only disadavantage connected to the inadequacy of American capital; while all those living receive, as wages, as commercial profit, or as interest on capitals an abundant share of the income such capitals create.[3]

But when existing capitals have been destroyed, be it by some great disaster, be it by the prodigality of the capitalists, or of government, the remaining inadequate capitals prove to be out of proportion, not only with the needs and demands of consumers, which does not impose very painful hardships; they stand also in no relation to the workers they ought to sustain, and who, raised in greater abundance, are deprived of the wages of labor which were to be their income; these workers remain thus exposed to misery or to hunger.[4]

When, on the contrary, capitals are larger than the needs of consumption, the first unpleasant result of such superabundance is that everyone fights over their use, and their owners come to be satisfied with a lower return; the interest rate falls, the income of those who hold this vital share of commercial wealth decreases, and diminishes their happiness.[5]

This is not all—the entrepreneurs, regulating from then on the production they manage, not by the needs of the society they should supply, but by the capitals at their disposal, create more goods than can be consumed; and everyone fighting over customers is satisfied with a lesser profit in order to sell. The decrease in mercantile profit diminishes the income of all who live from commerce and reduces their happiness.

Finally, capitals larger than needed have not only stimulated an excessive activity among merchants, they must have had the same influence on workers: new factories have been established, not because of the certainty that their output could be sold, but because there was enough capital to make long term investments;[6] by offering wages that could not be sustained, family fathers were called upon to raise children. A new population was born by showing them the expectation of work which would not always be in demand. The number of hands is soon above needs, as is capital; hence, the wages of every worker decrease; this third class, which also lives from commercial wealth, has less income, less enjoyments, and less happiness.

Thus, parsimony, which accumulates capital and which alone creates new wealth, is not always a blessing; it can sometimes be out of step if there is no profitable use for its savings. A nation is in a state of happiness when it finds itself in a progressive state, such that it can absorb all types of development at once; if it can, at the same time, expand to new lands or reclaim for cultivation those it had before neglected; provide plenteously to the basic subsistence of its population, and for the food of a larger population that will be born; pay amply for the clothes, the furniture, the housing, the amenities of all kinds readied for it, and demand more of the same for the future. If the nation is in this condition, it can accumulate capital without fear. Its savings will bring new blessings to a generation to come.

But a nation halted in its progress must stop the projects which bring about such growth and those who profit from it.[7] If the nation cannot increase the total amount of provisions, except by reducing everyone's standard of living, or by buying it with excessive labor, then it must not push any further its agricultural effort or the division of land; if it cannot increase its commercial population, except by forcing from everyone more work for the same wages, it must fear the growth of its industrial population. If it can trade the total of its goods only against an income which does not grow as quickly as its production piles up, it ought to set limits to its labor; if the undertakings which it ought to support with its capital do not render a much greater return, it must set limits to the accumulation of capital. A nation which cannot grow, must not save.[8]

As each effect becomes a cause in its turn in the growth of wealth, nothing is more difficult than to imagine when such growth ought to start, and when it must stop. However, it seems that commercial wealth is but of secondary importance in the economic order, and agricultural wealth, which furnishes subsistence, must grow first. That numerous class of people who lives from trade can only share in the fruits of the earth if they exist; it must not increase except as these fruits increase also. It rounds out the nation, but it does not constitute it. And if sometimes small nations were seen to exist by trade alone, acquiring great wealth, and even great power, without agriculture, and hardly any land, it must be remembered that political divisions which constitute independent nations do not always coincide with economic divisions born from mutual needs.[9] During the disorders of the Middle Ages cities alone preserved their liberty, while the countryside they depended on, and which depended on them, remained unfree; hence, major towns can be seen to separate themselves from their provinces to form, without them, republics. Their prosperity seems to rest on trade alone; however, Holland did have need, for just such trade, of the agricultural provinces along the Rhine; the Hanseatic cities, of the provinces bordering on the banks of the Elbe and Weser; and the imperial cities, of the feudal states of Germany.

National development always needs to be based on the progress of income; thus, we have already stated that all commercial revenues are created by human labor, while to agricultural labor, which is born from the same labor, is given a second revenue born from the labor of the soil. Hence, the progress of agricultural wealth, increasing the revenue more directly, seems to be destined to give an impetus to all other growth that must follow it. The economists of Quesnay's school have given too much weight to this principle; they did not want to recognize any other revenue than that which springs from the soil; and they had assumed that trade, arts, and manufacturing have no other goal than to serve the landowner. We do not regard agricultural revenue in such a narrow way; it is not unique, it is only more plentiful; and if it does not grow at the same rate as the others, there would soon be a disproportion between production and consumption.[10]

Translator's Notes to Chapter 1, Fourth Book

Unlike the first chapters of the preceding books, this chapter uses the first paragraph of the *Encyclopedia* chapter as an introduction, and then adds an extended theoretical discussion on the nature of commercial wealth. The chapter echoes some of the ideas in the second book, especially chapter 6. Its main idea is the postulate that production of commercial wealth must be proportioned to demand, as opposed to the assumption that production will create the demand. If production outruns demand, a decline in economic activity will inevitably follow. The responsible variable for such a development would be overinvestment, caused by an overabundance of capital, leading to satiation of markets. Sismondi asserts in this chapter that saving is no blessing if there is no use for its accumulation, a very unorthodox thought for the time. One can only speculate why Sismondi was so sensitive to market satiation—most likely his short experience in a merchant firm, his association with his English relatives, and his duties as a commercial secretary to the Genevese government during the Napoleonic era gave him an appreciation of the relative powers of production in the new age of steam-driven machinery and the available purchasing power of subsistence-wage recipients.

1. The concept is a direct extension of Sismondi's period model in book 2, chapter 6. The wages fund sustaining the workers this year is formed from the income of last year. It is represented by goods and an equivalent sum of money, as in the physiocratic *Tableau*. In the present period workers create new goods which will replace the goods used up in the present production cycle. A

corresponding money income will be formed which will generate in turn the wages fund for the next period. The sequence will lead to expansion if in each succeeding period aggregate demand is slightly larger than aggregate supply. If the latter overtakes the former, profits will fall because of declining consumption, and the wages fund will shrink, leading in turn to lower incomes for producers/workers and therefore to a further decline in consumption.

2. As noted in book 3, Sismondi should have discarded the term *reproduction*. He would have simplified his model to see that, in a continuous circular flow, sustained consumption supports the generation of incomes, which in turn allow the continuous creation of his wages fund, sustaining the workers and their consumption.
3. Sismondi consistently argues that sustained expansion of an economy requires a continued excess of aggregate demand over aggregate supply. Marx appropriates this idea in his crisis model, which ascribes to overinvestment (accumulation) and insufficient demand the accelerating decline of the capitalist economy.
4. It is not clear what exactly Sismondi meant by a *great disaster* (perhaps he had in mind the recent events during the Napoleonic wars), nor what he meant by the prodigality of capitalists, but this short paragraph describes a phenomenon of the business cycle that has recurred regularly with every new technology and investment in new real capital—displacement of labor and destruction of fixed capital as the economy adjusts to new production methods. Marx took this up in his business-cycle theory by postulating that accumulation will lead to overexpansion and subsequent destruction of capital values. The present problems with unemployables and the existence of a rust belt are contemporary manifestations of this cyclical and technological phenomenon.
5. Classical analysis would argue that a declining interest rate would increase consumption and diminish saving, but also increase investment, leading eventually to a new full-employment equilibrium. Sismondi argues, however, that a lower return on capital decreases consumption expenditures of profit recipients at the same time that the lower cost of capital leads to overexpansion of production and substitution of capital for labor, with subsequent declines in workers' wages and consumption. This omits price effects, but according to Sismondi's analysis lower prices, as a consequence of larger production, would accelerate the slide into a recession because they would lead to earlier satiation of demand and, therefore, a quicker decrease of factor payments.
6. The French term used is "longue avances." The analysis always returns to a guild-corporate market model, which sees direct knowledge of demand as a desirable organization and rejects any large market-oriented production. Curiously, despite the outdated idea advanced, the paragraph also seems to be descriptive of the merger wave now engulfing U.S. business—the availability of abundant credit is a prime condition for this activity.
7. This statement makes no sense in the conventional analytical approach. However, in Sismondi's cyclical period model it is entirely logical. If a business expansion crests, as for instance measured by inventory accumulation, any further investment made in response to available capital, and in the hope of future profits, must be disappointed, and will in fact contribute to the imminent decline. Sismondi would most likely agree with contemporary business-cycle policy, which would try to limit expansions through fiscal and monetary policy.
8. Sismondi clearly calls here for an expansion of consumption. By implication, he rejects the classical position that the fall of the interest rate due to lower

economic activity will automatically shift saving to consumption. Instead, he believed that capitalists will respond to losses in sales and revenue by cutting expenditures and/or expanded production to recoup gross revenue. Marx postulated the same mechanism in his theory of crises.

9. The reference is, as the next few sentences show, to the Italian and Hanseatic city-republics, but the sentence could equally well apply to the Netherlands and even Geneva, which was then not a part of Switzerland but an independent city-state. The reference to the noncoincidence of political and economic division clearly begs the question—if a city state can indeed become powerful and wealthy with little land, then Sismondi's primacy of agriculture does not really exist.
10. This explicit reference to physiocratic doctrine shows that Sismondi was aware of his physiocratic bias, as shown here and elsewhere in *New Principles*. However, his concern was really with his major theoretical preoccupation, namely proportionality between, and among, economic sectors. Since agriculture was, in his time, the dominant sector, he could not envision a well-functioning economy without prior and adequate expansion in that sector. To some extent he was indeed right—industrial revolutions presuppose larger agricultural outputs. Sismondi's insistence on the need for proportionality among sectors again anticipates Keynes—the stipulated equilibrium between leakages and injections in the various components of the domestic product is a more sophisticated utility version of Sismondi's required proportionality.

2

On Knowledge of the Market

While the management of landed wealth has given rise to many faults, to many wrong systems, it can nevertheless be regarded as very simple compared to commercial wealth. In the former, the goal to be achieved was steadily in view; those involved knew what they would demand from each other; the cultivator wanted to live off the produce of his land, and his needs were the first measure of his efforts. But he who lives from trade depends on a metaphysical public, an invisible power, unknown, whose needs he must satisfy, forecast their tastes, consult their whims and demands;[1] these he must divine without their saying anything, and he cannot afford to misinterpret them without risking his livelihood and his existence on each miscalculation. This condition, so critical to all classes who live from trade, is for the legislator already a strong reason to count much less on them for the stability and prosperity of the state than on the classes who live from agriculture.[2]

[The solitary man was used to labour for his own wants, and his consumption was the measure of his production; he fitted out a place to produce him provision for a year, for two years perhaps; but afterwards he did not indefinitely augment it. It was enough to renew the process so as to maintain himself in the same condition; and, if he had time to spare, he laboured at acquiring some new enjoyment, at satisfying some other fancy. Society has never done anything by commerce, except sharing among all its members what the isolated man would have prepared solely for himself.[3] Each labours,] afterwards, to keep up this provision, [according as consumption destroys a part of it; and since the division of labour and the improvement of arts allow more and more work to be done, each, perceiving that he has already provided for the reproduction of what has been consumed, studies to awaken new tastes and new fancies which he may satisfy.

But when a man laboured for himself alone, he never dreamt of those fancies, till he had provided for his wants; his time was his revenue; his time formed also his whole means of production. There was no room to fear, that the one would not be exactly proportioned to the other; that he would ever work to satisfy an inclination that he did not feel, or which he valued less than a want. But when trade was introduced, and each no longer laboured for himself, but for an unknown person, the different proportions, subsisting between the desire and what could satisfy it, between the labour and the revenue, were no longer equally certain; they were independent of each other, and every workman was obliged to regulate his conduct by guessing on a subject, concerning which the most skilful had nothing but conjectural information.

The isolated man's knowledge of his own means and his own wants, required to be replaced by a knowledge of the market, for which the social man was labouring; of its demands and its extent.

The number of consumers, their tastes, the extent of their consumption, and their income, regulate the market for which every producer labours. Each of these four elements is variable, independently of the rest, and each of their variations accelerates or retards the sale. The number of consumers may decrease,] if a war has ravaged a country to which trade is directed, if sickness, famine, or poverty have increased mortality there; if the government on which the country relies has placed, as a policy, obstacles in the way of communication between buyers and sellers; if these new obstacles are a consequence of nature, such that the roads are poorer, more dangerous, and more expensive,[4] so that goods cannot go as far for the same price; finally, if new producers have entered into competition with old ones; because the more sellers for a given number of buyers, each seller's share will be smaller.[5]

The [tastes of consumers may be changed by fashion,] by a longer or shorter interruption of old habits which have led to new ones; by the introduction into the country of new products, more elegant, more convenient, and less expensive than the old ones; by a change in religious beliefs in the majority of the population, which could, for instance, lead to a demand for fermented drink among Moslems, or terminate a demand for dried fish in Catholic countries.

The consumption of whatever commodity can decrease independently of the number, the tastes, and the income of the consumer, merely if that income has been given another direction. A country threatened by war would have to make provisions for arms; another, threatened by the plague, would have to make provision for hospitals, and would decrease its other consumption expenditures, even if the calamity which reduced them did not strike.

[Finally, their income may diminish without a diminution of their number, and with the same wants,] if they will not have the same means to satisfy them. Indeed, if the income does not proportion itself to the population, the latter will not be enough to provide a market by itself. In vain is corn grown for those who are hungry, or suits made for those who are naked, if they have no means to pay; buyers, not needs, make business. If the income of the wealthy diminishes, even if their numbers remain the same, their consumption must decrease. If the circulating capital of the rich decreases, while the numbers of the poor remain the same, the consumption of the poor must decrease also; because, as we have seen, labor being the income of the poor, it only acquires a commercial value by its exchange against circulating capital; it is given entirely for that capital, and it diminishes in value if that capital decreases. Thus, no calamity can strike the wealth of a nation without contracting at the same time the market that nation offers to producers; whether its capital or its revenues are affected, either its wealthy or its poor will be the worst buyers.

[Such revolutions in the markets are difficult to know with precision, difficult to calculate; and their obscurity is greater for each individual producer, because he but imperfectly knows the number and means of his rivals, the merchants, who are to sell in competition with him. But one single observation serves him, instead of all others; he compares his price with that of the buyer, and this comparison, according to the profit or loss which it offers him, is a warning to increase or diminish his production, for the following year.] Unfortunately, that comparison is made by all the producers at the same time, all strain to make it their policy, and all, ignorant of the extent of the efforts of their rivals, almost always overshoot the goal they had set themselves.[6]

[The producer establishes his price according to what the merchandise has cost, including his profit, which ought to be proportional to what might be obtained in any other kind of industry. The price must be sufficient to repay the workmen's wages, the rent of land, or the interest on the fixed capitals employed in production,[7] the raw materials wrought by him, with all the expenses of transport, and all the advances of money. When all these reimbursements, calculated at the mean rate of the country, are themselves repaid by the last purchaser, the production may continue on the same footing. If the profits rise above the mean rate, the producer will extend his enterprizes; he will employ new hands and fresh capital, and striving to benefit by his extraordinary profit, he will soon reduce it to the common level. If the buyer, on the other hand, pays a price too low for compensating all the producer's reimbursements, the latter will, of course, seek to reduce production, but this change will not be so easy as the other.]

Political economy has established as a principle that production will as readily diminish as it increases in relation to demand; however, one errs greatly in assuming that this movement should be so regular; while the demand which increases production spreads general well-being, the superabundance which must reduce it, causes long and cruel sufferings in the body politic, before it has produced the expected effect. There is no proportionality between the good created by calling forth new workers, and the evil which is created later when they are pushed out of existence.[8]

The workers employed by a producer who cannot make enough from the price paid by the buyer to pay all his advances, are seldom able to change their trade; they were trained in an often long and expensive apprenticeship; the skill they have acquired is part of their wealth, they would give it up if they would turn to another trade. A new capital would be needed, which most often they do not have, to pay for a new apprenticeship; to the extent that even if there were a constant demand in another trade, workers would not go at all from one trade to another, but they will continue [to work at a lower price; for less even than the necessaries of life;] the output will be cheaper, but its quantity, far from decreasing, may even increase. The worker who gains his subsistence by ten hours of labor a day, if he has suffered a diminution of his wages, will seek to earn the same amount which he needs to live, by increasing his working time. He will remain at work for fourteen hours, and he will not rest on holidays; he will deny himself the time devoted previously to pleasure and dissipation, and the same number of workers will turn out more goods.

In the same way [fixed capitals cannot be put to another use.] A cotton producer has raised at great expense vast buildings for his manufacture, he has his machinery turned by a stream of water brought from far away,[9] he has provided every worker with an expensive loom. One-half, three-quarters of his fortune are irrevocably destined to produce cotton cloth. The price paid by the buyer does not cover any more interest and his costs; will he, because of this, shut down his factory? No, without doubt. In agreeing to lose one half of the income of his fixed capital, he continues to produce, and he will realize the other half, but, if he closes his factory, he will lose all his income.

[Lastly, the manufacturer himself must live by his industry, and never willingly abandons it; he is ever disposed to attribute the decline of his last year's trade to accidental causes; and the less he has gained, the less he is willing to retire from business. Thus production continues almost always longer than demand;] and when it finally ends, it is only after it has caused a loss of capital, revenue, and human lives, to all those who contributed to its realization, which cannot be calculated without trembling. The producers will not retire from their work, and their number will not diminish till a number of the factory owners have declared bankruptcy, and a part of the workforce will have died from misery.

No other error is more generally propagated than the one we are going to expose; it maintains itself in the face of daily experience; it is being reproduced by a clever English author, Mr. Ricardo, who has based very rash conclusions on it. One type of experience confirms it, it is true: in the same manufacture, the manager changes very rapidly from a cloth which fashion abandons, to one that it begins to favor; from striped velour to single color; the same building serves one or the other, the same intelligence in the master and the workers accommodates itself to the new work as to the old one, and the profit connected with the novelty repays the expense on some new machines. But almost all the steelworkers would perish before they would be able to take up cotton manufacture.[10] The turnover of factory owners and their circulating capitals, without being quite as difficult in actuality, operates nevertheless only with extreme slowness; that of the greater part of fixed capitals is absolutely impossible.[11]

To be sure, what we have said should not be understood in an absolute sense: that the profit of the producer of every commodity ought to be proportional to what he might have obtained in any other industry. Everyone, in calculating the risks of a new investment, is guided in effect by that first rule. In every country there is a going profit in trade in the same way as there exists a going rate of interest; this profit becomes the same in all businesses which can be entered and left with ease, and it serves as a basis for general investment. But every old business, and above all, every industry which demands long training and much fixed capital, utterly avoids such competition. Its profits can be much higher or much lower, for a very long time, compared to those of an industry carried on in the same country by people who have no way of going from one to the other. Mr. Ganilh has even remarked, with reason, that the profits of farmers are not at all proportional to those of commerce, all risks and personal considerations being equal. Habits are a moral force which is not subject to calculation, and the writers of political economy have too often forgotten that they are dealing with people, and not machines.[12]

Through a great reduction of interest on fixed capital, a decrease of the manufacturer's profit and the workers' wages, the price of goods is reduced, they find new buyers, and the increase in activity which misery itself has caused, can sometimes be maintained. Events will let us know whether the renewed activity of the manufactures, of which we have just recently been told tales of ruin, is not related to this cause. Often, the convulsions of a dying man seem to show more force than he had at the peak of his health.

[The buyer's price, on the other hand, is fixed by competition. He does not inquire what the article costs, but what are the terms on which he may obtain another to serve in its stead; he addresses himself to various merchants, who offer him the same commodity, and bargain with him who sells cheapest; or else he considers which will suit him best, among several articles of a different nature, but capable of being substituted for each other. As each is occupied solely with his own private interest, each tends to the same object: all the buyers, on the one hand, all the sellers on the other, act as if in concert: the sums asked, and the sums offered, are brought to an equilibrium, and the mean price is established.

The seller's price should enable him to reproduce the article sold, with a profit, under the same condition, in the same quality. His market, therefore, extends to every country where the mean price established by commerce is not smaller than his. His production is not limited by the consumption of neighbours or countrymen; it is regulated by the needs of those who, whatever country they inhabit, find an advantage in purchasing his goods, or for whom his producing price is not superior to the buying price. It is this which properly constitutes the extent of the market.]

Translator's Notes to Chapter 2, Fourth Book

This chapter was perhaps originally intended to connect the criticism of Ricardian analysis with basic Smithian arguments, but instead Sismondi only succeeds in distancing himself further from the master. Several paragraphs from the *Encyclopedia* are used, but new arguments are added that are far removed from classical market analysis. Sismondi repeats two interrelated arguments—first, modern production has led to the separation of producer and customer/consumer with a consequent absence of reliable market information; second, it has created relative immobility of fixed capital, including skilled labor, which prevents the timely transfer of capital among competing uses. Classical analysis assumed that perfect market information was incorporated in the market price, which would lead people to make rational choices. In effect, the Smithian postulate of the invisible hand was assumed to limit free will whenever there was a rational response to market price. To Sismondi the individual consumer has a much wider range of choices, and the variables that determine consumer demand are independent and can change in response to factors that may, or may not, lie outside the system. Hence, market demand is, to the producer, an only partially known quantity which may misdirect the system to over- or underproduction. In addition, the relative immobility of fixed capital adds to the uncertainty, because the need to amortize fixed assets before transfer to other, more profitable uses, prevents timely adaptation of production to unexpected fluctuations of demand. Sismondi rejects quite consciously the basic classical assumptions that the factors labor and capital are freely transferable, and that the consumer is a rational economic man—assumptions that are crucial to Say's Law. His analysis is based on commercial experience, as opposed to Ricardo's frictionless banker's view of the economic world.

1. The text reads "consulter les volontés ou les forces . . ."

2. Sismondi gives the impression that he did not particularly like the life of a merchant, even though he was apparently a capable apprentice-worker in Lyon. The argument advanced in favor of political stability as being associated with agriculture is still a favorite with governments to justify support schemes for agriculture. The family farm is represented as a source of food and manpower, of love for the soil and the fatherland, as opposed to the cosmopolitan inclinations of merchants and money changers. The greatly reduced contribution of the agricultural sector to total output in industrialized societies has had no apparent effect on this argument. Sismondi, as a member of the patrician establishment of Geneva, and as a historian of the Italian trading republics with their very conservative ruling class, should have had a higher opinion of the conservative instincts of the middle-class city dweller.
3. This clearly physiocratic statement is a strange one to make for a citizen of Geneva, a city republic that had lived for centuries from trade.
4. Sismondi still experienced the delays and costs of the European toll system, which would disappear during the nineteenth century with the spreading Industrial Revolution. At the time of the publication of the second edition of *New Principles* in 1826, cities had toll gates, and most roads were toll roads and collection points for government revenue.
5. The last sentence does not really agree with the beginning of the paragraph; Sismondi altered the text of the *Encyclopedia,* apparently as an afterthought, without correcting the sense. Originally, the last sentence read: "and finally, their income may diminish without a diminution of their number, and with the same wants, the same means of satisfying them may no longer exist." Here, as elsewhere, Sismondi employs a mercantilistic market-share argument to make his case for the existence of business fluctuations. Experience would seem to have vindicated his analysis—the implied assumption of unlimited demand that is the basis of classical analysis is a special case. Returning to this idea again and again, Sismondi is the first writer to recognize fully the productive potential of the advancing Industrial Revolution and the consequences of market saturation.
6. The text from the sentence starting with "Unfortunately, . . . " to the end of the paragraph was added to the second edition. The analysis describes rather well the phenomenon of competitive imitation, that is, rival producers entering the same market because it is seen as profitable—for example, McDonalds, Burger King, and Wendy's all setting up fast-food outlets next to each other on a highway or in a mall.
7. The use of *or* could imply that fixed capital stands in for land, or that interest and rent are equivalent to each other.
8. Sismondi appears to be the first writer to postulate expressly an inequality between the ascending and descending phases of the business cycle. Marx uses the same model to develop the concept of the reserve army, the proletarianization of the petit bourgeois, and worker immiserization. The Keynesian model incorporates a similar inequality in the postulates of downward rigid prices and wages and the liquidity trap.
9. It should be noted that Sismondi assumes for his argument not a steam engine, but a water wheel. While already fairly common in England, steam installations on the Continent were apparently still rare enough to be excluded from the analysis of a writer who was preoccupied with the consequences of technical change.

10. The sentence was changed from the first edition to convey the idea that (1) not all workers would perish, and (2) that the workers would have to be trained (*se mettre en état*) to change industry.
11. To Sismondi, specialization of real capital as a consequence of the division of labor and its limited transferability was *the* main cause of business cycles. He raised an issue then that has lain neglected almost to the present day. Mainstream analysis has dealt with the problem by assuming that real capital will be translated into financial capital via depreciation and obsolescence allowances, and the production process itself will make fixed capital transferable. As Sismondi makes abundantly clear, this approach abstracts completely from the time dimension and the losses that will occur during the amortization process, which in turn will have a feedback effect on the level of consumption. Recent experience with a purely financial approach to production suggests that it may have a negative effect on goods production due to neglect of long-term profit planning from new products, and excessive financial manipulation (for example, leveraging) for short-run profits.
12. This should be compared with Keynes's *General Theory,* chapter 22, "Notes on the Trade Cycle," and book 4, "The Inducement to Invest." The last sentence in the paragraph is directed at the mechanical application of long-run analysis and its Newtonian philosophical ancestry.

3

How the Seller Extends His Market

We have said that when the price offered by the buyer is above the amount needed by the producer to repay all his advances, and also to give him a decent profit, the latter will increase his production, in order to gain from the offered advantage. He calls new capital to his assistance, which he will easily obtain by offering higher interest, and he will bring in[1] new workers. At the moment when the sons of workers choose a trade, the owner of a manufacture is always certain, by the offer of a higher wage, to draw to himself all those he can employ. He will speedily seize on the inventions of the trade which can multiply his products, and the profit he can expect encourages him to advance a considerable capital for the installation of new machines. This is the course of true business prosperity; everyone prospers with him; his business profits rise; the capitalist who has lent him money gets from him a much higher interest;[2] the worker, a much higher wage, the manufacturer of machines, new work.

But this beneficial activity has been set in motion by a demand greater than the preceding production; and this demand assumes a new income destined for consumption. Hence, the prosperity of the manufacturer is the result of the prosperity of others. It is because others have become wealthier that he becomes wealthy in turn. It does not matter that the new income which is going to be exchanged for his production be born from the earth, or from trade, that it belong to his countrymen or foreigners, that it arose near or far from him, or that it be in the hands of the poor or the rich; for him it is enough that the exchange be consummated with profit for him; and it is enough for the general prosperity that the income be new, and that it demand new work.[3]

On the other hand, [as the division of labour incessantly augments its productive powers, and the increase of capitals daily obliges the merchant to seek new employment for industry, and try new manufactures, the producer feels no interest more pressing than that of extending his market. If he cannot find new places of sale, it will neither suit him to enlarge his manufactory, when his capital has been increased by saving, nor to improve his fabrication by performing more work with the same machinery, or the same number of hands.] With a given quantity of consumption, all that he will have produced in the new factory he will have taken away from the old one; all that he will have produced with his new machines he will have taken away from his workers. [The whole progress of his fortune depends on the progress of his sale.]

No other truth is longer known among merchants, no other is tied as closely to daily experience; it is therefore strange that it has been lost sight of by the modern writers of political economy.[4] [Since all the talent of the merchant essentially tends to increase his sale; since the main object of all mercantile policy is the increase of the national sale; since every commercial calamity is explained by the diminution of sale, what is to be thought of that doctrine which reduces political science to the forming of a greater and greater number of producers more and more active, and which supposes that, by indefinitely augmenting production, sale will also be indefinitely augmented?][5]

Quite to the contrary, the interest of society in the increase of production and commercial wealth ought to be tempered by considerations which do not concern each individual producer. Society demands that a new income call forth new work; it is sufficient for the individual producer that an old income leaves its old course and come to him; that it leave his rivals whom it has sustained, and give life to his own workshop. Society always ought to desire that employment be regulated by demand so that sales be general, and that no producer be at a disadvantage; but every producer, instead of guiding himself by overall demand, proportions his activities to the capitals available to him. He will always guide himself by the productive resources available to him, and not those available for consumption. The slightest attention given to the movement of commerce is enough to convince a merchant not to relax in his efforts because there is little business on hand, but on the contrary this serves as a reason to make him work harder in order to attract all to himself.

Government, far from pushing production indiscriminately, then seems to have the duty to alertly moderate a blind zealousness, one which turns most often against fellow citizens, at the very least against other people. In the first instance, this is against the common interest,[6] in the second, it works against humanity.

The increase in the income of the society or market he serves does not rest at all with the producer, such that the increases could be exchanged for an increase in production; indeed, all his efforts are directed to attract to himself in exchange the greater part of those incomes he has seen as already existing. Among merchants, it is regarded as bad form to win over each other's customers; but the competition that each engages in against all others does not present such a precise idea; and a merchant is not any less in a hurry to extend his market at the expense of his fellow merchants, than he is eager to proportion it to increases in wealth, if this offers him the exchange of a new income.

He will sell more if he sells cheaper, because the others sell less; the attention of the manufacturer is therefore endlessly directed to the discovery of some savings of labor, in the use of materials, that will enable him to sell at a lower price than his competitors.[7] As the materials, in their turn, are the product of previous labor, his savings come down at all times, in the last analysis, to the use of less labor for the same product. Whatever labor he sets in motion in order to erect a new factory, to build new looms, to take into his service water, wind, fire, or steam, he will not push his extraordinary efforts unless he believes himself assured that the usual amount of labor used will be considerably decreased, and that, in the future, in common factory language, a child can now do what ten men did before.

However, the goal of the manufacturer has not been the dismissal of a part of his workforce, but to keep the same number and produce more. Let us assume he succeeds; he will copy from his fellow merchants their practices; he will sell more, they will sell less,[8] the merchandise will decrease a little in price. If all the participants in that market are fellow citizens of the same state, let us see what the national result will be.

The other producers will imitate, if they can, the actions of the first; hence it will become necessary that one or the other lay off their workers, and that they do this in the same proportion in which the new machine adds to the productive power of labor. If consumption remains unchanged, and if the same amount of work is done with ten times fewer hands, the nine-tenths of revenues of that part of the working class will be withdrawn from them, and their consumption of whatever kind will be decreased by as much. Old trades will be lost, and with them that part of the revenue of fixed capital which sprang from their value; the profits of commerce will be established by competition, precisely at the point where they were before. Finally, only consumers will have gained; they will make a small profit on the purchase of their needs.[9] But that benefit is in no way proportional to the diminution of labor which causes it. The first manufacturer, if he has only made a saving of 5 percent by substituting a machine for his workers, will have forced all his fellow producers to imitate him, and to dismiss, as he did, three-quarters, nine-tenths of their hands. The result of the invention, if the nation is without foreign trade, and if its consumption is unchanged, will then be a loss for all, a decrease in the national income, which will make the consumption of the following year less.[10]

In truth, if the inventor of a new process were sure to be immediately imitated by his fellow producers, he would probably not put it into operation, at least not if consumption needs did not greatly surpass production. Hence he seeks to keep the process a secret; and if he succeeds he will garner to himself alone what was previously the wealth of all.[11] His fellow producers are forced to give the same discounts he does; in most cases they will continue for some time to sell their merchandise at a loss; and they will most probably abandon their old machines and their trade only when they will stare bankruptcy in the face; their former incomes will disappear; their very circulating capital will be lost; their workers will have been laid off and will lose their livelihood. On his part, the new inventor will monopolize that part of that market; he will gain all those shares of revenue which the old producers divided among themselves save, however, those he will surrender to the consumer in the form of lower prices.

Up to this point, in both cases, the discovery of a new process has caused a great national loss, a large diminution of incomes, and consequently of consumption.[12] And this must be so; since labor itself makes up an important part of national revenue, the demand for labor cannot be decreased without making a nation poorer. Thus the profit which is expected from the discovery of a cheaper process almost always comes from foreign trade.

[As policy is wont to comprise the obligation of social duties within the circle of our countrymen, the mutual rivalship of foreign producers has more openly displayed itself. They have striven to exclude each other from markets, where they came in competition, by selling at a cheaper rate;] when in a country a new factory process has been discovered which makes for great savings, that country overnight sees the number of its foreign customers increase almost indefinitely. The stocking producers of England, before the invention of the stocking frame, had only Englishmen as consumers; since that invention, until the moment when they were imitated outside their island, they have had as their consumers the whole Continent. All losses have fallen therefore on the Continental producers, and all benefits came to the English; the number of their workers, instead of decreasing, increased; their wages increased, the manufacturer's profit also rose, and the invention has appeared to have as its effect a general well-being, because all those who suffered on its account were foreigners and lived far away, whereas those who were made richer by it lived together under the eyes of the inventor.[13]

Each improvement introduced into industry, if it has not been the result of a new demand,[14] and if it has not been followed by a greater consumption, has almost always produced the same effects—it has killed, far away, old producers no one saw, and which have disappeared unsung; it has enriched, besides the inventor, new producers who, because they did not know their victim, have regarded each new invention as a benefit to mankind.

[Yet if a single manufacturer has succeeded in making this saving, which extends his market; or if the exclusive use of it is secured to him by patent,[15] his countrymen, also manufacturers, against whom he has made this successful competition, must support all the loss of it,] if we assume that he had divided before with them the foreign market he now monopolizes; [while he himself and the foreign consumer] to whom he sells at a lower price [share all the profit. In an age, when communication among different countries is easy, when all the sciences are applied to all the arts, discoveries are soon divined and copied, and a nation cannot long retain an advantage in manufacturing which it owes but to a secret; so that the market, extended for a moment by a fall in the price, is very soon shut up; and if the general consumption is not increased, the production is not so either.] It must therefrom be concluded that a system of encouraging inventions in the trades by patents is hardly judicious. Before the expiration of the patent foreigners will have discovered the secret, and the nation which subsidizes invention by a sacrifice it imposes upon itself, will never reap the fruits thereof.[16]

The manufacturer who, by an invention, has made it possible to serve his countrymen heretofore served by foreigners, should undoubtedly be regarded with more leniency. The effect is nevertheless the same; he takes away the livelihood of workers far from him, and raises new ones in his neighborhood; but this is the inevitable consequence of the progress of civilization. The former, who had counted on a foreign market for their existence, which must be closed to them by advances in industry, have from the start placed themselves into a precarious situation, where they must soon expect misery. The government has to applaud the rise of a new class of citizens who obtain an adequate livelihood from their work, and the friend of mankind cannot gainsay these new efforts; but he must sorrow that competition between producers must always bring new suffering to one among them.

Must it then be concluded that every invention which economizes on human labor is always fatal to a part of mankind? Without a doubt, no.[17] Society has not advanced except with the help of such discoveries; it is through them that man's labor has satisfied man's needs, as well as his enjoyments, such that the work of only a part of society has been sufficient for the luxury of all society, and which, while feeding an immense consumption, has at the same time permitted the accumulation of immense wealth. Every invention in the arts which has multiplied the power of labor in man, from the plow to the steam engine, is useful, but it is not usefully employed except in its relation to consumption. If consumers have need of a larger product, the invention is useful by giving it to them with the same amount of labor; if the consumers do not have need of a greater product, the invention will nevertheless be useful provided it will give to the producers a longer rest. It is not the fault of the progress of mechanical science, but of the social order that the worker who acquires the power to make in two hours what he made in twelve before, is not any richer, does not, as a consequence, have more leisure, but produces six times more product which is not demanded from him.[18]

Society is not hurt at all from the greater ability to produce that it has acquired, but it can be hurt by what it puts to bad use from what it produces and does not know what to do with. All labor called forth by an increase in demand is useful for society; but labor which has as its only goal the nullification of some other's labor is most often dangerous and cruel. When consumption is limited and cannot grow, when workers are already in excess in factories, when by the use of all their capacities they obtain only an insufficient wage, the invention of a machine which replaces a number of hands by inanimate force is a calamity, because the inventor, instead of using it to assist his own workers, employs it to kill the workers of his rival.

The remotest provinces of western America, when they wanted to bring to market their immense production, would have found nowhere enough workers to harvest their crops, enough seamen to sail all the ships which could have been loaded therewith. Never was an invention more useful than that of the steamship which, plying the vast streams of America, opened to remote growers a market that would have remained closed to them for a long time. The work of several thousand men is done by a small number of machines; but far from their use leading to the dismissal of any workers, it is the cause of thousands of workers being called to a labor which, without them, would have remained impossible. It is in accordance with such results that the application of science to human labor ought to be judged;[19] they are always advantageous in a country where hands are scarce, and where a thousand expedients must replace workers who are not born early enough.

We have seen that each new process that saves labor is followed by a reduction in the price of the product. This is the goal the manufacturer had in mind; he has extended his market by it. From this reduction comes not only a small saving for the consumer, but also an increase in consumption which can be quite large. The buyer has destined a certain part of his income for a certain expenditure; if the income is neither increased nor decreased, the consumer will probably devote the same share of his income to buy the same goods; and for the amount so destined he will obtain, after the price reduction, either a larger quantity, or a better quality, of the same commodity. He will have a much larger number of suits for the same money, or better suits; in either case, he will add something to his enjoyment, without actually adding to his wealth.[20] However, in addition, new consumers will probably be attracted by the low price, they will then seek a benefit which has been brought within their reach while, when it was more expensive, they only dreamt of it. In order to obtain it, they will make every effort to increase their income, either by greater effort, or by greater savings. In this way we have seen certain pleasures that were once considered luxuries, descend step by step to classes who did not have them. Glassed windows, before reserved to palaces, are found today in the meanest cottages. The seller, by lowering his price for his goods, contributes therefore indirectly to an increase in the number of buyers, or to the total amount of sales.[21] It even happens sometimes that he will create a new revenue by the desire he awakens in those who want to acquire what he has to offer, and are therefore determined to increase their labor and effort. Nevertheless, it is not generally desire, but the means to purchase that the poor man usually lacks, and if the latter puts himself into a position to acquire the merchandise of the former through greater saving, he will withhold that sum from some other producer.

There is therefore an extravagant sophism in the proposition so often repeated triumphantly, that in diminishing the costs of production the produced goods are put within the reach of the poorer classes, and that thereby consumption is increased. Certainly, consumption of this or that article, but not total consumption, or the total return offered for the production. The family which has but one thousand francs income, or which earns only one thousand francs, will not spend more than one thousand francs for its purchases, be it that a decrease in the price of glass, or stockings, allows them or not to put glass into their windows, or have stockings for their feet. The nation which comprises a million of such families, each having one thousand francs of income, will only spend one billion[22] for its total consumption, to whatever price manufactured goods will fall, until such time that its income is increased.

The seller can also increase his sales, without new inventions, solely by contenting himself with a smaller profit on each sale. The most active, the most industrious, the most parsimonious, can by that method seize the market of their rivals, or as this is expressed in business, spoil the market.

The Jews, who permit themselves practically no luxury or pleasure, are generally accused by other merchants, above all in Poland, of making all competition impossible by such extreme parsimony. For the merchant who is satisfied with a small profit the result is undoubtedly favorable; he repeats these small profits on an ever-larger capital, especially the one which replaces the capitals of his rivals; but it is not easy to decide whether the nation gains anything, even if it does not lose by such saving. The consumer doubtlessly profits from all the reductions taken from mercantile profits; nevertheless, the enjoyment he gains, making the use of his income so much more pleasurable, does not actually increase that income; it merely permits the consumer a bit more elegance in his clothing, or his furniture. As most often the pleasure attached to such elegance resides in its rarity, he is no longer conscious of the progress he has made with all his peers; the required use of a finer cloth, where previously a coarser would have served, adds nothing to his enjoyments. On the other hand, the loss of business revenue by the Warsaw merchants, for example, who are forced by the Jewish peddlers to close their shops, is a real decrease in income that would have given rise to a new consumption in turn.

Translator's Notes to Chapter 3, Fourth Book

New Principles is discursive, polemical, and theoretically diffuse—this chapter is one major example. Under an innocuous heading Sismondi advances a macromodel of political economy that rejects Smith's and Say's optimistic view of the coincidence of individual and social interests as a fallacy. Here he supplies the basic arguments for Marx's theory of exploitation and anticipates Keynes, years ahead of his contemporaries. Here, as elsewhere, he starts from the viewpoint of the businessman-merchant and the connections between consumption spending, levels of economic activity, and production decisions, including the relation between the latter and spending on machinery, that is, investment. He is not concerned with value definitions, and does not use a faulty value theory to construct a revolutionary analysis of the industrial system. His foremost aim was, as was Keynes's, to make the system work, to spread its benefits as widely as possible by limiting or abolishing the business cycle. Sismondi shared the goal of the greatest happiness for the greatest number with his classical contemporaries, but unlike them his macroview of aggregate demand and aggregate supply does not assume automatic equilibria between them, as postulated by the invisible hand and Say's Law. The chapter is a major step in Sismondi's uncertain and diffuse process of constructing an alternative to contemporary microeconomic analysis. It shows that the development of these alternatives was difficult and extended over a considerable time—some of these ideas were already in the *Encyclopedia*, as shown by the sections incorporated in the new work. The notes to this chapter also show that extensive additions were made to the second edition of *New Principles*, undoubtedly inspired by the conditions Sismondi observed after 1819.

The resistance of Ricardian economics to contemporary criticism, its major role in the Marxian canon, and its continuing influence on econon now raises the question of what it is that makes Ricardian ideas s factor in the methodology of economic analysis? Judging by the diffe. Sismondi's and Ricardo's approach to economic analysis, the inf. from the determinacy of the conclusions, a perception that econon science, even if the conclusions are false or misleading. In additic ...our theory of value clearly shows how ideological content can be successf..ly masked by appropriate terminology—as Joan Robinson observed in *Economic Philosophy* (1962, 14): "economic terminology is coloured. Bigger is close to better; equal to equitable; goods sound good; disequilibrium sounds uncomfortable; exploitation, wicked; and sub-normal profits, rather sad." Classical analysis added to the value-laden terminology a method of logical deduction that made the conclusions appear to be scientifically unassailable, true by deductive verification—it often takes a great deal of ingenuity to find in an economic argument the flaw that reveals the conclusion as a convenient rationalization of ideological bias. And it seems that the more certain the conclusion looks, the more it will be accepted, not only as a conclusion, but as a guide to future policy, even though it may contradict common sense or experience. It is Sismondi's failing, as a theorist, that he never developed a method supplying the certainty of classical and, by extension, Marxian analysis—unfortunately, the historian was at all times in active debate with the political economist—to him the myriad variations of human institutions always put into question the general explanation. The banker/broker, and his later disciple, the Hegelian revolutionary, had no such reservations, and consequently they could offer seemingly permanent solutions, even though they were shown later to be wrong.

1. The text reads: "*et il forme de nouveaux ouvriers*." The verb *forme* is here ambiguous, because it could imply the then-prevalent belief that higher wages lead to higher birthrates, and therefore to a larger labor force, or the verb could mean the more restricted idea that employers would train more workers for their operation—an idea consistent with Sismondi's observations of migrations from the country to the city. The translation assumes the latter meaning as more in keeping with Sismondi's thought.
2. A clear distinction between the lender and the user of capital is made, foreshadowing the later standard separation between interest and profit.
3. The most distinctive feature of Sismondi's business-cycle model is the assumption that expansion can take place only if a new revenue is created to increase the demand for new production, and hence also a new demand for labor. While Say makes the same assumption in his Law of Markets, he also makes the additional assumption that new production will generate this demand because the factor incomes derived from the new production will be spent when received. Sismondi does *not* make that latter assumption. Rather, he assumes consumption is an independent variable that determines new production; then the allocation between saving and consumption must change in favor of the latter, a conclusion quite different from the standard determination of saving/investment by the interest rate with consumption a dependent variable. The discussion in this chapter suggests strongly that Sismondi believed in the existence of some kind of a normally fixed consumption function, quite compatible with physiocratic theory. On the other hand, he is quite aware that new production will put new purchasing power into the hands of the workers, but being essentially pessimistic about the permanence of such new demand, he

quickly comes to the downside; that is, he assumes that demand will decrease mainly because machines will displace workers and thereby destroy purchasing power. He clearly sees a multiplier at work which will magnify any decrease of aggregate demand. This chapter should be compared with chapter 22 of Keynes's *General Theory* (1956) and his emphasis on the collapse of business expectations.

4. Since *New Principles* is also a tract against Ricardo, the reference here is mainly to him, and possibly McCulloch. Again, Keynes comes to mind: "the methods of the early pioneers of economic thinking in the sixteenth and seventeenth centuries may have attained to fragments of practical wisdom which the unrealistic abstractions of Ricardo first forgot and then obliterated" (1956, 340).
5. This excerpt from the *Encyclopedia* was a footnote there.
6. The text reads *"il est contraire à la politique."* Clearly, Sismondi had an explicit macroeconomic model in mind, recognizing the fallacy of composition, as opposed to the microeconomic model of classical analysis, which has as a macromodel the postulate of the invisible hand.
7. This should be compared to the philosophically much more elaborate analysis of Marx in *Das Kapital*, volume 1, chapter 23, 2. Marx does not add any more substance to the argument despite the elaboration.
8. Sismondi always assumes a fixed market demand in the short run, necessitating a battle for market share. The model seems to assume a limited number of sellers, with market influence, rather than the great number of competitors without market influence stipulated by classical analysis. The description used here again suggests Sismondi's experience—a city with a small number of merchants (or manufacturers) who know each other well and divide among themselves a limited demand.
9. That is, they will profit by lower prices, but Sismondi seems to also have a consumer-surplus concept in mind—lower prices than expected by the consumer for what he would have bought anyway.
10. This paragraph is comparable to Marx in *Das Kapital*, chapter 13. Marx adds to the common sense and experiental concept presented here formulations like this: "Naturkraefte, wie Dampf, Wasser, usw. die zu produktiven Prozessen angeeignet werden, *kosten ebenfalls nichts*." (Italics added.) *Das Kapital*, vol. 4, 13, 2, p. 404. The statement is false, but the intent is quite clear—since all value is exclusively created by labor, all other resources must be costless. Marx's analysis is as logically rigorous as Ricardo's, but it is for that very reason far removed from economic reality.
11. General patent and copyright laws did not exist when Sismondi wrote.
12. Sismondi always tied consumption directly to income, although the nature of the connection was not analyzed in any detail. However, the connection suggests a kind of consumption function with the laboring classes having a 100 percent marginal propensity to consume.
13. A still-valid description of export-led growth, which could be applied to the present problem of Japanese-U.S. trade imbalances.
14. The clause, from here to the next semicolon, is an addition to the second edition.
15. This means a special grant by government, not general protection.
16. The last two sentences in this paragraph were added to the second edition.
17. The material to the end of this paragraph and the next paragraph were added to the second edition.

18. A foreshadowing of the later argument that the total remuneration of the worker must include leisure and provision for old age and sickness. Sismondi was greatly ahead of his time in clearly perceiving that larger output must lead to more leisure for the producers, that is, workers. In his time, the generally accepted idea was that the market demanded ever-increasing production; therefore the worker was to be at the machine for the maximum time allowable, consistent with sleep and eating. It should be remembered that the sixty-hour week in the U.S. steel industry was abolished only *after* World War II.
19. This sentence was added to the second edition.
20. The next two sentences are additions to the second edition.
21. The end of this paragraph and the next paragraph are additions to the second edition.
22. Sismondi uses the equivalent term ''milliards.''

4

How Commercial Wealth Is Regulated by the Growth of Income

The seller alone has no means of extending his market which does not affect his fellow merchants; he fights with them over a given amount of revenue which must replace his capital; and the more he secures thereof for himself, the less he leaves for the others. An increase in this revenue does not depend on him; but every time such an increase occurs, he profits, and he becomes one of the agents[1] by which general prosperity spreads. Now, as we have repeated many times, the national income is composed of, first, for the wealthy, the profits derived from all fixed and circulating capital, and second, for the poor, the price of their labor exchanged against circulating capital. All consumption not exchanged against an income is a loss to the state; all consumption exchanged against a new income is a source of new prosperity.[2]

New income is created for the nation from all fixed or circulating capital newly formed by parsimony, and appropriately employed to create a new and desired production.

A new income is also created from all new labor which a circulating capital employs in proportion to demand; this fully paid labor creates or employs workers who did not exist before, or had been idle.

All new circulating capital that finds appropriate employment, or which creates a production whose consumption is assured without detracting from any other, then profits society with two new incomes, one for the wealthy, through the increase this capital will experience in its circulation—the other for the poor, by the labor to which he will give value. Both incomes will be exchanged for new consumption, and will proportionately increase the market of the sellers.

But an income that has merely changed hands is not in any way a new income. The merchant who increases his revenue by what his competitors lose, does not make his nation any richer; the manufacturer who increases his revenue by the wages he takes from his workers, adds nothing to the national income; similarly, the public servant who raises his emolument from what taxes take from the taxpayer, in no way creates new wealth. Each of them, through their consumption, will give to commerce a new advantageous sale, and stimulate a given production; but they will replace only the consumption of other citizens, whose income has passed into their hands.[3]

Likewise, it is not unimportant for the well-being of citizens whether everyone's share of ease and enjoyment approximates equality, or whether a small number has luxuries while a great number is reduced to subsistence; these two distributions of income are also not unimportant to the progress of commercial wealth. Equality of benefits must result in the steady expansion of manufacturers' markets; inequality, always further contraction. The same income is used by the rich as well as the poor, but it is not used in the same way. The former uses much more capital and much less labor than the latter; he benefits the population much less and, as a consequence, contributes less to the reproduction of wealth.

[When cultivation on the great scale has succeeded cultivation on the small, more capital is perhaps absorbed by land, and reproduced by it; more wealth than formerly may be diffused among the whole mass of agriculturists, but the consumption of one rich farmer's family, united to that of fifty families of miserable hands, is not so valuable for the nation, as that of fifty families of peasants, no one of which was rich, but none deprived of an honest competence. So also in the towns, the consumption of a manufacturer worth a million, under whose orders are employed a thousand workmen, reduced to the bare necessaries of life, is not so advantageous for the nation, as that of a hundred manufacturers far less rich, who employ each ten workmen far less poor.

It is very true, that the ten thousand pounds of income, whether they belong to a single man, or to a hundred, are all equally destined for consumption, but this consumption is not of the same nature. A man, however rich, cannot employ for his use an infinitely greater number of articles than the poor man, but he employs articles infinitely better; he requires work far better finished, materials far more precious, and brought from a far greater distance. It is he who especially encourages the perfection of certain workmen, that finish a small number of objects with extreme skill; it is he who pays them an exorbitant wage. It is he also that especially rewards such workmen as we have named unproductive, because they procure for him nothing but fugitive enjoyments, which can never by accumulation form part of the national wealth.][4]

A hundred families living in comfort would have fed themselves with better bread and meat, they would have drunk much better wine, or the better beer of the country, and they would thus have encouraged national agriculture; they also would have clothed themselves in better textiles manufactured in the country; their luxury would have been the possession of many suits of clothes, and enough spare linen; thus they would have given strong encouragement to national manufactures.

If the same increase is distributed among ninety-nine wretched families and one very rich, the encouragement they will give to national industry will be infinitely less. The former live off potatoes and milk, and as a consequence will consume the fruits of a part of the land ten times less extensive; they will clothe themselves in cheaper textiles which, therefore, demand less labor, and they will own many fewer suits to change into; hence, they will keep national manufactures much less busy than the former.[5]

In order that there be no interruption of work and general suffering, the single rich family that has accumulated all the income formerly divided among the hundred, must make up to agriculture and manufactures all the consumption the ninety-nine do not have anymore. Doubtless, it will maintain a certain number of servants who will help in the consumption of the fruits of the land; however, they will encourage appreciably less domestic agriculture by their upkeep, than that of far-away climates. They will bring their wines from famous vineyards in France, Spain, Hungary, and Africa; their liqueurs from the islands,[6] their spices from the Indies, and instead of employing the lands whose crops cannot be consumed anymore by the ninety-nine families, they will detach from them a part where skillful gardeners exhibit their industry; the rest will be compelled to look for new consumers. Likewise, for its clothes and furniture, the rich family can never use for its needs all the textiles the ninety-nine other will not buy anymore; but it will bring in the carpets of Persia and Turkey, the shawls from Cashmere, the mousselines of India; it will employ embroiderers and fashion houses; it will remunerate magnificently the efforts, the elegance, and the taste of a single worker, and it will leave without work the nine-tenths of national manufactures which the once-comfortable families have ceased to employ.

Is it worthy of mention that [whilst the effect of increasing capital is generally to concentrate labour in very large manufactories, the effect of great opulence is almost entirely to exclude the produce of those large manufactories from the consumption of the opulent man.] Every time an object, heretofore produced by the skill of a worker, becomes the work of a blind machine, it loses some of its perfection, as well as its esteem, in the eyes of fashion. The invention of tulles can be of benefit to moderate wealth, but it does not replace in any way lace for the opulent; and this is the same for all machine products.[7]

It is thus, by the concentration of wealth among a small number of owners, that the domestic markets grow ever smaller, and industry is forced ever more to seek its outlets in foreign markets, where even greater changes threaten it.[8]

All nations whose production exceeds their consumption, turn their attention equally to foreign markets, and since its limits are unknown, its extent appears unlimited. However, since navigation has been improved, trade routes have opened and safety has been better assured, it has been discovered that the world market was circumscribed in the same way as previously each national market; that the general optimism of all producers who sold abroad has everywhere raised production above demand; and that offers of a great discount producers of one country gave to the consumers of another was at the same time a death warrant directed at the producers of the latter; resistance to this commercial warfare has been violent and disorderly, but almost always popular, however opposed it may be to the first concern, the interest of consumers, who after all are all the inhabitants of the country.

Thus, what we have seen at the beginning of this chapter, that the domestic market cannot expand except through national prosperity and increases in national income, comes to be true again of the world market for every nation that sends its goods to foreign nations and participates in world trade; an increase in global sales can only come from world prosperity. It is only when men acquire new incomes that they can satisfy new needs and buy what we want to sell them.

[The manufacturer's market may, in the last place, be extended, by what forms the noblest wish of a statesman, the progress of civilization, comfort, security, and happiness, among barbarous nations. Europe has arrived at such a point, that, in all its parts, there is to be found an industry, a quantity of fabrication, superior to its wants; but if a false policy did not incessantly induce us to arrest the progress of civilization among our neighbors; if Egypt had been left in the hands of a people requiring the arts of Europe;] if Greece and Asia Minor[9] [were extricated from the oppression under which they groan; if our victories over the inhabitants of Barbary had been profitably employed in giving back the coasts of Africa to social life; if Spain had not again been yielded to a despotism which destroys and ruins her population; if the independents of] Latin [America were protected, so that they might be allowed to enjoy the advantages which nature offers them; if the Hindoos, subject to Europe, were amalgamated with Europeans; if Franks were encouraged to settle among them, in place of being repelled,—consumption would increase in these different countries, rapidly enough to employ all this superabundant labour, which Europe at present knows not how to dispose of, and to terminate this distress in which the poor are plunged.]

If we glance at trade news, the newspapers, stories of travellers, we see everywhere proofs of that superabundance of production which exceeds consumption; of a manufacture that does not proportion itself at all to demand, but to capitals which seek employment; of the efforts of merchants which brings them to throw themselves in a mass into every new market, exposing them in turn to ruinous bankruptcies in every trade from which they expected profits. We have seen commodities of all kinds, but above all those from England, that great manufacturing power, abound in every Italian market, in amounts which so greatly exceeded demand that the merchants, in order to recoup a part of their capital, were obliged to give the goods away with a quarter or a third loss, instead of a profit. The torrent of trade, repulsed from Italy, has spilled over into Germany, Russia, Brazil, and soon has encountered the same difficulties there.

The latest newspapers tell us of similar losses in the new countries.*[10] In August 1818, complaints were heard at the Cape of Good Hope that all warehouses were filled with European goods, that they were offered at a lower price than in Europe, without being able to sell them. In June at Calcutta, the complaints of business were the same. Above all, a strange phenomenon was observed, England sending cotton cloths to India, and therefore succeeding in working cheaper than the half-naked inhabitants of Hindustan, by reducing its workers to an even more miserable existence; but this strange direction given to trade has not lasted long, today English goods are cheaper in India than even in England. In May, European goods had to be reexported from New Holland[11] which were sent there in superabundance. Buenos Aires, Colombia, Mexico, Chile, were similarly overflowing with merchandise. Mr. Fearon's journey in the United States, completed only in the spring of 1818, showed even more strikingly the same picture. From one end to the other of this vast and prosperous continent, there is not a town, a small village, where the goods offered for sale are not infinitely above the means of the buyers, while the merchants strain to seduce them by overlong credits and arrangements of all kinds for payment on terms, and interest rates. No other fact appears to us in more places, under more disguises, than the disproportion between the means for consumption and those of production; the inability of producers to leave one industry when it declines, and the certainty that their ranks will be thinned only by bankruptcies. How is it that the philosophers do not want to see what everywhere springs to the eyes of the common man?

*The latter, relative to the first edition of this work in 1819.

The error into which they have fallen stems entirely from the false principle that makes the annual output, in their eyes, the same thing as the income. Mr. Ricardo, after Mr. Say, repeats and affirms it. "M. Say has, however, most satisfactorily shown," he says, "that there is no amount of capital which may not be employed in a country, because a demand is only limited by production. No man produces but with a view to consume or sell, and he never sells but with an intention to purchase some other commodity, which may be immediately useful to him, or which may contribute to future production. By producing, then, he necessarily becomes either the consumer of his own goods, or the purchaser and consumer of the goods of some other person."*[12]

With this principle it becomes absolutely impossible to understand or explain the best demonstrated fact in the whole history of commerce: the satiation of markets. With this principle it is equally impossible to extricate oneself from the contradictions about the meaning that ought to be given to the words *value* and *wealth* with which Messrs. Say and Ricardo mutually charge each other; it is impossible to explain how the profits of capital and the wage rates often fall at the same time when production increases. The confusion of the annual income with the annual product throws a dense veil over the whole science; on the other hand, all becomes clear, all facts are in accord with theory as soon as one is separated from the other.[13]

It is essential to state that Adam Smith had avoided the errors into which his disciples fell; also that Mr. Ricardo, in the chapter we have just cited, is busy fighting against him.[14]

Seven years have passed since the first publication of this work, and the trade revolutions which have followed one another during this time have evermore confirmed in my eyes the doctrine that in wealthy nations production was often determined, not by needs, but by the abundance of capital, and that therefore, in quickly surpassing consumption, it created cruel distress.

The crisis which afflicted English trade in 1819 has subsided, and the reawakened prosperity of manufacturing has been presented to me, again and again, as a proof of my errors. I could have answered that a free, industrious, and enlightened nation like England, has almost always the power to recover from its disasters; that immense capitals had been lost in 1819, and numerous families ruined, but that the opulence of the rest of the world had increased since the peace,[15] and that a new and large income, exchanged by foreigners against the products of England, had revived its industries. However, another cause worked even more powerfully; it deserves some elaboration.

*Ricardo, ch. XXI transl., vol. II, p. 105.

The opening of the immense market Latin America offered to the industrial producers had appeared to me as the one event which could most relieve the English manufacturers. The British government thought so too; and in the seven years that have passed since the commercial crisis of 1818, an unheard of effort was made to introduce English trade into the most remote parts of Mexico, Colombia, Brazil, Rio de la Plata,[16] Chile, and Peru. Before the government had decided to recognize these new states, it took pains to protect English trade by frequent visits of men o'war,[17] whose commanders fulfilled more diplomatic than military functions. Afterwards, it has braved the clamorings of the Holy Alliance and recognized the new republics,[18] at the very moment when all of Europe, to the contrary, planned their downfall. But, however immense the market be that free America offers, it would have in no way sufficed to absorb all the goods England had produced above the needs of consumption, if the borrowings of the new republics would not have suddenly increased immeasurably their means to buy English goods. Each American state borrowed from England a sum sufficient to establish its government; and although this was a capital, it spent it immediately during the year like income; that is, it used it entirely to buy English goods for government account, or to pay for those which had been shipped for private account. Numerous companies were formed at the same time, with immense capitals, to exploit all American mines; but all the money they have spent is the same income in England that is to pay, either for the machines they use directly, or for the goods shipped to places where they were destined to work. As long as this peculiar trade has lasted, in which the English asked from the Americans only that they would buy, with English capital, English goods, and to consume out of love for them, the prosperity of English industry has appeared brilliant. Not income, but British capital has been employed to stimulate consumption; the English, buying and paying themselves for their own goods they sent to America, have foregone only the pleasure to enjoy them themselves. Never had English manufacturers more orders than during that train of speculations in 1825 that has so astonished the world; but as the capitals have been spent, and the moment of repayment has come, suddenly the veil has dropped, the illusion has ended, and distress has come back even stronger than it was in 1818. In effect, production has again excessively increased, the manufacturing population has not ceased to increase; but an enormous mass of capitals, employed in hazardous speculations, whose returns will be at best very distant, was withdrawn from industry; the foreign buyers who for one or two years have eaten these immense capitals, have fallen back into their primitive poverty which forces them to parsimony with an additional enormous debt.

The crisis has thus returned stronger than ever; no orders for industry, no sales, insufficient wages offered to the workers, of whom a great number cannot even find work; the capital of the manufacturers entirely tied up in their finished goods which fill their warehouses; these are the signs of actual distress, and a growing disproportion between production and consumption. The suffering inflicted on the people is great, and perhaps will be prolonged, because the false prosperity of the last year has much aggravated the situation of England. The cries of joy with which the arrival of some orders are celebrated, the employment given to some manufacturers, should not deceive us. England has advanced 40,000,000 sterling (a billion)[19] to several states who have taken up loans, and a similar sum to several companies who have undertaken huge projects. These two billions spent over the last two or three years, not only cannot be spent anew in the next two or three years; it is highly probable that the very interest for this imprudently spent money will have to be waited for, for a considerable time. Hence, there must be an immense deficiency in consumption, compared to the artificial activity the lent capitals created. Yet, I am far from saying that the evil cannot be remedied; the nation has great resources, and the government is very agile. Only an experience so dearly bought will finally extend enlightenment: it must force the recognition that consumption is not at all the necessary result of production; the satiation of markets is on the contrary the inevitable result of a system to which everyone rushes.

Translator's Notes to Chapter 4, Fourth Book

The chapter states the central concept that Sismondi brought to the understanding of the business cycle: income is not at all times fully exchanged against the corresponding output because spending is a discretionary variable, and therefore Say's Law of markets is false. Sismondi recognized earlier than any of his contemporaries that the new age of machine production had the potential to expand output faster than demand—his description and analysis of the worldwide crises of 1818–1819 and 1825 show that he had a better understanding of the causes of commercial distress than did Ricardo and his disciples. It seems peculiar that a writer-historian-pamphleteer removed from the daily competition of the marketplace should have a better grasp of this economic problem than the successful London banker and the equally successful French manufacturer. But as has been noted several times in these comments, Sismondi looked at the world globally from a merchant's point of view, that is, with much sensitivity to the extent of the market, and this viewpoint had been shaped and sharpened by a period of great uncertainty. It resembles mercantilism in its concern for market share and assumed fixity of demand. From it comes naturally an appreciation of consumption as a determining factor in production and, thus, it acquires the Keynesian flavor mentioned earlier. It is probably no accident that Keynes included in the *General Theory* a generally approving chapter on mercantilism. Sismondi also advances in this chapter the hypothesis, which became fully acceptable only much later, that the global economy expands by export-directed production and a parallel spread of technology, with worldwide demand satiation as the ultimate end.

1. "Canaux" in the first edition was changed to "agents" in the second.
2. Sismondi always postulated a direct link between circulating capital and the wages fund. Therefore, for him, the circular flow is closed by the workers using circulating capital as the wages fund. Workers are assumed to have a 100 percent marginal propensity to consume. The spending of the remainder of the profits is in the hands of the capitalists. Any decline in the wages fund or nonspending from the remainder of the income of the wealthy must lower total consumption and leave a surplus of produced goods, decreasing the wages fund because of reduced profits. Any increased demand from whatever source, such as an increase in the wages fund because of higher expectations of future sales, or a new market overseas, will have the opposite effect.
3. A classic early description of the *crowding-out effect*.
4. It is noteworthy that these two paragraphs were incorporated from the *Encyclopedia*. Sismondi here anticipates the concept of the average propensity to consume and clearly shows that a more equally distributed national income will lead to a higher propensity to consume, inducing in turn a greater demand for more production.
5. A rejection, by implication, of the "natural law" of subsistence wages, advancing instead a determinate relation between aggregate spending and income distribution.
6. The reference is obscure, but may mean Greece.
7. Sismondi was only partially right there. As machine production improved, turning out better-quality goods, it became chic to employ and display machine-made goods as inherently superior over the changeable quality of handmade goods.
8. This discussion anticipates most of Marx's theory of the decline of capitalism and foreshadows Lenin's idea of imperialism as the last stage of capitalism, that is, the logic of capitalistic overproduction and concurrent underconsumption would force the expansion of capitalism to secure markets in colonies.
9. The *Encyclopedia* referred to Turkey alone. Greece was liberated from Turkish rule in 1831 after a ten-year war. The next sentence refers by implication to the hostilities and reflects the general sympathy Europeans had for the Greek cause, causing Lord Byron to fight and die on the Greek side at the siege of Missolunghi in 1824.
10. The note was added to the second edition.
11. Australia.
12. The quote was not translated, but is taken directly from the *Principles*, Everyman's Library, no. 590, New York, Dutton and Co., p. 192. There are no quotation marks in the French text separating "he says" from the quote.
13. Sismondi's point is again that income, while arising from production, is not necessarily spent on that production.
14. This paragraph is the end of this chapter in the first edition. Sismondi added the subsequent material as a discussion of the events between 1819 and 1826. His account shows his intimate knowledge of English and European conditions, undoubtedly gathered from his in-laws during his visits and by correspondence.
15. Sismondi refers to the peace negotiated at the Congress of Vienna. The reference here to persons who disputed his views is most likely to his English

in-laws and their business friends who were most likely ardent supporters of classical analysis.

16. Argentina.
17. The text uses "*vaisseaux de ligne.*"
18. The Holy Alliance was the alliance between France, Russia, Austria, and Prussia to suppress all perceived revolutionary activity in Europe and elsewhere, but in reality directed against any nationalistic movements, such as the German unification movement and the independence movements in South America, and any other attempts to overthrow ruling dynasties. England was an intermittent member of the alliance, but France's insistence on intervening in the Spanish possessions in South America to defeat the independence movements led to the declaration of the Monroe Doctrine in 1823, with British support. Prince Metternich of Austria was the prime mover in the alliance, with the main support of Russia.
19. This apparently meant a billion *francs*, but is not so stated in the text. The description of the crisis shows some significant parallels to the present problems with South American debt.

5

Of Wages

Since the comparison between the average market price, or the price offered by the buyer, and the cost price, or the price demanded by the seller, must decide what kind of commodities suit every country—what production, divided between the manufacturer and the merchant, and all those to whom they give a living, provides an adequate income; what production favors general prosperity and ought to be encouraged—it is essential to review the various elements which make up the producer's price.

Labor is the most important; and up to a certain point it is the regulator of the others, because there exists a necessary wage below which even competition cannot for long reduce the worker; whereas a reduction of interest on money, or the profits of capital, which are the other components of price, seemingly has no limit.*[1]

A low price for labor usually permits the manufacturer to make his goods at a lower price; it enables him to find profits in an industry which would be in decline in a country where wages would be much higher. He thus increases the sales of his business and gives it an appearance of prosperity. Indeed, low wages have often been regarded as the effective cause of the success of industry in a country.

But the price of labor can be low, either in reality or nominally, according to whether labor exchanges for an insufficient or superabundant quantity of goods needed for living. Money is only the sign of exchange, the worker has no intention to hoard it; as soon as he has received it, he spends it for the provisions he needs.[2] If these have a low price, and if his

*Mr. Ricardo has pushed this reasoning to its limits; he has regarded wages as the only effective cause of price. In order that his theory be correct, it would be necessary that workers be reduced to subsistence, and that they could not leave at all; luckily this is almost never true.

daily labor exchanges after all, not only for his subsistence, but for a quantity large enough for some luxury, then wages are but nominally low. A feeling of comfort is solely tied to abundance; only because of it is life worth living, and work is mixed with pleasure. When the worker obtains abundance by his labor, the nation must desire that worker's existence, because his life will be a blessing to him, at whatever low price the value of his daily labor be represented in money.

If[3] provisions are dear at the same time labor is low-priced, if, as a consequence, the workers, forced by competition, content themselves with subsistence, or less than subsistence, when they curtail all their enjoyments and all their hours of rest, and their existence is a continual battle against misery, then prices are really low and their lowness is a national calamity. Yet these workers do produce a part of exchangeable wealth, they do indeed use the national capital, and they give to the manufacturer profits; but this increase in wealth is bought too dearly at the expense of humanity. It has been known for a long time that an excessive division of land leads, in the agricultural population, to a state of universal misery, in which the worker, with greatest effort, does not receive a living wage and, although the activity to which he was forced results in an increase of the gross product, it has been recognized that this wealth, inadequate to feed those it should sustain, was a national calamity. The same is true in the same way for industrial workers. The nation impoverishes itself instead of growing richer if its income increases as one, and its population as two.

If wages are low only in a nominal sense, if the workday of a man, for example, only pays ten sous, but if for these ten sous he will have all the provisions or objects of basic need he would get before for twenty, national prosperity not only permits, but demands the creation of new industries. The low price of provisions which has caused that of wages points to a state of misery for the farmer. Apparently he does not find an adequate market for his produce; the consumers are too far away, and the freight costs too high. To establish a factory close by is even better for him than to open a canal from him to market—this brings the market to him. The workers who have settled around his farm will consume the produce of which he has too much; and their products, always less bulky than produce, will be exported more easily. Thus everybody profits; the farmer turns his assets to good account, the worker lives in comfort, and the merchant thrives.[4]

Often the prevailing opinion has considered the low price of labor a national advantage, without stopping to inquire whether it was nominal or real; manufacturers who refused to raise the wages of their workers were lauded for their patriotism, and governments helped them sometimes by fixing wage rates and enforcing them. It is difficult to conceive of a law more impolitic and more unjust at the same time. It is not the profit of the manufacturer that makes up the national interest, but the benefits manufacturing distributes among all the classes that contribute thereto—the sharing of everyone in the national revenue that is born from labor. [If government should propose, as an object, the advantage of any one class in the nation at the expense of the rest, this class ought to be precisely the class of day labourers. They are more numerous than any other; and to secure their happiness is to make the greatest portion of the nation happy. They have fewer enjoyments than any other; they obtain less advantage than any other from the constitution of society; they produce wealth, and themselves obtain scarcely any share of it. Obliged to struggle for subsistence with their employers, they are not a match for them in strength. Masters and workmen are indeed mutually necessary to each other; but the necessity weighs daily on the workman; it allows respite to his master. The first must work that he may live, the second may wait and live for a time without employing workmen.][5] Who is not filled with deep pain when he sees the workers of a factory town leave their work in a body because their employers are determined not to raise again wages that a year of frightful distress had lowered; when one sees them resigning themselves to every privation in the hope of finally overcoming the obstinacy of the manufacturers, and if one considers at the same time that every day destroys the small nest egg of an unfortunate family, that nakedness, cold, and hunger already threaten, while years of stoppages would not suffice to make the factory owner feel the grip of poverty? And while these unfortunates fight for a wage on which their lives and that of their children depend, in their despair they still respect a system that oppresses, soldiers and constables who watch them, who await eagerly the first disturbance to hand them over to the courts and their severe retribution; who knows even if not some deserters mingle among them to goad them to the crime everyone is eager to punish?

Nations grow rich if they increase their income, but not if the income of one of their classes is usurped by another; they grow wealthier if they sell a greater quantity of their goods at the same price, because then, in producing more, the income of the poor increases as well as that of the rich; but not if the opulent gain only what the poor lose, because the profit of trade is nothing other than the lowering of the wage. Even if the lowering of the price of labor would allow a greater extension of national trade, the new production it would create would be paid for too dearly if it would bring forth a miserable and suffering class. It should never be forgotten that wealth is nothing but the symbol of the blessings and conveniences of life; it is taking appearance for reality to create a spurious wealth by condemning the nation to what truly constitutes misery and poverty.

A wage is not only compensation for labor, reckoned at so much per hour according to its duration—it is the income of the poor; hence, it must suffice not only for his livelihood while at work, but also for work stoppages; it must provide for childhood and old age, as well as for manhood; for sickness and health, days of rest to maintain strength, either prescribed by law or religion, as well as for days of work.

Far from being advantageous, it is contrary to national welfare to encourage work whose wages do not provide for all of these differing needs. New work will always bring forth a population who will agree to accomplish it. Such a suffering and unhappy population will always be restless and an enemy of public order, it will also be dangerous to others as well as a burden to itself. If it exists, it must be saved from despair; but one should guard against calling it into being.[6]

If a fund is created by government, and administered by law to come to the help of the poor in their sickness, during inclement seasons and work stoppages, in their childhood or their old age, then this fund, which actually exists in England as the poor rates, will soon be regarded as a supplement to their wages; and if, after a train of social upheavals the poor find themselves anew in dependence on the rich; if there is again more labor offered than demanded, the poor, assured of receiving help in their old age, or their sickness, and for their children, will content themselves with a lower wage, and will resign themselves to only a part of what rightfully belongs to them, administered by others rather than by them, to serve them as a reserve fund. Yet, it must be admitted that, in this situation, if there would be no poor rates, they would nevertheless agree to work for insufficient wages; only, that state of privation could not last because their class would rapidly diminish.

In the state to which the poor rates have brought England, the income of the poor can be presumed to consist of two quantities—one part the inadequate wage they receive for their labor, the other part the funds raised by a public tax to help them. These funds which, during the last year (the year 1818)[7] amounted to 8,168,430 pounds sterling, must give support to one-eleventh of the population, that is, to 516,963 individuals constantly supported, to 423,663 occasionally assisted, a total of 940,626 persons, out of a total population of 10,150,615 individuals, of which about six million have no property whatever. Those on welfare receiving about 8 pounds 14 shillings per annum per capita can content themselves to live from a wage by that much lower. These 8 pounds 14 shillings their masters save from their wages were then added to the profits these masters made from the work of the assisted workers. Together[8] with the injustices or calamities which resulted from this disastrous institution, one must not forget the absurdity that landowners were deprived of a part of their income, to be handed over to the manufacturers, such that the latter could sell their products to foreigners without profit to the nation, being paid by their misery, solely in return for the loss they will cause to other ranks of society.

In general it is believed that something has been done for the prosperity of a nation if means have been found to employ the energy of children, and to associate them, from the tenderest age onward, to the work of their parents in industry. However, the outcome of the battle between the working class and those who pay it is always that the former, in return for the wages granted to them, give all the work they can give without perishing. If children would not work at all, it would be necessary that their fathers had to earn enough to support them till their strength had matured; without that the children would die at an early age and work would soon come to an end. But since the children earn part of their livelihood, the wages of the parents could be reduced. No increase in the income of the poor classes resulted from their work, only an increase in work, which exchanges always for the same amount, or a decrease of the daily wage, while the total cost of national labor has remained the same. It is therefore without benefit to the nation that the children of the poor have been deprived of the only happiness of their lives, the enjoyment of an age when the forces of the body and the spirit would unfold in cheerfulness and freedom. There is no profit to wealth or industry if they are forced to enter, at six or eight years of age, those cotton mills where they work twelve or fourteen hours in an atmosphere of constant lint and dust, and where they perish, one after the other, of consumption before their twentieth year. One should have to be ashamed to reckon the amount which could justify the sacrifice of so many human victims; but this daily crime is committed gratuitously.[9]

Similarly, it has sometimes been thought that the working class could be helped if it would be freed from the observation of the rest day established by church legislation; this would only make the situation worse. Forced as it is to exchange all labor it is allowed to give against its subsistence, it gives six days of its labor for what will sustain it for seven, because it is not permitted to give more; from the moment that a rest day would not be mandatory, it would be forced to work without pause for the weekly price it receives today. The first nation that abolishes the day of rest would, truly, have an advantage in extending its market by lowering its prices; it would declare war on all the workers of other countries, and deprive them of their livelihood, till such time as they would find themselves in the same position. But from the moment that workers in other countries would have renounced their only enjoyment, the advantage of the innovator would end, the market would close again, and work would have become much more severe for everyone.

Sunday rest is therefore not only a naive Hebrew observance, and not at all a superficial rite that belongs only to a single nation, like purifications and sacrifices; it is a law of charity which would be well observed by the different faiths, Jews, Moslems, and Christians. Such rest was not at all prescribed for man so that he could devote attention to prayers and religious observances, but that he may taste relaxation and happiness, that innocent merriment, that dance and song, all the honest enjoyments of which man feels the need, would also from time to time come to the door of the slave and the worker. The Decalogue does not extend a day of rest to the believer only, but also to the slave and the stranger who are in the service of the Jew; it extends not only to man, but to cattle and the ass which work for man, so that the beasts might know the enjoyments of life.

It is difficult to understand why this benificent law has been changed among the Christian nations alone, why with them the day of rest and merriment has been changed to a day of sadness. More than one baneful consequence has come from this unnatural strictness. The prohibition of innocent enjoyments has given a dark, and sometimes cruel, tinge to the character of the mass of the people; the banning of noisy activities has made them seek refuge in drunkenness. The more the observation of a rest day is actually distorted by the suspension of all public amusement, the more will drunkenness become a public vice; thus the morality which was believed to be given to religious observances, will be lost.*[10]

But, it will be said, if all the workers of a nation labored seven days instead of six, they would turn out more goods and produce more wealth. If every man would work twelve and fourteen hours per day instead of ten; if instead of working for daily wages he would work by the piece, and hence with all the effort and zeal that self-interest would induce him to put into his work; if every child began to work from the earliest age; if every oldster would continue to the last moment of his old age, then production would be infinitely increased. This is somewhat how Arthur Young judged France, which he reproached for its laziness, and who calculated the lost time, or more properly the time gained for happiness by the small landholders, compared to the great farmers and day workers of England.

This sophism tends to forget the essential principle we have identified in

*Recently Catholic priests have imitated the strictness of the English Puritans and have endeavored to ban the entertainments of the rest day; they have thus gone away from the beneficial institution of Sunday, and the traditional customs of their church.

writing the history of wealth creation: man works in order to rest; there must always be a repose which corresponds to the work which created his enjoyments. We owe to the progress of civilization the accomplishment that one man can rest for ten, for a hundred, for a thousand, that is, to have contrived that in resting he could consume in one day what others will have produced in ten, hundred, and a thousand days of work.

This disproportion is neither the goal of society, nor of political economy, and the warrant given to wealth; this is on the contrary its abuse.[11] If the childhood and old age of the poor is deprived of rest, if the hours given over to work are taken from the nights of the worker, if the hours devoted to the battle for subsistence are taken from religion and the observance of his beliefs, then by the same token you will be obliged to add to the luxuries of the rich new pleasures and new indolences, so that he can consume what the new work will have produced. Surely he will not thank you for having procured these new enjoyments, so dearly bought and so little appreciated; he does not even notice that his linen is a bit finer, that the knife he uses is a bit shinier, because hundreds of human creatures have been deprived of their sleep to create in him first the new desire, and then to satisfy it.[12]

Besides, the wealthy are not the goal of the social order; wealth is only desirable in a society for the comfort it spreads among all classes. As much as an increase in work contributes to an increase of such comfort, that work is itself a national blessing; on the other hand, as soon as those who perform it are not taken into account, but only those who will enjoy it, it can transform itself into a frightful disaster.

Translator's Notes to Chapter 5, Fourth Book

This chapter incorporates a short and modified paragraph from the *Encyclopedia*. It was changed but little from the first edition. Sismondi addresses the relation between the daily cash wage, the worker's actual daily subsistence, and his need for rest, support in case of disability, education, and old age: questions of general welfare that were not considered by classical analysis, except perhaps in the sense that the worker was believed to make provision for these other expenditures out of his wages by saving, an unrealistic idea under prevailing conditions, as Sismondi recognized. It could be argued theoretically that the subsistence theory of wages excluded saving by the very assumption of subsistence as a living-minimum wage. In describing the living conditions of the working class, Sismondi uses impassioned language which reappears, with extensive additions, in Marx's *Das Kapital*. Discussing the benefits the wealthy would get from higher income, Sismondi again shows the influence of Italian utility reasoning—he clearly sees that such an increase would bring less satisfaction to the rich than the poor. Combined with his theory of consumption-driven prosperity, this analysis supports his consistent advocacy of a widely and evenly distributed national income. No value theory is connected to his macroeconomic concerns with full employment and economic instability, hence Schumpeter's dismissal of Sismondi's work in his *History of Economic Analysis*.

1. The French term is *aller à infini*.
2. As remarked earlier, Sismondi assumes a 100 percent marginal propensity to consume for the worker. Therefore, any change in the wages fund must have a direct and immediate impact on consumption, with an equally direct influence on production. To Sismondi wages make up the major part of total spending in a nation; hence, investment in machines as another part of total spending is assumed to be less significant as an influence in the determination of general economic activity.
3. The second edition omits *mais* at the beginning of this paragraph.
4. This is one of the easy oversimplifications that the pamphleteer uses to make a point dramatically. Although this contradicts Sismondi's monopoly assumptions in the agricultural book, the idea of widely dispersed small businesses is in consonance with his overall ideas of a wide distribution of income.
5. This short insert from the *Encyclopedia* is remarkable for two reasons: first, that it appears already there, a much stronger attack on masters than its model in *The Wealth of Nations*; second, it presents in a nutshell the heart of all exploitation theories—the unequal bargaining power of master and men. There is a strong hint here of government as the tool of the ruling class, although this concept was undoubtedly seen in connection with mercantilistic wage and hour legislation.
6. These two paragraphs define clearly, for the first time, the true economic extent of the wage bargain. They go far beyond what was in Sismondi's time (and in fact for a long time afterwards) the customary definition of a subsistence wage—the general description used by Ricardo: "The natural price of labour is that price which is necessary to enable the labourers, one with another, to subsist and to perpetuate their race, without either increase or diminution" (*Principles,* chapter 5). The more extensive view Sismondi had of what constituted a living wage was contrary to practice—no thought was given for a long time to the worker's needs for rest, treatment of sickness, or indeed any other needs that were not explicitly connected to the worker's job and the hourly wage. The social consequences mentioned here were painfully evident at the time in English cities—displaced workers from the country living in subhuman squalor in crowded tenements, crime in the streets, in short, conditions so well described in Dickens's *Oliver Twist*. Although as yet the extent is much less, the present computer revolution has created similar conditions among what is now euphemistically called an *unemployable underclass*, including the new wave of the homeless, drug dealers, and simply the long-term unemployed on welfare.
7. The term in parentheses was added to the second edition for clarification.
8. The second edition leaves out *mais* at the beginning of this sentence.
9. This paragraph should be compared to Marx's discussion of the working day, *Das Kapital*, bk. 3, chapters 7 and 8, also the footnote on page 236 (Dietz, Berlin, 1937).
10. The note was added to the second edition. Sismondi was reared in the Calvinist tradition of Geneva, which had very strict Sabbath observances. It would seem that this particular opinion was influenced by the Catholic customs of northern Italy.

11. The last clause was added to the second edition. The idea that wealth is held as a special dispensation in trust for society, and as a matter of contract that imposes special obligations on the wealthy, accords with Sismondi's Calvinist background. It was already mentioned in the previous book in connection with landholding.
12. A prophetic description of *consumerism*. The brief paragraph again shows that Sismondi was ahead of his time in fully understanding the increased powers of production the Industrial Revolution brought with it.

6

Of the Rate of Interest

Wages and profit are the elements making up the price of every commodity. Wages represent the immediate labor by which it has been produced. Profits represent the advantage flowing from past labor by whose assistance production has been facilitated. In such profit, two parts are always distinguished—the interest of the capitalist which represents the pure rent of capital, stripped of all labor and all compensation for the talent of the person who uses it, and business profit, which is that very compensation, and which, while adjusting itself to the sum of capital used, yet shares its character with wages inasmuch as it grows with ability and decreases with mismanagement.

Merchants who are rarely able to distinguish whether they gain[1] by the loss of others, or by the common advancement of wealth, by setting their profits in opposition to the interests of the capitalists, have regarded commerce as much more favorable to the state when the interest rate was lower. Indeed, when a business deal brings them 10 percent on the employed capital, it seems better to them to put 6 or 7 percent into their own pockets, while giving only 4 percent to the capitalist, or even 3, rather than give 5 and only keep 5. But it is obvious that the advantage of one class is gained at the expense of the other, and that the national income is in no way increased.

A decrease in the rate of interest results only from one of two causes: either capital is increased for a given need, or the need is decreased for the same capital; one of these two circumstances is a means to prosperity, the other a calamity; and till one knows exactly which of the two prevails, and just at what point they unite with each other, it can only be concluded from a decrease in interest rates that capitalists lose a part of their income. If the decrease is the result of abundant capital,[2] the total income of society is increased; a greater capital produces a greater income to the capitalists, even though the interest rate may be low. On their part, the merchants profit doubly, both on the larger amounts and the lower rate of interest. A share of the income of the capitalists goes to the merchants; and taking the place of the profits they could make, permits them to sell at a lower price and extend their business. If the decrease is the result of a recession,[3] that share of the income of the capitalists is[4] cut off, because the merchants make no more profits; nothing is added to their income, and there is a national loss.

Accordingly, it should be clear that the efforts of many legislators to lower the rate of interest, or to fix it, [or to suppress it altogether,] are preposterous. The attempts at suppression and prohibition of all interest, in the name of usury, [has generally been the consequence of religious prejudices, and of mad attempts to adapt the Jewish legislation to modern Europe. The effect of these laws,[5] so opposite to the general interest, has always been either to force contractors to envelop themselves in a secrecy which they must require payment for, and may use as a snare for the unsuspiciousness of others; or else to force capitalists to employ, in other countries, that capital which they could not lend in their own neighbourhood, with the same safety and advantage.] Fixing the rate of interest is foolish because the profits capitals may yield being variable and dependent on the demands of the marketplace, the charges which have to be allowed for their use must vary with these demands and profits. Finally, the mere attempt to lower the rate of interest is impolitic. Such interest is part of the national income, and considered by itself, it is advantageous that it be large. Conversely, [a diminution in the rent of the national capital, is a national evil.[6] Most frequently, indeed, this evil is the sign of an advantage greatly superior to it, namely the increase of capitals themselves; but, in forcibly producing the sign,[7] we cannot at all forcibly produce the thing, any more than by turning round the pointers of a watch we can alter the flight of time.]

When the low price of interest is the consequence of abundant capital,[8] national prosperity is increased by the interest earned by all the new capitals, since the national income is larger even though the proportional revenue produced by every thousand écus be less. But aside from the greater wealth of the owner of such capitals, the business which borrows them increases because of the ease with which capitals can be obtained. [With more capital, the manufacturer and the merchant transact their purchases and sales at a more favorable moment; they are not pressed by either operation, or compelled to provide for the present by a sacrifice of a future advantage. Executing all kinds of labor more on the great scale, they save time, and all those incidental charges, which are the same for a great and for a small sum.]

These are perhaps the only advantages which flow from the use of larger circulating capitals for manufacturing, given a finite demand.[9] But more often need, or the market demand, is capable of expansion, and the augmentation of circulating capitals permits the production of a larger output, on which total profit will be larger, although proportional profit will be smaller. Thus, if a society that had twenty million circulating capital, yielding 10 percent, half on capital, half on profit, now has forty, which yields but 8 percent, divided in the same manner, the incomes of capitalists on the one hand, and merchants on the other, are not any less with 1.6 million instead of a million each.[10] A decrease in the rate of interest almost always leads the manufacturer to employ a larger fixed capital, and to advance further the division of labor and machines, leading to a new reduction in the prices of his products, which will be the subject of the next chapter.

An increase in circulating capitals, resulting in a decrease of the interest rate, and a saving in the conduct of manufacturing, is an advantage for each nation compared to all others, since it permits it to reduce its production costs, extend its markets, and to increase its sales at the expense of its rivals. But if a nation is considered in isolation, or if the entire business world is considered, increases in capitals are only desirable if the use to be made of them increases at the same time. Now, every time their interest decreases, it is a certain sign that their use diminishes proportionally to their quantity; and this decrease in interest, which is always an advantage to somebody, is also always tied to the harm of someone else, either among fellow citizens, whose incomes are diminished, or among foreigners, whose labor is terminated.

Translator's Notes to Chapter 6, Fourth Book

This very short chapter should be compared to Ricardo's chapter on profit and Say's chapter "Of the Revenue of Capital," book 2, chapter 8, of the *Traité*. Sismondi is closer to Say than Ricardo in dividing the return on capital into profit and interest, clearly labeling the latter as a return to capital alone, the former as a return to individual ability and effort. Both Say and Sismondi look at this distributive share from a businessman's point of view, while Ricardo, intent on establishing a comprehensive value theory, loses sight of the realities of the market place.

The chapter incorporates three small segments from the *Encyclopedia*, and some small changes from the first edition. The very brevity of the chapter can be taken as a preparation for the substance of the following chapters. One of the major points of Sismondi's theory of business cycles, the overabundance of financial capital leading to overexpansion of production is made here again, and will be elaborated in subsequent discussion.

1. The preceding clause was changed from the first edition, which read: "Les

marchands, auxquels il est toujours indifférent de gagner par la perte d'autrui, . . .''

2. The remainder of this sentence and the next sentence were added to the second edition.
3. The French term is ''suspension des affaires.''
4. The following clause, to the semicolon, was changed from the first edition, which read: ''passe aussi aux negocians *(sic)*, pour compenser le profit qu'ils ne font pas; mais . . .'' The first edition left out *t*'s in words like *negociants*.
5. The *Encyclopedia* text was changed for *New Principles*. The French text here is ''Elles n'ont jamais eu d'autre résultat que de forcer . . .'' The *Encyclopedia* version has been retained to maintain the integrity of the citation.
6. Sismondi uses the term ''la rente des capitaux nationaux.'' Above he used ''*le loyer*,'' which was translated as 'the charges.' It is noteworthy that he clearly equates rent and interest as charges for the use of a factor of production, in contrast to Ricardo's view of rent.
7. Sismondi translated ''en augmentant le symptome'' as ''in forcibly producing the sign.''
8. The material from here to the bracket, indicating *Encyclopedia* text, is changed from the first edition. It reads there: ''il en resulte de grands avantages pour le commerce, et une augmentation de débit, qui est accompagnée d'une augmentation réelle de revenues.''
9. The French text reads: ''lorsque le besoin est borne.'' Sismondi was at all times preoccupied with the extent of the market relative to production, and he was a pessimist as far as the ability of the market to absorb all goods offered was concerned.
10. No money denomination is used, thus making the example quite general, although it can be assumed that francs were meant.

7

Of the Division of Labor and Machinery

[Abundance of capital and a reduction in the rate of interest][1] almost always lead the manufacturer to use two devices which generally go together, division of labor and machinery. Both tend to reduce his cost of production, and therefore extend his sales. The division of labor presumes an operation conducted on a much larger scale; because every worker is restricted to a single operation, he will find it possible to engage in it at all times; it therefore demands more circulating capital; on the other hand, the proliferation of machines which replace or reduce human labor always demands an initially high investment, which will only be returned in small instalments; it therefore also presupposes possession of idle capital that can be withdrawn from present needs in order to provide a kind of perpetual rent.

[The increasing divison of labour forms, as we have seen, the chief cause of increase in its productive powers; each makes better what he is constantly engaged in making, and when, at length his whole labour is reduced to the simplest operation, he comes to perform it with such ease and rapidity, that the eye cannot make us comprehend how the address of man should arrive at such precision and promptitude.[2]

Often also this divison leads to the discovery, that as the workman is now worth nothing more than a machine, a machine may in fact supply his place. Several important inventions in mechanics applied to the arts,[3] have thus sprung] from a similar observation of the worker, or he who employs him; [but, by the influence of this division, man has lost in intelligence], in bodily strength, in health, in enjoyment, [all that he has gained in the power of producing wealth.

It is by the variety of its operations that our soul is unfolded; it is to procure citizens that a nation wishes to have men, not to procure machines fit for operations a little more complicated than those performed by fire or water. The division of labour has conferred a value on operations so simple, that children, from the tenderest age, are capable of executing them; and children, before having developed any of their faculties, before having experienced any enjoyment of life, are accordingly condemned to put a wheel in motion, to turn a spindle, to empty a bobbin. More lace, more pins, more threads, and cloth of cotton or silk, are the fruit of this great division of labour; but how dearly have we purchased them, if it is by this moral sacrifice of so many millions of human beings.][4]

When division of labor exists, a part of national capital has always been fixed, not in a machine, but in the worker himself who operates the machine.[5] He had to serve a stated apprenticeship, a prescribed use of his time, a certain[6] consumption of subsistence without income, in order to acquire that competence by which he excels the average. The pinmaker, the weaver, the worker in a spinning mill, know how to produce more than the unskilled[7] manual worker; they have acquired the knowledge of their trade by much labor and much longer privations. No one comments on the use and waste of the capital they have created, because it is built on their small advances, or the small savings of their parents. Yet, it has really cost a certain amount, and their work ought to pay an annuity on sunk capital, over and above the usual wage.[8] Most often in business recessions, the opposite happens; one sees the factory worker labor at a lower wage than that earned by a farm worker, or a bricklayer's helper; the skill he has acquired has only served to confirm the insufficient value of his work, so as to make it equal to the price of his subsistence.

Although the uniformity of operations to which all workers' activities in a factory are reduced, seemingly ought to harm their intelligence, it is only fair to say that in England, according to the observations of the best judges, the factory workers are superior in intelligence, in knowledge and morality, to farm workers. They owe these advantages to the numerous means of instruction which, in that country, have been brought within the reach of all ranks of the people. Living continually together, less tired out by fatigue, and much more able to engage in conversation, ideas have spread much faster among them; since they have been awakened, emulation has put them soon well above the workers of any other country. This moral advantage is in other ways more important than the increase in wealth; just as, on the other hand, the spiritual degradation which has been observed to follow the establishment of many manufactures is an evil which no increase in production would be able to compensate.[9] It is a calamity to have called into existence a man who has been at the same time deprived of all enjoyments which make life worth living, to have given to a nation a citizen who has no love for it, and no attachment to the established order; at the same time, this is a poor economic speculation, since if that man will create by his work a revenue equal to his cost, he will not replace the capital which had been stored to fashion him.[10]

The employment of machines to replace human labor is an operation similar to the call for, and creation of, new workers. In the same way, a decrease in the rate of interest begins a search for a productive use of superabundant capital. Similarly, an increase in production flowing therefrom is an advantage if it were called forth by demand, and if it would only correspond to an increase in consumption; but it is a cause of general misery if it were only caused by increases in capitals, and not by increases in incomes, because this gives to the innovator merely a means to wage war on his fellow-members, taking away their business.[11]

[At the renovation of arts and civilization, there was so much work to be done, and so few hands to do it; oppression had so far reduced the poor class; there remained so much uncultivated land in the country; so many ill-supplied trades in the towns; and sovereigns required so many soldiers for war, that it seemed workmanship could never be economized enough, since an artisan, sent away from one trade, would always find ten others ready to receive him. Circumstances are not now the same; our labour is scarcely sufficient for the labourers.] We have already shown some causes for that, and we shall see others elsewhere; [in the mean time, surely no one will maintain that it can be advantageous to substitute a machine for a man, if this man cannot find work elsewhere; or that it is not better to have the population composed of citizens than of steam-engines, even though the cotton cloth of the first should be a little dearer than that of the second.]

A greater division of labor, always tied to a greater circulating capital, and to the use of a larger fixed capital, can give an advantage to the entrepreneur and make his manufacture flourish, without having to again conclude that this leads to a social benefit. If he was led to such an expansion by a greater demand, then benefit is certain; since he will pay the same wages to his workers, even though a larger circulating capital be employed to support a larger number of them;[12] he will pay the same interest to the capitalist, even though the machines he will have built employ new capitals; he will reserve the same proportional profit to himself, although it is now taken from a much larger amount.

If the manufacturer was not at all led by a new demand, but by an offer of overabundant capitals, whose owners agreed to have them employed at a much lower return, the use of these capitals to build new machines that will enable him to sell at lower prices and, consequently, to look for new consumers farther away, may still be a national advantage, acquired at the expense of foreign producers. He will create an income for capitals which, without him, would have remained idle; he will not decrease the wages of his fellow-citizens, even though he makes his foreign competitors lose their wages; and he will have created a mercantile profit for himself from the same new capital that will pay interest to the lender.[13]

But if the manufacturer, without an increase in demand, and without an increase in capitals, merely converts a part of his circulating capital into machines, and lays off a number of his workers proportional to the work he has done by his blind servants, and without extending his sales, only increases his profit because he produces what he sells at a lower price, the social loss will be certain whatever the advantage he finds there for his own account. These three different cases nevertheless do not occur at all in a clearly isolated way; a small increase in demand is often followed by production that far surpasses it; the capitals devoted to new machines can be partly new, partly taken from circulating capital that paid wages; and the result of these various combinations is further complicated inasmuch as the manufacturer himself can rarely know if he has created the demand, or it has come to seek him out.

In a country where provisions are dirt cheap, a manufacture which employs much labor is proper, because it multiplies consumers of its provisions. Similarly, in a country where capitals are cheap, a manufacture that uses up much capital, that demands very large investments, can be proper, because it will make capitals fruitful which did not find any employment. However, it is still easier to shift capital than industries. The capitals which do not find employment in a wealthy city can go and seek it in a poor city; but the workers who have been laid off because their work will be performed by a machine will run the risk of dying of hunger.

Abundance either of provisions, or of capitals, is a good indication of the direction that is proper to give to the working population of a country. Generally the same areas do not give to manufactures both these advantages at the same time. In opulent cities where capitals are abundant, even though provisions may be cheap, life is expensive, because rents are high. If any manufacture is established here, it must be of the kind which employs much capital, much science, and few hands. Conversely, in poor countries where transport is difficult, where provisions cannot be sold, where agriculture languishes for lack of consumers, if manufactures are established, they ought to be of the sort that employs many hands, little capital, and few scientific forces. Thus, the manufacture of watches and jewelry is very proper for Geneva; the more it is perfected, the more it demands funds and skills, the more it fits a wealthy city where life is expensive; therefore, on the other hand, that same city ought to give up the manufacture of lace, of linen and the wool trade, where unskilled manual labor enters into the price in a greater proportion than the profits of capital.[14]

Translator's Notes to Chapter 7, Fourth Book

This chapter raises for the first time in clear form in economic analysis the problem of incorporated skills, and the cost to society if these skills are wasted because of the advancing division of labor, that is, the increased use of machinery. In effect, the costs of such waste represent a social expense that is laid on society as a whole and therefore not incorporated in the market price. The extent of such unaccounted costs may be one cause of market failure. Sismondi has also quite modern ideas about the type of development that should be followed by societies that have different resource endowments.

1. In the *Encyclopedia*, this sentence reads as follows: "Abundance of capital, and the consequence of this, a low price of interest . . ."
2. The paragraph is a straightforward reference to Adam Smith and his famous pin factory. However, the following text shows that Sismondi emphasizes the negative implications of the division of labor, and the substitution of machines for labor.
3. *Arts* is used here and elsewhere in the sense of craft skills.
4. The paragraph already appears in the *Encyclopedia*, in an essay intended to explain the system of Adam Smith, an essentially optimistic view of the Industrial Revolution. Already, here, Sismondi is too pessimistic about the disadvantages of industrial development to repeat the conventional wisdom about the benefits of the division of labor. He had had, of course, much more direct experience with the darker sides of the Industrial Revolution than Smith could have had, but it also seems that he was much more sensitive to individual consequences of social actions than either Smith or, indeed, his own contemporaries. Smith had harsh words for the masters, but his essentially optimistic view of human interaction determined him, and his disciples, to accept the negative consequences of industrial development for the sake of more production.
5. This statement is a substantial departure from classical analysis, which tacitly assumed that the factor *labor* is essentially undifferentiated, that is, composed of unskilled workers. To Sismondi, the destruction of incorporated skills by technological displacement is one of the main causes of the business cycle. Declines of long-term living standards, with attendant declines of aggregate consumption, are a direct consequence of technological unemployment. Recovery will occur only after the work force has been restructured, with new skills and wage patterns. The skills lost are a direct investment loss to society. Marx incorporated this idea in his definition of *socially necessary labor*, and makes it a causative agent of his theory of crises.
6. This sentence uses *certain* three times. The first two instances were translated as *stated* and *prescribed*, respectively.
7. Sismondi used the term *ordinaire*.
8. This idea is an early version of Marshall's *quasi-rent*.
9. From the beginning of this paragraph to here is new to the second edition. It represents a significant modification of Sismondi's pessimistic view of the consequences of industrialization expressed elsewhere. Like other references to English conditions that were added to the second edition, this is most likely due to reports he must have received from his English in-laws. Some of these reports may have been self-serving and presented conditions in an unduly favorable light. On the other hand, Sismondi was an astute observer, and it is

quite probable, based on his other, negative remarks, that he supplemented hearsay with his own inquiries.

10. For the second edition, Sismondi dropped the ending of this paragraph from the first edition: "Telles sont les funestes consequences de l'ardeur avec laquelle chaque producteur, cherchant a étendre son débit, fait la guerre en même temps à ses rivaux et à ses ouvriers, et convoite un profit nouveau qui ne peut être pris que sur la vie des hommes." Clearly, the paragraph has been moderated in its pessimistic assessment of the results of industrialization. The concept of "the cost of a worker," as stated here, is the central idea in Marx's exploitation theory, and receives a similar dire interpretation in *Das Kapital*.
11. This is one of the many references to the inventor-innovator that appear in *New Principles*. The term is clearly used in a Schumpeterian sense, and was undoubtedly suggested to Sismondi by his observation of the hectic economic change in England and on the Continent. It is ironic that Schumpeter had a rather low opinion of an author who, in many respects, was quite close to his own views.
12. Circulating capital is defined narrowly here as a wages fund, with a close correspondence to Marx's definition. To define it in this way establishes direct connections between the labor force, investment, and consumption spending, a theoretical necessity for any underconsumption theory. It should be noted that Sismondi, in the preceding sentence, rejects the idea of the invisible hand, and again enunciates a version of the fallacy of composition.
13. In the light of recent experience, Sismondi's observations on export-led expansion have a prophetic ring. It should be noted that he is quite aware that one nation may beggar its neighbors, again a rejection of Smith's invisible hand and Ricardo's foreign-trade assumptions, especially his famous example of trade between Portugal and England. Friedrich List would later take up this line of thought to show that there is not necessarily an advantage to all partners in free trade.
14. Sismondi advanced here, for his time, a novel argument for the international division of labor in the sense that he disaggregated the classical theory of comparative advantage and substituted therefore technical development categories of labor and capital-intensive industries.

8

Results of the Struggle to Produce Cheaper

We have seen that the struggle instituted among producers to take customers away from each other leads to production at an ever lower price, without regard to the needs of the business world; and we have shown that, if those needs did not increase, the competition that enriched some individuals, caused a certain loss to others. It can be justly objected that new production creates in its turn a new income, and that, even though the demand which flows from that income comes only after the production, this would not prevent it from absorbing it. True, but the new income that results from the producers consenting to work more cheaply, must be less than the new production.[1] This proposition appears to us as self-evident; however, we will expand on it again with some examples.

The first effect of competition has been a lowering of wages, increasing at the same time the number of workers. Supposing that one hundred workers earn each, in a cloth manufacture, 300 francs annually; their annual product can be represented by ten thousand ells of cloth, their income and their consumption amounting to 30,000 francs. If, within ten years, there would be in the same manufacture two hundred workers, whose annual wages be only 200 francs per year, their production will be surely doubled, they would produce twenty thousand ells of the same cloth; however, their income and their consumption would amount to only 40,000 francs. There is therefore no corresponding increase to their production in the workers' incomes.[2]

In the same manufacture, a circulating capital of 100,000 francs yields annually to the manufacturer 15,000 francs, from which he pays 6 percent interest to the capitalist, or 6,000 francs, and keeps 9,000 francs for himself. The increase in capital and the decrease in the rate of interest has allowed him to enlarge his business, and to be satisfied with a smaller profit for himself, because he uses a larger capital. He has put 200,000 francs into his factory, he pays only 4 percent to the capitalist, or 8,000 francs, he keeps for himself only 8 percent and still believes to have managed his business very well; because his income has increased from 9,000 to 16,000 francs, and that of the capitalist from 6,000 to 8,000 francs. However, their production has doubled, but their incomes, and consequently their consumption, have only increased in the proportion of five to eight.

Still benefiting from an abundance of capital, the manufacturer has added to his factory new and sufficiently improved machines to double his annual output. He has invested 200,000 francs which he calculates to have placed to great advantage, because he makes from them the same profit as from the first 200,000 francs he has put into circulation, that is, 8 percent for him, 4 percent for the capitalist, in all 24,000 francs.

But here the decline in consumption will surely make itself felt. Ten years ago, the output was ten thousand ells of cloth, and the income representing consumption was 45,000 francs as follows: 30,000 to the workers, 6,000 to the capitalist, and 9,000 to the manufacturer. Today, the output will be forty thousand ells of the same textiles, and the total income, representing consumption, will be only 80,000 francs, as follows: 40,000 to the workers, 8,000 to the capitalist who has lent the circulating capital, 8,000 to him who has lent the fixed capital, and 32,000 to the manufacturer, of which 16,000 are profit on circulating capital, and 16,000 profit of fixed capital. Production will have quadrupled and consumption will not even have doubled. There is no need to bring into the calculation the consumption of the workers who will have built the machines. That is covered by the 200,000 francs which were invested in them, and thus are part of the account of another manufacture where the same facts can be imagined to have occurred in the same way.[3]

However, because production quadrupled, and the incomes it generated increased only twofold, it is necessary that there be somewhere an industry whose income quadruples while its production increases only twofold; or there will be a business glut, distress in the market, and finally loss.[4] Every manufacturer counts on the unknown, on the foreigner; he fancies that in some other trade, new incomes are created of which he has not yet taken account; but all industries resemble each other, all foreigners communicate with each other and compare their prices, and the calculation which has been made before for a single manufacture can be quickly applied to a whole nation, and finally to the market of the known world.

The facts we are presenting are universal; each manufacturer who will have expanded his business, not because of need, which would have permitted him to maintain for each worker the same wage while hiring new ones, to maintain for every capital the same interest while employing a larger amount, will discover the same results if he calculates the profit and loss of his factory. If, instead of merely thinking of himself, he makes the same calculation for the national sector of his business, he will see the same calculation again confirmed. Business can expand; but if its expansion leads to a shrinkage of what was previously paid as a wage, and as interest on every thousand francs, consumption will not stay in step with production, and the overall result will never be a greater prosperity.

This argument contradicts, by its fundamental assumptions, one of the axioms on which political economy has above all insisted: that only the freest competition determines the most advantageous course of industry, because each one understood his interests better than an ignorant and indifferent government could understand it, and that the interest of each is the interest of all. Both axioms are true, and the conclusion is nevertheless not right. The interest of each checked by those of all others would truly be the interest of all; but everyone seeking his self-interest at the expense of others, as well as in the development of his own means, is not always checked by forces equal to his own; therefore the strongest finds his interest in taking, and the weakest finds his in not resisting him; because the smallest evil, like the greatest good, is the policy of man. In this battle of all interests against each other, injustice can often triumph, and injustice will be, almost always in this case, helped by a public power which will imagine itself impartial, and which will indeed be so, because, without examining the causes, it will always be on the side of the stronger.[5]

To return to our factory, and we will see the interest of everyone, a compelled interest, lead him to an end manifestly contrary to the interest of the greatest number, and perhaps, in the last analysis, against the interest of everyone.[6]

From the natural progress of society comes a steady increase of capital, and from a fault in social organization which we will examine elsewhere,[7] comes a steady increase in the working population, and a supply of hands as a rule greater than the demand for labor. The manufacturer stands between these two progressive forces with his factory where he employs only 100,000 francs and one hundred workers at 300 francs wages.[8] Another capitalist offers him another 100,000 francs; it is in his interest to take them, because, as we have seen, it will bring his revenue from 9,000 to 16,000 francs. It is to the benefit of both capitalists to accept a reduction in interest because, without it, one half of the capital will remain idle, whereas by accepting 4 percent annually instead of 6, the combined income will increase from 6,000 to 8,000 francs. It is in the interest of the working class to submit to a reduction of wages, be it that it has really increased in numbers, or that demand for its labor has been decreased by machines. If it would take advantage of its numbers and destroy the machines, the police and army would drive them away. Everyone, in his self-interest, gives up part of his income, till he for whose benefit all sacrifices seem to have been made, and who appears ready to gather its fruits, finds in turn that when incomes decrease, less is bought, and that industrial production is not anymore in agreement with market demand.[9]

From whatever viewpoint one considers the progress of wealth, one comes always to the same end. When it is gradual, when it is well-proportioned, when no one of its parts follows a precipitous course, it spreads universal well-being; but if any one of its gears completes its actions earlier than all the others, there will be suffering.[10] We have seen what flows from a consumption that proceeds faster than the creation of income, and what flows from a production larger than consumption;[11] we are going to see what happened to an economy that created more capital than the needs of industry could absorb; an even greater suffering results from an increase in population greater than the demand for labor. On all sides it seems therefore that the action of every individual tends to jam the functioning of the machine. Perhaps the task of government should be to moderate these movements, in order to equalize them.

It is not that there is no room for the progress of human effort in the creation of wealth every time it exerts itself to add to the general fund, rather than fight over it; and every time that man battles against nature, and not with another man. Thus, [the application of science to art is not limited to the invention of machines] which, in themselves, were very useful because more production was demanded than the population was able to produce. Science has also served in [the discovery of raw materials, dyeing ingredients, preservative methods more sure and economical. It has produced better work at a cheaper rate; it has protected the health of labourers, as well as their produce; and its effect in augmenting wealth has almost always been beneficial to humanity.][12]

Likewise, when nations have done nothing but follow the guideposts of nature, and profit from their [advantages of climate, soil, exposure,] the possessions of raw materials, they have in no way put themselves into an unnatural position; they have in no way sought a sham wealth which turns to real misery for the masses of the people. [There is also a natural advantage in the superiority] of the capabilities of the people that compose these nations. Nature itself, bountiful in certain climates [seems to have reserved for those who inhabit them a superiority of industry, intelligence, strength of body, constancy of labour, which do not even require to be developed by education. But other qualities, other virtues, which appear to contribute more effectually still to the increase of riches, as well as to the happiness of society—the love of order, economy, sobriety, justice,—are almost always the work of public institutions. Religion, education, government, and principles of honor, change the nature of men; and as they make good or bad citizens of them, they advance or retard their approach to the object proposed by political economy.][13]

The intelligent and industrious nations will turn out more labor with the use of the same resources; the sober and virtuous nations will have more enjoyments with the same income; the free nations who love order will have more security with the same capital. No social virtues are ever lost, provided they are not put up for auction. The most wisely constituted nations will be the happiest, as long as they will not lose sight of the fundamental proportion between demand and labor; but once they descend to the wretched practice of working at a discount in order to take away customers from rival nations, neither intelligence, nor sobriety, nor freedom will save them from misery.[14]

Translator's Notes to Chapter 8, Fourth Book

This chapter elaborates and continues the basic macromodel that Sismondi introduced in book 2, chapter 6. He is seeking an analysis of the business cycle that will account both for social behavior and technological change. He anticipates many of Marx's conceptual "inventions," such as the creation of a reserve army as a consequence of technological displacement, the increasing organic composition of capital, and the reduction of consumption as a consequence of declining factor payments. However, he fails to address some of the important concepts of classical market analysis, in particular the influence of falling prices on consumption, and thus appears as failing the test of analytical competence in established contemporary economic theory. Sismondi is, indeed, more of a pamphleteer than a theoretical economist, but it would seem that his main problem is simply a different analytical viewpoint—he is above all a macrotheorist and this book nowhere addresses what was dear to the hearts of his contemporaries or later writers, value theory. Hence, price formation is only of concern to him inasmuch as it affects consumption and investment. In this regard Marx was much more astute—he made sure that his exploitation thesis was connected to a value theory, however flawed it may have been.

1. This sentence is theoretically false—the payments of the factors of production must add up to the value of the product. But this is not what Sismondi had in mind. He was concerned with competitively forced decreases of wages (the term *producteurs* must be taken as referring to workers) during the production period that would result in a decrease in net incomes, a likely increase in profits, and hence a decrease in consumption, that is, a failure to buy back total output. The main assumption is always that the worker will spend 100 percent of his wages for consumption, but not the capitalist. If the capitalist can shift income by simultaneously lowering wages because of competition among workers for limited work spaces, and raising thereby his profits, overall consumption will decline.
2. The implied conclusion is of course that the workers will be unable to buy back their production, thus creating a general deficiency of demand. Despite Sismondi's disregard of the effect of lower prices, the beginning of the chapter implies

that market competition, through lower prices, forces manufacturers to lower their factor costs. If it is assumed that market prices do not decline, that is, that manufacturers have market power, then the Marxian conclusion must be reached: profits increase, and the system will suffer from a permanent deficiency of demand because of overinvestment. However, if it is assumed that prices decline because of overproduction, the manufacturer will suffer a loss and discontinue his business, again leading to a downturn of the economy. The latter case is preferred by Sismondi, but Marx also uses this solution.

3. The example suffers from the same disability as its predecessors in this chapter—ignoring what must surely be, under these assumptions, falling prices. However, it can be argued that even *with* falling prices consumption will fall behind production because the *rate* of increase in production is faster than the rate of increase in income. Sismondi assumes no saving either by the workers or the capitalists; if he did, his argument would be identical to Keynes's. As it is, his argument can be interpreted to mean that expanding production will lead to saturation in the absence of rising incomes even in the presence of falling prices. Measured against the seamless argument of Say, the model is clumsy and easily refuted, but on the other hand it is the first instance in political economy of an explicit macromodel dealing with total spending.
4. The argument can be used to explain the rise of service industries to add to total demand, a point that Malthus makes in his *Principles*.
5. This paragraph is a conscious rejection of Say's law *and* Adam Smith's assumption of economic harmony in a free-trade economy. There is again the implication here that Sismondi had a notion of the fallacy of composition, but he bases his argument mainly on perceived inequalities of market strength, the basic argument of Marx's exploitation theory. The last sentence in this paragraph clearly foreshadows Marx's argument of government as a tool of the governing class and oppressor of the proletariat.
6. An anticipation of Marx's argument that the capitalist cannot help himself acting as he does because the market compels him to do so in his own interest.
7. Sismondi refers to the seventh book of *New Principles*.
8. The two progressive forces are, on the one hand, an increasing population, and on the other, displacement of workers by machines; see below in this paragraph.
9. The discussion fits well into Keynesian analysis. The example employed is "cooked" in the same way as any of Ricardo's, to which Sismondi objected again and again. To assume that two capitalists are only too glad to hand over their money to the manufacturer, one has to imagine that there are no other opportunities for investment, as stated at the beginning of the chapter. That in itself would already indicate a depressed economic condition, in which case it is likely that the manufacturer would not be overly eager to expand his operations. In fact, the conclusion of the paragraph describes precisely such a situation—a general pressure on factor prices that eventually translates into a general depression. It should be noted that two major Marxian concepts appear in this paragraph: the reserve army, depressing wages, and the increasing organic composition of capital, increasing the reserve army. It was perhaps Sismondi's fault that he failed to give his concepts concise and catchy names that would have engaged the imagination of the general public. It may also have been to Marx's advantage that, by the time *Das Kapital* was published, a workers' movement was in existence, ready for theories of exploitation.

10. The statement parallels present-day economic policy prescriptions, which propose to moderate expansions in order to prevent deep depressions.
11. Sismondi did not consider saving in this argument even though, superficially, this statement would suggest that the imbalance is caused by precisely the withholding of income from consumption.
12. This somewhat incongruous statement was taken from the *Encyclopedia*. Sismondi may have inserted it to preempt criticism of his excessive gloominess, or to ward off those comments that would inevitably point to the perceived benefits of machine production and the application of science to wealth creation.
13. The paragraph reflects more than anything else Sismondi's Genevese educational background, the enlightened humanitarian instruction he received in the gymnasium.
14. These words would appeal to any present-day defender of regulation and protection. They reflect a parallel between Sismondi's time and the present, the relatively high rate of technological change that was transforming society at a rapid pace. It is on the basis of this and similar sentiments that Marx denounced Sismondi as a petit bourgeois, implying (unjustly) that he was wedded to an outdated status quo.

9

Of Government-Created Monopolies

We have just said that it was not at all true that a government had no need whatsoever to involve itself in the development of commercial wealth; in leaving it to the free play of competition it is not at all certain that oppression and excessive suffering for many individuals will not result therefrom, and perhaps, by the very progress of wealth, universal want and the ultimate ruin of those who had elevated themselves the most. If the government practices a regulatory and moderating influence on the pursuit of wealth, it may be infinitely beneficial; only, it is not at all easy, in the state of ignorance in which this science still exists, for it either to know clearly the ends it should have in mind, or to modify its course according to circumstances that may arouse adverse behavior; and when one examines what various governments have done for the advancement of wealth, one can seldom see anything but the consequences of wrong methods, or the effects of chance.[1]

Generally, governments, with respect to commercial wealth, have only considered merchants; they have believed that their interest always agrees with that of the nation; and it is almost always in accordance with their advice that they have made their laws.[2] They have sought to make merchants wealthy as quickly as possible; they have often given them a direct monopoly, or the exclusive right to buy and sell, in order to better assure them the advantage of buying cheaply and selling dear; and when the clamoring of those who wanted to sell even dearer, of those who wanted to buy cheaper, and of those who were sorry that they could neither buy nor sell, have forced governments to renounce such biased and impolitic laws, there have remained nevertheless, in that part of commercial legislation that was permitted to survive, some traces of monopoly.[3]

All such legislative systems were always described as intended to favor progress for commerce, industry, and the capital that nourished them. From this point of view, there exist hardly any laws, even in nations considered the most competent,[4] which cannot be proven to act exactly to the contrary.[5] But we have just declared that if a government could be at the same time sufficiently enlightened, sufficiently benevolent, and sufficiently impartial to be trusted, the occasion would arise where, in moderating the march of industry, and halting a disordered expansion, it would render a great service to society. Some of the trade regulations, today prohibited by common consent, if they merited their condemnation as thorns in the side of industry, could perhaps be justified as restraints.

In barbaric ages, governments were seen to give to individuals, for a monetary consideration, to reserve for themselves, either the right to sell certain provisions, or certain merchandise, on which the monopolist made exorbitant profits. With more enlightenment, it was soon realized that a monopoly of that kind was nothing but a tax, and they have ceased to be among the favors that could be given to trade.

However, those monopolies which in former times were granted by the great barons in their fiefs, and which even today Turkish pashas sell to the highest bidder, are altogether of the same type as the trading privileges of the trading companies,[6] to which a certain public warranty is given, sometimes to pursue without competitors some type of venture, like a bank or an insurance, sometimes to trade alone in some country, like India or China. The particular nature of the trade subject to the monopoly, the need for large credits, large capitals, or large forces to gain the respect of barbaric governments or people, have been advanced as motives for the favors given to a small number of privilege holders, to the cost of their whole class. Perhaps one would only have to talk of the profits returned from such difficult commerce, in order to disgust the public. In another book, at the very least, we shall identify this profit in the banking monopoly.[7]

Public opinion has generally made a judgment on the reasons that were believed to be a basis for trading-company monopolies. It was shown that such a [monopoly has never failed to heighten the price for the consumer, to diminish production and consumption, to give the national capital a false direction; sometimes by attracting it prematurely to a branch of trade which was not yet suitable, sometimes by repelling it when fruitlessly seeking an employment.] It has also been noted that despite the privileges of these companies that allows them to buy cheap and sell dear, [by nature they are so ill suited for economy and trading speculations, that although amazingly rich, and sometimes sovereigns of countries[8]] they have ended almost all in bankruptcy, lacking, if not in honesty, then at least in the vigilance of their administrators.[9] The experience of the last half-century has added nothing to what Adam Smith had already taught to statesmen about the vices of privileged companies.

Trading companies could hardly be established other than for trade with countries unacquainted with European politics; nowhere else would their monopoly have been tolerated; but sometimes advantages could be obtained for the traders of one nation in preference over all others, either by the favor of a foreign government, by fear, or by hopes for an alliance, which gave them a kind of monopoly in the country that yielded to such arrangements. This is the aim of trade agreements which, for a half century, have been an important object of European politics.[10]

An exemption from import tariffs paid by all other nations, or a reduction of such tariffs, gives unquestionably to the nation obtaining it almost all the foreign trade of the nation granting it. Whoever produces at the same cost, but can sell 5 or 10 percent cheaper than another, because he pays less tariffs, is nearly sure to sell alone. But the government which grants such an exemption gives foreigners the right to tax its subjects. The exchequer or the consumer lose whatever the foreigner gains.

[When a treaty of commerce bore a concession of mutual exemption, each state should have discovered, that a monopoly granted to its producers was too dearly purchased by a monopoly granted to foreigners, against its consumers; and the more so as there existed no kind of relation between the two favored branches of trade. Some show of reason may be discovered, why the consumers of cloth should be taxed for the advantage of cloth manufacturers; but there is no shadow of reason why the consumers of wine in England should experience a loss, in compensation for an advantage to sellers of goods in Portugal.]

It would be pointless to pursue the errors of the old system of trade agreements; no one today could hope, in Europe, to create such a system on an unequal basis, and it is probable that the first treaties that will have to be negotiated, will be based on more liberal principles; that they will have as their goal the breaking of the shackles of the prohibitive system which industry will not be able to support much longer,[11] and by beginning to abolish the barriers between neighboring nations, they will habituate men to regard each other as brothers, even though they are not fellow citizens.[12]

[No treaty of commerce can fully satisfy the greediness of merchants desiring a monopoly; and therefore governments invented the fantastic expedient of creating in a colony a nation expressly to be purchasers from their merchants. The colonists were prohibited from establishing any manufacture at home, that so they might be more dependent on the mother country. They were carefully prevented from following any species of foreign trade; they were subjected to regulations the most vexatious, and contrary to their own interests; not for the mother country's good, but for the good of a small number of merchants. The infinite advantages attached to a new country, where every kind of labour is profitable, because every thing is yet to do, enabled colonies to prosper, although they were continually sacrificed. As their raw produce was fit for a distant trade, they had it in their power to support a most unequal exchange, in which nothing was taken from them that the buyer could procure at home; but their rapid increase itself bears witness against the system which has founded them; they have prospered by a system diametrically opposite to that followed by the mother country.[13] The exportation of all raw produce, the importation of all wrought produce, have been encouraged in colonies, and have presented to such as believe in the existence, and calculate the state, of a commercial balance], a balance sheet according to which their losses, in their trade with the mother country, the only one that was permitted to them, have been increasing every year.[14]

If, on the other hand, we measure the colonies by the principles we have so far stated, we will see them as[15] a forced means to enable old nations to share in the advancement of a new one. Industry did not find anymore growth in France, capital no more employment, labor no demand; or at the least, the progress of the economy, of labor, and of consumption had declined; Santo Domingo[16] absorbed all this excess; an immense effort was necessary to create a new country, for the benefit of men who did not work at all themselves; violence gave them slaves for their lands; and French trade built their villages, furnished them, filled them with shops, and fed their inhabitants. Without doubt, there were advantages to be gotten for the nation which involved itself thus in the development of its colony, and turned it all to its profit; but the injustice was so great, that the gain could not last very long. On the other hand, the incomes with which the colony could buy French labor showed that agricultural business, even though it be conducted in a very costly manner, such as slavery, suffices to enrich a nation. Nowhere in old Europe do we see agriculture raise great fortunes, because all profits are absorbed by the rent of land. In a new country where land is plentiful, and rent nonexistent, the profit of agriculture is the richest of all.

In their colonies mother countries have reserved to themselves all the advantages of a monopoly, but at the same time they have strongly circumscribed their market[17] [whilst the free trade of all Europe, with all its colonies, would have been more advantageous for both, by infinitely extending the market of one, and accelerating the progress of the other.] Despite total liberty, the colonies would have refrained for much longer from competing with Europe in manufactured goods. [What justice and policy should have taught, force will obtain, and the colonial system cannot long continue.][18]

When all other expedients for extending the market of their manufacturers have proven insufficient, some governments have gone so far as to pay their merchants in order to enable them to sell at lower prices; and the more this strange sacrifice is contrary to the most simple considerations, the more it is ascribed to great statecraft. [A bounty is a reward which the state decrees to the manufacturer, on account of his goods, which comes to him in the shape of profit], hence it encourages the pursuit of an industry which has no income, and since it is given on exportation [a government pays merchants, at the expense of its own subjects, that foreigners may buy cheaper than them.][19] It has been assumed that this maneuver has often been pursued in order to ruin foreign firms whose competition was feared. The sacrifice appears to be out of all proportion to the goal sought; the nation which, for ten years, has paid a bounty to discourage its rivals, risks, if it discontinues the payments in the eleventh year, to see them ready to begin again; on the other hand, industries whose sales generate such small profits that a bounty suffices to ruin them, cannot have been very important, and the rivals to which such was to be done, perhaps were quite pleased that their capitals and their workers were retired from such a risky business.[20]

A bounty can only be justified for a political reason, if it is granted on the production of goods that are deemed necessary for defense, for the subsistence of a people, or to assure at all cost such production, such as arms, ropes for ships, medical supplies, or produce suited to the country, if its cultivation is still unknown. The gathering of riches is not the main goal of a nation, and it must be sacrificed to everything that secures its safety and health.*

Restitution of taxes, called "drawbacks" by the English, which often bear the same name, should not be confounded with bounties. At the moment of exportation of a merchandise produced within a country it is proper to return all the taxes which were levied on its production, similar to those which were levied on all imported merchandise that was reexported. To levy a tax on the consumption of foreigners who can provision themselves wherever they please is never successful. A tax on production which would not be refunded, would then limit the market of the national

*To my great astonishment, Mr. Ricardo justifies bounties, which I believed had been abandoned by all economists (chap. XXII). But, on the whole, his system tends to conclude that all is the same, and that nothing hurts anything else; this simplifies greatly the science; it is but a step form this doctrine to denying the existence of evil.

producer; and in giving it back to him on export, the government puts him [on a footing of equality with all his rivals.]

Translator's Notes to Chapter 9, Fourth Book

This chapter is a quasi-historical survey of mercantilistic practices and a strong polemic against restrictive trade practices similar to Adam Smith's condemnation of the mercantile system. It is very likely that Sismondi's position was strongly influenced by his experience with the Napoleonic Continental System. During the Napoleonic period, he opposed the system in his capacity as secretary to the Genevese city government, at that time an "independent" republic.

1. Reading these comments about 170 years later, one is struck by the thought that not much has changed in the meantime. It would seem that political economy is still an uncertain guide to economic policy, or, alternatively, that governments seldom agree on what should be done for the common good.
2. This refers to Jean Baptiste Colbert, Louis XIV's (*Le Roi Soleil*) finance minister, who was known to have shaped his policies in close consultation with the merchants of Paris. (See the discussion in chapter 5 of the first book.) It probably also refers to the two most powerful trading companies of the mercantilistic period, the English and the Dutch East India Companies, who were a law unto themselves, both at home and in their overseas possessions.
3. At the time Sismondi wrote, that is, after the conclusion of the Napoleonic wars, most European states followed very restrictive trade policies, with high tariff barriers and prohibitions on exports. Moreover, France, Russia, and Prussia had actual state monopolies in salt, playing cards, tobacco, and alcohol, some of which are still in existence.
4. The reference is probably to England, not free-trading, but economically the strongest nation in Europe, and moving in the direction of free trade.
5. Sismondi has the Corn Laws in mind. The following observation, that *if* governments could be sufficiently trusted, they could make a contribution to the control of economic instability, has a contemporary ring in the Keynesian age of governmentally generated deficits.
6. The preceding clause was altered from the first edition. It reads there as follows: "Cependant il n'y a aucune différence entre ces monopoles, accordés autrefois par les seigneurs de châteaux, aujourd'hui par les pachas, et les privilèges des compagnies de commerce, . . ."
7. Book 5, "Of Money." The last two sentences in the paragraph were added to the second edition. They indicate Sismondi's total opposition to paper money.
8. The reference here is specifically to the English East India Company, which was the de facto government of India. Most chartered trading companies were self-governing in their possessions, subject only to periodic reviews from the home office, due to the vast distances involved (that is, vast for the average speed of transportation at that time). The history of New Amsterdam under Peter Stuyvesant is a good case in point.
9. Sismondi changed this sentence from "faute de vigilance, si ce n'est de probité, . . ." in the first edition.
10. The reference is to the Methuen and Eden treaties, as shown by the argument of the next paragraph. The Methuen Treaty of 1702 between Portugal and England gave favored status to Portugal for its (port) wines, and to England for

its textiles. The treaty had the effect of making Portugal an economic dependency of England because of the superior economic position of the latter and the unfavorable terms of trade for the former. The arrangement served as a model for Ricardo's example on international trade in the *Principles*. The Eden Treaty of 1786 between England and France was intended to make the same arrangements for these two nations, but was soon abrogated by the Revolution.

11. It would seem that this refers to the post-Napoleonic period, when most European states pursued a policy of strong protection. The sentiment expressed also indicates how closely economic and political concerns are connected—the post–World War II development of the European community bears witness both to Sismondi's perspicacity and the reason that *political economy* is indeed the proper title of the discipline.
12. Like many others, Sismondi apparently believed in the peaceful effects of free trade, all historical evidence to the contrary notwithstanding. This remark may also point to his belief in a united, peaceful Europe without frontiers, an ideal that had currency with the French Revolution and after.
13. This paragraph from the *Encyclopedia* was obviously influenced by the events in America, both North and South, then still very recent.
14. In the first edition, the clause after the bracket read: "un résultat aussi désavantageux pour elles, qu'avantageux à la métropole."
15. The first edition read: "En rapportant au système que nous avons exposé nous-mêmes le regime des colonies, on voit que c'etait . . ."
16. Sismondi refers here to the French part of the island of Hispaniola, now known as Haiti, whose Spanish portion is known as the Dominican Republic, or Santo Domingo.
17. The first edition reads: "mais dans un marche fort resserré . . ."
18. One could wonder what Sismondi would have said if somebody had told him that this system would last through the nineteenth century and into the middle of the twentieth.
19. Little seems to have changed in this policy from Sismondi's day to the present, as can be seen, for instance, in the sales of subsidized grain at (lower) market prices by the United States to the Soviet Union, or of butter by the European community to India.
20. In the first edition, the conclusion of the paragraph, starting after the semicolon, reads: "dans intervalle, il avait empêche de nouveaux ouvriers et de nouveaux capitaux de s'engager dans une manufacture dont le débit présenterait si peu de benefice, il leur aurait fait plus bien que de mal."

10

Restrictions Imposed by Legislation on the Proliferation of Producers

The monopolies we have just reviewed are not by any means the only ones merchants had successfully been able to establish; they had formed themselves into corporations and guilds, under the authority of the government; they had their statutes and privileges sanctioned by law; and the general result of their organization had been limitation of their numbers, and of the activities of everyone, such that the production never exceeded the demand, or even never equalled it.

All the trades had been organized, and no one could work or sell, if he did not belong to one of the associations that were called guilds, and had as their heads delegates of corporations who exercised the *wardenship*. They policed the corporations and levied the fines for each infraction of their rules. Normally, the number of *masters* was fixed in each guild, and only a master could maintain a shop, and buy and sell for his own account. Every master could employ only a prescribed number of apprentices to whom he taught his trade; and in many guilds he could only have one. In the same way, every master could employ a limited number of workers who were called *journeymen*; and in those crafts where only one apprentice was allowed, only one, or two, journeymen could be employed. No one could buy, sell, or work in a craft if he was not apprenticed, journeyman, or master; no one could become a journeyman if he had not served a stated number of years as apprentice, or become a master if he had not served a similar number of years as journeyman, and moreover had not also made his masterpiece, or done a prescribed work in his craft, which had to be judged by the guild wardens.

It is obvious that such an organization puts the renewal of the craft corporation entirely into the hands of the masters. They alone could accept apprentices, but they were not at all obliged to take them on; also, they let themselves be paid for such a favor, and often at a high price, such that a young man could not enter a craft if he had not, first, the amount he had to pay for his apprenticeship, and whatever was necessary to maintain himself for the duration of the apprenticeship, because during four, five, or seven years, all his labor belonged to his master. His dependence on that master was therefore for a long time absolute, because a single order, or even a whim of the master, could close to him entry into lucrative trades.

The apprentice, having become a journeyman, acquired a little more freedom; he could hire himself out to any master, going from one to the other; and since entrance into the status of a journeyman was only open through apprenticeship, he began to profit by the monopoly from which he had suffered, and he was at least certain to have a labor well remunerated no one else could do. However, he depended on the guild wardens for a master's shop;[1] thus he did not at all regard himself as assured of his future, or of having a position. Normally, he did not marry if he had not become a master.[2]

To secure the laws which placed one part of the population into absolute dependence on the other, governments had been told that the statutes of apprentices, and all the guild regulations were necessary to keep unqualified workers from practicing a craft of which they knew nothing, or deceitful masters from cheating the consumer.[3] These pretenses cannot stand up to even the slightest examination; it is proven that competition alone can give to the craftsman proper instruction; that the length of apprenticeship stifles the spirit and discourages industry; that the consumer has the sole right to judge what suits him, and to abandon products encouraged by guild rules, in order to seek those which are opposed to them; and that finally, fraud is never better prevented, or punished, than by the purchaser.

The progress of industry had already emasculated the guild wardens before their abolition; their statutes were mainly in force in closed cities; the suburbs were considered as privileged areas, where industry was free; the crafts created since the last statutes had remained independent; the greater share of the large manufactures, either in France, or England, from that time on found themselves freed from apprenticeship and dominations of the wardens, and this hodgepodge increased the ire of those who, in their own country, were refused the free possession of their labor, and the exercise of talents they felt they possessed.

The guild wardens were abolished in France by the Revolution, and their reestablishment is generally only desired by the defenders of old prejudices and old abuses, who reject scrutiny, and who, in political and religious questions, were always ready to say: *placet, quia absurdum*.[4] However, the influence of all these privileges, how they impede increases in population, and the swift development of industry, has never been investigated, and are not easy to assess. These institutions were born in small free-merchant republics, and in franchised communities where the legislators themselves were engaged in the trades they subjected to these regulations. It is true that they had an interest in the monopolies they established; but the experience of free men always deserves a closer scrutiny than the legislation of ministers, strangers to the matters they pretend to regulate.[5]

The misery of the poorer classes is never prevented if one waits for the coming of a superabundant population to then provide for it. As soon as it exists, despite all the attention it receives from the legislator, it will depress the worker's wages through competition. If its labor will not be enough to support it and enjoy its life, the only means to keep it from suffering, is to keep it from being born.[6] No government, however enlightened, however energetic, however charitable it is assumed to be, ever recognizes fully enough the connection of the demand for labor with the number of workers, in order to take upon itself regulation of population increases. The wisest course of action would be to leave this care to parental love, and the sense of honor of fathers of families, by giving them at the same time all means to fairly assess their status. Under no circumstances would citizens dream of marrying, if they would not see before them the means to keep their children alive, during their early years, without suffering and degradation,[7] and to establish them in the standing they themselves occupy when they will be able to work. The pauper has an income, just like the wealthy; if he would know this income fully, he would proportion his family to it.[8]

When talking about agricultural wealth, we have seen that the peasant proprietor pushed population, and the division of land, to the limits where he could bequeathe to his children ease through work, but that the division of land and population stopped there; whereas the day laborer, who lived only from a wage, believed he could leave to his children an income equal to his own, if he raised them to a working age; and that the population in this class increased out of proportion to the demand for labor. The same observation is repeated among those who live from business wealth.

When the craftsman has an ownership interest in his work which gives him a determinate income, he recognizes it, and proportions his family to it; whereas, to the contrary, if the value of his labor should be determined by competition, this value could diminish endlessly; he knows only his work on which he counts and which he bequeathes to his children; but he is deceived in his estimation: the workday of his two sons will not equal two of his, and, in believing that he leaves them in a position equal to his own, he will place them in a much worse condition.[9]

The self-interest of the craftsman demands that his daily bread not be disputed by those who have nothing but strong arms and eagerness, and will offer to do his craft at a cheaper price than his; in the same way that the interest of the peasant proprietor demands that his land not be disputed by those who, having nothing but strong arms and eagerness, offer to draw from the land more food than he. The interest of society is not to put up everything for auction, and draw the greatest possible work from each trade, the greatest amount of food from the land; because society is made up of members who would enrich themselves at each other's expense, and who would bring each other finally to the last degree of misery, in order to divide a sum four times greater between a number ten times greater.

Truly, the interest of one who would be an artisan but has no trade, and of one who would be a farmer and has no land, is opposed to the guarantee given by law against unlimited competition. Society had to choose between these opposed interests; but its best reason to decide in favor of property is, that in so doing it hurts only those it prevents from being born, whereas in establishing universal competition it hurts those it condemns to death.[10]

It is well established by facts and theory that the founding of trade guilds prevents, and had to prevent, the birth of a superabundant population. It is equally certain that such a population exists today, and that it is the necessary result of the existing order.

According to the statutes of almost all guilds a man could not become a master till after reaching the age of twenty-five; but if he had no capital of his own, if he had not saved enough, he continued for a long time as a journeyman; many, and perhaps the greater number of all craftsmen, remained journeymen all their lives. Therefore, it hardly ever happened that they would marry before being made master; if they would be imprudent enough to so wish, no father would have wanted to give his daughter to a man who had no position in life.

Total births are not only regulated by the number of marriages. A father knows that he must settle his children, and he fears fertility that would be his ruin. Every son he had to apprentice remained totally his dependent till the age of twenty; he had therefore to find a capital to pay for the apprenticeship, and settle his son in his trade;[11] hence, he avoided having more children than his wealth permitted him to provide for. The population of cities was therefore not renewed by the lowest classes, but by the highest among the artisans, because only masters marry, and the increase in their families always proportioned itself to their wealth. Therefore, the population of cities, far from being overabundant, had always to replenish itself from the countryside.

Today, on the contrary, the factory hand, living from day to day, and just getting by to the last day of his life without ever receiving a better guarantee of his income than what he could obtain by his work, sees no proper time when he must choose between celibacy and marriage; and as he has accustomed himself to such uncertainty and regards it as the natural lot of his class, he marries during his first good year, when his wages are high, instead of foregoing all his pleasures and domestic comforts.[12] Moreover, his marriage is made easy for him; his wife also works in the factory; both lived separately, both believe they can live together. The same factory looks forward to their children, and will give them employment at the age of six or eight; because the worker has spent little in the initial upkeep of his child, every new child who reaches the age at which its work is paid will appear to add to his income—a bonus appears to be given to the multiplication of poor workers. In the worst years, when there is no work in England, the parish and the workhouse, elsewhere the hospital, maintain in a state of misery, between life and death, a family which need not have been born.

In truth, the multiplication of population caused by marriages of poor workers is today the great distress of the social order. In England, agriculture only employs 770,199 families, commerce and manufacture 959,632, other occupations 413,316. Such a great part of the population maintained by commercial wealth, out of a total 2,143,147 families, or 10,150,615 individuals, is truly frightening.*[13] Luckily, France is far from having such a great number of workers, whose subsistence depends on the chances of a distant market, who in their highest prosperity can barely enjoy life, and see it menaced by every advance of a rival industry, or by every scientific discovery that threatens to replace their hands by blind energy.[14] Meanwhile, the textile workers of the Dauphine earn only eight sous daily; they earn perhaps even less in the cotton trade; in the latter, pickers have been observed to receive less than four sous a day. Is it not the proper duty of humanity to prevent a new generation from being called to such a miserable existence?

It is not in any case the guilds that should be reestablished; it was only by chance that they produced in some way an advantageous effect which the lawmaker had not had in view. Besides, since the great perfection of machines, all those who worked almost like machines have had their influence diminished.[15] But it is in the effects which the guilds produced

*Since the publication of the first edition of this book, the population in England has continued to increase with distressing rapidity, the more so because wealth is far from having made the same progress. It is London and the large manufacturing towns which allow these rapid increases; but at the same time the number of people who have nothing increases, the number of people who have something seems to decrease.

that we have to find the lessons on how to fight the calamity with which society is afflicted today.

It is in the study of that experience that the legislative authority must find the limits it can impose on competition, such that it assures to each worker a certain property right in his work,[16] that in one part of his life he can count on his income, and that he knows the risks he will brave if he raises a family. We will return to the results of this experience when we talk about population.[17]

Translator's Notes to Chapter 10, Fourth Book

This entire chapter was new to the first edition of *New Principles* and was not substantially revised for the second edition. In the manner of the preceding chapter, this is a quasi-historical survey of the guild system, a content that could not be deduced from the title. On the whole, the chapter is critical of guilds, as behooves a professed disciple of Adam Smith, but one senses a certain kind of nostalgia for a less chaotic period of production. Sismondi's ambiguity about the Industrial Revolution begins to show here, more than in earlier chapters on agriculture. At the end of the chapter he begins what is his first plea for an evolutionary merging of the capitalistic industrial system with the "good" aspects of the guild system, in particular the perceived certainty of the market, and the limitation of family size. There is also a first hint in this chapter of a later argument that it is the absence of property rights in his work that makes the proletarian such an intractable problem in industrial society. Much of what is said here and later is derived from an eighteenth-century rational-historical vision infused with a good deal of romanticism for an idyllic economy of smallholders in agriculture and artisans in the cities. But it should be kept in mind that Sismondi wrote between 1819 and 1826, Marx between 1848 and 1863, and later. By the time Marx came out with *Das Kapital,* the Industrial Revolution had made enormous advances and had fully revealed some of its drawbacks. Given that Marx derived a great deal of his reasoning from Sismondi, one has to credit the early romantic with superior insight into human motivation. Also, the eventual development of unions and *their* development towards guild institutions supports Sismondi's vision of human motivation, as opposed to both the classical view of an undifferentiated labor factor, and its direct derivative, the Marxian view of the proletarian as an undifferentiated *class*.

1. Sismondi uses the term *maîtrise,* a master's position that includes the shop, a term not fully translatable.
2. The term used is *passe maître,* meaning both the advancement to a master's position and the passing of the examination that was tied to presenting a masterpiece.
3. The arguments have a familiar ring to anyone acquainted with union history. It seems to be human nature to try to monopolize the source of income, both for the business owner and his employees.
4. This is a pejorative reference to the returned Bourbons, who were characterized as having learned nothing and having forgotten nothing. Sismondi wrote during the time of the Holy Alliance, which tried valiantly to erase all traces of the French Revolution, not only in France, but everywhere in Europe.
5. The last few sentences in the paragraph reflect Sismondi's familiarity with the

history of the Italian republics, and his unfavorable opinion of contemporary bureaucrats, mostly acquired during and after the Napoleonic period.

6. Due to the population movement from the countryside into the city, repeated now in the underdeveloped countries, there was a perception of overpopulation. The most famous statement on this matter is of course Ebenezer Scrooge's remark: "Are there no prisons?" Sismondi's discussion should be taken as mainly applying to England, because in the Continental nations the problem was not as acute, due to later industrial development.
7. This clause was added in the second edition.
8. Perhaps the major difference between Marx and Sismondi is the former's abandonment of all middle-class standards as a basis for understanding the economic system, and seeing the proletarian as somebody to be led by a version of the Platonic guardians, a position clearly consistent with Marx's Hegelian vision and his view of himself as being in possession of the final *scientific* explanation of the capitalistic system. Sismondi, on the other hand, assumes here that workers have middle-class values and will act on them if they are given a chance to do so, a position consistent with his own status as a self-supporting writer. As a consequence, Sismondi is meliorative, Marx revolutionary. In retrospect, the Marxian system is flawed *because* of that basic assumption—Marx was unable to foresee the rise of a new middle class. As will be seen later, Sismondi advocates a solution that is much closer to the reality of a developed industrial society than Marx's utopian classless society. It may be no accident that Marxist societies have become totalitarian class societies with feudal characteristics because of this difference. See Milovan Djilas's *The New Class* (1957).
9. This paragraph reflects Sismondi's childhood experience—the precarious position his family had during the Revolution and the financial problems his father experienced after the default of the Necker loans. It is reasonable to assume that Sismondi's preoccupation with security for the worker had its genesis in the days when he had to leave school and become apprenticed in a Genevese business in Lyon because his father had lost most of his fortune.
10. To characterize property as a device to limit competition must have struck Sismondi's contemporaries as an unusual way of looking at that social institution. However, it is very apt, and Sismondi, at least, did not avoid the question of property rights, as did most of his contemporaries in political economy.
11. Today, the middle class has to make similar sacrifices for a college education.
12. In reading this, one should keep in mind that Sismondi married late in life, and then only after he had established some financial security for himself and his mother and sister in Tuscany.
13. The note is new to the second edition. It is not clear where the cited figures were obtained, but it should be noted that Great Britain now has a population at least five times as large.
14. The term used is "une force aveugle."
15. Sismondi left out "protectrice" after "influence" in the second edition.
16. This is the main theme of the work. It is interesting in this context to consider that an important part of union legislation in the United States (the Clayton Act) is part of antitrust legislation, that is, legislation concerned with monopolies in property.
17. Book 7 of *New Principles*.

11

Of Customs

[These different expedients] we have just reviewed, to which governments have recourse to protect business, [are now generally decried, though almost all governments yet agree] in regarding customs with which they line the frontiers of their states, as providing needed protection to their industries. Their most common approach is to use customs to stop the exportation of raw materials which national industries use, because the producer who resells them will make a profit by buying them cheaply; and, [in repelling[1] from their states the produce of foreign manufactures, or at least loading it with heavy duties,] giving [the national producer an advantage.]

This principal distinction between raw materials and finished goods, which seems quite simple when expressed in general terms, is not at all simple in practice. There exists no absolute raw material, except the marble in the quarry, the ore in the mine, the timber in the forest. When they are taken from their original location, their price already includes human labor. The price of all agricultural products is mostly composed of it. Nevertheless, each later worker considers all those who came before him solely as providers of raw material. Flax is a finished good for the retter, and it is a raw material for the spinner; the former, as a general principle, favors exports, the latter that they be prohibited; the yarn is again a finished good for the spinner, raw material for the weaver; cloth is a finished good for the weaver, and raw material for the calico printer; calico, or printed cloth, is a finished good for the printer, and raw material for the milliner, the decorator, and the tailor. The last one will always demand to be sole master of the market with respect to all those who worked before him. He retards their industry by export restrictions, and as a consequence he reduces the total output they could produce. If a customs code is considered as a whole, it is almost always found that the prohibitions given successively to various levels of industry are in direct contradiction with each other.

Besides, it could not be otherwise, because the very principle on which the successive export prohibitions are based is false. Trade does not make its profit on production, but only from consumption. Every advantage which is alone obtained by a levy on the profits of the producers,[2] is but a shifting of income and not a real profit. If the weaver sells his textiles at a higher price, business profits; but if, selling at the same price, he makes a greater profit because he pays less for the yarn, then it is not anymore trade, or the country, that profit, but he alone, and his profit is offset by the loss of the spinner. This rule holds at every level of production.*[3]

Raw materials of industry are originally derived from the soil; therefore they form a part of the landlord's wealth, or of the cultivator's. If there is no advantage in their export, no one would dream of prohibiting their export. The prohibition shows clearly that producers were paid more selling them abroad, where they made a profit, and the law restricts their markets, in contradiction of the principle which we have set forth above as a basis for commercial advantage, which is to receive for every good the highest possible price. From export prohibitions must follow, first, a reduction in the price of raw materials, because that price is no longer determined by the free competition of buyers; then, a reduction in the quantity produced, because it will proportion itself henceforth to the domestic demand alone; and finally, a decline in quality, because an industry which is badly paid is[4] always negligent.

But if every new processor concludes that all operations preceding his have only supplied him with raw material, and if he obtains new export prohibitions, it becomes difficult to foresee where the repercussions will stop that he thus brings to production. The decorator, if he succeeds in prohibiting the exportation of calicos, would strike at one and the same

*With respect to the lowering of prices of raw materials which tariffs are to accomplish, this rule applies in all cases; but, with respect to a lowering of prices which can be brought about by more economical and expeditious processes, it is much more difficult to foresee the results. There is a gain to society if, despite lower prices, each producer draws from his output an income equal to what he received before; the saving of the consumer is then the net benefit; there is even more of a gain if the producers realize a larger income from an increase in production when the consumer saves at the same time. But if, through a more expeditious and economical system, the share that one class of society draws from the product, and which constitutes its income, is diminished, or if one of the classes is forced to give for the same share a larger quantity of work, the gain of the consumer is exactly counterbalanced by the loss of the producer, while morally the loss of the producer is in another way quite as painful, quite as fatal to society, as the saving is without profit.

time at the printer, the weaver, the spinner, and the bleacher; the income he believes he makes, is taken from theirs; but he is not at all sure if he can use all of their output; the damage he does to them is much larger than the good he expects for himself, because he gains merely the discount on the price he pays to them; but he gains nothing on what he makes impossible for them to produce.

Import prohibitions are as imprudent and ruinous[5] as export prohibitions; they have been invented to give to a nation an industry it did not yet have, and it cannot be denied that they constitute, for a beginning industry, the strongest source of encouragement. [Perhaps this manufacture scarcely produces the hundredth part of what the nation consumes of such commodities; but the hundred purchasers must compete with each other to obtain the one seller's preference, and the ninety-nine rejected by him will be compelled to obtain goods by smuggling. In this case, the nation's loss will be as a hundred; its gain as one. Whatever advantage may arise from giving a new manufacture to a nation, certainly there are a few which deserve such a sacrifice, and even these might always be set agoing by less expensive means.[6]

Besides, we must also take into account the weighty inconveniences of establishing the vexatious system of duties, of covering the frontiers with an army of custom-house officers, and with another not less dangerous army of smugglers, and thus of training the subjects to disobedience. We must remember, above all, that it is not in the interest of a nation to produce every thing indifferently; that it ought to confine its efforts to such goods or commodities as it can manufacture at the cheapest rate;[7] or to such as, whatever price they cost, are essential to its safety.] Finally, the goal that was sought by encouraging commerce should never be lost from view: to increase the income of the nation proportionally to population, and thus provide more comforts to it. A new industry, no matter to what degree of perfection it has brought its products, and even if it provides some profit to its main entrepreneur, cannot be considered prosperous if the wages of its workers do not keep them in some comfort, or if it can maintain itself only at the expense of a population whose very existence is misery.

[If the prohibitive system gives a very powerful, though very expensive encouragement to rising manufactures, it can offer, in regard to such, no advantage to those which are already prosperous; the sacrifice at least which it imposes on consumers, is entirely useless. If the manufacture was destined for exportation, government, by granting a monopoly of the interior market, causes it to abandon its ancient habits to assume others which probably are less advantageous. Every manufacture destined for exportation gives proof of not fearing the competition of foreigners. From the moment that it can support competition abroad, notwithstanding the expense of transport, it has still less reason to dread this competition in the very place of production.[8] Thus nothing is more common than to see goods prohibited which never could have been imported with advantage, and which gained credit solely by being so prohibited.

By the prohibitive system, governments had proposed to increase the number and productive powers of their manufactures. It is doubtful if they rightly knew the price they paid for this advantage, and the prodigious sacrifices they imposed on consumers, their subjects, to bring into existence an unborn class of producers; but they succeeded much more rapidly even than speculators on political economy expected. For a time they excited the bitterest complaints on the part of consumers; but even these complaints ceased afterwards, because sacrifices in fact had also ceased, and manufactures so powerfully encouraged, had soon provided with profusion for the national wants. But this emulation of all governments to establish manufactures every where, has produced two strange and unexpected effects on the commercial system of Europe; one is the disproportionate increase of production without any relation to consumption; the other is the effort of each nation to live isolated, to suffice for itself, and refuse every kind of foreign trade.

Before governments had been seized with this manufacturing ardour, the establishment of a new manufacture had always to struggle with a crowd of national habits and prejudices, which form as it were the *vis inertiae* of the human mind.[9] To overcome this force, it was necessary to offer speculators a very manifest advantage; hence a new species of industry could scarcely arise without a distinct previous demand, and the market was always found, before the manufacture destined to occupy it. Governments, in their zeal, have not proceeded upon this principle; they have ordered stockings and hats beforehand, reckoning that legs and heads would be found afterwards. They have seen their people well and economically clothed by strangers, and yet have caused them to produce clothes in the country itself. During war, this new production was not capable of being too exactly appreciated; but when peace came, it was found that all things had been made in double quantity; and the readier the mutual communication of states had become, the more embarrassed were they to dispose of all their works executed without orders.

Consumers who at the beginning had been sacrificed,[10] afterwards found themselves called to unexpected gains, because merchants, eager to recover their funds, were forced to sell a very great quantity of goods with loss. Manufacturers gave the signal for these sacrifices; resigning themselves to a cruel loss of their capital, they induced extensive merchants[11] to furnish themselves with goods beyond their custom or ability, in order to profit by what appeared a good opportunity. Several of the latter have been forced to experience a similar loss, before their excessive supply could be introduced to the shops of retail dealers; and these again before they could make them be accepted by consumers. A universal embarrassment was felt by manufacturers, merchants, and retailers, and this was followed by the annihilation of the capital destined to support industry. The fruit of long saving and long labour was lost in a year. Consumers have gained certainly, but their gain is scarcely perceptible even to themselves. By laying up a stock of goods for several years to profit by their cheapness, they have also included themselves in the general embarrassment, and still farther retarded the period when the balance can be re-established between consumption and production;] by providing for their clothing and furnishings with goods of better quality and style, they do not see themselves as richer, because for all of these enjoyments of vanity, the only value lies in their rarity, and not in the quality of the goods.[12]

[According to the former organization of Europe, all states did not make pretences to all kinds of industry. Some had attached themselves to agriculture, others to navigation, others to manufactures; and the condition of these latter, even in prosperous times, could not have appeared so worthy of envy as to demand prodigious efforts to attain it. A miserable and degraded population almost always produced these rich stuffs, these elegant ornaments, this furniture which it was never destined to enjoy; and if the men who directed these unhappy workmen sometimes raised immense fortunes, those fortunes were as frequently destroyed.[13]

The development of nations proceeds naturally in all directions; it is scarcely ever prudent to obstruct it, but it is no less dangerous to hasten it; and the governments of Europe, by having on all hands attempted to force nature,[14] are at the present day loaded with a population, which they have created by requiring superfluous labour, and which they know not how to save from the horrors of famine.

The existence of this manufacturing population,[15] and the duty of providing for its wants, have constrained governments to alter the aim of their legislation. Formerly, in the real spirit of the mercantile system, they encouraged manufactures, in order to sell much to foreigners, and grow rich at their expense.] Today [perceiving that a prohibitive system is everywhere adopted,] or is demanded by the producers, [they cannot any longer count on the custom of strangers, and therefore study to find, in their own kingdom, consumers for their own workmen; in other words, to become isolated and sufficient for themselves. This system of policy at present, more or less strictly followed by all the nations of Europe, destroys all the advantages of commerce; it hinders each nation from profiting by the superiorities due its climate, to its soil, to its situation, to the peculiar character of its people; it arms man against man, and breaks the tie which was destined to soothe national prejudices, and accelerate the civilization of the world.

According to the natural progress of increasing wealth, when capitals are yet inconsiderable, it is certainly desirable to direct them rather to some neighbouring branch of trade, than to one which is very remote; and as the trade of exportation and importation] employs its funds to replace alternatively the capital of foreigners and of natives, [a country which has little capital may desire to employ it entirely in the trade of its interior, or for its own use; and the more so, because if the market is near the producer, the same capital will be several times renewed in a given period, whilst another capital, destined for a foreign market, will scarcely accomplish a single renewal.]

But we have seen that capitals can exceed present needs as well as remain below them; such that, if they are in excess, the nation suffers first by the loss of a part of the incomes of the capitalists, and is moreover open to even more damage, because the capitalists, in order to employ their funds, will set afoot industries which will not find an adequate market afterwards.[16] It is therefore quite dangerous for a nation to close its door to foreign trade; it is thereby drawn into a false activity which will encompass its ruin. By leaving to capital the greatest freedom, it will go where profits call it, and those profits are the signposts of national needs.

[Besides, nations, on reckoning up their produce and their wants, almost constantly forget that neighbouring foreigners are much more convenient and more advantageous producers and consumers than distant countrymen. The relation of markets on the two banks of the Rhine is much more important, both for the German and the French merchant, than the relation of markets between the Palatinate and Brandenburgh is for the former, or between Alsace and Provence for the latter.

The ardour, with which all governments have exited every species of production, by means of their restrictive system, has brought about such a disproportion between labour and demand, that perhaps it has become necessary for every state to think first, not of the comfort, but of the existence of its subjects, and to maintain those barriers which have been so imprudently erected.] One can never rely with any certitude on even the best-established theories to dare to prescribe an immediate evil, with the assurance that it will result in a future benefit. Such a decision can be made even less if it must be feared that it will result in misery and death for numerous families that were raised, and who have adopted their trade, under the guarantees of existing laws and the established order; first, one has to think of saving those who suffer, and then worry about the future.

But if one contemplates the march of industry in Europe, it can hardly be doubted that the immediate result of this universal battle can only be the impossibility of continuing it in any way. Every day one learns of the opening of a new factory, or of the improvement of an old one that allows increases in production; but every day one also learns that some market has been closed to free trade, and that another nation which never before had ever dreamt of industry, has in turn decided to become self-sufficient, and not anymore, in the vulgar expression, *pay tribute to foreigners.* Every manufacturer, instead of thinking of his own country that he knows, has contemplated the world that he cannot know, and that world closes itself off against him evermore. Misery is everywhere, every manufacturer has lost a part of his capital; everywhere workers are reduced to a wage that is barely enough to let them live in wretchedness. One hears, it is true, sometimes from one canton, sometimes from another, that production is reviving, and that all workshops are busy; but this sporadic activity is more often the result of risky speculation, of misplaced confidence, and of superabundant capital, than of new demand; and appraising the business world at a glance, one cannot dismiss the suspicion that the profits of industry diminish even faster than its products multiply.

What can be done if one will not be able to sell abroad anymore? What can one do if everyone, forced to compare the output of his people with their needs, and not anymore counting on the illusions of foreign trade, will clearly understand that the people cannot buy all that one wants to sell? How do you put it to the craftsmen, whose numbers were increased by procreation with so much effort, who were employed by much industry: we have been mistaken, we do not have any need for you; you should not be alive? The coming unmasking of a false system is perhaps imminent, and such a disaster makes one tremble. When this moment will have come, all the barriers erected among nations will fall again because the impossibility of keeping them will be clear; the deadly competition of those who seek today to steal from each other their daily bread will cease, everyone will attend to such industry as the nature of the soil, of climate, and the character of the natives will make most profitable, and will not further regret the need to depend for all other products on foreigners, and not make everything at home; but before this will come to pass, who knows how many lives will have been sacrificed in the pursuit of an error?[17]

Translator's Notes to Chapter 11, Fourth Book

This chapter is mainly composed of paragraphs from the *Encyclopedia*. Sismondi rearranged the sequence of material used in this chapter and the previous one—the material in this chapter preceded the material in the previous chapter. Since most of the material is from the *Encyclopedia,* the argument is mainly an extended rehash of Adam Smith. However, the pessimistic Sismondi appears in a few places, notably in a note and at the end of the chapter, where he returns to the theme of misery because of overproduction.

1. "En même temps" was inserted in the first edition, but the excerpt from the *Encyclopedia* has been used as originally written.
2. "Sur le prix de production" in the first edition was changed to "sur les gains des producteurs" in the second edition.
3. This note was added to the second edition. It should be noted that an elasticity concept is employed in analyzing the gains from enlarged sales. The end of the note again incorporates an exploitation idea very similar to Marx's.
4. "Aussi" was omitted here in the second edition.
5. The first edition reads "Les prohibitions à l'entrée n'ont pas un effet si immédiatement ruineux que les prohibitions à la sortie."
6. The *Encyclopedia* has no paragraph here, but the break Sismondi introduced at this point for both editions of *New Principles* was retained.
7. This was changed in *New Principles* to "qu'elle peut manufacturer mieux que ses rivales. . . ."
8. This is obviously not correct, because a firm may compete abroad against less-competent producers.
9. In *New Principles,* Sismondi rendered the Latin as "la force d'inertie."
10. In the reprint of the *Encyclopedia* this reads "satisfied," an obvious mistake, since in *New Principles* the word is "sacrifiés."
11. Wholesalers.
12. Sismondi provides here an almost classic description of the business cycle as an inventory recession. His experience is with the first post-Napoleonic depression of 1817, when British goods flooded the Continent at cut-rate prices because British producers wanted to get rid of their production accumulated during the blockade years. Many industries that had been established during the Continental System experienced severe difficulties in staying alive against this competition. However, the argument is clearly polemic: during the duration of the blockade, demand was certainly there and the new industries filled that demand, thus meeting the major condition for an expanding economy. What Sismondi had in mind was the obvious inferiority of the new industries as measured against the more advanced British factories, and the sacrifices consumers had to make to establish these industries. There is also another tacit assumption that was evident to Sismondi, but is not evident anymore: the Napoleonic Wars, although fought on the French side by national mass armies, were still in certain respects wars of the eighteenth century, when wars were considered the business of the military and civilians were more or less left alone. During the existence of the Continental System there was considerable intercourse between the two main combatants, France and England, both as to travel and, of course, smuggling of goods, often winked at by the French authorities. Sismondi could therefore take the implied position that it was unnecessary under the circumstances to create import-substituting manufactures because the goods could have been procured at less cost from abroad. The existence of these new manufactures was directly responsible for the prohibitive system he condemns, since every state wanted to preserve what had been acquired at great cost. It should also be noted that the states involved, mainly France, but also Austria, Russia, and to some extent England, followed what was in effect an employment policy by protecting their new and estab-

lished older industries. Sismondi clearly sees that extensive buying of durable goods will depress future consumption and production till stocks have been worked off. Similarly, he lays out the mechanism of capital destruction that Marx uses in his crisis theory.

13. Sismondi changed some of the text for *New Principles*. In the second sentence, the second "others" was rendered as "troisiemes aux manufactures." In the last sentence, "immense fortunes" reads "fortunes rapides." There is no paragraph break here in the *Encyclopedia,* but the paragraph break in *New Principles* has been retained.
14. The *Encyclopedia* copy has "nations" here, which is most likely a typing mistake.
15. In *New Principles* this reads "La naissance de . . ."
16. This ia an often-repeated assertion in *New Principles*. Sismondi clearly disregards here that holders of capital will invest only in projects that promise above-average returns. However, he probably assumed that in a period of slack economic activity capital owners may take higher risks. The argument resembles some modern development analysis, which holds that in underdeveloped countries capital may either lie idle, or be invested in risky or prestigious ventures, because of the absence of worthwhile investment opportunities.
17. Sismondi returns here to Smith's free-trade argument and, be it noted, to that of Ricardo. He is not consistent in his analysis—earlier he condemns the world market as an engine of overproduction inasmuch as its demand is unknown. The pamphleteer has run away from the political economist. The recurring theme of disorderly markets and his dread of instability engendered by rapid industrialization, expressed mainly as a fear for the living standards of the workers, is strongly expressed each time it is raised, probably as an unconscious response to early insecurity. A parallel to Marx seems to exist: both writers made a living as free-lance writers, but though Sismondi was able to maintain himself in modest comfort with his pen, and careful management of his inherited assets, Marx was unable to support himself and his family, mainly because of his total disregard for such obligations and his revolutionary preoccupations. If the situation had been reversed, would Sismondi have been the radical writer, and Marx the ameliorative one? There exists no analysis of the influence on Marx's personality of his financial dependence on Engels, but it is at least conceivable that such dependence may have contributed to his condemnation of the "capitalist system" as a displacement mechanism for his guilt feelings at his own inadequacy as a breadwinner. This is beside the clearly demonstrated debt that Marx owes to Sismondi's ideas, never acknowledged except in footnotes. Both writers are clearly disturbed by rapid change, both praise what Marx calls "idyllic" relations, but, as will be shown in the seventh book, Sismondi has a more realistic approach to the problem. The classless society Marx postulates at the end of the dialectical process is a utopia, a return to the idyllic relations the bourgeoisie had destroyed. Marx creates the heavenly yonder after the revolution—Sismondi confesses eventually that the ideal solution eludes him, a confession intellectually more honest, but also most unsatisfactory from a policy standpoint.

12

On the Influence of Government on Commercial Wealth

We have presented enough arguments in the preceding chapters to let statesmen ponder anew one major question: "Is it proper for governments to speed up the growth of commercial wealth?" Trade creates much greater wealth than that derived from the soil, and above all makes it much more easily disposable; therefore, it supplies for warfare and emergency needs sources of strength that could not be found in a purely agricultural nation; but in increasing such wealth, it increases also the number of the needy; it makes the life of a numerous class of human beings more precarious, their dependence more cruel, their character even more degraded, their attachment to the nation and the established order even weaker. Trade finds abroad resources which nature denied to the country, but in turn it places the nation at the mercy of foreigners, and instead of leaving to everyone the confidence that by his own wisdom he can provide for his own existence, it leaves our welfare at the mercy of errors and faults of others.[1] Trade is a bond between nations, and it contributes to universal civilization, but commerce also excites a hidden rivalry of everyone against all, and it only builds the prosperity of one producer on the ruins of his brother.[2]

We have seen no society governed with such wisdom that its agricultural or commercial wealth would have given to its citizen all the happiness one could expect therefrom. In every nation we can point out glaring faults, crying injustices to which we can attribute the misfortunes suffered there; it is not easy to delineate precisely the extent of their consequences, and experience has not yet taught us which effects one of these riches could produce without the other, and how one is born from the other at the proper moment. But at this moment the nation whose prosperity surpasses all others is without a doubt the federation of North America; the happiness enjoyed there is founded on the rapid development of agricultural wealth.

It has been predicted that many emigrants will bring England's industries there; should we cheer for the Americans? Is it quite obvious that it would not be better for them to be served by the peoples of the Old World, who agree for a pittance to perform work scarcely fit for humans? Are the buyers payers of tribute, or on the contrary, are the producers employees of the foreigners?[3]

The last work destined to acquaint us with the United States, a work we have already cited several times, answers this question in a way that may dispel all doubts. In June 1817, Mr. Henry Bradshaw Fearon had been dispatched by thirty-nine English families who, constrained in their civil and political liberty,[4] weighed down by taxes and wanting change, wanted to know in which part of the United States it would be suitable for them to settle. Mr. Fearon, with great good will, has sent to his principals a series of eight reports with his observations. The last is dated from April 1818.[5] Mr. Fearon arrived in the United States full of zeal and enthusiasm for the new country he wanted to adopt, and with a mind embittered by his memories of the sufferings of the poor in England. By degrees his illusions vanished, yearnings for the amenities of civilization, and those connected to the cultivation of the mind, replaced his former feelings, and he returned to England, determined to end his days there.

In part, his decision can undoubtedly be attributed to force of habit which must be overcome, to the realm of prejudices he did not suspect in himself, and which were offended by opposing biases. However, the picture of the United States he presents to us is one of the most important[6] lessons in political economy we could receive. He shows us what the consequences have been of the almost total adoption of what are habitually called wholesome doctrines of government, in the one country in the world that seemed to be the most suited to receive them.

The Americans have taken to their heart the new principle to work to produce without regard to the market, and to produce always more. Since they have behind them an immense continent, traversed by a prodigious number of navigable rivers, their population could increase and spread in an always-new land, almost as fast as their wealth; lands[7] cost them almost nothing, the rent of the most fertile ones was almost zero, the growing products of the fields seemed to be always ready to buy the growing products of the cities; and the growing population, always well paid for its labor, seemed equally ready to buy one or the other.

Yet, the outstanding characteristic of United States business, from one end of the country to the other, is the superabundance of commodities of all kinds over the needs of consumption. The English, above all, send there infinitely too much of all goods. They extend fairly long credit for which all the merchants, all the retailers, in turn burden themselves with too much merchandise. Their warehouses are always full enough beyond any possibility of depletion; and daily bankruptcies are the consequence of such oversupply of mercantile capital that cannot be converted into income. The last list of insolvent debtors published in New York in the year 1817 comprised more than four hundred names.*[8]

Industries in great number have already been established, above all during the course of the last war;[9] but since all machine improvements were introduced there from their inception, and since they acquired a double importance in a country where labor is dear, these industries employ to this day only a comparatively small number of workers. Pittsburgh in Pennsylvania, the most important manufacturing city in all of the United States, which is called the *American Birmingham,* only employs in forty-one different trades, turning over a capital of almost two million dollars, 1,280 workers. However, industry there is already in great distress; there is no balance between demand and supply for labor, and from everywhere petitions are addressed to Congress to institute a *protective* system of tariffs, similar to the European one.**

But the most remarkable consequence of this rapid growth in population and wealth in America, and of the tendency of all social institutions to speed up this hurrying over again, is the influence which this mad universal auction has had on the character of the inhabitants. The conservative[10] part of the nation, the part that guards established customs, has been totally suppressed; there exists no American who does not intend to make his fortune, and a quick fortune at that. Profit making has become the first aim in life; and in the freest nation in the world, liberty itself has been cheapened relative to profit. The calculating business spirit extends down to the children; it subjects real estate to constant speculation; it snuffs out the development of the mind, an inclination for the arts, letters, and sciences; it corrupts the very agents of a free government, who show a not-very-respectable avidity for office, and it imparts to the American character a blemish which will not be easily removed.[11]

The enterprise of some several hundred thousand emigrants who are summoned to populate a beautiful country, created for as many as hundreds of millions, is such an extraordinary event, or rather such a unique one in the world, that one would not know either to prescribe the rules to follow, or to blame what seems distressing. Perhaps, at this moment, the Americans could do only what they did. But they will not begin to know

*Fearon, p. 209.
**Fearon, pp. 206 and 209.

all the virtues, all the high ideals, all the noble thoughts of long-civilized nations until they have become, if not stationary, at least slower in their progress, until they will have other goals than those of populating and profiting. During that time, until this too-rapid development will have been moderated, they will suffer cruelly, before they will be persuaded to follow another road. This is a great and instructive experience that old nations must always have in view. But, while waiting for its results, they must not lose sight that they possess none of the advantages of the Americans; and since these advantages would not be offset by any of the drawbacks mentioned by Mr. Fearon, the old nations must not pretend to an activity that is not meant for them, and which has no such vast scope in which to unfold.

One can question whether government ought to encourage businesses, such as to establish them before their time, or to outstrip agriculture; but many famed economists have doubted that it can do so, or that it should do anything more than nourish them. [Thus, nearly all the favours which governments confer on trade and manufactures, are contrary even to sound policy and justice; and,[12] judging of them by the law of profit and loss] seem destined to have results opposed to those expected. [But political economy is, in great part, a moral science. After having calculated the interests of men, it ought also to foresee what will act upon their passions. Ruled, as they are, by self-interest, pointing out their advantage will not be sufficient to determine their pursuit of it.[13] Nations have sometimes need of being shaken, as it were, to be roused from their torpor. The small weight which could suffice to incline the balance, with a calculating people, is not sufficient when that balance is rusted by prejudice and long continued habits. In such a case, a skillful administration must occasionally submit to allow a real and calculable loss, in order to destroy an old custom, or change a destructive prepossession.[14]

When rooted prejudices have abandoned to disrespect every useful and industrious profession, when a nation thinks there can be no dignity except in noble indolence; when even men of science themselves, carried away by public opinion, blush at the useful applications made of their discoveries,[15] it perhaps becomes necessary to grant favours, altogether extraordinary, to the industry which it is necessary to create, to fix incessantly the thoughts of a too lively people on the career of fortune which lies before them, intimately to connect the discoveries of science with those of art, and to excite the ambition of those who have always lived in idleness, by fortunes so brilliant as, at length, to make them think of what may be accomplished by their wealth and activity.]

To those who recommended[16] such efforts Adam Smith has cautioned that [the mercantile capital of a nation is limited in a given time, and those who dispose of it, always desiring to put it out to the greatest advantage, have no need of any new stimulant to augment it, or to turn it into new channels where it best produces profits. But all the capital of a nation is not mercantile. Inclination to idleness, which public institutions have fostered among certain nations, not only binds men, but also fetters fortunes. The same indolence, which makes those people lose their time, makes them also lose their money. The annual revenue of territorial[17] fortunes] from the moment it is reaped to the moment it is spent,[18] [forms of itself an immense capital, which may be added or deducted from the sum devoted to support industry,] and which by and large is so constantly squandered that it would be so much more desirable that it would not be so used. [In southern countries], while there was not enough capital for an industry the country needed, [the whole revenue of the nobility][19] after having lain idle in their coffers for many months, [was annually dissipated in useless pomp; but to recall the heads of noble families into activity has likewise been found sufficient to give them habits of economy. The great French, or Italian proprietor, becoming a manufacturer, has, at once, given a useful direction to the revenue of his land, and by adding his own activity to that of a nation becoming more industrious, has added likewise all the power of his wealth, which formerly lay unemployed.

The torpor of a nation may sometimes be so great, that the clearest demonstration of advantages, which it might derive from a new species of industry, shall never induce it to make the attempt. Example, alone, can then awake self-interest. French industry has found, in the single little state of Lucca, more than ten new branches, to employ itself upon, with great advantage both for the country and those engaged in them.[20] The most absolute liberty was not sufficient to direct attention to these objects. The zeal and activity of the princess Eliza, who called into her little sovereignty several head-manufacturers, who furnished them with money and houses, who brought the produce of their shops into fashion, has founded a more durable prosperity in a decaying city, and restored to a beneficent activity much capital and intellect, which, but for her, would forever have remained unemployed,] a prosperity that has only ended with the contrary action of a new government.[21]

[When government means to protect commerce, it often acts with precipitation, in complete ignorance of its true interests; almost always with despotic violence, which tramples underfoot the greater part of private arrangements; and almost always with an absolute forgetfulness of the advantage of the consumers,] whose welfare is identical with that of the nation. [Yet it must not be inferred, that government never does good to trade. It is government which can give habits of dissipation or economy; which can attach honour or discredit to industry and activity; which can turn the attention of scientific men to apply their discoveries to the arts; government is the richest of all consumers; it encourages manufactures by the mere circumstance of giving them its custom. If to this indirect influence it join the care of rendering all communications easy; of preparing roads, canals, bridges; of protecting property, of securing a fair administration of justice; if it do not overload its subjects with taxation; if, in levying taxes, it adopt no disastrous system,—it will effectually have served commerce, and its beneficial influence will counterbalance many false measures, many prohibitory laws,] many monopolies, [in spite of which, and not by reason of which, commerce will continue to increase under it.]

End of Fourth Book and of the First Volume.

Translator's Notes to Chapter 12, Fourth Book

As in preceding chapters, the title of this chapter does not in any way prepare the reader for its contents, a fairly extensive survey of conditions in the United States, as based on the account of an English traveller who scouted opportunities for what appears to have been a group of dissenters contemplating emigration from Great Britain to escape discrimination. In some of its passages, Sismondi sounds like John Stuart Mill in his chapter on the stationary state in the *Principles*. It seems that the United States was regarded with a great deal of ambiguity at that time. On the one hand, the United States was seen as a new world in which ideal societies could be realized (New Harmony, for instance); on the other hand, it was seen as harboring a population that was exclusively, and vulgarly, devoted to money and profit, bent on amassing wealth at all cost, particularly at the expense of the unsuspecting immigrant, so graphically described by Dickens in *Martin Chuzzlewitt*. The chapter reveals once more Sismondi's ambiguity towards orthodox Smithian doctrines. He sees the possible benefits of a free-market system, but he is too much of a historian and, more important, a realist not to see the blemishes of the new system. This chapter in a most graphic way reveals that he is an intellectual of the eighteenth century, a rationalist who has to devise an analytical system to deal with a world in very rapid change. His task was in many ways akin to that faced by Keynes in the interwar years, and that confronts the economic profession at the present time—to account for technologically induced and accelerated transformations of social institutions. Because Sismondi was neither a revolutionary nor a visionary it was extremely difficult for him to envision a new economic and, above all, technological order. Here and later, he tries to apply to the problems he sees the rules he acquired as a youngster in Geneva. Given the difficulty of fully appreciating the change that overtook Europe then, he did not do so badly.

1. Sismondi touches here on the major problem of classic free-trade doctrine: the contradiction between individual freedom, as exemplified by the market and a monetized economy, and the interdependence between individuals that is powerfully fostered by the division of labor. Adam Smith solved the problem by postulating an invisible hand that would harmonize the contradictory ends

of individuality and interdependence. A half-century later, Sismondi has legitimate doubts about the realism of that solution—he has seen too many failures. In purely theoretical terms Sismondi is the first writer who has some idea of the fallacy of composition that invalidates Say's Law, but his analytical acuity is not equal to making the case clearly. It should also be taken into account that the theoretical equipment of the time was on the one hand dominated by the labor theory of value, and on the other had not had the time to develop many of the analytical categories that are now part of the standard tools of the political economist.

2. Sismondi uses the limited-market argument often, mainly to explain exploitation of the working class. Even as a self-proclaimed follower of Adam Smith, he was still wedded to mercantilistic and Thomistic ideas.
3. The first edition read: "Doit-on appeler les acheteurs, les tributaires, ou les producteurs, les salariés de l'étranger?" This paragraph, very briefly, recapitulates the debate between Jefferson and Hamilton on the future economic course of the United States.
4. These were most likely Quakers, or some other dissenters.
5. In other words, just a year before the publication of the first edition of *New Principles*. It is possible that Sismondi saw these reports through the agency of his brother-in-law Josiah Wedgwood, who was a prominent dissenter.
6. In the first edition this reads "imposantes."
7. In the first edition, the singular "land" was used.
8. Sismondi had a great aversion to bankruptcy because of his childhood experiences. He strove all his life to maintain himself in a modest, but financially secure position.
9. The War of 1812.
10. The French term is *la partie stationnaire*. Apparently Sismondi equates *conservative* with reluctance to engage in profit seeking.
11. This should be compared to John Stuart Mill's brief discussion of United States society in his chapter on the stationary state, *Principles of Political Economy*, 1848.
12. Sismondi rearranged this short clause from the *Encyclopedia* for *New Principles* by omitting "are contrary even to sound policy or justice; and . . ." after "manufactures."
13. This is a straight contradiction of Adam Smith's dictum that it is the self-interest of the individual that governs economic activity. Sismondi implies here that self-interest may also defend established institutions, a notion made popular later by Thorstein Veblen under the name of *the vested interest*. The idea came to Sismondi most likely from utility considerations.
14. There is a paragraph break here in *New Principles*, but not in the *Encyclopedia*.
15. Sismondi omitted here from the *Encyclopedia* "and in such applications see nothing but what they call *cookery* of the sciences."
16. "Those who recommended" was added in the second edition.
17. The French text reads "fortunes nationales."
18. This was added to the second edition.
19. The reference here is most likely to southern Italy, the *Mezzogiorno*, which at that time was the reactionary Kingdom of The Two Sicilies, feudal, agricultural, and with immense landholdings that gave to the owners large incomes and left the agricultural population in great poverty. The problem of the Mezzogiorno has persisted till the present time, even though successive governments have

tried to change the economic climate there. The description is a good example of development analysis. The next clause in the sentence was added in the second edition.

20. As noted, Sismondi had a farm in the state, and his mother and his sister lived there.
21. All the prejudices of the Calvinist show here, at the same time losing from sight, conveniently, the previous critical assessment of industrial development as a creator of a numerous miserable working population. The historical reference is to the difference between the Napoleonic era, and the return of the previous dynasty after the Congress of Vienna.

Fifth Book

Of Money

Introduction

This book corresponds to the fifth chapter of the *Encyclopedia* article. In monetary matters, Sismondi is an arch-conservative who takes an uncompromising stand against paper money and what he sees as its association with government debt. Given his experiences and the prevailing practices of almost all governments right after the Napoleonic Wars, his total opposition to the Scottish school of money, including Adam Smith, is not surprising. All countries were afflicted with war debts that had been converted into paper money, and therefore sustained constant inflation in various degrees. Sismondi had written a pamphlet on the Austrian currency during his German travels with Madam de Staël, but his horror of governmental deficits is of course also a function of his father's experience with the French debt peddled by his copatriot Necker just before the Revolution. Some historical awareness of the John Law *bubble* of 1719–1720, and direct experience with the assignats of the French revolutionary government and the ensuing inflation can be safely assumed to be also involved in this position.

1

Money, Sign, Pledge, and Measure of Value

[Wealth incessantly circulates from producers to consumers, by means of money. All kinds of exchange are accomplished under this form, whether the means of producing wealth are transmitted from one proprietor to another, or when land or movable capital changes its owner, or when labour is sold, or when the object destined to be consumed reaches the hands that are to use it. Money facilitates all these exchanges; it occurs among the different contractors as a thing which all desire, and by means of which every one may find what he immediately requires; as a thing, moreover, submitted to invariable calculation, and by means of which all other values may be appreciated, this alone being their scale.

Money performs several functions at once: it is the sign of all other values; it is their pledge and also their measure. As a sign money represents every other kind of wealth; by transmittimg it from hand to hand we transmit a right to all other values. It is not money itself which the day-labourer requires; but food, clothing, lodging, of which it is the sign. It is not for money that the manufacturer wishes to exchange his produce, but for the raw materials, that he may again begin to work; and for the objects of consumption, that he may begin to enjoy. It is not money which the capitalist lends the merchant to profit by;[1] it is all that the merchant will purchase with this money, immediately afterwards; for so long as the merchant keeps it in its original shape, he can draw no advantage from it;] and it is only at the moment that the money has left his hands, or that the sign has been exchanged against the reality, that his capital will bear fruit. [By an abuse of language, which has caused much error and confusion, the words money and capital have become almost synonymous. Money indeed represents all other capital, but it is itself the capital of no man; it is always barren by nature, and wealth does not begin to increase] till the moment one has gotten rid of it.[2]

[Money is not only the sign of wealth, it is also the pledge of it. It not only represents wealth, it contains the worth of it. Like wealth, it has been produced by a labour which it wholly compensates. In work and advances of all sorts employed in extracting it from the mine, it has cost a value equal to what it passes for in the world. It furnishes to trade a commodity which is expensive; because, purchased like every other, it is the sole kind of wealth which is not increased by circulation, or dissipated by enjoyment. It issues, still without alteration, from the hands of him who employs it usefully, and of him who squanders it upon his pleasures. But the high price at which society acquires money, though at first view it appears an inconvenience, is precisely what gives it the merit of being an imperishable pledge for its possessions. As its value was not given by arbitrary convention, arbitrary convention cannot take its value away. It may be more or less sought after according as it occurs more or less abundantly in the market; but its price can never deviate very far from what would be required to extract an equal quantity from the mine.

Money, in the last place, is a common measure of values. Before the invention of money, it must have been very difficult to compare the value of a bag of corn[3] with that of a yard of cloth. Dress was equally necessary with food; but the processes, by which men procured them, seemed scarcely susceptible of being compared. Money has furnished a common and invariable unity to which everything can be referred.]

Under certain circumstances, these three properties that define money can be seen to exist separately in the trade of some peoples. Bank notes and bills of exchange are but the sign of values without being their pledges;[4] a confusion of these relationships has induced more than one government to convert the former to paper money; the real difference which exists between them has almost always brought in its train the ruin of the country that has mistaken the sign for the pledge of exchange.

On the other hand, the gold dust used as a general medium of exchange in the trade of Guinea, can be thought of as representing the pledge of values without being their sign; it has no numerical unit; it does not in any way represent to the mind in any precise manner the value of any single item, or the value of all things; it is only always equally desired by everyone, and it offers thus to everyone a trustworthy medium of exchange.

The lack of a unit of account in the gold dust has prompted the Mangigues, a people of Africa, who use it in place of money, to create a measure of value, entirely separate from this universal commodity; it is an abstract quantity they call *macute* which does not refer to anything in particular, and has no bodily existence, and is not at all, like our moneys of account, the sum of many real moneys; but it is only conceived of in the mind as an ideal term of comparison. This ox is worth ten macutes, this slave fifteen, this glass pearl necklace two; these items are exchanged immediately one against the other; and the macutes that cannot be given nor received, serve but to count the values of what is really received. The macutes are the measure of values, even though they are neither their sign nor their pledge.[5]

Translator's Notes to Chapter 1, Fifth Book

The introductory chapter is taken almost entirely from the *Encyclopedia*. At the end Sismondi embellished it by referring to monetary practices in Africa. As one of them he cites "macutes," a monetary institution that was prominently mentioned by Montesquieu in *L'ésprit des lois*, book 12, chapter 8, although spelled *macoutes* there. This example was apparently popular because it appears elsewhere in the literature. An attempt is made to clarify the term *pledge* (paragraph 3); it would seem to mean that the money commodity (gold, silver) has an inherent value of its own derived from the labor incorporated in it, and the market price of it must approximate at all times the cost of its acquisition. Sismondi sees this characteristic as necessary to guard against a depreciation of all other values. It is interesting that a writer otherwise attuned to utility considerations and the role of demand in, for example, the price of labor, can forget them when dealing with money. This is a particularly clear example of the idiosyncratic nature of all social theorizing. See also note 2.

1. The words "to profit by" do not appear in *New Principles*, but have been retained to save the integrity of the quotation from the *Encyclopedia*.
2. Sismondi takes here the orthodox Aristotelian position that money has no utility, as opposed to utility concepts applied to demand questions. The idea is also opposed to his concept of gold being a *pledge*. In the following discussion of money as a pledge, he disregards his own view that wages are a variable determined by negotiation and market power, and assumes that gold has a stable value that represents the labor incorporated in it, a view that is shared by Marx. Historically, this is clearly not true, and Sismondi, as a historian, should have known that gold and silver can have widely varying purchasing power, depending on the supply of the metals.
3. The term *corn* designates always the most common cereal. Here it stands for wheat.
4. In other words, they contain no inherent value, as representing the cost of mining the gold, but are merely the representatives of "real" money.
5. Sismondi's terminology is confusing, and because of his preconception that money must be full-bodied coin he fails to see that money can indeed be anything that is commonly used as such. He also fails to see that gold dust must, like full-bodied coin, incorporate, by his view, real value and therefore be a pledge within his meaning of the word.

2

Of the Proportion That Arises between Wealth and Money

We have observed the creation of wealth by labor and thrift; we have seen that its constant end is the happiness of man; we have traced step by step the wealth that comes from the soil, and what is created by toil in commerce; we have shown how it is distributed among citizens, and how it fulfills its role through consumption, followed immediately by reproduction.[1] But all things labor produces and enjoyment consumes, we have seen pass from hand to hand by exchange; and money is almost always the intermediary and common measure of that exchange. No possession passes from seller to purchaser without some coins of equal estimated value passing from purchaser to seller at the same time. These same coins, indeed, do not remain at all with the seller, as the commodity stays with the buyer; the seller must in turn become a buyer; his coins pass to others, who will transfer them to others again. There is no bar to these very same coins accomplishing one or two hundred different payments during the year. However, the movement of the sold goods shows at all times an equal movement to, but in the opposite direction of, the money which pays for them.

Some writers in political economy, struck by this main equality, have concluded that the money circulation must be of equal value to the sold goods, forgetting that a coin changes masters ten or twenty times for every time that goods are sold.[2] This assumption cannot stand up to even cursory examination: it is like observing that goods are transported in bundles from one warehouse to another, and that there should be as many porters as bundles to keep trade going. This comparison is more appropriate than would seem at first blush; each bundle is transported from one warehouse to another by the intervention of the coins for which it sells, just as much as by the shoulders of the porters who carry them; but the same coins, like the porters, repeat, day after day, the same service for new bundles. However, there ought to be a certain proportion between the number, or rather the movement of bundles, and that of the porters who carry, and the coins that pay for them. Merchants increase, or decrease, these exchanges of bundles in accordance with the wishes of the buyers and sellers, and not in accordance with the means of transport. No more vigor is given to buying and selling by adding coins, which are one of the means of transport, than by adding porters, who are the other.

Equal amounts of wealth do not use in any way an equal amount of money for their distribution, because the frequency of exchanges is much more related to the nature of wealth than its value; hence the abundance of money in a country does not indicate, of necessity, the wealth of that country. Scarcity of money is not at all a sure indication of poverty; but the proportion of money which each particular wealth sets in motion deserves some comment.[3]

Agricultural wealth is of all types that which demands the least amount of money to accomplish its circulation. Actually, a large part of the income produced by agriculture is consumed by those who produced it, without having been the object of any exchange. The peasant-owner, who lives from his corn and the meat of his flock, who drinks his wine, who dresses in the cloth which his wife has spun from his hemp, his wool, who pays no rent for his cottage, hardly ever sees a shilling, unless he needs it to pay his taxes; whereas the city worker, in a much more confined condition, with many needs, less enjoyments, and constantly threatening poverty, never procures for himself food, clothing, housing, except with cash in hand. His miserable existence sets in motion an amount of money ten or twenty times larger than that of the peasant.[4]

Perhaps one half of all provisions passes from the soil to the consumer without having occasioned the movement of even one shilling; the other half is rarely purchased to be resold; a single exchange brings it usually from the original producer to the consumer. It is but a small part which, gathered as an object of trade, and passing through many hands, demands many times the services of money.

But the income which springs from the soil is again but a small part of territorial wealth; landed property itself, with all its improvements, truly makes up the common wealth. Now, this property demands only an infinitely small sum of money because of its very slow circulation. An inherited attachment, most often strengthened by prejudice, keeps a landed estate most often in the hands of the same family for many generations. Whereas the value of landed estates in France comes to several tens of billions[5] it needs hardly some millions, perhaps some hundred thousands, to settle all the payments to which the buying and selling of these estates gives rise every week.

Independently of the annual harvests and the estates, one can also include, as part of territorial wealth, the circulating capital intended to improve the land, which consists of cattle, agricultural machinery, and seed; but even this capital of the farmer does not in any way turn over very quickly, and does not at all require the services of a large money supply; it is consumed and reproduced on the farm with few exchanges, and it would be a lot if it caused in four years the movement of as many pounds as its own value.

After this review of all the parts of territorial wealth, it is clear that purely agricultural countries need to maintain only a very small quantity of money; they have no call for it; and if, instead of coin, they are given paper money, or bank notes, they would be even more hampered by it. Nevertheless, with such a small amount of money they can be very rich, keeping all their inhabitants in great comfort; make annual savings; create greatness for posterity; pay into the public treasury generous contributions, yet they will have enough money to settle their accounts; from the moment they have a surplus they can spare to give to the treasury, they can also export it to obtain their medium of exchange. If they have a small amount of money, that is so because of the nature of their wealth, they need no more of it. Under these circumstances, if they would have gold or silver mines, they would export the entire output.

It should be noted that, in a wholly agricultural society, it is not only money that is not needed, but also circulating capital. Land is improved by fixed capitals; they are bound to the property, and are never separated therefrom. As to circulating capitals, those which buy and replace the annual harvest, the country has soon enough of them; the advance in wealth will be quite helpful to the progress of agriculture, but not to a proportional progress in the grain and cattle trade. Also, the peasant farmer who has saved a little capital, most often lays it by as a reserve in the form of money; and at the same time that the circular flow is completed with many less coins, it is on the other hand much slower.[6]

After all we have just said it is now understandable that, in a purely agricultural country, it is very difficult to levy suddenly a new tax, raise a large loan, to sell all at once a great number of estates, despite its wealth; neither wealth nor confidence are lacking, but only money and circulating capital at the same time, because this country has no need for either one or the other for the development of its industry. To force on it money, either real or representative, will have no effect on its prosperity, not any more than providing it with porters to transport the goods it does not have. *Mobilize the lands to improve them,* as is often said without understanding, proposes to exchange fields against fields; this will leave the nation with precisely the same proportion of lands and circulating capital as before. Circulating capital is not *mobilized land*, but consumable wealth, and one profits and enjoys it only by consuming it.

The small amount of circulating capital, and consequently of money, that agricultural wealth needs, explains also the difficulty that is always encountered in selling land, not only in purely agricultural countries, but even in those which combine the two industries. Land is only sold for circulating capital; and if this capital is relatively scarce in purely agricultural countries, it is also very difficult, in countries which combine both industries, to change the direction of its application, to make it pass from trade to agriculture. Generally not enough account is taken of the power of habit; human habits tie down capital, and an advantage must be well advertised and of long standing, to deflect even a small part of such capital from its accustomed ways.[7]

Business wealth causes an altogether rapid circulation of both money and capital. That part of the annual output that is consumed by its producers is so infinitesimally small, that it can hardly be taken into account; all the rest is distributed through exchange, and exchange requires money. The journeyman hatter barely makes one hat for himself in the course of a year, whereas his everyday subsistence demands the sale of his labor, the purchase of his bread, and the use of money for both.

This is not all; agricultural exchange affects only a part of all agricultural income; business exchanges comprise the totality of all commercial capitals, and they renew themselves without end. In textile manufacturing, the wool merchant must have a circulating capital equal in value to the shepherd's fleeces it takes the place of, and the exchange which consummates this entirely is made with the help of money; the manufacturer must have another circulating capital, larger than the previous one, to replace that of the wool merchant; the wholesaler must have a third one, the retailer a fourth, without counting the additional capitals of the carder, the cloth-shearer, the dyer, the teamster, the broker, who finish the processing of the cloth and bring it to the consumer. Each of these capitals consists of consumer goods that are for the most part not yet finished, and pass from one processor to another by means of money. Undoubtedly, the value of money is very far from being the same as the value of the capital it circulates, but ultimately a certain proportion between the value of both must exist; likewise, if business should experience stringency, if it were lacking money proportional to such movement, it could not attract any share of money that would be superior. Business needs to achieve the transfer of goods from the producer to the consumer without delay and hindrance. If transport facilities are lacking, it will call them in from the outside; if they are overabundant, it will send them back, because it would have no use for them, and it is not the means of transport that determine the movement.

Translator's Notes to Chapter 2, Fifth Book

This chapter is entirely new, without reference to the *Encyclopedia*. Sismondi's description reflects an economy not yet fully monetized in the agricultural sector. Producers have no need for money except for taxes, and the peasant lives from what he produces on his farm. The observations made about the differing needs for liquidity in the two main sectors distinguished, trade and agriculture, are examples of astute institutional analysis, which set Sismondi apart from his contemporaries. Unfortunately, it also leads him into considerations of details that make it difficult to construct a coherent theory of economic behavior.

1. As in previous chapters, Sismondi refers here to the replacement of consumed goods by the next cycle of production.
2. It is not quite clear whom Sismondi had in mind. Almost every known writer in political economy of the time knew that the money circulation was not as large as the goods circulated by such money. He may have used this as a straw man to explain his main point, the separateness of capital and money.
3. This short paragraph refutes mercantilistic doctrine that abundance of gold and silver in a nation is always a sign of wealth. As Sismondi properly notes, a large part of Europe had only partially monetized economies. The largest economic sector, agriculture, incorporated a large number of subsistence farms, providing mostly for local needs in direct market sales. There were farming entities that produced for the market, for example, Italian rice farmers in the Po valley; estates in England, northern Germany, and Poland for cereals; and of course sheep farming, mainly in England. On the other hand, cities were the major part of the money economy, and Sismondi describes this economic dichotomy very well, including the still-prevailing craft nature of industry.
4. This is one more example of Sismondi's romantic vision of country life versus city life. One cannot help, when reading this paragraph, of thinking of his first work, the *Tableau*, and it is not farfetched to assume that his nostalgia for his Tuscan metayerie never left him. He takes a consistently pessimistic view of the city worker, which may also be explainable by his acquaintance with the sometimes-appalling living conditions in cities, like London, that had absorbed a large influx of workers from the countryside. On the other hand, in his chapters on agriculture in book 3, he has a more realistic view of the joys of country life.
5. The text reads "milliards," the European equivalent for billions.
6. Sismondi seems to have had a good understanding of the importance of money velocity. One wonders what he would have said about modern agriculture with its massive investments in machines. However, his observation about the low need for circulating capital is still relatively true today. His observation on gold and silver mining in agricultural societies could, in his time, be applied to the United States.
7. This observation anticipates Veblen's analysis of institutional inertia by about eighty years. It also falls entirely outside the basic assumptions of classical political economy, which stipulate quick responses to market changes, for example, the influence of the interest rate on investment.

3

Fundamental Differences between Money and Capital

[The important part which money performs in political economy, and the various properties by which it animates exchange, and protects and serves to measure them, explain the illusion which has misled, not only the vulgar, but even the greater part of statesmen, and exhibited this commodity in their eyes as the efficient cause of labour, and the creator of all wealth.[1] It is essential for us, however, to pause here, that we may both display those errors in a clear point of view, and firmly demonstrate the principles which follow. In the epoch of civilization, at which we are arrived, no labour can be accomplished without a capital to set it in motion; but this capital, though almost constantly represented by money, is yet quite a different thing. An increase of the national capital is the most powerful encouragement to labour; but an increase in the circulating medium has not of necessity the same effect. Capitals co-operate powerfully in the annual reproduction of wealth, giving rise to an annual revenue; but money continues barren, and gives rise to no revenue. Indeed, the competition between those capitals, which are offered to accomplish the annual labour of the nation, forms the basis for the interest of money; but the greater or less abundance of the circulating medium, has no influence in the fixing of this interest.][2] Accumulated capitals can finally be borrowed by the government for the benefit of the nation; but the money which serves as a transport, is but the agent of that contract.

[Painful experience has shown all the inhabitants of Europe what a dearth was, and a period of general penury among a civilized people. At these mournful epochs, every one has heard it a hundred times observed, that it was not corn or food which was wanting, but money. Indeed, vast magazines of corn have often remained full till the next harvest; those provisions, if proportionably shared among the people, would have almost always been sufficient for their support; but the poor, having no money to offer, were not able to buy them; they could not, in exchange for their labour, obtain money, or at least enough of it, to subsist. Money was wanting, natural wealth superabundant. What phenomenon could appear more proper to confirm the universal prejudice which looks for wealth in money, not in consumable capital?

But the money, which is wanting in a time of scarcity, is the wage offered to the workman to make him labour; the wage, by means of which he would have purchased a subsistence. The workmen never labour, except when some of those who have accumulated capitals, or in other words, the fruit of preceding labours, can profit from capitals, by furnishing, on one hand, the raw material, on the other, a subsistence for the artisan. Labour cannot be carried on so as to produce any material fruit, any fruit capable of becoming wealth, without raw materials on which to operate; the workman cannot labour without food to support him; and therefore, every kind of labour is impossible without a capital previously existing in objects of consumption, to furnish his materials and his wages; and, if the workman himself lay out these advances, it is because he combines for his little object, the two characters of capitalist and artisan.][3]

What is lacking then in a time of scarcity is consumable capital that would have been transmitted by money; but not that money itself. This has not diminished in Europe at all; it had even increased in many places which experienced pressing want, but it circulated no longer as quickly as capital; be it that this real capital was destroyed by various calamities, by war, bad harvests, be it that it had not yet been released so as to perform its functions. Since, after having nourished labor, capital must wait for the consumer and replace itself with the income of the latter, it cannot begin again the former function if it has not accomplished the second.[4] But the calamities which had not harmed capitals, had affected incomes. These did not replace at all, in their usual way, the circulating capitals; consumption shrank, work had to shrink also; no money at all came in to pay the wages.

[As the workman requires a capitalist, so the capitalist requires workmen; because his capital will be unproductive if it continues idle; and the revenue which he expects and has to live upon, springs from the labour which he causes to be executed. Hence, whenever he is occupied in a productive enterprise, he employs all his capital in causing labour, and leaves no part of it in idleness. If he is a clothmaker, and has devoted ten thousand pounds to his manufacture, he does not stop till his ten thousand pounds] are entirely converted into merchandise, [and he no longer has new sums to employ in the operation. If it then be asked why he stops, he will answer, like the workman, that money is wanting, that money does not circulate.

It is not, however, money which is then wanting any more than in the former case; it is consumption, or the consumer's revenue. On commencing his manufacture, the capitalist studied[5] to adjust it to the demand; and he reckoned that as soon as his cloths should be ready, they would be purchased by the consumers, whose money, the sign of their revenue, would replace his capital, and become the sign of subsistence to new workmen, to whom he would pay new wages. It is not money which the consumer is in want of, but revenue. Some have had inferior harvests this year; some have gained a smaller interest on their capitals, a smaller share on the annual re-production of the fruits of industry; others, who have no income but what arises from their labour, have not found employment; or else the whole three classes are not poorer than they were, but the manufacturer has imagined them to be richer, and regulated his production according to an income which does not exist.[6]

Income, of which we have seen all the different sources, is a material and consumable thing; it springs from labour; it is destined for enjoyment; it is exactly of the same nature with the advances in wages and raw material, laid out by the manufacturer;] and these advances, to those who receive them, become themselves an income. [Money is but the sign and measure of it. The capital it should replace is also composed of material objects, destined for consumption, and incessantly renewed. Money serves but to represent it, and always forms the smallest part of each merchant's funds. We have supposed the clothmaker to possess 100,000*l*,[7]] but we can very well understand how these funds, renewed by continuous turnover, will leave in his hands, in cash, only the output of one week, and how this output will not be more than the hundredth part of his capital. For this purpose, we will assume that 50,000 francs be employed in buildings, machines, and other fixed capital, and that his total profit ought to be 10 percent, or 10,000 francs income; that on the other hand, the weekly work product will go entirely to the merchant, who will pay cash for it. It is enough under the circumstances that the fiftieth part of his circulating capital, or 1,000 pounds be used by him each week for salaries and advances; that the same sum, with a profit of 20 percent, be reimbursed to him every week by the merchant, as he delivers his pieces of cloth. Of these 1,200 pounds,[8] he will retain each week 200 pounds for himself, which will be his income; he will pay out 1,000 pounds that will constitute the income of his employees; and the entire circulation will have been accomplished, without his ever having seen in actual cash the 100,000 pounds that make up his fortune.

[An increase of the national capitals is the most powerful encouragement of labour; either because this augmentation pre-supposes an augmentation of income, and, consequently, of means of consumption; or because these capitals, not being profitable to their proprietor, except as they are employed, each capitalist incessantly endeavours to create new production by their means] which would have a market. [In distributing them to his workmen, he gives to those workmen a revenue which enables them to purchase and consume the preceding year's production; and he sees those capitals return increased by the revenue, which he is to expect from them in the following year's production. But though he distributes and afterwards recovers them, by means of the circulating medium, which serves for all exchanges, it is not the circulating medium which forms the essential requisite in his operations. The same clothmaker, labouring each year on an equal quantity] has sent during the year 2400 ells of cloth to the cloth merchant, who has bought them at his price; they were [valued at 60,000 pounds, or 25*l* a piece. He exchanges 400 pieces for such objects of consumption as are needed to supply the wants, the enjoyments, the luxuries of himself and family. He exchanges 2000 pieces for the raw-materials, and the labour which, within the year, are to re-produce an equal quantity; and thus next year, and every following year, he will have, as before, 2400 pieces to exchange on the same conditions. His capital, equally with his revenue, is actually in cloths, not in money; and the perpetual result of his commerce is to exchange] produced cloth against cloth yet to be produced.

[If the consumption of cloth is increased, if by this means his trade, in place of comprehending 2400 pieces annually, comprehends 3000, more labour will, no doubt, be ordered by him, and executed by his workmen; but if the money alone is increased, and not the consumption or the income which determines it, labour and production cannot increase.][9]

We have assumed that every eight days the producer received from the merchant, for whom he worked, the value of the finished goods, and that therefore it was enough for him to draw 1200 pounds, employing thereof 1000 in his business. If, through a change of routine by the merchant, his cloths are picked up only every fortnight, he will need to be paid 2400 pounds to enable him to maintain his factory at the same level of activity; if the manufacturer has no merchant, who, after having given him an order in advance of his work, takes it off his hands as soon as it is produced, then he must wait for buyers; if he sells his output, as is the case in many manufactures, at the fair, which is held every three months, then, in order to maintain the same level of activity, every fair must pay him 15,000 francs.[10] He will thus have much more cash in his trade, without having more business, and hence he will have less profits. In the first case, the entire turnover of his factory can be accomplished by the same 240 crowns of 5 francs each that returned to his hands after they left them; in the second case, he needs 480; and in the third, he needs 3,000 to turn out exactly the same output. Interest on the former was hardly important in the accounting he makes of his profits; interest on the latter is already a heavy charge. He has always the same fixed capital, 50,000 francs; he needs the same 50,000 francs, in started cloth, in wool and stock, to supply every week his workers; the former are always represented by the same structures; the latter, by the same 2,000 ells of cloth; but he needs also 15,000 francs in cash, waiting in the register, from the moment of sale to that of expenditure; and if his profit is always the same 10,000 francs annually, it will not be more than 8 and two-thirds, instead of 10 percent, on his capital.[11]

Whether we consider in turn the merchant or the consumer, we will not find that the increased use of money, given the same turnover, adds the least little bit either to the wealth of the business, or to productive activity. [Let us take separately each one of the customers] of the merchant. [There is not one of them who does not levy a greater or a smaller portion of his income in kind, but all may arrange matters so as to receive the whole of it in money.] One can lease out the farm he had cultivated himself; the other can place at interest the capital he had in his business. [They are not, however, more rich on this account; they will not be at more expense; they will not buy more cloth from him, and his trade will experience no kind of augmentation.

What happens to individuals may equally happen to nations. The revenue of a country, or the sum total of profits arising from the different kinds of labour, amounted, we shall say, last year, and this year, to fifty millions; but last year, the country levied all its profits in goods, in merchandise destined for its consumption; this year, from some mercantile circumstance, some arrangement of exchanges, it has levied the fourth, the third part, in money imported through the frontiers. It is neither richer nor poorer, for this alteration; its consumption will, as formerly, be fifty millions; and with regard to the money imported, apparently its industry required this money,] because of some slowdown in its circulation, [otherwise it will be again exported. To increase the circulating medium of a country, without increasing its capital, without increasing its revenue, without increasing its consumption, is to do nothing for its prosperity, nothing for the encouragement of labour.][12]

We have seen that every time private interest is involved, in almost all cases where a felt need is expressed by saying that there is a lack of money, it is capital that is lacking, and not money. What is true of private individuals concerning their prosperity, is equally so of governments in the administration of public prosperity. Money is but a sign of their finances; by its means they dispose, in normal times, of a part of everyone's income, and in times of crisis, when the state must be defended or saved, of a part of the capital accumulated by everybody. Now, this revenue, this capital, are material things, consumables, suited to sustain life, and to set work into motion. What matters to the state is that its administrators, its judges, its soldiers, its sailors, its armorers, its munition makers, all those who perform for it a public task, be fed, clothed, housed, according to rank, during the time of their labor; that raw materials be given to those who make arms for the others, that everyone receive all the consumables that must be used up in the public service.

All these goods exist in the hands of individuals, they are the result of their labor; control over them must be given to the government, so that it can, for its part, turn them over to the different agents it hires. This transfer is facilitated by the use of money; it might be, and is sometimes, accomplished instantly. The more or less of the goods transferred does not change its essence. Men are ruled and defended, not with money, but with commodities and labor, the same things that enable them to live. Government needs to take these things in one place, and give them in another. Usually it does this with money; but if money be lacking, it can still accomplish its task; if it lacked the goods, even having the money, the administration and defense of the nation would be impossible.

In normal times the expenses of government ought to be only a part of national expense; therefore it ought to come from revenue; but in times of emergency, when survival is more precious even than wealth, that expense must come from capital or the wealth accumulated by many generations. This dissipation of capital is accomplished by loans which appear to be only demands on those who have money. However, those who hold money are not at all those who lend the capital, neither are they the ones to whom it will be returned.

The state borrows leather to make boots, cloth to make uniforms, powder and lead to make ammunition, iron to make guns, provisions to feed workers and soldiers. It borrows and dispenses all these accumulated commodities, normally without reproduction, or at least without saleable reproduction.[13] It does not oblige itself to return them all at once, but only to return annually a part of the annual production of similar things, or others of equal value, in the ratio of interest to capital it has received. Money, in this borrowing and its repayment, is but a means to facilitate the transaction and to keep the accounts. It does nothing but pass quickly, first from the hands of the lender, then to the government and its agents, then to those who sell to the government the goods and labor it employs; and anew it passes, by repayment, from the taxpayer to the government, and then to the lender. More of it is not necessarily needed for large loans than for small ones, it needs only to move faster.

All that we have said about a manufacture at the beginning of this chapter can be applied to this circulation. If the state borrows 400,000,000 francs, but with such a regular and quick circulation that it will use the money it receives in the same week, safe in the assumption that in the following week it will receive as much again, and will be able to use it in the same way, then the same coins will be constantly shuttled back and forth, and the entire loan will be raised, and spent with 8,000,000 in money, or 1,600,000 crowns at five francs. If the slowness of payments, of provisioning, of repayments, prevents that the same coin make more than four circuits during the year, or three months pass from the moment it enters the till of the lender, to the moment it leaves the treasury of the government, then 100,000,000 in money will be needed, or 20,000,000 crowns at five francs, to raise the loan of 400,000,000, and spend it. If, finally, this loan is raised all at once, if the 400,000,000 are accumulated in their entirety before they are spent, if they are paid to foreigners in such a way that it takes much time for the coins to complete their circulation and return to the country, then actually 400,000,000 coins will be needed to raise a loan of 400,000,000.[14]

On the occasion of the decline of government obligations, we have seen entirely bizarre theories advanced on the supposed relations between the mass of rents owed by the state and the money circulation, as if each crown owed by the treasury ought to have somewhere its counterpart in money, and as if there were some ratio resulting from the nature of things, between the crowns that have been used once to make a single payment, and which may then have been exported, melted down, or replaced by others, and the coins that are necessary every day for every market, between all buyers and all sellers of everything in the world. It is impossible to contend against this incomprehensible theory, since it had been founded on very specious reasoning.

The error of those who consider lenders as the true owners of the great mass of money, is more common, and somehow more tempting; it has no better basis in fact.

In our days colossal fortunes have been made in Europe, and they have secured the trade to which the loans have given rise.[15] These bankers, whose credit has become a new power, have placed themselves as intermediaries between governments and capitalists. They purchase the loan to resell it before they have paid it, and they undertake to find the lenders, those who have stocks of accumulated goods, and are willing to have them consumed by the government, in return for annual interest, rather than have them consumed by productive workers who will return to them next year an even greater amount of commodities.

The medium of all these contracts is always money; but the bankers themselves, who appear to be nothing but merchants of money, possess proportionally hardly more thereof than other citizens. Let us assume that it be true that the richest of them has a fortune of 50,000,000; if we could see his balance sheet, we would perhaps find that this sum is made up of 10,000,000 in English obligations, as well as those of Holland, France, and Vienna, of 8,000,000 to 9,000,000 in bills of exchange on all markets in Europe, and at most a million in cash. A like fortune is created to command an immense credit; it is easily converted to cash, but it does not consist of money after all; and, at the moment where the banker underwrites a new loan, he must buy the cash he does not have by selling the assets that make up his portfolio. In order to do so, he counts on the crowns every citizen has in his pocket; they will not at all be difficult to find; but he also counts on accumulated goods, on real capitals that people would rather put out at interest than to employ them in working businesses, to repay him eventually; and if these capitals do not exist in the country, or if they do not exist in a quantity equal to what the loan requires, unless it utterly paralyzes all industry, government obligations will fall, and the loan will not be taken up, whatever sureties may be offered.[16]

Translator's Notes to Chapter 3, Fifth Book

A major part of this chapter is taken from the *Encyclopedia,* showing that already there Sismondi was very concerned with what he considered confusion between capital and money, that is, the notion that business activity could be stimulated by the injection of money into the economy. As a firm believer in the benefits of a full-bodied currency and strongly opposed to any form of paper money, he viewed any step in the direction of making bank liabilities money as economically disastrous. This opinion ties in with his other opinion on capital, namely, the idea that oversupply of capital in the absence of effective demand leads to overexpansion of production and eventually to economic recession. This, like the other chapters in this book, is not a very clear discussion of money, but in one respect the analysis is very perceptive, namely, in his understanding of money velocity. Unlike many of his contemporaries, he does not assume that velocity is constant, but, on the contrary, he gives the strong impression that he considers it to be a variable, and moreover a variable that has some influence on economic activity.

1. The reference here is to mercantilistic doctrine and practice.
2. This straight Aristotelian statement is of course true, but only under the assumptions Sismondi admits. He takes the view that money is a veil of real economic activity.
3. Sismondi could still assume that the artisan could combine these two roles, although he restricts such action to a "little object"; with Marx this assumption is gone, and in fact has been converted into its opposite, namely that the small

entrepreneur will be destroyed and forced into the proletariat by massed capital.

4. Sismondi is consistent in linking consumption to business activity and the circulation of resources. One of the questions that arise for a modern reader, accustomed to a diet of data, is the origin of the information that is used and cited by writers like Sismondi. Here, one would have to ask how he knew that money had increased in Europe with an accompanying decrease of velocity.
5. The French text reads "le chef d'atelier avait cru la proportionner aux besoins du marché . . ." It is not quite clear whether the copy of the *Encyclopedia* article omitted some words here or not; the original of the article was not available.
6. This clearly uses a circular-flow model with lags and expectations. The approach should make it quite evident that Keynesian analysis is based on business experience, specifically merchants' experience. Sismondi did not have Keynes's developed categories of marginal utility analysis at his command, but it is noteworthy just how much his broad divisions resemble those of Keynes.
7. The *l* stands for *livres,* that is, pounds.
8. This is one thousand pounds output at net labor cost plus 20 percent profit. It simply assumes that the manufacturer adds his profit margin, with the clear implication that if the market does not take the merchandise off his hands, the profit margin will be wiped out. Marx, on the other hand, locates the margin with the worker and makes it an integral part of the value of the commodities, leading to the exploitation hypothesis. Sismondi can argue that if the consumer is willing to pay an extra 20 percent for the merchandise, the worker has not received his full share, as indeed he will in later chapters. But he also sees that the profit margin is as much a measure of risk and investment, and that there is nothing sacrosanct about the margin, being entirely subject to market evaluation. Sismondi's argument here should be compared to Marx, *Das Kapital,* 7, chapter 21. Marx uses some of the same numbers Sismondi uses in this example, raising the question whether an assumption of 20 percent profit on a capital of one thousand pounds was common at the time, or whether Marx liked the example, which appears among other quotes from Sismondi in this chapter. See also Marx's following chapter 22 for an example that is very similar to Sismondi's.
9. This is a particularly good example of Sismondi's disregard of price effects in favor of macroeconomic categories. It is obvious that he would not have favored monetary policy in whatever manner it might have been conducted. Yet, as later chapters in this book show, he knew English and Scottish banking very well.
10. A quarter year of 12.5 weeks (15,000 divided by 1,200) is assumed.
11. This could be considered as an example of transactional liquidity preference. The discussion is very similar to a discussion of transaction velocity in any standard textbook of money and banking.
12. Apparently, the example assumes exports. In *New Principles* Sismondi left out "without increasing its capital." The full citation from the *Encyclopedia* is used here.
13. Here the meaning of the term *réproduction* becomes quite clear. It means production with following replacement by consumption goods, in other words, without interruption of the circular flow. The production of war goods is obviously such an interruption, and therefore has to lead to the dissipation of capital.

14. Sismondi has a clear appreciation of the relation of money velocity to total money circulation. On the other hand, his example is based firmly on the assumption of a full-bodied coin circulation, an assumption that, after the end of the Napoleonic Wars, was hardly in keeping with reality.
15. The reference may be to the Rothschilds and the Hambros.
16. The paragraph is a graphic reminder that Sismondi had an early exposure to government loans, which he apparently never forgot. He clearly understood how bankers operate.

4

Interest Is the Fruit of Capital and Not of Money

[Since no labour can be accomplished without a capital to set it in motion; since no reproduction of wealth can take place without raw materials for the work, and subsistence for the workmen, it follows that the furnisher of those wages and materials has taken the most intimate share in the re-production; he is, in a great degree, the author of its profits, and has the most evident right to participate in them.[1] But he who lends a capital lends nothing else but those wages and raw materials represented by money. He lends a thing eminently productive; or rather the only one which is productive; for since all wealth proceeds from labour, and all labour is put in motion by its wage, he lends labour itself, or the first cause of production in all kinds of wealth.

Hence, whenever] theologians[2] have attached [an odious sense to the word *usury*, meaning by it any kind of interest paid for the use of a sum of money, under pretext that as money produced no fruit, there could be no lawful share of profit where there was no profit;] they have made an absurd distinction. There would be [just as much reason to prohibit the renting of land, or the wages of labour, because without a capital to put land and labour in exercise, both would remain unfruitful.[3]

Theologians, however, were right in saying that gold and silver were barren by nature; they are barren so long as kept in their own shape; they cease to be barren, the instant they become the sign of another kind of wealth, which is emphatically productive. Theologians, if they determined to abide by the single principle on which their prohibition was founded, should have been contented with declaring usury criminal, every time the lender obliged the borrower to keep the deposit in its primary form, locked up in a strong box, from the moment of borrowing to that of payment. For it is quite certain that money, whilst locked up, produces no fruit; and neither borrower nor lender can get good of it except by parting with it.]

However, it cannot be concluded from the actual tolerance of the theologians that the church had not expressed itself in the most precise and absolute manner against all types of interest taken for the lending of money; today, it escapes from the decrees it had thundered during centuries of ignorance, only by subtleties one has trouble understanding; and the prohibition of all interest, taken literally by pious persons, has had a marked influence on the creation of wealth in Catholic countries; it has resulted in a much greater habit of dissipation among the people, because parsimony did not lead in any way to comfort, and accumulated capital was but one more occasion to dissipate, if one wanted to put it to use.

[But, if money is of itself barren; if it produces no fruit but in so far as it is the sign of other values, then it is evident that no good can be done by multiplying the sign and not the thing. It is true, if you multiply the sign in a single country, you give this country the means of commanding] the goods the money represents, and can be found in other countries. [But when you multiply the sign in all countries at once, you do nothing for any. At present, there exists such a proportion between the sign and the thing, that a pound sterling[4] is worth a bag of corn; but if, by the stroke of a magic rod, you should instantly double all the money in the world, since every thing to be obtained in exchange would continue the same, the two pounds[5] in place of one would be required to represent a bag of corn. The quantity of corn consumed by a workman, in food, would not be altered, consequently his wage must be doubled. With twice as many guineas,[6] exactly the same work would be done, and nothing would be changed but names and numbers.

Capitalists require their capital to be employed, that it may gain a revenue; and hence they offer it for a certain price, to such as wish to cause labour; workmen on the other hand, and those who employ workmen, have need of capital for their labour; and, after reckoning up the profit expected from it, they offer a certain share of their advantage to capitalists. The necessities of money-lenders and of money-borrowers, come thus to a state of equilibrium in all markets; those classes of men agree upon a medium rate.[7] The regulator of their bargain is always the quantity of labour required by consumers, compared with the quantity of capital, representing raw materials and wages, to be disposed of in executing this labour. If the want is great, and the means of labour small, the interest of money[8] will be considerable; if, on the contrary, there is much capital in circulation, and little employment for it, interest will be very low. It must always be regulated by what is called the quantity of money offered in the market, because money is the sign of capital, though not capital itself.][9]

If money were multiplied by a wave of a magic wand, without cost to a nation, or if suddenly new mines were discovered where large amounts of gold and silver would cost nothing more than the trouble to gather them in, and that would double the amount of money in circulation, the rate of interest would in no way be changed.[10] It is true that double the amount of guineas would be needed; twice the weight of metal would be needed to get the same work done and represent the same value; but these double weights will not make the textile factory we have taken previously as an example, go any faster or slower; it would not need less than the value of 2,000 ells of cloth for paying its workmen who would have produced 2,400 during the year; it would matter little whether the ell sold for twenty-five or fifty francs, whether the account of the manufacturer with his workers is settled every week with 240 guineas at five francs or with 480; the profit would always be at ten per hundred of the capital employed; the division between the capitalist and the manufacturer would be always equally based on a comparison between the labor the one can command, and the labor for which the other can find an advantageous market; and if, before the sudden multiplication of money, this division was fixed at 4 percent for the capitalist, it would remain at the same rate after such enlargement.

But we have assumed a free addition to the national money supply that would diminish its value by just as much as it would increase its quantity. The rate of interest would not be further changed, if the money, bought at its proper value, either by trade with foreigners, or by work in mines, came to such places in much greater abundance, not having lost any of its relative value; because then the same capital would not be increased in quantity at all, it would have merely changed its form.

[Nearly all the circulating capital of each manufacturer and trader is successively presented to him under the shape of money, in its return from the buyer to the seller; but the part of his funds, which the merchant actually has in money, forms, in ordinary cases, but a small portion of the capital employed in his commerce; an infinitely greater portion being kept in its original state in his own warehouses, or in those of his debtors. On the other hand, it is almost always in the power of each merchant instantaneously to augment the quantity of money at his disposal, by selling his goods at a less profit, or by discounting the debts which are owed him.[11] In this way, he has money when he wants it without being therefore richer; the money, far from adding to his capital, is purchased with it. If such operations are performed at one time by several merchants in the same town, that town purchases money from its neighbours; if by a greater number of French, English, or German merchants, we say that

France, England, or Germany buy money. There will, in reality, be found much more in the market to make payments with; guineas will be much more abundant; but there will be neither more nor fewer stores offered to lend, and the rate of interest will not be affected in any way by the change. Such as are acquainted with the movements of trading places, know well that guineas may abound in them while capitals are scarce, or guineas may be scarce while capitals abound.

It is a gross error, then, to believe, that, in all cases, a considerable importation of the circulating medium will make the rate of interest fall, or an exportation make it rise. Money is a kind of wealth; and like any other kind of wealth] acquired by labor, [it forms part of circulating capital. If the money imported is a gift, or a tribute; if it costs nothing to the nation,] and if it loses nothing of its value, [it will certainly augment its circulating capital, and must certainly contribute to lower the rate of interest on the spot,] in the same way it would contribute to raising it if it were paid as tribute, or an expense without repayment; [but the same sums paid to the nation in goods would equally contribute] to lower interest; and would equally raise it, if it were the nation that gave its goods for free. [If, on the other hand, this money has been purchased with any other portion of the capital, in that case the sum total of the latter will remain the same, and the rate of interest will not be affected.

Upon these principles, it is easy to see how mines of silver and gold do not enrich a nation more than any other kind of industry. The precious metals drawn from the mines are goods purchased, like all other goods, at the price of labour and capital.[12] The opening of the mine, the construction of its galleries, the establishment of refining furnaces, require large advances, independently of the labour by which the ore is drawn from the bowels of the earth. This labour, and its fruits, may be exactly paid by the metal produced, and the state will gain by the operation, as by any other manufacture.] This labor may also yield an output much larger than the advances of the entrepreneur, and what its true costs were; but by the same token the output may also be much above the market demand, and the mine entrepreneur finds himself in this case in the position of a manufacturer who, through the discovery of a more economical process, has produced an output so much larger than the consumption of his neighbors, that he is obliged to lower the price, so that he can also sell to more distant consumers.[13] In reality, the purchaser of the precious metals is all of society. It needs to be provided each year with a quantity of precious metals equivalent to what is used in the goldsmith and jewelry trades, plus what the use of money destroys by abrasion. If it is given more, the total amount will decline in price, like any other merchandise whose production outstrips consumption. Finally, the mine may pay back to the entrepreneurs less than they have expended, and the money they produce may come dear to them. It is said that this is generally their fate. [The profits of mines are irregular. As the head price in a lottery seduces gamesters, an unlooked for advantage encourages miners to continue their exertions, although the usual returns be inferior to those obtained by any other kind of industry; and nearly all of them are ruined, just like gamesters, because they were at first successful.][14] Then the fixed capital used in the opening of the mine, lowered in price, and the labors expended by the first developer, are sold at a discount, and a new miner can again make his fortune, not because the mine becomes richer, but only because he has not repaid all the advances it had cost.

[From these principles, we may also conclude, that the blame so frequently imputed to Frederic II. and the Canton of Berne, for having hoarded up and withdrawn from the country a large portion of the natural circulating medium, is without foundation.] It has been asserted that, by so hoarding, the two governments had delivered a fatal blow to national industry, because they had decreased the capital that was to sustain it. A parsimonious government indeed decreases the consumption it would have made in the name of the nation, and as a consequence the reproduction that would have followed; this is no reason to blame governments for their parsimony. Since they have no income of their own, but only share in the incomes of their citizens, the less they dissipate of those, the more means to spend they leave to each citizen.[15] If governments save from their revenues in one year to provide for the expenses of the next, they still leave to everyone, during that next year, a freer disposition of their incomes, and such parsimony, profitable to each individual, is so to all. It is not in any way for diminishing national consumption that parsimonious governments could be blamed.

They can be still less blamed for decreasing the circulating capital. Money, as we have seen, does not constitute the national capital; it is but such a small part thereof, and it is not difficult to replace it either in this form, or in any other.[16] When Frederic removed these guineas from circulation, they were soon replaced by others, since the need that was felt for them had not diminished. It is true that one part of the national capital remained idle by being appropriated to the next war; but that part had been withdrawn from revenue, without exhausting anything; it had moreover been accumulated during a time of prosperity, whereas, since nations today always conduct war with their capital and not their revenue, Frederic, without such saving, would have had to raise in a moment of need and distress the same sum on the capital and industry of his state, by loans, and pay thereon the high price with which such a service is always sold by the lenders. The parsimony of the sovereign had created a new capital with which he provided for expenses that could never have born fruits. If he had relied on the expedient of loans to provide for the same expenses, he would have diverted to this end business capitals.

However, the Swiss republics that had recourse to the same expedient, could be blamed, but on principles of safety or liberty, not on those of political economy. Their treasure, which they were not strong enough to defend, was an object of envy to their neighbors, and it most likely provoked the attack they were victim of, and it then indeed fell into the hands of their enemies. Moreover, this treasure strengthened the usurpations of the aristocracy by freeing governments from demanding anything from their people in taxes, and to render an account of their finances. The citizens of the Swiss cantons will do well to bar their governments from hoarding, and they will probably have no difficulty in succeeding therein; but for that they should not invoke the principles of political economy.

Translator's Notes to Chapter 4, Fifth Book

Sismondi takes up the thorny question of the origin and use of interest. Since he was most concerned to show that money and capital are not the same thing under any circumstances, his analysis is far from clear, and in places self-contradictory. Some of the paragraphs would indicate that his business experience was at odds with economic theory, as he saw it. In that respect, it should not be forgotten that his basic ideas were strongly influenced by physiocratic concepts and utility notions acquired from eighteenth-century Italian writers, coupled to a classical labor theory of value. Utility ideas influence him to make a strong case for profit as a legitimate return to the provider of wages and raw materials, in accord with J. B. Say, but not in agreement with the labor theory of value, and certainly entirely opposed to the later doctrines of Marx. A substantial portion of the chapter comes from the *Encyclopedia*, indicating that his ideas on the subject were already fairly well developed before he started to write *New Principles*.

1. This takes the position that the entrepreneur is an active factor of production, and as such is entitled to his share of the product. This is diametrically opposed to Marx's position. This paragraph reflects Sismondi's experience in Lyon, as well as his experience as an owner and operator of a métairie in Tuscany. He would naturally feel that his role as owner-entrepreneur entitled him to a part of the product. Marx, on the other hand, had never successfully conducted any type of business, had had no other experience and therefore reflects in his writings the disdain of the academic philosopher for the world of profit, and the sympathy of the financially dependent for what he sees as the underdog of the Industrial Revolution, the worker.
2. The French text uses here, and in the next paragraph, "les casuistes." Since Sismondi translated the term as 'theologians' in the next paragraph, this translation was used here. It should be noted that he disregards, in this defense of interest, the Aristotelian origin of the church concept of usury.
3. This short clause shows that Sismondi used the utility-derived idea of the equality of the factors of production to analyze interest. However, he also quite

clearly equates money to capital, a position he just criticized in the previous chapter.

4. The French text reads here: "qu'une pièce de vingt francs."
5. The French text reads: "il faudrait deux pièces de vingt francs."
6. Sismondi translates "écus" as 'guineas.' The term has been translated as 'cash,' or 'crowns,' or 'shillings,' depending on the context, elsewhere in this translation.
7. This short paragraph is remarkable for, first, its clear separation of the capital lender from the entrepreneur, and second, for the notion of a market equlibrium that determines interest. It should be noted that it had already appeared in the *Encyclopedia*, in other words, at about the same time that Ricardo advanced a much more cumbersome profit theory.
8. *New Principles* omitted "of money."
9. If Sismondi had seen that the distinction between capital and money was unnecessary for his analysis, he would have been much more successful in enunciating a cohesive theory of business cycles.
10. This contradicts the analysis of the previous paragraph and assumes, in contradiction of his own analysis of consumption and production, that the injection of gold (or silver) into the economy operates without lags equally in all sectors.
11. The clear implication here is that profit is a variable, dependent on market conditions. Based again on experience, and utility reasoning, Sismondi was on the verge of a much more useful analysis than his contemporaries, and certainly a better one, even in this rudimentary state, than the Platonic philosophical explanation of value that Marx had constructed, with its implication of an inherent, unalterable value of labor incorporated.
12. One is here reminded of Keynes's description of the gold standard as an unemployment-insurance scheme.
13. Sismondi apparently never thought of the possibility that lower prices might actually stimulate consumption in the same market. Here his analysis clearly implies constant consumption.
14. This was written before the great gold discoveries were made, but it could have served, perhaps, as a guide to many who were lured by gold. Some of the largest fortunes in California were made, not by gold miners, but by butchers and bakers who provided the miners, at a price, with their provisions.
15. Sismondi has a clear, if as yet not fully and consistently developed, national accounting scheme as an analytical framework. In this instance, the implication is that government and consumers are interchangeable, a far cry from Adam Smith's aversion to any but minimal government expenditure. This may be a reversion, conscious or not, to mercantilistic ideas about the role of government in the economy. It is in general agreement with other proposals on the role of government in regulating fluctuations in economic activity.
16. Given this sentence, one wonders why Sismondi did not see the similarity between paper money and full-bodied coin as a medium of exchange.

5

Of Coinage

The precious metals are the common standard that serves to measure all values of the business world, but every government makes them specially suitable for this function by coinage. Thus, the weight and the fineness of the precious metals is regulated in an entirely uniform manner, with a public guarantee, so that by simple inspection of the impress everyone can tell the quantity of precious metal and the degree of fineness, or alloy, which, under a common standard, are offered in exchange for whatever things are to be sold.

The labor of refining the precious metals to uniformity, of converting them to coins perfectly alike in weight, of clothing them with a national seal that guarantees them, and gives the certainty that no particle has been detached from them, this task is a manufacture every government has reserved to itself as a monopoly. This labor is rightly used for social wealth, and the coined precious metals are actually worth more than an equal weight in gold and silver in ingots. To the producer, they are worth the cost of the ingot, plus the labor of converting them to coin; to the buyer, they are worth the convenience he would find in the ingot, plus the convenience of finding the ingot already weighed and assayed to the most scrupulous uniformity.[1]

Since the minting of coins is always a monopoly guaranteed to the government, it has found itself under the necessity to set the remuneration for this useful labor, instead of having it established by competition; and as is usual in all cases of arbitrariness, this has degenerated in turn into two opposite extremes.

Sometimes a government has levied on coinage a profit totally disproportionate to its advances; it has altered either the weight, or the fineness of the coinage; for each mark of silver, it has issued only seven ounces in guineas, and declared that these seven ounces are fully equal to the eight it had received. If the precious metals could only circulate within the borders of the country in which this government exercises its monopoly, this arbitrary setting of profit on the coinage would have to be respected; but money ought to facilitate trade with foreigners, as well as among citizens; the legal guarantee given by the government to the coinage is taken by foreigners only for the actual value; the loss experienced by the natives when they send their guineas abroad teaches them quickly their real value, and every commodity bought with these guineas will soon rise in price, proportionally to the discount which the government has imposed by exacting too large a profit.[2]

At other times governments have made a gift to the public of all the costs of coinage, and have issued against the ingots brought to the mint a number of coins equal in weight and fineness. This is falling into the other extreme. Coins combine the two qualities that ought to make their price higher than the ingot, a much greater labor to produce them, and a much greater ease, or a much greater enjoyment, for him who uses them. When a government does not repay itself for its proper costs, two appreciable disadvantages flow therefrom; one, that the smallest differences in the exchanges are sufficient to lead to an exportation of the coinage, to be sold to foreigners at the price of the ingots; the other, that all goldsmiths in need of precious metals are always tempted to melt it down. In either case, the labor is lost if the coinage is free. The melting and exportation of specie is prohibited; but why offer the temptation of doing a thing which must be prohibited; and why make public a prohibition which cannot be enforced?[3]

Experience proves that the foreigner does not hesitate at all to take into account the real value of refining and coinage. Dutch guilders, Venetian and Florentine sequins command a premium over their real value as ingots, because of guaranteed gold without alloy. Spanish piasters, and French écus, circulate in half of Europe, despite the seigniorage they carry, because they are a convenient money, well struck, that inspires confidence.[4] Every time a foreigner is willing to pay the *fashion* of the coinage, the citizen has no reason to reject it; and if the charge is moderate and does not exceed the costs of minting, it is a perfectly justified tax, easily paid.

To this question has been attached more importance than it really merited, particularly at those times when it was believed that the major goal of political economy was the retention of the precious metals within the borders of a nation. It was said very well that, if seigniorage gave to fifteen ounces of guineas the same value as to sixteen ounces of ingots, it would remain in circulation, at the same value, at a sixteenth less weight of silver. It is not easy to grasp what would have been lost here, but it is even more difficult to imagine how the same people who feared this loss could have applauded at the same time a system of bank notes whose admitted goal is to satisfy the need for money with the least possible quantity of precious metals.[5]

Coinage gives rise to another problem, and one which, for a moment, baffles the mind. It concerns the proportion of the two precious metals, and the motives which can determine the choice of one or the other, or both, at the same time, as the monetary unit.

Gold and silver are both infinitely divisible, and capable of being rejoined without loss; they do not spoil during storage, and they can be refined to such a degree that they are perfectly homogeneous, perfectly alike in similar amounts. These are the qualities that make them eminently suited to become the common standard, the measuring rod for all other values. To this must be added yet another quality in which all other values are wanting, their rarity, or the difficulty of extracting them from the mine, and the costs involved therein. The third precious metal, platinum, has the same advantages, and if it would ever be used as money, the monetary order of the world would not be upset thereby.[6]

If the world market demanded precisely equal amounts of gold, silver, and platinum, or if only its demand were independent of production, the value of each of these metals would proportion itself exactly to its scarcity, and to the labor necessary to extract it from the mine.[7] If then silver were twelve, fourteen, or sixteen times as abundant as gold; twelve, fourteen, or sixteen times easier to extract from the mine, its price would then be uniquely set by that circumstance, and one ounce of gold would be worth twelve, fourteen, or sixteen ounces of silver. But the difficulty of production, or the rarity of raw materials, make up but one of two elements of the price of everything; the other element, namely, demand, does not depend at all thereon, and in the particular case of the precious metals, demand itself is such a complicated measure that it is very difficult to judge.

The influence of demand on price determination is most clearly seen in one of the three precious metals: platinum. The mines for this metal are probably rarer and less productive than those of gold; if large quantities would have to be extracted, they likely could be gotten only at a higher price than that of gold. But platinum has no glitter, it is hardly used as an ornament; it has not been introduced into the monetary system of any nation, and consequently its use is very limited; deposits nearest to the surface, or the least costly mines, are alone worked, and platinum is, relatively, the least costly of the precious metals.

Gold and silver, on the contrary, are the objects of a double demand, and a twofold use, both of which are, and become, perhaps every day, larger. As ornaments and even as utensils, gold and silver are useful to man, and the demand that renews itself without end, or perhaps increases, serves as a gauge to production, and induces the use of less or more labor, digging more or less in the bowels of the earth, not halting these exploitations till such time as the costs they entail surpass the value of the product. Precious-metals mines watch goldsmiths, in exactly the same way in which all other mines watch those who employ their output, or even the entire industry. Consumption, in the last analysis, determines production,[8] and the proportion between gold and silver, leaving aside its monetary use, will depend, on one hand, on the larger or smaller use goldsmiths will make of either, on the other hand, on the larger or smaller costs which depth or scarcity of one or the other type of mines necessitate.

However, an even greater amount of the precious metals is devoted to another use, namely to serve as money; and the demand for the metals as money is much more complex and settles the components of their price in a much less precise manner.

Human society, considered abstractly in the world market, is the demander for the precious metals, from which money must be made; however, humanity is indifferent to the amount produced, as well as to the proportion between the two metals that enter circulation. Society values the metals as money only because of their absolute scarcity. A million pounds of gold would suffice as well for world circulation as a million hundredweights. Each pound of gold would buy, in the first case, exactly ten times more goods than in the second, and everything would go just as well. Again, if gold, instead of being fifteen times rarer than silver, were thirty or sixty times rarer, the proportion between the two metals would be the only thing to change, and everything would go again just as well. Thus society, though it be the only consumer of metals in the form of money, makes nevertheless no demand on their account; it remains almost indifferent to their production.[9]

But the owners and operators of mines do not share at all this indifference. While their labor tends to lower the price of their output, they are on the other hand sure of its sale. The gold they extract from the mine lowers the total value of money in circulation, but it gives them with certainty command of an aliquot part of that money. He who discovers a rich zinc mine, incurs the risk of producing more than is demanded thereof, and as a consequence his zinc will remain unsold. But he who discovers a gold mine, buys with that gold any good whatsoever, and as a consequence can put it into circulation before society could form a demand, or reject what is has no use for.[10]

Let us suppose that the world market only contains five million pounds of gold, and seventy-five million pounds of silver, used as money,[11] and let us suppose these two amounts to be equal in value, as they would be today; that the labor of miners brings to market an additional quantity of either one million pounds of gold, or of fifteen million pounds of silver, or in such a proportion between one and the other that equals fifteen million pounds of silver, without having for this new output any new outlet. Though the sum total be increased by a tenth,[12] its value will not have changed at all; each pound of gold, each pound of silver previously in circulation will be worth only nine-tenths of what it was before, and the million pounds of gold that the miners will have produced will be taken from their hands only for a price which, before their labor, would have bought nine hundred thousand pounds of the same metal. No matter; if what was expended for their output is worth less than nine hundred thousand pounds, they will be encouraged to continue; and although society may not demand an addition to the precious metals, the promptness with which it takes them into circulation is clearly equivalent to a demand.[13]

The annual product, which we have assumed to have been increased by a tenth of the total mass of money, could be all in gold; it could be in silver; it could be half gold, and half silver, but it does not follow necessarily therefrom that the relation between the value of one and the other metal be changed. These metals are employed subsidiary to each other in circulation, and the mints do not follow a precise rule for their annual production, such as not to strike too much of one or the other. In the case we have assumed, it is necessary that the precious metal cost no more to produce than nine-tenths of what it was worth before in the circulation. The work of the gold mines, or those of silver, will be more or less active, as the costs of their operation remain more or less below this proportion, and the quantity of gold or silver that will come to market will be regulated by the cost of production. Whatever it may be, it will be coined and will enter circulation. In certain years, the government will coin more gold pieces, in others more silver pieces, and business will take them up indifferently. Silver is handier for all small transactions, gold for all the transmittals of large sums; but in the majority of all payments, business will use one or the other metal without distinction. According to the size of annual mine output, one or the other in turn will obtain superiority in the markets, without causing a change in the general standard of values.[14]

If there exist troublesome variations, they are those that make business unstable, and which change commercial transactions into speculative ventures. Irregular work in the mines would cause such changes, if they sent to market a quantity of metals sometimes very much larger, sometimes very much smaller, than needed. If silver were sometimes worth 10 percent more, sometimes 10 percent less, all calculations of commerce, relying on a fixed exchange rate, would be overturned. By using a common standard, men are obliged to abstract from all variations it may experience. They disregard all fluctuations in the prices of gold or silver, in order to concern themselves only with commodity prices, just as in measuring their cloth, the merchants disregard the accidental lengthening of the measuring rod, caused by heat or humidity, in order to see only that of the cloth. But, in order to make such an abstraction without danger, this amount must be small.[15]

In reality, it is always infinitely less important than we have here assumed in order to make ourselves understood. Not only are the mines far from producing in one year a tenth of the precious metals actually in circulation, they must moreover replace a considerable consumption, whereas we have assumed none exists. This consumption is the result of the wear and tear, and loss of coins, and, one can assume, of the obsession to bury them, common in all the despotic countries of the East, to which enormous sums have been sent without ever reappearing; it is also the result of employing the precious metals in many ways of life, and these are the losses which make it today very difficult to decide whether the output of the mines offsets them, remains below, or adds to the mass of precious metals in circulation.

Nevertheless, society will be constructively served by trying to diminish further the probability of such fluctuation, and one of the means to accomplish it is to use gold and silver indifferently for the common standard, by fixing a legal ratio between them. This would almost be like combining strands of different metals to form a shaft in order to construct a pendulum of unvarying length, such that the expansion of one by heat corrects that of the other.

If a government chooses a single metal as a standard and declares the other a commodity, as has been proposed over and over again, that standard will be found to be affected by all the yearly variations in mine output. If, on the contrary, it adopted and legalized that proportion which will appear to it the dominant one in world trade, for example, today that of 15 to 1; if it declares that any debt of one ounce of gold could be legally paid with fifteen ounces of silver, and vice versa, as is French practice, then the common standard of business will not be established by the annual output of gold or silver mines, but on an average proportional to the variations these two quantities experience, and the desired standard will thereby acquire more stability.[16]

In reality it appears that money circulation is achieved without trouble equally whether perhaps a fourth, or an eighth of the money supply be in gold and the entire remainder in silver, or, on the contrary, a quarter or an eighth be in silver and the rest in gold. As long as the proportion between the two metals will not deviate from these wide limits, the mint will strike coins indifferently either of gold or silver, depending on which ingot price of either will offer it the better profit, and which can be bought relatively cheaper; but, if the disproportion becomes such that no silver can be found for change, or gold for overseas trade, business would offer a premium for one or the other type of money, as it is quite commonly offered for gold in Italy; and by its persistence in offering this premium, it would warn the government that it is time to change the legal proportion, and to adapt itself to the proportion that would secure the relative profit of the mines.[17]

Let us return to our first assumption of a total circulation of five million pounds of gold, and seventy-five million pounds of silver; then, that in a given time period, a million pounds of gold are consumed, and that fifteen millions pounds of silver are produced by the mines. If the two metals have both a legal par value, in a ratio similarly established by law, the total value of the money supply will not have changed at all, and neither will the proportion between the two metals, because within these limits the public being indifferent to the use of one or the other, the consumption of silver will increase in direct ratio to its production. Henceforth, payments will be made with ninety million pounds of silver, and four million pounds of gold, which suits business just as well as the previous ratio. But if one of the metals is designated as money, and the other a commodity, the consumption of both will no longer be regulated by their production; gold will rise in price compared to silver; because governments, obliged to maintain their coinage in gold, will offer a higher price to miners, so that they continue to extract it from the mines; and if gold is the common standard, all goods will appear to be cheaper; if it were silver, all goods will appear dearer.

The advantage of using both metals simultaneously as a standard is therefore in allowing mints to proportion consumption to the production of one or the other metal, according to which one has become more abundant; so that despite any differences occurring in the costs of production, the ratio between their base prices really remains the same. On the other hand, the disadvantage associated with the standard proposed by many economists, declaring one of the metals a commodity, is that the mints strike each year unvarying quantities of gold or silver specie, without worrying about variations in mine output, and that as a consequence sometimes one, sometimes the other metal being in greater supply, the fluctuations in their relative prices will be so much greater.[18]

Independently of the precious metals, all peoples have also used copper as a subsidiary money, for the payment of small amounts. But copper does not have any of the advantages which make the precious metals suited for coinage. Since copper mines are much more abundant, and their exploitation much less costly, the price of copper is so much lower than that of silver, that it has become very difficult and costly to transport it from one country to another. Nevertheless, these shipments are absolutely necessary to the money supply so that the quantity remain proportional to the needs of the circulation. Hence, copper coins are not at all equalized in the markets of the business world; if there are too many of them in one place, there is no chance that they will flow off by themselves. Copper no longer has the advantage of being capable of regular and easy refining which would make it always equal to itself. It may be of better or lesser quality, which would not be possible to say of gold or silver. These two reasons take away all fixity of value. Thus, it can never be considered by itself as a common standard, but only as a conventional representation of fractions of real money.

A copper coin is therefore really nothing but a little costlier bank note, but also a bit more substantial, and a little less easy to counterfeit than those made of paper.[19] In order that a copper coin can always be freely converted into specie, it is necessary that government issue them only in such quantities as are needed for the smallest transactions, and that it decree that copper is never a legal payment for more than the smallest silver coin in circulation. With these precautions it has only the advantages and disadvantages of a good bank note. If, to the contrary, a debtor can discharge himself with copper for large amounts due in silver, and if government, in order to make a greater profit on its coinage, increases its emission thereof, then copper, or copper coin, can only be regarded as paper money of a kind that is both costly and inconvenient.

There have been discussions on whether it is appropriate for a nation that its small coinage be composed of pure copper, or copper containing silver. This is hardly a question of political economy; it ought to be decided by its convenience or suitability. Copper money containing silver can be more exactly proportioned to its value, without overloading the purse, and without making it so small that it be easily lost: it is therefore more convenient. On the other hand, it either gives to the counterfeiter more profit, or at the least an easier way to hide the fraud. Generally, the purity of metals can be ascertained by a single glance, whereas, if they are alloyed, even the experienced eye has much greater difficulty judging their proportions. The righteous reason not to offer under any circumstances a temptation to commit a crime ought to have great weight;[20] but, if a country indulges in bank notes, which give rise to a much greater temptation, it is hard to understand why it would deny itself the use of convenient one- or two-pence coins.

It is true that governments themselves have often inspired justified mistrust, and it is perhaps to escape the abuse of authority that a money has been excluded from business which can be so easily altered in value. In Piedmont, the Austrian provinces of Italy, in the Papal States, and in many others, silver-alloyed types of money of unknown fineness have been seen to multiply. The authorities, who make on their minting a profit of 60 and 70 percent, declared these entirely debased coins equal to the old ones. Hence the old coins were melted down or exported; gold and silver disappeared, and the currency comprised only copper coin of a fictitious value. This money was based much less on confidence than on deceit, since the public was in no way advised of the decrease of fineness that had taken place in coins which always bore the same stamp, and had, when new, the same luster. It is not strange that the people have complained that the authorities themselves thus committed the crime they punished in counterfeiters. If a repetition of such a scandalous abuse can be prevented only by excluding from trade all moneys of inferior fineness, then without a doubt there ought to be no hesitation. But it seems that we should have come to a time when governments could be guided by reason and justice, instead of treating them like children to whom the most innocent games are prohibited since they could hide much more dangerous ones.[21]

Translator's Notes to Chapter 5, Fifth Book

This chapter was written for the first edition. Most likely Sismondi felt a need to establish a basis for his preference of full-bodied money that put him into opposition to his acknowledged master Adam Smith, and the whole Scottish school of monetary thinking, whose most famous disciple was John Law. It is also likely that his historical research reinforced his personal experience, and led him to the belief that only a strict regimen of full-bodied coinage would ensure stability. But his understanding of monetary matters is colored by local custom—he advocates a bimetallic standard (the official policy of the Latin Monetary Union, which comprised France, Belgium, Italy, and Switzerland), but he ignores what he must have known from his historical investigations, that the gold-silver ratio varied over time, depending on new discoveries. He could not have foreseen the gold strikes in California, twenty plus years in the future, but in the context of the present chapter that was not really necessary. Sismondi must be classified with those thinkers who, again and again, starting with Aristotle, have insisted that money has no utility, but in order to function it must possess full value as a commodity. On the other hand, he sees that supply and demand determine the use of either of the precious metals. The most likely explanation for this split monetary personality is his belief, reinforced by experience, that paper money, easily produced, will lead inevitably to overissuance, where such a course of action in coinage is more difficult. Here, again, he had to ignore his own historical information, showing abundantly that governments had no trouble debasing the currency whenever they needed it.

1. Sismondi most likely started the chapter with this idealized description as a

heuristic device to establish the basics on money as he saw them. It should be noted that he holds a cost-of-production theory on the supply side, and a utility theory on the demand side.

2. There are echoes here of the (wartime) discussion in England over the value of the pound after the Bank of England suspended convertibility, which led eventually to Ricardo's famous tract *The High Price of Bullion a Proof of the Depreciation of Banknotes* that established his name as the foremost political economist of his time.
3. There is some advice for the present here. Again, the remark is based on utility considerations and seems eminently practical. Below, Sismondi returns to the same idea in connection with alloyed coinage and counterfeiting.
4. If Sismondi had drawn the right conclusion from this fact, he would have seen that money can be anything that meets the needs of the users. The sentence, with a few alterations, could have been adapted to paper money. The paragraph illustrates the mélange of currency that circulated in Europe at the time.
5. The reference is most likely to John Law and the Scottish monetary school, and, by implication, to Adam Smith, who advocated the use of paper money.
6. It is an interesting question why platinum has never been used as a monetary standard, even though this could have been a possibility in recent times, if not in antiquity. However, Sismondi again seems to overlook here the role of relative scarcity in the unit of account—it is likely that the monetary system would have been affected by the addition of platinum to the total money stock. In the next paragraph, he considers supply and demand separately, which may also support the interpretation that he meant: that platinum would fit structurally into the monetary system he had always in mind—full-bodied coinage.
7. Like most of his contemporaries, Sismondi mixes a cost-of-production theory with utility considerations. In this sentence, the transitional nature of his analysis is highlighted most clearly. If he had consistently opted for utility and relative scarcity, he would probably have come up with a much more rigorous analysis.
8. This is a the usual total inversion of Say's Law and repeats the position Sismondi took earlier with respect to production of other goods. It raises the question whether the value of the precious metals is really as unvarying as he would have it in earlier chapters.
9. Again, this could have been adapted to paper money. While Sismondi acknowledges that a doubling of the money supply would double price levels, a straightforward application of the quantity theory, he does not consider that increases in the money supply may have differential effects in the economy.
10. The preceding two sentences, starting at "He who discovers . . ." were added to the second edition. The analysis clearly assumes an initially totally elastic demand for the precious metals.
11. A ratio of 15:1 is used, later the official ratio of the Latin Monetary Union. The standard of the union was the Napoleonic silver five-franc piece, which was also based on a 15:1 ratio, and which Sismondi calls the ecu.
12. Fifteen million pounds silver (or one million pounds gold), relative to five million pounds of gold *and* seventy-five million pounds of silver of original circulation.

13. The argument is very ambiguous, and it is difficult to see what Sismondi actually had in mind. He seems to say that as long as production costs are below market price, gold and silver will be taken up for monetary purposes, even though there is no need for them as money.
14. This states the basic position of the Latin Monetary Union. The standard, the five-franc piece, was assumed to be fully interchangeable with gold coins without distinction. This bimetallic system was essentially based on the theory that the prevailing ratio between gold and silver was in fact stable, an assumption that was proven wrong after the great gold finds in California and, later, Australia. Even before these finds, there existed irregularities in the exchange ratio. On the showing of Sismondi's own argument here, this should be expected, because if relative supply changes while demand remains the same, the price of the product must change.
15. This remark should have been pursued further. The observation that changes are the important variable in experiencing inflation (or deflation) is perceptive. His reference to the change of the measuring rod because of heat or humidity is an interesting proof that Sismondi either had a broad view of the sciences or, more likely, drew on his apprentice experience.
16. This was one of many arguments that were advanced for a bimetallic standard. Another was the increase in liquidity that would follow, used mostly in the United States by the Silver Movement.
17. The observation above, that changes must be small to allow business to make its calculations without regard to the standard, is tacitly ignored. Also, it does not conclude that the merchants might use credit facilities to overcome the shortage of the circulating medium, that is, paper.
18. This paragraph was added to the second edition. It seems to represent a reappraisal of the preceding discussion and conclusion.
19. The remark reflects the undeveloped state of bank-note printing of the time. Banks printed notes ad hoc, without safeguards, either as to design or paper, and counterfeiting was in most countries a lucrative trade. Before the passing of the 1863 bank legislation in the United States, merchants in New York City and elsewhere would have almanacs that listed bank notes of banks that had gone out of business, counterfeits thereof, bank notes of banks that were still current, and counterfeits of those, with discounts against specie. European countries also had a good deal of paper money in circulation that was discounted against specie, a consequence of the Napoleonic Wars, and Sismondi's remark reflects this experience.
20. See note 3, above.
21. Sismondi alludes here to the debasement of the coinage that the Austrian government practiced during and after the Napoleonic Wars in order to pay its debts. Evidence of the inflation can be found in the *Austrian Statistics,* which were compiled for the emperor from 1823 onward. Receipts and other monetary data are listed in *Konventionsmuenze*, a fictitious unit of account that corresponded to a prewar guilder. The varying types of circulating medium were discounted at various rates against this unit. Austrian debt, and others, for example, Prussian, consisted mostly of floating circulation, either in paper, or in debased coin. Sismondi had an intimate knowledge of the conditions because

of his Italian farm, and also because of his extensive travels with Madame de Staël in Austria and Germany during the war years. See his 1810 pamphlet *Memoire sur le papier monnaie dans les Etats Autrichiens et des moyens de le supprimer*.

6

Of Bills of Exchange

The export of specie from one country to another is almost always prohibited by suspicious governments, which, seeing in gold and silver the entire wealth of the state, believe they would be ruined if all their guineas would be carried outside their frontiers. However, the merchant who buys, or exchanges his specie against merchandise, knows generally what he is about, and one need not believe that he makes only[1] bad deals in buying; one is hardly ruined by paying one's debts; and specie is rarely ever exported except for purchases, or for paying.

This prohibition, almost universal in Europe during the Middle Ages, hastened the invention of bills of exchange, which have developed into some kind of money for world trade, and whose use would have been only a little less profitable, if the transport of specie would not have been forbidden. Such transport would always have been a costly matter to undertake; it would have been exposed to a thousand dangers; whereas bills of exchange provided an easy and safe means to settle debts, not only between two countries, but many, and they performed the function of money, better than even money could have done it.

A Bordeaux merchant had sold wine in Paris, and had bought lace there; he gave to the seller of the lace an order to pay on the buyer of wine, and thus paid his debt with his receivable. This is not yet properly a bill of exchange, but a simple transfer of credit. It was a lucky invention that made this transfer retransferable by the will and the single signature of the bearer. This invention has been attributed either to the persecuted Jews in France in the twelfth century, or to the Ghibellines persecuted in Tuscany during the thirteenth; both wanted to hide their possessions from the searches of the authorities, and they succeeded in this by circulating their credits in half of Europe. The Bordeaux merchant whom we have assumed to have sold his wine in Paris, having no payment to make, sold to some of his fellow merchants his credit on Paris, represented by a draft, payable at a date certain, or he availed himself of it to pay other debts. His credit on Paris was 1,200 francs; he signed it over to pay an equal sum he owed to a merchant in London; that one in turn remitted the same letter, with his signature affixed, or *endorsed*, to a merchant in Amsterdam, whose debtor he was; the Dutchman then to a German, the German to an Italian, and the bill of exchange made perhaps the rounds of Europe, settling many successive debts of 1,200 francs, before being returned to Paris by someone who had a payment to make there, and who left it to his creditor to receive the sum from the hands of the original debtor.[2]

In this sequence of transactions, the draft represents always the money due to the first maker; and it does not matter if that money be the original value of the goods first shipped, or a preexisting credit, perhaps created by another bill of exchange, or guineas deposited in specie. What gives value to the draft is the sole belief of the recipient that the drawee will have the will, and the ability, to pay, and if he does not do so, the maker will reimburse him. This belief, which has been called *credit*, is strengthened by each endorser, who assumes towards his transferee the duty to pay the entire value of the draft with all costs, if it is not paid on maturity.

The greater part of all monetary transactions in Europe is made today through bills of exchange; more payments are probably made in this way than by money, at least in all those instances where larger amounts are involved.[3] Since bills of exchange are payable at time, by transferring them before maturity, interest for the time they are still outstanding is usually deducted from their face value; this is called a discount. The recipient of a bill for 1,200 francs due in three months will have purchased it only for 1,185 francs, deducting 15 francs as interest at 5 percent for three months. He has then no reason to hurry to part with it, as if it were money; because, if he keeps it in his portfolio, it will bring him interest as regularly as if he had lent the same sum for profit. Thus, the majority of capitalists, instead of lending to bankers and merchants, discount bills of exchange; while a draft has become an easy way to borrow for merchants. A draws on B, his correspondent, a bill of exchange for three months, which the latter accepts, and which the capitalist C discounts and keeps in his portfolio. B, in turn, draws on A an equal bill, for the same period, which the same capitalist, or another, discounts in the same way, and also keeps in his portfolio. This transaction comes to exactly the same as if A and B would have become cosigners for each other, borrowing from C the value of their two bills at three months. Thus it is that bankers raise, as they call it, cash for currency, and how their credit transforms itself into capital for them.

Bills, being purchased and settled in specie, performing the service of money, and appearing to have no other existence than through the money that settles them, have often been considered as equal in quantity to the money they replace. The wealth of capitalists is estimated in cash, or in good bills, as if they were one and the same thing; and when the money supply of a nation is to be estimated, that information has almost always been sought in the quantity of bills held by capitalists in their portfolios. However, no other idea could be as erroneous; no proportion of any sort, no relation, can be established between the money circulating in a country, and the bills of exchange which, in the same country, perform a similar function; the abundance of one does not presume at all the abundance, or scarcity, of the other. Bills of exchange are but a claim on the property of another. This claim can have as its collateral any type of property, goods, other credits, even real estate, as well as cash; and although at maturity the draft will be settled with money, that money was perhaps not in the hands of the payer on the very eve of the payment; during the three months the bill ran, the money which in the end settles it, has perhaps discharged thirty similar bills. In general, bills of exchange are but claims easier to transfer than all others; but like all claims, they presuppose a debt, as all claims are but a right to share in a material asset; if all claims and debts would be abolished, real capital, the wealth of the human race, would remain the same.

Without being part of the wealth of the human race, bills of exchange form an important part of the wealth of this, or another nation. The Genevese capitalist, without leaving his small territory of two leagues in diameter,[4] finds himself having a property right, or participation in, the ownership of spices stored in warehouses in Amsterdam, in linen goods of the East India Company of London, the wines of Bordeaux, the silks of Lyon; and all that is locked up in his portfolio in the form of so many drafts on these different places. Is there in Geneva a money supply corresponding to all of these values? Have these values been sent by money from Geneva? Not any more.[5] The Genevese is co-owner in Amsterdam, London, Lyon, Bordeaux, of a real, personal, and business capital, and we have endeavored, in the preceding chapters, to clarify that such capital is not at all money. He sent it from one place to another with drafts; he still owns it through bills of exchange; and, as soon as he converts them, he will hasten to exchange them for new bills.

In business, bills of exchange are found to accomplish two circulations in opposing directions; they are sold in the same city, like commodities, for money; they are transferred from city to city, and sometimes in the same city, in payment for goods, just like money. In the first instance, they make a much larger amount of money necessary to accomplish the exchanges of which they are the object; in the second instance, they make that part of the money supply superfluous which they replace in the exchanges they settle. The second effect appears necessarily to be farther reaching than the first; and it is probable that, without the invention of the draft, it would have been necessary, for trade needs, to have a much larger sum of money than the one that is needed today.[6]

While bills of exchange replace money, and while they are in some way the universal money of the business world, they differ from it fundamentally because of their fixed maturity date, which makes them subject to discount, and consequently assures to their holder interest.[7] The actual money standard, the bank note, and paper money, of which we will speak presently, have a faster circulation, because their holder loses the amount of interest as long as he holds them in his till; whereas the bill of exchange stays usually in the hands of some capitalist, who finds it more advantageous to keep it till maturity, rather then to send it on its way.

Translator's Notes to Chapter 6, Fifth Book

This chapter, as the previous one, has no precedent in the *Encyclopedia*, except for a short reference to the clearing system of the Lyon merchants, which may have served as an inspiration for this discussion. However, the chapter shows Sismondi's intimate knowledge of business practices from his Lyon apprenticeship. Although there is no biographical evidence to support it, his writings also intimate a later close acquaintance with business practices, particularly export trade and financing that was a Genevese specialty. Sismondi was for a while the secretary to the Genevese Chamber of Commerce (1801 and after), and in this capacity he must have been associated with mercantile interests in the city. In any case, this chapter is a short and clear explanation of what a bill of exchange is and how it is used in international trade. In it, Sismondi comes close to admitting that this negotiable instrument serves as money, but he remains faithful to his monetary view of the exclusive role of full-bodied coin, and to a sharp distinction between credit and money. In this chapter the terms *draft* and *bill of exchange* are used interchangeably.

1. "Only" was added in the second edition.
2. The sequence of draft remittals is a fair representation of the channels of trade then existing, and what nation was most likely to trade with what other nation.
3. One wonders why, after this description of the European money market, and Sismondi's obvious clear understanding of the uses of the trade bill of exchange, he steadfastly refuses to acknowledge paper as a possible medium of exchange. However, his position was not unique. The controversy between the banking and the currency school in England (and in the United States) reflects the same division. The nineteenth century in this respect must be seen as a transitional period between specie-oriented monetary theories, and credit-oriented macroeconomics. It also reflects the fact that monetary theories were not then, and have not been since, well-integrated into general economic theory.
4. Geneva was a city-republic that joined Switzerland only after the publication of *New Principles*.
5. This alludes here to the, for Sismondi, still recent practice of actually shipping

specie in settlements of debts. Actually, drafts were already a major instrument of long-distance trade in the Renaissance, as DeRoover has convincingly shown with respect to the Medici and Florentine trade.

6. Sismondi is entirely correct that the money supply would have had to be much larger in the absence of drafts, an admission that drafts are the equivalent of money.
7. This remark is in line with Sismondi's view of money as having no utility, hence not able to earn interest. He sees interest as a time premium on real capital, as represented by the draft.

7

Of Banks

[From confounding money with capital, has arisen the general mistake of attempting to increase the national capital by a fictitious capital, which, not having been created by an expensive labour, is not, like gold and silver, a pledge of the values it represents; and which, after having delighted nations with the illusions of wealth, has so frequently left them in ruin.]

The banks were the first to start the idea of paper money, and the very invention of banks has been the fruit of successive happenstances and observations. [It will be more easy to follow the] reasonings and illusions [by which so many states in our time have endeavoured to replace their money by paper, if we previously direct our attention to the manner in which one of the most ancient trading cities of France made a few crowns perform the functions of a considerable medium.

At Lyons, it was agreed upon in trade, that all payments should take place only at four fixed periods,] which every three months followed the famous old fairs. [During the three days which the payments took up, all the accounts of the city were settled at once. Each, at the same period, had much to receive and much to pay. But, on the days immediately preceding the payments, all the merchants used to meet on the exchange, to make what they called *virements,* in other words, to assign one to another, such sums as would settle their accounts. A owed B, who owed C, who owed D, who owed E, himself indebted to A; and the five accounts were settled without any payment. If E was not indebted to A, it was agreed that A should pay E, and the other four were acquitted by a single payment. Every merchant bought but to sell again, therefore, but to pay; and if those assignments were extended to their utmost limits,] it would have been astounding to see how little money was needed to settle immense transactions*[1]

[But all mutual debts are not equal, and bankruptcies occasion difficulties, and sometimes errors in the assignments. The invention of banks has supplied this deficiency.] Some have been seen to come into existence independently for the benefit of the merchants who wanted to rely on them. The banker was but the cashier of the merchants; he received and paid for them; and since he performed this office for a great number of merchants at the same time, it happened very often that he paid himself. Hence he had no need at all to keep idle in his vault all the funds it was supposed to contain. If for each 100,000 francs of payments he made, there were regularly 50,000 francs he paid to himself, and whose payment was settled by crediting B with the sum that stood before to the credit of A, he could use the 50,000 francs that were not needed for his payments better elsewhere. Thus, he settled with one half of the money the circulation of his fellow merchants, and he placed the other half out at interest. By arranging to have prompt and easy repayments with closely spaced maturities, he was assured that he would not let demanders for money wait, even though, by an unusual occurrence, all his payments during a certain period, would have to be made to others than his depositors. Thornton tells us that the number of bankers in London comes to seventy, and that they pay daily between four and five million sterling; this assumes at least 1,500 million yearly, and that nevertheless this prodigious circulation is accomplished with twelve or thirteen million sterling in specie or bank notes.**

This business has not been left to the bankers alone; in the majority of the trading nations, public enterprises, started under governmental protection, have taken a share of it. The more a banker extended his operations, the more he had to diminish his payments.[2] Conversely, all those who still make up the seventy bankers of London would be eliminated if all their business would be conducted by a single bank; therefore, the substitution of a single national bank for several bankers was deemed to bring about a great saving in money, and a great benefit. It acted like an open office where transfers are constantly made. [Every trader pays, or receives, by a line which is written down in the bank's books on the debtor or creditor side of his account, without any money being disbursed. Among merchants, who have all an open credit with the bank, the operation of the bookkeeper supplies with the utmost ease that of the cashier; and no

*It seems, after Thornton, Chapt.III, that a similar operation occurs every day between the bankers of London.
**Henry Thornton, *Inquiry into the nature and effect of credit,* Chapt.IV, p. 154.

difference of amount, or days of payment, prevents sums from being reciprocally balanced.][3]

However, it ought to be said that, if we have represented the practice of *virements* as pioneer transactions, followed by those of bankers who merely acted as cashiers, we have done this to facilitate the understanding of this business, rather than relate the facts in the order in which they really occurred. The oldest banks in Europe, at Genoa, Venice, Amsterdam, Hamburg,[4] have been founded, not with the intention of making transfers, but only to accept deposits, in order to safeguard them better in their original state than each trader could do at home, and to avoid that mixture of foreign, or debased, specie which, above all in the smaller states, constantly altered the currency.

The public banker had undertaken, in the most solemn manner, a clearly defined obligation to keep in his coffers, in its original state, the sum total of money or bullion that each trader had deposited there, thus acquiring a credit on the bank, and to pay, on demand, to those to whom the credit had been transferred. The bank denied itself the natural profit connected with this trade; and it provided for the costs of the institution with a levy which the depositor[5] paid. But it seemed that this was placing too much trust in an institution which was under the absolute control of a government, by counting on it to forego such a considerable profit that appeared to be deductible without hurting anybody. The Bank of Amsterdam, chartered in 1609, continued at least till 1672 to execute religiously its commitments, maintaining intact in its coffers the immense deposits that had been entrusted to it; hence it was seen to pay without difficulty all the moneys which the quick advance of Louis XIV induced all depositors to draw out at once. This event merely affirmed its credit, and led it to abuse it towards the middle of the next century. From that moment, it began to loan the capital that remained dead in its vaults, to the East India Company, to the provinces of Holland and West Friesland, and to the City of Amsterdam.[6] At the time of the French invasion in 1794, when it had to reveal its long-kept secret, the bank was found to have lent to these four corporations 10,624,793 guilders. The corporations were insolvent, and the bank was dragged into their bankruptcies.

The Bank of Hamburg, founded in 1619, remained more faithful to its charter; the deposit which represented the reserves of the bank was conserved there intact till the night of 4 November 1813, when it was seized by order of Marshall Davoust, to defray the costs of the siege. It amounted then to 7,489,343 Marks Banco.

The ruin of the two most famous deposit banks in Europe shows at what price, in modern times, that power of credit was bought to which we trust perhaps too much now, and how many pitfalls are connected even with its most moderate use. An invention which followed closely on the heels of deposit banks and banks of account, extended soon beyond all bounds both the use of credit and its dangers.

[A bank like that of Amsterdam, however, is of use only to such as have a current account in it. Many traders may have no account; and few or none who are not traders ever have any, though called, as well as others, to pay and to receive. To extend the advantage of assignments also to the business of such persons, those note-banks were invented which have since become so common in all parts of Europe. Their notes are assignments on the bank, payable to the bearer on demand. Everyone, by combining several notes, may make his odd payments himself;] and he is not called upon to settle them with currency.[7] [Hence, it is generally most convenient for him to transmit the notes to others, as he received them, without having drawn any money; and even though each may require payment at his pleasure, no one thinks of it, just because each feeling that he may do so at any time, feels always that it will be soon enough afterwards.

Up to that period, banks had done nothing but simplify payments, and save the employment of money, and render circulation easy with a smaller sum than would otherwise have been required. But some one must profit] from the fact that a smaller quantity of sterile money was employed in business. A share of capital that before drew no interest, could be changed to profit-bearing investment, and someone had to realize that profit. [In arranging the assignments in Lyon, each profited according to his share in trade; each needed to have money in his coffers only four times yearly, for three days. He, of course, gained interest for the remaining 353 days; and as those assignments simplified all his operations, a smaller sum performed for him the office of a greater.] In London, and everywhere where bankers have set themselves up to be merely cashiers of the merchants, these bankers profited from the resulting saving of money, and that was the gain from their trade. In Amsterdam, Hamburg, Rotterdam, and Nuremberg, where deposit banks where founded,[8] this profit was solemnly relinquished, and since currency did not circulate, less of it had to remain in the country, immobile, and not yielding interest; but this condition was not always faithfully observed. When note banks[9] were founded they openly proclaimed that they would profit from such interest, and that this was the gain on which they counted.

The banks issued to the trade their notes as perfectly equal in value to specie, because in effect they could be converted to specie at the will of each depositor, and from one moment to another; as a result they demanded interest equal to specie, and received it without trouble. Usually, [it was by discount on such of the proceeds of trade as were payable at long dates, that banks pushed their notes into circulation.] The merchant bearer of a bill of exchange at three months received its value in bank notes, less the interest for three months. He thus exchanged paper against paper; but what he received was payable at sight, although most often he was not paid earlier than the draft against which he had exchanged it.[10] The specie it represented belonged from that moment really to him who had transferred his bill of exchange; however, the banker, speculating on the fact this asset would not be claimed immediately, lent it during the interval to others, and herein alone lay his gain, or the service he rendered to society.

The banks drew interest, not on the specie they really paid out, but on the specie every note holder believed to command at any moment, which however were not at all in the banks' tills. The art of the banker consisted of judging to a nicety the current needs of the market, in order to have in his safe an amount equal to the daily demand, and prudence required of him to have, besides that amount, also a sufficient reserve for all extraordinary cash demands, plus regular repayments, prompt and safe, since an accidental inability to pay would induce most of the note holders to demand payment.

It is always astonishing that the will and the passions of mankind can be subjected to calculation, and that, every time a larger number of people are concerned, an average for them can be found with certainty. Nothing seems to be more arbitrary than the intent of someone unknown who will have received tomorrow a note for a thousand francs, to exchange it, or not, for specie. However, since this concerns the intent of not only one, but of two thousand individuals who will be in the same position,[11] such intent can be predicted, and the amount of necessary specie to serve them can be judged with great certainty.

The great body of currency flows at the same time through many channels of circulation. Among them, all cannot be filled equally with bank notes; these latter are uniquely destined to avoid the trouble and dangers of possessing and transporting large sums; this is the only advantage the merchant finds in them who uses them. He makes his payments more safely and better with five hundred- and thousand-franc notes; he transports them with less cost, and they are promptly accepted; but from the moment he is obliged to accept his payments in smaller notes, the time lost becomes almost equal to what he would experience with the acceptance of specie; the danger of counterfeiting increases with the multiplication of denominations; the danger of tearing or losing the notes is much greater; a certain concern about the value of a sign which is not a standard weighs on them; everybody prefers a twenty-franc coin to a twenty-franc note; there are few people who prefer five twenty-franc pieces to a hundred-franc note. As long as the bank redeems its notes, few of the small notes will remain in circulation for whatever amount it seeks to issue.*[12]

Now, we have seen that a profitable operation begins, in the general course of exchanges, with a developer of projects, either industrial or agricultural, who pays the wages of his workers. This entrepreneur, be he farmer or factory owner, may well have received his capital in bank notes; but he cannot use it in this form to pay his workers. He will bring it soon to the bank to change it to currency. Therefore it will not do to make bank notes part of that circulation. Their prompt return will cause loss and not gain.

The worker exchanges, by pennies and farthings, the silver of his wages for his subsistence; no bank note can enter this part of money circulation.[13]

Wages are the income of the worker; but the worker is not the only one whose income is expended in small amounts. The wealthiest as well as the poorest provides for his subsistence with a number of small purchases which must be made in cash. If some large landowner receives his income from his farms, or his capitals, in bank notes, even if he pays the invoices of his suppliers with bank notes, the circulation of the bank note would not go far; either the landowner or his supplier hasten to bring it to the bank for exchange. Hence, bank notes ought not to enter the circulation of incomes.

But production does not enter immediately into the hands of consumers; it is the object of two, three exchanges between merchants of different countries. These exchanges are on account, and the sum of their settlements gives rise to a new trade, that of traders of bills of exchange, who are also called bankers. All deals between these traders are made for large sums; every one of them takes in, in order to pay out almost the same value; every one of them has in his vaults a reserve, or value, almost evenly divided between bank notes and specie to make such settlements; and if no one of them feels any uneasiness about the bank, it is likely that no one of them would dream of exchanging his notes against specie. This is the channel of circulation which can be filled with bank notes without inconvenience and unease. From there some will flow back to the exchanges that are made between capitalists and bankers, for the placement

*It must be admitted that the contrary has occurred in England, and even more in Scotland; habit has triumphed over the aversion which must be inspired by those dirty and dangerous rags, compared to gold coins. The large circulation of the provincial banks consists of one-pound notes, even though the poor are more likely to lose them, or to be taken in by counterfeits which require to be paid for in gold. The shareholders in these banks have succeeded in inducing in their fellow citizens this habit that has recently caused enormous losses.

of capitals by the former, for the payment of interest by the latter. In the remainder of all business transactions, bank notes cannot stay in circulation; and those that fall accidentally into the hands of others, will return soon to the bank for payment.[14]

It is true that there exists, outside of commerce, a circulation that absorbs a certain quantity of bank notes, the revenue of government. It is convenient for government that all remittances of collections from the provinces to the treasury be made in bank notes, that all payments of the treasury to its suppliers and contractors be made in the same form. Government needs for its business more money transfers than all of commerce together; it gave rise to a new branch of banking, and it can use for that bank notes with as much profit as the bankers. But, after the circulation of great sums, the revenue of government comes also to the consumer; and for settling the pay of its troops, or the board of its prefect, the bank note must be changed into money; because now it is used as income by all those who receive a stipend.

Whenever banks are prudent and cautious, the manner in which they put their notes into circulation will make them enter naturally the two channels to which they are suited. They discount bills of exchange; but they are properly the result of large transactions that trade causes between traders and bankers; and except in the case where the bill is fictitious, or but a speculation of persons in distress, or of developers too far extended, who, according to an old saying, raise cash by passing paper, the total of bills represents fairly closely the total of currency that ought to circulate in large amounts, solely in the hands of merchants, and which can be replaced by bank notes.

Again, banks discount government securities, the obligations of provincial tax collectors; and they generally advance loans before the collections are received. If such advance is made only for a short time, for example, three months, it can correspond to the time during which the notes remain in the circulation of the major agents of the treasury, and there will be no need to exchange them; but there hardly exists a bank that does not find itself more or less dependent on the government that protects it, and does not discount its issues for a much longer time than the circulation of large amounts of public revenue takes. All that happens then is that a part of the notes issued in this manner return quickly to the bank, as soon as they have come into the hands of those who have a need for smaller denominations, to be converted to currency. The Bank of England, which discounts the tariffs for the government, was obliged, because it made its payments in silver, to maintain a reserve in its vaults of one-third to one-half of the face value of its notes. The Bank of France, although much more cautious, discounting only the value of three signatures,[15] and whose maturity is not further away than three months, is nevertheless constrained to maintain a reserve quite as large, probably because of sudden turnovers that may cause in money markets a large discount on public issues. If the bank would make sure to discount only business paper, it would be very likely that a cash reserve of one-tenth of its circulation would be sufficient for its liquidity.

Translator's Notes to Chapter 7, Fifth Book

This chapter summarizes Sismondi's opinions on banks. He is quite knowledgeable about their operations. but he does not disguise the fact that he is also extremely suspicious of them. The first paragraph is worth noting, inasmuch as he reiterates his position that gold and silver are money because labor was incorporated in them, a position later taken by Marx. Sismondi consistently identifies money as full-bodied coin, assigning to bank notes an inferior status. It is clear that he has no experience with, or knowledge of, checking deposits, although the operation of a giro bank, like the Bank of Amsterdam, is but a step away from that development. To him the saving grace of a giro operation lay in the absolute duty of such a bank to keep all specie in its vaults, that is, 100 percent reserve banking. On the other hand, he is quite aware of the fact that most banks do not need 100 percent reserves, that banking's great service to trade is economy in the use of specie, and that reserves of a fraction of total circulation can be sufficient. But his experience with inflation and destroyed financial assets is the major determinant of his monetary views. He restricts such fractional banking to the needs of wholesale trade and, significantly, to the government. One wonders what he would have said about present-day financial arrangements in most industrialized nations and the rest of the world.

1. This description of the Lyon merchants' clearing system was cited in the translator's comments introducing the previous chapter as a possible inspiration for the discussion of the bill of exchange. Sismondi had already described the system in the *Encyclopedia*. He may have had actual experience with it—from the description of this arrangement, and others, it would seem that he had great insight into the operations of clearing arrangements.
2. This assumes that the banker would be limited in his deposits, even at that time not a very realistic assumption. But Sismondi appears to be preoccupied with lack of liquidity as well as with his major fear, inflation and devaluation of the circulating medium.
3. An accurate description of the functioning of a giro bank, such as the Bank of Amsterdam.
4. Sismondi should have included the Swedish Riksbank as an early issue bank.
5. Here and below the term *prêteur,* 'lender,' is used, which makes it quite clear that he regarded, correctly, the depositor as a lender to the bank. The *Amsterdamsche Wisselbank* charged its depositors a yearly fee for account keeping.
6. The Bank of Amsterdam was controlled by a commission of trustees, some of whom were also members of the city government and, in addition, the most prominent merchants in the city; many of them were involved with the Dutch East India Company in top positions. Lending started secretly to the company

and then expanded to the other borrowers mentioned by Sismondi. Whether the bank could have survived during the Napoleonic Wars is questionable. If it would have been in full possession of its gold, it would have been confiscated, in the same way that the assets of the Bank of Hamburg were confiscated by the Napoleonic generals, as Sismondi relates in the next paragraph.

7. This sentence clearly defines the distinction Sismondi made between bank notes and currency-specie. To him, all notes were representatives of real money, that is, specie. However, it should be noted that he was quite aware of the advantage bank notes had for the average person who had no deposits with a giro bank.
8. What is here called a deposit bank would be called a giro bank today.
9. They would later be called banks of issue.
10. As the next sentence makes clear, this means that the recipient of the bank notes did not receive specie before the maker of the draft received his payment in specie. Sismondi was aware that holders of notes may not want to "cash" their notes, as he makes clear above, but to classify them therefore as "money" was apparently contrary to his view of specie as the only money.
11. This sentence from "However . . ." was added to the second edition. It is not clear why two thousand was chosen as a basis for his statistical explanation. It may be that he had some insight into the numbers required for predicting, for example, withdrawals, at a particular level of confidence.
12. The note was added to the second edition. It was probably based on information Sismondi received from his in-laws, and refers to the fact that in Scotland paper money was in general circulation through the country banks. During the depression of 1825, many of the banks failed and their notes became worthless.
13. This describes an economy that is still at a very low liquidity level, with a sharp division between the everyday expenditure of the worker and the large transactions of wholesale merchants. The description is reminiscent of the two-tier monetary system of Florence in the Renaissance, where two currencies existed side by side, copper and token coin for the workers, silver and gold for the merchants.
14. The analysis was made at the beginning of the nineteenth century and probably represents a reality observed right in Geneva. Sismondi made this observation on the threshhold of a new age. Within 150 years of the publication of the second edition of his work, a mere blink in history, specie would have disappeared from circulation and credit would reign supreme. His remarks about the suitability of bank notes for small payments reflect his own bias as well as the reality of an economy not yet fully monetized for the working classes. The following description of government finance indicates that these operations were quite sophisticated.
15. Three endorsements.

8

Credit Does Not Create the Wealth of Which It Disposes

[Bankers, in virtue of their credit alone, seemed to have capitals of almost immense extent, to offer in the service of merchants. Credit soon appeared to have a creative power, and speculators, persuaded that by emitting a bank note, they add as much to the public wealth as by importing an equal sum of money, delivered their minds to dreams dangerous for themselves, and for the states that gave ear to them. They proposed the establishment of banks to multiply the funds of trade, to provide for the enterprises of agriculture, to set labour everywhere in motion, to increase the general capital, and redouble the activity of industry.]

The theory of banking has been thoroughly investigated since Adam Smith, and it cannot be said that this branch of the science has made, after him, any kind of progress, or perhaps there was none to make. Nevertheless, since the publication of his writings, enterprises reckless with credit have followed each other with even more rapidity than before; one after another they have pulled almost all nations into a frightful abyss of calamity and ruin; and despite this sad experience, not a year passes where one cannot see another project aborning, equally dangerous to the public weal. Since we cannot add anything to the analysis Adam Smith has made of the operation of banks and credit, we will try at least to expound his principles with more clarity.[1]

Above all it is essential to establish that credit never creates any new wealth; that it adds nothing to the capital of society, and that all it can do is to make profitable a part of such capital which was not so. In general, credit only shifts wealth; it gives to one person the disposition of what belongs to another, but it leaves everyone as rich or poor as before. Credit is the ability to borrow. But nobody can borrow without finding a lender; what does not exist cannot be borrowed. A decree which would abolish all debts, would turn society topsy-turvy, but it would not destroy it. It would amount to universal robbery; all creditors would be robbed of their property by their debtors; but the assets of the nation would be precisely the same as before. The possession of all real things is divided today among two or more individuals; one owns the thing, the other, the right to it; but the thing will be worth less as much as the right is worth more; in abolishing the right, the thing will regain all that the right to it has made it lose. The abolition of debts, by shaking trust in property, would truly destroy all sense of order and economy,[2] as would universal robbery in a country whose government would not give any guarantee against violence. A nation would ruin itself by the bad use the robbers would make of their wealth, and not because property would have passed, in the one case, from the robbed to the robbers, and in the other, from the creditors to the debtors.

One can quite well understand that if a man has a field that is worth twenty thousand francs, and he owes on it ten thousand francs to another, the property of the creditor joined to that of the debtor is but twenty thousand francs; but no one wants to reason in the same manner if it concerns banks and the public credit; nevertheless the analogy is perfect.

A bank, by means of its circulating paper, finds itself in effect holding a new capital of which it can make use; but this capital does not belong to it, it belongs to those who have the right to withdraw their guineas from its vaults, and who leave it there on trust. Generally, in order to earn and get this trust, the bank offers a pledge to the lenders. The Bank of England has given as a pledge the original value of its shares, deposited in specie. When the bank was founded in 1694, this came to 1,200,000 pounds sterling; but its operations were of such a nature as to make the specie come into its vaults, without letting it leave; and then the pledged trust funds were lent to the government, and only its shares continued to guarantee the holders of its notes against the losses the bank could make. For this price it had obtained an exclusive privilege, for a fixed number of years; at each renewal, it increased this primary deposit, and it amounted in 1797 to 11,686,800 pounds sterling.

This capital of the bank, that serves as the basis of its credit, is the cause thereof, and not the effect; it consists of a part of the wealth of the shareholders, and it ought not to be confused with the money that is on deposit with the bank, till such time as the holders of its notes demand it back, and which it has turned to good account beforehand, by way of its credit.

This latter is the only part of the capital the bank adds really to circulation—the money which rested idly in the coffers of the great merchants, and which it has coaxed out by replacing it with its notes, in order to lend it out in turn. The bank borrows with one hand in order to lend with the other; it borrows without interest in order to lend at interest. Speculation would yet be tantamount to the creation of new wealth if it were unconstrained, but it is on the contrary uniquely restricted to these idle sums in its vaults, otherwise always circulating in one lump, that are necessary to trade, and which are nevertheless a loss to it. There are some cities where it is customary to give and to receive always bags of 1,200 francs by weight, without counting them.[3] These bags, all similar, pass from merchant to merchant without ever being opened. Well, a bank can only bring into its vaults, through credit, and lend afterwards, the specie contained in these bags that were never untied.*[4]

*The reports of the committees created by the two Houses of Parliament for the Scottish and Irish banks give us, under the date of the 1 June 1826 precise data on the circulation of bank notes for these two kingdoms.

But the committees seem to believe that the credit of the Scottish banks creates capitals that favor industry; thus they give great praise to this system so admirably conceived, as they say, to husband capital, develop a spirit of enterprise, and to support in the nation moral habits. However, these very reports show us that the Scottish banks borrowed with one hand in order to lend with the other, without adding anything to the capital of the nation.

There are thirty-three banks in Scotland, among which are three which French law would call corporations. All the wealthiest banks have established inferior offices, or branches, in smaller cities. One hundred sixty-five banks issue notes in Scotland. Their total circulation, at the time of the report, amounted to 3,309,000 pounds sterling, of which 2,079,000 were in smaller notes from 5 pounds, or 125 francs. In order to put into circulation this large sum which has driven out all other currency in Scotland, and with a small number of shillings as a reserve, the Scottish bankers engage in three operations. They discount bills of exchange with their notes, as we have explained above; they take in small deposits from all workers and the poor who have some savings, in exactly the same way as savings banks, and they open cash accounts, for a limited amount, to any hardworking man who, even without any collateral, gives in exchange his note guaranteed by two good signatures. The total amount of deposits in the banks is estimated at twenty to twenty-one million sterling. The banks pay 4 percent. This same amount is advanced in cash accounts with an interest of 5 percent.

It is clear that in this double operation the Scottish banks are nothing but lending and borrowing agencies, which is without doubt very useful to the nation, and above all in giving to the small capitalist a use for his money, as well as to the industrious borrower those sums which he needs; but this business could be carried on without bank notes, the difference between the interest received and interest paid would be enough to assure a profit. However, it is above all through this lending service that the Scottish banks have succeeded in driving specie entirely from their country, and making at the same time their interests national ones. The whole class of lenders, large and small, and the whole class of borrowers, are interested in maintaining the banks' credit; both persist in preferring pound notes to a gold coin named a sovereign, and while Parliament, alarmed by the violent shocks that have unsettled not only the credit of banks, but of all commerce in

Actually, the accounts published by the Bank of London, at the time of the suspension of its payments, 26 February 1797, surprised and astonished by showing of what small importance this always grandiosely touted resource is for business. The bank of the largest and richest city in the world, the bank that belongs to all of England, and not only to London, now discounts only 3,000,000 sterling annually in trade bills. The bank was indeed more occupied with serving the government than the public; however, its total circulation, during the last five years preceding its suspension of payments, has never risen above 11,497,095 pounds sterling, and during the same period it had in its vaults, in specie or ingots, 6,272,000 pounds. Thus, all the capital it has succeeded to add to the currency of the nation, by virtue of its credit, has never amounted to more than 5,225,095. Then again, its advances to the government were much above what the circulation of the public revenue could use in bank notes; thus the notes issued came steadily back to the bank to be exchanged; and because this decreased its cash reserves, the bank saw itself soon forced to suspend its payments.[5]

Similar calculations for the Bank of France give results not far different from those above: it has seldom at any one time a value of more than a hundred million francs of its notes in circulation; it employs a fund of about forty-five million in specie to back them. All the capital it borrows from trade, in order to lend it back, amounts then, at most, to from fifty to sixty million. That is probably the highest limit of services it can render to the public.*

Such a conclusive experience, in the two most powerful and business-oriented nations of the world, should have enlightened speculators, and quite convinced them that a bank is not at all a dispenser of new wealth, inexhaustible, which it can pour forth at its pleasure for the encouragement of industry; that the capital it is able to put into circulation, the capital that comes from bags never counted, is infinitely limited, and that every attempt it would make to attract to it any other part of the currency would be ruinous to the bank as long as it would freely honor its notes, and would

England, has wanted to bring gold back into circulation by prohibiting the issue of bank notes of less than five pounds, all of Scotland has become angry, as if a great injustice had been done to it, and the committees of the two Houses have decided to leave the Scottish banks in status quo, and to limit the reform to the English banks.

*The trade of Paris is not at all comparable to that of London, and the amount of discounts by the Bank of France is nevertheless higher than those made to business by the Bank of London. This difference is due probably to the sixty-six bankers who replace the Bank of England in a part of its operations at London, and the even larger number of bankers who carry on a similar business in the provinces.

be ruinous to the country from the moment the law would force it to accept its notes.

However, the mania of lending banks, regional banks, of banks that are pretended to be a resource by furnishing industry with capital to stimulate it, is not at all over. Every day some new speculator comes forward with a gigantic project; that he will ruin himself together with those who will trust him, is already a great misfortune; but, if he succeeds in drawing into his project the wealthiest capitalists in the nation, he will perhaps succeed in turning his speculation into a national cause; then, at the moment where his circulating paper will come back to him from everywhere to be exchanged for specie, the legislature will interpose itself to save him from bankruptcy; like all those who have preceded him, he will perhaps adopt the dangerous expedient of giving his notes forced circulation, and the nation will fall into the abyss of paper money.[6]

The developers of a bank intended to support manufactures should consider fully that, if they will lend ten thousand francs to a manufacturer, the latter will not at all spend them in one payment, or in ten payments of a thousand francs; but, that as of tomorrow, he will need to change his notes in order to pay the masons who will build his factory, or the workers whom he will employ there; if the ten thousand francs are to be used in their entirety, not in gold coins, but in small change, and if the bank has put into circulation even hundred francs notes, it would still be necessary to change them, before the manufacturer has converted his capital into goods. Now, there is no advantage to keep as paper bank notes one will not use till they have been converted to currency. They will all be carried back to the bank to be converted to specie before they have entered the manufacturing circulation, at least if the notes are not for such small sums that they replace specie in all domestic transactions, which it is hoped the government will never permit.

The developers of a regional bank should take into account fully that the great landowners, on whom they count to make loans, borrow either to clear land, or to build, or to pay other debts. They demand at all times a circulating capital to change it to fixed capital. Hence they find themselves in an even more unfavorable situation at the bank than the manufacturer. Money does not circulate for them, it passes once through their hands, never to return. The manufacturer who has taken in, in one year, one hundred thousand francs in currency, will take in again, in the next year, one hundred thousand francs in currency, and so for each succeeding year. But the most solid, the most parsimonious landowner who has used this year one hundred thousand francs in agricultural projects, will have done a good business if he has invested the money at 10 percent, if he has increased in that way by ten thousand francs the income he draws every year in currency. If then the bank has given one hundred thousand francs to the landowner in notes of a thousand francs, from the first day the latter will have exchanged, or cause to exchange, his notes into specie to pay his workers; and should he remain for a century the debtor of the bank, no bank note will ever reenter circulation between him, his peasants, and the markets where he sells his produce.

Finally, the government ought to remember that it is its bounden duty, as trustee of the common weal, to prevent that the currency, which is a national asset, be ever borrowed by insolvent debtors. The business of a bank is always to borrow the currency circulating in a nation, replacing it with notes that are but promises to pay, and then lending the former in turn to foreigners in order to collect interest. Every bank note put into circulation sends guineas of equal value across the borders. The bankers who have borrowed guineas in order to represent them in this fashion, can be what is commonly called very liquid, that is, they can mortgage a great real estate fortune upon completion of their pledges, although it may not suit the nation to entrust to them its existence; because the time may come, where, even with the greatest sacrifices, they would not be able to bring back the specie they have exported.

If a corporation in every respect similar to that of banks, came, after the harvest, to propose to the government that there are in the granaries a stock of wheat that will only be consumed in stages in six, eight, ten, and twelve months, that this stock were idle during this time, and without profit, almost like the specie in the bag of the banker; and if the government would lend to the corporation during that interval, the latter would leave in each granary as many mortgage notes on good lands, and it would undertake meanwhile to bring back, every Saturday, enough corn to feed all people during the next week; surely the government would be quite mad to believe that there was ever enough collateral to extend so much trust to it; it would be hardly less foolish if, trusting to the mortgages a land bank offers, it permits the bank to ship all currency abroad, with the promise to reimport it as soon as a need for it would be felt.

Currency, in quiet and normal times, can be represented by a token; but it is necessary to the security of society that, when needed, it can reappear in its natural form, be it for being employed in the national defense, because in a time of danger, all credit notes become useless, be it to serve only as the standard of all values in domestic transactions. The elimination of the standard, leaving nothing but the tokens in trade, exposes all contractants to much more dangerous errors, and changes all transmittals of property into hazardous bargains. A nation that has no more currency, knows not anymore what it owns; in times of war it lays itself open to see all that it considered its wealth being changed suddenly into useless rags;

in times of peace, it risks basing all its foreign trade on fallacious calculations, selling at a loss when it believes it will make a profit. Even today, Russia, Austria, Denmark can teach us what happens to a trade whose common standard is a paper endlessly variable.

Impounded currency cannot be retained in a country by export prohibitions; it remains if it is not driven out, it returns when exported without replacement; but from the instant it is made useless, it will become impossible to keep it. Of the various channels that replenish its circulation, sometimes one or other can be overfull, and directly the surplus escapes abroad; on the contrary they can be reopened; it is then enough to leave them empty, and forthwith currency hastens from abroad to fill them again.

It is but filling one of these channels, we have said, in setting bank notes in place of the bags that always remain full. Government gives its consent to this operation when it permits the issuance of notes of one thousand and five hundred pounds. But by stopping there, and prohibiting making any smaller notes, it prevents any effect on the currency which, in order to circulate, is divided into smaller amounts. On the day after it permits the issuance of hundred-franc notes, it authorizes, and forces, the exportation of all currency that circulated in amounts of more than one hundred francs. Finally, on the day it allows the issue of five-franc notes, it authorizes and forces the exportation of all silver coin, and it leaves only copper money to pay the small change of the paper. It is true that, as long as the circulation of these small notes is voluntary, it may happen that no one wants them, and there will be no consequences; nevertheless, the government should not even permit such an experiment; if it fails, it will ruin the businessmen; if it succeeds, it will ruin the nation; and if its success is doubtful, if the zeal of those concerned, who wish to borrow from the bank, supports a semi-circulation, then, after having ruined one and the other, the government will finally be drawn in to intervene, in order to protect credit, in a way that has never failed to be disastrous.

Mr. Ricardo has said of banks: "A currency is in its most perfect state when it consists wholly of paper money, but of paper money of an equal value with the gold which it professes to represent. The use of paper instead of gold, substitutes the cheapest in place of the most expensive medium, and enables the country, without loss to any individual, to exchange all the gold which it before used for this purpose, for raw materials, utensils, and food; by the use of which, both its wealth and its enjoyments are increased."*

Admiral Anson, in his travels in China, observed that the fortifications

*Chapter XXVII, p. 242, translation; chapter XXV of the original.

standing along the Canton River, intended to inspire in him respect for Chinese might, although they looked very well from afar, were only made of papier-mâché, and were armed only with paper cannon. The Chinese had reasoned somewhat like Mr. Ricardo. *The use of paper instead of copper for cannon, replaces a very expensive resource with another that is much less so; this enables the country, without loss to any individual, to exchange all the copper previously used for cannon, for raw materials, utensils, and food, by the use of which, both its wealth and its enjoyments are increased.*[7] This will go very well as long as there is peace; but with the first war and danger, it will be observed that the paper guineas and the cardboard cannon are not equal to those of silver, copper, and bronze, and that public safety was sacrificed to shabby parsimony.

The United States of America on their part have also experienced this dangerous ordeal; during the War of Independence their paper money depreciated rapidly, and they got rid of it only by a complete default, whereas they discharged punctually the bonds given for provisions, and which hardly lost any value. Today trust in their government is absolute, and their prosperity is so swift that the bank notes which have replaced the old notes had to feel the effects thereof; nevertheless, serious objections are connected to them because of the immoderate use that have been made of them. *The Bank of the United States* continues to pay its notes on presentation, so that they cannot be regarded in any way as paper money. But, other than that this bank has branches in almost every city, while it honors its notes only in the major ones, Americans have regarded the right of every citizen to found a bank and to issue notes on its credit as part of their liberty. In the quite new city of *Cincinnati*, in the state of Ohio, a city with barely ten thousand inhabitants, one can find already two banks guaranteed by charters, a third one without a charter,* and a branch of the Bank of the United States. These four institutions issue notes in competition with each other, and this for such small denominations, that notes equal to seven French sous, thirteen, twenty-six, and fifty-two sous are in general use; they have driven out all specie, except some Spanish piasters, not as whole coins, but at will cut up into halves, quarters, eighths. It also happens often that a note is cut in half with a scissor, because the half is sufficient to make payment.**[8]

When bank notes have been reduced to such small denominations, above all in a country where the wages of a general laborer amount to

*In chartered banks, bankers put at risk only their stock, as in a joint stock company; in the unchartered banks, they are liable with their person and their entire property.

**Fearon, Vth report, p. 253.

more than five francs per day, paper must have entered the smallest channels of circulation. America experienced from them painful troubles in the first emergency, and has experienced them in 1812; but even in the midst of peace and prosperity, it has thus deprived itself of the most precious of guarantees in its business relations. Failures of bankers are frequent; and with the immense variety of notes that circulate, one is always in danger of receiving worthless notes, or of being ruined by an unexpected bankruptcy. Moreover, since each note will be cashed only at the place where it was issued, it loses value in proportion to the distance from the issuing bank, and this loss amounts to from 10 to about 40 percent.[9] Thus, by having removed all precision, all stability from the standard destined to measure all other values, all trade of any kind, and every type of property, is exposed to perpetual speculation. This daily and universal game with values is perhaps one of the main reasons for the defect all travellers agree on, and charge Americans with, the business greediness that measures all things by the profit that can be made from it. Without a doubt, bank notes are a more economical means than specie to effect circulation; but it is such an inferior means, as to safety, as to uniformity, and as to integrity, that a nation is quite unwise if it endangers everything it holds most dear, by such parsimony.

Furthermore, the principle that the law ought not regulate private banks is totally false. These banks borrow the national currency, a public property, that is, and always ought to be under the watchful eye of the supreme authority. Land, in a large city, has a high price; what is used for streets and public squares has a great value that can be viewed as lost as that of the common currency; neither one nor the other yields any income. Should it then be nevertheless permissible for anyone to excavate under the streets and squares to construct storages? and should the magistrate, guardian of public safety and property, not forbid any such digging he would not have expressly authorized? Ought he not, before allowing it, assure himself that it could never result in any danger, any cave-ins that would damage the public road? Currency is the great highway of commerce; every private bank that replaces currency with paper, excavates a mine under this great highway. There are market savings, but diminution of safety; and the government must never permit this usurpation of its property without an assurance that the public highway is safe from all danger of collapse.

American banks would have very little business if they would limit themselves to discounting bills of exchange; it is understandable that these cannot be very plentiful at the frontiers of the new western territories; but they lend in various disguises the capital they acquire by public trust; thus they engage their debtors to assist in supporting their credit; in turn they spur them on, with capitals easily obtained, to speculative projects on which they would have hesitated if they would have had to commit their own funds. This spirit of imprudent project making, this overabundance of all types of commerce, that increases so much the bankruptcies in the United States, is without any doubt due to the proliferation of banks, and the ease with which false credit has replaced real wealth.

Not only in America, but in England and on our continent, general experience has shown that those banks that imagine themselves to be lending institutions, march constantly to their ruin every time they want to replace a real capital with their credit; yet they must not be confused with banks that, like the Lombards and the municipal lending institutions[10] in Italy, borrow currency at interest, in order to lend it out again as currency with interest. If, in transferring the capital of a wealthy region to a poor one, they gain the spread in interest, the business can be profitable; it is only charitable if it has for its only goal saving the poor from the hands of usurers. Some issuing banks, those of Scotland for instance, could have been advantageous from this point of view, although they were bad as note banks; they profited almost nothing from, and perhaps lost on, their notes; but they profited from giving the poor Scots, at 6 percent, capitals which cost them only 4 in London; and at the same time they provided earnings to the Scottish entrepreneur who would not have found lenders; and to the London capitalist who would not have found borrowers; the circulation of their notes only disguised the real reason of their business, and perhaps deceived everyone involved. As much can be said about some banks opened in several northern provinces.

But everyone knows what disasters the John Law system has brought to France in 1716. Law had begun with a bank of issue whose notes were payable at sight, and he announced then that he would double the capital of France with his notes, in order to encourage trade, manufactures, and agriculture. The first assignats, created in 1789, carried a promise that they were payable at sight by the emergency fund; the truth is that no funds were ever provided to pay for them. The Bank of Vienna, founded by Maria Theresia during the Seven Years War[11] paid then its notes at sight, and it was believed that in this way circulating capital was increased by twelve million guilders; it was forced, in 1797, to seek an order to suspend its specie payments.[12] The Bank of Stockholm, founded in 1657, as long as it was content to borrow at 4 percent in order to relend at 6, made good business. But once it was merged, after the death of Charles XII, with a second bank, and once it had begun to issue notes, and to make loans to the government and the aristocracy, it was soon obliged to go to the legislature to obtain exemption from payment. It was really only under the obligation to redeem its notes in copper coins, which are the currency of that kingdom; but, in 1762, by successive reductions in even that money, was only obliged to redeem the ninety-sixth share of its original obligations. The old Bank of Copenhagen, founded in 1736, which suspended payments in 1745; the new one, founded in 1791, which also suspended its payments a few years later, had both undertaken to pay their notes at sight; both believed they were affluent enough to lend their imaginary wealth to government and individuals; both ruined themselves and the country; and in October 1813, 1,800 guineas in Danish paper were offered for one guinea specie. The bank founded in Russia by Catherine II in 1768, which then issued forty million rubles in assignats payable at sight in copper coins, has maintained itself for eighteen years with tolerable prudence, without making new issues. But in 1786, the Empress created the *Loan Bank*, intended to lend assignats on mortgages to owners of land and houses in the cities; it increased the total assignat circulation to one hundred million rubles; it reserved thirty-three million to the Loan Bank. The latter has lent therefrom twenty-two million to the great nobles, merely increasing thereby their luxury, and eleven million to building contractors in the two capitals. Industry or the wealth of the state were in no way increased by these ill-timed loans. But from then on the bank has not ceased to make new issues. By 1810, it has reached a sum of 577 million rubles outstanding circulation; and although it is always supposed to redeem them at sight in copper coin, the exportation and melting of that currency being forbidden, and having moreover sustained considerable conversions, the Russian ruble in bank notes is only worth a quarter of a silver ruble.*

So many frightening examples of the fates of banks, even those that were founded on an entirely voluntary contract, could be an inducement to forbid them entirely. However, those which limit themselves to the only service to which they are suited, the discount of trade bills with short maturities, give a very legitimate benefit to entrepreneurs, and are reasonably useful to business; they decrease in some degree the interest rate, and above all they contribute to its regulation and uniformity. All the notes discounted by the bank, if it did not exist, would probably be discounted by various merchant houses; but the borrowers would not be sure to find lenders in time of need, and above all they would be much more at their mercy through circumstance.

However, a bank is much more a great machine for the use of government than a help to business; it alone is in the position to make the great

*An excellent description of the history of banks, and in particular those of Russia, can be found in the work of M.Storch, *Cours Économie Politique,* Vol VI, pp. 119–252.

loans governments are so often in need of, to discount the obligations of the provincial tax collectors, to facilitate loan treaties, and finally to interpose an intermediary between the state and its creditors. Among the public accounts, a bank is of the highest importance; a finance minister could only with difficulty dispense with its assistance; but it is precisely because it is a power in the state that it can become dangerous. It is because it renders to the government immense services, that the government may also want to favor it. There is no other country where the theory of political economy in general, and that of money in particular, is more widely disseminated than in England, and yet Mr. Pitt has demanded, in 1797, the suspension of bank note redemption; an English Parliament has agreed thereto, an English Parliament has decreed that the bank note had lost nothing of its old value, at the very moment where it lost 25 percent against gold; and since that time, during twenty-four years, even England herself has found itself with paper money instead of trustworthy bank notes.

Translator's Notes to Chapter 8, Fifth Book

This chapter is a direct continuation of the previous one. Here Sismondi brings in all of the examples he apparently left out of the preceding chapter, to reinforce the point that there is a vital distinction between credit money and real currency. An interesting addition is a lengthy note on Scottish banking, taken from parliamentary committee reports, and a later discussion on the state of U.S. banking, much of it unfavorable. It is Sismondi's position that bank notes drive out specie, but apparently he never entertained the possibility that paper money came into use because the country lost its specie paying for needed imports. The chapter incorporates only the short introductory paragraph from the *Encyclopedia;* all other material is new.

1. The dutiful reference to Adam Smith is not followed up in the rest of the chapter.
2. This short remark is the major theme in Sismondi's analysis of economic motivation. It appeared in the preceding books, and will reappear as a policy foundation in the seventh book. It is the exact antithesis of Marx's view of social production. Sismondi's opinions reflect a variant of the Protestant ethic, the firm belief that property holding engages the best instincts of laboring man, and is the basis for any prosperous civilization. It is again likely that the sentiments expressed here can be traced back to his experiences during the French Revolution. Marx was a romantic admirer of the French Revolution, but had had no significant experience with it, while Sismondi did, and as a consequence became totally opposed to any revolutionary restructuring of society.
3. In the heyday of Florentine banking, the florins from the mint were passed from hand to hand in this way. The bags were sealed, and since the mint was known to keep its coinage at full weight and fineness, nobody opened the bags.

4. This note was added to the second edition, clearly representing material that became available after the publication of the first edition of *New Principles*. It is a very good description of the Scottish system which at that time was probably the most advanced in the use of paper money. The description also shows that the Scottish bankers had advanced beyond mere note issue to attract deposits to their banks in other ways. Sismondi is ambivalent about this operation; on the one hand he sees the usefulness of the banking service, but on the other hand he is very much concerned, probably with some justification, about the perceived instability of the system. It is interesting to note that he is very much aware of the influence of what Veblen would call later "the vested interest." Like Veblen, he was very sensitive to the influence of institutional structures.
5. Payment suspension in this context means *not* cashing bank notes for gold or silver. The suspension was necessitated because the English government used the bank to raise funds for subsidies to its allies against Napoleon, and to equip armies and ships. In effect, the government used deficit financing to pursue the war.
6. Sismondi will later in this chapter mention John Law, but it is most likely that this paragraph refers to Law's Mississippi scheme. There may have been in his mind also the memory of Necker's financial machinations, but Necker's attempts to save the finances of Louis XVI were not in any way connected to the issuance of paper money. It is interesting that French economic history was apparently decisively influenced by the Law episode and the revolutionary assignats. The average French citizen in the nineteenth century, and well into the twentieth, did not trust banks, and as a national policy, France always kept larger gold reserves than, for example, England. General de Gaulle's postwar policy of exchanging dollars for bullion and bringing it to France was most likely another manifestation of this mistrust.
7. This is one of the most ironic passages in this work. Seen from his historical perspective and his experience, Sismondi had a valid concern—the continuous propensity of governments to overissue currency, leading to inflation. It is not clear whether he saw that strict adherence to a full-bodied circulation had the opposite effect, that is, deflation, unless new supplies of specie were brought to market.
8. Apparently it never occurred to Sismondi to regard such actions as conclusive evidence of a scarcity of currency that the citizens of Cincinnati tried to relieve by these expedients. The reference to cut-up Spanish coins is an interesting footnote to the American usage of "two bits."
9. See book 5, chapter 5, note 19. The American banking system of the time was known to be utterly chaotic.
10. *Monts-de-piété*.
11. The war lasted from 1756 to 1763. Austria, Russia, and France were allied against England and Prussia. England gained Canada in 1763, in the Treaty of Paris; Prussia gained Silesia in the Treaty of Osnabrueck.
12. By then the Austrians were heavily engaged in the war against the French, and they paid for their war expenses with borrowings from the bank. Eventually, most of the war expenses became floating debt in the form of paper money.

9

Of the Crises Which Convert Bank Notes into Paper Money

The safety of every type of property, in a country with a national bank of issue, demands that the ever so smooth transition from bank notes to paper money, and the sophisms that are used to justify this change, be subjected to the most severe examination. Governments imagined that in banks they had found an open mine, from which they might draw without hesitation.[1] [At each new season of need, they struck new bank notes. But they soon perceived, with astonishment, that notes were no longer received with the same confidence, and were speedily carried back to the bank for payment; and next, as their custom generally is, they substituted their authority for the nature of things. They refused payment on demand, but they ordered each citizen to receive as ready coin, those notes which had thus become *paper money*; and they authorized every debtor to pay his accounts with it.[2]

The money of a country has a determinate relation to the wealth of that country, and to the activity with which its wealth circulates. The same guineas serve, in the course of a year, for a great number of different bargains; yet still there is a necessary equation between the mass of values, and the sum of guineas which serves to pay them, multiplied by the rapidity of the circulation.] If, in the course of a year, all transactions amount to five hundred million francs, this sum in ready cash will have to pass from buyers to sellers, while an equal value in merchandise, or labor, will have passed from sellers to buyers. But, in the first amount, the same guineas that had served for one transaction, serve again for a second, then for a third. Since they are not consumed by anyone, everyone passes them on after receiving them; it is not so with goods. If every guinea has served in ten transactions annually, five hundred million of goods sold will have to be bought with fifty million guineas; if every guinea has served in fifty transactions, the same amount could have been paid with ten million guineas.*[3]

In any country, neither the sum of all transactions concluded during one year, nor the quantity of currency with which they are consummated, nor the speed of circulation of the latter, is ever known with certainty; it is likewise astonishing to see to what extent the speculations on these different matters diverge, this being one of many examples that ought to make us cautious of conclusions drawn from what is called political arithmetic. But whatever these amounts may be, it is certain that they do not in any way depend on the quantity of currency existing in a country. There will not be less or more output finished, nor more or less output demanded, because the currency, or what stands for it, will be abundant. Those who hold currency will not be, because of such abundance, either more or less eager to get rid of it in order to avoid having dead capital resting in their coffers without interest.

Whatever this proportion may be, it will nevertheless be established with certainty, without government intervention, and without it having any knowledge of it. [If too many guineas are in the country for the wants of the circulation, this is not a reason why the person holding them in his coffers should keep them longer than he has occasion so to do. All useless stagnation would be so much interest lost for him; and, therefore, he

*I have thought that I ought to simplify the statement of this equation in order to make it easier to understand. In reality, goods are also bought to be resold; but a piece of cloth hardly ever passes in the course of a year through the hands of more than four persons, whereas a guinea changes hands sometimes more than a hundred times. The value of all the goods sold, divided by the number of transactions of which they were the object from the producer to the consumer, is equal to the value of the guineas used to buy them, divided by the number of times these guineas have been exchanged in the same amount of time.

Bills of exchange bring also a certain modification to this equation. All that is bought and paid with bills of exchange ought not to enter in this general reckoning of the movement of currency; it is a direct exchange almost as if cloth were exchanged for corn; but as the bills are bought and resold in specie, which is the object of the banker's trade, they therefore act as merchandise, and ought to be counted as such. We have said elsewhere that the circulation of bills, if they perform the function of currency, is not at all as quick as that of currency, because of the interest they yield.

It is not uncommon to hear discussions on political economy by people sufficiently ignorant not to have noticed this difference in the speed of the circulation of currency and the goods for which it pays; to see them even write on these matters, and basing banking projects that must enrich the world on this error. To hear them,currency which circulates in business is, or ought to be, equal to the value of all it buys. The passage of one guinea through ten hands, while a good passes only through one, is however such an obvious fact, that it is enough to state it in order to prove it.

continues still to give them circulation, and some one is always at hand, who not finding any profitable use to make of them in the country, takes them out of it. If exportation is forbidden, a greater mass of idle guineas will be kept within the country, till the loss of those unable to employ them be great enough to pay the risk of smuggling. If precautions are so well taken that exportation is entirely impossible, the whole money circulated in the country will fall in value till it be reduced to the equation which it cannot pass, that is, to the numerical value of all the sales and payments made within the year, divided by the rapidity of circulation.][4]

An issue of paper money does not add a single purchase or sale to those that were made before in the country. However, if money velocity is merely ten times that of goods, then for each thousand-franc bank note issued, an additional ten thousand francs worth of transactions must occur. As that never happens, each thousand-franc note makes two hundred guineas at five francs useless. Such inutility causes them to be offered at a discount, and this discount is known as the depreciation of the exchange.[5] When the pound sterling is quoted at only twenty-four or twenty-three francs in Paris, this is because the English guineas, made superfluous by bank notes, are cheap in London, and sell for less there than they would sell in Paris. Somebody can always be found who computes the difference between the English exchanges and the price of gold in Paris; and if this difference is enough for smuggling, and leaves a profit, smuggling will occur, till the last supernumerary guinea has been exported.

This theory of the equation of the currency with commodities had already been expounded by Adam Smith, with a degree of clarity that seemed to leave no further doubt; it has nevertheless been attacked, at the end of the last century, by a ministerial writer, Mr. Henry Thornton, M. P. By attempting to prove that the Bank had acted prudently in advancing enormous capitals to the government, that Parliament had acted wisely in authorizing the Bank to stop redemption, and that all those who had discharged their business, had shown great patriotism in this, he believed he had victoriously refuted Adam Smith, whom he accuses of many errors.

Mr. Thornton relies on a true fact, namely that the velocity of the currency is not in every way equally quick. When confidence is high, everyone holds only the least possible amount, so as to not lose the interest on a dead capital; from the moment confidence declines, money becomes tight, as is said; everyone prefers to lose interest on a certain amount, and preserve it in the safe, rather than expose himself to being taken unawares, if the debtors on whom he counts do not pay at maturity. Thornton concludes properly that, the movement of goods remaining the same, it will be necessary to have a much larger amount of specie for currency to make a corresponding movement, when there is bearishness in business, than when there is confidence. The equation we have already given is perfectly in agreement with this theory.[6]

But, adds Thornton, it is therefore proper, in a period of anxiety, to issue new bank notes or, as was done in 1793, bills of exchequer, (government obligations similar in nature to liquidation tickets), to take the place, in the circulation, of those that every individual holds back. I do not deny that this expedient may not succeed in a crisis; it is for all that not any less dangerous.

Mistrust can have many causes, it must also have many different effects. If it is solely connected with business difficulties; if a great number of bankruptcies, following each other suddenly, have spread fear, and make it believable that the firms that are still holding on, are ready to fall in turn, then money will get tight, everyone will increase his reserves for the unforeseen circumstance; but as there will be no more reason than before to doubt the solidity of the government or the bank, everyone will amass indifferently in such reserve bank notes, bills of exchequer, or specie. The new issue the government will have made in order to help business, if it only replaces exactly the notes and specie withdrawn from circulation, will not in any way contribute to discrediting the paper, and could save merchants from a grievous crisis.[7]

But if suspicions are directed against the bank or the government; if a revolution, an invasion, make a public bankruptcy believable; if unwise projects, or unjust laws make it imaginable that all rights are not protected anymore, contracts not enforced, among them those bankers have undertaken, then everyone will want to build a reserve for a feared emergency, and he will want to create it from specie, not bank notes; everyone will have that right, because the specie left in the reserves of the bank were his asset before. Under such circumstances, the bank must entirely cease using a credit that does not belong to it; it must, to the extent demanded, redeem all its notes, to the last one, with specie, and not lend a single one by discount. Doubtlessly, there will be some distress among the holders of bills; this is a misfortune, but it is unavoidable; it is in no way connected to the existence of the bank, which can only lend what is lent to it, but from the existence of the capitalists, who lack entirely a sufficient fund for the needs of the moment, or who do not believe that the collateral offered is in any way adequate to secure them. The bank merely acts as an intermediary between the borrowers and the lenders; to force it to put its credit at the service of business when credit shrinks, is like forcing a moneychanger to find specie for paper, when no one offers any specie.

The bank had substituted its notes for the reserve that each merchant had in his till before, for unforeseen emergencies; from the moment that every merchant wants to rebuild his reserve, the service of the bank terminates, and its notes must be retired. It profited from the guineas left with it till its creditors would come to reclaim them. From the moment they are again demanded, its duty is clear, it must hand them over, without considering whether they could, or could not be, useful to those to whom it would have lent them.

However, it should not be believed that a decrease or discontinuation of bank discounts creates hardships proportional to the complaints that will be heard. The number of merchants, holders of drafts they had intended to discount, is never large enough that their distress, when the bank decreases its discounts, can be considered a public calamity; they will make shift as is done in many places where there is no bank; and, if the paper they would offer for discount is good, they always find means to bridge the two or three months that must be waited; thus, it is not they who scream, but those who have counted on withdrawing specie from circulation for some new speculation, and to whom the means to use the capital of others is suddenly denied.[8] If a new loan is offered, either at home, or abroad, or a new market is opened to business, and it shows possibilities of a very good profit, there will be a great demand for capital in that place. The poor as well as the rich will want to profit from an investment that appears lucrative, and they will borrow immediately if they can; if they have credit, they will find it much easier to draw on their business accounts,[9] and to accept from them in return drafts on themselves; we have explained this process in a preceding chapter, and we have shown that, when a capitalist discounts such drafts, he thus invests usually, easily and safely, his money. In that he is not the same as a bank. A capitalist puts out at interest an amount he wants to lend, and that he intends to use successively to discount other drafts, forever. A bank lends only what does not belong to it, what can be demanded back from it from one moment to the other, and what ought to constitute its reserves, for the movement of large sums of merchants with whom it does business. It does not matter to the capitalist whether the ten thousand francs he advances on a draft be used to make ten or ten thousand payments; his investment would not be any worse if all the guineas he handed over would be changed in their entirety into shillings; but it matters to a bank that its borrower does not borrow to change his notes into guineas; it matters to the bank that its discounts are limited to the only channel of circulation for which its notes are intended; and if the draft presented to it was not born from trade; if it is an expedient to borrow at a time when the everyone borrows and no one lends, it behooves the bank to refuse.

Such refusal will, indeed, contribute to make the raising of a loan difficult, and will lower the price of public obligations; better put, it will maintain them at their real price, which is the result of their proportion to offered funds. It is not at all proper to sell the obligations to those who cannot pay for them, but to those who wish to establish in this manner a perpetual trust. If the bank, at the moment when an enormous amount of loans has been put up for sale, had not decreased it discounts, not only would all its notes have come back in a few days to be redeemed in guineas, but all those who would have borrowed from it, finding themselves at the end of three months unable to pay, would have sold with a loss the public obligations they had taken on, and would thus have caused a new shock on the Stock Exchange.

While the suspension of payments by the Bank of England is for us only a foreign incident, it is very important to analyze and understand the sophisms that were used, with success, to accomplish this in a country where finance is so well understood. Similar cases will arise in all countries where a bank exists, and in all countries the holders of discounted drafts, and the bankers who do not wish to make a loss, will argue as they have done in England. Analogous cases have also occurred in France; and the bank there has taken, despite all outcries from business, the only wise and honest decision; it has immediately reduced its discounts. Its rule is not to take paper for longer than three months; in a time of stringency it has reduced this to forty-five days; it would have limited itself to thirty, to fifteen, to no discounts at all, if the distrust continued; the holders of bills could be embarrassed; that is the result of bearishness, and not of the stopping of payments; but the bank, which cannot force confidence in itself if there is none, would at least honorably discharge all its obligations and, after the return of calm and abundance, it would be richly rewarded by having honored its notes to the very last one, and having shown that, in the most violent crisis, they were always equal to the specie of which they were the promise. If, on the contrary, it shies away from this course, if ever it is forced to continue discounts while its credit diminishes, and its reserves decrease, or it is given an out, any subterfuge to dispense with the redemption of its notes that are payable on demand, then paper money is inevitable.

But, finally, it is not enough that the promise of the bank to redeem its notes on demand be formal; that in guarantee of this promise the stockholders have given mortgages on all their property, or that they have deposited a large capital into the hands of the government; that the profits they made while they held this privilege be only justified by the risk of loss such an event might occasion for them; that the suspension order they seek clearly is equivalent to bankruptcy; it is moreover necessary, in order to force them to meet their obligations, to examine whether they are practicable. This is the truth; and it is a major reason to interpose the authority of the legislature in the founding of any bank of issue; it is a major reason not to allow bankers in any way to make specie disappear that belongs to the public, if they give no certainty that they will bring it back in time of need; this is a major reason for not allowing them to put into circulation small denomination notes that drive the last gold coin from the country, and soon the last silver coin; and finally to prohibit provincial banks that have so mightily multiplied in England.

Still, the difficulty of bringing back specie for redeeming bank notes, at a time when everyone wants to exchange them for coin, is very far from being so great as it has been made. We have seen that the amount by which the notes of the Bank of France in circulation exceeded its reserves, was never more than fifty to sixty million francs; that in England it was never more than five to six million sterling. These are large sums, no doubt; but, if they are compared, either to the annual output of precious metals of the American mines, which comes to nine to ten million sterling, or to the annual revenue of either nation, or to their annual tax collections, or the expenditures the least little war makes them pay abroad, it is seen that it is not difficult to retire all the notes of a bank, provided one is not so imprudent as to advance them anew as long as the crisis lasts.[10]

If the Bank of England had proceeded in good faith to such action in 1797, it would have devoted to such purchases, not its notes, which was doing nothing, but a share of the public funds it holds; the buyers of these funds, in order to pay for them in gold, would have demanded ingots on the Continent, and these ingots would have been sent to them immediately on their credit, before they would have even dreamed of offering anything in exchange; who doubts that the London merchants cannot command, alone on their credit, in the various trade centers of Europe, an amount in excess of ten and fifteen million sterling; that this very sum is not usually due them in these places?

Then the exact opposite of what happened would have taken place: gold would have been valued at 2 or 3 percent, perhaps 5 percent, more in London than at Hamburg, Amsterdam, and Lisbon, whereas it was 4 or 5 percent less there. At the very moment when the bank suspended payment, an active smuggling operation carried, despite the war, guineas from London to Paris. If the bank would have repurchased in good faith gold and silver to redeem its notes, louis d'or, napoleons, Spanish piasters, and écus of five francs would have taken the opposite course, and gone from France to England. Neither one of these operations would have needed more time or effort, and the bank would have settled its affairs in a very short time. The English merchants would not have had much trouble in settling with Continental merchants who would have supplied them with specie on credit. The drafts of these merchants, in payment of their advances, would have declined abroad by 5 percent; that was precisely equal to a premium of 5 percent on any kind of English goods exported. More goods would have been sold as a consequence; the Bank, properly so, would have reimbursed the merchants for this 5 percent difference. That would have been the total sum of its losses, or the price at which it would have repurchased its money. Assuming that it had to redeem ten million sterling, above its reserves, this did not amount to more than a 500,000 sterling loss, truly minimal compared to its capital fund, or the profit of 3,800,000 pound sterling it was about to make.

It is true that what complicates this operation, and will undoubtedly persuade the Bank to fail its obligations, is the absolute necessity to first restrict, and afterwards suspend absolutely its discounts as long as the crisis lasts. As long as the notes do not stay in circulation[11] it would be much better for the bank to discount in écus or guineas than in notes. It would earn nothing on such a discount; it would lose with certainty on a discount in notes. It is likely that the Bank of England, before deciding to suspend its payments, for a long time made a loss on the gold it repurchased at the rate of 4 pounds and 4 pounds 2 shillings the ounce, while it returned it to business, in the form of guineas, at the rate of 3 pounds, 17 shillings, and 10½ pence sterling; and perhaps its loss exceeded greatly what it would have had to give up to retire its notes from circulation.

The skill of bank directors is essentially the ability to anticipate such business crises. When they lead to numerous bankruptcies in business, they soon stop of their own accord; if they are the effect of a sudden demand of new capital, the banker must school himself to never provide these new capitals, to lend nothing to those who remove specie from circulation, and to restrict his operations to those who discount real bills and not fictitious ones; if, finally, they result from distrust of the country's political situation, the banker ought to refuse all emissions till such mistrust has abated, and he himself will contribute more than anybody else to such abatement by his promptness to meet all his obligations.[12]

Since the first publication of this work, a new crisis, much more violent than any of its predecessors, has shaken the banking trade in England, has precipitated the bankruptcies of more than half of the provincial bankers, has caused immense losses to the rest, and has finally determined the government to recall the currency and to prohibit the circulation of the smallest notes. But, in this prudent course, it had to fight a mob of private interests, and prejudices and habits even more powerful than those interests.

Since the suspension of payments by the Bank of England, provincial banks had multiplied infinitely. Since nothing but paper was seen everywhere, people were disposed in every county to prefer the paper of a known banker to that of the Bank. The banks had, with discounts, with cash accounts, engaged all the small merchants to receive their paper; and although the Bank had resumed its payments, they had continued their trade with profit. Their bank notes, most of which are one pound sterling, constitute almost alone the currency of the consumer, the shopkeeper, the craftsman; hence, though the pound sterling is worth about twenty-five francs, everything is so expensive in England that a consumer hardly values a pound note, as a Frenchman did once with an assignat of five francs. The result has been that the mass of notes issued by private banks has risen to eight million, while the circulation of the Bank of England is twenty million sterling.

This all-paper currency has not raised any complaints as long as everything remained quiet. The banks kept the accounts of all the small merchants, of well-to-do individuals, of a great number of farmers, and their lending paper every time the latter were in need of money seemed to everyone a most convenient invention. It is not only that the banks gave much too easy credit, that they thus promoted the entrepreneurial spirit to an often dangerous extent by giving everyone the feeling of a great overabundance of capital, but they pushed business to such imprudent speculations, to that gambling with public obligations that has had finally such sad results. But those whose passions were catered to by the bankers applauded, even though these passions led them to their fall; often, the bankers declared bankruptcy, in consequence of their misplaced trust, but others soon took their place.

However, gambling in government obligations that had been pushed in a kind of mania, and that in stocks of North American mines, have suddenly ruined all the players, now that the moment has come to resell what they had bought at a higher price. The speculators only succumbed after having exhausted their credit with the bankers; consequently every bankruptcy from stock speculation damaged some bank; every failure increased also the need for specie on the Exchange, and the demands made on bankers; and some of them have been ruined. Since then fear has been everywhere, everyone wanted to change his bank notes into gold, everyone has demanded his gold back, and it was really his, because, as we have seen, it belonged to the bearer of the bank note, and what was left with the banker is only in storage.

However, all the gold that was so claimed had been sent abroad; to bring it back at once was in that case impossible. The bankers, with the greatest of sacrifices, strove to meet the demands of the public; they sold what they held in English and foreign government obligations, all the shares of companies that so madly proliferated, and they thus precipitated the fall of those securities speculation had driven up, and which have fallen today below their actual worth. Immense sums have been lost on that occasion by metropolitan and provicial banking houses; with a loss of 20 and 25 percent the heads of these houses, and often even their friends, strove to provide for the immediate need, to bring together enough specie to redeem the notes. The disaster must not be judged solely by the number of failures; those who have survived have for the most part lost as much as those who went under; the latter have come down to their last penny, the others still had something left.

Nevertheless all classes of society were struck together; the trouble, the loss, the shock equaled what would have been experienced in the greatest political upheavals; about seven hundred of the richest families in the nation have been thrown into poverty, all the savings of the poor, which they had held in provincial bank notes, were wiped out; all the reserve funds of the wealthy that were kept in the till for current expenses, vanished suddenly; and the majority of the manufacturers laid off their labor because they had no more cash to pay wages. Next to such distress, the loss of eight or ten million sterling national capital, that was suddenly destroyed, is nothing but a subsidiary misfortune.[13]

Undoubtedly, the invention of banks has allowed great savings to be made, adding to the productive capital of the nation the whole value of its currency. But what are then the advantages of such saving, of increasing production? Is wealth the goal of society, or the means to attain its goal? And if it is only the means, if it ought to be devoted in its entirety to purchase happiness, what better use can society make of it, than to buy security for everyone, the stability of all property? A metallic currency of a nation is, of all public expenses, the most useful, of all its luxuries the most reasonable. It is said that it produces nothing; but are security and stability nothing? It produces nothing, but the immense parks the English have preserved within the precincts of London, produce nothing as well; they occupy an area that could be made productive, and are perhaps worth as much as the total money circulating in London; yet the inhabitants have felt that clean air, a stroll, enjoyment for the eyes, were also goods, and that wealth which gives health and pleasure is not unproductive.[14]

If increase of wealth is taken as the goal of society, then the end will be endlessly sacrificed for the means. More production is secured, but it is purchased with a larger population and greater misery; more wheat is harvested in the fields, but the peasants are lost who lived there in happiness and were ready to defend it; the most beautiful cloths are produced in the mills, but the workers who weave them are clad in the coarsest clothes; to stimulate industry all gold and silver is used and replaced with bank notes; but everyone, going to bed rich in the evening, may awaken in the morning ruined without it being his fault. Hearing these national economies discussed, one would believe that man has joined together in society, not to assure his happiness, but to produce more cheaply metal buttons, or cotton textiles.[15]

Translator's Notes to Chapter 9, Fifth Book

This chapter is an elaboration of the previous banking analysis. At the same time, it is a very severe critique of banking, bank notes, and generally of excess credit creation. Sismondi regards government funds and shares of corporations as speculative paper wealth. The chapter was extended for the second edition by several long paragraphs on English financial conditions and the depression of 1824.

1. This sentence reads in the *Encyclopedia*: "Governments, on their side, imagined that in banks they had found an open mine, from which they might draw at discretion."
2. Obviously, Sismondi sees that bank notes are money, but he will not agree that they are *legitimate* money. As he makes clear, they are against *nature*.
3. In trying to clarify what he considered a difficult argument, Sismondi apparently made a mistake. In the associated text paragraph, and below, he states correctly the equation of exchange, namely GDP (Gross Domestic Product) 500 million divided by velocity of 50 times is equal to a money supply of ten million (500/50 = 10). Transactions are the same as velocity in this example. In this footnote, he *divides* the GDP by the number of transactions (T), and the money supply (M) by its velocity (V), to come to a supposed equality, or GDP/T = M/V. If it is assumed that the GDP is equal to PT (that is, price times transactions), then the left-hand side of the equation simplifies to P, which makes no sense if it is equated to M/V. Even if it is assumed that he meant the equation to read GDP/T = MV/V, the operation would yield P = M, which makes sense only if it is assumed that he wanted to demonstrate that an increase of the money supply will always increase prices, provided that T and V are equal, a heroic reinterpretation of what he wrote.
4. Here Sismondi states the equation of exchange correctly. He consistently assumes that once bank notes enter circulation they will drive out specie. He believes that notes are in forced circulation after suspension of specie redemption; however, he is not clearly stating his conditions. It would seem that he employs a version of Gresham's law with respect to bank notes, which to him are an inferior medium of exchange.
5. Historically, paper money was offered at a discount on the exchanges against gold, rather than the other way around, as is evidenced by Ricardo's pamphlet on the depreciation of bank notes. The assumption that bank notes will displace a determinate quantity of specie can only be accepted if output will not increase proportionately to increases in the money supply, triggering price rises and hoarding of specie, that is, an instance of Gresham's law. This is consistent with Sismondi's view that consumption is a very stable variable, if not a constant, which is not amenable to short-term manipulation. Why he should believe this is not clear; however, it may be based on actual observation of the general population, and farmers in particular. Given levels of income in the general population, and the relative inflexibility of income structures, sudden changes in consumption patterns would have been very unlikely. Also, the variety of goods was much less in his time, the productive machinery of the

Industrial Revolution had not yet changed the consumer sector, and hence inducements to "consumerism" were infinitely less. Also, his residence in Calvinistic Geneva may have contributed to this view.

6. This paragraph describes an early version of the precautionary motive for liquidity preference, with decreasing velocity if liquidity preference increases.
7. This is good monetarist reasoning, given the assumption that liquidity will be restored by the injection of new money. However, the analysis throws doubt on this assumption, because Sismondi believes that new money does not in fact stimulate consumption, and would therefore have no effect on solvency and profitability of business. The Keynesian model postulates a liquidity trap which would simply swallow the new money. Sismondi suggests something similar here and in the next two paragraphs. But it is important to keep in mind at all times that he is concerned with a deterioration of the standard by overissue of currency. In his view, monetary manipulation to cure business fluctuations is worse than useless, because it will inevitably lead to depreciation of the currency, that is, inflation. Without the restraining influence of specie, governments are always eager to overissue bank notes and are thus the generators of economic crises.
8. The paragraph is a commentary on Necker's ill-fated issue of French obligations. It may also reflect Sismondi's later experience with postrevolutionary speculators, although there is no evidence that he was ever involved in such schemes. He may, however, have observed such projects both in Paris and in London during his extended visits to these cities. Then again, his English in-laws may have acquainted him with such schemes. The end of this chapter has an extended description of English conditions after the crisis of 1818 that he could have gotten firsthand only from his in-laws. He takes here a fairly detached view of business distress, even though later he makes much of the far-reaching consequences of a business collapse.
9. The text uses the term "correspondent," which in Sismondi's times meant a business connection, either a supplier or a customer.
10. The prescription would be a severe restriction of credit, which would further aggravate the depression. The argument is, of course, that the redemption of notes will restore trust in the currency, and therefore lead to reexpansion. Sismondi is apparently unable to see that bank notes have already become an integral part of the commercial scene, and that their removal would force a liquidity crisis that would bring many additional businesses to bankruptcy.
11. That is, they are redeemed by the holders as soon as received, which is equivalent to stating that there was a run on the bank. The Bank of England suspended payments because it had issued too many notes in relation to its reserves to accommodate the government. Sismondi's advice amounts to raising the bank discount rate to attract foreign funds, an expedient the Bank of England used frequently during the nineteenth century to stabilize the pound rate.
12. In the first edition the chapter ends here. The following material is a description, and appraisal, of English financial conditions during the second major crisis after the Napoleonic Wars. Unfortunately (and for a historian, inexcusably) Sismondi does not provide any dates for the events he describes, probably assuming that his readers knew what he was writing about. The time referred to is probably 1824. The advice he gives in this paragraph, like most of the preceding advice, shows that Sismondi understood banking, but had little understanding of the role liquidity played in a business crisis.
13. This is a classic description of a banking panic. However, it is debatable whether the overissue of bank notes because of share speculation was respon-

sible, as he claims, or whether, instead, it was due to a contraction of credit connected to an inventory recession. The description has some similarity to the recent banking crisis in the Sunbelt, except that the existence of a "safety net" has shielded the depositors from the consequences of overspeculation. It should be noted that in England and Scotland all money was apparently paper issue of local banks, probably a consequence of increased economic activity and consequent need for liquidity.

14. Sismondi makes a point here that was only appreciated much later in the century: the increased productivity of the new age eventually had to be consumed not in goods, but in leisure, qualitatively rather than quantitatively. He will return to this point at greater length in the last book, where he will couple it with a demand that the worker share in the property of productive means, and hence profit.
15. Here, one can almost hear Charles Dickens and his severe critique of the new industrial order in *Hard Times*.

10

Of Paper Money

What distinguishes paper money fundamentally from bank notes is that the circulation of the former is by fiat, while that of the latter is voluntary. Many government obligations, payable to bearer, whether they carry interest or not, as the exchequer bills in England, or the evidences of liquidation in France, are not in any way paper money, although they would be payable anywhere at sight, because everyone takes them only voluntarily, and for a price at which he values such a security; likewise they do not have the quicker circulation of money, and they give it no competition; they can be exchanged directly against chattels and land, as wheat can be exchanged against cloth, or a house against a rent; but they make no part of the global equation we have established between the money stock divided by the velocity of its circulation, and all the goods it buys, divided likewise by their own circulation, the equation which gives to a country the necessary value of its money stock.[1]

On the other hand, all paper in forced circulation must be regarded as paper money, though it be cashed on demand; since such a payment is really illusory from the moment that the forced acceptance of such paper was seen as necessary, and it was declared by law as equivalent to specie. In fact, the banks of Russia and Sweden continued to redeem freely the paper money of these two countries; but they paid in copper money which is, after all, nothing but a type of token money whose value, outside the borders, is hardly more real than that of paper. It is not even permitted to melt this copper money down, or to export it, so that it confers no real value on the paper against which it is exchanged.

Similarly, it is worth examining how parts of the paper money, and copper coin,[2] that have been put into circulation in Austria, and in other countries, have an exchange rate much above their intrinsic value. Such money is but a token which derives all its value from the law that forces its acceptance. Everything we shall say about paper money is equally applicable to it.

Every new issue of paper money renders superfluous an equal quantity of specie, till all specie has been driven from the country. If a government stops there, the paper circulation can still maintain itself. In such a situation there would be more risk than suffering, and this is where England stopped for twenty-four years. It gave itself a paper money; and if it is considered how little profit is attached to such a great risk, it is astounding that it would have committed such an error; but it had well avoided the dangers of a superabundant currency, multiplying its notes beyond what the circulation could absorb.*[3]

Other governments have been less prudent, or better, they had to fight against more difficult circumstances. There is not one which has not sacrificed to the needs of the moment the security of the future, and the justice it owed to its citizens; not one which did not multiply its paper in such a way as to exceed three or four, often ten and twenty times, the nominal value of its money. Other than the states we have mentioned when considering banks, paper money can still be seen in Spain under the name of *vales-reales*. In 1805 there were up to 120 million piasters in circulation, and they lost 58 percent. As they had lost 88 percent in 1819, it must be assumed that there are now at least 280 million in circulation. Sardinia, the Papal States, and Naples, had also had their paper monies, from which the Revolution freed them.

However discredited the expedient of paper money be, one is never sure that a government will resist the temptation to impose a tax on those people who will not see right away that they are paying it, and who, as a consequence, offer no resistance. Since there is no more currency to export, this tax will be collected from those who are holding paper money at the moment of a new issue. If the circulation of a country is accomplished with fifty million francs, and if the government issues twenty-five million more, the seventy-five million are only worth precisely the same as the fifty. All those who had notes in their pocketbooks lose really a third of their value, which the government pockets; but as the market price does not establish itself immediately, these notes pass from hand to hand some more times, undoubtedly declining in value, but without being reduced to their true value; so that any one of the losers does not see all at once what is taken from him. This illusion is maintained some time; perfidious minds

*When this work appeared, the Bank was still exempted from redeeming its notes on demand. The Act of Parliament that calls on it to resume its payments, was however under debate from February 1819, and became law two years later. Still, the currency to the present time consists almost entirely of paper.

and bought writers work to keep it up; the loss is laid to speculation, to lack of confidence, whereas on the contrary a blind confidence accepts constantly the notes for more than they are worth; and a second, then a third issue comes, most often to reduce again their real value, before the notes have found in their depreciation the rate to which the first issue should have carried them.

Nevertheless, the circulation of paper money is always equivalent to a general bankruptcy.[4] Everywhere [paper fell every day in its proportion to silver or to goods. The bearers of it, feeling they had no pledge for their values, the sign of which they were always presenting, dreaded lest the paper should undergo a new deterioration in their hands, and made haste to get rid of it. Each lost and caused loss, each having no longer any common measure of value, became unable to distinguish the gain from the loss, and always selling with advantage, he ended in ruin. During this time, coin disappeared, goods themselves were exported from the country without giving any return; and the expedient, which promised to create immense wealth, produced nothing but ruin and confusion.]

The circulating capital of France has been destroyed almost entirely twice by paper money, the first time by Law's bank, the second time by the assignats. During the depreciation of the paper one never sold without buying at a higher price what had been sold, and hence no exchange took place without loss; all labor accumulated in earlier times, being subjected, step by step, to a similar exchange, ended in annihilation. Therefore everyone has endeavored to shield what had real value from such constant depreciation. During the second time, we have seen that everything that was capable of being sold, however far removed from trade it had heretofore been considered, became an object of exportation. All the warehouse stocks of merchants of all descriptions, even libraries, have been emptied; antique furniture in its turn has been sent abroad. Trade had acquired a false vitality. The nation seemed to sell much, but it was paid for its sales only in paper without value; finally it found itself to have exchanged all its material wealth against 45,579,000,000 francs in assignats which, at the moment of their abolition on 7 September 1796, sold for no more than 3 sous 6 deniers per 100 francs.[5]

Exportation on the same scale has been the consequence of the depreciation of Austrian paper, and at the same time it gave a false vigor to manufactures, it has been the main obstacle to the progress of an empire that seems to combine all economic advantages, and that loses all of them by mismanagement. The error resulting from the exchanges, for Russian merchants, has similarly brought them to sell at a loss, and Mr. Storch shows, with an interesting list of articles exported from Petersburg, that, while the nominal price in assignats seemed to have doubled from 1803 to

1811, the merchants really sold almost all their goods a third cheaper in the second year, which implies that they sold them at a loss.[6]

It is quite likely that the British government, when it maintained the suspension of redemption of bank notes, having thus left the country under the dangerous sway of paper money, has had as a secret motive the stimulation of large exports, but bought with a national sacrifice to which Parliament probably would have never assented if it had been demanded openly. The forced circulation of the bank notes maintained the English exchange rate always below par. This was a discount of 2 to 5 percent offered to all foreign buyers on all goods taken out of England. This discount without a doubt increased their demand, but it was exactly in the nature of a bounty; it was a sacrifice the nation made so that its merchants could profit, or continue their sales.*[7]

When a nation has the misfortune of having fallen into a system of paper money, it cannot escape from it except by a violent shock; all palliatives will merely prolong the disease and make it more ruinous. Paper must be demonetized; and there is no doubt that specie will rush almost instantaneously from everywhere to fill the void the paper will have left in the circulation. The government must at the same time repair as much as it can of the wrong it has committed, and of those even more numerous ones it has allowed to be committed. The paper has become its debt; it is sacred like any other private property that it may have seized for national need. It is quite clear that it cannot restore it,[8] except in England, where the note issue was confined to proper limits, and where a much smaller sacrifice was sufficient to make the bank capable of resuming redemption; but it can everywhere convert its debt and pledge to pay interest thereon.[9] To forego such action is deceiving the public confidence. However, whatever wrongs such a violation of promises and national honor may bring to society, the continuation of a paper that diminishes in value every day is an even greater evil. France recovered quickly from the shock it experienced with the abolition of the assignats on 7 September 1796. But the time of their circulation had carried grief into all families, and ruin to all estates.

The government's second duty is to regulate, by a depreciation scale, the value of contracts that had been made in this deceiving money. The

*Another intent moved, without doubt, and with greater force the directors of the bank; but since it is quite personal, it is not likely that the ministry was privy to it. The bank, having ceased to keep a reserve in its vaults, had increased its profits, and with it its dividends, from all the interest on that reserve. We have seen that the reserve was usually six million pounds; hence, three hundred thousand pounds sterling were gained annually by the stockholders with the suspension of payments in specie.

law has almost always authorized the discharge of debts in paper that were contracted in specie, and it has thus become an accomplice in all private bankruptcies, all bad faith payments that are the necessary consequence of the substitution of a nominal value for a real value in currency. But it would be most likely beyond its powers to force the settlement of all obligations contracted in nominal values, in real values. The creditor can be forced to lose, but the debtor cannot be made to pay what he does not have. If this could be done, the injustice would be equal to that of the first operation, and social injury would perhaps be even greater. England has experienced the first injuries from it in the Continental peace of 1813. She was not fully convinced that she possessed a paper money; the sale and exportation of gold being prohibited, the mass of the people had not in any way calculated, and made little of, the decline of paper. Looking upon it at all times as an unchangeable value, not giving any attention to the declining foreign exchanges, she merely believed that everything had become dearer.[10] All term contracts had been entered into after the rise in price of real goods. The farmer had promised 125 pounds sterling rent for land that was worth only 100 before, and he was in this like all other contractors. The bank notes, not having been issued in a quantity beyond the needs of circulation, appreciated almost to par, when peace rekindled trust and above all stopped the enormous subsidies England paid to the Continent. This rise, not being in any way the consequence of the abolition of paper, was not followed by an intervention of the legislature to change past contracts to another standard; no depreciation scale was published. Whoever had promised to pay 125 pound paper, worth 100 pounds in specie was held to paying 125 pound paper, worth 123 or 124 pound sterling. No legal remedy could be obtained against such crying injustice, which was not even well understood by those who suffered from it. But, also, no power would be able to extract from an industrious man a capital he most often did not have. In the course of two or three years, almost all farmers were seen to have been forced into bankruptcy, and almost all landowners were obliged to lower the rents on their estates. During that time agriculture experienced a shock from which it will not recover for a long time; by as much as a government compromises the public weal by varying the standard intended to measure all other values, by that much the fluctuations in the value of money, inevitable when paper is substituted for specie, will be fatal, and they are uniformly so, whether the paper rate of exchange indicates profit or loss.[11]

End of the Fifth Book

Translator's Notes to Chapter 10, Fifth Book

This chapter is the last in what should be considered a trilogy on paper money, namely chapters 8, 9, and 10. They mainly analyze the inflationary consequences of the Napoleonic Wars, ascribing every problem to the use of paper money. Sismondi was most likely aware that the need for increased spending led to the use, and abuse, of paper money, but he does not connect the two explicitly. Whether he would concede that gold and silver would have been insufficient to meet all expenditures of the combatants is unanswerable, but he would probably take the position that the available specie would have sufficed, given a decrease in prices. As pointed out elsewhere, he could not foresee the gold discoveries and the following changes in liquidity and production they would bring. He has an idea that an increase in the money supply increases business activity, but he believes that such benefit is dearly bought by the monetary instability it must inevitably engender. Looking backward from our present experience one cannot help but agree with him to a certain extent.

It should be noted that Marx has no analysis of this problem. His academic approach lacked the personal experience Sismondi brought to the subject.

1. This goes back to the formulation in the note of chapter 9. The repetition of the error must lie in some assumption about the relationship between the money velocity and the number of transactions that occur.
2. The text reads here: "le numeraire de cuivre ou de billon," which translates as "the copper money or copper coin," a duplication that was judged to be awkward.
3. The note was added to the second edition.
4. This sentence was changed from the *Encyclopedia*. There it read: "The circulation of paper money became, in a short time, nothing less that a general bankruptcy."
5. This is a classical description of the consequences of hyperinflation. However, Sismondi's insistence that everything was exported has to be taken with a grain of salt. It is more likely that specie disappeared into private hoards and remained in the country. On the other hand, some of the other things he describes may indeed have been removed from the country. During the German hyperinflation of the early 1920s, foreign capital acquired a great number of German assets, and in this sense the national wealth was indeed "exported."
6. It should be noted that this really discusses the inflation caused by the huge costs to all combatants of the Napoleonic Wars, and the antecedent French Revolution. Measured against available resources of the time, these wars were at least as destructive and debilitating as the later World Wars.
7. Sismondi is quite perceptive about the effects of exchange-rate depreciation on external trade. It should be noted that his analysis of the external effects of inflation clearly implies a recognition of the worsening terms of trade that follow. His preceding analysis of inflation as a tax on, mostly, the poorer part of the population, is equally incisive.
8. In specie; that is, they cannot redeem the paper currency.
9. This proposes to convert all paper money into long-term government obligations that carry interest, a device used by the British government when the Bank of England was founded—the consols (consolidated debt bonds of the British crown) had no maturity date and constituted a government debt in perpetuity. While the argument makes sense, especially seen from the viewpoint of the holder of paper currency, it is impracticable from a government viewpoint. The outstanding monetized debt is usually much too large to be converted in this manner, if only for the reason that interest payments would be impossibly large. Besides, it must be assumed that governments chose this

route precisely because it relieves them of later obligations. It should be noted that Sismondi's argument is *always* on the side of preserving property at any level of society.

10. Sismondi gives here, and in the preceding paragraphs, a convincing description of the money illusion. Whether all Englishmen were in fact so deceived as he makes out, is questionable.
11. The description of agricultural problems due to inflationary-deflationary money variations is an early observation of a dilemma that recurs with every major change in credit and money. Agriculture in the United States experienced the same combination of overfinancing of expansion during an inflationary period after World War I, and again after World War II, and is experiencing the same problems now, after the inflation of the late 1970s. Sismondi ascribes the problems to monetary reasons alone, without taking into account that expansion of production to meet higher demand may be a contributory factor. In fact, in an earlier chapter he makes the point that the farmer uses loans to increase his fixed capital, thus immobilizing his assets, which can be withdrawn only very slowly after every harvest. Agriculture is therefore much more affected by monetary fluctuations due to its inherent illiquidity.

Sixth Book

Of Taxation

Introduction

The first chapter of this book on taxation starts with the beginning paragraphs of chapter 6 of the *Encyclopedia* article. There, Sismondi had already expressed policy positions far removed from the standard individualism of the contemporary classical literature, being acutely aware that social expenditure must reach beyond the limits Smith had set for them. There can be little doubt that many governments had reached and surpassed the limits of bearable taxation by this time, mainly because of recent war expenditure, but also because of the natural extravagance of royal, ducal, and other courts. Sismondi reflects a contemporary entrepreneurial sentiment, just as much as his master did before, but unlike Smith he had experienced a more fully developed industrial society, and recognized the greater scope that social action would have to have to correct the dysfunctions of the new order. In other words, in Smith's society individual effort with a minimal government role was still a viable alternative as a corrective for social dislocation; in Sismondi's world it became progressively clearer that such was not the case. The progression actually invites the idealistic, Platonic extreme of the communal state that Marx envisioned as the utopian solution to the social shortcomings of the Industrial Revolution and capitalistic, machine dominated, production.

1

Who Ought to Pay Taxes?

[The primary object of political economy is the development of national wealth; but the object of all governments, since they began to bestow any attention on this subject, has been to participate in this wealth, and to acquire the disposal of a greater share of the nation's annual revenue. The ever increasing necessities of governments, and the excessive expense of wars, have forced princes to load their people with the weightiest possible yoke. Taxation, of itself always an object of repugnance to the subject, has become a nearly intolerable burden; the question is no longer how to make it easy; it is not to do good, but to do the least possible evil, that all the efforts of governments in this respect are limited.

Quesnay's sect of economists, who discovered in the net revenue of land the solitary source of wealth, might also believe in the advantage of a solitary species of taxation. They rightly observe, that government, in justice, ought to apply to him who is destined to pay the tax in the long run;[1] because if this tax is paid by one citizen, reimbursed by a second, who again is reimbursed by a third, not only will there be three persons instead of one incommoded by this payment, but the third will be so much the more incommoded, as it will be necessary for him to indemnify the preceding two for their advances of money. Upon the same principle, the economists called the tax which weighs on the revenue of land a *direct tax;* to all others they gave the name of indirect, because those taxes arrive indirectly at the person who pays them last. Their system has fallen, their definitions are no longer admitted, but their denominations have remained in general use.

We have recognized but a single source of wealth, which is labour; yet we have not recognized but a single class of citizens, to whom the revenues produced by labour belong. These are distributed among all the classes of the nation;[2] they assume all manner of forms, and therefore, it is just that taxation should follow them into all their ramifications. Taxation ought to be considered by the citizens of a state as a recompense for the protection, which government grants to their persons and properties. It is just that all support this, in proportion to the advantages secured them by society, and to the expense it incurs for them.

The greater part of the charge arising from social establishments, is destined to defend the rich against the poor; because, if left to their respective strength, the former would very speedily be stripped. It is hence just that the rich man contribute not only in proportion to his fortune, but even beyond it, to support a system which is so advantageous to him; in the same way it is equitable to take from his superfluity rather than from the other's necessaries.] Nevertheless, the poor on his part finds protection in the social order; from the moment that he has any property, an income from the fruits of his labor, he enjoys them under the protection of government. The tax he pays is for him a measure of freedom; he has a claim on the political order he contributes to support, and the sacrifice this contribution lays on him is the proper price of the enjoyment he must find in the rule of law.[3]

[Most public labours, most charges for defence and for the administration of justice, have territorial rather than movable property in view; it is hence farther just, that the landed proprietor be taxed in proportion higher than others.] However, if the poor himself shares in the benefits of the social order, the wealthy capitalist, the wealthy merchant, the rich manufacturer share therein even more. They are, if such be possible, even more exposed to the envy of the poor than the landlords, and a moment of anarchy would destroy their wealth much more quickly. In order to employ this wealth, they are, either themselves, or through their agents, or their debtors, always in a battle with the poor they make work; they impose on them sometimes onerous, sometimes even unbearable conditions. It is not their own power which makes this possible, it is that of society they borrow; industry, from which they derive all their incomes, directly or indirectly, could not survive if the government, which most often protects the established order without even examining the rights of the parties, gave not at all times powerful support to the haves against the have-nots.[4] The landlords must contribute, over and above the share of their incomes, to discharge the expenses incurred directly in their favor; but the capitalists are bound to contribute also over and above that proportion, for a government to which they owe their very existence.

With these slight modifications, the general rule can be accepted that everyone ought to contribute to the maintenance of society in proportion to his income. Of the different parts of wealth only incomes ought to be taxed; because government will use the tax revenue in a nonproductive way; it will spend it; that is, it would impoverish society as much, if all of what it spends were not taken from the funds which are reborn of their own, and which are only destined to be spent. That share of wealth governments will take, will have been, without a doubt, income for one and capital for another, since we have seen that these two embodiments of wealth change into each other without end; but it is important that government take it from the one who considers it income, and not from the one who looks upon it as capital, because the first, holding it for expenditure, economizes by as much on the remainder, no one wanting to impair funds destined for reproduction.[5]

Taxation provides for the annual expenditure of the state; and for each taxpayer, taxes are also a sharing of common expenses made for him and his fellow citizens. This expenditure is not much different from any other. The goal of wealth is always happiness; if everyone's capital is used to bring forth new riches, the income is used, and ought to be used to consume, to give happiness. Now, there are also enjoyments that every taxpayer purchases with taxation: the enjoyment of public order, of justice that guarantees person and property; enjoyments public works give with good roads, spacious walks, clean waters; public instruction is an enjoyment, whether it addresses itself, under the name of education, to children, or under the name of ritual, to adults; finally, there is enjoyment, this being the complement of all the others, in a national defense that safeguards for everyone the sharing of advantages the social order ought to secure.

Therefore, taxation is an evil only to the extent that is evil to purchase by a sacrifice the thing which we need or desire; but it is also a good, if that thing is worth more to us, and gives us more enjoyment than the sacrifice by which we have obtained it, takes away. If society were well organized, then it would always be like thus, because it must then always have the good sense to bring together the efforts of the many for a common end, rather than seeking to achieve it by a train of individual efforts.[6] Every taxpayer, through his money, ought to obtain more enjoyments from roads, canals, public fountains, the security of his person, the education he received, than if he would have sought to provide all these things at his own cost. The money the tax takes from him will then be well used if, on the one hand, all that is taken in the name of social happiness is really devoted to social benefits, and not to satisfy or pamper the passions of the rulers; if, on the other hand, those to whom such benefits are to be secured are capable of purchasing them with their incomes. For many a citizen a carriage would be a very great enjoyment; nevertheless he must forego it because his income would not suffice, and if, for once, he would take from his capital, he destroys the source of all his future enjoyments. Similarly, a beautiful theater would perhaps be a great enjoyment for all the citizens of a nation; they must forego this also if, in order to purchase this benefit, they have to encroach on their capital, to renounce for a present enjoyment future subsistence.[7]

The measure of everyone's enjoyments ought to be at all times everyone's income; in the same way, sharing in the communal benefits taxation ought to bring us, must be at all times proportioned to the general income.

Translator's Notes to Chapter 1, Sixth Book

New Principles shows the influence of physiocratic thought almost everywhere, but despite Sismondi's conscious or unconscious leanings in that direction he rejects the physiocratic idea of the single tax. In this chapter he establishes two connected rules for taxation—first, that income is generated by labor, and that therefore taxation must follow such labor wherever it generates income, and second, that taxes generally benefit the rich since they have a greater need for protection of property; therefore a larger share of the tax should be paid by the wealthy. That Sismondi had a benefit theory of taxation is evidenced by his idea that the poor should also pay a share of taxes because they consume the services of the state in such general services as personal security and education. Significantly, he again differs from Smith in viewing taxes as a necessary evil, but *also* as a benefit because they provide services the individual could only obtain by communal action. The formulation at the end of the chapter differs from Smith insofar as Smith's version generally implies large undertakings, while Sismondi clearly has such individual services as education, recreation, and transportation, as well as personal security, in mind. The argument is moreover couched in utility terms and therefore less dogmatic about the scope of government action than is Smith's—as long as the individual obtains benefits commensurate with taxation, government action is justified. This does not preclude Sismondi's viewing most governmental efforts with the same suspicion as did Smith.

1. Sismondi's own translation of his English version is a bit obscure here. The sentence reads in French: "Ils observaient avec raison que le gouvernement doit s'adresser en droiture a celui qui payera l'impôt en dernier résultat;" which should translate to 'Government, in all justice, should impose the tax on whoever must ultimately pay it.' Since the first paragraphs of the chapter were obviously taken from the *Encyclopedia*, the original version was used.
2. This short sentence incorporates a fundamental difference between Sismondi and Marx. Clearly, Sismondi's approach is more realistic in the sense that in any social structure there must exist people who are not workers, but who must be supported by society because they render essential services to society. Obviously, the question turns on the definition of *worker*, but the experience of so-called socialist societies would suggest that the Marxian formulation is defective. Again, it would seem that Marx's academic orientation and philosophical training preordained an idealistic theory, even though he maintained that he had stood Hegel on his head, and reversed philosophical idealism to realistic socialist materialism.
3. This clearly is a benefit theory of taxation, coupled to, and moderated by, an ability-to-pay principle.

4. This sentence immediately recalls Marx's dictum that government is always the representative of the ruling class, that is, the bourgeoisie in the capitalistic state.
5. Sismondi advances an intriguing reason for saving, namely, that taxation levied on income forces the taxpayer to cut down on spending from income in order not to impair capital. It seems that he has a very definite idea that taxation is an alternative to private spending, an idea he derived from Smith, but he is not certain of the dividing line between investment funds and consumption income.
6. This viewpoint is clearly opposed to Smith, and more important, to Sismondi's contemporaries. Like Keynes, Sismondi, being concerned with an economic malfunction—the business cycle—sees the need, under certain circumstances, for collective action. As mentioned before, Sismondi gives the impression of understanding the fallacy of composition, and its applicability to the limitations of individual effort. It is possible that he knew the *Fable of the Bees*; Smith knew it and indirectly inveighed against it in *The Wealth of Nations*; in any case, the discussion between advocates of collective action and pure individualists has not ceased to the present day. As a practical man and historian, Sismondi clearly saw the need for both under different circumstances.
7. This expresses perfectly the Protestant ethic of Calvinistic Geneva. Obviously, Sismondi had not yet experienced the benefits of credit cards, but the previous chapters (and the very next paragraph) show that he condemned any enjoyments on the cuff.

2

How Taxation Ought to Affect Income

It is beyond dispute that taxation must be levied on income only, and be proportioned to it; but after conceding this principle, it is still difficult to determine just what is properly taxable income, and in which way this income can be assessed on a proportional scale.

In the second book we have seen that income is an increase in wealth, a product of the earth and the labor of man, which can be consumed without reproduction, and without diminishing the original stock of wealth; we have also seen how, if consumption exceeded income, and encroached on capital, the land was found to be reduced to a lower state of cultivation, or indeed how past stored labor was not in any way replaced, in step with its consumption, by an equal amount of labor or, finally, how the men who have lived working lives, were not any more in a condition to begin anew and achieve the same work.

A share of the annual product must then be used to maintain land in the same state of cultivation, another to replace the accumulated stocks of human effort, to keep them at the same level; a third to sustain the laboring part of the nation, to maintain them at the same level of strength; if any part of this necessary allocation of the annual product is diverted, the nation will be quickly impoverished, it will destroy itself, and it will perish.

It is therefore essential not to confuse in any way with income, neither to waste, nor encroach upon, that part of the gross product which is consumed in maintaining the improvements of the land in the same condition; nor what replaces the fixed and circulating capitals with which all work is accomplished; nor what sustains the men by whose efforts these works are done. But how are these shares to be identified?

Will only the rent of land be considered as the net product of agriculture, and interest on money as the net product of capital? But the tax base will thus be much reduced, and numerous classes to whom the state guarantees benefits will be exempted from the duty to contribute to the expenses of the state. The farmer is not an inferior to the landlord, the merchant not an inferior to the capitalist, objects of the protection of the laws and the charitable action of government. The very day laborer lays claim to a share of all the public institutions; and it is for him, as for every other citizen, that justice is administered, that national honor is defended, that public works improve the country, and contribute to the well-being and enjoyments of all its inhabitants.

Labor is the source of public wealth; from labor springs income, and this annual increase is not in any way limited to the share that goes to the owners of land, or capital, as rent and as interest. The income of the farmer, or the profit he obtains by his industry, can be just as important as that of the landlord whose estate he cultivates; the profits of the merchant are generally larger than those of the capitalist whose funds he employs; the very wages of many workers, above all when they have acquired an important skill, or when they pursue higher careers, the fine arts, the learned professions, suffice for a life of opulence. These different members of society do not in any way object to making pecuniary sacrifices to obtain luxurious enjoyments; why would they object to contributing to the first of all benefits, that of order, justice, and security?[1]

It is true that in many countries the working class has been reduced to the bare subsistence level; everything that could be taken away from the remuneration of its work has been regarded as profit; the net product is seen as favorable to wealth, the sole end of society, while in the eyes of some writers laborers are no more than a means to the production of wealth, who could be dismissed as soon as they were useless. Under this deplorable social arrangement, while a subsistence is calculated that may sustain life at least cost, and limits of effort that may be demanded every day without exhausting physical strength, there would be doubtless mockery in demanding from the poor worker, who knows not any enjoyments, to pay for the benefits of an order and justice that does not protect him in any way, of a national honor to which he is indifferent. But it is after all not the sharing of the exchequer in the income of the poor that is faulty, but the degradation of the poor brought to a state in which his income does not exceed his subsistence.

After all, citizens are not classified as poor or wealthy according to the sources of their income. If the wages of many workers' families are just enough for subsistence, there exist also many families of poor landowners, poor capitalists, who do not obtain more from the rent of their lands, or from their capital, than the workers obtain from their work.[2] If members of one group are entirely exempted, it will become necessary to lay a heavier hand on others; taxation may well cut into subsistence by striking the net product, rather than the output of industry; it is as unjust and cruel to let landlords die of hunger as wage earners.

Every annual increase in national wealth, every addition that is consumable without reproduction ought to be therefore taxable; it may be spent entirely, and all spending ought to contribute in a certain measure to a guarantee of all benefits. The national income arises from the simultaneous action of four classes of individuals: landlords, capitalists, all those who employ capital for any industry whatever, and the workers; it is divided among them under the several names of rent, interest, profit, and wages;[3] everywhere it is equally destined to purchase enjoyments; everywhere it must contribute to the public good of social order; everywhere it ought to be levied in a proportional relation to such other benefits as it may bring; everywhere it must be treated with caution, because taxation, when encroaching on subsistence, would not leave to the taxpayer the means to live.

While it is essential, for humanitarian reasons, to never impose taxes on such income that takes from the taxpayer a share of his subsistence; because it would be absurd to talk to a man of the benefits of the public order when this order would condemn him to die of hunger; it is not any less important to observe that, in any kind of income, there is always a share that must remain inviolable, and which the exchequer cannot reach without compromising the very tax base, without depriving itself of future resources.

This necessary and inviolate share of income which alone gives value to property, and which induces its holder to conserve it, to improve it, and instills in him the reproductive impulse, is not at all the same in every type of wealth; and the abuses of the power to tax have not in any way for everyone the same disastrous effects.

The net income of land is, of all incomes, the one that has the least need to spring from the actions and will of its owner; it is also the one which governments have felt least obliged to treat with circumspection. In reality, however trampled on landlords might be, they cannot remove their lands to another country, nor can they destroy them; and the sole result of their oppression is that they cease to improve their possessions. No other class of citizens is so completely at the mercy of the exchequer. Thus the despotic governments of Asia have plundered them completely, taking over the ownership of land, and already, in many parts of our Europe, the weight of taxes is sufficiently heavy, so that the landlords are no more than farmers of the exchequer.

The most despotic government could not treat the net revenue of capitalists in the same manner. They have almost at any time the ability to remove their assets from vexatious taxation, and the exchequer, if it would have the facilities to assess their income that it now lacks, would have to observe the rule never to collect for itself such a large share thereof as to cause them to remove their wealth elsewhere.

Merchants, industrialists, farmers, all those who turn capital to account, are a bit more attached to the land than the capitalists;[4] at least the last two classes find it very difficult to leave a country; but in return their profits are their only encouragement to work, and if the exchequer found a means to collect a large part of the profits of commerce, manufacturing, and agriculture, so that the remainder would barely compensate the risks of the business, industry would first slow down, and soon cease entirely. Under the ministers of Charles V and his successors, it was seen to disappear from countries which flourished before, and idleness came back into vogue. Who would actually want to work with dedication, if his labor, instead of increasing his comfort, would only lead him to chance the little he has?

But if there is one part of the national income the exchequer must touch only with extreme care, from fear of impairing what is a necessity in recreating it, it is undoubtedly wages, or the income of all those who live from their labor. This income the workers should consume, but only in sustaining themselves, who are the living capital of the nation.[5]

In wages there is a needful portion which ought to sustain life, strength, and the health of those who receive it, so that labor continue, so that wages which is to them an income, but a capital to those who pay them, can give to the latter the fruits they expect, and to continue, from year to year, to impart to the social machinery this impulse. Woe to the government that touches this portion, it sacrifices everything, both the human victims and hopes for future wealth.

This distinction leads us to understand how faulty the policies of governments are who have reduced the working classes to a subsistence wage in order to increase the net incomes of industrialists, merchants, and landlords. The exchequer does not limit its claims in order to share in the net income of the latter three classes; it demands from every citizen a portion of his *enjoyments,* proportionate to his income, in order to secure the benefits of order, justice, the preservation of the national honor; but would it ask of one to whom it has not left any enjoyment? and when the entire work of the nation will be performed by machines,[6] or by men reduced to the state of machines, where will the exchequer find again that important portion it raised at other times on the income of a class of the nation it will have allowed to be destroyed?

These distinctions have not yet led us to recognize in a precise way the object of taxation, and even less to find the means to reach it. Nevertheless, from what we have just said, we can deduce a small number of rules that will serve us to judge the various forms of taxation.

1. All taxation must be levied on income and not on capital. In the first case, the state expends only what the individuals were bound to spend; in the second case, it destroys what gives life to individuals and the state.
2. The tax base must not confound the annual gross product with the income, because the former includes, in addition to the latter, all circulating capital; and a portion of this production must remain to maintain and renew all fixed capitals, all accumulated labor, and the lives of all productive workers.
3. Taxation being the price the citizens pay for benefits, it should never be asked from anyone who enjoys nothing; taxation should never reach that share of income that is needed to sustain the life of the taxpayer.
4. Taxation should never drive out the wealth it strikes, it must therefore be more moderate as such wealth is of a more elusive nature. It must never touch that income portion which is necessary to its preservation.[7]

Translator's Notes to Chapter 2, Sixth Book

This chapter is an addition to the basic *Encyclopedia* article; it contains no paragraphs from that work and hence presents Sismondi's developed ideas, after he had reappraised his views. The argument is clearly directed, not to any basic analytical solution of taxation, but to an equitable working policy of this forever-vexing problem. In line with his previous arguments on unaccounted costs, Sismondi stresses at the very beginning that, out of the yearly product, the three factors land, capital, and labor (in that order) must receive shares of the product to maintain their original strength, implying clearly from the beginning that taxation must not encroach on such shares. In this he differs from classical analysis inasmuch as he *includes* maintenance of the worker as a necessary part of what would today be called replacement investment. It should be noted that in the body of the chapter, Sismondi identifies four factors: landlords, capitalists, entrepreneurs (although he does not call them that), and workers, and names the shares rent, interest, profit, and wages. He anticipates a later classification—Ricardo does not yet distinguish between interest and profit, nor does he make a distinction between the entrepreneur and the capitalist.

1. The preceding discussion illustrates Sismondi's greatest strength and weakness, his constant pursuit of an equitable and rational organization of society that would recognize the merits and contributions of all its members, and at the same time engage their best efforts to improve and advance such a society in their own interest. He knows that classes have conflicting interests, but his aim is to engage these conflicting interests to their *mutual* benefit. His views were most likely decisively shaped by his participation in the administration of a small city-republic, the necessarily close knowledge of, and communion with, cocitizens, and, in addition, his experience with English institutions. In his time, England was the beacon of hope for all liberally minded Europeans, a safe harbor for

revolutionaries like Mazzini, and last, but not least, Marx. Sismondi's devotion to the ideals of rational discourse and his belief in the icons of Calvinistic betterment, hard work and frugality, are however the major reasons why his work, seminal in many respects, never attained the status of an important contribution to economic thinking. He lacks the single-minded focus of either the theoretician (for example, Ricardo) or of the fanatic revolutionary who projects his own frustrations and failures into his work, like Marx. What Keynes said about Malthus applies even more to the immediate forerunner of Malthus, namely that economics would have been better off if it had not heeded the unrealistic abstractions of Ricardo. But to the present day there exists a fascination with idealized systems of analysis, however remote they may be from actual experience. The Marxian system derives its power not from the accuracy of its theoretical structure, which was obsolete at the time of its publication, but from its seeming ability to provide a simple answer to complicated problems. Sismondi does not provide simple answers anywhere, only indications of directions that reasonable men might explore; the last sentence in this paragraph is an excellent example—unfortunately, there are men who are definitely not interested in the public benefits of order, justice, and security.

2. One wonders, on reading a sentence like this, whether Sismondi was thinking of his own Tuscan farm, and the straitened financial circumstances of his mother and sister when they lived there.
3. It is remarkable that this distinction was already made in the first edition of *New Principles*, that is, in 1819. Alfred Marshall is usually credited with introducing the entrepreneur into economic analysis, and separating interest and profit from each other.
4. The distinction made here also illustrates the peculiar way French economic institutions were structured. Whereas in England the industrialist was also for the most part his own capitalist, that is, the provider of funds, in France the rentier, the individual who lent his savings at interest to others, was a major source of funds, as he was also elsewhere on the Continent. The observations on the oppression of the landlords by the taxing authority again reflect Sismondi's close, and undoubtedly antagonistic, experience with such taxation. His realistic understanding of the ability of chattel owners (merchants, industrialists) to eventually remove their possessions from onerous taxation recalls mercantilistic doctrine and practice, especially the use of tax incentives to attract new industry, a practice that is still used today by governments professing a thorough devotion to pure market principles.
5. Sismondi will elaborate in the next book on this idea (which was raised before) namely, that the working population incorporates investment in skills and experience that must be preserved. This view is diametrically opposed to the classical view of labor as, mainly, a lump of undifferentiated workers. The Smithian and Ricardian formulation that the market will have determined the proper payment to different types of labor does not invalidate this view—the formula is equivalent to stating that for purposes of income-share analysis labor force *structure* is unimportant. Marx, interestingly enough, goes even further in abstracting from labor so-called *labor power,* thereby sweeping under the theoretical rug most problems that have to do with labor-force structure and technological displacement, a philosophical sleight of hand that is also connected to his definition of *socially necessary labor.*
6. This short sentence anticipates the famous note, in the next book, about the king of England turning a crank.

7. This balanced appraisal of taxation, however tentative, is very realistic, but it certainly does not offer any cut-and-dried answers to idealists and reformers of human society. Neither is it theoretically as well founded, or as analytically compelling, as Ricardo's analysis, another explanation of why the author failed to become a major force in the development of political economy. On a practical level, the four points give only marginal instruction to a tax assessor, but they also reflect the absence of viable classifications of product shares, an absence which probably explains the prominence of tax analysis in all works of political economy of the time.

3

Of a Single Tax Proportional to Income

It is a natural habit of the human mind to seek to reduce all its processes to the simplest formula; to generalize all its rules, and to bring out, by a uniform procedure, all it can abstract from more complicated behavior. This habit, which tends to simplify everything, to generalize everything, is no doubt the cause of all basic advances in many sciences. However, one must not surrender to it in a thoughtless manner; it springs more from our weakness than our strength, and abstractions exist less often in the nature than in the limits of our mind.[1]

Thus, almost always more suffering than relief has been given to society by the search for a single tax. It is undoubtedly better to simplify the exchequer's relations with the taxpayers, and it is undoubtedly desirable to substitute a fixed rule for arbitrariness, and certainly, all citizens being obliged to contribute to the national expenditure in proportion to their income, a single tax, proportioned to such income and equal for all would seem at one and the same time more equitable and simpler than the variety of taxes the artifices of finance have invented. However, most of the rules on taxation we have just proposed would be inapplicable to a single tax. The majority of incomes we have judged proper for assessment would not be reached by it. The more inflexible the rule, the more it must be held in esteem, if it is not to offend all those it would come to touch; and the single tax, even if it were feasible, would yield much less, and cause much more distress than the diverse taxes that accommodate themselves to different kinds of wealth.

If it were feasible, we have said. Actually, the first doubt that comes to mind is to know if it is possible to reach all incomes by a single legislative act, a proportional tax. For that it would be necessary either to seize the individual income at its source, at the moment when every citizen receives it, or else take it at its conversion to consumption, at the moment when every individual expends it. Both methods would be almost equivalent to each other, since expenditure is properly the most precise measure of income; if some misers spend less, if some spendthrifts spend more than they have, in yearly incomes, these small differences are unimportant for society. But if, as I believe, these two methods are equally impracticable, no other than the one actually followed would remain, to fit taxes to each kind of wealth, and to compensate, by their variety, for the inequity of each, considered separately.

The first approach would have to reach incomes at their inception. This will be the only one we will address in this chapter. After having examined, in the next two chapters, taxes on some specific sources of income, we will return, in the sixth chapter, to a general tax on expenditure or consumption, and we will show that, when wishing to allow only that one, it is equally inequitable or impracticable.

Let us assume that in the relation between private and public expenditure we allocate to each citizen nine-tenths of his income for his other enjoyments, and that we impose on him the obligation to contribute, with the remaining tenth, to the benefits government[2] provides for him; it will then be necessary that every income arising in that society in whatever manner pay to the exchequer a tenth. How would one go about assessing it, given the different kinds of wealth?

We have seen that the main income is that of the landlords. Yet, that will not cause difficulties, at least not in a system of lease farming; it differentiates itself clearly enough from capital, annual investment, and any other part of wealth; the contract which gives rise to it is often easy to recognize; even if it were disguised, the land itself could not escape scrutiny; and in reality governments have rarely spared the landlords; almost all have come to participate in their income at its source, almost all have gone beyond the tenth we have assumed they ought to demand.

The income created by fixed capital, from machines and factories of all kinds, comes close to the foregoing, and is hardly more difficult to tax, although the repayment of the original investment that is used up, is confused here with income. The owners of this capital will be more exposed to abuse by the authorities than the landlords; in overburdening them, more damage will be done to a nation, because more obstacles will stand in the way of the reproduction of wealth; but they will be hardly more difficult to reach.

The difficulty is greatly increased as soon as incomes that flow from circulating capital are considered. These, as we have seen, are divided into two parts: one, under the name of interest, goes to him who lends capital; the other, under the name of profit, remains with the one who has put it to work, whether he be contractor, farmer, industrialist, or merchant. To share in these revenues, the exchequer first needs to identify them, then be able to compel those who receive them to yield a proportionate share.

Interest is a fixed quantity, most often equal in all similar markets, independent of events,[3] which, in its similarities with land rent, would seem to be a good object of taxation. But the transfer of capital is a private transaction that government has almost no means to discover, it cannot even seek out without vexatious regulations; which it cannot assess without creating a multitude of fictitious contracts, frauds and subterfuges of every kind which, in order to evade the tax, will compromise the peace of families and the safety of all property; and which cannot be maintained without driving a large share of all capital abroad.

The profits of capital are an even more elusive wealth. The same enterprise, the same business that has given a profit last year, may make a loss this year. However, if the businessman regards his entire profit as income, and adds no portion of it to his capital in the good years, whereas the loss must be made up from his capital in bad ones, he will be soon ruined. His true income then comprises the average of the good and bad years; but this average is unknown even to him; how much more impossible is it for a watchful government to estimate it? Moreover, if the other taxpayers are interested in hiding their incomes only to escape the claims of the exchequer, businessmen have a special reason to deceive. However well established their fortunes may be, they always need potential credit; their failure would always depend on the good will of their competitors, if they, knowing the full extent of their resources, and being able to ascertain easily the nature of their undertakings, were the judges to choose the most critical moment to refuse loans, or to demand payment. Business is a jealous profession, where the interdependence of each and everyone is so great, that it can be counterbalanced only with secrecy. Every tax, on the contrary, is public by nature; a tax on income, on the profits of business, would give the public a measure of the fortunes of all businessmen, and this is what they fear the most; generally they would not hesitate to submit to the most arbitrary taxes, rather than to expose themselves to an inquiry into their fortunes which would bring their secret to the light of day.[4]

We come finally to the last source of income, the one that is divided among the largest number of citizens, and which, consequently, makes up the largest portion of the national income and, although the aliquot share of each be quite small, cannot be left out of taxation without depriving the exchequer of its most important resource: the wages of any type of labor. A share of income is always intermingled, in many ways, with other types of income. The landowning farmer must get from his land rent, profit, and wages at the same time; the contract farmer, profit and wages; the farmhand, wages alone. Thus wages are part of the income of whoever raises the fruits of the earth, and this class makes up, in France alone, five-sixths of the nation. The majority of artisans in the cities mix in their income the profits of retail trade with their actual wages; the factory owner, the merchant and all his clerks, all their employees, live from the wages their care and intelligence deserve, as much as from profit; the unproductive worker, finally, to whatever class he may belong, and by whatever channel he draws his own income from the income of others, finds it also in his wages.[5]

But how would wages be assessed directly as a source of revenue? When would they be taxed? To what vexations would the poor day laborer be subjected if every day one would demand a tenth of that day's wages? To what certain ruin would he be brought if, taking as his yearly income the wage he is not sure to receive except day after day, he were forced to pay fifty francs annually, while he makes ten francs per week? And if the tax would be raised in step with the diligence, the skills which really increase a worker's wages, what encouragement would one not give to laziness and vice, as against order and industry?

Thus, only incomes from land, houses, factories, and other fixed capital can be taxed directly; all other income escapes at the source from the scrutiny of the government, and it is only at another point of its existence that the exchequer can hope to share in a good which in reality it protects only under the condition that it obtain a portion thereof.

As a result the government has seen itself obliged to multiply taxes, so that each is lighter, and that with the failure of one, another reaches the various classes of individuals. On the one hand, it has taxed receipts with direct taxes, on the other hand expenditures with consumption taxes;[6] it has taken wherever it has found something to take; but it is almost always impossible for it to appreciate how much it asks from each class, and consequently to maintain the proportional equality that justice would have required. However, tax payers like better to submit to this considerable inconvenience than to the obligation to render an account of their incomes they often have never even made for themselves.

Striking thus almost blindly at wealth wherever it is found, there are still some rules on taxation Adam Smith has advocated, and which all governments ought to follow, if they do not want to increase the already grave evils caused by taxation, stirring up a resentment out of all proportion to the benefits derived from it.[7]

Every tax is by so much worse as it costs the people more than the receipts it brings into the treasury. It is by so much worse as its collection time causes more inconvenience to the taxpayer; so much better as the moment of payment has been tied to the time when the taxpayer has the means to do so.

It is by so much worse as its collection requires a more vexatious surveillance, a greater invasion of a citizen's liberty; it is by so much better as it gives less temptation to commit fraud, as it requires less surveillance, and as its discharge appears to be more voluntary.

These rules ought to be added to those we have given at the end of the last chapter. By observing them, even if one would not know how to make a tax a boon, at least one would make it less of an evil.

Translator's Notes to Chapter 3, Sixth Book

This and the following chapters on taxation are an example of conceptual limitations grounded in technical limitations. Taxation was a favorite subject of writers at the time, and most had difficulty in coming to a clear analysis of it. Even Ricardo's prose is hedged around with qualifications; Sismondi was handicapped, as were his contemporaries, by the absence of technical means to reach all citizens equally and equitably, some mechanism that would make, for instance, a withholding tax on wages possible. In this respect the citizen of a modern state is much more under the control of his government than a citizen of France in 1820, even if it is assumed that a modern democracy responds to the wishes of the voters, and a monarchical government does not. The truth is that taxes are collected by bureaucracies that have their own agenda, and their utility is determined not by legislation, but by their technical efficiency. With advances in communications, tax collection has become much more intrusive than even Sismondi could have imagined, or would have tolerated. At the end of this chapter he raises, in passing, the question of "vexatious surveillance." It would have been interesting to hear what he would have had to say on the present scope of taxation in all industrial countries.

1. His historical writings made Sismondi quite aware of the complicated nature of human relations, and the influence of what would be called much later *institutions*. In any case, *New Principles* is full of warnings against abstractions, this being one of them. This approach to political economy, discursive and undogmatic, vitiated much of what Sismondi had to say. There were just too many facets of a problem to consider, too many possible solutions to be explored, to allow a clear policy position.
2. The text uses the term "*l'ordre public*." It should be noted that Sismondi simply uses the customary tenth that was originally associated with contributions to the church.
3. This apparently assumes that interest is tied to medium-term and long-term contracts with fixed interest rates. Given the undeveloped nature of money markets at Sismondi's time, interest rates would have been determined either with reference to government issues or, more likely, mortgage contracts, both of which would be long term with fixed rates, hence the comparison with land rent. Petty made a similar comparison in his *Treatise*.
4. The text generally uses here the terms "*negociants*," "*marchands*," and "*commerce*," indicating that Sismondi had mostly the trading fraternity in mind, his former associates, who were prominent in Geneva. Since the text is quite general, the terms *businessmen* and *business* seemed to be more appropriate to express the spirit of the argument after the time lapse of 160 years since the publication of the work.

5. Despite many indications that Sismondi held a utility view of the factors of production, here the Smithian-Ricardian dichotomy of unproductive-productive labor reappears. In retrospect, the division may have more justification than we are prepared to admit today. Is the service job of a lawyer or accountant really as "productive" as that of a blue-collar worker? Is financial manipulation as productive as building new factories? Thorstein Veblen raised this question at the turn of the century in his *Theory of Business Enterprise*, and answered it with a resounding *NO*! The Marxian canon that the Soviet Union follows divides the economy into two sectors in accordance with the labor theory of value, A and B, classifying in the former all "productive" activity, in the latter all services. It may be that such a national accounting scheme may give a better view of the economy than those in use in the non-Marxist industrial world.
6. The following sentences to the end of the paragraph are a modified version of the *Encyclopedia*. Sismondi changed "governments" and "they" to the singular mode, and slightly altered the sense. Since the break comes in the middle of an integral argument, the *New Principles* text was translated.
7. The next two paragraphs summarize, in a somewhat more literary style, the four canons of taxation from *The Wealth of Nations*.

4

Of Taxes on Land

[The revenue most easily collected by taxation is that which proceeds from land; because this species of wealth cannot be concealed from sight; because, without the proprietor's declaration, the value of it may be known, and because, in gathering the produce at the moment when nature grants it, we are sure exactly to meet the proprietor's convenience for paying it. But economists are divided in opinion as to the two modes of collecting this tax, the one in kind from the unaltered product, the other in money from the proprietor's net revenue.] Both methods have been used more than once simultaneously in Europe, under the names of *tithe*[1] and *land tax;* they are met with in antiquity, and among almost all agricultural people who have acknowledged the authority of a goverment.

The tithe is a tax [levied at the moment of abundance, before the producer has in any shape taken possession of his property.[2] The rule, according to which tithes are established,] when it applies only to the major crops, [is so] simple and [universal, that few discussions or vexations arise from it, and this gives it a great appearance of equality. The collection of a tax in kind requires a great]er [number of clerks and warehouses] than one in money; however, its utmost simplicity makes it less costly; moreover, it would be enough for a government, not being pressed, to have the use of it, to find a benefit in the storing of the provisions, till a time favorable to their sale, or giving the use of them to farmers; hence, the tenth is, because of its simplicity, the tax most easily leased out. The cultivator, pressed by his obligation to pay the taxes in cash, sells his harvest almost always out of season. The government, by granting the tax farmers[3] a rent, would perhaps cover, by that single advance, all the collection costs.

[Combining such advantages, a national impost in the shape of tithes has seduced many political speculators. Tithes have also been defended with obstinacy by the powerful body to whom they are in general abandoned.][4] This body, which revives at its pleasure, from Jewish customs, those it judges to conform to its interests, while it abandons the others to oblivion, has often declared the tenth as an inalienable right, founded on divine law, whereas it has never aspired to renew ablutions and burnt offerings by standing on the authority of these same books. The tenth, on the other hand has been attacked with ever so much bitterness by the enemies of the clergy, and its restoration or abolition has almost always been a partisan matter.

The tenth has been distorted, by a mixture of Judaic superstition, and greediness, in all countries where it has been divided into large and small. The tenth can be applied without great difficulty to the annual field harvests, to the hay harvest, the corn harvest, the grape harvest, because these harvests occur at the same time, and thus are in their entirety before the eyes of the tithe-owner;[5] but tithes on successive crops, on products from the animal kingdom, the tenth on fruits, gardens, poultry, the stable, the milk shed, which are collected, in England, by an ecclesiastical fraternity called vicars, are an unavoidable occasion for disputes, vexation, and bitterness; they have fostered strife in each village between the vicar and his parishioners, and are the main cause for the rise of the sects dissenting from the established church.[6]

The great tithes, if they were claimed by the state, would doubtlessly be a quite productive tax, easy to assess, neither causing much discontent, nor much cost. But these advantages [are more than compensated by their real inequality, and the obstacles they oppose to industry.][7]

This is not how Mr. Ricardo judges them; he sees the tenth as a neutral[8] tax, paid entirely by the consumer, not at all detrimental to industry. As the reputation of Mr. Ricardo has infinitely risen since the publication of the first edition of his work, I believe it necessary to examine his opinion in greater detail, and to refute his arguments.

The principles according to which Mr. Ricardo claims that *tithes fall wholly on the consumer*, and that, *by proportioning themselves even for the worst lands to the quantity of the product, tithes are an equal tax*[9] are not at all stated in the chapter devoted to this tax. (Engl. Ch. IX, p. 225; Transl. Ch. XI, p. 290.) As a consequence, this chapter appears to me almost unintelligible. Explaining it in accordance with those that precede it, one sees that Mr. Ricardo does not in any way believe that the tenth could be paid by the landlord, because he sees rent as representing only the difference between a better and a worse piece of land, a difference the tenth does not change. This argument appears to me doubly erroneous, because rent, as we have stated elsewhere,[10] stands for other things than this difference, and because the tenth increases very noticeably this difference to the disadvantage of the poorer lands.

Mr. Ricardo also believes that tithes would not be paid by the farmer because "If the price of raw produce did not rise so as to compensate the cultivator for the tax, he would naturally quit a trade where his profits were reduced below the general level of profits; this would occasion a diminution of supply, until the unabated demand should have produced such a rise in the price of raw produce, as to make the cultivation of it equally profitable with the investment of capital in any other trade."[11]

I have shown, on the contrary, that there exists no average profit at all, though every trade always tends to approximate it; this is so because the profits of every trade change every year, whereas it takes twenty or thirty years to leave a trade in which fixed capital has been sunk, and for which masters and workers have performed a long apprenticeship. I have shown that, in particular, agriculture was an industry which could not be put on a par with any other, because all the capital that was invested in it, either fixed, or circulating, could never be employed in any other industry; because the agricultural laborers could not transfer to the trades of the cities, because the farmers themselves were incapable of pursuing any other type of employment. They may well change lands, but not the trade; and as the number of farmers is much larger than that of any men engaged in any trade, the profits of capital employed in agriculture are always inferior to those of the capital employed in any other industry with similar risks, considered separately.

Mr. Ricardo, in his entire book, talks of nothing but corn growing, as if this were the only product of the soil, whereas for the cultivator it is never a question of producing corn, or leaving the land idle, but to choose among all the agricultural occupations, of which some demand much larger investments than corn, others much less, and tithes treat them quite equally. The very cost of corn growing is a matter hardly calculable by the cultivator. In the course of four yearly harvests, when he has produced in succession wheat, turnips, oats and clover, manure and tillage have produced these four harvests together, but do not belong properly to one or the other.

However, the farmer of whom this year the tenth would be demanded that he was not usually paying, makes his profit-and-loss calculation. He cannot expect to obtain from the owner a proportionate rebate, his leases are long-term, and many years will pass before he will have to negotiate with him again.

He has no occasion to reimburse himself for the tenth from the consumer till the harvest has decreased, and since he will pay the tithe on the hay which demands less investment than corn, and on hops which demand more, it is not in his intent that he will decrease his plantings to escape the tithe; his only aim is not to have his capital subject to the tenth as well as his income. The annual crop must in reality reimburse him for his seed, his fertilizer, the workdays that have made the harvest grow, a compensation for the deterioration of his teams and his herds, the hire of his granaries and barns, the rent he pays to the landlord, and finally his own profit. On all that the tenth is taken from him. If he had only meadows he would not in any way be taxed on his sowing, his labor costs, his plows, his granaries and barns; but he has already acquired this agricultural equipment; if he does not use it at all, he would lose more than what the tenth asks of him; so he contents himself with letting them deteriorate, and not renewing them. Production decreases, but slowly; he has less need of day laborers, and the wages of agriculture decline, while on the other hand the price of corn increases. Thus, the tenth paid first by the farmer is by and by passed by him to the day laborer, whose wages decline, on to the consumer, whose cost of living is raised, and finally to the landlord who received from his land a monopoly price, and who must be content with a lower rent, because the advantage from this monopoly declines. The share of what each one suffers is unequal, and can hardly be predicted in advance.

Still, the tenth strikes agriculture in an unjust as well as an unequal manner. A tax ought to be assessed only on income, tithes are levied on the income together with the circulating capital of agriculture. They affect not only the profit of the farmer, and the rent of the landlord, but all the investments the farmer has made to obtain the harvest that is tithed.[12]

[In good years, and good soils, two sheaves in ten may represent all these advances; in bad years or soils, eight in ten will scarcely cover them; it is not very rare even that the whole crop is insufficient to pay the expenses. Tithes, however, are equally levied in all those cases; from the first they take an eighth part of the land revenue; from the second a half; from the third, which is nothing, they take a portion of the capital destined to produce the following crop; and their inequality is the more cruel, because it is always the poor whom they oppress, taking most from the very persons whose necessity requires most moderation.

Again, the more productive a mode of cultivation is, the more advances does it need to have committed to the ground. Tithes, which are but the seventh or eighth part of the revenue in a pasturage, become the fifth in a field of corn, the third in a vineyard, the half in a hop-yard or in a field of hemp,] or tobacco, [and the whole in a garden. Thus whilst the national interest incessantly requires the raw produce to be incessantly increased by committing larger advances to the ground—tithes instruct the cultivator incessantly to diminish his advances, and follow that species of culture which gives back least to the nation, but which also least exposes him who undertakes it to be punished for his industry.]

The cultivator subject to the tenth is obliged, every time he wishes to devote his field to a more productive culture, to negotiate in advance with the assessor, to accept a fixed assessment instead of a tenth of the crop. This fixed rent is exactly the land tax. In order to be equal to the tenth, it must be raised from a fifth to a fourth of the net income; because the *recaptures* of the farmers, as the physiocrats called them, comprise at least one-half of the gross product.

The land tax is designed to let the exchequer share in the income of the single proprietor, and it affects usually nobody but him. Based on a general assessment of lands, and sometimes on a land survey, it obliges every farmer to advance, in the name of his landlord, a proportional share of the net income, such as it had been calculated at the first assessment. But this assessment being invariable, the more the farmer pays to the exchequer, the less he pays to the landlord. This fixity still allows him to enlarge his cultivation, to improve the soil he tills, without the public demanding from him to share income coming from investments this public has not provided. The same reason makes this tax less costly to collect. Every cultivator knows exactly what he must pay; he has no hope of escaping the assessor, and he employs no trick to do so.*[13]

*Mr. Ricardo, always starting from the same principles, claims that the land tax is paid only from the income of the landlords when it varies with each variation of land rent; otherwise it will be reimbursed by the consumer. He says: "If No. 3 be the land last cultivated," (this means that land of the third quality is put under cultivation, because lands of the first and second quality do not suffice to feed the nation), "although it should pay no rent, it cannot, after the tax, be cultivated, and afford the general rate of profit, unless the price of produce rise to meet the tax. Either capital will be withheld from that land . . . to seek a more advantageous employment. The tax cannot be removed to the landlord, for by supposition he receives no rent."

In order for this argument to be true, one must believe with the author that pastures pay no rent at all, that the worst lands sown do not pay it either, that the landlord receives no compensation at all, either for his property rights, or for all the capitals he has applied to the land to bring them into cultivation, that soils are cultivated one after the other in the order in which they are the most productive, that all farmers' profits are equalized among them, and that those of agriculture are leveled with those of any other industry, and that, finally, it is as easy for a farmer to become a silk manufacturer, and employ his oxen, his plow and his granary to make velours and satins, as it is easy for a tailor to make frock coats when French dresses change. These are always the same abstractions whose futility can be sensed as soon as one sees the world as it is, not as it is created in a book.

To explain how the capital of the farmer will help him to become a manufacturer, it is not enough to say that he will sell his oxen, his plow, and his barns, because in order to sell them, there must be somebody who buys them, and that somebody

[On the other hand, this territorial impost often requires] the taxpayer to pay cash at the moment he has none. In that case, [it forces] the landlord or the farmer [to sell their commodities to obtain the quantity wanted, perhaps at the most unfavorable moment, and it thus contributes to cause a glut in the market at the moment of harvest, and a scarcity at the year's end.] In this respect, Tuscan legislation is worthy of imitation. Instead of collecting the land tax all at once, which would force the cultivator to sell at the same instant as all his colleagues; or month after month, which would force him to find money at harvest time as well as at spending time; it demands the tax in three installments, which follow, after some time, the three principal harvests of the country, those of wheat, wine, and oil, that is, the month of August, the month of November, and the month of February. Whoever pays the annual tax in March, the time when it is assessed, receives a rebate of 5 percent. To the contrary, whoever does not pay on the due dates cannot be prosecuted till after the year has ended; but, from the due day in each term, say, the last day of the month, that has passed for him, his debt is increased by 10 percent for the period he has failed to pay. This addition is a profit for the collector, but it is quite seldom that a landlord lays himself open in such a manner.[14]

The heavier the land tax, the more it will bring disorder to markets and all of the rural economy, by forcing the cultivator, or the landlord, to sell at any price in order to raise cash. At the same time, it separates him in some way from his property, and takes from him the desire as well as the means to make such permanent investments that increase, for many generations, the fruits of the soil.

The first estimate on which a land tax is based can often be unjust or unequal; and, if it should not be so, it can be troublesome in that, with the passage of even a little time, great inequities may spring from the progress of agriculture made in one region, its decline in another, the opening of new roads, of new canals, of new harbors, or shifts in population that give access to new markets; an assessment which appeared first as very equitable, will then demand a new land survey, and a new, more equitable allotment. However, the land tax has, in this type of uniformity, not the same qualifications as the others.

At the moment when a land tax is imposed in a country which was not subject to one before, the evil it brings to those it strikes is more serious than even they can imagine. It takes not only from them the income for a year, it takes from them also the capital the income stands for. If the tax is fixed at a fifth of net income, this is almost as if a fifth of the land were

will continue to use them in agriculture—the individual will have changed, not the intended use.

confiscated for the benefit of the state. From then on, every farmer has two masters; the one who has that name, for four-fifths of the income, and the state for the other fifth. If the landlord wants to change the farmer, if he wishes to mortgage his land, if he wants to sell it, if he wants to divide it among his children, the share of the exchequer is always deducted in the same way, and only four-fifths remain for him.

Without a doubt, such despoiling of everyone's property is hard to take; but it is already in the past; there are few countries in Europe which have remained to the present day free of the land tax, and the tenth, at the same time; one or the other had the same effect, and the right of the exchequer on the fifth from the income of land is established by old custom.

From then on, what will be the result of an adjustment in the land survey? Will it be more equitable? Will it be more equal? Two estates have been equally taxed at 1,000 francs annually; however, one yields only 3,000 francs, the other yields 12,000; one pays a third net, the other a twelfth. The inequality appears shocking; but one, as a consequence of that very inequality, has been sold, or received as an inheritance, for the price of 40,000 francs, and the other for 220,000, both on the twentieth penny of net income. To whom then must equal justice be done? to the land or the man? If it is the land, one cannot doubt that by taxing the two estates on the fifth of their net income, one should be reduced to 600 francs, and the other brought to 2,400. This will be equivalent, to the owner of the first, to a capital gain of 8,000 francs, he has never bought by buying the land, not ever inherited from his father, never counted on having as his portion in the division of the inheritance with his brothers. The second at the same time will lose a capital of 28,000 francs, which he had paid, or received in division, and on which perhaps weigh mortgages in favor of his brothers, or the sellers.[15]

If the law is to give justice to the individual, the law must not in any way change the division of estates, under whose trust everyone has lived and contracted. He from whom the correction of the land survey takes away a portion of his property, experiences a severe injustice, and that injustice is not in any way compensated by the unexpected benefit of his fellow man.[16] There is no more reason to give to one than to take away from the other, and the equal division of the domains of the exchequer, among the co-owners, is hardly better based on justice than the equal division of any other property.

One can add as another reason, not of justice, but political, that the equal division, instead of satisfying the owners, would probably give rise to general claims because, in the estimation of every man, there is not as much enjoyment in the gain of a thousand francs, as there is pain in their loss.[17] Those who find themselves burdened today would receive only very small relief for their waiting; those who to the contrary are spared would believe themselves terribly imposed upon after the reassessment.

Hence, there is no general calculation by which the inequality that is complained of can be remedied. Since we must not lose sight of the obligation we have discussed in another chapter, to respect the needful income, so that the owner does not become indifferent to his property, then government has to come to the relief of those truly aggrieved through partial abatements of taxes, and it has to reestablish equality among the landed taxpayers, with the same slowness and consideration which it brings to filling the tremendous gap that exists among its subjects, between extreme wealth and misery.[18]

Translator's Notes to Chapter 4, Sixth Book

While this chapter incorporates some material from the *Encyclopedia*, it became in the second edition a major critique of Ricardo and Ricardian rent, as applied to the incidence and payment of land taxes. The rent concept is a contentious one; the differential rent of Ricardo is a theoretical curiosity with little relation to reality. Sismondi refutes Ricardo's analysis that the incidence of land taxes is on the consumer, instead arguing that the farmer-contractor, the landlord, and the farm-hand would all have impaired incomes. The reason for the difference of views must be sought in different conceptions of markets and time. Ricardo assumes at all times that the market will liquefy capital for the individual at once, transferring resources from surplus to deficiency industries. Sismondi, on the other hand, argues that real capital is not transferred in a financial transfer, that its continued existence has an effect on the industry, and that resources in agriculture are particularly immovable. Therefore, taxes in the agricultural sector are not passed on. The difference may reflect a real difference in economic organization between France and the rest of the Continent, and England, where the latter may in fact have had greater mobility of agricultural resources than the former. In the last analysis, taxes are indeed paid by the consumer, mainly because everyone is a consumer, but the objections Sismondi raises against Ricardo bear importantly on the question whether political economy should be abstract, or be concerned with explaining reality in all its messy ramifications.

1. This tax is also known as the *tenth*. The terms will be used interchangeably in this chapter.
2. This apparently means that the tax is levied on the harvest before the producer has taken it off the fields.
3. A reflection on French practice and experience. France was divided before the Revolution into *les cinque fermes*, 'the five farms,' regions that were economically separate, that served as administrative units, and that were usually leased to tax farmers. Originally, the tax farmers would pay for their privileges in advance, and then reimburse themselves from the helpless taxpayers in their district, a practice that led to vast abuses, that was probably a major cause of the French Revolution, and that may have been one of the reasons why taxes were such a prominent topic of discussion at the time.
4. The Catholic church.

5. The French term used is *décimateur,* which the dictionary declares is obsolete. The reference here again is most likely to the church, which was the largest owner of tithes in Europe.
6. It should be remembered that Sismondi's in-laws were dissenters.
7. The next eight paragraphs were added to the second edition. They are a lengthy refutation of Ricardo's views on taxation, and were apparently developed from a footnote in the first edition.
8. The French term is *égale,* 'indifferent.'
9. This paraphrases the first paragraph of chapter 11 of the *Principles*, no. 64. The source citation that follows is apparently, for the English source, a transposal of the chapter number. It is not clear whether it is a misprint or an error by Sismondi.
10. Book 3, chapter 13.
11. The quote is from para. 56, chapter 9 of the *Principles*. Sismondi changed the quote slightly in translating it for *New Principles*. The translation quote was taken directly from the Gonner edition, p. 137.
12. This paragraph is the last in the addition made to the second edition. It is clear that Sismondi has an entirely different view of rent than does Ricardo. Although Ricardian rent is still an item in the theoretical paraphernalia of economics, there can be little question that Sismondi's concept of rent as a payment for the use of a resource eventually became the standard. It took the utility revolution to accomplish this task, but Ricardo's abstraction had a hardy life even after that revolution. This phenomenon refers back to the question that was asked above about the success of Marx and the failure of Sismondi. The labor theory of value was a dying doctrine because of its inability to explain anything at the time Marx began his studies, but he knew little of that, and Ricardian labor economics suited his political and philosophical preconceptions fully; Ricardian analysis was simple to grasp, it had all the answers, even those Ricardo did not bring out, and so a realistic analysis of a complex phenomenon was lost to an ongoing political controversy.
13. The note was added to the second edition. Sismondi altered the quote selectively. In the last cited sentence he left out "until the price of corn shall have risen, in consequence of demand, sufficiently to afford the usual profit; or if already employed on such land, it will quit it, . . ." The quote was taken directly from chapter 12, para. 66, p. 159, of the Gonner edition.

    The note continues the main argument of the work, namely that the assumptions of classical theory with respect to capital are unrealistic, that invested capital cannot be moved quickly because of specificity. Here, another observation is added—even if capital is sold to be transferred to another sector of the economy, the *monetary* transfer does not do away with the *real* capital; that is, the real capital will have an effect on the market. If the industry, in this case agriculture, is depressed, the overhanging fixed capital will depress activity further, and make, in the context of this chapter, land taxes more onerous. While the individual may escape from the industry, this is not possible for the nation as a whole. The idea is close to Keynes's view that the return on fixed capital is partially a function of all capital in the market. A short reflection will show that Ricardo and Sismondi differ in their focus—the former looks at individual transactions in the market, the latter at classes and a national market—the former is microeconomic, the latter macroeconomic.
14. On the testimony of Sismondi, Tuscany must have been at that time an

enlightened state, at least where economic and financial matters were concerned. Tuscany had several advantages not accorded to other states at the time. Being the land area that coincided with the Florentine city holdings, it had a rich tradition of business acumen and industry; it is quite fruitful, with a very temperate climate; and it had the undoubtedly fortuitous advantage of having rulers who were eighteenth-century ''enlightened'' despots who did not try, after the Napoleonic Wars, to roll laws and society back to the ancien régime. As a consequence, Tuscany was probably in Sismondi's time one of the more prosperous states in Europe. The legislation mentioned, as well as previous observations on Tuscany, would indicate that the government knew how to engage individual self-interest in a constructive way. It also shows that raw individualism was tempered by a concern for the community, a necessity in a state that was heavily populated for the time.

15. The sentence is a bit confusing, but Sismondi assumes two possibilities, sale *or* inheritance for either piece of land, leading to the assessment, and two ways of taxation, tenth or a land tax of one-fifth, leading to different *land values*.
16. Sismondi would most likely reject a Pareto optimum that is achieved by redistribution.
17. Utility reasoning is used here, or so it seems. On the other hand, this observation may be based simply on self-observation and common sense.
18. This last remark must be taken as an ironic comment on the governments of his day in particular, and all governments of all times in general.

5

Direct Taxes on Other Sources of Income

The land tax reaches only one type of income, and levies of various kinds that reach citizens in proportion to their expenditures, weigh anew on landowners; the taxes on sales of properties that are assessed, not on income, but on the national capitals, weigh also on real estate, in a ratio five or six times heavier than on chattels. Thus, landowners pay three times, whereas other citizens pay only once; and, if the different ways of paying are combined, one will find quite generally that they pay up to a third of their income, whereas others pay hardly a thirtieth.[1]

We have seen that there exist some reasons why they should contribute a little bit more than others to the support of a government which, on its part, expends more for them; but there is no reason for such a vast disproportion, and if one could reach the capitalist as easily as the landowner, it would be just to make him pay directly to support a government that protects his property. In the great states this has hardly been attempted; it was felt that the wealth of every citizen could only be ascertained by an irksome inquiry; it was feared that capital would be driven out and thereby deprive industry of necessary support, and a mine was voluntarily abandoned that was almost impossible to exploit. But Europe has seen, above all in the Middle Ages, great numbers of small trading republics rise amid the fields that fed them and which did not depend on them. The imperial and Hanseatic cities, the Italian republics, and those of Switzerland, were the centers of a vast trade, the home of wealthy capitalists, whose hoards tempted the greed of their neighbors. These cities, called upon to defend themselves against mighty princes, would have never been able to raise sufficient tax revenue in the small surrounding territory that depended on them. Moreover, their movable assets were often the cause of their danger; it was up to them to defend themselves. Those who came there to enjoy a freedom, a status they found nowhere else, had to pay for their freedoms of the city. These republics sought means to reach directly the incomes of the rich, while respecting freedom and commercial credit.

Often they were satisfied with the declaration that everyone would make of his fortune; often they did not even ask to know it; but required that every citizen, after having computed his accounts, pay to the coffers of the state what he would estimate as his due, without being permitted to identify the amount of this sum. At Hamburg, the declaration a citizen had to file, was equivalent to a quarter percent of his capital, and received under oath. At Geneva, the tax named the *gardes,* amounting to a mil of capital, with some modifications, is also left to the veracity of the citizen. Everyone reckons his accounts without witness and then pours his bag into the coffers of the government, without anyone having the right to see the coins; afterwards he signs a declaration, to the effect that he has paid his share. During the first years after the establishment of the tax, he was not even required to take an oath.

This way of paying taxes can only exist in such republics, and it is a creditable accomplishment for those who are able to maintain it, even though it is necessary that it be very moderate. At Geneva the capitalist pays barely the fiftieth of his income, whereas the landowner pays at least the twentieth. This proportion is undoubtedly inequitable, but it is the only one possible; and the first requirement of a tax is that it be collectible.

There are, in the great states,[2] a class of capitalists who own great fortunes. These are the holders of government obligations,[3] of whom we will say more when we deal with loans. Their wealth is entirely related to the conservation of society; they are more interested than anybody else in defending it; it is quite fair to make them contribute thereto more than anyone else, because they often are the true owners of almost all public wealth, and besides, it is easier and less expensive, since it is sufficient to withhold merely a portion of the income the exchequer has already in its hands.

But it is precisely the ease of withholding government rents that makes it so much more dangerous. There are few governments burdened with debts that have not abused it sometimes. Now, when government is at the same time debtor and legislator, it is not easy to decide where the tax ends and the bankruptcy begins; or, better said, every time when, under the pretext of assessing the income of its creditors, it defaults on the obligations it has undertaken towards them, it is really a bankrupt.

Nevertheless, I do not in any way believe that it would be impossible in a country where the rights of the citizen are not an empty title, or the prerogatives connected therewith, and where they are an object of concern, to assess bond holders a voluntary contribution that could become a productive resource. In France, every citizen who pays direct taxes of 300 francs, is an elector; every citizen who pays 1,000, is eligible to be a national representative. These duties are already highly honored and they will become even more so. Why should one not give to the bond holder the right to transfer his claim of 5 percent on the national debt to a new issue of 4 percent? The owner of a payment of 1,500 francs who, by this transfer, would have reduced it voluntarily to 1,200, would be an elector. The owner of a rent of 5,000 francs, voluntarily reduced to 4,000 francs, would be electable. The rents of the 4 percent issue would be transferable like the others, and with their ownership, would transfer all the freedoms of the city.[4]

At the time such a law would be enacted, perhaps there would not be a large number of voluntary reductions; but the approach of every election would multiply them, and all would be irrevocable; all would extinguish the debt without cost; all would have at the same time the advantage of settling it earlier, of moving it to the provinces,[5] of interesting most of the people of the nation therein, and of extinguishing the jealousy the provincial taxpayers feel quite naturally against the creditors in the capital, or abroad. As to the political effects of the admission of this new class of electors, it would be equally reassuring to order and liberty. These people, who have entrusted to the state their wealth and their means of existence, are not inclined to upset the state; on the contrary, they are the firm defenders of order, of thrift,[6] of good faith in dealings, and of that respect for the rights of everyone on which their credit rests. Few people deserve more to be citizens than the creditors of the state who have voluntarily contributed to the discharge of its debts.

Attempts were made to tax directly the incomes of trade and industry by dividing into classes those who practice the various kinds, and obliging everyone to pay in accordance with the class to which he belongs. In this way license fees were introduced in France, which encompass not only trade and the manufactures, but also the majority of the professions. This is therefore a share in incomes that arise from profits, and of those that arise from salaries, that has been sought. But there exists such a great distance between the ability to profit from a profession, and assured gain, that it would be quite unjust to tax a man for what he could earn, and what he has perhaps lost; so that, despite the invention of the proportional tax based on house rents because these were believed to be an index of wealth, there is no equality between the share of the profits a merchant hands over to the exchequer, and the share of land rents a landowner gives up. There exists none between the yields; licenses do not bring in the fifteenth of what the land tax produces.

Personal taxes and personal property taxes are established on such arbitrary grounds that the majority of cities have preferred to substitute for them some consumption tax.

Thus, incomes from capital, trade, and industry are as yet but very weakly affected by direct taxes. Those which arise directly from work have not even been taken into consideration; it is felt that to tax every worker by reason of the wage he could earn, was either to lay oneself open to rob him of his subsistence, or giving him a means to obtain an increase in wages which would have raised the prices of all goods and would have stopped their sale. Moreover, to tax a man because of his ability to earn a higher wage, is to punish in some way his efforts, his intelligence, qualities by which he has become superior to his coworkers. It is in a much more indirect manner that one must obtain from him a share in the income that flows from these many qualities, if one does not want to discourage them.

In France, the tax on doors and windows is also reckoned among the direct taxes. This is rather a tax on the consumption of houses. Counting windows was believed to be easier than getting a true declaration of the amount of rent.[7]

Almost all governments have imposed a heavy tax on inheritances, sales, and all transfers of property; again attacking capital rather than income, they diminish the productive base of wealth, almost like levying the tenth on the seed instead of levying it on the harvest. However, as this tax is usually collected at the time when it is most convenient to pay; as the same person is rarely called upon to pay it more often than once on his entire wealth, and as it is easy to eliminate all arbitrariness from its mode of assessment, the *enregistrement,* one of the most productive taxes in France, causes not nearly as many complaints as others that are much less onerous; and it is probable that those from whom it takes at once a share of their capital, always manage to recover from their income, by their frugality, an amount equal to what they have lost, so that the effect on national wealth is almost the same as if income had been taxed.[8] But the tax on mortgage loans, and the stamp duties on judicial acts do not merit in any way the same indulgence because they are collected on incidents that could be taken as signs of poverty, or at least of need and not of wealth. To levy a tax on the debts of a man, or his trial, seems to be hardly less reasonable than to levy it on his illnesses.

Thus, despite the fervor of the financiers, their constant activity, their gift for invention, and the swiftness with which a discovery in their art, in whatever country it may be made, is spread in all civilized nations, it has remained impossible for them to reach directly the greater portion of incomes, and it is because of this failure that they have tried to levy a tax proportioned to expenditure.[9]

Translator's Notes to Chapter 5, Sixth Book

In this somewhat tedious ongoing discussion of various types of taxes, Sismondi advances a rather remarkable scheme to reduce the national debt of a country by giving the debt holders the privilege of becoming legislators when they voluntarily renounce some of the debt they hold. The scheme is fanciful and would hardly be practicable for present-day conditions. It reflects, however, the much simpler conditions he had to consider, although it should be kept in mind that for the resources available at his time, governments were as indebted, if not more so, than governments today.

1. No justification is given for this statement. It must be assumed that it was made with reference, again, to his own experience with his Tuscan farm. However, his viewpoint may also have been influenced by his observation that industry escaped taxation because of its newness, and by what he has described, and will describe again in the next paragraph, as the inherent difficulty of reaching commercial and industrial income, that is, business profits, because of their private nature. This reflects the fact that most businesses were proprietorships then, and chartered companies were not required to disclose details of their operations. The argument is also reminiscent of physiocratic ideas about the ultimate incidence of any tax.
2. This probably refers to England, France, Austria, Russia, and Prussia, these being the major European powers of the time.
3. The text reads "les rentiers de l'Etat."
4. The scheme is based on French practice, but is more likely to succeed in a small, easily administered political entity. While the scheme sounds wonderful, no modern national government could adopt it, for the obvious reason that the creditors of the state would then run the state, a condition no democratic elective government could tolerate. On the other hand, this raises indirectly an interesting question, namely the relationship of governmental oversight and the size of the political entity. In political economy, Sismondi is consistently on the side of the smaller unit, which permits direct participation of the worker in decision making and profits; he is not as clear on political matters, but it would seem that he would prefer the smaller political unit to the larger one. The scheme he advocates here could conceivably have worked in the city-republic of Geneva, where everyone of any consequence was known to everybody else. However, he clearly overlooks the capacity for mischief an oligarchy may have. The term *electeur* was translated literally as 'elector' since the term 'voter' in this context eliminated the sense of property-related exclusivity that was connected with voting at the time.
5. The text reads *"de la faire passer dans le départements."* The reference is not quite clear, but it seems that Sismondi believed that his scheme would extinguish the debt and at the same time disperse ownership of the debt from the capital to the provinces. It would create more provincial electors and legislators and loosen the political monopoly of Paris, as is indicated in the next sentence.
6. The text reads "de l'économie," which could also be translated as 'the economy.' In the context, the chosen reading made more sense.
7. A reference to a tax that was imposed by the tax farmers in France to recoup their advances after they had almost exhausted any other sources of revenue. The discussion illustrates the difficulties governments had in assessing certain classes, and, by implication, shows just how unequal taxes must have been.

8. Sismondi could also have applied this reasoning to the land tax.
9. This anticipates the next chapter. ''Financiers'' most likely stands here for tax farmers, but could also refer to bankers like Necker who ran finance ministries in times of fiscal emergency.

6

Taxes on Consumption

[Those different kinds of income, which cannot be appreciated for taxation,[1] at their origin, are always employed in consumption; and this is the moment when taxation can reach them with far less inconvenience. By taxing every kind of goods, in the purchasing of which wealth may be employed, we are sure to make that wealth contribute, and we need not know to whom it belongs. For such a contribution there is not required any declaration of fortune, any inquisition, any distinction of poor and rich; it does not attach taxation to labour; it does not punish what ought, above all other things, to be encouraged. Besides, each contributor pays his taxes on consumption, as it were in a voluntary manner, at the time when he has money, and finds himself enabled to purchase the thing taxed; he reimburses the merchant, who has already advanced the impost, and he scarcely perceives that himself has paid any.[2]

Taxes on consumption are, however, very far from being able to reach the revenue in a correct manner, by means of the expenditure.] If [it is required, for example, that every kind of fortune, every kind of industry, protected by the state, should pay the treasury ten percent of the revenue which they give;] to do this, it would be necessary, first, that every citizen pay 10 percent on the rent of his housing, whether it belongs to him, or whether it were rented. Housing is the slowest of all consumptions; nevertheless it is one, and rent represents its annual value. But the collection of a tax on housing rent is not at all like the remainder of consumption taxes; it has no advantages; it engenders a hateful inquisition; and in order to avoid stooping that low, taxes on windows and doors, on chimneys, and other stand-in taxes were invented. However, generally this has remained quite far below the proportion that was to be assessed, and this share of expenditure has not been put in any way on the same footing as all others.[3]

Second, every man would have to give to the treasury the tenth part of what he spends on wages for domestics, and in salaries for unproductive workers. The services performed by unproductive workers ought to be regarded as quick consumption that follows immediately on production; but, though they do not give rise to taxable goods, they are benefits guaranteed by society, and whoever enjoys them ought to reimburse society for the costs of that guarantee. Even if these unproductive workers would pay in their turn a tax on a share of their income, there would be no duplication, because as all other citizens, they would pay because of their benefits.

Third, yet other things that have never been counted among goods, but which make a part of the expenditures of the rich, and of his benefits, must be taxed in the same way. On the one hand, these are the dogs, the horses, the carriages; on the other, all art objects, paintings, statues, and finally everything the rich man buys, and pays, for his amusement.

Fourth, all goods intended for the use of man, of whatever nature, ought to be subjected in the same manner to a proportional tax of 10 percent, whether they come from abroad or have been produced in the country,[4] even if they are the output of a domestic industry. But it was quite possible to subject foreign goods to a tax at the moment when they crossed the borders of the state; this was then a well-defined taxable matter; and although the collection of tariffs be very costly and often quite annoying, it could be complied with; whereas it is difficult to imagine the degree of tyranny that would have to be employed to stop the circulation of all manufactures, of every industry in the country till they have paid the tax. This is not all; it would be necessary also to look into households to make them pay taxes on every article of clothing, every textile that would be made for one's own use; not only because it is a portion of the expenditure and enjoyment of every individual, but also because, [by making exceptions to this rule, each would be induced to serve himself, to the prejudice of manufactures, trade, and the division of labour, which much increases its productive power.]

Fifth, all provisions destined for consumption and the subsistence of man must finally be taxed in the same manner, be it in the country or in the cities; whether they have been purchased or sold; whether the user has produced them on his own field, his own vineyard, his own garden. If such a tax were to be levied, not one citizen would, for even one hour in a day, be safe from the harassment of the tax officials.[5]

However, only in this manner could all the types of expenditure we have just reviewed be assessed, so that consumption taxes would be true proportional taxes on income. Every one of them that is omitted creates a very unfair inequality among consumers. In the actual condition of our civilization, all the cleverness of financiers could only invent [a fourfold division of duties on consumption,[6] the *gabelle*, custom, excise, and tolls; the gabelle comprises those commodities of which the government claims a monopoly, salt and tobacco, for example;] it has them produced for its own account, [it sells them alone, at a high price, by its agents or favourites,[7] and prosecutes by rigorous penalties all such as attempt to take a share in their manufacture or trade. Customs are destined to levy a proportionate duty on goods imported from foreign countries;] the excise strikes a very small number of national and industrial goods, from which it collects a tax at the moment of production; in France it only covers liquors, and is known under the name of *droits reunis*. Tolls, instituted at the gates of towns, collect a tax on the provisions of the country, as they come to the door of the town consumer.[8]

From this it can be seen that the expenditures of the wealthy, that cannot be listed under the two classes of provisions and goods, do not pay any consumption taxes; that, among provisions, all those consumed outside of towns, except salt and liquors, and even more those that are of own production, do not pay any tax whatever; that among goods, all those that are produced in the country, pay no tax;[9] and in accordance with the prohibitive system adopted today everywhere, they constitute by far the greatest number. Even among those subject to customs, the [goods destined for the consumption of the rich, presenting, in the same bulk, a much greater value than goods consumed by the poor,] have been subjected to much lighter duties, so that fraud might not conceal them from the tax, or, when one wanted to exclude them, they are not smuggled in. If the trouble is taken to enumerate the different parts of the income of the rich that have thus been shielded from taxes, it will be found that at most he pays on a tenth of his expenditures some consumption taxes; as these duties always increase more in their ratio to incomes, and in proportion as one descends to the poorer classes, and those most unfortunate of all, the factory workers, whose expenditures comprise almost entirely purchased provisions brought into town, not one part of their income escapes.[10]

Therefore the most unjust and inhumane proposition is the often repeated one to abolish all direct taxes, and to raise the total of all state revenues from consumption taxes; since the former would be nearly equivalent to the latter, it would dispense almost entirely with taxes on the rich, and levy taxes only on the poor. In many ways this would bring us back to the old feudal system in which the noble paid nothing; but there would be then in this invention an improvement for the aristocracy, since, to become rich, it would be sufficient, because of this arrangement, to be exempted from payment.

It seems that the proposal to raise consumption taxes in such a way as to provide for the entirety of pubic expenditure, to bring them, for example, in France from 222 millions to 800 millions, already presented enough difficulties, even when retaining all the various existing taxes on consumption. Nevertheless, one has seen, in an assembly distinguished by talent, men who in other respects have shown great political understanding, adopt the strategy that a single tax on consumption would suffice for everything, if such tax would be imposed on the most universal consumption of all, that of bread.

A frivolous calculation has led them into temptation. France counts thirty million inhabitants who are assumed to eat, on the average, three hundred pounds of bread annually, totalling nine billion pounds of bread; a tax of two sous per pound of bread would yield nine hundred millions; if one hundred million are deducted for the costs of collection, the required amount is obtained.

This calculation is false and inapplicable in all its parts. First, by rejecting its basic assumptions: every individual, man, woman or child, rich or poor, having some means of subsistence, or perishing in misery, would have to pay thus equally to the state for the right to exist, six hundred sous, or thirty francs anually. No matter that such payment would be collected sous by sous, or all at once, its very equality among persons so unequal, would not be any less than the most glaring of all injustices.

Already the salt tax, although it was not nearly as onerous, had been conspicuous for its unfairness, and for the misery to which it brought the poor. In the same way this so-called consumption tax had become a type of head tax, weighing on all subjects, without regard to the wealth of the taxpayer, or his means of payment. The poorest household consumes as much salt as the wealthiest; but it takes for the purchase of its greatest necessity a sum the rich in his abundance hardly notices.

But, whatever injustice the salt tax inflicted, it could be collected; the tax on bread would be impossible to collect. Has it been taken into account that five-sixths of the inhabitants of France do not buy their bread, but that they eat their own harvest, or that of their landlords? All the peasants are in this situation, all the landlords and all of their servants; and the latter two classes encompass at least one-half the inhabitants of small towns. Then, all the workers must be subtracted who are fed by their masters who are at the same time craftsmen and landlords, and this class is much more numerous than has been assumed. Hence, there remain the residents of some large cities, further all the most miserable among the proletarians, altogether perhaps five million people, who buy every day their bread at the baker's.

How would one propose to levy the head tax of thirty francs per head, on the twenty-five million remaining residents? A head tax which for a poor sharecropper family in the Auvergne or the Poitou, where the peasant rarely sees a guinea of five francs, amounts to the enormous sum of 180 to 240 francs; because a family comprises at least six to eight individuals, above all among the peasants who lose many children at a tender age; for that reason even more than half, perhaps two-thirds of the population is not of working age, and the remaining third comprises women as well as men. It is from these unfortunates that one would have to demand the money they do not possess at all; undoubtedly one would wait for them at the grinding of their corn, and without inquiring whether there exists any proportion between the tax demanded from them, and their income, without any means of exchanging any portion of that income against cash, without any means to live after having taken the smallest part from it, they would be told while their corn is held at the mill: "You will not eat if you do not pay!"

Two sous a day seems to be such a small matter to the political accountant[11] that it seems to him all but impossible that all those who buy their bread from the baker would not pay, without complaint, such a light tax; but these two sous are eight, ten, twelve for the father of the family; but among the five million Frenchmen who buy their bread from the baker, one-half are perhaps factory workers. The miserable wages of the textile workers in the Dauphiné, the cotton workers in the north, do not exceed eight sous a day; it is doubtful that they can live with such a penurious wage; if bread were raised in price by a tax of two sous per pound, it is certain that they would have to die.

It is therefore absurd to reduce all taxes to a single tax on the consumption of corn, it is impossible to assess proportionately incomes with consumption taxes which can be used only as supplements to direct taxes; they reach as best they can the incomes that have escaped the former, but they always weigh unequally on society, and in this inequality, the poor are always sacrificed to the wealthy. Consequently, these taxes can only be as equitable as other, unconnected, taxes assessed on other principles, that rest on the rich alone.

[It is a great inconvenience of taxes on consumption, that it never can be known at their establishment who is to pay them in the long run. The legislature always proposes to make them be reimbursed by the consumer; but sometimes they do not reach his distance;[12] at other times, they do not stop at him, and the consumer] finds on his part means to be [reimbursed for them by those for whom he labours. To make the consumer pay the whole tax, the nation must be in a state of increasing prosperity; for otherwise, as the consumer is not richer than before the tax, he cannot devote more money than formerly to his enjoyments, and must, therefore, in some shape, diminish his consumption. The producer, on his side, no longer selling the whole of his goods, must diminish his production, or consent to pay a portion of the tax. If a public calamity happens, a scarcity or even a state of embarrassment in trade, consumption still further diminishes; and the producer, compelled to dispose of his goods, pays the whole tax; till, no longer finding any profit in his labour, he abandons it entirely.[13]

On the other hand, when taxes on consumption have raised the price of every thing, industrious men, who form a numerous class among consumers, no longer find in their industry sufficient resources to support them. His wages no longer furnish the day-labourer with those limited enjoyments which are to be reckoned among the necessaries of life, since life, or the power of labouring, could not long be maintained in an individual deprived of every pleasure. He struggles, therefore, with all his strength, to get his wages increased; the manufacturer and merchant, in like manner, to get their profits increased. As the total sale diminishes, it is necessary for their subsistence that they obtain more for each separate article. Their joint efforts soon succeed in raising the price of all goods coming from their hands, but especially goods of prime necessity, because the sellers of these give the law to buyers, who cannot do without such goods. A rise in the price of those commodities reacts anew on wages and profits; the disorganisation becomes complete; national productions cost much higher than those of countries not oppressed by a similar system; they cannot support a competition in foreign markets; exportation ceases, demand is not renewed, and the nation sinks under a frightful distress.][14]

Mr. Ricardo devotes a chapter to taxes on agricultural products, and generally he is quite willing to approve of them, for the same reason which brings other economists to reject them. He is convinced that they will immediately raise wages in the same proportion, and consequently will not cause any distress to the poor. Mr. Ricardo never abandons the abstractions on which he has based his entire system, and it is difficult to bring them into conformity with the facts we have sought to lay before our readers. We have tried to show elsewhere[15] the error of his principles; we stop here for a moment to consider the very consequences of his argument.

"If the price of raw produce did not rise so as to compensate the cultivator for the tax, he would naturally quit a trade where his profits were reduced below the general level of profits; this would occasion a diminution of supply, until the unabated demand should have produced such a rise in the price of raw produce, as to make the cultivation of it equally profitable with the investment of capital in any other trade."[16]

What? will husbandmen turn themselves into lawyers or doctors, or even watchmakers or mechanics, because their wages are no longer enough to live on? Would husbandmen, who in almost every country make up four-fifths of the nation, and even in England almost one-half thereof, find a profession ready to receive them, if only a tenth of them, a number hardly noticeable out of the total, and which would be immediately compensated for by an increase in the work of the others, tried to change their career? Farmers, whose bodies are accustomed to the outdoors, whose hardened hands have been made incapable of any delicate work, whose health requires strong exertions, whose souls need the pleasures of the fields, are they going to shut themselves up in a cotton mill? What! finally, would farmers leave the fields because a tax on flour would raise bread from four to six sous the pound, and go and imprison themselves in towns till the wages of agricultural labor were increased?[17] Is it not evident that all workers, in the towns as well as the countryside, would have the same need to raise their wages, and that, if their proportion were not changed, would not leave their trades? Because, to bring about the result which Mr. Ricardo expects, it would be necessary that they cease to work rather than change their trade.

Let us beware of this dangerous equilibrium theory that reestablishes itself of its own accord! Let us beware of believing that it does not matter on which side of a scale one puts or takes away a weight, because the other will quickly adjust itself! Let us beware of the belief that an imposition of a tax on basic necessities will finally rest on the wealthy, even though the poor may advance the tax! It is true that a certain equilibrium will reestablish itself in the long run, but this will be by great suffering. It must be regarded as an established fact that capitals leave an industry only through the bankruptcy of owners, that men do not leave a trade except by the death of the worker; all those who change from this trade to another more easily must be regarded as exceptions rather than the rule. The slightest attention to what happens every day before our eyes in the factories will teach us that, whatever the decline of a branch of industry, one never sees a factory close without the ruin of the owner. One never sees a worker quit his trade till such time as he is, driven by the agonies of hunger, trying anything to escape death, as a shipwrecked man clings to a plank while he sees his ship sink.

If a tax on basic agricultural products is charged, however high it may be, some type of equilibrium will one day reestablish itself between the wages of the worker and his necessary expenditures; because, if it is never reestablished, the nation would perish entirely. But, before this equilibrium be established, the bankruptcies of all merchants, in those branches of industry they would have had to abandon, would have robbed the nation of more capital, in pure losses, than the tax would have brought in revenues to the treasury. Similarly, the mortality among the workers who cannot find a livelihood, would have robbed the nation of more lives than the most disastrous war. It is by such frightful means that political balance is restored; and if one comes down from abstractions that should never clothe a science which determines the fortunes and lives of men, this is how the adjustment is accomplished, and which Mr. Ricardo describes in these words: "From the effect of the principle of population on the increase of mankind, wages of the lowest kind never consume much above that rate which nature and habit demand for the support of the labourers. This class is never able to bear any considerable proportion of taxation."[18] His argument would have taken a different meaning, if Mr. Ricardo had added "because a frightful epidemic has then wiped out one part thereof, and sent the rest to languish in hospitals."[19]

[The establishment of taxes on consumption] and their division between tariffs, salt tax, excise, and tolls, [has covered Europe with four hosts of clerks, inspectors, agents, who, by incessantly struggling with each citizen about pecuniary interests, have contributed to render authority odious to the people, and accustomed men to elude the law, to violate truth, to disobey, and to deceive. The more heavy and multiplied these taxes are, the more rapidly will immorality make progress; the most unjust inequality has been established among contributors; liberty has been encroached on by vexatious inquisitions; the manufactures, the trade, even the existence of those who labour and who should create every kind of wealth, have been endangered. Those countries which have enjoyed the highest prosperity are exactly those in which this aggravation of indirect taxes threatens every kind of industry with the most complete ruin.

Governments have not been contented with taxing revenues and expenditure; they have gone forth to seek out all the acts of civil life which might afford them an opportunity of asking money. Some have established capitations, which, weighing equally on the poor and the rich, force the man to pay who has nothing, for whom society does nothing, equally with him who has too much; for whom society lays out enormous expenses;] they have encouraged the most dangerous games, lotteries, ruinous vices, so that they might draw some profit from them; they have sold exemptions, monopolies, privileges, titles, judicial offices. It is unnecessary for our purpose to explore this sad labyrinth; the principles we have enunciated suffice to judge the different taxes, those that have only arbitrary bases, as well as those that are regulated by everyone's income and expense.[20]

Translator's Notes to Chapter 6, Sixth Book

The maze of indirect taxes that were the lot of the long-suffering consumer in most Continental states is analyzed in this chapter. Economically, most states were divided by internal tariffs; rivers were used as convenient devices to collect fees from shippers; entries into cities served the same purpose, as well as a police control on the movement of citizens, and in particular, foreign travellers. As noted, one major reason for this state of affairs was the poor control central governments could exercise over their citizens, making the collection of income taxes a difficult and, as Sismondi points out, an expensive matter. To this must be added the arbitrariness of taxes imposed by a government desperate for revenue, and we can understand the heat shown in the argument. In this chapter, Sismondi again takes the opportunity to attack Ricardo's analysis. Comparing the two approaches to taxes on consumption, it is quite clear that Ricardo eliminated most of the difficulties in the analysis by resolutely focusing on the long run, describing the human consequences with a good deal of cant.

1. Sismondi, in taking this paragraph intact from the *Encyclopedia*, left out "But" at the beginning. Also, in his translation he used "appreciated" for "appreciés," which means 'to value,' but in this context should be translated as 'assessed.'
2. The sentence reads: "et il aperçoit a peine qu'il paye un impôt." It is likely that a misprint crept into the reprint, and the translation should read: "that he himself has paid any."
3. The reference here to a share of *expenditure* is somewhat obscure, but probably refers to rent and stands for the income, the assumption in the previous paragraph.
4. The *Encyclopedia* text reads: "the commodities produced in the interior of families by domestic industry . . ."
5. This passage recalls the well-known Prussian practice in Berlin under Frederick II during the Seven Years War (1756–1763), of sending so-called coffee-sniffers around who would spot households that illegally roasted contraband coffee. The preceding discussion illustrates vividly how much more households were self-sufficient, apparently producing a wide variety of goods for internal consumption and thereby escaping the taxing authority.
6. Sismondi omitted from the Encyclopedia "which are adopted in almost all countries." The word *gabelle* immediately following is italicized in the *Encyclopedia.*
7. The French text reads *"ou ses fermiers,"* 'tax farmers.'
8. Many large cities in Europe still have monuments to this form of taxation, either as actual gates, built of stone, or as names attached to toll houses, now mostly located in parks. Examples are the Toledo Gate in Madrid, the Hallesche Tor in Berlin, and the numerous *portes* that surround Paris.
9. The text is ambiguous here. It reads "qui sont manufacturées dans le pays," which can mean both countryside, that is, out of town, or country, that is, all of France.
10. This describes very accurately the regressive tax systems generally used in all European nations at the time. The French Revolution had done away with some of the inequities of the ancien régime, but it was the Third Estate, the middle class, that had profited from those reforms; the new Fourth Class, the *proletarians,* as Sismondi calls them, had neither the political nor economic power at the time to force further changes in the tax system.
11. The French term used involves a double meaning—*calculateur* means both 'accountant' and 'schemer'.
12. The French text reads: "mais quelquefois ils n'arrivent pas jusqu'à lui." Sismondi seems to have translated literally here, although he would have

expressed the thought better by "but sometimes they fail to reach that far." This instance raises the interesting question whether Sismondi wrote the *Encyclopedia* article in French, translated it, and kept his notes. It is the first instance in *New Principles* of a quote from the *Encyclopedia* that shows evidence of translation from French into English, and back. Since the quote clearly comes from the *Encyclopedia*, it was kept for this translation.

13. Sismondi sees taxation as a leakage from consumption that can be compensated only by rising income. However, as a disciple of Adam Smith, he does not draw the opposite conclusion that negative taxes, that is, government expenditure, can be used to counteract a decline in business conditions, mainly because he is against increasing government involvement in the private sector. It is evident that he understands very well the conditions that determine the incidence of a tax—his discussion is a literary textbook description of how consumption taxes are shared by the buyer and the seller.
14. Sismondi uses an elasticity concept; interestingly, he combines it with the assumption that sellers have some control over the market, and that monopoly power will lead to recession because it curtails consumption. His reference to the day laborer and his necessities should be compared to Marx, *Das Kapital*, Part III, Chapter 8, on the length of the working day, p.242.
15. Chapter 4, pp. 122–129.
16. Ricardo, *Principles,* Chapter 9, p. 137, Gonner edition.
17. Sismondi clearly overestimated the attractions of the countryside over those of the towns, a consequence of his own favorable opinions on country living. In his time, the movement of workers from the country to the cities was already well under way in England. It came later to the Continent, and from the viewpoint of Chêne it could probably be dismissed as irrational. He obviously does not consider the possibility that wages in the mills were indeed better than those in the countryside, especially at a time of diminished demand for agricultural goods.
18. *Principles,* chapter 9, p.140, Gonner edition.
19. Actually, Sismondi cut off the quote at a semicolon. Ricardo goes on to say: "and, consequently, if they had to pay 8s per quarter in addition for wheat and in some smaller proportion for other necessaries, they would not be able to subsist on the same wages as before, and to keep up the race of labourers. Wages would inevitably and necessarily rise; and in proportion as they rose, profits would fall." Sismondi is closer to economic reality in assuming, first, that wages do not inevitably and necessarily rise, as Ricardo assumes and, second, that Ricardo's abstract reasoning closes its eyes to the transitional difficulties that would occur. Sismondi makes the argument, repeated over and over, that changes engendered in the short run may completely invalidate the long-run results predicted by the analysis. As Keynes put it so succinctly: "In the long run we are all dead."
20. The paragraph seems to speak quite forcefully to the state of most countries today. It is evident that this was written at a time when military expenditure still took a very large part of all taxation, just as it does today. As productivity increased in most countries with progressing industrialization, and military expenditures declined absolutely and relatively during the century, tax loads on the individual declined, fueling in turn the huge capital expansion that became the hallmark of the middle and the end of the nineteenth century. After two world wars, the pendulum has swung to the other side, and the symptoms

Sismondi observed can be seen in almost every nation with a large military commitment. On the other hand, those nations that were forbidden at the end of the last war to engage in major armaments, for example, Japan and Germany, show economic growth and few of the abuses here castigated.

7

Of Loans

The numerous disadvantages connected with every type of tax, the impossibilty of finding among them one that is truly equitable, truly proportional, and will not become ruinous to the country when a great amount is needed, must increase in our eyes the importance of parsimony, and make us realize that this is one of the first virtues a nation can demand from its government. This virtue is not, in any way, as many others, a necessary consequence of a free constitution. It is true that it is found in republics, but it is as common in aristocracies as in democracies. Stinginess, which is often blamed on old age, is ennobled when in *senates*, or assemblies of elders, it has as its goal the preservation of the public wealth. The constitutional democracies to which Europe seems to be inclined today, appear, to the contrary, among all governments, the least frugal, because the obligation to provide for expenses has been separated from the desire to spend. The excutive power, alone charged with foreign relations, what is called the honor of the nation, its defense, finds it much easier and safer to accomplish everything with plenty of money. The multiplication of offices, honors, and pensions, facilitates the task of the government abroad; it makes its influence at home that much more quick; it guarantees supporters, and it justifies proportional increases in stipends, prerogatives, and the civil list, for ministers, princes, even the monarch himself. A taste for pomp, the belief that politics rests on magnificence, has to exist in constitutional monarchies as in absolute ones; but in the former the government is never stopped, as in the latter, by the impossibility of making expenses and revenues balance; it is not in any way its business to find the money. It suffices that it have shown, or made the representatives of the people believe, that the money is necessary; it thus burdens them with all that is most painful in its office; it is not any more responsible for the irritations the people may experience, and it awaits quietly that its expenses be met, much like a prodigal son who counts on the assets of his father's estate, without taking the trouble to look at them closely, and who believes that he has only one concern, that of justifying the accounts that will discharge him.[1]

Far from concealing from oneself the disadvantages of a chosen government, it is essential to fully recognize all their consequences, before they carry us too far. We have seen[2] [states, in the vigour lent them by freedom, in the full enjoyment of all their advantages, give way to all the dreams of ambition; they listen to all the suggestions of pride, of jealousy, or of vengeance; under the pretext of being on their guard against distant or imaginary dangers, they rush headlong, with light hearts, into ruinous wars, and persist in them with obstinacy; though the voice of humanity calls for peace in vain, the superiority of their nation does not yet appear sufficiently established, their enemy is not yet sufficiently humbled; the work which they thought accomplished has been overturned; it must be re-established at any price. Present resources, however, are exhausted; and recourse is had to borrowing: credit is still entire; the national capitals are drained away from commerce, and placed, one after another, at the disposal of a minister, who dissipates them, and replaces them by assignments on the future; and the passion which blinded] the nation and its parliament [for a few months, condemns their posterity to suffering for ages.

Perhaps no invention was ever more fatal than that of public loans; none is yet enveloped with more illusions. The passions excited by politics are so violent; the questions to be decided by negotiations or by arms so important; all sacrifices become so natural, when the prosperity, the existence, the honour of all are at stake, that governments and the people, before yielding, are to exhaust every resource to the very uttermost. They will send out the last man to battle, they will expend their last shilling, if they can possibly dispose of either; and they will do this not alone for the safety of the people, but for any war, any quarrel in which they happen to engage, because there is no one in which their offended pride may not be confounded with honour, in which they cannot honestly say what is true only in extreme cases, that a nation had better cease to exist than exist dishonoured.

If the possibility of making such preternatural exertions could be furnished to nations, and reserved at the same time for an extraordinary necessity, no doubt a great service would be done to human society, which is shaken to its foundation every time that one of its members is overthrown. But each means of defence becomes in its turn a means of attack. The invention of artillery, happy for society if it could have been employed only in the defence of towns, has served to overthrow them; the invention of standing armies has opposed discipline to discipline, and talent to talent; the invention of conscriptions has opposed all the youth of a nation to all the youth of another; the invention of *landsturms* and *levées en masse*, has made even women and old men descend to the field of battle to assist regular troops: the invention of loans has attacked and defended the present generation, with all the hope and all the labour of posterity. The strength of nations, though becoming still more formidable, has continued still in the same proportion. The state, in danger, has not found deliverance more easily; but humanity herself has been sacrificed, and, amid those gigantic combats, it is she that must perish.[3]

As, after those destructive expenses rendered possible by loans, there remains an apparent wealth, which has been named the public funds,[4] and which figures as an immense capital, the different portions of which constitute the fortunes of opulent individuals.] Also, it has been believed, or some have sought to convince us, [that this dissipation of national capital was not so great an evil, but rather a circulation, which caused wealth to spring up again under another shape; and that mysterious advantages existed for great states in this immaterial opulence, which was seen to pass from hand to hand on the market of the public stocks.

No very powerful logic was needed, to persuade ministers of the advantages arising from dissipation; stock jobbers, of the national profit attached to their commerce; state creditors, of the importance of their rank in society; capitalists, eager to lend, of the service they did to the public, by taking from it an interest superior to that of trade. Thus all appeared amply satisfied with regard to the unintelligible doctrine, by which it was pretended to demonstrate the advantage of public funds.[5]

In place of following this subtle reasoning, we shall endeavour to show that stocks[6] are nothing else but the imaginary capital, which represents that portion of the annual revenue set apart for paying the debt. An equivalent capital has been dissipated; it is which gives name to the loan; but it is not this which stocks represent, for this does not anywhere exist.[7] New wealth, however, must spring from labour and industry. A yearly portion of this wealth is assigned beforehand to those who have lent the wealth already destroyed; the loan will abstract this portion from its producers,[8] to bestow it on the state creditor, according to the proportion between capital and interest usual in the country; and an imaginary capital is conceived to exist, equivalent to what would yield the annual revenue which the creditors are to receive.]

If everyone could follow the history of those shares of the public revenue he receives, the capitalist, who believes that all his wealth is in the national debt,[9] would have to say, on seeing the field where land taxes originate, the shop where indirect taxes are collected, that must pay his interest:"*Here is my wealth! From here comes my rent that I believed I received from the treasury.*" This capitalist is in effect co-owner with the husbandman, the merchant, the craftsman, who are taxed to pay him his interest; the capital he believes to have in government bonds is a mortgage on their real estate, or their industry, and the income they will bring forth from their labor is but like that of a métairie that is cultivated at half-shares between them and the creditor.

[As, in lending to a merchant or a landed proprietor, we acquire a right to part of the revenue which arises from the merchant's trade, or from the proprietor's land, but diminish their revenue by the precise sum which increases our own; so in lending to government we acquire a right to that part of the merchant's or proprietor's revenue, which the government will seize by taxation to pay us. We are enriched only as contributors are impoverished.]

Some political writers, some ministerial orators have believed, or at least have put out that the national debt was a vast disposable capital, a monetary force, an essential portion of the circulating capital that sets industry in motion. That is not far from saying that the immense trade of England is the consequence, the rich product, of its vast debt; this is almost as if a merchant would try to satisfy his creditors by handing over to them his liabilities, instead of his assets. The capital that is held in public funds is employed at nothing as such; to its owner it is only a bearer claim to the work of others. If it is withdrawn to give life to trade, only some other's is put into its place, and nothing is repaid; what was in the public funds is left there, and what was in industry is left there; merely the names of the two owners change. The former rentier who has sold his bonds to use the proceeds in industry, does not devote to such productive use the capital of the rents, but the capital of whoever bought them, and which was perhaps employed in a bank or agriculture, which was at the least a circulating capital, since it could be transferred to him. It will change its particular destination, but not its general purpose to enliven trade. The old capitalist who has become a rentier, as long as he will remain a rentier, will do nothing with his capital in the public funds; because nothing can be done with what has no real existence.

It was believed that there was no need to deal with a question that contains a self-contradiction; because, how can a debt be mistaken for wealth? But the authority of some famous names obliges us to dwell further on a prejudice that language supports, that a confusion of ideas makes always difficult to analyze, and a multitude of vested interests works hard to make respectable.

With respect to the benefits of the public debt, it is impossible to create a greater illusion than the one that seems to have come from Alexander

Hamilton, first Secretary of the Treasury of the United States, honored statesman, still, and truly deserving of such esteem. In his reports addressed to the House of Representatives, he exhorts Americans to devote themselves to the establishment of new industries, and he vouchsafes that in such undertaking, they will not lack capital; and how strange! the resources he offers them for this new enterprise he wants them to undertake, are their debts, the seventy million dollars on which the treasury pays annual interest. "There is, he says, a type of capital actually existing in the United States, which lays to rest all unease about a lack of capital: the funded debt;" and he devotes some twenty pages to confuse a negative quantity with a positive quantity, the liabilities and assets of a nation.*

If a distinguished statesman falls into such a crass error, one owes it to him to at least look for the cause of his illusion. Hamilton has perceived that state creditors can usually sell their holdings at any moment they wish, using the proceeds in new enterprises. He has therefore concluded that the public debt was the disposable capital that would fertilize them. This is not so; the capital ready to purchase the public debt is the only one that can be used. But the capital of buyers who cannot buy, leaving their funds in the industry where it was before, this capital that can be transferred to sellers to be used anew in industry, this capital is not at all that of the debt, and is not in any way measured by it. The American nation owes seventy million dollars, and the price of its bonds in the market stays perhaps at four or five per hundred of loss. What does that prove? Only that, out of the owners of the seventy million of debt, those of two or three million were disposed to sell, and that there were also buyers for these two or three million. It is the latter two or three million which are alone available; but if they are employed in a new enterprise, if they are withdrawn from the exchange where they sustained total credit, the owners of the remaining sixty-seven million could very well not find any buyers, even though no doubt would be raised about the solvency of the nation. The claims on income remain always the same; but the consumable wealth, that could perhaps be employed for reproduction,[10] does not come forth anymore to exchange itself against this contingent wealth.

The problem of the public debt is made complicated by introducing foreigners, but is not changed thereby. At the time when Americans borrow seventy million dollars, foreigners will perhaps lend them the largest part. If, afterwards, Americans redeem their obligations circulating abroad by means of the capital they have formed from their savings, they will thus repay their national debt; if, later, they sell their obligations again

Report on the Subject of Manufacture, t. I, p. 201; *Works of Alexander Hamilton*, New York, 1810.

to foreigners, they will borrow anew. In this case, buying means paying; selling, borrowing; because, in purchasing, a national creditor is substituted for a foreigner; in selling, a foreign creditor is created in place of a national one.

It is true that government securities provide a convenient means of creating, in the name of the public, a debt it would be much more difficult to secure in the name of every individual. We do not deny this in any way; but, in return, this way of borrowing is much more costly; we shall clarify this comparison by an example.

An American owns a $200 annuity in U.S. government obligations; he also pays to the treasury $200 in real estate taxes on his property. Equivalence between these two sums can be stipulated, and it can be assumed that he pays his annuity to himself. His wealth is then limited to his real estate; his debt to the treasury, and his claim on the treasury cancel each other; if they would be abolished simultaneously, he would neither be richer, nor poorer, thereby. Nevertheless, he regards his $200 income from the securities like a capital of $4,000, and he does not even dream that the $200 he owes annually, can, on their part, be regarded as a negative sum of $4,000 he ought to deduct from his property. If he is pressed by a sudden need, he will sell his annuity of $200; and since it is negotiable on the world market, it will perhaps be bought by an Amsterdam merchant who does not know him, and is in no way concerned to know what his rights are, but who nevertheless will take over the mortgage he had on his own property; therein lies the unrivalled advantage of government securities—they are more easily converted than private debts. If the taxes and the debt had been cancelled at the same time, he would have lost an imaginary capital of $4,000 in government securities; he would have gained $4,000 on the value of his property, the imaginary capital for the $200 in taxes he pays; and, as regards the sudden need that made him sell his rent, he would have borrowed $4,000 on his own account, without being either richer or poorer than by the sale of his claim.

But a government never raises $200 without loss to pay $200. It needs an assessor, a collector, a treasurer, a controller, to take from the taxpayer a share of his property; it needs a cashier to pay him; the government does not perform these operations free of charge; it cannot do them without occasioning inconvenience, delay, and loss, proportionate to such double effort. The expenses of taxing and administration are not overestimated when it is assumed that the government collects with one hand $240 from the taxpayer to give him $200 with the other, as an annuitant; hence, if he estimates his share in the public debt at $4,000 at 5 percent, he ought to estimate at $4,800 the mortgage burden on his property in favor of the treasury, that pays for the same claim. Far from losing a $4,000 capital by the cancellation of his claim and the tax that pays for it, he would really gain in this off-set a capital of $800, represented by an annuity of $40.

Generally it can be stated in principle that a nation which has twenty million francs in revenues and owes nothing, is richer than a nation which owes ten million on an income of thirty million, because the expenses of administration increase with gross revenue and are a loss for everyone. This would be the same for an individual; but for either, a colossal and encumbered fortune often commands a false credit which a smaller, but entirely free one could not obtain.

Private claims, just like the public claims, are a part of individual wealth, and are nevertheless in no way a part of national wealth, since they do not increase the annual income of the nation, but change only its distribution. The nation owns all its material wealth, plus the claims of one part of its citizenry on the others, minus the same claims the latter owe to the former; and two equal quantities, positive and negative, being offset one by the other, nothing remains but material wealth. [If all public and private debts were abolished in a day, there would be a frightful overturning of property; one family would be ruined for the profit of another, but the nation would neither be richer or poorer;] its income would be exactly the same, [and the one party would have gained what the other had lost. This has not, however, in any case, been the result of public bankruptcies; because governments, whilst suppressing their debts, have maintained a taxation which belonged to their creditors; or rather they have broken faith to the latter,] and it is the property of the latter they will afterwards demand with the others.

However disastrous public borrowing be, it needs only that one of the modern nations that exerts much power be engaged in it, to drag all others along. Weapons are not suited to new warfare, and it is equally impossible for a nation to resist with its income the capital of others, as to limit itself to bayonets when the others use artillery. Not even the choice of borrowing in the least onerous manner is left; he who pushes the time of repayment back the farthest will be able, with the same interest, to raise the largest sums. Everyone in turn gives in to this forbidding competition; and the art of public finance, in perfecting itself, has only served to make ever heavier the burden that weighs down the people.

The first public loans, those that were raised at the time of Charles V and Francis I were time loans. The king mortgaged a determinate revenue to those who advanced a large amount; but, in a few years this income had to pay them interest and capital. The subsidy was insufficient and the interest high; but finally, a short time after the peace was concluded, the state had discharged its debts; it regained the enjoyment of all its rights, the people were relieved, and the generation whose passions had dragged it into war paid its expenses alone.[11]

Borrowing with life annuities was an improvement of finance, and a refinement in credit. The revenues of the state were not handed anymore to the tax farmers; the disposition and regularity of the public accounts were much easier to maintain, and a much longer time was given to repayment; it was accomplished by an imperceptible liquidation: every creditor discharged the state from its debt by his death; and although life annuity interest was much higher than the perpetual one, loan terms were nevertheless not unfavorable for the treasury, and its basic condition that the debt be extinguished with the life of the lender guaranteed an entirely just principle, namely that the total repayment of the debt rest alone on the generation that had profited therefrom.

Because afterwards, through a new advance in finance, life annuities were changed into perpetual ones, the present generation brings in some degree bankruptcy on its descendants; it borrows, dissipates all that has been lent to it, and it burdens the coming generations, to whom it leaves nothing, with the repayment.

Sophisms have been invented to make a conduct that does not radiate in any way good faith, appear more righteous. It has been asserted that the government must not encourage investments that cause the destruction of fortunes; that this amounted to bribing family fathers, and bringing them to prefer their own advantage to that of their children; that this was tantamount to the annihilation of national capital, and sacrificing the future to the present. Oftentimes this was not far from saying that it was for the love of later generations that we let them be burdened with a huge debt, instead of repaying it ourselves.

The accusation of destroying capital by a life annuity falls of its own if it is quite clear that a loan is not capital. The land burdened with a life annuity becomes free at the death of the creditor. All the capital value it had before, it still has; but a portion of that value represented the rent with which it was encumbered, and that portion returns to the owner. Similarly, the nation regains precisely in capital and interest what its creditors lose, and it finds itself not in the least impoverished by the extinction of the fictitious capital of its annuity debt.

It is truer to say that, through life annuities, the nation encourages egotistical tendencies, almost in the same way as by the institutions of canonries and prebends, and all sinecures and life pensions. Whoever enjoys such an income, if he is not married, will undoubtedly only think of himself; if he is married, the ties of nature are stronger than the attraction of a profit that can always be obtained, even if the state would not offer it;

and those who invest in a life annuity know well how to restore, by their parsimony, the capital the treasury will not give back to them.

When governments substituted perpetual loans for life annuities, they believed themselves to be absolutely released from the obligation to repay what they had borrowed, and they assumed to have satisfied their duty if they regularly saw to the payment of interest. However, new needs soon forced every year an increase in the funded debt; and the ministries who would have resigned themselves gracefully enough to the accusations of posterity, began to think of their own interest when they discovered that the burden they threw on the future finally made them lose their own credit. An enormous debt, which could only increase, without any probability of any decrease, was tailor-made to frighten the new lenders who were needed; it had to be proven to them that it was intended to discharge this debt; citizens had to be shown a time, however far removed it might be from the sacrifices that were asked of them, and amortization was invented.

This system, an ingenious scheme of interest compounded from an initially small fund, intended to discharge every debt, growing through its own savings, almost gave to the state the advantages it had found in the successive liquidation of the life annuities. That was a type of natural amortization which also operated without interruption. But the extinction of each life annuity brought an immediate relief to the treasury, whereas every saving and every repurchase made by the amortization fund in no way decreases taxes; the amortizing power is merely strengthened thereby.

It can happen that, in dealing with lenders, a larger capital is obtained than would have been possible with a life annuity, by way of appropriating the same revenue to pay the annuity and the amortization, even though both were to be liquidated in the same number of years; doubtlessly this would be a reason to prefer amortization to life annuity. But, whatever independence is claimed to be given to an amortization account, it is always a part of the state, it is always subject to the law; and experience has already proven that, in times of need, in crises, a loan from the amortization fund, an illegal use of its capital, is such an easy expedient, that no government would trust itself to have the necessary firmness to never touch it.

The government which borrows dissipates the capital it has so obtained, and at the same time makes posterity a perpetual debtor [in the clearest part of the profit arising from its work.[12] An overwhelming burden is cast upon it, to bow down one generation after another. Public calamities may occur, trade may take a new direction, rivals may supplant us, the reproduction which is sold beforehand] can never be recouped; no matter, we will not be any less burdened by a debt exceeding our capabilities, a debt mortgaging what does not yet exist, our future labor, [which we shall not perhaps be able to accomplish.

The necessity of paying this debt begets oppressive imposts of one kind or another; all become equally fatal when too much multiplied. They overwhelm industry, and destroy that reproduction which is already sold beforehand. The more that it has paid already, the less capable does the nation become of paying farther. One part of the revenue was to spring from agriculture—but taxation has ruined agriculture; another proceeded from manufactures, but taxation has closed up those establishments; another yet from trade, but taxation has banished trade. The suffering continues to increase, all the resources to diminish. The moment arrives at last, when a frightful bankruptcy becomes inevitable. And doubts are entertained whether it should not even be hastened, that the salvation of the state may yet be attempted. There remains no chance to shield the whole subjects of the state from ruin; but if the] idle [creditors are allowed to perish first, perhaps the] working [debtors will escape; if the debtors perish from penury, with them will be extinguished the last hope of the creditors, who must soon perish in their turn.][13]

Let us beware of seeking some pleasure in national hatreds, resentments that between people are always senseless, because governments and not people take offense at each other, to see our fellow men suffer.[14] If the time really approaches when a great nation, that has given to the world shining examples, and has enlightened us by its experience, is on the point of suffering the consequences of the license it has permitted to its government*[15] when the painful situation in which it finds itself already, amid many outward signs of opulence, indicates to us only the danger we will run following too closely its path; when all free people remind themselves that, not having, like absolute monarchs, the ability to abrogate all their undertakings, parsimony is to them almost as necessary as freedom; that wars without reason, gigantic projects, absurd extravagances, necessitate

*Despite the new losses England experiences today, and while the illusions to which its merchants had given themselves over are dispelled all at once, its financial situation is much better than it was seven years ago, since the first edition of this work, because an able and parsimonious ministry has undertaken in good faith to remedy old extravagances, because it has greatly decreased expenses, and abolished at the same time the most onerous taxes on industry. But, despite all its ability, the ministry could only carry out the reforms with the help of the increase of the national income that had been caused by the opening of South American trade. Today, when the unchecked activity of English industry has swamped all markets, and the trade that enriched them has become for them a cause of ruin, new dangers threaten the nation, and new difficulties beset the ministers. Perhaps they see already the road that will carry them over the reefs; but for those who are not privy to their secrets, nothing is visible but the dangers of the voyage.

unlimited loans; that such loans must be followed by ever increasing taxes, and that there exists no opulence, however shining, however well established it may appear, which will not finally succumb under the tax burden.[16]

Still, civilized society seems to be subject, just like inanimate nature, to those general laws that maintain the whole by the sacrifice of the individual, and which propel the whole toward a common end, by disasters that pitilessly strike the different parts. The end we have to this point kept in view as being properly that of political economy, has been the growth of wealth, the accumulation of capitals. We have shown that these capitals call man to work, and shower him with abundance; we always called their increase *prosperity*, and their destruction *calamity*. Still, it could be seen already that capitals may accumulate faster than the demand for the output they produce may increase; that in that case their yield decreases, and therefore they increase output while at the same time they decrease consumption; that every conversion of circulating capital to fixed capital entails the creation of a future output without corresponding consumption; and that, if a society continue some time in its progress of prosperity, without being able to expand into new regions, raising a new nation on new territory, it would soon have, by the very reason of its capital accumulation, a frightful disproportion between its production and its consumption.[17]

It seems that frightful calamities are called to the task of returning human societies to order, just as lightning, hail, and storms purify the air; as plague, war, and famine maintain equilibrium between coming generations and the food the earth can provide.

The ruinous extravagances of mad ministries, the ravenous luxuries of some governments; the military spending without limit, and the destruction of wealth war brings in its wake, are perhaps necessary to reestablish the threefold equilibrium between production, consumption, between capitals and demanded labor, between these and the income that must be born from them. Hence, the efforts that are made to divide ratably the loss among all members of society, are fruitless; the mutual security they have pledged one to the other only serves to spread the suffering more widely. Where the hand of destiny wields its frightful rod, men and wealth must perish together; man, too weak to understand these frightful laws, must bend his head and submit. It does not fall to him to channel the calamities that, striking blindly, are in the nature of things, like sickness, age, and death, and which, guided by cartels,[18] would become crying injustices. At a time of famine, a plague would be an advantage for the survivors, by ridding them of a portion of those whom a limited quantity of food must sustain; yet woe to him who, in this expectation, would bring it to his fellow-citizens! Similarly there exists perhaps a time in the progress of nations when the destruction of wealth is necessary so that creative activity can begin to stir anew. Yet woe to him who, to that end, burns the town of his fathers! Woe to him who stirs the waste of government and its mad prodigalities. It is not for us to seek the evil, even though it would be useful to us. Let us seek for nations wealth, health, liberty, happiness. If poverty, sickness, oppression, misery be necessary for them to reawaken their energies, regenerate their populations, revive their courage, and strengthen their character, the great laws of nature will bring to them enough misfortunes without us.[19]

End of Sixth Book.

Translator's Notes to Chapter 7, Sixth Book

This chapter should be compared with Adam Smith's *Wealth of Nations*, book 5, chapter 3. Sismondi generally follows closely Smith's argument on the public debt, but his personal experiences with governmental debt constantly enter the discussion. He displays considerable familiarity with the technicalities of govermental finances, probably developed during his official position with the government of Geneva during the Napoleonic era. Some of the financial instruments governments used to borrow, such as life annuities, have disappeared, but on the whole many of the caveats advanced in favor of a balanced budget are as true now as they were then. Sismondi's considerable capacity for irony is well displayed in his discussion of Alexander Hamilton and the various arguments advanced in his time in favor of expanding public borrowing.

1. This paragraph has a most modern ring, but why Sismondi believes that absolute governments must be more disciplined financially is not clear, and in fact a most surprising observation by a historian of France. The reign of Louis XIV was as absolute as anything ever experienced in Europe, and it spent prodigal sums for pursuing *la gloire*, so much so that his policies of war and spending were in part responsible for the subsequent collapse of the ancien Régime in the French Revolution.
2. The following text was taken from the *Encyclopedia,* which uses the plural "states"; in *New Principles* this was changed to "a nation" and uses the singular throughout. The reference is undoubtedly to France and the immediate past. However, the *Encyclopedia* text was used because it is quite evident that it was taken from there with only this slight alteration, and it was thought better to let the author speak in the original English version.
3. These paragraphs cannot be read in the 1980s without a recognition of how much things have remained the same, even though they have changed so much since 1826. One need only add, or substitute, atomic warheads on intercontinental missiles to bring the argument up to date.
4. *New Principles* italicizes "the public funds," but as the quote is from the *Encyclopedia*, that reading has been retained.
5. As elsewhere in the work, Sismondi's aversion to government borrowing is clearly related to his own experience. One wonders what he would have said

about the debt most nations now carry as a result of wars, armaments, and plain mismanagement.

6. Sismondi uses "les fonds public" in *New Principles*. Since "public funds" appears in the preceding paragraph, it must be assumed that he used the two terms interchangeably. "Stocks" as a term for corporate equity was not current in France at the time.
7. This takes, here as elsewhere, the strict position that only *real* capital can be called that; financial capitals are mere obligations that modify ownership. Sismondi is aware that the existence of such obligations influences the distribution of income, but he agrees with Aristotle that all financial instruments, including money, have no inherent value.
8. The French text reads "*cette portion sera oté par les impôts a ceux qui les produiront.*"
9. Sismondi uses the term "l'emprunt."
10. This means again the use of factors to replenish the flow of goods.
11. The passage "it [the state] regained the enjoyment of all its rights" refers to the fact that the king ceded to the tax farmers royal prerogatives to regain them only after the loans had been paid off.
12. Sismondi reworked this paragraph from the *Encyclopedia*, but the reference to profit is not clear. He may have meant that expenditures for defense and general infrastructure are a proper part of the debt.
13. This paragraph concludes the *Encyclopedia* chapter on taxation. It should be noted how it was changed for *New Principles* by the insertion of *idle* before creditors, and *working* before debtors, changing the original meaning subtly against the rentier class. While the entire chapter follows fairly closely Adam Smith's argument, the much less detached analysis is clearly influenced by his father's ruinous experience with the Necker debt. A large part of this chapter comes from the *Encyclopedia*, indicating that already there Sismondi took a determined stand against government borrowing. The additions serve only to further support the argument.
14. This sentence is very close to what has become the stock-in-trade argument of socialist governments against so-called capitalist regimes, namely, that the latter do not represent the people, but warmongering cliques, whereas the socialist governments as true representatives of the people are only concerned with peace. The argument arose first during the French Revolution and has proved quite durable, despite the obvious and well-attested fact that people, as a mass, are quite capable of atrocities against groups who are perceived as different or alien. In addition, it should be quite clear by now that a goverment is a government, regardless of its political position, and acts accordingly.
15. This note was added to the second edition. The government referred to in the note is the liberal Tory cabinet of Lord Liverpool, which, after 1822, included Robert Peel as home secretary, and William Huskisson as president of the Board of Trade. Both were liberals in the Smithian sense; Huskisson was a free trader.
16. This could, perhaps, have served as a warning to some present-day governments. However, the pessimistic assessment was written at the beginning of what must be considered the great period of expansion and prosperity that came to be known as the Victorian age. Obviously, Sismondi did not foresee the vast increases in national income that the Industrial Revolution made possible, and that formed the basis of the political preeminence of England in the nineteenth century, up to World War I.

17. A comparison should be made here to the extensive discussion of capital accumulation in *Das Kapital,* vol. 1, chapter 23, 2, and chapter 25. Clearly, Sismondi (and Marx after him) had a view of the domestic market that was, perhaps subconsciously, mercantilistic in its assumption of an essentially limited ability to absorb new production. On the other hand, the new capabilities of machines to increase output must have appeared as so far out of proportion to customary living standards, that overproduction and underconsumption would appear as natural consequences. Also, Sismondi and Marx rule out, either by implication (Sismondi) or openly (Marx), the possibility that increased output would be absorbed by increased leisure, or a different division of the product. Sismondi could not have foreseen this development in his time; Marx should have seen it, because at the time of the publication of *Das Kapital* the first signs of a reduction of the workday could be seen in England.
18. Sismondi uses *combinaisons*, which can mean monopolies, trusts, syndicates, and in general any business arrangement in restraint of trade.
19. These concluding sentences point to the next book on population. Sismondi seems to refer here to Malthus's population theory, which he will attack in the next book. As noted before, Sismondi was related by marriage to Charles Darwin and saw, after the publication of *New Principles,* the manuscript of *The Origin of Species*.

Seventh Book

Of Population

Introduction

The last book of *New Principles,* in its very first paragraph, sets the tone for what must be taken as Sismondi's culminating effort to develop a workable definition of political economy as the science of attaining the greatest happiness for the greatest number of individuals. The balance between a population and its means of subsistence is the focus of his analysis. He rejects Malthus's population theory and its assumption that the working population especially will always increase pari passu with an increase of food, providing the theoretical justification for the subsistence theory of wages. He substitutes the idea that an increase in population will be governed by income, such that a higher living standard will *reduce* population, because parents will not want to dissipate their possessions among many children, a thesis now accepted in development economics. It is obvious that Sismondi knew that people practiced birth control, and there is little doubt that, unlike Malthus, he approved of the practice. He also considers the relation between the increased use of machines, the displacement of workers, and the associated problem of *relative* overpopulation leading to his famous simile of the King of England turning a crank, which most likely served as a model for Marx's idea of the reserve army. This book corresponds to the seventh chapter of the *Encyclopedia*.

1

Of the Natural Progress of Population

[We have defined political economy, as being the investigation of the means, by which the greatest number of men in a given state may participate in the highest degree of physical happiness, so far as it depends on the government. Two elements, indeed, must always be received in connexion[1] by the legislature: the increase of happiness in intensity,[2] and the diffusion of it among all classes of subjects.] It seeks wealth, provided that it benefits the population; it seeks population, provided that it participates in the wealth; it seeks only so much of each that it may increase the total happiness of its subjects. [It is thus that political economy, on a great scale, becomes the theory of beneficence; and that every thing which does not in the long run concern the happiness of men belongs not to this science.

The human race, originating in a single family,[3] has multiplied, and spread itself by degrees over the globe; and much time was of course required, before it could be adjusted to the means of subsistence, which different parts of this globe are capable of supplying. We see this work of nature repeated in new countries, or in a colony established in a desert region. A state which passes from barbarism to a higher state of civilization, cannot all of a sudden become covered with as many inhabitants as it may comfortably support; as the earth has been wasted several times; as the greater part of its provinces has been by turns plunged into a state of desolation, to arise from it slowly afterwards, we have often had the opportunity of witnessing this spectacle of a growing population. We are accustomed to consider it as the mark of prosperity and good government; and hence our law and constitution all tend to favour this increase, though to increase the symptoms of prosperity is very different from increasing prosperity itself.

Nature has attended to the multiplication of races with a kind of profusion. Although that of man is among the slowest in its progress, it may increase, when all circumstances are favourable] with a swiftness of which no history in the world can provide us with examples, because no nation, at any time, has ever mustered all favorable circumstances together. [When every man has a great interest in bringing up a family, and has the means of doing so; when all marry, and all as young as nature permits; when they continue to have children till the approaches of old age,] a family would soon become a nation, and a nation would soon cover the earth. The human race would without doubt increase fourfold, perhaps tenfold in the course of a single generation.

But between this power to multiply, considered in the abstract, and reality, there is, and there must be a vast difference. Not all men have the wish to have a family; not all have the means to raise one; they do not all marry; among those who do marry, the majority greatly postpone the age at which they would begin to have children; a great number stop having children long before their old age;[4] in any human endeavor ability should not be confused with will. The propagation of the species depends on the will, and it finds therein its limits.

In discussing society, all causes that determine men to have, or not to have families, can be reduced to two: the pleasures of married life and fatherhood, or its congeniality, call men to marriage; its cares, fear of privation, or egotism, cause him to live alone. He weighs his tender affections against his own needs; thus a regard for his livelihood is for everyone, as it ought to be, to the advantage of society, the deciding motive for fatherhood or celibacy.

If one takes a wife, if one hopes to find happiness in her love and that of her children, it is also necessary to make these individuals happy who will be dependent on oneself. We have already said elsewhere that a customary symbol, wealth, stands for all the physical welfare a person may provide for another person; and everyone forms his own idea of such well-being, in accordance with the amount of happiness in the state in which he has lived. Without a doubt, many other circumstances contribute to happiness; often, virtue, health, disposition, are perhaps more important; but no other is for us so clearly esteemed; for no other it depends more on us to know whether we have it or not. That is to say, poverty, for every station in life, is a descent from that station a man would choose to live in, and a real evil, well understood, and to which no man will voluntarily expose those he loves, if he seeks his happiness in their affection; to which he will not expose himself, if he wants to secure his happiness through egotism. A husband undertakes to provide for the sustenance of his wife and children; this undertaking is enough to set limits to his discretion. Before marriage, before becoming a father, he always counts the income he can share with his family, what he can leave them after his death. If a spendthrift marries without thinking about the family he ought to have, his imprudence is offset by the timorous prudence of him who never marries, out of fear he may never have enough; and looking at the entire society, one can state that the bachelor will not become a husband and father unless he feels assured that his income will suffice for his new station. Hence, population will be solely governed by income; and, if it exceeds this measure, it is always because fathers have deceived themselves on what they believed were their incomes, or often, because society has deceived them.[5]

[Thus, every nation very soon arrives at the degree of population which it can attain[6] without changing its social institutions. It soon arrives at counting as many individuals as it can maintain with a revenue so limited, and so distributed.[7] If a great transient calamity, a war, a pestilence, a famine, have left a great void in the population, should those events be followed by a period of general security and comfort,] income will exceed population, be it for the well-to-do, enriched by the inheritances of their kin, be it for the poor whose labor will be paid so much more because there are so fewer arms. Thus, [this renewing power of human generation is speedily developed; and an observer is astonished to see how few years are required to obliterate all traces of a scourge, which seemed to have unpeopled the earth.]

In many countries, civil law gives command of all income of every family to the oldest brother; only he will marry, while the others will grow old as bachelors; however, the population will not in any way decrease; a single son from four, by marrying, will leave in turn four sons; their income not having changed at all, there exists no reason for the population to change; only a fourth of the individuals in it is quite sufficient to renew it, as long as the means of livelihood do not lack.

But if, for whatever reason, the citizens of a state have counted on nonexistent income, or on income which has ceased to exist, to raise their families; if the population increases while the means to sustain it do not, the nation is struck by the cruellest of calamities. [The earth soon consumes those whom it cannot feed;[8] the more numerous births are, the more will mortality display its ravages, to maintain constantly the same level; and this mortality, the effect of misery and suffering, is preceded by the lengthened punishment, not of those who perish only, but of those who have struggled with them for existence.]

The national income can be stationary, decrease, or increase; not only must one be prepared that the population follows naturally these same changes, and will do so if the social organization is not faulty; but it is essential to the happiness of such a population that it does follow them;

and if some fault in the social order prevents some classes of citizens from knowing their income, then it is at least necessary that the legislator be attentive to such variations, so that he would not augment a population that ought to be stationary, or declining, and that he not bring down on the state, as has often been seen, the calamity he must fear most. For the losses of battle, the ravages of the plague, are a lesser evil for humanity than the lost income of the poor. Those who languish and die of misery will envy those who have been gathered in by the sword.[9]

Translator's Notes to Chapter 1, Seventh Book

The chapter title reads: "Des progrès naturels de la population." The singular 'progress' was judged to be a more appropriate translation in the general context of the work. The chapter examines the basic Malthusian assumptions of the potential of population increases and opposes to it, in typical Sismondian fashion, the obstacles this potential faces, especially social ones. By implication, Sismondi rejects the foundation of the subsistence theory of wages, and with it one of the pillars of Ricardian analysis.

1. The French text reads: "Deux éléments, en effet, doivent toujours être considérés ensemble par la législateur . . ." Since this is Sismondi's *Encyclopedia* text, and the sense is the same, it has been retained even though the choice of words appears somewhat old-fashioned.
2. The phrase appears to echo Bentham, but it is more likely that Sismondi took this sentiment from Italian writers like Beccaria.
3. It should be noted that Sismondi, like Malthus, bases his argument on the veracity of the biblical account.
4. Sismondi probably alludes to his own experience. He married Jessie Allen when he was forty-six and she was forty-two, and they had no children. Sismondi had an unhappy love affair in his youth, but this postponement of marriage may also be attributed to his always precarious financial circumstances. He married when his economic position was secure, though not affluent. The reference to old age should be taken as relating to menopause and infertility.
5. Sismondi here leads up to his later argument that the wage system gives no clue to the worker of what his income will be, and therefore removes any restraints on procreation, leading to the Malthusian and Ricardion subsistence theory of wages. Sismondi evidently advocates here a distinctly bourgeois viewpoint whose validity depends on the assumption of property possession. Again, he will argue later that the worker ought to share in the ownership of his workplace in order to induce these bourgeois virtues. As noted above this argument is now a standard part of developmental economics; that is, rising incomes in underdeveloped countries are expected to eventually lead to smaller families. Marxism rejects Sismondi's argument for the worker's ownership in his workplace, calling it petit bourgeois, because Marx accepted the subsistence theory of wages under capitalism together with the labor theory of value. Events in capitalistic economies and Marxian socialism over the intervening 150 years seem to have justified Sismondi's view over that of Marx.
6. The French text reads: "qu'elle peut nourrir."
7. Unlike Malthus, and particularly Ricardo, Sismondi takes a much more complex

view of the limits of population. This sentence clearly assumes that populations change if the institutions change which determine the existing income distribution. One could speculate that this view was influenced by his experience with the consequences of the French Revolution, which indeed changed income distributions by changing the feudal matrix of most of Europe. The next few sentences point to the great plague of the mid-fourteenth century which killed close to 50 percent of Europe's population. Sismondi, as a historian of the Italian Middle Ages, must have been familiar with those events.

8. Compare this to Malthus's "At nature's mighty feast there is no vacant cover for him. She tells him to be gone, and will quickly execute her own orders, if he do not work upon the compassion of some of her guests" (*Second Essay on Population*). One wonders what both Malthus and Sismondi would have said if they could have seen the population levels in their own countries today.
9. It is quite evident that the population question makes the tacit assumption of small increases in production and output. The flowery language Sismondi employs at the end of the paragraph appears to deny what he has assumed at the beginning, namely that national income may also increase. However, he is right in assuming that it is possible that even with increasing incomes population may outrun the product, as is indeed the case in some underdeveloped countries today.

2

How Income Sets a Limit to Population

When we represent income as the natural, and necessary, limit to population, it should never be forgotten that we have given this name to that part of wealth which, produced[1] annually over and above the advances made by everyone, can also be consumed annually without the consumer being any poorer therefore; also, income is for some the product of the soil, after they have reimbursed themselves for the value of their land and all expenses of cultivation; for others, the product of capital, after reimbursement for circulating capital and compensation for the help of fixed capital; for again others, it is this compensation of the fixed capital; for others again, it is their labor power whenever it is demanded.

It is the very nature of income, distinguishing it from all other forms of wealth that, after being consumed in its entirety, it leaves no gap.[2] The landowner, if he contents himself with the rents of his land; the capitalist and the merchant, if they content themselves with their interest and profit; the craftsman, if he contents himself with his wages, will not ever impoverish the nation when each consumes his income in its entirety. But, if the landowner neglects his land,[3] destroys his forests, instead of cutting them over in an orderly manner, if he sells his cattle without replacement, if he prunes his vineyards to destruction, if he does not fertilize his fields, he eats as income a share of his capital. The merchant also impairs his capital, if his expenses exceed his profits, if he decreases his advances, or he increases his debts without increasing his gain. Both do not only hurt themselves, the nation becomes poorer with them, and because of them. The craftsman, much closer to poverty, even if he has the entire enjoyment of his income, can also, by injudicious use of that income, impoverish the nation if he spends it in such a way that he does not keep himself in proper health, and fit for work. In him, life is productive power; if he wears it out, if he loses his life,[4] he destroys national capital, needed to employ circulating capital, against which the very use of his life must be exchanged. If, on the other hand, the worker offers in exchange for this circulating capital, not one life, but many; if, instead of working alone, he labors himself with many children for the wages intended for him alone, the productive power connected to this life, that is, his income, will fall in value through competition, even though his work be the same. It is not sufficient that he wants to work; his labor must be demanded in order for his income to exist.

It can be seen that, in whatever way a disproportion between income and population arises, it is always capital, or the demand for labor, which diminishes,[5] and it is always the working class that suffers, and is deprived of its income. If the landlord consumes his property, if he ruins his soil, he decreases his income that must be exchanged against labor, or the fruits of labor; if he borrows, he obtains a circulating capital he consumes, and which will never again breathe life into labor; if he sells part of his estate, it will be to eat the capital he has gotten in exchange for a share of his rights in his property. Less capital will then be left to exchange for labor, and the worker will suffer the next year.[6] If, on the other hand, the landlord loses his income through some misfortune and then cuts back on his expenses, and lives with what is left to him, what hail and frost have spared, capital will not diminish, but will only circulate more slowly, because the consumption of the rich will not hasten to replace it; demand for labor will decrease and the worker will suffer in the same year.[7]

Similarly, if the merchant, or the capitalist, eat their capital, since this is the capital which must pay for all offered labor, those who offer such labor will suffer the next year. If, on the other hand, having suffered losses, they do not eat an income equal to that of the last year, then as consumers they slow down circulation and demand for labor, and those who offer labor will suffer the same year.[8]

If the income of landlords and capitalists is exactly consumed during the year, and if the capital is in no way diminished, such that its value and velocity of circulation have remained the same, but if, at the same time, workers who offer labor have increased in number, the workers will again suffer, because they give the whole of their work for the same capital,[9] which was destined to pay only for a smaller quantity.

This discussion shows that the poor, as well as the rich, have an income to which, more than any other class of society, they ought to proportion their numbers, but whose value does not depend at all on them, and that each of the higher classes of society may alter or destroy it, without their knowledge. The great fault of the existing social organization is that the poor may never know on what demand for labor he can count, that his labor power will never be a fixed and certain income for him.[10]

The progress of wealth, by concentrating workers in large factories, and in subordinating their industry to the direction of powerful capitalists, has in this respect been singularly unfavorable to the poor. It has taken from him every means to estimate the market demand for which he works, and has absolutely alienated him from the consumer who will have need for his output. As long as artisans, divided among small shops, have counted on selling the results of their work in the next town, they knew their customers, and they learned almost instantly when their customers' incomes declined and, consequently, the demand for their labor decreased also. In hard times, the worker who worked but a half week suffered hardship; he then had care not to marry, or increase his family. But since large capitals brought together in large factories, not craftsmen, but factory hands, they could no longer know the consumers who may live perhaps hundreds of miles distant, and who knew nothing of their distress, or the decline in demand, till the moment when, suddenly, their master dismisses them, perhaps as they are just about to marry, or to increase their family.[11]

The village cobbler, who is at the same time a small merchant, manufacturer, and craftsman, will not make a pair of shoes which are not demanded of him; and, if he sees his customers can employ only one shoemaker, he will not propose that three or four of his sons follow his trade; he will see in advance that there is no place for them in this world; but if a shoe factory is built in the big city; and if it, in the course of several years, calls for six pairs of shoes per week from twenty journeymen, they will believe that they have a position, doubtless inferior to that of a master of a shop, but at least certain, returning for their work a settled income; they will marry, relying on this assurance. If then the owner of the business has badly planned, gone bankrupt, if he lays his labor off, they and their families will perish as victims of an error not of their making.[12]

The owner, or farmer,[13] of a small estate, however limited his knowledge may be, knows quite well what quantities of corn, wine, and vegetables he can sell in the market; and if there is no population around him, if he is far from canals and main roads, he will not increase his land clearings, so that later he would not know what to do with his produce, unless his family increases. If, on the other hand, he has only a limited amount of land, not enough to give employment to all his children, he will not seek to have many children, and to marry them all off. But if a large farmer, or a great landlord, undertake expensive cultivation that demands much labor; if, during several of the following years, he employs a score of workers in his hop plantations, weeding his fields, and in his vineyards, and then asks for more from them; these workers, undoubtedly less happy than the small farmer, will nevertheless believe that they have a secure income from their work; this income will appear to them to be available to them and their children in proportion to their ability to work; they will marry relying on that assurance. If then the owner has made a mistake in his plans, if he finds it more advantageous to cancel all his advances and content himself with grazing, and those products the earth will give him with hardly any work, these workers, with their families, will perish as victims of a mistake they have not made.

Thus, the more property is taken from the poor, the more he will be in danger of miscalculating his income, and contributing to a population increase which will not in any way match the demand for labor, and will not find any subsistence. This observation is sufficiently old to have become part of daily speech, having been transmitted from Latin to the modern languages. The Romans called proletarians those who had no property, because they, more than any others, were called upon to have many children. *Ad prolem generendam.*[14]

It seems perhaps astonishing that, income acting as a limit to population, a lesser income would be just what would encourage a population without limits. But it must not be forgotten that poverty and wealth are relative to every class of individuals. Everyone's needs are determined by custom and the obligations society imposes on his station. To fall from this station, and not be able to discharge its obligations, is what every man calls suffering from poverty. A man who marries, prior to providing for the well-being of the many with what was heretofore set apart for a single person, will always do well to cut down on his expenses; but he will lose nothing of his status, because society expects such a change, and does not demand the same obligations from him. Yet,[15] from the moment his income would not be sufficient to support him and his wife and children in the manner to which he is accustomed, he would experience all the pangs of poverty, even though a man born to the station to which he would have come down, will look upon the same situation as one of ease. Indeed, we never see an estate owner turn his sons into farmers; and they their sons into farmhands; we never see the wholesaler propose that his sons become retail shopkeepers, and they their sons to be craftsmen, and the craftsmen doom their sons to be day laborers. Every time a young gentleman has only a choice between living as a bachelor, or taking up a profession truly inferior to that of his father, we can take it for granted that he will forego marriage. Despite the frequency of revolutions that unsettle national prosperity, and every day impoverish a rich family in its station of life,[16] nothing is so rare as to find families that have voluntarily descended from one station of life to another; the population of the upper classes of society would on the contrary tend constantly to die out, if it were not replenished from the lower classes.

But when it has been admitted that there exists a class that customarily possesses nothing, whose idea of wealth is simple existence, whose idea of poverty is to die of hunger; when it be allowed that its subsistence is so neatly measured that nothing can be taken therefrom, then those who live in such conditions will conceive for the objects of their affection only the desires they have for themselves. If they have lived from day to day, they will be content provided that their children live from day to day; if they have never tried to know the market which requires the use of their labor, they will never gauge it for their children. The wretched factory worker who earns a mere eight sous a day, and who often suffers from hunger, will not forego marriage; he has been habituated to know no future further removed than next Saturday, when his weekly wages are paid; thus his moral character, and feelings for his fellow man, have been deadened; much too often he has experienced present sorrow to be afraid of the future sorrow his wife and children might experience; if his wife also earns eight sous, if his children, as long as they are of tender age, are entitled to receive help from the hospital, from public charity, or, in England, from his parish through the poor rates; if, upon attaining the age of six or seven years, they begin already to earn something, his children, far from diminishing his income, will seem to add to it; as his family will become more numerous, the more it will be a charge on society; and the nation will groan under the burden of a population disproportionate to the means of sustaining it.

Translator's Notes to Chapter 2, Seventh Book

This entirely new chapter, without any material from the *Encyclopedia*, is Sismondi's first detailed discussion of the causes of the so-called overpopulation that was the subject of Malthus's *Essay*. Sismondi begins to lay the groundwork for his idea that workers should participate in the ownership of their workplaces, and that their wages ought to cover not only their daily subsistence, but also illness and old age. (See note 4.) Sismondi had the firm conviction that property holding, even on a small scale, is the best remedy to what is now called *alienation*, a position that earned him the contemptuous epithet petit bourgeois from Marx; properly so, because Sismondi, in taking this position, drew on the experiences of his Genevese past, which were in all respects strongly bourgeois.

1. Sismondi uses here as usual *reproduced*. If it is kept in mind that he uses the term in the special sense in which it was used by the physiocrats, the term *produced* is more appropriate to a modern reading.
2. This clearly means that the productive endowment of the nation remains unimpaired after consumption. The reference here is again to reproduction, meaning that the total productive process recreates all that has been used in production first, and then proceeds to produce a surplus, which is consumed under the heading of "income." The appropriate contemporary categories would be saving, gross domestic investment, and consumption, where ex-ante saving would be equal to ex-ante investment.

3. Sismondi inserted the next three sentences in the second edition, to "do not only hurt themselves." The insertion shows that he was very aware of the consequences of depleted capital on production, a point he made before and will apply again to the skills of the worker.
4. This argument will be used later in the book to justify the demand that the wage of the worker must not only provide for daily subsistence but must cover the entire life span, including sickness and old age. The view of the worker as living capital would appear to be derived from experience with Swiss skilled craftsmen. The English experience of an unskilled labor force coming into the cities from the farms would tend to predispose writers like Ricardo to the prevailing classical view of the labor force as an undifferentiated assemblage of individuals with few skills.
5. Sismondi, the classical economists, and Marx are all in agreement that it is capital that, in an industrial society, determines the demand for labor. Both Sismondi and Marx derive their cycle theories from fluctuations in capital utilization, which are coupled to underconsumption. Ricardo, of course, eventually considered the question in the famous chapter 31 of the *Principles,* "On Machinery."
6. This statement follows from the spiral model of book 2, chapter 6, which stipulates that the income of this year buys the production of next year.
7. In Keynesian terms, this sentence means that losses, leading to decreased investment, and not compensated by increased consumption, must lead to a lower level of production and unemployment.
8. Sismondi sees consumption as a variable which influences production, implicitly rejecting Say's Law. The subsistence theory of wages must be taken as a subvariant of Say's Law because it postulates that labor will always consume a particular minimum, subject to change only by population movement. The distinction made as to the period in which labor will suffer from a diminution of capital is again related to the time model of the business cycle.
9. This clearly assumes the existence of a wages fund as a part of circulating capital.
10. The observation has a contemporary ring. Union demands for job security in contract negotiations in the 1980s are a reflection of a work environment that is changing as fast, or faster, than the one Sismondi observed.
11. This paragraph was rewritten entirely from the first edition. There it reads: "Cette incertitude sur la demande annuelle du travail est à peu pres nulle lorsque l'ouvrier est associé à la propriété; elle est aussi grande que possible lorsqu'il lui est absolument étranger. L'estimation du capital employé chaque année à la reproduction passe les calculs, non pas d'un pauvre artisan seulement, mais du premier homme d'Etat, dans le pays de monde le plus eclairé; mais l'estimation des besoins du marché pour lequel chacun travaille est heureusement à la portée de chaque chef d'atelier. Si l'atelier est petit, lorsque la demande de travail diminue, le chef travaillera moins et s'imposera des privations; si l'atelier est grand, il en imposera seulement à ses subordonnes, qu'il congédiera. Dans le premier cas, il n'y a pas lieu de craindre qu'il augmente sa famille comme son revenue diminue; dans le second, ceux qu'il avait engagés, qui peut-être s'étaient mariés, comptant sur ses calculs, perdent tout leur revenue quand il les congédie, au moment peut-être où leur famille augmente."
12. Sismondi always describes the consequences of market failure in the darkest

terms, but in the absence of social safety nets the fate of the unemployed was dire indeed. Marx, in denouncing capitalism, made the most out of the descriptions of poverty he had culled from parliamentary investigations. Sismondi's view was probably based on actual observation, as he indicated in the foreword to this work.

13. This means an entrepreneur who leases a farm from the owner.
14. This is the first use of the term in this sense. It is likely that Marx took it from here and generalized it for his exploitation theory.
15. This was added in the second edition.
16. Again, an echo of Sismondi's youthful experience with the Revolution in Geneva.

3

It Is Not the Amount of Subsistence the Earth Can Produce That Acts as a Limit to Population

An English philosopher, Mr. Malthus, who combines strength and breadth of knowledge with a conscientious study of facts, and who is moved in his inquiries by a strong sense of compassion, has first awakened public attention to the calamities to which a superabundant population, struggling with extreme misery, was exposed. He has surveyed all nations, barbarous and civilized, ancient and modern, and has shown that everywhere suffering and death are struggling with the generative principle, decimating society whenever population had expanded too quickly. Mr. Malthus published his work on population in 1798, directing the attention of statesmen to dangers which before him Plato and Aristotle, Montesquieu, Franklin, Sir James Steuart, Arthur Young, and Townsend had pointed to in vain. He showed that civil and religious institutions of many countries tended to increase already unbearable suffering, and he thus gave an entirely new direction to an important branch of political economy. Five successive editions of his work, expanded, modified, and corrected, have spread his influence, and developed his system as much as possible. But even in its most perfected state, this system does not appear to us to be correct. Mr. Malthus has seized onto a proposition that seemed to him evident, but which is merely commonplace; he has made it the foundation of his argument without analyzing it, and as a consequence has fallen into errors which seem to us dangerous, and which, we believe, for all the respect we bear him, call for a refutation.[1]

[Mr. Malthus established as a principle that the population of every country is limited by the quantity of subsistence which that country can furnish. This proposition is true only when applied to the whole terrestrial globe, or to a country which has no possibility of trade; in all other cases, foreign trade modifies it; and, farther, which is more important, this proposition is but abstractly true, true in a manner inapplicable to political economy. Population has never reached the limit of subsistence, and probably it never will.] All those who would be in need of subsistence have neither the means, nor the right, to draw it from the soil; those, on the other hand, to whom the law gives a monopoly over land, have no interest whatever to call forth all the sustenance it could produce. In all countries landlords have opposed, and can be expected to oppose, a system which would solely tend to multiply provisions without increasing their income. [Long before the population can be arrested by the inability of the country to produce more food, it is arrested by the inability of the population to purchase that food, or to labour in producing it.

The whole population of a state,[2] says Mr. Malthus, may be doubled every twenty-five years; it would thus follow a geometrical progression; but the labour employed to meliorate a soil, already in culture, can add to its produce nothing but quantities continually decreasing. Admitting that, during the first twenty-five years, the produce of the land has been doubled, during the second we shall scarcely succeed in compelling it to produce a half more, then a third more, then a fourth. Thus the progress of subsistence will not follow the geometrical, but the arithmetical progression; and in the course of two centuries, whilst the population increases, as the numbers 1, 2, 4, 8, 16, 32, 64, 128, subsistence will increase not faster than the numbers 1, 2, 3, 4, 5, 6, 7, 8.

This reasoning, which serves as a basis to the system of Mr. Malthus, and to which he incessantly appeals, through the whole course of his book, is completely sophistical. It opposes the possible increase of the human population, considered abstractly, and without regarding circumstances, to the positive increase of animals and vegetables in a confined place, under circumstances more and more unfavorable. They ought not thus to be compared.]

Speaking theoretically, the propagation of plants follows a geometrical progression infinitely faster than that of animals, and those in turn multiply infinitely faster than men; a wheat grain produces 20 of its kind the first year, which in turn produces 400 the second year, 8,000 the third, 160,000 the fourth. But in order that such multiplication actually occur, it is necessary that nourishment, cultivation, and land be provided; all this applies also to man.[3]

The propagation of animals which live from these plants is quite slower; sheep double in four years, quadruple in eight; and, doubling every four years, they will produce the numbers 8, 16, 32, and in the twenty-fourth year or, according to Mr. Malthus, when the human generation would not in fact be doubled, that of the sheep would already be as sixty-four to one.

But this power of propagation is potential in plants, animals, and man. This real and active power is limited for all three by the will of man alone; and in our social organization, not by the will of any one man, but by that of the owner of the land. As long as there remains uncultivated land, he is the master of letting the multiplicative power of plants work, or contain it; as long as the former are not consumed in their entirety by the animals, he is master to let the multiplicative force of the latter work, or restrain it; hence he will hold back one, or the other, if the people who demand from him the fruits of the soil do not offer him in exchange an income.

If the history of mankind is studied, it can always be found, at all times, in all places, that the will of man, or what is the same, the laws to which he submits, and which are an expression of that will, have alone arrested the growth of subsistence, and with it that of human procreation. Frequently, wretched workers have been seen not to have found wages for their labor, or insufficient wages; they were seen to languish, bereft of bread, and perish; but in no country has the human species ever been seen reduced to the starvation rations of a population in a besieged city, or the crew of a ship in distress. Nor has humanity ever been seen, not because of bad harvests, but because of the impossibility of producing more, to have less subsistence than was needed to feed the living amply, even at the very moment when that population decreased rapidly through misery, or through the lack of an adequate wage offered to the working classes. Humanity has never been seen to be halted by the impossibility of making the earth produce new fruit in perfect proportion to its needs; nor has it ever been observed to come to the point where it could not make the fruits of the earth multiply in that very geometric progression that is for them, as for humanity, a potential power man never uses.[4]

A famine[5] caused by inclement weather is not the hindrance to population as Mr. Malthus would have it. He assumes an inability to produce, and not the loss of crops that were going to be produced. The destruction of crops by rains or drought does not in any way mean that next year it would be impossible to grow corn in a proportion much greater than that of human births.

However,[6] subsistence, or the means to purchase subsistence, is lacking to the poor classes, and halts the quick multiplication Mr. Malthus regards as a law of human nature; but there is no lack of food to the rich class, there is no lack for the noble, whose name and prerogatives command attention amid his fellow citizens, such that one can always be sure of the progress of procreation in that particular body of the nation.

The nobility has everywhere possession of adequate subsistence; it ought to multiply then, till its descendants are reduced to extreme penury. Yet, this is precisely the opposite of what happens; in all countries of the world the old families can be seen to die out after the passage of a certain number of generations, and the nobility is ever replenished by recruits from commoners. Every head of family avoids an increase of his race he would regard as a degradation of his renowned name. If some houses divide themselves into several branches, the number of those who disappear is again much greater, and the descendants of those who lived at the time of Henry IV are not as numerous as were their ancestors. This well-known fact should calm those who are today agitated over the impoverishment of a nobility whose perpetual entails would not protect their fortunes. Tracing the origins of the Montmorencies to at least the time of Hugh Capet, one would not doubt that from that time on all those who had the right to carry that name have carefully guarded it. The Montmorencies have never lacked for bread; their procreation, according to Mr. Malthus's system, should never have been halted by a lack of food; hence, their numbers should have doubled every twenty-five years. By this calculation, and assuming that the first Montmorency had lived in the year 1000, in the year 1600 his descendants should have amounted to 16,777,216. France, at that time, did not have that many inhabitants. Their increase continuing in the same manner, the entire universe would contain today only Montmorencies; because their number would have increased to 2,147,475,648 in 1800. This calculation seems to be facetious; it nevertheless shows with clarity, on the one hand the possible increases of a single family, if only the potential inherent powers of the human species are taken into account; on the other hand, the obstacles the human will always opposes to such increases; a hindrance quite independent from the amount of subsistence; because it halts before others the highest ranks of society, or those who are most sheltered from misery.

[In a state absolutely savage, men live on the produce of hunting and fishing. The fish and the game are multiplied like man, in a geometrical progression;] as with man, this progression is halted as soon as their numbers have reached a certain level. The hunter who wars on them, has almost never a need for social laws; it is through his own will that he avoids, in this condition, the increase of a family which would be burden on him.[7] The income of hunters is so uncertain that they are often exposed to famine, but this is not at all because of an unlimited increase in their population; it is on the contrary quite stationary till such time as savages come into contact with a more civilized people, when they can be seen to diminish rapidly in number.[8]

[The progress of civilization substitutes the pastoral life for a life of hunting; and the natural produce of the ground, better managed, is sufficient for a much more numerous population of men and of animals. The deserts, which scarcely support five hundred Cherokee hunters, would be sufficient for ten thousand Tartar shepherds, with all their flocks; the multiplication of the latter is always much more rapid than that of men; whilst the production of a man requires twenty-five years,[9] that of an ox requires but five, of a sheep but two, of a hog but one. The number of oxen may be doubled in six years, that of sheep in three, that of hogs may be rendered ten times as great in two years. Whenever a shepherd gains possession of a country formerly abandoned to hunting, the multiplication of his flocks will greatly precede that of his family.]

A Tartar tribe, soon after coming into being, multiplies indeed rapidly; but the flocks of the Tartars have never been seen to consume all the grasses of the Tartary steppes; an isolated family in these wildernesses would wither away in its solitude, and would be crushed from the moment it came into contact with other people. It would therefore wish to become sufficiently numerous to find support in itself, and it soon so becomes; achieving the most favorable size, it stops of itself. The pride of descent which is found again and again in all pastoral people, in Araby, in Tartary, Afghanistan, and in the Scottish Highlands, is opposed to the division of inheritances and families.[10] The youngest sons would find new pastures in going away from the patriarch chief of their clan; they prefer to remain together and not to marry. Prejudices and habits make marriages late and of low fertility. War, which all pastoral people have always waged with passion, thins their ranks even more; and though the pastoral life has many charms, as among the Afghans, where one half are husbandmen, and the othes are herders, it happens often that the husbandmen become herders, while there is no example that herders become husbandmen; the clans who drive their flocks are never seen to exhaust their pastures.

However, there is a progression in civilization that leads the herders to an agricultural life, or perhaps rather one that makes an agricultural tribe prosper in a country where the herders have left. From that moment, the people, [instead of trusting to the natural productions of the vegetable kingdom, they produce and multiply them by their labours. It is calculated that thirty families may live on the corn] and the cattle [produced by a piece of ground, which would have supported only a single family by its produce in cattle. At the time, therefore, when a nation passes from the pastoral to the agricultural state, it in some sense acquires a country thirty times as large as the one it formerly occupied. If the whole of this country is not cultivated, if even in the most civilized kingdoms, there remains a vast extent of fertile land still employed in unprofitable pasturage,] then it is ever the will of man and his laws which are opposed to drawing from the soil all the subsistence it can give.

[The multiplication of vegetables follows a geometrical progression much more rapid still than the multiplication of cattle. In common tillage, corn increases five-fold in the course of a year; potatoes ten-fold in the same space of time. The latter vegetable, to produce a given quantity of food, scarcely requires the tenth part of ground which corn would occupy. Yet even in the most populous countries, men are very far from having planted all their corn fields with potatoes; from having sown all their pasturages with corn; from having converted into pasturage all their woods, all their deserts abandoned to hunting. Those things are a fund of reserve remaining to every nation; and, by means of them,] if its mind be changed, it could suddenly, from one year to the next, multiply prodigiously its subsistence; it could multiply it in a geometric progression, such that it would surpass by a great deal all possible progress of the human ranks.

If its mind be changed, we have said, because the will of agricultural people has handed over to the landlords the right to raise or not, according to their interests, the sustenance the earth gives; and the landlords, in all countries, have never allowed that this sustenance be drawn from their land, if those who demand it cannot purchase it with their income. It is in vain that there exist twenty thousand individuals in Rome who suffer from hunger, and who ask for work, and four hundred thousand acres at the gates of Rome that are not cultivated, and which that work could cover with harvests;[11] the day laborer who, by his work, would merely grow his subsistence, would give nothing to the owner. Even if he would give him something, he would not give him any more than what the owner obtains from his land without work; and so, no work being done, no subsistence is created, no population can increase, because the national will, expressed in its laws on property, has set itself against such an increase.[12]

Translator's Notes to Chapter 3, Seventh Book

Chapter 3 is a refutation of Malthus's population theory. Part of the chapter was already contained in the *Encyclopedia*, but was greatly amplified for the first edition, and then rewritten again for the second edition. In trying to refute Malthus, Sismondi relied mainly on the argument that social conditions limit population, particularly the inability of the poor to buy subsistence because of unequal income distribution. The causative factor, unequal income, is seen as an adjustable *social* variable. To Malthus it was the result of an economic law that always operated in the same manner, hence not adjustable by noneconomic action. In addition, for Malthus adjustment by political means, as, for example, in the English Poor Laws, ran counter to sound economic practice, and could therefore only aggravate the gap between rich and poor. Sismondi and Malthus differ on the ability of the social system to change. The former sees no natural law determine social arrangments, while the latter sees social organization as a consequence of innate human propensities, hence not accessible to deliberate social adjustment.

1. The first paragraph was entirely rewritten from the first edition, where Sismondi had modified the *Encyclopedia* version (p. 116, second paragraph). The rewrite reflects reaction to the various editions of Malthus's *Essay,* which had been published since the *Encyclopedia* article appeared. It should be noted that Sismondi takes pains to point out that Malthus reiterates what many others had said before him. The name of the mercantilist Sir James Steuart is spelled "Steward" by Sismondi.
2. The French text reads: "La population humaine. . . ."
3. Sismondi had apparently misread Malthus. It is precisely the point of Malthus's work that these three items are not available in sufficient quantities.
4. A distinction is made here between famines brought about by bad harvests, and a general incapacity to produce enough food for all. If Sismondi's position is compared to that of Malthus, for example, in the first *Essay,* they will be found to be in close agreement, except that Malthus postulates the subsistence of the poor, or lack thereof, as a general law, while Sismondi sees it as a consequence of social organization. With respect to the bounty of nature, Sismondi is an optimist, Malthus a pessimist; with respect to social organization Sismondi is a historical relativist, and Malthus takes a natural-law position. However, Sismondi admits at the very beginning of the chapter that Malthus's proposition is true for the earth as a whole.
5. This paragraph was inserted into the second edition.
6. The paragraph starts in the first edition with "La subsistence proprement dite, ou le pain, a pu manquer à la classe pauvre . . ."
7. Sismondi, like other writers before him (and after), constructs an ideal primitive society as a reference point. This particular picture seems to have been influenced by his co-Genevese Rousseau. Anthropological research has shown that so-called primitive tribes have usually very complex social regulations.
8. Seventeenth- and eighteenth-century European exploration carried infections into populations that had no immunity to them and were therefore decimated.
9. In both editions of *New Principles,* Sismondi substitutes twenty years. The figure twenty-five years used in the *Encyclopedia* is most likely based on Malthus, who in turn used a generally agreed figure derived from American experience.
10. The *New Principles* uses *Cabul* for Afghanistan. Malthus would attribute the static size of pastoral tribes to the inability of the families to nourish more children, who die in early infancy as a consequence. Sismondi appears to attribute this fact to active birth control. Malthus, as a clergyman, considered birth control a vice; Sismondi, while laying major emphasis on late marriages, still refers to prejudices and habits which make for low fertility, thus reflecting a cultural difference between English and French attitudes toward birth control.
11. This recalls Sismondi's sharp criticism of large-scale agriculture in the Roman Campagna in the third book.
12. Sismondi obviously oversimplified in the same manner that Malthus did, to prove his point, although in the context of his time he was probably more nearly correct on what total populations could be accommodated within the boundaries of European states than was Malthus. The basic argument that population size is not necessarily the result of an immutable law, even among the poor, but a variable depending on social conditions, and particularly on

property distribution, is still an important argument in modifying Malthusian theory. It incidentally supplies a major reason for the socialization of land, the breaking up of estates usually associated with Marxian revolutions. Sismondi would have supported such action, up to a point, because of his insistence that the landlord holds his property in trust for, and the benefit of, society and can be relieved of it if he does not serve the interests of the community. He would advocate that smallholding supersede large estates to make every cultivator a holder of property and thereby engage his self-interest.

4

What Population Increase Is Desirable for a Nation

There are some countries, as we saw when we discussed territorial wealth, where the system of cultivation is so oppressive, where the safeguards given to family pride are so contrary to the public interest that the conduct of landlords, when they oppose improved farming methods, is at one and the same time unjust, inhuman, and opposed to the very goal for which landed property was instituted; but, in general, when we have characterized it as detrimental in its relation to population increases, we meant to speak of it less as a hindrance than an encouragement. Landlords sometimes prevent a productive enterprise when they should have allowed it; but there is certainly a time when they must refuse it. This would be when a nation is so unfortunate that it would take from the soil all the sustenance possible, and has, in consequence, brought itself to the very worst type of subsistence; one that would have put into production all its reserves, and consequently would not have left to itself any resources for an unforeseen need. Landlords are the guardians of society against this type of competition men would conduct against each other, when, all having been reduced to a class of workers in an ailing industry, they put their existence up for auction, and content themselves with the largest amount of work and the smallest amount of subsistence they can reconcile with maintaining their life. It is fortunate that landlords make this competitive folly impossible for everyone; it is perhaps already the greatest flaw in our institutions that they have made this necessary for some, by calling forth a population society had no interest in seeing born, and deceiving certain classes about their incomes and means of existence.

[So long as a great part of the country is uncultivated; as land proper for liberally rewarding rural labour is covered only with spontaneous production; as even the part under tillage is imperfectly worked; as the soil is not rendered healthy,[1] the marshes drained, the hills protected against precipitations, the fields defended against the ruinous forces of nature; so long as all this is not done merely for want of hands—it is desirable for the happiness of agriculturists, and for that of the nation living on their labour, that the classes of cultivators should be increased, and enabled to accomplish the task reserved for them,] as long as an ample reward is still connected to it.

[So long as the objects produced by the industrious arts are imperfectly supplied to the consumer, or at least as he cannot procure them except by a sacrifice disproportionate to their value; so long as he is constrained to furnish himself coarsely by domestic industry, for want of opportunity to buy furniture, effects, clothes, proper for his use; so long as his enjoyments are restricted by the inconveniences of all the utensils with which he is obliged to content himself,—it is desirable that the manufacturing population increase; since, from the need there is of such a population, it might evidently live in comfort, and contribute to the enjoyment of other classes.

So long as all hands are in such a degree necessary for agriculture, and manufactures, or trade which serves them, that the guardian professions, equally useful to society, are badly filled up[2]—it is desirable that population continue to increase, that so interior order, security of person and property, may be better protected, health better attended to, the soul better nourished, the mind more enlightened; and that society may be externally defended with sufficient force, comprehending even the recruitment of a sea and land army, which consume population.

This population, indeed, whenever it is required, will quickly be replaced.[3] But it is not enough that it be replaced, if it cannot find the niche, to which it is destined. Sometimes a fertile soil is in vain abundant, and remains uncultivated. There is no chance of the most numerous population assembled in its neighbourhood coming to profit by its resources. This soil has become the property of a few families; it is declared indivisible and unalienable; it will always pass to a single proprietor, according to the order of primogeniture, without the capacity either to be subjected to an emphyteutic lease, or burdened with a mortgage. The proprietor has not the capital necessary for its cultivation; he can give no security to such as have this capital, that will engage them to employ it in his land. Thus the idle population of Rome in vain calls for labour; the waste Campagna di Roma in vain calls for labourers; the social organization is bad; and so long as this shall remain unchanged, the day-labourer will perish from penury, on the surface of fields which, for want of culture, are turning to their wild state; and the population, far from increasing, will diminish.]

Similarly, in the manufactures, [the rich proprietors of Poland,] Hungary, Russia, [will in vain require all the produce of luxury; the bad condition of the roads, prohibiting every distant transport,[4] will in vain present superior advantages to national industry; oppression and servitude destroy all energy, all spirit of enterprise in the lower class. Elsewhere, ruinous monopolies, absurd privileges, affrighting] insults,[5] [ignorance, barbarity, and want of security, will render the progress of manufactures impossible; no capital will be accumulated to animate them. In those cases, to increase the population will not increase industry. The births will in vain be doubled, be quadrupled, during a certain number of years; they will not afford an additional workman, they will only be followed by a proportionably quicker mortality. The social organization is bad; so long as this shall remain unchanged, population cannot increase.

The guardian population is fed as well as recruited by the other classes. It is not sufficient that many children are born] so that society may have many defenders; [unless their parents enjoy a certain degree of opulence, they can never bring them up to the age of men; the prince can never make soldiers of them. In this case, wars by land or sea will devour the population; while they employ only its superfluity, the social organization is good.

The population is always measured, in the long run, by the demand for labour. Wherever labour is required, and a sufficient wage offered, the workmen will arise to earn it. The population, with its expansive force, will occupy the place which is found vacant. Subsistence will also arise for the workmen, or in case of need, be imported. The same demand which calls a man into existence,[6] will likewise recompense the agricultural labour which provides him with food. If the demand for labour cease, the workman will perish, yet not without a struggle, in which not he alone will suffer, but all his brethren and his rivals. The subsistence which enabled him to live, and which henceforth he cannot pay for, and he cannot demand, will, in its turn, cease to be produced. Thus national happiness rests on the demand for labour, but on a regular and perpetual demand. For, on the contrary, a demand which is intermittent, after having formed workmen, condemns them to suffering and death: it would be far better if they had never existed.

We have seen that the demand for labour, the cause of production, must be proportional to revenue which supports consumption; that this revenue, in its turn, originates in the national wealth, which wealth is formed and augmented by labour. Thus, in political economy, all things are linked together, we move constantly in a circle, since each effect becomes a cause in turn. Yet all things are progressive, provided that each movement is adjusted to the rest; but all stops, all retrogrades, whenever one of the movements which ought to be combined is disordered. According to the natural march of things, an augmentation of wealth will produce an augmentation of revenue; from this will arise an increase of consumption, next an increase of labour for reproduction, and therewith of population; and, finally, this new labour will, in its turn, increase the national wealth. But if, by unreasonable measures, any of these operations is hastened without regard to all the rest, the whole system is deranged, and the poor are weighed down with suffering, instead of the happiness which was anticipated for them.

The object of society is not fulfilled, so long as the country occupied by this society, presents means of supporting a new population, of enabling it to live in happiness and abundance, whilst yet those means are not resorted to. The multiplication of happiness over the earth, is the object of Providence; it is stamped in all his works, and the duty of men in their human society is to co-operate in it.[7]

The government which, by oppression of its subjects, by its contempt for justice and order, by the shackles it puts on agriculture and industry, condemns fertile countries to be deserts, sins not against its own subjects alone; its tyranny is a crime against human society, on the whole of which it inflicts suffering; it weakens its rights over the country occupied by it, and as its troubles the enjoyment of all other states, it gives to all others the right of controlling it.] It is not only because the Barbary kingdoms arm pirates in their privateering against the Europeans which gives the latter the right to hold them to account for their robberies; it is because they have doomed to desolation a country whose trade is necessary to Europe: it is because they have destroyed liberty, security, agriculture, trade, and the population. Europe would find immense resources for its subsistence in that bountiful region, so happily positioned to exchange with it all its products; Europe would find in the wealth of Africa, if it were to become again what it was at the time of Hadrian, a vast market for the products from which its factories overflow. The tyranny of the Dey of Algiers or the Emperor of Marocco, is not only felt in Africa; its repercussions are felt in our workshops.[8]

Today, men take pleasure in asserting a principle which, in fact, is constantly set aside in practice. The philosophers, the friends of liberty have asserted that nations have no right to interfere in the governance of each other, and that, however frightful the abuse of authority be in a country, foreign nations could only take notice of the deeds of that government against other countries. The common needs of humanity, the good and the bad they can do to each other by breaking off their intercourse, deny this principle, so much more advantageous to tyrants than to free nations. It is because the people at home suffer hunger that we have a right to take cognizance of the abuse neighboring nations commit with the gifts of nature. A false application of respect for property has extended it to sovereignty. But, [the institution of property is the result of social convention;] public authority has taken it under its protection, because, [in a society subjected to laws and a regulating government, the interest of each may be implicitly relied on for producing the advantage of all, because the aberrations of this private interest are, in every case of need, limited by the public authority.[9] But in the great human society formed among independent nations, there is no law or general government to repress the passions of each sovereign: besides, the interest of those sovereigns is not necessarily conformable to that of their subjects;[10] the one is contrary to the other, whenever the object of the rulers is to maintain their tyranny;] and even if the right of property of the Barbars over Barbary would be considered as unlimited, it could not be mistaken for the inherent rights of those they oppress.

[But whilst more than three quarters of the habitable globe are, by the faults of their governments, deprived of the inhabitants they should support,] many of the countries of Europe seem to be threatened, in repeated instances, with [the opposite calamity, that of not being able to maintain a superabundant population, which surpasses the proportion of labour required, and which, before dying of poverty, will diffuse its sufferings over the whole class of such as live by the labour of their hands.] Wherever this calamity has been experienced, wherever labor was offered in vain by those who have but their labor to live, and who perish of poverty in the middle of superabundant subsistence they cannot buy, it is our laws, our institutions that have caused such disproportion. By an imprudent zeal our governments have disturbed the equilibrium nature had established. [Religious instruction, legislation, social organization, every thing has tended to produce a population] the needs of society did not call for, even as the legislators, seeking the goal of increasing wealth, not the happiness of man, studied ways of economizing the amount of human labor needed to produce the demanded output. At the very time consumption was so limited, when all markets were saturated, governments were seen to seek, with equal ardor, increases in births, and decreases in the number of hands that were needed in all the trades. Thus, [the proportion which should subsist in the progress of the different departments of society has been broken, and the suffering has become universal.][11]

Translator's Notes to Chapter 4, Seventh Book

Together, this and the previous chapter illustrate one of the problems of Sismondi's approach to economic analysis and his construction of *New Principles*. Chapter 3 is a straightforward rejection of Malthusian population theory, and it is entirely new material. This chapter, which ought to be a follow-up and reenforcement of the preceding argument, contains up to two-thirds material from the *Encyclopedia*. Apparently, Sismondi wanted to analyze the more difficult question of the most desirable population growth, most likely to provide a positive answer to the pessimistic Malthusian theory and the classical subsistence theory of wages. It seems he also wanted to summarize in support once more the main points of the preceding books. He could have taken the position that only a minimal population growth is desirable, or reiterated, in more detail, his view that individual income would regulate such growth. Instead, he reverts back to the much more diffuse arguments of his earlier article, which amounted to not much more than general condemnations of social organization and governments, and are admittedly an exposition of ideas he now opposed. His thoughts on the subject had then not yet been fully developed, and as a consequence, he weakens his position by reusing the old material. The first paragraph is a reference to a proposal published in the first edition and dropped from the second edition because of protests, that is, that poor workers be prohibited from marrying until they have acquired some property.

1. The term used is "assaini," meaning in this context 'improved', or 'made arable'.
2. The expression is awkward, but Sismondi apparently meant that the nation has not yet developed professional services, either in the private or the public sector. The term *guardian professions*, used earlier, is of physiocratic origin.
3. The French sentence reads: "Cette population naîtra aussitôt qu'elle sera demandée." In the *Encyclopedia*, Sismondi referred, previous to the preceding three paragraphs, to the destruction of population because of overpopulation (see chapter 1 and 2 of this book). In *New Principles,* the argument has been altered by the sequence, hence Sismondi uses "naîtra" rather than "replaced." Since the paragraphs follow each other, except for this change, the *Encyclopedia* version has been retained.
4. The French term used is "rencherissant" for 'prohibiting'. The sense is slightly altered; the proper word here would have been 'make prohibitive'.
5. The *Encyclopedia* reprint reads here "advances," which has a superficial resemblance to *"avanies"* used in the French text. It is likely that a misprint occurred. It was thought advisable to insert the appropriate translation to preserve the sense of the sentence.
6. This hurries things along a bit, since it takes several years from birth to manhood. However, it should be remembered that Sismondi was familiar with the fact that five-year-old children worked in factories. Also, movement of workers during the early nineteenth century was less constrained by national borders. Alternatively, one could assume that Sismondi postulates that the working of the labor market would draw individuals to the open positions. This would assume that there exists a reservoir of idle labor that could supply the need. Clearly, this would then merely describe the conditions he experienced at the beginning of the nineteenth century, when, especially in England, great numbers of unskilled individuals, Irish peasants and Scottish crofters, left the land for the cities and factory work. He also seems to assume that once the workers had made this decision they could not return to the land.
7. Much of the preceding argument and, in particular, this sentence, echoes Quesnay's views, as expressed in, for example, *Rural Philosophy* and the *Tableau*. (See Meek 1963.)
8. This can be interpreted as a justification for the white man's burden, but it has to be kept in mind that Sismondi took the general position that landlords and

governments had a social duty to promote happiness, failing which, they were subject to removal. He would have been just as willing to do away with European governments, or landlords, if they failed similarly.

9. While the beginning of the sentence echoes Adam Smith, its end is more in keeping with cameralistic philosophy. Sismondi reflects his familiarity with French *etatisme*, even though he condemned the total control over economic activity practiced by Colbert.
10. Sismondi omitted here "or, to speak more correctly." It should be noted that he adopts Hobbes's position of nations living in a state of nature.
11. The paragraph was rewritten for the second edition. The first edition used the *Encyclopedia* text for a straightforward translation. The paragraph reads in the *Encyclopedia:* "But whilst more than three quarters of the habitable globe are. by the faults of their governments, deprived of the inhabitants they should support, we, at the present day, in almost the whole of Europe, experience the opposite calamity, that of not being able to maintain a superabundant population, which surpasses the proportion of labour required, and which, before dying of poverty, will diffuse its sufferings over the whole class of such as live by the labour of their hands. For our part, we owe this calamity to the imprudent zeal of our governments. With us, religious instruction, legislation, social organization, every thing has tended to produce a population, the existence of which was not provided for beforehand. The labour was not adjusted to the number of men; and, frequently, the same zeal with which it was attempted to multiply the number of births, was afterwards employed, in all arts, to diminish the required number of hands. The proportion which should subsist in the progress of the different departments of society has been broken, and the suffering has become universal."

5

Of the Religious Encouragement Given to Population

[Religious instruction has almost always strongly contributed to destroy the equilibrium between the population and the demand for labour which is to give it subsistence.][1] Religion, having been presented to us as the work of the Divinity, is always assumed to be perfect and unalterable. Its priests reject with all their might every change which would accommodate it to circumstance; yet, when civil and political laws are part of a religion, such immobility amid the progress of society has often set them in opposition to their original goals. The aims the legislator had set himself have been forgotten, while the precept has remained; and, intended to produce a certain benefit, it has become pernicious after achieving it. [Religions began with the origin of the human race; and therefore at a time when the rapid progress of population was every where desirable; their principles have not yet changed, now when the unlimited increase of families has given birth only to beings, of necessity condemned to physical suffering or moral degradation.

A Chinese knows no greater misfortune, no deeper humiliation, than not to leave sons behind him to perform the funeral honours at his death. In almost all other creeds the indefinite increase of families has ever been represented as a blessing of heaven. On the other hand, whilst religion repressed irregularity of morals, it attached all morality of conduct to marriage, and washed away, by the nuptial benediction alone, whatever was reprehensible in the imprudence of him who inconsiderately contracted the bonds of paternity.

Yet, how important soever purity of morals may be, the duties of a father towards those whom he brings into existence are of a still higher order. Children born but for wretchedness, are also born for vice. The happiness and the virtue of innocent and defenseless beings are thus sacrificed beforehand, to satisfy the passions of a day. The ardour of casuists in preaching up marriage to correct a fault,] and even to prevent it; [the imprudence with which they recommend husbands to shut their eyes upon the future, to entrust the fate of their children to Providence; the ignorance of social order, which has induced them to erase chastity from the number of virtues proper in marriage, are causes which have been incessantly active in destroying the proportion which naturally would have established itself between the population and its means of existing].

According to the viewpoint from which population is considered, the Catholic faith has sometimes been sharply attacked for having kept from marriage a certain number of individuals by religious vows; sometimes its prudence has been highly lauded for placing an early obstacle to such a dreadful increase of the human race. Neither the praise nor the blame are justified; if three-quarters of mankind would enter orders, the remaining fourth would be amply sufficient to maintain the population at the same level; an income being assured in advance to those who, from religious zeal, consecrate themselves to celibacy, every household produces, to profit therefrom, some children over and above those needed to maintain the population; just as every household produces some more in countries habituated to war or sea duty, so as to compensate for the losses of these dangerous professions. Since they were not expected to maintain the population, they would disturb the equilibrium if they had children like their brothers.

But much less attention has been given to [another very important part of the legislation of casuists, with regard to all that they have named the duties of husbands.* Considering marriage as solely destined for multiplication, they have made a sin of the very virtues which they enforce on single persons. This morality is enforced[2] by every confessor on every father and mother of a family.] It fights continuously the universal principle of interest and sympathy[3] of which we have spoken, as being the safeguard of society, which will not expose to suffering those beings who ought to be cherished and protected; which will not bring into the world offspring to whom it cannot assure a status equal to oneself, a subsistence that does let them suffer, an independence that preserves them from vice and

*These different casuistic authors, even those who have written in the vernacular, have generally rendered in Latin that part of their rules. A lay author would profit little if he followed these priests in this discussion. I limit myself to refer the reader to *Istruzione e pratica, per li confessori di M.Alfonso de Liguori, vescovo di S. Agata de'Goti.* The author, canonized two or three years ago, is one the Curia of Rome considers the most unerring of the casuists. Moreover, he cites the opinions of all the others. See particularly Vo;. II, Chapt. XVIII, para. II, of *Usu licito Matrimonii;* para. III, *Usu praecepto Matrimonii.*

corruption.[4] Confessors are no longer consulted in the reformed religions; but the morals they asserted have persisted with so much force that it is rarely tolerated to touch on these delicate questions, for fear of offending modesty, and of exposing oneself to abuse. Especially in the Anglican Church the influence of this old casuistic doctrine on conjugal duties opposes in a very baneful manner the natural sentiments of love and protection all fathers feel for their children.[5]

[When fatal prejudices are not honoured; when a system of morality contrary to our true duties towards others, and above all towards those indebted to us for life, is not taught in the name of the most sacred authority, no wise man will marry till he is in a condition that affords him a sure means of living, no father of a family will have more children than he can conveniently maintain. The latter expects his children will be satisfied with the lot in which he has lived; hence] when he cannot in any way increase his income, [he will wish the rising generation exactly to represent that which is departing; he will wish that a son and a daughter arrived at the age of marriage, should fill the place of his father and his mother; that his children's children should fill his place and his wife's, in their turn; his daughter will find in another house exactly the lot which he will give to the daughter of another house in his own; and the income which satisfied the fathers will satisfy the children.[6]

When once this family is formed, justice and humanity require that they submit to the same constraints which single people undergo. On considering how small is the number of natural children in every country, it ought to be admitted that this constraint is sufficiently effectual. In a country where population cannot increase,] or at least in which its progress must be so slow as to be barely perceptible, [where new places do not exist for new establishments, the father who has eight children should reckon either that six of his children will die young, or that three contemporary males and their contemporary females;[7] or in the following generation three of his sons and three of his daughters will not marry on his account. There is no less injustice in the second calculation than cruelty in the first. If marriage is sacred; if it is one great means of attaching men to virtue, and recompensing the chagrins of declining years, by the growing hopes of allowing an honourable old age to succeed an active youth, it is not because this institution renders lawful the pleasures of sense, but because it imposes new duties on the father of a family, and returns him the sweetest recompense in the ties of husband and father. Religious morality ought therefore to teach men, that marriage is made for all citizens equally; that it is the object towards which they should all direct their effort; but that this object has not been attained except so far as they are able to fulfill their duties towards the beings whom they call into existence; and after obtaining the happiness of being fathers, after renewing their families, and giving this stay and hope to their declining years, they are no less obliged to live chastely with their wives, than single persons with such as do not belong to them.[8]

Self-interest powerfully warns men against this indefinite multiplication of their families, to which they have been invited by so fatal a religious error, and no one ought to be disquieted if this order is observed remissly. In general at least three births are required to give two such individuals as arrive at the age of marriage;[9] and the niches of population are not so exactly formed, that they cannot by turns admit a little more and a little less. Only government ought to awaken the prudence of citizens deficient in it, and never to deceive them by the hopes of an independent lot] to raise their family, [when this illusory establishment shall leave them exposed to misery, suffering, and death.]

Translator's Notes to Chapter 5, Seventh Book

In this chapter, Sismondi shows that he is a child of the Enlightenment. While the attack on religion in general, and the Catholic Church in particular, is connected to his views on a harmonic relation between population and the economy at large, the tone is essentially anticlerical in a Voltairian way, even attacking Calvinistic teaching. Remarkably, the greater part of the chapter is derived from the *Encyclopedia,* and is thus also in opposition to the sentiments on the subject of procreation that prevailed in the Victorian age. The controversy that swirled around Malthusian doctrine for most of the nineteenth century, and still generates a great deal of heat in the late twentieth century, shows that the subject touched deep convictions, probably because it is associated with sex, and contradicted received theological doctrine on the origins of man.

1. An amplification was inserted here in the first edition, which, in turn, was taken from the *Encyclopedia*. The material from here to the next bracket is new. This insertion and a translation below (see note 7) appear to support the previously noted possibility that the *Encyclopedia* article was translated from a French manuscript which appears to have been the first version of this work.
2. The text has "enseignée", 'taught', a weaker verb than 'enforce,' implying that Sismondi changed the harshness of the attack for *New Principles*.
3. Clearly, this alludes to the teachings of Adam Smith, as expressed in the *Theory of Moral Sentments*.
4. When referring to independence, Sismondi meant an adequate income. The tenor of the chapter again would suggest that he must have always felt very keenly his modest circumstances, and what must have been at times a struggle to make a living by free-lance writing, even though he occupied a comfortable villa on the outskirts of Geneva. His strong condemnation of Catholic Church teachings may be due to his Calvinistic background, but it is also possible that his experiences in Tuscany may have influenced his judgment. His discussion of agriculture above points to the possibility that he saw the shortcomings of, for example, métayage as partly rooted in the large families of the Italian peasants favored by the teachings of the church.

5. This short sentence shows Sismondi's familiarity with British conditions and a forceful rejection of the Victorian cant that surrounded sex.
6. The sentiments expressed here point in the direction of practices that must have been prevalent in Geneva as a city-state with limited land and constant competition. Most city-states, especially in Italy, were distinguished for their arranged marriages between families, and the associated limitation of children. Sismondi's family, with two children, one boy and one girl, can be assumed to express the prevailing sentiments of his upbringing.
7. This was apparently translated literally from a French text. The meaning is that either six of his children, the equivalent number in the population at large or six of the next generation will not marry, that is not have children. Since this is the text from the *Encyclopedia*, no alteration was made. The assumption of six deaths, with a remainder of two, together with the previous discussion, shows conclusively that Sismondi considered two children replacements for the parents.
8. Again, Sismondi must have had his own life in mind when he wrote this paragraph. He had as a youth a very active life, he married late, his wife survived him, and he had no children, supporting the assumption that he practiced what he preached.
9. That is, two adults of marriageable age require three infants, with one assumed to die before reaching that age.

6

Of the Encouragements Given to Population by Politics

Governments have almost always regarded increases in population as a means to power or national defense; in their eyes excess of births over deaths has always been a sign of prosperity; and, without troubling themselves greatly over how these new citizens they desired so much to get, would live, without reckoning whether there would be any income that could sustain them, any industry that could make them useful; they have done everything they possibly could to encourage marriage, and to enlist every household to bring into the world as many children as possible. To this end, honorific titles, pecuniary rewards, or at least tax exemptions, have been promised to fathers of large families. Yet, it was not possible that the favors handed out by the government compensate for the costs connected with the education of numerous children; and this type of encouragement would have had little influence, if it were not strongly supported by the clergy.

The obstacles raised to emigration by government constitute a much greater real evil. The love of men, and above all of the poor, for their customs, their native soil, is quite powerful; it is only with a strong feeling of fear, and a fear almost always well-founded, that they venture into unknown lands; the burden of their needs, the impossibility of finding in their fatherland enough work, an adequate livelihood, can alone resolve them to do so. The craftsmen who emigrate are men who suffer, and who make others suffer; they do not know how to render a greater service to their country than by leaving it; the ports should be opened to them, every help ought to be given to these unfortunates who, most likely victims of legislative error, sacrifice themselves for their brothers by leaving them.[1]

However, we have seen that a harsh policy was followed almost everywhere against emigrants, repeated efforts by governments to prevent them from crossing the borders; and, during the scarcity that afflicted Europe during 1816,[2] when every nation could not feed its citizens, precautions redoubled against the hiring agents who wanted to direct them to America and Russia, and the official press repeated with care the false promises of these agents, the sufferings of those who had listened to them; whereas the government ought to have undertaken the protection of these children of the nation it could not feed, ease their passage, and guarantee their well-being.

These errors are still less important besides those, more general and dangerous, which encourage production that is not in any way demanded by the consumer, to create to this end a new class of paupers, whose families are multiplied with care, whose industry is maintained for some time by prohibitions and an entirely artificial system, and who must finally be abandoned in their battle against need.

There exists in every nation a class of individuals who have been expelled from their niches in society, who have lost their inheritance, or their metayage, if they were husbandmen, their small capital if they belonged to trade or industry, and who have no more for their livelihood than the daily labor they render to unknown masters; happy the nation where this class is small; there is none where it does not exist at all.[3] These unfortunates, as long as they are unsure of their own livelihood, think little of marrying, and of undertaking the burden to provide a livelihood to others. [But whenever a new demand for labour raises their wages and thus increases their revenue, they hasten to satisfy one of the first laws of nature, and seek in marriage a new source of happiness. If the rise of wages was but momentary; if, for example, the favours granted by government suddenly give a great development to a species of manufacture, which, after its commencement, cannot be maintained, the workmen, whose remuneration was double during some time, will all have married to profit by their opulence; and then, at the moment when their trade declines, families disproportionate to the actual demand for labour will be plunged into the most dreadful wretchedness.

It is those variations in the demand for labour, this sort of revolution so frequent in the lives of poor artisans, that gives to the state a superabundant population. Already brought into the world, that population finds no longer any room to exist there; it is always ready to be satisfied with the lowest terms on which it may be permitted to live. There is no condition so hard that men are not found ready to engage in it voluntarily. In some trades, the workmen are obliged to live in mud, exposed to continual nausea; in others, the labour engenders painful and inevitable maladies; several stupify the senses, degrade the body and the soul; several employ none but children, and after introducing, abandon to a horrible indigence the being] they have allowed to live only twelve or fifteen years. [There are callings, in fine, which public opinion brands with infamy: there are some which deserve this condemnation. Yet the ranks are always full; and a miserable wage, scarce sufficient for existence, induces men to undergo so many evils. The reason is, society does not leave them any choice; they are compelled to be contented with this cruel lot, or not to live.]

If by uncalled-for encouragement government sometimes deceives the unfortunate workers about the income they can expect from their industry, it even more often brings them to deceive themselves; this happens if it encourages a social organization that multiplies the numbers of those who possess nothing, who live from day to day, who are not called upon to have any knowledge of the market for which they work, and who are consequently at the mercy of their masters. When we discussed landed wealth we have seen how this state of dependency grows, in proportion to which the worker has a lesser direct interest in the soil he works; how the condition of the peasant was never more precarious than when he was reduced to the status of a simple day laborer, and how it was also then that the agricultural population grew without any relation to the demand for labor. In discussing commercial wealth, we have seen in the same way that the more the condition of the artisan became precarious, the less he knew about the market for his industry; and the more it was impossible for him to judge the opportunities he would leave to his children, the more he increased his family without proportion to the demand for labor. We still will have occasion to come back to the effects of this precarious state of the lowest class, we recall it here merely in passing.[4]

Finally, public charity can be considered as an encouragement society gives to a population it cannot sustain. The more such charity is sustained and well organized, the more efficiently this encouragement operates, as in England, to the prejudice of society. The unfortunate creatures who seem to enter life only to suffer, who, from earliest childhood have known only want and misery, are objects who deeply stir pity, and bring forth the help of charitable souls. Unfortunately, beggars recognize this quickly; children are for them a tool of their trade. Far from being embarrassed by raising them, it is by them that they live, and the more they expose them to suffering, the more alms they receive. Public establishments, when they exist, supplement individual pity; hospital aid proportions itself to the number of children of poor families, and, in England, or even in the maritime cities of America, where the poor have a right to weekly assistance from their parishes, the poor rates are a sort of pump for the multiplication of the indigent population.

When social organization has not in any way divided the working class from that which owns some property, and when the great mass of people always joins to the fruits of its labor those of any other wealth, either landed or commercial, public opinion alone suffices to contain the scourge of beggary. There is always some shame attached to the husbandman who has sold the inheritance of his fathers, to the artisan who has squandered his small capital. If one or the other fall into poverty, at least he will suffer enough from this degradation that he will make every effort to escape therefrom; if he is then a victim of a temporary misfortune, the charity of his neighbors, who have not yet become indifferent by a constant repetition of similar events, will soon come to his assistance. But in the state in which Europe finds itself today, above all where England finds itself, with such a numerous population of day laborers that they have almost entirely replaced both peasants and artisans; when all the work, be it in the fields or in the cities, is performed by some type of manufacture, by people condemned to never own anything, never to be masters of their own fate, who cannot feel any shame for having fallen into beggary; why would they blush if their master has dismissed them from today to tomorrow? Perhaps he has done it either because he has closed his shop due to bankruptcy, or he has replaced their industry with a machine. The public is right, it does not attach anymore any shame to a calamity it has caused itself.[5]

While public opinion can no longer condemn beggary, and the causes of misery multiply every day, charity, even if beseeched by ever more genuine misfortunes, by ever more innocent victims, will soon wither. Moreover, the excessive bonus given to the multiplication of paupers makes the help ever more insufficient. The evil is almost at its peak in England: more than eight million sterling have been appropriated in one year to help more than nine million paupers: every year this sum and the number of paupers run the risk of increasing, till this system is changed by a terrible disaster.

Today there is talk of abolishing these parish helps, and of leaving the indigent to public charity. However energetic such charity may be, it is not in any way ready to take over a burden that is to be placed on it; the change in the system would bring on frightful misery; the number of those who would perish of hunger is much greater than one can imagine; whether or not they died quietly, would such a great number of people, expelled from social protection, not succeed in shaking a state that permitted such misery? A remedy must be found at higher levels. It is not the class of paupers, it is the class of day laborers that must be made to disappear, that must be brought back to that of property owners.*[6]

*In the first edition I called here for the authority of the legislature to put an obstacle to the marriages of paupers who count on making their children a tool of begging, and that in general it demand some guarantee from those who proposed to

There will be no rest for England, there will be no happiness for the working classes, there will be no real and lasting progress towards prosperity until a means will have been found to create a community of interest, instead of opposition, between the entrepreneur and all those he puts to work;[7] until the workers in the fields will have been called to share in the harvests, and the factory workers in their output. Until the master, feeling at one with the workers he employs, will recognize that he cannot gain anything by reducing their wages and, to the contrary, will seek on his own to share the profits of his enterprise with them to make certain of their cooperation. But though we seem to see the goal that ought to be attained, we cannot venture to take upon us to show the means of its realization.[8]

[The guardian population presents the same species of suffering in another rank of society.] War accustoms fathers to the belief that it is necessary, for the preservation of their family, to have one or two more children; the foreign service to which the Swiss are accustomed, has raised in their country an overabundant population that is in need of such an outlet. The Scottish Highlanders were raised for public and private warfare; births had to be increased sufficiently in those savage mountains so that the number of those who perished in daily battle would not halt the cultivation and pasturage by which the nation lived. When more peaceful days follow the rule of the sword, the nation is for some time weighed down with an overabundant population, because customs are settled and deeply entrenched, and it becomes necessary that everyone should have suffered because of them before one dreams of reforming them.[9]

[War multiplies the commission of officers in the army and navy; the complicacy of administration multiplies] the places of civil servants of all kinds. [Religious zeal multiplies the places for pastors. All of them live on pensions with a certain degree of opulence; none of them knows, or is able] to measure [the fund which affords him subsistence. They reckon on ushering their children into the same career with themselves; they bring them up, multiply their families in proportion to their actual opulence, and blindly repose on the future. Their pension, however, finishes with their life; and at death they leave their children in a state of indigence, the suffering of which is farther aggravated by the possession of a liberal education. The laws,] the administrative and military rules [which obstruct the marriage of officers,] civil servants, [clergymen, and generally of all

raise a family, who were without the means of feeding it and shielding it from misery. These extreme measures, intended to halt a calamity which at that time appeared extreme and universal, has been misunderstood. It seems to me pointless to develop an idea whose use is possibly today not desirable.

such as live on pensions, how hard soever those laws may appear at their first establishment, are justifiable, because they save from poverty the class to which its torments would be most piercing.][10]

Translator's Notes to Chapter 6, Seventh Book

Sismondi's writings are ambiguous on the role of government in political economy. On the one hand, he professes to be an advocate of economic freedom, a disciple of Adam Smith. On the other hand, a major part of his work is a call for governmental restraint on unfettered economic instincts. Nowhere is this split political-economic personality more evident than in this chapter. Sismondi lays major blame for unbalanced population increases on ill-advised government actions. At the same time he calls on them to restrain such population increases. He eliminated from the second edition a remarkably autocratic proposal to prohibit marriages to paupers which apparently had been attacked by other writers; the proposal exhibits a naive belief that children will be born mainly in marriage. Sismondi cannot have been ignorant of the fact that even in his time many children were born out of wedlock.

However, in the light of later experience and analysis, the chapter fully develops the idea, hinted at several times earlier, that property owners tend to limit their offspring. He therefore calls for restoring to the working classes their share in productive property, not as a class, as Marx would have it, but as individuals, engaging the self-interest of labor in the working of industrial production. In all industrial countries the postdepression reforms have in fact mostly accomplished this goal. The latest developments in many nonsocialist countries, which bring worker participation directly into production, would argue that Sismondi was greatly ahead of his time. The petit bourgeois idea of small property owners at all levels is of course opposed by Marxists, but it is clearly in consonance with Adam Smith's ideas of a competitive system dominated by small economic units whose self-interest leads to a stable economic equilibrium. If Jefferson envisioned an America of small landholders, Sismondi envisioned an industrial nation of small producers and shareholders. Quite clearly he knew that large industrial production units were here to stay—what he wanted was a diffusion of economic power through worker participation.

1. Sismondi's physiocratic tendencies come again to the fore. The policy he advocates here was also the policy of the physiocrats, as opposed to the mercantilistic practice of prohibiting emigration. The paragraph also foresees the beginning of the major population migrations that became a hallmark of the nineteenth century.
2. In the first edition, this reads "il y a deux ans," in accordance with the publication date of 1819.
3. Again, it must be remembered here that Sismondi's father lost everything in the default of France, and because he became a dealer in milk and produce he was regarded as déclassé by his former peers. This reference, of course, precedes by about forty years Marx's well-known argument that the petit bourgeoisie would be forced into the proletariat by the development of monopoly capitalism. The next sentence is also a clear reference to Sismondi's own condition and an explanation for his late marriage.
4. An earlier argument that a large family, given the employment of children, was

a source of additional income seems to be forgotten here. Also, the assumption that a knowledge of the market would limit families is farfetched. Most workers, contrary to his views, did not know the market in his sense even before the Industrial Revolution. Sismondi overlooks (what he most certainly knew as a historian) that precapitalistic production in countries such as Holland and Belgium, and in cities such as Florence, even in the Middle Ages, produced a large proletarian population that had no idea what the market was.

5. This is an early version of the Marxian reserve army, even to the extent that it assumes that it lowers wages below the subsistence level.
6. Sismondi eliminated here from the first edition two very long paragraphs that discussed in detail measures to prevent paupers from having children they might use to beg. The main thrust of the argument was to ban marriage to paupers. In addition he writes "le mariage de tous ceux qui n'ont aucune propriété devrait être soumis à une inspection sévère; on aurait droit de demander des garanties pour les enfants à naître; requérir de lui un engagement de conserver à ses gages, pendant un certain nombre d'années, l'homme qui se marie . . . en même temps qu'on ne permet jamais le mariage à ceux qui demeurent dans le dernier degré." Sismondi defends this position in the next paragraph as follows: "Mais le même obstacle qui arrêterait la multiplication indéfinie des pauvres ouvriers, arrêterait aussi dans les ateliers la production indéfinie et sans rapport avec la consommation. Il diminuerait donc la masse des produits commerçables, mais il augmenterait en fin de compte les profits du marchand aussi-bien que ceux de ouvrier." In other words, he believes that a deliberate reduction in the birthrate will reduce the reserve army and confer on the worker a monopoly position that will assure him a greater share in the product. Sismondi had history (and theory) on his side, even though the suggestion was badly received. Whenever sickness, such as the Great Plague, reduced the working population sufficiently, wages rose and the position of the workers improved. The subsistence theory of wages makes the same, often overlooked, point.
7. This also, is a major difference between Sismondi and Marx. Marx saw the solution to the problem in confrontation, and eventual defeat, of the capitalist, with communal ownership of productive capital the ultimate foundation of the state. Sismondi wants to make the worker a participant in the capitalistic system, as the Marxists contemptuously say, "co-opt" the worker by giving him a share in the ownership of capital. A Marxist would point out that in a communist system the working class "owns the means of production"; hence there would be no need for sharing in Sismondi's sense. This conveniently overlooks what he knew quite well, namely that if everybody owns something, nobody owns it, and the power of decision making will revert to those in political power or managerial control. The lessons of the Genevese Revolution were not forgotten by its victim. The institutional ownership of corporations by pension trusts, and mutual funds, with computerized trading of shares, is a more effective socialization of capitalistic ownership than Marxian socialism.
8. This sentence has been held to show that Sismondi was an undecided scribbler who lacked the fortitude of his convictions. It is probably the reason why *New Principles* did not make more of an impact on on his own and subsequent times. Unlike all of his contemporaries, he prefers to persuade, to point to answers, without the panacea of a total solution, a comprehensive system of explanation and salvation. Sismondi was too conscious of the many pitfalls of human error to trust any of the nostrums that were advanced.

9. Sismondi always saw population increases as a function of social institutions, and therefore subject to human will and change. This contrasts vividly with Malthus's assumption, so quaintly put: "That the passion between the sexes is necessary and will remain nearly in its present state."
10. This last paragraph seems to have served as the takeoff point for the two paragraphs in the first edition that were subsequently eliminated in the second edition. Sismondi argues by analogy from his position on landholding (which he regards as a social grant and therefore subject to social regulation) to marriage, which he characterizes also as an act taken by social consent, and therefore subject to social inspection and regulation.

7

Of a Population Made Expendable by the Invention of Machines

[But an inordinate increase of population is not the only cause of this national suffering] by breaking the equilibrium between the supply and the demand for labor. [The demand for labour may decrease, and the population continue stationary. Consumption may be arrested, revenues dissipated, capital destroyed, and the number of hands formerly occupied may no longer be able to find sufficient employment. The population immediately follows the revolution of the capitals destined to support it.[1] As day labourers are more eager to receive even the smallest wage, than merchants to employ their money, the former are laid under conditions more and more hard, as the demand on the capital diminishes; and they conclude by contenting themselves with so miserable a remuneration, as is scarcely sufficient to maintain them alive. No enjoyment is any longer attached to the existence of this unhappy class; hunger and suffering stifle in them all moral affections. When every hour is a struggle for life, all passions are concentrated in selfishness; each forgets the pain of others in what he himself suffers; the sentiments of nature are blunted; a constant, obstinate, uniform labour, debases all the faculties. One blushes for the human species, to see how low on the scale of degradation it can descend; how much beneath the condition of animals it can voluntarily submit to maintain life; and, notwithstanding all the benefits of social order, notwithstanding the advantages man has gained from the arts, one is sometimes tempted to execrate the division of labour, and the invention of manufactures, on beholding to what extremes of wretchedness they have reduced beings created equal with ourselves.[2]

The misery of the savage hunter, who dies so frequently of hunger, is not equal to that of millions of families, whom a manufacturer sometimes dismisses; because at least there remains to the former all the energy, and all the intelligence, which he has put to proof during all his life. When he dies for want of finding game, he yields to a necessity which nature herself presents, and to which he knew, from the beginning, he must submit, as to sickness, or to old age. But the artisan, dismissed from his workshop, with his wife and children, has beforehand lost the strength of his soul and body; he is still surrounded with riches; he still sees besides him, at every step, the food which he requires; and if society refuses him the labour by which he offers, till his last moment, to purchase bread, it is men, not nature, that he blames.[3]

Even when persons do not actually die of hunger; even when the aids of charity are eagerly administered to all indigent families, discouragement and suffering produce their cruel effects on the poor, the diseases of the soul are communicated to the body, epidemics are multiplied, children die in a few months after their births, and the suppression of labour causes more cruel ravages than the cruellest war; besides, fatal habits, either of mendicity or idleness, take root in the population; another course is given to trade, another direction to fashion, and even after death has cleared the ranks of workmen, those who remain are no longer in a condition to support the competition of foreigners.

The causes of diminution in the demand for labour often belong to polity, properly so called, rather than to political economy.[4] There is, perhaps, none more efficacious than the loss or diminution of liberty. When a nation begins to alienate this precious possession, each citizen thinks himself less secure of his fortune, or the fruits of his labour; each abates something of the activity of his mind, and his spirit of industry.[5] The virtues which accompany labour,—sobriety, constancy, economy,—give place to the vices of idleness, to intemperance, dissipation, and forgetfulness of the future. Trade, industry, activity are regarded with contempt, in a state where the people are nothing, whilst all the distinctions, all honours, are reserved for noble indolence. Favour, intrigue, flattery, and all the arts of the courtiers, which debase the soul, are roads to fortune, much more sure and rapid than strength of character, bold and enterprising activity, or a spirit of speculation.[6] Intriguers are multiplied daily; they regard with contempt those who follow the only honourable path to fortune, that in which none makes progress except by his merit or his labour.

One cause of depopulation is, however, presented, which lies within the narrowest range of political economy. The progress of the arts, the progress of industry, and hence even that of wealth and prosperity, discover economical methods of producing all the fruits of labour, by employing a smaller number of workmen. Animals are substituted for men in almost all the details of agriculture; and machines are substituted for men in all the operations of manufactures. So long as a nation finds within its reach a market sufficiently extensive to secure for all its productions a prompt and advantageous circulation, each of these discoveries is an advantage, because, instead of diminishing the number of workmen, it augments the mass of labour and its produce. A nation which happens to originate discoveries, succeeds, for a long time, in extending its market in proportion to the number of hands set free by every new invention. It immediately employs them in augmenting the produce, which the discovery promises to furnish at a cheaper rate. But the period arrives at last, when the whole civilized world is but one market, and when new customers cannot be found in new nations. The demand of the universal market is then a precise quantity, which the different industrious nations dispute with each other; if one furnish more, another must furnish less. The total sale can only be increased by the progress of general opulence, or because conveniences, formerly confined to the rich, are brought within the reach of the poor.

The invention of the stocking frame, by means of which one man does as much work as a hundred did before, was a benefit for humanity, only because at the same time, the progress of civilization, of population, and of wealth, increased the number of consumers. New countries adopted the customs of Europe; and] this footwear, [formerly reserved for the rich, has now descended to the poorest classes.] It was for the poor, for the artisan, more economical than the leggings he gave up in its favor. The poor used that part of his income he had used before to buy leggings, to buy stockings. [But if, at the present day, some new discovery should enable us, by a single stocking frame, to do the work which ten years ago was done by a hundred, this discovery would be a national misfortune; for the numbers of consumers can scarcely increase, and it would then be the number of producers which would be diminished.]

As a general rule, every time that the demand for consumption exceeds the means of production of the population, every new discovery in the mechanical and other arts is a boon to society, because it provides the means to satisfy existing needs. Every time, on the contrary, that production fully meets consumption, every such discovery, in our existing social organization,*[7] becomes a calamity, because it adds to the enjoyments of

*We have said it already elsewhere, but we think it to be essential to repeat it: It is not the improvement of machines which is the true calamity, it is the improper distribution we make of their products. The more we can produce with a given quantity of labor, the more must we increase either our enjoyments, or our leisure; the worker who is his own master, when he would have produced in two hours, with the help of a machine, what he had made before in twelve, would have stopped after two hours, if he had no need, and could not use a larger product. It is our

consumption nothing but to satisfy them at a lower price, while it cuts off the very life of the producers. It would be invidious to weigh the advantage of a lower price against that of existence; moreover, the former is completely illusory for all expenditures governed by vanity; since nothing is sought but distinction, nobody will enjoy such distinction by obtaining for the same price better and more beautiful clothes, yet remaining in the same position with respect to all others. It must be remembered that in political economy only that is understood to be in demand which is accompanied by the offer of sufficient compensation for the thing demanded. Yet, it often happens that there exists a great demand in a society, with a corresponding offer, for a needed commodity, although the offer made is not enough to pay for the total needed labor. When this demand and offer bring about an invention which will most likely satisfy them, then the invention is again a great advantage to society, even though it may momentarily make those suffer who worked at a higher price, for a lesser number of buyers.

When, from the eighth to the tenth century, Arab traders brought from China to the West the art of making paper, if the same Arabs had also brought from the same country the art of printing,—which would seem so natural, that one is almost astonished that it did not happen,—printing, brought to Europe at a time when there was no eagerness to study, no demand for books, would have plunged Europe into even greater barbarity than that in which it already wallowed, because it would have totally extinguished the copier's trade.[8] These men preserved then the feeble remainders of a love for letters. They lived by copying missals and some religious books; they were thus compelled to studies that gave them a taste for other, more refined studies. After having copied many pious books, they also copied some classics, so as to provide in that way for the demand of a very small number of men who, in all of Europe, were capable of reading them. The printer, with two typesetters and two printers much less learned than the copyists, would have produced what a thousand copyists could have done. Therefore, one printshop would have supplied all religious books, and perhaps some trade posters; but, by making all copyists die of hunger, it would not have let them continue to serve the small number of scholars who demanded other things, and who could not have, alone, supported the trade.[9] One would find in Italy and Spain more than one province where printing has had really no other effect. In the tenth century, printing would not have taught reading any more than the art of making paper taught to write.

actual social organization, it is the dependency of the worker that brings him to work, not less, but more hours per day, for the same wages, while the machine enhances his powers of production.

Happily for learning, happily for us, and happily also for the breed of copyists of the Middle Ages, printing was discovered only in a century where the love of learning had made universal progress. Everybody wanted books, even though few were in a position to buy them; the supporters of learning set aside a considerable income to obtain for themselves literary enjoyments, though this income was not in any way sufficient to pay for the immense efforts of the copyists. A wonderful invention enabled those who replaced the copyists to produce in the same time 250 times more output than they, at the very moment when that output was demanded by a new public, disposing of a new income. The number of printers in Europe is much larger than that of the copyists in the tenth century. This number of printers has been often cited as proof of the effect of machines to increase demand as well as output; but the effect should not be mistaken for the cause.

Even if demand is not quite as marked as that for books, at the time of the invention of printing; [whenever a discovery, economizing labour, brings within the reach of a poorer class what was previously confined to the rich, it extends the market; and whilst benefiting undertakers, and poor consumers, it does no harm to workmen. But when the discovery cannot increase the number of consumers, though it serves them at a cheaper rate; either because they are already all furnished, or because the thing produced can never be useful to them, however low it may fall,—the discovery] made for the profit of the factory owner[10] and not for his workers, creates merely a monopoly, and [becomes a human calamity; because it is advantageous but to a certain manufacturer, and that only at the expense of his brethren, or it benefits a single nation, and that only at the expense of others. This national benefit, if purchased at the expense of wretchedness and famine to foreign artisans, would not in itself be much worth coveting; it is, besides, very far from being certain. From the progress of communication between different states, from the skill of manufacturers, a discovery in one country is initiated in every other before the former has gained any great profit by it.][11]

It has been answered [that whoever introduces a saving in any article of this consumption, preserving still the same revenue, will consume what he saves from the fall of price in such and such an article, by a new expenditure, for which he will put in requisition a new labour. But there never will be any proportion between this new demand and the labour suspended on account of it.

On one hand, consumers make use of goods a little finer, a little prettier, at the same price. The clothes with which the poor workman is dressed, are a little superior in quality, are really worth a little more than those which covered his father, at the expense of the same part of his wages.

But he himself does not perceive this advantage;] it is in some way a social obligation [to dress like his equals, without finding more enjoyment; he makes no saving in this article, he cannot apply it to any other expense.*

On the other hand, the price of goods is not always established in direct proportion to the labour they require, but in a very complicated proportion subsisting between this annual labour, the circulating capital, and a primary, unrenewed labour, consumed in building the manufactory, constructing the machinery with expensive and often foreign materials. Hence, even when a hundred workmen are dismissed, that the work may be done with one by means of machinery, the goods are not reduced to the hundredth part of their price. The stocking-frame economizes work nearly in this proportion, yet it scarcely produces stockings ten percent cheaper than those made with the needle. Notwithstanding the invention of large mills for spinning wool, silk, cotton, women continue to be employed in spinning with the wheel, or even with the distaff; a certain proof that the saving] made by employing water and fire in their production instead of people [does not exceed ten percent. The same observation may be extended to all improved manufactures; they have never diminished the price of their produce, except in arithmetical progression, while they have suspended workmanship in geometrical progression.

Let us compare this saving in workmanship with the saving in price, according to the most simple calculation on the commonest manufacture;] let us assume, for more clarity, that a worker, with the stocking frame, produces exactly the output a hundred workers produced before. If he does not, the defenders of machines would want that he did, and the argument will not be any less conclusive. [A hundred thousand women, who knit with the needle each a hundred pair of stockings annually, produce ten million pairs; which, at 5s a-piece, would sell at 2,500,000*l*: the raw material is worth a fifth of this. There remains 2,000,000 to distribute among 100,000 workmen, or 20*l* pound a-head.[12]

The same work is done at present on the frame by 1000 workmen, and comes in ten percent cheaper, 4s.6d a pair, or 2,250,000*l* in all.] The

*It is said that the Emperor Alexander, astonished to see, in England, that the entire population that surrounded him was wearing stockings, shoes and dress tolerably similar to that of a proper burgher, exclaimed in surprise: "Where are the poor? Are there no poor people in this country?" However, more than one-half of these individuals, whom custom forced to spend a good deal for their clothing, had no other property than the wages they would receive that Saturday for the entire week; and more than a tenth of them were helped by their parish. There would be more independence and more happiness for the poor, to walk barefoot, or in wooden shoes, and owning a cottage, some fields, a garden and two cows, like the majority of the peasants on the Continent.

consumer [therefore saves 250,000 pounds. If employed solely in workmanship, this sum would be sufficient to maintain 12,500 of the workers who have been dismissed] and there would be only the seven-eighths who remain in the street; [but this is not what happens; the consumer, accustomed to buy stockings at 5s a pair, pays still the same price; but, by reason of the progress of the art, he merely wears them a little finer. This progress in his luxury gives subsistence to a tenth more stocking manufactures, that is to a hundred more; to these add still farther a hundred workmen employed] every year [in repairing the machines, or constructing new ones, and you have in all 1200 workmen living on the sum which supported 100,000.]

The price of ten million pairs of stockings produced does not contain, as before, four-fifths of manual labor. This can be broken down only by a guess, and we do not attach any importance to this hypothetical calculation.[13] Five hundred thousand pounds will always pay for the raw material; 1,500,000 pounds will pay the interest and profit of the fixed capital invested in the frames and the buildings where they stand; 100,000 pounds will be used annually for repair and replacement of machines; 100,000 will be profit of circulating capital, which must always be larger when the enterprise is conducted on a large scale, and the remaining 50,000 pounds will pay the worker's wages. Thus the income created by the production will be diminished rather than increased.

[The same calculation is applicable to all improved manufactures; for the manufacturer, in adopting a new machine, and dismissing his workmen, never troubles himself with inquiring whether he shall make a profit equal to the diminution of workmanship, but merely whether he shall be enabled to sell a little cheaper than his rivals. All the workmen of England would be turned to the street, if the manufacturers could employ steam engines in their place, with a saving of five percent.

Besides, the improvement of machinery, and the economy of human labour contribute immediately to diminish the number of national consumers; for all the ruined workmen were consumers. In the country, the introduction of the large farming system has banished from Great Britain the class of peasant farmers, who laboured themselves, and yet enjoyed an honest plenty. The population has been considerably diminished, but its consumption is reduced still farther than its number. The hands perform all sorts of field labour, are limited to the scantiest necessaries, and give not nearly so much encouragement to the industry of towns as the rich peasants gave before.

A similar change has taken place in the population of towns. Discoveries in the mechanical arts have always the remote result of concentrating industry within the hands of a smaller number of merchants. They enable men to perform with an expensive machine, that is to say, with great capital, what was formerly performed with a great labour. They discover the economy which exists in management on a great scale, the division of operation, the employment common to a great number of men at once, of light, fuel, and all the powers of nature. Thus small merchants, small manufacturers disappear; and our great undertaker supplies the place of hundreds, who, all together, perhaps, were not as rich as he. All together were, however, better consumers than he. His expensive luxury gives far less encouragement to industry than the honest plenty of a hundred households, of which his household supplies the place.]

As long as always-new demands have made manufactures prosper, one has seen, [the number of labourers, in spite of augmented powers of labour, increases likewise; and such as were dismissed from the country found still an establishment in manufacturing towns, the population of which continued to increase. But now when at last the market of the universe has been found sufficiently provided for, and new reductions of workmen have occurred; when hands have been dismissed from the fields, spinners from the manufactories of cotton, weavers from those of cloth; when each day a new machine supplies the place of several families whilst no new demand offers them an occupation or a livelihood; distress has reached its height, and one might begin to regret the progress of this civilization, which, by collecting a greater number of individuals in the same space of ground, has but multiplied their wretchedness, whilst in deserts it could at least but reach a small number of victims.][14]

The moment has finally come to ask where we want to go. According to the latest census, agriculture employs in England 770,199 families; this is in proportion, not only to the amount of territory, but also to the size of the product, infinitely less than in any other part of Europe; should a reward be offered to him who will find a means to produce the same output with 70,000 families, and to him who will do it with 7,000?

In England, trade and manufactures employ 959,632 families, and this number is sufficient to provide all manufactured goods, not only for England, but further for one half of Europe, and half of the civilized inhabitants of America. England is a vast manufacture which, in order to maintain itself, is obliged to sell to almost the whole known world. Must a reward be offered to whoever will find a way to produce the same output with 90,000 families, and to him who will produce it with 9,000? If England would succeed in performing all the work in its fields, and that of the cities, by steam driven machinery, and have no more inhabitants than the Republic of Geneva, while maintaining the same output and the same income, such as it is today, must one regard it as richer and more prosperous?*

Well, such reward is offered continually through the competition of all manufacturers, of all farmers, to him who will teach how to dispense with people. This reward is offered in the same way on the Continent, by all the nations which believe themselves obligated to follow England on its course in manufacturing. Governments have in this respect supported with all their powers the zeal of manufacturers, and the political writers, far from pointing to the dangers of such competition, have made it their business to spur the nations on.

After a discovery in the arts has increased the productive powers of man, it would doubtless be desirable that it be prevented from turning against those it ought to serve.[18] If it is not prompted by any new demand for labor, if it does not put the goods produced within reach of new consumers, it would be desirable that at a minimum it would not replace, and not render useless, a given number of producers, either national or foreign. But there exists no means to raise a direct obstacle against the revolution it will bring about; it would be both useless and dangerous to try and suppress the invention itself. If we hinder in our factories the introduction of a new machine, our neighbors would not be as scrupulous, they would make war against our workers with their steam engines, their

*Mr. Ricardo answers firmly in the affirmative; and, although this be the necessary consequence of the system he follows, I am still confounded that in facing it, he has not shrunk from such a conclusion. His very words must be quoted to be quite sure not to attribute to him ideas he would disown. "The whole produce of the land and labour of every country is divided into three portions: of these, one portion is devoted to wages, another to profits, and the other to rent. It is from the last two portions only, that any deductions can be made for taxes, or for savings; the former, if moderate, constituting always the necessary expenses of production.[15] To an individual with a capital of £20,000, whose profits were £2,000 per annum, it would be a matter quite indifferent whether this capital would employ a hundred or thousand men, whether the commodity produced, sold for £10,000, or for for £20,000, provided, in all cases, his profits were not diminished below £2,000. Is not the real interest of the nation similar? Provided its net real income, its rent and profits be the same, it is of no importance whether the nation consists of ten or of twelve millions of inhabitants? and so on." Indeed? Wealth is everything, men are absolutely nothing? What? Wealth itself is only something in relation to taxes? In truth, then there is nothing more to wish for than that the king, remaining alone on the island, by constantly turning a crank, might produce, through automata, all the output of England.[16]

It can be noted that Doctor Quesnay, in distinguishing the net product from the gross product, and by giving credence to the opinion that only the former had importance, has been the first author of a doctrine so fatal to mankind: at least he has never drawn such grievous conclusions.[17]

spinning machines, and all their new inventions; this is a war to death where one is forced to defend oneself, but where one is imprudent to begin.

No spectacle is perhaps more astonishing, more frightening, than that presented by England, in the midst of that wealth that at first dazzles the eyes. If one is not content alone to judge it by the colossal fortunes of its peers of the realm, to whom twenty thousand pounds in rents is but a mediocre income; if one appraises at its proper value, and in accordance with the benefits it provides, the offensive luxury they display, with their magnificent coaches, their numberless lackeys running through the streets, their staffs elevated, their fox-hunting suites, in which twenty horses and forty dogs cost them more than one hundred thousand pounds a year, one feels some indignation in comparing this extravagance to the sufferings of the poor. Bands of beggars fired from the factories tramp along the highways, alternating with bands of ragged Irishmen, who go from farm to farm, offering to perform all the tasks of agriculture at the lowest wages. Neither ask for alms unless they are denied work, but all places are filled. The farmworker, the *cottager*, sees with bitterness these strangers dispute him a task which before was barely enough to support him. In the towns, in the capital, at the corner of Hyde Park, where the most magnificent coaches follow each other with lightning speed, troops of ten and twenty factory hands sit, motionless, despair in their eyes, fever draining all their limbs, and draw not even a moment of notice. A third of all factories is already closed, another third will have to close soon, and all warehouses are overfull; on all sides goods are offered for sale at a discount that leaves not even enough to pay one half of invoice cost:[19] and all letters from South America declare that the huge cargos trade had brought there, can scarcely be sold for a price that covers the freight; in this worldwide distress, where the worker is thrown out everywhere, and the English nation has given over his place to the steam engine that performs the work done before by men, rewards are still offered to the inventor of new machinery that would make those workers useless who still find a livelihood. Surely, it seems that, in the midst of so much suffering, one ought to refrain from encouraging those who, at this moment at least, cannot but increase it again. The suppression of privileges given to the inventor of new processes in industry, would perhaps not change much the progress of *scientific capability*, as it has been properly called, but it would relieve the poor workers of the feeling that, in their misery, the government is also in league against them.

We have seen elsewhere that the consequence of the privilege conferred on an inventor is to give him a market monopoly against his fellow producers. This results in national consumers gaining very little benefit therefrom, the inventor gaining a great deal from what the other producers lose, and that their workers die from misery. According to business policy, which is hardly Christian, one saw this evil so to speak offset by the consequences of the invention in foreign markets. The new producer gained much there, the foreign consumers gained therefrom a little; but the foreign producers lost by it, their workers perished, and thus a formidable competition was gotten rid of.[20]

Without going into this question from the moral viewpoint, it will be enough for us to say that the pecuniary calculus has changed. The sciences have made too much progress for an invention to remain hidden from the scientists of another country, who, informed of its existence, will undertake to research it. Foreigners will imitate our inventions before our own compatriots, hindered by the patent of the inventor, can adopt it; thus the evil we will do to others, will not compensate us for what we will do to ourselves; this would be sinning from an inclination to disregard evil.

If, on the contrary, all inventions are immediately made public, immediately given over to imitation by all the rivals of the inventor, the zeal for similar discoveries will be cooled, and then they will no longer be regarded as an expedient by which one can steal from one's competitors new tricks, but solely as a means to supply to their very own all the work they will ask for when demand will begin to increase.

However, nothing can prevent that every new discovery in the applied mechanical arts decreases by as much the manufacturing population. This is a danger to which it is constantly exposed, and against which the social order offers no remedy. At least this is a potent reason to wish that in a state such a population not be numerous, and for not raising a people with the intention to make them the manufacturers and shopkeepers of the world.

Translator's Notes to Chapter 7, Seventh Book

It was Sismondi's declared intention to point the way to a more humane social order, an order in which human happiness would be maximized. To that end, he stressed again and again the need for developmental balance between population, capital, and land. In this chapter, almost at the end of *New Principles,* he undertakes to analyze technological change, and its impact (mostly negative, in his estimation) on that balance. About half of the chapter is taken from the *Encyclopedia,* indicating that Sismondi, far from merely expounding settled principles of political economy there, as he would have it, was already then much concerned with dynamic change and its perceived deleterious effects on established social institutions. Drawing on English experience to further support his arguments against rapid and uncontrolled technological change, he pulls together diffuse concepts from preceding books and chapters in *New Principles* to describe all basic Marxian categories of capitalistic exploitation—the reserve army, the descent of the small producer into the proletariat, surplus value, and the so-called *dialectic* movement of society, showing them to be responses to the tensions arising between technological change and established property relationships. In this chapter, also, the much quoted sentence about the king of England working a crank, creating the entire product of the nation by robots, appears (in a note). The chapter, written between 1818 and 1826, has a contemporary ring because it adresses a condition quite similar to the present, second technological revolution, of the computer, and the associated changes in resource uses. Sismondi offers here no remedy for technological displacement, except to suggest that the abolition of patent protection might slow the pace of technological change. He recognizes, rightly, that technological invention is unstoppable once it is set in train; hence the remedies will have to be sought elsewhere in the social order, such as the increase of leisure in step with the increase of productivity that he mentions in passing in the first note of the chapter. His failure to advance a comprehensive alternative to capitalistic production must be seen as the major reason for his failure to change the course of political economy.

1. The term *"revolutions"* refers to movements of capital. 'Turnover' is the most appropriate English word. In the French text, "revolutions" is used, hence his translation.
2. This does not view the worker as the noble proletarian that later became the standard view under the influence of Marxism and socialism in general. The last sentence clearly indicates that Sismondi is an eighteenth-century rationalist who looks upon mankind as an entity which is divided by accidents of birth and employment.
3. The remark points up the major difference between Sismondi and the classical writers, that is, Ricardo, Say, and McCulloch. The latter looked upon political economy as a manifestation of natural laws to be discovered. It is Sismondi's position everywhere that society does not operate like a physical universe, but its operation is a function of human will, and therefore alterable. His rejection of the Malthusian theorem as a basis for the subsistence theory of wages in the first chapter of this book is one programmatic statement of this position. In human affairs there is nothing determined by unalterable laws; effects may follow logically from preceding actions, but the actions themselves are human choices; compared to Ricardo, Say, and later Marx, Sismondi is the champion of free will. This position is mainly responsible for a less-than-rigorous theoretical analysis, but it brings out views of human relationships that are original and insightful.
4. The distinction made here became of course, in time, a general separation that culminated in Marshall's *Economics*. Sismondi sees this from the continental European point of view which was essentially different from English ideas. Especially, the French tradition of juridical administration favored a separation of political and economic concerns.
5. Again, echoes can be heard of the Genevese Revolution and the terror Sismondi experienced, but historical knowledge of the disorders that had accompanied the ancien régime is very much in evidence.
6. Philosophical inquiry and inquisitiveness were most likely meant, but the sentence could also refer to entrepreneurial vigor and risk seeking.
7. The note was added to the second edition. Sismondi condensed into this note two ideas, one of which was destined to make an illustrious career with another author, the other to become a tenet of modern consumption economics. First, Marx's analysis of the source of surplus value is clearly outlined, including the idea that it is the power of the capitalist that keeps the worker at his task over and above what he would have produced otherwise. Second, the idea that

leisure for the worker must be increased with increased productivity, a commonplace enough idea now, was most revolutionary for Sismondi's time. It should be noted that no value theory is used to make this point; this should make it clear that the labor theory of value Marx considers the analytical basis of his work is irrelevant to the problem.

8. Sismondi, as usual, overstated the case in order to make a point. Printing was known in Europe, probably brought in from China; however, it was not printing with movable type, but woodblock printing, only minimally suited to producing books. Woodblocks were used to produce broadsheets where an illustration of a curious event was accompanied by some text, for example, the appearance of a comet. The copiers in the monasteries exerted great political pressure to keep even these manifestations of mass production from the market, usually on the pretext that holy texts should be reproduced only by hand with ink and quill. It is possible that the copier's trade would have disappeared quickly, but a greater supply of books would have stimulated more reading, if printing with movable type had come on the scene earlier. This particular narrative is one more example of historical construction that was not only used by Sismondi, but equally by Adam Smith, Ricardo, and other writers in social thought, including Marx. The analysis uses here and elsewhere in the chapter the essentially mercantilistic idea of a limited demand that is totally inelastic. Only autonomous changes in tastes are assumed to change this condition.
9. This gives an almost classic description of the dilemma modern publishing houses face, as, for example, in the publication of this translation. The market for such books is very limited, and the costs must be defrayed by books that have mass appeal, if the price of the specialty items is not to become prohibitive. Again, Sismondi assumes the most extreme result. It is very unlikely that the copyists would have died of hunger, because they were monks, worked in monasteries, and would have continued their existence as monks, even if copying had stopped from one day to the next.
10. The text reads "chef d'atelier." Sismondi makes the tacit assumption here, quite appropriate for his time, that the owner came to manufacturing because he had some invention of his own he wanted to produce and sell.
11. This offhand remark on the transferability of technology shows that Sismondi was a free-trader who knew from his historical researches that inventions cannot be bottled up in any one nation for any appreciable amount of time.
12. In *New Principles*, Sismondi uses the amounts 5 francs, 50,000,000 francs, 40,000,000 francs, and 400 francs per head, respectively, making a franc equal to one shilling.
13. The same ratio of francs to shillings was used here to make this paragraph correspond to the previous one, which came from the *Encyclopedia*.
14. This paragraph is the last one in the *Encyclopedia*. In the next chapter, Sismondi goes back to use some earlier material from the *Encyclopedia* regarding population, but essentially, all that follows from this point on is new material. The beginning of the next paragraph clearly indicates that Sismondi is prepared to begin a summing up, and an exposition of his own ideas.
15. Sismondi's reference to Ricardo is to his *Principles*, chapter 26, pp. 336–37. Ricardo appended here a footnote indicating that the allocation may change and the laborer may receive part of the net produce of the country. Sismondi omitted any mention of the footnote.
16. This is one of the most quoted remarks from the *New Principles*. It seems to

have special applicability to every period when deep-reaching technological changes transform production methods and social relations. Sismondi could not foresee, or indeed imagine, that new production methods might create new jobs which would absorb not only the existing labor force, but indeed a much larger one. On the other hand, he is more sensitive to the human costs incurred in such fundamental shifts, and seeks to minimize them.

17. The last paragraph was added in the second edition.
18. This paragraph was rewritten, probably to make a better transition to the following discussion to the end of the chapter, which is entirely new to the second edition. These paragraphs are clearly related to English visits after the appearance of the first edition, and to the developments there that Sismondi could follow from Geneva by correspondence with his in-laws, and of course from reports in the daily press.
19. This is the earliest description of a typical inventory depression in a full-fledged business cycle, the first of the Industrial Revolution. It is basically not different from descriptions of later ones, supporting the thesis that industrial business cycles are based on a combination of overproduction and underconsumption, leaving open the crucial question of the main causative factor. Sismondi tends to blame overproduction, due to increased productivity through the introduction of new technology, but the repeated stress on the importance of demand brings in the question of market satiation. He would seem to be the first writer who recognized the possibility that consumption had temporary limits that, in the short run, circumscribed saleable output, even though Say's Law suggested that expansion of production expanded pari passu also consumption. The mercantilists and Adam Smith recognized the limitations inherent in the "extent of the market," but their discussion proceeded in the context of a merchant-craft economy in which demand is of lesser importance, or can be assumed to be limitless vis-à-vis limited production. Sismondi is the first political economist to introduce the notion of "unwanted production," output made possible by new machinery, but not saleable due either to limitations of income, or unfavorable consumption habits. It must be remembered that he postulates at the beginning of the work that the income of the previous year buys the output of the current year, hence there may be inadequate income to clear increased production.
20. This remark anticipates Lenin's idea of imperialism as the highest stage of capitalism, and the need of capitalistic economies to colonize foreign markets. (*New Principles* was translated early into German and Russian, and there existed in Russia groups that advocated Sismondian principles.) To Sismondi, there is nothing conspirational or deliberate about such a movement of goods; it is merely a consequence of an assumed increased interdependence brought about by increased productivity allied to improved transportation. He assumed at all times that eventually an integrated world market would establish itself, with global limitations on consumption and production.

8

How Government Must Defend the Population against the Effects of Competition

The reader will have noted that the main difference between the ideas we are advancing, and those Adam Smith has expounded, is that the latter has always rejected government intervention in everything connected with the increase of national wealth, and we have often asked for it. He had proven in principle that the freest competition would force every producer to sell at the lowest possible price, and consequently allow every consumer to make the largest savings on his purchases. He had considered wealth in the abstract, without reference to the people who ought to enjoy it; and, in this system, he had perhaps reason to conclude that in producing the largest output possible, and selling it at the lowest possible price, the first action would increase incomes, and the second would decrease the expenditures of society.[1]

The most perfect competition must have inevitably one or the other of these results. But, if one begins to consider political economy as relating to population as well as to wealth, if one has sought, not what leads to the greatest opulence, but what would give humanity the greatest happiness through opulence, one must be frightened by the very thing that had been wished for from the very first. To work as much as possible. and sell at the lowest price, means to forego all the benefits of the wealth that has been sought; it means adding to one's toil, and taking away from one's enjoyments; it means changing citizens into slaves, so as to have the benefit of adding ever greater sums to the balance sheet of the nation.

Government has been established to protect, by the authority of the whole, everyone against the abuses of everyone else. It opposes the public interest to all private interests. It does so, not because the men who compose it derive from their superior rank any superior knowledge, but because it has called to its service everyone's knowledge, as it has everyone's authority. Justice is the expression of such enlightenment. The will of all those who are enlightened enough to understand what constitutes the good of all, concurs to consecrate the rights of everyone, to protect them by the establishment of laws and courts. However, justice, at the same time it is the greatest good of all, is opposed to the private interest of each, because that interest would always teach one to usurp the possessions of his neighbor. Political economy is another expression of social enlightenment. In the same way, it teaches to separate the interest of all, namely, that no one be worn out by labor, no one be deprived of his reward, from the self-interest of each, namely, to attract to himself all the rewards of labor, and while producing the most possible, to make it at the lowest possible price.

Thus, the task of government, as protector of the population, is to set everywhere limits to the sacrifices which everyone could be forced to make on his own; to prevent that a man, after having worked ten hours daily, would agree to work twelve, fourteen, sixteen, and eighteen hours; to prevent, likewise, that after having demanded substantial nourishment, animal as well as vegetable, he content himself with dry bread, and finally with potatoes and thin gruels; to prevent, finally, that in always outbidding his neighbor, he lowers himself to the most frightful misery.

This task is difficult; it is complicated; it must be joined to the greatest respect for individual liberty. But it must never be forgotten that, among the rights which constitute that liberty, there are many which are social grants, which would be unknown to the savage, and which ought to be tempered by the same public authority that guarantees them. We have indicated, while discussing the progress of each type of wealth, the protection against competition the government owes to the people. We shall, in this chapter, only briefly recapitulate these diverse functions.

[When peasants are proprietors,] and when there are no more uncultivated lands which can be cleared by the first holder, [the agricultural population stops of itself, when it has brought about a division of land, such that each family is invited to labour, and may live in comfortable circumstances.][2] From then on, [when two or more sons are found in one family, the younger do not marry till they can find wives who bring them some property.] If they leave their father's house, [they work day-labour; but among peasant-cultivators the trade of day-labour does not afford a rank;[3] and the workman who has nothing but his limbs, can rarely find a father imprudent enough to give him his daughter.

When the land, instead of being cultivated by its proprietors, is cultivated by farmers, métayers, day-labourers, the condition of the latter classes becomes more precarious, and their multiplication is not so necessarily adjusted to the demand for labour. They are far worse informed than the peasant proprietor, and yet they are called to perform a much more complicated calculation. Living under the risk of being dismissed at a day's notice from the land they till, it is less a question with them what this land will give, than what is their chance of being employed elsewhere. They calculate probabilities in place of certainties, and commit themselves to fortune with regard to what they cannot investigate. They depend on being happy, they marry much younger; and they bring into the world many more children, precisely because they know less distinctly how those children are to be established.] Thus, with respect to the agricultural population, government's main task consists of[4] assuring to those who work a share in the property, or of giving preference to the cultivation I have called patriarchal over all others. The very great estates can never be cultivated in this way. Legislation therefore ought to lean towards their division, taking care of the general interest by halting an infinite division, and the efforts of cleverer men to continually reestablish great fortunes. However, since out of regard for liberty, the legislator can use only general and indirect means, the task limits itself to give to real estate the greatest possible salability, to maintain the division of inheritances in families, to prohibit all reservations, all perpetual entail that tie down estates, and to give to ownership of land advantages that would make every peasant resolve to make the acquisition of a small patrimony the goal of his ambitions.

These indirect measures, helped by the vigorous support of society, will have by themselves a great influence in repairing a disorder which, until now, has been protected by the full authority of governments. But, when this disorder is already deeply entrenched, when lands are united in immense estates, as in the Roman Empire in its decline, in the Papal States, and in England; when the landlords use the power of monopoly against the day laborers, whom they compel to outbid each other, and to finally offer to work for the most pitiable wages; when, at the same time, they profit from the advantages of massed capital, production planned on a large scale, and economic management, to make the position of the small proprietors and farmers untenable, legislation must come more directly to the help of the latter. It must do this in the interest of the working class, the whole nation, the great landlords themselves, who will find themselves ruined in turn when they will have succeeded in destroying the people they harry out.

An Elizabethan statute, not enforced, forbids to build, in England, a cottage without allocating to it at least a parcel of land of four acres.*[5] If

*Cited by Malthus, *Principles of Population,* Book IV, Chapt. XI, and Fifth Edition, Book IV, Chapt. XIII.

this law had been enforced, no marriages would have taken place among the day laborers without their having a cottage, and no cottager would have been reduced to the ultimate degree of wretchedness. This is something, but it is not in any way enough; in England's climate, a peasant population would live in poverty with four acres per family.*[6]

In a last chapter, we will inquire whether there is no general rule which ought to protect the working population, on the land as well as in the cities, against the competitive folly to which the actual organization of society exposes them. But, before having found this remedy, we feel already that the difficulty to provide for the fate of the poor workers of the land is not at all insurmountable, even in England, where today the confusion is the most threatening. It is very much more difficult to provide for the existence of the poor city workers. The imagination recoils from their number and misery; and, among the calamities that afflict them, there are some which seem to be beyond remedy.

[The industrious[7] population which inhabit towns have still fewer data than those of the country, for calculating the lot of the succeeding generation. The workman knows only that he has lived by his labour; he naturally believes that his children will do likewise. How can he judge of the extent of the market, or the general demand for labour in his country, whilst the master who employs him is incessantly mistaken on these points? Accordingly, this class, more dependent than any other on chances of every kind for its subsistence, is exactly the class which calculates those chances the least in the formation of a family. They are the people who marry soonest, produce most children, and consequently lose most; but they do not lose their children, till after being themselves exposed to a competition which deprives them successively of all the sweets of life.][8]

We have shown elsewhere the protection that this unhappy class found at other times in the establishments of guilds and masters; and the type of certainty it acquired when a worker was made master, and found himself from that moment on in a position to maintain a family. It is not the guilds' strange and oppressive organization whose reestablishment is here at

*Today, the English cottagers have for the most part only an acre and a half, or two acres of land, for which they pay a fairly high rent; in Scotland, where the land is poorer and the climate more unfavorable, their portion is hardly larger, and it is again less in Ireland. This subdivision of land is not at all the result of divisions of inheritances, it is entirely the work of the lord; in Ireland in particular, it is the result of the wishes of the lords to have a large number of poor freeholders[11] who vote in accordance with their orders in the county elections. This is another reason that the law ought to oppose the creation of such a wretched population, engineered by the aristocracy for an entirely political end, to force the lord, when he divides the land among many cottagers, to give to each enough land for a livelihood.

stake. Experience's lessons would be of little value if, after having misled us, we only seek to pursue blindly the old paths of our fathers, without seeking a better way. But what the legislator must seek above all, is to raise the wages of industrial labor, to extricate day workers from the precarious conditions in which they live, to finally ease for them the achievement of what they call a *status;*[9] because a universal experience has taught us that in every situation the majority of the poor as well as the rich does not marry unless each has attained that measure of independence at which it can reasonably aim. The son of the farmer or sharecropper only marries when he has secured a farm or shareholding. The son of the cottager or day worker, only when he has a cottage; the small shopkeeper, when he has opened a store; the craftsman when he has started his workshop. If we will offer to the factory worker a higher status, where he may and must naturally advance by his labor, we can be almost certain that he will not marry till after he has obtained that advancement.

The most detrimental change occurred in the condition of the day worker, be it because of the abolition of the guilds, or because of the establishment of large manufactures that employ vast amounts of capital, as well as all the sciences and many hands; it is since then that workers live and die as workers, whereas before the status of a worker was but a preparation to achieve a higher status. It is opportunity of advancement which must necessarily be reestablished. Masters must be given an incentive to help their workers achieve a higher position; it is essential that the man who, indeed, begins work in a factory for nothing more than his wages, has before him at all times the hope to share, through his good conduct, in the profits of the enterprise.

The manufacturing class would, without a doubt, be much happier if, after a probationary period, it would come to possess a right of ownership in the business to which it gives its sweat, as salesmen finally come to have an interest in the firm of their employer; if one half of the profits were thus distributed among the employed workers, the other half going to the providers of capital, and if the workers aspiring to such progress would never marry till they were made partners. But this utopia may very well be the object of the legislator's wishes; it will be with difficulty that of his legislation.[10]

It remains to us then to search, for the workers in the cities as for those on the land, what principle of law and justice society must protect in the worker, against the forces of competition that tend forever to reduce him below his subsistence. This principle must be common to all types of labor, and it must set just bounds between the claims of the worker and those who employ him. If we can discover it and make it known to everyone, we shall believe to have done well by humanity.

Translator's Notes to Chapter 8, Seventh Book

A great deal of mercantilistic thought appears in Sismondi's writing, moderated by physiocratic and Smithian ideas. This chapter finally makes clear that, all along, he had advanced ideas different from either Smith or mercantilism. Sismondi, obviously inspired by what he remembers as ideal Genevese conditions, wants to create a society of freeholders both on the land and in the city, small property holders who take an interest in their political and economic condition. Since he does not believe in the truth of Say's Law, or the self-equilibrating powers of the market, he must again turn to government as the representative of the collective will that is responsible for the maximization of social happiness. But, importantly, he feels government can use only indirect means and must respect individual liberty in its efforts to regulate the economy. As a constant opponent of economic concentration Sismondi wants what today would be called agricultural reforms, that is, the division of large estates, and what in the twentieth century has become one of the latest innovations of industrial progress, worker participation in manufacturing. He comes to this solution from his appreciation of guild organization, but goes beyond it in recognizing that the new age of increased division of labor demands new institutions. Trade unions did not yet exist when *New Principles* was published, but this chapter leaves little doubt that Sismondi would have favored them as a counter to capital concentration. He becomes, therefore, a champion of economic individualism, tempered by a regard for collective happiness. Today he would likely feel most at home in nations like Sweden, Denmark, or Holland (and of course, modern Switzerland), that combine a regard for individual freedom with limitations of economic markets. Not accidentally, these nations resemble Sismondi's Geneva—they are small and have representative-democratic political structures with broad direct participation of the individual, and with economic arrangements that protect citizens against undeserved hardships. In 1826, such ideas were either quite unfamiliar, or were rejected as hopelessly romantic or revolutionary. In the next chapter these ideas will be further extended.

1. Smith is obviously right, as stated, but Sismondi wants to make a point here, and in doing so he misrepresents the man he considered his mentor and guide. Adam Smith rightly believed that increasing the wealth of a nation by competition would benefit every individual by providing a higher living standard and greater satisfactions, because each consumer would be free to arrange his life in accordance with his own preferences. So does Sismondi. But the difference between him and Smith lies rather in Smith's assumption that "what is prudence in the conduct of every private family, can scarce be folly in that of a great kingdom" (book 4, chapter 2, *Wealth*). Sismondi rejects this assumption, but he does so in an ambiguous way, never clearly stating that such a transition from individual to society is not permissible on logical grounds. Here lies the main reason for the accusation that Sismondi lacks analytical rigor, but it also reflects the difficulty he had as a pioneer in freeing himself totally from the received wisdom of classical analysis. His main target is Ricardo, because Ricardian analysis posed the problem of individual versus society in stark contrast by stripping away the accommodating language Smith used. But the categories are nevertheless those of Smith, and Sismondi in a way acknowledges this with this remark.
2. In the *Encyclopedia* this sentence is followed by: "This is the case in almost all the Swiss cantons, which follow nothing but agriculture." This approach

stands in stark contrast to Malthus's theorizing, and is a clear reflection of a quite different cultural environment. Birth control was widespread on the Continent among the peasant population, as is attested by population figures, especially for France after the Revolution, and Sismondi was apparently well aware of it. As noted before, his own late marriage must have appeared to him as a particularly valid example of happiness limitation due to economic considerations.

3. Status in the community, associated with landed property.
4. The following text was extensively changed from the first edition. The paragraph reads from here: "a réunir sans cesse la travail avec la propriété, à accélérer cette reunion par tous les moyens indirects de la législation, à donner la plus grande facilité pour les ventes d'immeubles, à maintenir la division des héritages dans les familles, a interdire tous les réserves, toutes les substitutions perpétuelles qui enchainent les propriétés, et à attacher à la possession des terres des avantages qui fassent que chaque paysan se propose l'acquisition d'un petit patrimoine comme but de son ambition."
5. Sismondi uses "cabane rustique," and supplies the translation in the text as 'cottage'.
6. The note is new to the second edition, another instance of a revision inspired by English experience since the first edition. Sismondi reflects in his writings again and again the severe dislocations in agriculture brought about by the Industrial Revolution in England. At the time of the publication of the second edition continental Europe was just beginning to receive English technology; the great movement from the land to the city had not yet begun. The Continental System had kept English goods and techniques out, but the Continental manufacturers had nevertheless not been able to transform substantially their production methods. Post-Napoleonic protectionism isolated countries' economies, with the result that, for example, Germany, with perhaps the exception of the Rhineland, was a romantic agricultural and preindustrial economy. *New Principles* also reflects this reality in its emphasis on agricultural examples, and concern with agricultural institutions.
7. The French text reads "La population industrielle," but since the paragraph is undoubtedly taken from the *Encyclopedia,* that reading has been retained. It may be a misprint because Sismondi was obviously quite fluent in English and would have known the difference between *industrious* and *industrial.*
8. This is the end of the last material used from the *Encyclopedia.*
9. In the first edition, Sismondi continued here: "et de leur interdire le mariage jusqu'à ce qu'ils y soient parvenus." This was another reference to his proposal, stated in chapter 6 (see note 6 there) to prohibit marriage to the poor. The remainder of this paragraph is new to the second edition.
10. Sismondi returns by indirection to his first thought of postponing marriage among the working class at all cost, finally recognizing that this is wishful thinking. However, it should be noted that his proposal to make the worker a shareholder in the business in which he works, revolutionary for his time, would hardly raise an eyebrow today. His most cherished goal of worker participation has become a widespread reality in most industrialized nations, with the notable exception of Marxist economies.
11. Similar to note 5, above, Sismondi uses "francs-tenanciers" and supplies his own translation.

9

The Worker Has the Right to Receive Job Security from His Employer

It is not a natural consequence of man's nature, or that of work, that the cooperation of the two classes of citizens oppose their interests,[1] in order to produce all kinds of output. I mean the class of proprietors of accumulated labor who do nothing, and the class of men who have only their natural strength, and who offer to work. Their separation, their opposition of interest, is a consequence of the artificial organization we have given to human society. All of our actions are subject to our review, and the authority of the legislator extends necessarily to the grievances flowing from his laws.

The cooperation of capital with labor is not the relationship I want to discuss here; it is the very nature of the matter, and does not depend on us.[2] But the natural order of social progress does not tend in any way to separate men from things, or wealth from labor. On the land, the owner could remain cultivator; in the cities, the capitalist could remain a craftsman; the separation of the class that works from the one that does not was not in any way essential either to the existence of society, or to production; we have introduced it for the greater benefit of everyone; it behooves us to regulate it so that we may truly reap its advantages.

In the social organization we have chosen, all work is done by the constant cooperation of these two classes, those who own wealth, and those who put it to work. No output is produced without wealth and labor. The worker is necessary to whoever pays him, as the payor is to the worker. One provides the livelihood of the other; hence, there exists, there ought to exist, at the least, a type of solidarity between them.

The land can be cultivated by its owner. He unites in his person the ownership of land, the ownership of capital that cultivates it, the ownership of labor that fertilizes it. We have seen sufficiently numerous examples to doubt that the land will be well cultivated in this way, that the farmer is happy, and society is abundantly supplied with provisions.

But the owner, in order to enjoy the leisure of wealth, prefers not to cultivate the land himself; he farms it out; the farmer, in turn, who became a great lord, does not want to work as a peasant anymore, he has his chores done by day laborers. Early on, society does not oppose itself to this in any way; it refrains from interference in individual transactions, but it need not accept in any way the damages therefrom. It has allowed idle landowners, fat farmers, to create, for their own use, as an accomodation to them alone, a new class in the nation, that of day workers on the land; it must not ever allow that this class becomes again a charge to the nation.

It is evident that there would not be any day workers, and consequently, no poor on the land, no poor rates on agriculture, if every landowner would cultivate his own land with his own hands; if his strength were insufficient, he would divide his lands among his children; and the class of peasant owners would grow to its natural limits, that is to say, just to where its manual strength would be adequate for the cultivation of the land.

When this order has been changed, and the owners have given their lands to another class of men to cultivate, and if these men have been themselves either farmers, or métayers, and have done all their work with their own hands in return for an enduring contract that gave them a right in the property they had cultivated, then again, there will not be any, or hardly any, poor on the land, and no poor rates on agriculture.

The great landowners, the large farmers, have brought into being the day workers they cannot do without. The property of the former is worth nothing without the latter; the latter are of no use to any other class of society, if they are not to the former. Thus there exists a commonality between the two, and the day workers ought to live solely from the wealth they create on the large estates. They can be left to negotiate the price of daily labor with the owners; but if this price is insufficient, if the family of the worker, after having received its wage, still finds itself forced to demand a supplement, the estate owner, or large farmer*, to whose benefit this class exists, is called upon to provide this supplement. In the entirely barbaric and inhumane society of feudal countries, of slaveholding countries, this basic principle of justice has not been ignored. Never has a lord

*I do not in any way distinguish between the landlords and the farmers when discussing the subsistence of the poor day workers. They act in concert; but the farmer pays his rent only in proportion to the net product, all costs of cultivation deducted, and the poor rates, being a supplement to the wage, must be counted as part of the costs of cultivation.

dreamt to make his vassals, his serfs, his slaves a burden of the province in their misfortunes, their old age, and their sicknesses; he has strongly felt that it was up to him alone to provide for the needs of those who experienced them only for his own benefit. Often, indeed, he has discharged this duty with the hard-heartedness and parsimony that must flow from such a heinous social organization; but in the system of large estates, the actual debtor throws this sacred obligation on to the backs of his compatriots.

Can one imagine a more unjust policy than to make the small landowner, the small farmer pay, under the name of poor rates, a supplement to the subsistence wages of workers who cultivate the fields of the wealthy? How do these day workers benefit the owners, the farmers, who hold the bars of their plows themselves, and who, without outside help, perform all the work in their fields with their children? How, on the contrary, can those who do not want to work themselves in any way, be deemed to be day workers? And is the wage subsidy the parish gives to their workers not as unjust as if the same parish were charged to furnish oats to their horses?

The large estate holders, the large farmers, make perhaps no real profits from the day workers, who exist only for them, and who ought to be paid only by them alone, being partly maintained by the parish; because that same parish of which they are members in turn, supports other day workers, for whom the landlords never ought to be responsible, those of the arts and crafts. It is indeed essential, above all, to separate the administration of charity for the rural poor from that for poor craftsmen; they were not plunged into misery by the same people, and they should not be helped by the same people.

But in the disorder that exists today, when all the poor are thrown on public charity without distinction, whether such charity is regulated by law as in England, or is left to humanitarian instincts, as in other countries, every wealthy man pushes the poor onto society, and actively worsens their condition, without taking into consideration that, as a member of that society, he will be called upon later to come to their help, either through parish taxes, or by voluntary contributions he will impose upon himself for the love of mankind. If everyone would experience in his own person the results of his own efforts, everyone would forego saving that part of wages he would soon be called upon to repay.

There exists a natural unity between the large farmer and all the workers needed to cultivate his farm. Once this is recognized, once the farmer knew that he alone would be called upon to provide their subsistence during their illnesses, their old age, or their misfortunes, he will soon seek that way of support that will be the least costly to him or society, and he will soon find that it is the one that will give them the most enduring interest in life, that will tie them in the best way to their own tillage, that will sustain their spirits, their health, their physical strength the most, and therefore comes closest to ownership.

Today he seeks to reduce their wages to the lowest possible rate, to receive for that wage the most work possible. If such labor exhausts them and they fall sick, the parish will care for them; if, during the course of employment there are dead seasons, the parish will provide for them; if the fields do not give suitable work to the women, children, and old people, the parish will care for them. By means of competition, the large farmer obtains the greatest possible amount of labor from the strongest men, in the best season, and for the least price, while he shares with the small farmers, and the freeholders, the obligation to provide income to the families of the workers, for all the labor he does not put to work. In these circumstances, it is impossible that the small farmer can withstand the competition of the large cultivator, and the system of large farms must spread.[3]

But if the large farmer or the estate owner knew that they will alone remain responsible, through the entire year, for the family of the farmhand they need, they have no more incentive to reduce his wages to the lowest level, or to extract from him more labor than his strength permits; it would not suit them anymore to select the most profitable season to do all work at once, but on the contrary, to distribute it over the course of the year, so that there be less idle time. It would not suit them to employ only the strongest worker, but to the contrary the whole family equally, and in accordance with their strengths. That being so, it will be better to have retainers rather than workers, to hire families by the year, rather than men by the week. It will be better for the landlord to have métayers, or working peasants, rather than large farmers; and perhaps it will again be better to hand over a share of the fields to those who cultivate them. Thus a direction diametrically opposed to what England follows today, would be impressed on all rural production; and everyone, having only his best interest in mind, would come closer to the systems we have shown previously to be the most appropriate to spread happiness among all classes of the nation.

We make no pretension whatever to advance a proposal on the poor laws, for a foreign country we know only imperfectly, and which would be moreover hardly inclined to accept such counsel; we limit ourselves to showing that exemption from the poor rates can be used as an encouragement for homesteading, and its increase for the large landlords can to the contrary offset for the state the ruinous advantage the latter possess in the system of large estates.

Welfare for the poor in agriculture should be completely independent from that for the poor in industry and trades. If the extent of the market in which every poor day worker offers his labor is the same as that of the parishes, the limitation of the rural poor to the parish could be maintained. The support of these poor would be exclusively laid on the taxes of the large farmers who employ them; they would have to provide everything the rural poor would need, but they would be completely exempt from contributing to the support of the poor industry has thrown on society. Every man who would cultivate by himself an inheritance of less than twenty-five acres, being entirely his property, ought to be exempt from the poor rates. Every farmer who would cultivate with his hands, with his family, or with his retainers, a farm of less than fifty acres, ought to be similarly exempt; and every encouragement must be given, by new laws, to the large landowners to transfer, through leasing of small plots, by emphyteutic leases, and by long-term sales, a share of their holdings into the hands of their day workers. These latter are already partly at their expense, but they would be so much more directly, if everyone who has his lands worked by day workers would be obliged singly to support, in their wretchedness, the hands he needs for this ruinous system of agriculture. On the other hand, whoever has ownership of ten acres of land, or holds twenty on lease, would not have any right to be helped by the parish; and if he proceeded to divide this small inheritance among his children, they, to whatever small share they were reduced, would have no right either.

Such a proposal will likely arouse the indignation of the great landlords who today, in England, alone exercise legislative power; it is nevertheless only just. The farmers and owners who cultivate their small farms with their own hands have no use for day workers; the great landlords alone have a need for their employment; they have created them, so they ought to support them. They would discover quickly that the most economical way would be to let them regain their status as owners;[4] since the system of large estates is only profitable because of the unfair division that was established between those who work and those who employ them, and because the real wages of those who work are paid, not only by those who employ them and advance their daily wage, but by the rest of society which is forced, at all times of need, to make up for the shabbiness of the wages. One would see almost immediately a leasing of small holdings, and the sale of large estates in small parcels, so common today in France, supersede the daily absorption of small farms into large ones in England.[5]

Perhaps there would still exist some difficulty to make the entire existing population of farm workers owners again, above all since the customary importation of Irish workers has increased its distress. But England luckily has the means to do much for its rural poor, by dividing among them its huge parish commons. In general the English today are reluctant to do that, fearing that they will again increase a wretched population. This is because they only know farms of four hundred acres, and the cottages to which belong only one or two acres. If their commons were divided into freeholds of twenty to thirty acres, they would witness the rebirth of this independent and proud class of countrymen, this yeomanry they mourn today as almost extinct.*

The same principle of commonality between the one who works and the one who puts him to work, can be extended to the industries of the cities. When guilds began, every man owned the capital with which he worked, and almost all the craftsmen lived on the income that comes equally from wages and profits. The blacksmith himself supplied the iron and the coal he used; the shoemaker the leather, the cartwright his wood. The division of trades would not even have made the separation of the worker from the masters necessary; one sees manufactures where everyone manages for his own account the raw materials he uses. But ultimately, this division of trades, if it has not caused such a state, it has at least led naturally thereto. From then on, in the production of every commodity, instead of comparing simply the costs of production to those of consumption, to see whether it be proper or not to produce the demanded good, the capitalist has been asked to calculate if he could not get the profit the consumers withheld from him, from his diligent workers.

It is thus, by setting the producers against each other, that they have been brought to follow a course diametrically opposed to the interest of society. For society an industry is not worth the effort to be supported unless it can maintain its workers in a state of reasonable ease; for the owner of the industry it suffices that it bring profits, even though his workers should languish and finally perish in misery.[6]

The cotton manufacturers have reduced the wages of their workers successively from twenty sous a day to fifteen, to twelve, and finally to eight. Their interests having been absolutely divorced from that of their

*Mr. Ricardo argues, in his entire book, from the assumption that the noncultivated lands are inferior in quality to those which are; such that, in the present state of society, it is a bad investment to make them arable. I believe I can state as a fact, after repeated observations in all of Europe, that the commons are of the same quality as the adjacent cultivated land, and that the only risk of ownership was to decide what part of the land would or would not be, under the plow. Almost all the commons of Europe are the result of the feudal system. These are the ancient pasturages of the lord, *vastum domini*, but the lands destined for grazing are generally not at all the worst of the estate. Undoubtedly, some investment must be made for their cultivation, after being so many hundred years without manure; but afterwards there will be no part of the commons that will not be equal to some share of the land brought to cultivation by the same parish.

workers, they have had only to think of the means, in dealing with them, by which they could secure their services at the lowest possible price, at a time when they needed them; they lay them off when they are sick, in their old age, or in the dead seasons, so that public welfare, the hospitals, in England the parish, attend to their wretched existence. They fight, in concert with each other, against their workers, over who leaves this burden most fully to society; every trade is committed to the same battle, everyone advances the interests of his group against the common interest, and everyone of them forgets that he will have to provide in his turn, through private charities, by his contributions to hospitals, or through the poor rates, for the support of the wretches he labors to create.

In this constant battle to lower wages, the common weal, even though everyone shares in it, is forgotten by all. But if every trade takes up its own burden, every manufacturer will soon see whether it is in the interest of his business or not to lower wages; so that, if the subsistence of a man may demand twenty sous a day, it would be a hundred times better to give them to him directly, as a prompt reward of his labor, than to give him eight, as wages, and make him receive twelve under the title of alms.

However, it must be acknowledged that, although the principle be the same, it is much more difficult to put into practice for the industries in the cities, than for rural ones; but it is also much more needed, and even more urgent, to use it there. England is, until now, the only country where farmers need to be supported by public charity, while there is no country in Europe, this being, in truth, partly the work of England, in which the workers of every manufacture do not see themselves endlessly threatened of being deprived of their livelihood, or being reduced to a wage insufficient to meet their needs.

It is quite clear that if the trades could be reconstituted as guilds, for charitable purposes only, and if the masters of the trades were under the obligation to provide help to all the poor of their trade, on precisely the same footing on which the parishes furnish such help in England, one would soon set a limit to the sufferings to which the working class finds itself exposed, as well as to the overproduction that is today the ruin of trade, and also to the overpopulation that brings the poor classes to despair.

Today the manufacturer believes that he can profit either by selling at a high price to the consumer, or by paying a lower wage to the worker; then he would learn that he can make no profit except by selling, and that all he takes away from the worker, will no longer be provided by society, but by himself, as support for the worker. Today the manufacturer ensnares the worker with a miserable wage, and makes him endanger his health in a hellish atmosphere, in cotton dust, or mercury vapors;[7] then he would learn that for every sickness that brought him a profit, he will have to pay for the worker as many days in the hospital. Today the manufacturer, after having hired many families, leaves them all of a sudden without work, because he has discovered that a steam engine can do all of their work; then he would discover that the steam engine would not produce any savings, if all the people who worked find no other means of working again, and he were bound to support them at the hospital while he stoked his boilers. This cost, which would fall on his shoulders alone, would be in strictest justice; because he makes a profit today from the life of these hands, and all the injuries this causes he puts back on the shoulders of society. If the wages he pays are adequate, if they provide not only for the productive age of his workers, but for their childhood, their old age, their sickness; if the work he tells them to do is not unhealthy, if the machines he invents[8] provide only, as he asserts, an occasion to produce a larger output, then the responsibility that will be placed on his shoulders alone will not be a cost at all; he will have no occasion to complain. If it is onerous then his industry is a declining industry; it would be better that he gave it up, rather than make society support its losses.[9]

But it is not enough that this standard be of the most rigorous justice to dispel the very great difficulties it presents in its execution. On the one hand, the extent of the market for manufactured goods would lay open the workers of one region to become again charges to their employer, as a consequence of a change in production that happened a hundred miles away; on the other hand, changes in trade often ruin the very masters from whom help would be demanded; lastly, one runs the danger of seeing the new guilds revive the privileges of the old ones, and exercise like those their tyranny on their subjects.[10]

After having shown what, in my opinion, the principle is, where justice lies, I confess that I feel powerlesss to sketch the means of its implementation.[11] The distribution of the fruits of labor, between those who cooperate to produce them, appears to me fallacious; but it seems to me to be almost beyond human capability to imagine an arrangement of ownership entirely different from the one we know from experience.[12] The suffering of the most numerous classes, and perhaps the most essential ones of society, has been lately so overwhelming, that in the most civilized countries the mind of many philanthropists has been impressed with the necessity to devise a remedy. Men filled with perhaps more zeal for humanity than knowledge of the human heart, or experience, have proposed, under the name of the cooperative system, a completely new organization of society, that would replace personal interest by that of guilds,[13] created with the aim of accomplishing all the work society needs. Mr. Owen of New Lanark is the best known author of this school that counts a large number of adherents in England, France, and America. However, it would be idle to attack its principles; till now they have not been stated in an adequate manner to make much of an impression, and one feels always a kind of guilt in disclosing all the errors, all the inconsistencies of individuals whose writings breathe so much goodwill for their fellow man, and whose views are so virtuous.[14]

But if there exists a similarity between the system in the writings of Messrs. Owen, Thompson, Fournier,[15] Muiron, and the reforms towards which, I believe, we must lead, I feel obligated to say clearly that we are in agreement only on one point, and on all others we have nothing in common. Like them I would wish that there were a partnership between those who cooperate on the same output, instead of setting them in opposition to each other. But I do not view the means they have proposed to reach this goal as ever capable of leading thereto.

I wish that the industry of the towns, as those of the land, be divided among a large number of independent businesses, and not brought together under a great single head who commands hundreds or thousands of workers; I wish that the ownership in manufactures be divided among a large number of average capitalists, and not concentrated in a single man, master over many millions; I wish that the industrious worker have before him the opportunity, almost the certainty, to be a partner to his master, in order that he will marry only when he will have a share in the business, instead of growing old, as he does today, without hope of advancement. But, in order to bring about these reforms, I only ask for gentle and indirect legislative measures,[16] only the administration of a thorough justice between the master and the worker, which would lay on the former all the responsibility for the injury he does to the latter. The law ought to favor at all times the division of inheritances and not their accumulation, it should give the master a monetary and political incentive to bind his workers ever closer to himself, to hire them for longer periods, to have them share in his profits, and then, perhaps, will private interests, better guided, mend on their own the injuries that private interests have inflicted on society. Then the heads of manufactures would occupy their minds with devising schemes to lift their workers to their level, to interest them in ownership and economy, to make of them finally men and citizens, whereas today they labor incessantly to turn them into machines.

Unfortunately, no legislation can shield the poor from all cares, all suffering and even from all unjust dependency, but perhaps much has already been done for his happiness if hope has been rekindled for him, and if instead of that uniformly precarious condition to which he is condemned today, one shows him as the object of his desires a period of rest and ease his good behavior can procure him.[17]

Without a doubt, such an extensive change in legislation, by diminishing quickly that class of workers who fight with each other over who will be better at doing without what is necessary for life, and by forcing each trade to support with its own resources the losses it would have brought upon itself by untimely production, would soon reveal that many manufacturers, believed to be profitable, are really losers, because the help given each year to their workers by society amounts to more than their profits. Undoubtedly, it would follow that many a country that lives only by industry, would see many of its factories close, and the city populations that have grown without limits, would soon decrease, whereas the countryside would begin to grow again.[18]

A state must welcome with gratitude a new industry created by the needs of the consumers, but it must also let go the industry that leaves, without any effort to keep it. All the subsidies the government gives to it, all the sacrifices it makes to support it in its decline, only serve to prolong the suffering of either its masters or its workers, and it saves the declining industry only at the expense of those it ought to keep alive.

Only one nation, really, finds itself today in such straitened circumstances; only one nation sees at all times its apparent wealth contrasted with the frightful misery of a tenth of its population, reduced to live on public charity. But that nation, so deserving of imitation in some respects, so dazzling even in its faults, has seduced by its example all the statesmen of the Continent. And, if these thoughts can be of no use to it, at least I will consider to have served humanity and my countrymen by pointing to the dangers of the course it follows, and establishing by its very experience that basing all political economy on the principle of unfettered competition means to sanction every person's actions against society, and to sacrifice the interests of humanity to the simultaneous action of everyone's individual greed.

End of the seventh and last book.

Translator's Notes to Chapter 9, Seventh Book

This is the last chapter of this book and of *New Principles* proper. (Sismondi later added three appendices.) It summarizes Sismondi's ideas on the workers' role in the productive process. He reiterates his belief that the worker must be made a participant in, and owner of, the factories he works in, the same principle applying to the ownership of land. In a very real sense he takes up Adam Smith's idea of a perfectly competitive society of many small proprietors without control of the market, but by his time this society had to be recreated from the concentrations that had already occurred. Actually, Adam Smith's market had not really existed even in 1776, because at that time concentration in industry and agriculture were already in existence, although they would be dwarfed by what was to follow. Sismondi has an almost religious belief in the efficacy of ownership as a retardant on population growth, in his time nowhere supported by factual evidence. He deduced this from his own experience, and possibly from the experiences of friends and the Genevese citizens he met. On this point, as well as others, the chapter is clairvoyant: it seems to be true that societies with higher per capita incomes have lower birthrates, eventually; in the last half-century, Western industrial society has "socialized" ownership of the means of production through direct and, particularly, indirect stock ownership in pension plans; workers are moving into the boardrooms of large corporations, and even the staunch pro-business *Business Week* calls in an editorial for worker participation in managerial decision making (14 December 1987). This, of course, years after Germany introduced worker participation, and after various other forms of cooperation between management and workers were tried elsewhere. Thus, despite his famous disclaimer in this chapter, Sismondi may have had a better understanding of economic motivation than his better-known successor, Marx. Certainly, experience would seem to have vindicated Sismondi and not Marx. The other point worth noting is Sismondi's insistence that all costs of production be accounted for explicitly and be charged against the output. There can be little doubt that the success of the Industrial Revolution was due in part to the widespread existence of external costs that were passed off to society at large, thus making the product cheaper than it actually was. Some of these costs are now coming back to haunt industrial society; Sismondi is the first writer to discuss this subject in detail, and to call for, in the case of labor, what would be called today a lifetime income. The fact that such arrangements are still considered today a curiosity is a measure of how much he was ahead of his time, or alternatively, how much of a dreamer he was.

1. This is diametrically opposed to Marx's basic assumption that the technical-mechanical nature of the production process determines absolutely the social conditions of society, particularly the exploitation of workers by capital under conditions of capitalistic production. Marx calls the production process *cooperative*, but he denies that such cooperation can be achieved outside of a socialistic political structure.
2. Compare this with Marx, *Das Kapital*, 4, 11: "Die *Kooperation* bleibt die *Grundform* der kapitalistischen Produktionsweise, obgleich *ihre einfache Gestalt* selbst *als besondere Form* neben ihren weiterentwickelten Formen erscheint" (cooperation is the fundamental mode of capitalistic production although its simple form appears separately as a special mode alongside the more developed areas).
3. Here, the major question of the Industrial Revolution, the problem of externalities borne by society at large, is raised. While the discussion is confined to agriculture, and below to industry, and considers exclusively wages for workers, the principle is obviously applicable to other externalities. Sismondi proposes in effect that such externalities be borne by whoever causes them, that if such were the case, the use of labor (and by extension of other resources), would be less exploitative. As a consequence, the apparent advantages of large-scale production would disappear, giving every producer, so to speak, an equal chance in the market. He puts his finger on the major reason why the perfectly competitive model of his mentor Adam Smith is not representative of reality. If any one producer can shift part of his costs preferentially on to society, he will gain in the marketplace. Sismondi recognizes that forcing

every producer to account for all costs of production will work in the direction of maintaining the competitive model of many smaller producers Adam Smith had proposed. In this, Sismondi was greatly ahead of his time, although his thinking was quite likely influenced by the writings of eighteenth-century authors, such as Carafa; Marx, fascinated only by his discovery of exploitation, did not consider the concept from this viewpoint; eventually welfare economics concerned itself with the problem at a much later date, but as current debates about acid rain make clear, it is far from being solved.

4. It is worth noting that Sismondi quite consistently assumed tacitly that the day workers were once owners of farms and were driven from that status by the competition of the large estates. Evidently he anticipated Marx's idea of the descent of the petit bourgeois into the proletariat.
5. The next paragraph was substituted in the second edition for the following paragraph in the first edition: "En même temps, il est vrai, pour protéger contre la multiplication d'une population indigente, et la classe pauvre, et ses enfans à naître, et les riches tenus à les assister, je ne répugnerais pas à interdire le marriage a l'ouvrier de terre qui n'aurait pas ou dix acres de proprieté, ou vingt acres à ferme. Cette loi, toute bienfaisante qu'elle serait pour les ouvriers, pourrait, a son premier établissement, leur paraître infiniment rigoureuse; heureusement que l'Angleterre possède un moyen d'en adoucir la sévérité, par le partage de ses immenses communaux. Le journalier qui n'aurait point réussi à obtenir en propriété ou en fermage un bien suffisant pour élever un famille, pourrait encore, par sa bonne conduite, mériter que les magistrats du comte lui accordassent, avec la permission de se marier, une portion de terre communale en propriété. Cette esperance soutiendrait et consolerait une classe nombreuse d'hommes à laquelle on enlèverait ces douceurs du mariage et la paternité qu'elle considère sans doute comme des droits, mais qu'on ne peut séparer du devoir de maintenir sa femme et ses enfans, que contracte chaque homme qui se marie." This is another instance of Sismondi's belief that marriages among the poor should be restricted by law until such time as they had the ability to support themselves and a family. He owned property in a suburb of Geneva and therefore must have paid taxes. His late marriage was partly a consequence of his limited means, which certainly did not greatly increase after his marriage. It is likely that in the excised paragraphs of the first edition the resentment of the careful householder against the proliferating impecunious poor found literary expression. The spelling of *enfans* instead of *enfants* is taken directly from the first edition. As noted, this edition, printed in Geneva, left out t's in some words. Sismondi uses the partial sentence beginning with "heureusement que l'Angleterre possède . . ." in the next paragraph.
6. This again takes the macroeconomic welfare viewpoint, which sees in consumption the main engine of economic progress. Every worker who lives in misery because of low wages is of necessity a nonconsumer, or a minimal consumer, and must therefore make it impossible to keep up with the ever-increasing power of capital to turn out commodities. The formulation is again one that opposes the gross product, all payments to the factors of production, against the net product, the profit of the owner.
7. Mercury was used in hat making. The vapors affected the brain and produced a form of dementia. The Mad Hatter in *Alice in Wonderland* is a literary example of the effects of mercury, as explained by Martin Gardner in the

annotated edition of *Alice*. It appears that Sismondi had some connection with the hat industry. He uses hat making as an example of his business-cycle theory. Most likely his apprenticeship in Lyon introduced him to the industry, and it is apparent that he kept an interest in it later.

8. This clearly assumes that the factory owner is his own inventor of machinery, an assumption that in 1826 was entirely reasonable. Many of his English in-laws, like Josiah Wedgwood, were in fact manufacturers because they used their own inventions of new processes.
9. This argument has a very modern ring. If an industry cannot carry the direct costs and the external costs of its operation then it is not competitive and should be abandoned. By this criterion, which Adam Smith would have approved whole-heartedly, every industry that is subsidized either directly, or by being able to dump its refuse into the environment in the widest sense, would have to be abandoned. It could be argued that this standard is much too restrictive, but the history of the Industrial Revolution from Sismondi's day to the present proves that only by such indirect subsidization was it possible to create the industrial plant of the world. If all external costs of, for example, a power plant had to be internalized, the costs could well become prohibitive, as is shown by the history of the power industry. It is significant that Sismondi was the first writer to recognize that human labor, and human unemployment are in no way different from other resources in this respect: unemployment was an unaccounted cost of production.
10. Since in Sismondi's time remnants of guilds were still around, and still powerful both in England and in France, he had a practical appreciation of how they could hinder economic progress. This has to be noted, because some of his proposals have been characterized as a turning back of the clock. His observations here are of course applicable to the growth of unions, both as a necessity in the beginning of the Industrial Revolution, and later when many of these unions became in fact undemocratic sanctuaries of privilege, opposed to free trade and competition, and very often in cahoots with management.
11. This and the next three paragraphs are new to the second edition. In the first edition, this paragraph substitutes for a repeat discussion of the possibility of regulating marriages among the workers; the next paragraph starts with the words: "Il me semble aussi que c'est faire beaucoup que d'indiquer où est le principe, où est la justice. Il y a loin bien encore de la à une loi sage, mais l'on sait du moins vers quel but doit se diriger la législation." These words point to the starting words in this paragraph, but it is also clear that Sismondi must have felt strongly that after widespread criticism of his marriage prohibition proposal other solutions would be equally unacceptable. On the other hand he could not accept the schemes of Owen simply because he did not believe in the efficacy of cooperation as an economic motivator. As a consequence, he admits his bafflement and lays himself open to the criticism of indecisiveness, a mistake Marx avoided.
12. It seems safe to say that Sismondi exhibits here in its purest form the difficulties an innovator faces at all times. He is acutely aware that the present view of the economic process, the classical approach, is vitiated by the changed structure of property relations brought about by new technology, but he cannot make the step to new arrangements. Marx started at this same point, with the same assumptions, but he knew in advance how he wanted to change society, that is, radically, to communal ownership. Comparing Sismondi and Marx, it is

clear that Marx's use of the labor theory of value to *prove* exploitation is a smoke screen for his preconceived political solution; Sismondi at this point could have proposed what Marx did later, but did not choose to do so because he did not believe in radical solutions, because of his experiences during the French Revolution.

13. The French text reads *"corporations"* which could mean 'corporation', 'guild', or 'associations'. Since he talked about guilds just above, this meaning was chosen, but Sismondi may also have had in mind what later became known as "the corporate state" of fascist Italy. It is also likely that the reference is to Fourier's *phalanges*, since he refers to Fourier in the next paragraph.
14. This should be taken as the sly stab of a pamphleteer against an opponent rather than a serious disclaimer. The major writings of Owen were published between 1813 and 1821, and Sismondi must have become acquainted with them during his stay in England, as well as in Geneva.
15. The reference here is, in addition to Owen, already mentioned above, to William Thompson, who published in 1824 *An Inquiry into the Principles of the Distribution of Wealth Most Conducive to Human Happiness*, which drew the conclusion Ricardo had avoided, namely that labor was entitled to the whole product if labor alone created value. In 1827 he published *Labour Rewarded* in which he took a position quite similar to Sismondi's, that is, that capital was an agent of production and was necessary to labor.

    The second edition of *New Principles* has *Fournier*, but the reference is most likely to Charles Fourier, the French associationist, who published in 1808 *The Theory of the Four Movements*, and in 1822 *The Theory of Universal Unity*, in which he advanced the utopian community of the phalanges. Claude Juste Muiron was a follower of Fourier who in turn brought Victor Considérant to the ideas of Fourier. The similarities Sismondi mentions refer to cooperation in the industrial process and the effect the new machine industry has on the worker.
16. The previous (and excised) legislative proposals to bar marriage to the poor till they had a sufficient competence to support a family were not gentle or indirect at all.
17. Sismondi repeats several times in this chapter the condition that the worker earn the improvements with his good behavior. Clearly, his Calvinistic antecedents show here—rewards, particularly economic rewards, are earned by application and exertion. By implication he rules out generous welfare schemes, as he had indicated previously in his discussion of the English poor laws.
18. This shows a distinctly physiocratic bias. The passage could have been written by Thomas Jefferson in defense of his ideal of a republic of yeoman farmers. On the other hand, the call for deconcentration of industry and agriculture is quite consistent with his adherence to Smithian principles. His quarrel with received classical theory is then not alone with Ricardo, but also with the fact that Smith's world of *manu*-factures was changing radically in his time that is, small industrial establishments where production was accomplished with few or no machines by craftsmen working with their hands. Smith's nail factory is one example of a *manu*-facture. Mainstream economics had not adjusted to the institutional changes.

Appendix

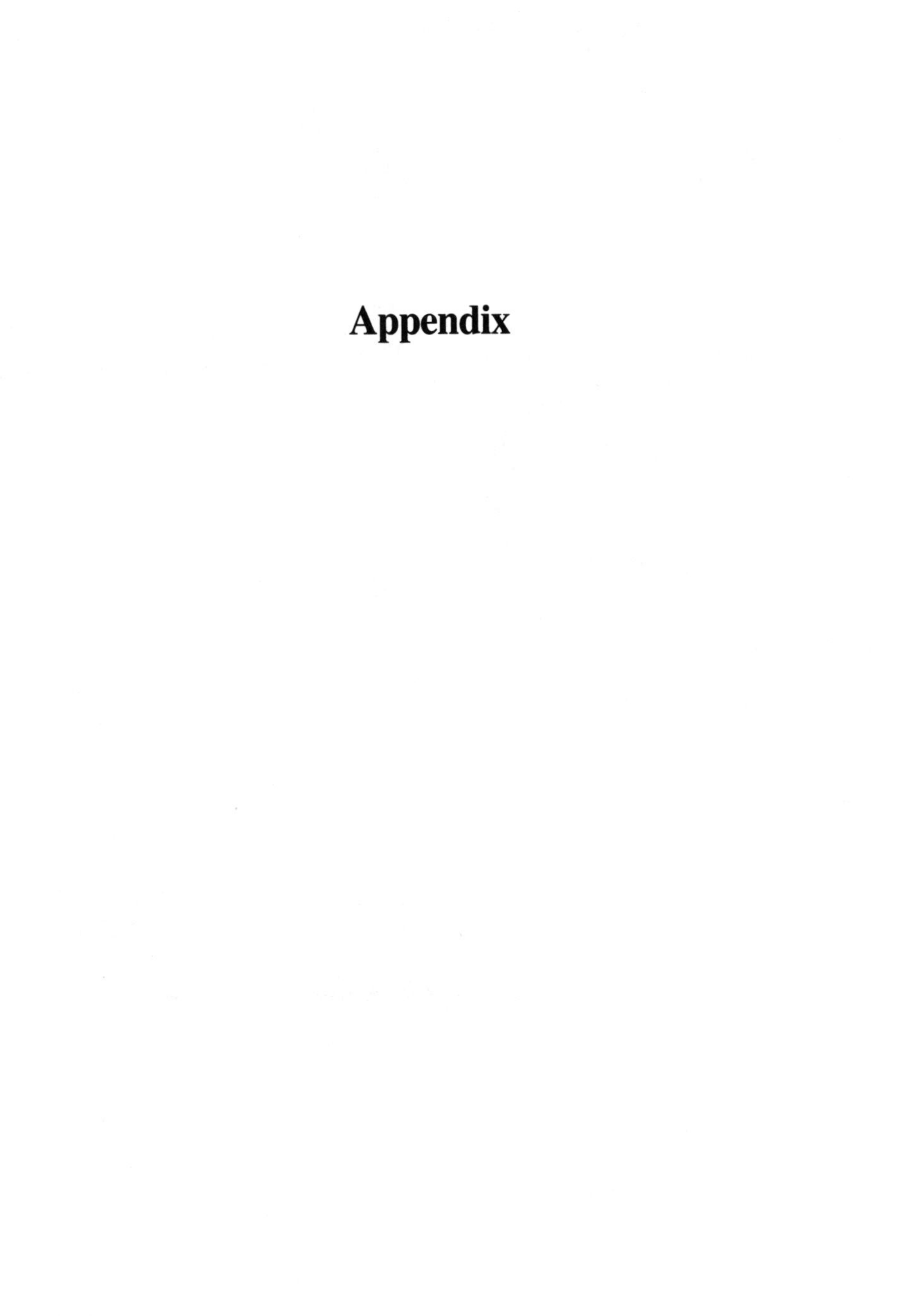

Introduction

Most of what follows in this *Appendix,* as it should be called, is self-explanatory and/or a restatement of what had been written in *New Principles*. All the pieces appear to have been written between the publication of the first and second editions of *New Principles,* although no date can be ascertained for the last one, apparently unpublished. In addition to the demonstrated changes between the first and second edition of *New Principles,* these writings throw a further light on the evolution of Sismondi's thoughts.

Clarifications Relative to the Equilibrium of Consumption with Production

Among the new principles of political economy I have sought to establish in this work, there is one that offends more than the others conventional wisdom, which nevertheless appears to me more important than any other to acknowledge, because it explained the violent crises that have without end plagued industry for ten years, and which would make a start in preventing their return. I have endeavored to prove that increases in the production of all objects of our needs and desires are a blessing only when they are followed by an equivalent consumption; that similarly savings in all factors of production are a social benefit only if everyone who contributes to production continues to obtain from it an income equal to what he received before such savings had been introduced; this can only be done by selling more products.[1]

I have therefore concluded that increases in production, in a given nation, could be a benefit or an evil, depending on circumstances, whereas all other writers on political economy have regarded them invariably as a benefit. Mr. Say, whom Europe esteems rightly as having completed, explained, and clarified the noble system of Adam Smith, declares: "Products exchange for each other, and their multiplication has no other effect than to multiply the enjoyments of man and the population of states."* Mr. Ricardo, regarded by the English as having founded a new era in political economy, and whose numerous disciples repeat today his maxims with unquestioning belief, went even further; he made man altogether an abstraction and proposed as the only goal of the science the unlimited increase of wealth. The means he specified to achieve this goal were an always increasing production, and a steadily decreasing consumption, so

*See his *Traité d'économie politique*, Fourth edition, chapter on markets.

that material wealth would be doubly increased by the actions of those who create wealth, and the savings of those who ought to enjoy it.*

A school founded by M. Saint-Simon in France, inflaming its imagination with the powers of industry, and looking upon the fastest creation of wealth, and the use of the sciences to help the productive arts as a revelation of superhuman powers found in man, proclaimed the *manufacturers,* the *producers,* as the new masters of the world, and proposed to bestow all the political powers of the state on those whom industry would place at the head of a new oligarchy.[2]

These three schools of political economy, at odds over fundamental principles, were far from acting in concert, but all three agreed in their opposition to me; I attacked what in their eyes was the glory of industry. At the same time the question I had raised was so obscure, so abstract, that I laid myself open to the most absurd interpretations; I had to expect to be constantly refuted by people who had not understood me; I had to expect to be told that I opposed every progress in the arts, all improvements of industry, despite the fact that I had declared that improvements were useful, but that their use, depending on circumstances, could be beneficial or harmful; I had to expect that my distinctions were condemned as unintelligible, because I separated what had never been separated before me; finally, I had to expect that reform plans, or absurd and tyrannical restrictions would be attributed to me, because it was impossible for me to state them in a few words, and to reduce to simple ideas those I believed to be appropriate.

However, I have never believed that I must forego the defense of what to me appeared to be the truth, because that truth was abstract, difficult to grasp, difficult to encompass, and because it lent itself to false interpretations. I have returned to the attack several times in the hope that in presenting the problem from ever new viewpoints, I would succeed in making it understood. Today I believe I have the duty to reprint some of these short pieces, so to speak constituting the continuation of my work. The first is an answer to a refutation a famous disciple of Mr. Ricardo[3] had made of my principles; the second is a statement of these same principles as I had made them orally to Mr. Ricardo himself.[4] Finally, the third consists of some notes on a refutation of my principles by M. Say. I believe it stated in a precise manner what the question between us is.

Translator's Notes to Clarifications

1. Sismondi has been characterized as an underconsumptionist pure and simple, for example, by Schumpeter, but this sentence shows again that he was more

*See *Principles of Political Economy and Taxation,* chapter 7.

than that. His concern was income as a share of total production, and relative to consumption. Looking at this sentence alone, one could infer that he would have wholeheartedly supported Keynesian analysis.

2. This refers specifically to *L'Organisateur* (1819–1820), *Du Système Industriel* (1821–1822), and *Catéchisme des Industriels* (1823-1824). *L'Organisateur* contains the famous simile of the loss of scientists, bankers, manufacturers, et cetera, of France as a calamity, versus the loss of the court and the entire aristocracy as a sad, but by no means important, loss to the nation.
3. Sismondi refers to McCulloch, who reviewed *New Principles* unfavorably in the *Edinburgh Review*.
4. Ricardo met Sismondi in 1822 at Coppet, the former estate of Madame de Staël, now in the possession of her son-in-law, the Duc de Broglie.

First Article

Analysis of a Refutation of *New Principles of Political Economy* Published in the *Edinburgh Review* by a Follower of Mr. Ricardo*

We see with regret that political economy in England adopts a terminology which every day is more sententious, wraps itself in speculations ever more difficult to follow, loses itself in abstractions, and becomes, to some degree, an occult science, at the very moment when a suffering humanity would have the greatest need that this science speak a popular language, that it comes to deal with the needs of everyone, that it comes closer to common sense, and that it finally deals with reality. Political economy ought to teach us the theory of everyone's well-being; it was never more necessary than now, when a general debility has afflicted commerce, when all industrial crafts hear cries of distress, when, at least in most countries, agriculture itself seems threatened.[1] It is then that humanity must be watchful against all generalizations of our ideas that make us lose facts from sight, and above all against the error of seeing public happiness in wealth, by abstracting from the sufferings of human beings who create this wealth.

It is said that the head of the new school, Mr. Ricardo, has stated himself that there were no more than twenty-five persons in England who had understood his book. Perhaps it is the result of having made this profession of obscurity that those who have understood him, look upon

*This little piece had been published the first time in 1820 in the *Annales de Jurisprudence* of Doctor Rossi under the following title: "Examen de cette question: Le pouvoir de consommer s'accroît'il toujours dans la société avec le pouvoir de produire?"

themselves as experts, and have brought a most stubborn sectarian spirit to the support, almost solely with his own words, of the whole of his system. One of his disciples has printed in article 11 of no. 64 of the *Edinburgh Review* a summary of his doctrine on the question which seems to us today to have the greatest importance. It is said that the master himself has approved it, and that the other disciples acknowledge it to be the clearest statement of their belief.

Mr. Owen, of New Lanark, one of the men who have shown the most ardent zeal for the welfare of the needy, and the greatest compassion for his misfortunes, had advanced the idea that when industry were left to itself, the use of machines and their gradual improvement could increase the production of goods of all kinds that constitute wealth, beyond the demands made by the consumers, thus causing an overabundance of all goods, a glutting of all markets, which could force manufacturers to lay off their workers, thus depriving of employment those classes of society who live only from their wages.

Without agreeing in any way with the opinions of Mr. Owen about the means to deal with this calamity, I have recognized, like him, in my *New Principles of Political Economy,* the fact of such a general obstruction, and I confess that I had some difficulty understanding how this could be denied today, against the evidence of world trade. I have explained it with a theory I believe to be new, on the nature of income that puts everyone in the position to buy his share of the annual product. I have sought to make it clear that the income of all is not the same thing as everyone's output, so that it would be possible that the product increases and the income decreases; that warehouses fill up, and the exchanges default, till finally there is a lack of buyers for the goods, because too much work was done; whereas the other economists assume that buyers cannot lack unless they have refrained too much from working. The piece in the *Edinburgh Review* to which I refer, is especially intended to fight against my *postulate* which the author declares to be *fundamentally mistaken*, and to prove that *the power to consume increases necessarily with each increase of the power to produce*.

I ask leave to examine in turn, and to refute, this refutation; but first it behooves me to assert that no author's vanity, no blind commitment to my opinions, made me take up my pen. On my part, I feel honored by the attention of a scholar whose name I do not know,* and a famous journal, to my opinions. I feel strongly that nothing matters less to the public than to know the author who has found the truth; what is important to it is to

*I have since learned that it was Mr. McCulloch who can therefore be regarded as the head of the school founded by Mr. Ricardo.

know that truth, whoever it was who may have told it. This truth, which we both seek, is of the greatest importance in present conditions. It can be considered as fundamental to political economy. General distress is felt in trade, industry, even agriculture, at least in many countries. The suffering is of such long standing, so extraordinary that, after having brought misfortune to innumerable families, unrest and frustration to all, it threatens the very foundations of the social order. Nobody can question that in England, for instance, the needy condition of the entire working class of the nation is the true cause of the hostility shown with regard to two questions which should be to them almost unimportant, the sweeping reform of Parliament, and the trial of the queen.[2] Two opposing explanations of this public distress, which causes so much agitation, are given. You have done too much, say the ones; you have not done enough, say the others. Equilibrium will not reestablish itself,[3] say the former, peace and prosperity will not revive till the entire surplus of goods that remains unsold in the market will have been consumed, and till production in the future is regulated by the demand of buyers; stability will return, say the latter, provided that efforts are redoubled to invest everything for production. It is a mistake to believe that our markets are glutted; only one half of our warehouses are filled; let us fill also the other half, and these new goods, exchanging for one another, will revive trade.

Perhaps a question of greater importance has never been discussed, never have been more serious consequences connected to the adoption of the affirmative or negative, because it concerns, at least as much as practice can be joined to theory, the comfort, all enjoyments, the very existence of the great mass of the population that lives by its labor, not in any particular country, but in the whole world. Let us then carefully pursue truth for its own sake, and not for ours. I would have wished that the author of the article had refuted me by using my system, and discussing it step by step. This is what I shall do with his. I will translate it without changing anything, or omitting anything, and I will answer him paragraph by paragraph.

"Demand and supply are truly correlative and convertible terms. The supply of one set of commodities constitutes the demand for another. Thus, there is a demand for a given quantity of agricultural produce, when a quantity of wrought goods equal thereto in productive cost is offered in exchange for it; and, conversely, there is an effectual demand for this quantity of wrought goods, when the supply of agricultural produce which it required the same expense to raise, is presented as its equivalent."[4]

First, we shall say that the author assumes that as far as price is concerned, it is understood that it is uniquely determined by the costs of production. All economists, beginning with Adam Smith, have recognized two elements of price, production and competition. Whoever wants to sell a good properly sets his price by his costs; but whoever wants to buy that product, he who *demands* it, is guided by two reasons that have no connection with costs of production, namely first, need, then ability to pay. The combination of these two elements and their relation to the commodity constitute a demand that can be stronger or weaker than the price of production. There will be no demand if whoever has a surplus he wants to exchange, has no desire for the good, be it that he cannot use it, be it that he has been provided with it already. Likewise there will be no demand if whoever wants the product has no surplus to give in exchange, or does not want to make the sacrifice that is demanded of him, in order to have it. There is a demand, but below production, when the need or means of payment do not equal the produced quantity. To the contrary, demand exceeds production when needs combined with ability to pay cannot be satisfied by what is available.

I will further say that the author, by assuming in every exchange two reciprocal demands, confounds two very different things, trade and consumption. Trade, in distributing the produced goods, serves demand, but does not create it. It changes the holders of the goods, but it leaves them always in the market, where they always compete with production of the same kind, till such time as trade comes to the final demand, that of the consumer, who takes them from the market, puts them to his own use, and makes the chosen goods disappear. When two producers come to the market with the same need to sell the produced article, they can very well make an exchange among themselves to increase their opportunities, without having any reciprocal need of what they offer, just as in the familiar game of chance, that actually has the name of *trade*, the players exchange their cards without looking at them, till one of them cries *enough*. But this exchange of goods without final demand, without effective demand, is almost always a symptom of a market glut.

At the booktrade of Leipzig, every bookseller from every part of Germany comes to the fair with four or five editions of books he has printed, each one comprising forty or fifty dozens of volumes; he exchanges them against collections, and he carries home with him two hundred dozens of volumes, as he had brought two hundred dozen. Only he had brought four different works, and he carries away two hundred. There we have the demand and the production which, according to the disciple of Mr. Ricardo, are correlative and convertible; one buys the other, one pays the other, one is the consequence of the other; but, by our lights, according to the bookseller, according to the public, demand and consumption have not yet begun. The bad book, even though it had been exchanged in Leipzig, remains not any less unsold; it does not any less cram the merchants' shops, either because nobody wants it, or because everybody has already one. The books exchanged at Leipzig will not move out until the booksellers find individuals that not only desire them, but who will make a sacrifice to get them out of circulation. Only they constitute an effective demand. But let us proceed.

"As long as commodities are brought to market in such proportions, that the things offered to be bartered against each other are equal in productive cost, and therefore in value, an increase in the supply of one class of goods will afford increased equivalents for the purchase of an increased supply of another class."

Yes, but is there any reason that the want, the need, for one or the other class of goods increase in the same proportion? The example of the booksellers of Leipzig applies point for point to this argument. If they return to the fair with a second edition of all the works they have exchanged at the first fair, the past year, each one constitutes *an increase in the supply of one class of goods, and will afford increased equivalents for the purchase of an increased supply of another class;* but will this exchange and this equality of production matter to a public that is already oversupplied with such books and wants no more of them?

"Supposing, for the sake of illustration, that a cultivator advanced food and clothing for 100 labourers, who raised for him *food* for 200; while a master-manufacturer also advanced food and clothing for 100, who fabricated for him *clothing* for 200; then the farmer, besides replacing the food of his own labourers, would have food for *100* to dispose of; while the manufacturer, after replacing the clothing of his own labourers, would have clothing for *100* to bring to market. In this case, the two articles would be exchanged against each other; the supply of food constituting the demand for the clothing, and that of the clothing the demand for the food."

There is perhaps no other method of reasoning that is open to more errors than that of constructing a hypothetical world altogether different from the real one, in order to use it for one's hypothesis. The mind, already confused by the impossibilities that are part of the hypothesis, can no longer distinguish those that imply contradictions, and which, as a consequence, will render the argument false. There are many in the example we criticize.

First of all, the author assumes work without profit, a reproduction which will only replace exactly the consumption of *the workers*. For there are in all two hundred workers, of which one hundred produce the subsistence of two hundred, and one hundred others produce the clothing of the same two hundred; but if they produced more than that subsistence, or the clothing of these two hundred, where would the consumers be? At the same time, he assumes a division of labor which never establishes itself except for gain; he assumes masters and workers, but he leaves no share for the masters. However, if the latter have no share, no profit, they can have no interest in continuing the work; they will lay off their workers, and unless the workers can continue their labor for their own account, all work will end. The whole argument rests on this false assumption. At the moment when we seek to find out what happens to the surplus of the workers' production over their consumption, one cannot exclude this surplus which constitutes the necessary profit of labor and the required share of the master.

This is not all: the argument is based on the necessity of an exchange between things equally necessary to life. The farmworker cannot do without clothing; the craftsman cannot do without bread. Agreed. But the perfect exchange, equal, without a remainder on one side or the other, does not happen unless the food and clothing of a man are always equal and indivisible quantities, and are always also procured with an effort, or sacrifice, similarly equal, so that they can be regarded as a unit.

To come as close as possible to the argument and the abstract hypothesis of Mr. Ricardo's disciple, we assume only three grades for the food, clothing, and labor of the worker, assuming that these three divisions exactly equal each other;[5] whereas there are, in reality, more than a hundred categories between the poorest worker and the individual enjoying the greatest comfort; and the subsistence expenditure of the worker, in each of these categories, does not in any way correspond exactly to his clothing expenditure.

The worker can feed himself with potatoes and milk, as in Ireland; he can feed himself with bread and soup, with meat one or two times a week, as the French peasant did formerly. He can feed himself with better meat, as the English peasant did formerly, or as the Swiss peasant does today.

The worker can clothe himself solely to hide his nakedness, and that is almost the state to which the factory workers have been reduced today; he can acquire a suitable garment, simple, warm, and comfortable, and that is the state in which we have formerly found these same workers. Finally, he can provide for himself, in addition to his everyday clothes, finer garments for holidays; that is the state of well-being we have observed in more than one trade, and more than one nation.

In order to acquire all of these things, the worker is finally called upon to make smaller or larger sacrifices. He can only work six hours a day, and devote the other six hours to enjoyment, to leisure, or to the cultivation of his spirit. He can work twelve hours a day, and care well for his body, but neglect his mind, or the moral side of his existence. Finally, he can sacrifice, not only his mind, but his very health, to work, either by devoting more than twelve hours a day to it, or by overtaxing his powers during the course of his labor, either in places, or with materials, dangerous to his health. The world shows us everywhere only too many examples of this latter worker's condition, and we see also that, however fatal this be to individuals, it does not prevent in any way the renewal of the species; more numerous births offset a higher mortality, and the ranks are always replenished.

At present, is whoever looks only to the requirement of exchange, as assumed by the disciple of Mr. Ricardo, really aware that the worker, with respect to these three relations, is reduced to the worst of the three assumed conditions; giving the greatest possible amount of labor for the least amount of food and clothing possible? When he is not reduced to such a state of wretchedness, the cultivator, before considering what trade he will make with the craftsman, will weigh first what trade he will make with himself: whether he prefers a frugal subsistence together with time devoted to the training of his mind, as formerly the Greeks, or leisure and enjoyments, like the savages; or whether he chooses steady work with a more substantial subsistence. The craftsman will choose in the same way between leisure with coarse clothes, and labor with holiday suits. Both will further weigh how much labor they are prepared to offer in trade. The cultivator may demand to be well fed, but worry little about being well dressed, or vice versa; and everyone, in this decision, will be totally independent of his neighbor. The hundred craftsmen could choose to provide the third quality of labor in order to obtain the third class of food and clothing, while the cultivators would choose to give only the first class of work, and would content themselves with the most frugal life and the coarsest clothes. What then becomes of the necessary exchange assumed by the disciple of Mr. Ricardo?

In the same way one cannot know beforehand what will be the choice of each of the hundred cultivators, of the hundred tradesmen; if they are entirely free, as the writer assumes, one would have a great deal of trouble predicting what choices they ought to make for the benefit of society. All labor is not an advantage, all leisure is not a loss. A nation much worse clothed, much worse fed than another, can neverthelss be much superior, if it has advantageously used the time taken from the labor in the fields and the trades. Even if it has devoted it only to leisure and pleasure, as if wealth were not intended to provide any other thing but pleasure and leisure, it is not at all certain that such a nation had not been happier. There exists between the extremes without a doubt a middle course, but moral principles must trace it; it can never be decided by numbers.

Mr. Malthus, in the excellent work he has just published on the principles of political economy, has already remarked, p. 358,[6] "Another fundamental error into which the writers and their followers appear to have fallen is, the not taking into consideration the influence of so general and important a principle in human nature, as indolence or love of ease." But it is with even greater satisfaction that I see this kind philosopher raise doubts about the social benefit of the unlimited increase of labor by the working class.*

"Now, let us suppose," continues the disciple of Mr. Ricardo, "that there are 1,000 farmers, *each* of whom advances food and clothing for 100, and obtains in return food for 200; and also 1000 master-manufacturers, each of whom, by advancing food and clothing for 100, gets clothing for 200;—In this case, each of the 1000 farmers will feel the same necessity for exchanging his surplus food which the single farmer formerly felt; and each of the 1000 manufacturers the same necessity for exchanging his superfluous clothing. Food and clothing for 100,000 will reciprocally purchase each other, just in the same way that food and clothing for 100 formerly did. The demand for each is increased a thousand fold, because the supply of each is increased a thousand fold."

This hypothesis, which is but a repetition of the preceding one, is nevertheless even more impossible to accept, because instead of separating a few individuals, it represents an entire society; but a society where the workers alone make a livelihood in return for uninterrupted labor; a society where labor does not bring leisure and abundance to anyone; a society where everyone is forced to exchange with his peers all he can produce, under pain of fasting or of staying naked. This state of universal want is the necessary condition for this assumption; because, if there would be a surplus, if every individual is not constrained to trade either to feed himself, or to clothe himself, the first farmer who will wish either to conserve his corn for another year, or to rest, will upset all equilibrium; the first who will prefer study to pretty clothes, or a walk to a full table, will leave the production of his neighbor without a demander. But if this is, in this hypothesis, the unnatural state of this society, how can it then accommodate judges, soldiers, doctors? what will they give, what will they receive in exchange? and what will become of the manufacturer who must exchange corn with the farmer, if that farmer is away at war, or if he will prefer to buy either justice or health rather than beautiful clothes?

"But let us suppose, once more," continues our author, "that in conse-

*I hasten to take this opportunity to express my regrets to have judged the work of Mr. Malthus on population, in my first edition, from his first edition, while the author, in the meantime, had developed, clarified, and corrected his principles in later editions of which I had no knowledge. I also blame myself for not having sufficiently indicated how I admire the insight, how much I love the character he has exhibited in all his works.

quence of more skilful applications of labour, and of the introduction of machinery, each of the 1000 farmers, by advancing food and clothing for 100 labourers, obtains a return consisting of ordinary food for 200, together with sugar, grapes and tobacco equal in productive cost to that food; while each of the 1000 master-manufacturers, by advancing clothing and food for 100, obtains a return consisting of ordinary clothing for 200, with ribands, cambrics and lace, equal in productive cost, and therefore in exchangeable value, to that clothing."

Often, an appearance of great profoundness and of great powers of abstraction is created by jumping over intermediary steps in a chain of reasoning. Our author even seems to take pleasure in astounding thus his reader, by disguising an esoteric meaning in a proposition which, at first sight, is judged absurd. But by restoring the intermediate steps he suppresses, it will be almost always found that they hide some error of reasoning.

Thus we know very well that no improved use of labor, no improvement of machines will produce sugar, spices, or wine in England, for which the author writes. That is understood, I am going to be answered; this is but a quicker way of stating it. I beg pardon, this is not understood at all. If the improvement of labor and machines of which he speaks will have doubled the powers of the thousand farmers who each employ one hundred workers, the product of their lands will be doubled in corn, in meat, and in fodder, all things for which, by the very assumption of the author, neither they, nor the manufacturers will have any need. The latter, in turn, when, by the improvement of machines, will have doubled the powers of the stocking trade, the cloth trade, the shirt trade, will not see come forth ribbons, laces, embroideries, but an amount of the same stockings, the same cloths, the same shirts, double of what the country can consume. How are all these things changed into those luxury goods for which our author is going to tell us the use? by trade, no doubt, by foreign trade. But is this not begging the question? How is it going to be proven that the tropical countries which, with less labor, produce more foodstuffs, will have a need for the corn of England, against their sugar and their spices, that France will trade its wines for muttons, or Virginia its tobacco against potatoes? or indeed how has he proven that one-half of the workers will leave the stocking trade, the cloth trade, the shirt trade, to change over to the trades that make ribbons, cambrics, and laces? We seek a cure against an excessive production; how has he proven that, the consumption of these necessities being so limited as he himself assumes, those who produce them will stop just at that proper point, and devote the rest of their time and their means to luxury items?

It is quite odd that the most erroneous part of our author's argument is the one he has glossed over in his statement with an evident absurdity. One would say that he has expected that no one would venture to reveal the contradiction in terms when he speaks of the English farmer who, by improving his plow, will make his fields produce sugar.[7] Nobody can believe that that was his idea, nobody will dare admit that he does not understand it; but couldn't we ask him whether he has properly understood it himself?

The first consequence of all increases in labor, machines, capital employed in whatever branch of agriculture or manufacture, is an increase in the products of that branch beyond preceding demand; it is therefore necessary that either demand increase, or that labor, machines, capitals be redirected to some other production. But how does such a shift come about? what is the *demand* that determines it? This our author has not told us at all.

"In this case," our author proceeds, "the supply and demand with respect to the food and clothing will remain, it is obvious, exactly as before; while the sugar, grapes and tobacco, which the farmers do not wish to consume themselves, will be offered in exchange for the ribands, cambrics and silks, which the manufacturers do not wish to consume themselves. These different articles, therefore, will be reciprocal equivalents and purchasers of each other; and there will be an increased demand for commodities, exactly proportional to their increased supply."

Again, we are asking here from our author not to suppress the intermediate steps in his argument. Who will demand? Who will enjoy? The masters, or the workers, either from the country or from the city? In his new hypothesis, we have an overabundance of product, a profit from labor; to whom will it belong? The question is important, first of all as an ethical one, to know who will reap the benefit of a new improvement in labor, and what the nation will gain in happiness; further as an economic one, because the number of consumers ought to have a decisive influence on the extent of consumption.

Since he has not made himself clear, we must follow both assumptions. First, by conceding that workers' wages rise as a consequence of the increase in their output, it follows that they could earn, by six hours of labor, the wages they earned before with twelve; they will be called upon to decide whether they want to devote the time they do not have to give anymore to the procurement of basic necessities, to leisure, enjoyments, or cultivation of the mind, or whether, on the contrary, they want to work as much as before to buy for that price the benefits of luxury. Wines, we have been told, will purchase laces, and tobaccos will purchase silks; but what kind of proportion can be established between the drunkenness of one part of consumers, and the frivolity of the other? what guarantee is there that a taste for the pleasures of life that divert the mind from work, will grow exactly as the growth in labor? what if each of the luxury articles, to the extent they are successively acquired, gives a lesser enjoyment; will then everyone be nevertheless prepared to obtain them with a greater sacrifice? Who indeed has shown that a cultivator, for the pleasure of wearing a cambric shirt embroidered with lace, and a coat of silk while guiding his plow, will agree to expose himself to unwholesome morning dews, to the burning noon sun, to the frosts of winter, when he could, by foregoing these trifles, get up later, exhaust himself less, care better for his health, in short lower his output, without worrying about the correspondent output of the manufacturer?

But we know well, and the history of the business world teaches us over and over, that it is not the worker who gains from the multiplication of the products of labor; his wages do not increase at all; Mr. Ricardo himself has said elsewhere that this can never be, if it is intended that public wealth should not ever cease to grow. A disastrous experience has taught us to the contrary that wages are almost always decreased because of such multiplication. But then, what is the effect, as far as public happiness goes, of the growth of wealth? Our author has postulated a thousand farmers who enjoy, while a hundred thousand farmhands labor; a thousand factory owners who grow rich while a hundred thousand craftsmen are regimented by them. Whatever happiness could come from the increase in frivolous luxury pleasures is consequently felt only by a hundredth of the nation. Would this 1 percent, called upon to consume the excess output of the entire working class, be equal to the task if, through the improvement of machines and capitals, such production increases continually? With the author's assumption, every time the national product doubles, the owner of the farm or factory must increase his consumption a hundredfold; if the national wealth is today, thanks to the invention of so many machines, one hundred times of what it was when it barely covered the costs of production, every proprietor ought to consume today goods that would suffice to sustain ten thousand workers.

We believe, strictly speaking, that a rich man can consume the manufactured goods of ten thousand workers; this is how the ribbons, laces, and silks come about whose source the author has shown to us. But a single individual would not be able to consume, in the same proportion, agricultural goods; and the wines, sugars, the spices which Mr. Ricardo has created as exchange, are too much for the table of a single person. They will not sell, and soon the proportion between agricultural and manufactured goods, which seems to be the basis of his entire system, could no longer maintain itself.

"It may be objected, perhaps," continues the writer,[8] "that on the principle that the demand for commodities increases in the same ratio as their supply, there is no accounting for the gluts and stagnation produced by overtrading. We answer very easily—A glut is an increase in the supply of a particular class of commodities, unaccompanied by a corresponding increase in the supply of those other commodities which should serve as their equivalents. While our 1000 farmers and 1000 master-manufacturers are exchanging their respective surplus products, and reciprocally affording a market to each other, if 1000 new capitalists were to join their society, employing each 100 labourers in tillage, there would be an immediate glut of agricultural produce;—because in this case there would be no contemporaneous increase in the supply of the manufactured articles which should purchase it. But let one half of the new capitalists become manufacturers, and equivalents in the form of wrought goods will be created for the raw produce raised by the other half: The equilibrium will be restored, and the 1500 farmers and 1500 master manufacturers will exchange their respective surplus products with exactly the same facility with which the 1000 farmers and 1000 manufacturers formerly exchanged theirs."

We have already been able to observe in our short excerpts, and one can see this even better in the work of Mr. Ricardo, that he and his disciple take pleasure in presenting impossible examples. This manner of reasoning has a serious drawback, which is that one is not anymore struck by the impossibility of the devices they then advance to remedy all the difficulties. Capitalists who all of a sudden double the extent of cultivated acreage in a developed country, who double the number of men employed in agriculture, and stamp from the earth this new nation, who double the mass of agricultural goods, are occurrences that seem to happen only in the realm of fairies; and when they have been accepted by hypothesis, it would perhaps be bad manners if one dwells on the difficulty to be experienced in reestablishing an equilibrium by inducing one half of these capitalists, and one half of the workers, brought into being by a wave of a wand, to leave agriculture in favor of crafts and trades.

However, we are just now at the juncture where this agricultural revolution, which seemed fantastic, is occurring, and we can judge the means that must serve as its corrective. The extent of the fields in the developed[9] world cannot be doubled; but the underdeveloped countries have been brought into cultivation, and political revolutions, a change in the financial system, peace, have all of a sudden brought to the ports of old agricultural countries cargoes that equal almost their entire harvests. The vast provinces on the Black Sea that Russia has recently developed, Egypt, which has changed her system of government,[10] the Barbary Coast where piracy has been abolished, have all of a sudden emptied the storage silos of

Odessa, Alexandria, and of Tunis, into the ports of Italy, and have brought to the markets such an excess of wheat that, for the entire length of its shores, farming has become an unprofitable industry. The rest of Europe is open to a similar revolution, caused by the vast extent of the new lands on the banks of the Mississippi that have been suddenly brought under cultivation, and which export all their agricultural products. The very ascendancy of New Holland[11] could one day be ruinous to English industry, if not with respect to the price of provisions whose transport is too costly, then at least with respect to wool and other agricultural products easier to ship. Without a doubt, the time will come, and it is the desire of mankind, when the industrial arts will follow the agricultural arts, when these new lands will supply their own markets; but this will be the task of many generations, perhaps that of many centuries.[12]

At this very moment, what is the advice the disciple of Mr. Ricardo gives, so that there be no excess of production over demand, no glut, no hardship? *that one half of these new capitalists become manufacturers.* This advice cannot in all seriousness apply to the Tartars of the Crimea, and to the fellahin of Egypt. Indeed, the time has not yet come to establish new manufactures in the transatlantic regions, or in New Holland. It falls therefore to the old cultivators to give way, and to reestablish equilibrium. But is it a simple or easy matter to bring a landed gentleman from Italy or Provence to understand that the patrimony he has inherited from his fathers is worth nothing anymore, absolutely nothing; that he has no other recourse but to leave it fallow, withdraw all the capital used for its cultivation, and start a factory? Rather than do this, he will wait till the capital has been eaten up to the last penny by a ruinous competition, and he will not give up agriculture till he dies in misery. Yet, in order to use the formula we have been given, the number of European cultivators who leave agriculture would have to be equal to one-half of the number of the new cultivators on the Black Sea, in America, or Africa who send their corn to the markets of Europe. All the workers they employ would have to change their calling at the same time.

But most often it is not agricultural output that gets ahead of manufactured goods, and which causes the glut business denounces; today at least, we are struck by the number of manufactures which, without awaiting the needs and the demand of the public, pour onto the markets goods that exceed infinitely the purchasing power of that public, even if it would be true that there is such power, unrelated to consumer need, which limits demand. However, would it be quite easy, in a fully cultivated country, to apply to the land for new clearings as much of the capital as is in excess in manufacturing, to reestablish equilibrium? These disturbances in every industry of a country, which can hardly resolve themselves in a century, do they ever arrive at a time when they can rectify annual fluctuations? and when gluts succeed each other, in whatever sector of industry, is their effect not equal to a constant excess of production over demand?

Furthermore, if the exchange of agricultural goods with those of the city is the main business of all countries, it is not nearly the only one, and the postulated equality in this trade does not merely simplify the picture of the overall industrial activity of a country, it misrepresents it. Every single product ought to be proportioned to the wants, the needs, and the means of payment of some class of purchasers. But these wants and needs change endlessly; the buyers, far from the eyes of the producers, are spread over the face of the earth. No philosopher,[13] with all his inquiries, no government, with all its powers, has yet known precisely the extent of any market: how would producers come to know it? They do not even look for it. They only strive to steal each other's customers. This battle, carried on from one end of the known world to the other, would be by itself enough to prove the superiority of production over demand. As long as it lasts, trade, engrossed with selling at lower prices, but not with producing less, has no inclination whatever to reestablish equilibrium.

"When an increase takes place in the supply of some particular commodity, or class of commodities," our author finally states, "then a glut, or want of sale, is experienced; but when an increase takes place in the supply of commodities in general, the different articles are employed in the purchase of each other,—and augmented supply is identical with extended demand."

No doubt, a general glut in trade is much rarer than a partial glut; perhaps it was left to our days to provide a severe and somber example thereof. But, after all, if the disciple of Mr. Ricardo had looked around him, he would have seen that such a glut was possible. A cry of despair rises from all the industrial cities of the old world, and all the plains of the new reply. Everywhere commerce is afflicted with the same apathy, everywhere does it meet with the same inability to sell. The suffering began at least five years ago; far from abating, it seems to have increased during that time.[14] In all the trades we know there is an overbundance of hands; how would the equilibrium that has been mentioned, be reestablished, when there is no trade that asks for the use of more manual labor?

The distress of manufacturers is the most cruel, because in contradistinction to the farmers, their subsistence is entirely dependent on trade. It is greatest in England, because England has proportionately a greater number of manufactures than any other European country. One cannot read without shuddering the petition of the producers[15] of Lower Nottingham. They say: "After having worked fourteen to sixteen hours a day, we earn only four to seven shillings a week to feed ourselves with our wives and families. We substituted bread and water, or potatoes and salt, for healthier food which at other times was always plentiful on English tables; in the meantime we protest that after the tiring work of an entire day, we have, many times, been forced to go to bed, and to put our children to bed, without an evening meal, so as not to hear their hungry crying. We declare in a most solemn manner that during the last eighteen months, we have hardly known what it means to be free of the pangs of hunger" (*Edinburgh Review*, May 1820, p. 334).

Many times it has been said that the equilibrium reestablishes itself, that work begins again;[16] but every time an isolated demand created an activity in excess of the real needs of trade, this new activity was soon followed by an even more painful glut. The patriotic organizations that we see being founded in Belgium, in Germany and elsewhere, for the purpose of keeping out foreign goods, are also a fatal symptom of such universal distress. The system that governs public opinion now is neither that of the philosophers, nor that of governments; it is the misery before everybody's eyes that has led to its adoption. The oversupply of agricultural goods is less noticed, mainly because the cultivator who does not sell the surplus of his wheat, suffers less than the manufacturer, who does not begin to eat till he has sold all of his handiwork; then also because agriculture did not have as great a development as industry; nevertheless, the agricultural sector is also generally distressed: the prices of provisions hardly compensate for the costs of production; in England general bankruptcies among farmers have shown that it would be better to curtail rather than increase agricultural undertakings; and against the assertions of Mr. Ricardo, the very foundations of his system, a general glut has been felt, an increase in production which, far from increasing, has decreased demand.

This great European calamity cannot be viewed without turning, with all of our hearts, our minds, to a search for cures that will put an end to so much suffering; but to our eyes the remedies we have attempted to point out in the preceding work, are all indirect, and work only slowly. Yet, already we believe to have accomplished something, if we have shown what *should not be done,* and what advice *should not be followed*; if we have proven that the power to consume does not necessarily increase with the power to produce; if we have, finally, raised a doubt in the minds of those who believe they serve their country and mankind by giving greater scope to all trades, at the very instant when perhaps they help to overwhelm us evermore under a mass of false riches for which we have no use.

Translator's Notes to Appendix, First Article

The *Annales* were a joint venture of Sismondi with Rossi, and lasted only three years. As Sismondi points out in a subsequent note, the follower of Ricardo is

McCulloch, who became the most prominent spokesman of what Marx would call *Vulgaeroekonomie*. This article represents a further development of Sismondi's thoughts between the first and second edition of *New Principles*. Some noteworthy ideas occur: utility reasoning is employed to question McCulloch's assumption that goods exchange for each other in equal proportion; Say's Law is again refuted by explicitly stating that the consumer has alternatives to the consumption of commodities, and that therefore fluctuations in demand, especially for agricultural output, will occur. The concentrated argument of this shorter piece highlights the fact that Sismondi came close to Keynesian analysis, especially with respect to one fundamental assumption, namely that as a country grows richer, its consumption will lag behind supply.

1. In agreement with the general discussion in the main work, Sismondi here clearly shows that he considers agriculture the rock-bottom base of the economy, the one sector that will be always the most important and most stable of all in the economy.
2. Sismondi makes specific reference here to two major controversies that were exacerbated as a result of the disturbed economic conditions in the British Isles after the end of the Napoleonic Wars: the drive for parliamentary reform led by William Cobbett, and the trial of Queen Caroline at the instigation of her husband, George IV, who came to the throne in 1820. These had been preceded by serious disturbances and repressive legislation that were in turn tied to the first post-Napoleonic depression. The Tory government under Castlereagh had aggravated the distress by passing protective legislation, among them the Corn Laws, which generally raised prices on subsistence goods and favored the great landlords and merchants. Sismondi's assessment is most likely a reflection of his own liberal views and those of his English relatives, who were liberal Tories.
3. This literal translation could also be rendered as "stability will not return." McCulloch employs *equilibrium* in the article cited here by Sismondi, but its use was not general. Say, although he uses utility reasoning in the *Traité,* does not use the term *equilibrium*. It does not appear in the index of Ricardo's *Principles*.
4. The cited text, translated by Sismondi for his article, was taken directly from the cited article for this translation. It appears under the heading "Mr. Owen's Plans for Relieving the National Distress," and is a review of several tracts written by Robert Owen. McCulloch cites Sismondi on p. 470 and then proceeds to review (unfavorably) *New Principles,* book 7, chapter 7.
5. He means that each grade of the three corresponds to its counterparts in the other two in quality. The concept is obviously fraught with difficulty, as is made clear in the next sentence.
6. *Principles of Political Economy with a View to Their Practical Application,* 2nd Ed., Reprint Augustus Kelly, 1951, p. 320.
7. This remark shows that technological innovation falsifies the best laid arguments of pamphleteers. The article was written in 1820; the sugar beet industry had gotten its start in Germany during the Continental Blockade, but it began to grow decisively only after 1830, invading in the process France and England. It is not clear whether McCulloch in writing what he did, had the fledgling sugar industry in mind or not. Most likely the mentioning of tobacco, sugar, and grapes was indeed merely a shorthand for the notion of a diversified agriculture—McCulloch was not known for great originality of thought. Sismondi's attack sounds specious—what he had in mind becomes clear below

where he uses utility reasoning to question the postulated equality between production and consumption, raising the possibility of a mismatch which McCulloch apparently does not even contemplate.

8. The term used here is "journaliste," which in the context must be taken as a derogatory term, indicating that the author of the article was not regarded as a serious political economist.
9. Sismondi uses "civilisées," as opposed to "barbare." The terms are translated as 'developed' and 'underdeveloped', although some of the implications that are present in the terminology are lost.
10. This refers to Muhammad 'Ali, who in 1805 was appointed governor of Egypt by the Sultan, and proceeded to open the country to Western, at first mainly French, influence. In 1811, Muhammad 'Ali massacred the Mamluks, the former rulers of Egypt, at a banquet, to eliminate opposition, and then proceeded to extend Egyptian rule to the Sudan and the east coast of the Red Sea. He introduced the cultivation of cotton and hemp to Egypt, and developed an irrigation system.
11. Australia; this name had been given by its discoverers, the Dutchmen Willem Corneliszoon Schouten and Abel Tasman, in the 1600s. England claimed the territory after James Cook explored the east coast. He called his find New South Wales. Matthew Flinders circumnavigated the continent during 1802–1803 and proved that New Holland, the western part, and New South Wales, the eastern part, were part of the same landmass. Flinders suggested the name Australia, from *Terra Australis,* but the name came into general use only very gradually. Sismondi obviously still considered the old name appropriate.
12. Sismondi, like many of his contemporaries, underestimated the speed with which the Industrial Revolution would spread, even though he had a very realistic and accurate notion of the development of world trade in the coming age of steam. In this he was much more perspicacious than his economic colleagues in England.
13. This term could also be translated as political economist, or scientist, or investigator, but it was retained as the more comprehensive term that reflected Sismondi's view more accurately.
14. The depression described so vividly started at the end of the Napoleonic Wars in 1815 and lasted till 1820. Its main cause was the inability of English producers and merchants to sell the accumulated output of the war years, which had waited for the end of the Continental System. In the economically weakened condition of the Continent, only very limited purchasing power was available to buy these goods. In addition, most Continental governments had imposed high tariffs on imports to reserve the home market to domestic producers, thus making it even more difficult for England to create an export-led revival of trade. As mentioned before, England had also closed its borders to trade, raising prices of basic foodstuffs, and thereby greatly aggravated the distress of the working population. At the same time, the technological transformation of English industry made labor redundant, reducing further the ability of the domestic market to absorb increasing output. This depression is usually seen as the first global endogenous fluctuation of the Industrial Revolution.
15. The text uses the word *fabricants,* meaning manufacturers, but the tenor of the petition points to factory workers. On the other hand, it is possible that the petitioners were small producers who suffered as great a distress as their workers.

16. This remark foreshadows Herbert Hoover's *Prosperity is just around the corner,* and is, of course, based on the same theoretical assumption, namely the one that is attacked here. It should be noted that the article also clearly describes beggar-my-neighbor policies, similar to policies followed during the Great Depression of the 1930s.

Second Article

On the Balance of Consumption with Production*

Economists are divided today on a fundamental question, and on its answer depend in some degree the first principles of their science. We have already dealt with it elsewhere; we ask leave to take it up again, and perhaps it would be proper to return to it once more. A small number of pages would be neither enough to move those with settled opinions, nor to establish a new doctrine with others. All that we can hope to do is to show the importance of the question to be decided, and to bring those who have perhaps formed their opinions too quickly, to ponder it anew.

Here is the question. Mr. Ricardo, in England, and M. Say on the Continent, have maintained that it is enough for the economist to be concerned with the production of wealth, because the greatest prosperity of nations is always likely to produce more. They have said that production, by creating the means for exchange, creates consumption; that one should never fear that wealth will glut markets whatever the quantity human industry might have produced thereof, because the needs and the wants of man will always be ready to turn this wealth to his uses.

On the other side, Mr. Malthus, in England, has held, as I have tried to do on the Continent, that consumption is not at all a necessary consequence of production; that the needs and the desires of man are indeed without limit, but that such needs and desires are not satisfied by consumption unless they are tied to the ability to exchange. We have asserted that it is not at all sufficient to create such means of exchange in order to let them pass into the hands of those who have these desires or wants; that it happens quite often that the means of exchange increase in a society

*This small piece was published the first time in the *Revue Encyclopédique*, May 1824, Vol. XXII.

while the demand for labor, or the wage, decreases; that then the wants and needs of one part of the population could not be satisfied, and consumption also declined. Finally, we have claimed that the one unmistakable sign of a society's prosperity was not the growing production of wealth, but a growing demand for labor, or an increase in offered wages that rewards it.[1]

Messrs. Ricardo and Say have never denied that a growing demand for labor is a sympton of prosperity; but they have asserted that it is the inevitable result of increases in production.

Mr. Malthus and I deny this; we regard these two increases as flowing from independent causes, and sometimes capable of being opposed to each other. According to our view, when the demand for labor has not preceded, and determined, production, the market gluts, and then a new production becomes a cause of ruin, and not of happiness.

On this question, the greater number of economists have embraced the opinions of Messrs. Say and Ricardo; but almost all business men behave in accordance with the principles advanced by Mr. Malthus and myself. In industry as well as agriculture, it is sales that appear to them to be the immediate cause of their prosperity or their distress; they wish to guide their productive efforts by their sales, even though they may not always be successful at it.

Mr. Ricardo, whose recent death[2] has deeply grieved, not only his family and his friends, but all those he has enlightened by his wisdom, all those he has uplifted by his noble sentiments, stopped at Geneva for a few days during the last year of his life. We discussed in a friendly fashion, two or three times, this basic question on which we held opposing views. He brought to his arguments the courtesy, good will, and love of truth that characterized him, and a clarity of thought which even his disciples would not have expected, accustomed though they were to the flights of abstraction he demanded from them in their study; but a spoken discourse cannot do justice to a question which calls for a difficult reconciliation of practical arguments with, in some way, metaphysical considerations; consequently I have undertaken to reproduce here, with some more order, and with the help of some additional reflection, the arguments I used in these sessions whose memory is dear to me.

We acknowledged to each other (and how not to acknowledge it), that all types of industry, agricultural and manufacturing, have in turn complained, in every country of Europe, of glutted markets, the impossibility of selling, or of selling except at a loss; I saw in this overproduction, or its mismatch to consumption; but such overproduction or mismatch were equally impossible according to Mr. Ricardo, who attributed this result to defects of the social organization, to constraints imposed on the circulation of goods, and to tariffs.

We moved away from the question which engaged us, the case of a nation that would sell more to foreigners than buy from them, that would seek a larger foreign market for an increasing domestic production. A majority of statesmen, from a remaining sympathy for the mercantile system, have strongly advocated, similarly to what Messrs. Ricardo and Say have recommended, to increase production without end in the nation they govern; but this was for exportation's sake, not domestic consumption; and these two systems, while they agree on some measures, are opposed to each other in their axioms. Thus, the English cabinet has intended to make England the workshop of the world; it has intended the people of Europe, of America, of India, to become the customers of English merchants; so that every new advance in national industry be linked to the opening of a new market abroad. But, instead of counting, for consumption, on trade between expanding sectors, it has prided itself on pushing foreign producers successively out of foreign markets, at the same rate as the English came in with either higher-quality goods, or lower-priced ones.

In that system nations are rivals to each other; industrial prosperity in one causes the ruin of industry in the others; and, if all adopt this system at the same time, if all consign each year a greater amount of exports to foreign markets, if all, by offering discounts on their goods, strive to steal from each other their customers, and to sell more than they buy, their competition, that will embrace the world market, will be injurious to everyone; or else one alone will be able to succeed at the expense of all others, and that one alone will gain from free trade; the others, on the contrary, will have to defend themselves against an industry that kills their own.[3] Thus, the same cabinets that have pushed increasing production, have adopted the prohibitive system.[4]

Mr. Ricardo, to the contrary, as a supporter of absolute freedom of trade between nations, has had to prove that his system, instead of being a special case, could be followed by everyone at the same time; that the producers, instead of being rivals, help each other as customers. Also, his entire theory rests on the basic principle that a nation cannot sell more than it purchases, that there exists a necessary balance between production and consumption, that the latter always increases with the former, that foreign trade does not alter the exchange that establishes itself between the two amounts, that it merely satisfies the many different tastes of consumers by bringing to these markets equal, but more varied values. If, for example, the production of cloth in England is going to increase by one hundred thousand pieces yearly, all that foreign trade would do, would be to allow Englishmen to consume in wines and spices, or any other form trade might make possible, the value of these hundred thousand pieces, instead of consuming them directly. In the eyes of Messrs. Say and Ricardo, by creating objects of trade, trade is created, and as a consequence consumption; and the equality of consumption with production seems to them equally shown, by either looking at the entire world market, or by postulating that every nation exists in isolation from every other.

It is quite important to have this principle constantly in view, so as not to draw false conclusions from the upheavals that have occurred in our days in the industrial conditions of several nations. The manufactures of the most industrious nations of Europe have been for several years in a state of frightful distress, because they have been unable to sell their products; today (in 1824) they have recovered, and it is agriculture that suffers everywhere, because it cannot sell its harvests; but the relief manufactures have obtained is not at all a proof of Mr. Ricardo's system; when agriculture will experience similar relief, the truth of his theory will then not be any better established. We know that a new market, an immense market, has opened itself to the Europeans in Spanish America. Now, for us the question is not to determine whether the chances of war, or politics, cannot give to a nation new consumers; it must be proven that it creates them itself when it increases its production. There are, at the least, strong reasons to assume that the improvement in the state of European markets is due to the fortunes of politics, and not to the natural progress of wealth.[5] All the strong demands have come from Spanish America, where no obstacle hinders anymore the introduction of European goods, where the war, blazing up in all provinces, consumes much and produces little, where strong popular passions, stirred at the same time, sacrifice capital instead of income to the purchase of arms and goods provided by England.*

Mr. Ricardo does not in any manner count on colonial wars, the liberation of America, on Colombian and Chilean loans to provide customers to English manufacturers; according to him, these manufacturers generate their own customers. He said: "Suppose a hundred cultivators produce a thousand bags of corn, and a hundred wool manufacturers produce a thousand ells of cloth; viewing only them in the world, abstracting from all other goods useful to men, of all middlemen, they exchange their thousand ells against their thousand bags; let us then assume that

*We have seen above, Vol. IV, chapt. IV, what the consequences of such artificial activity have been, how the English have themselves provided the money with which their goods have been bought and consumed by foreigners, and how, since they have stopped lending to their customers, the latter have stopped buying.

with the successive progress of industry the productive powers of labor increase by one-tenth; the same men then exchange eleven hundred ells against eleven hundred bags, and everyone of them will find himself better clad and fed; a new advance will exchange twelve hundred ells against twelve hundred bags, and so forth; the increase in products will always increase the pleasures of those who produce them."[6]

To my mind the abstraction we are asked to make with this argument is by far too strong: we are asked to neglect details; but this is not simplification, this is misleading us by hiding from our view all the successive operations by which we can distinguish truth from error.

Returning to the same exchange that Mr. Ricardo describes in so few words, we will be astounded by its complexity; let us follow the various markets a producer attends or may attend, and admitting, like Mr. Ricardo, that from small to large the same operations are performed by everyone; let us separate the causes from the effects and, leaving out ourselves a great number of intermediaries, let us see how much the producers of one half of wealth must be the consumers of the other.

In order to study this social mechanism we will choose agriculture as an example, and we will look in agriculture only at tilling, abstracting from all its other products; we will begin with its infancy, when the industry had made as yet little progress, and the productive powers of labor left very little surplus, over and above the subsistence of the worker; this is a hypothesis and analysis presenting the least difficulty, and will force us to deal with the least detail; but at the same time, we will look at society in its actual organization, with workers without property, whose wages are fixed by competition, and whose master may dismiss them at the moment when he has no more need for their labor; because it is precisely this social arrangement to which our objections apply. Finally, we will abstract from money, like Mr. Ricardo.

Let us postulate a cultivator who, on a given area of land, maintains ten members of his family, servants and farmhands working for him, and who produces annually on his estate 120 bags of corn. So as not to complicate too much our numbers, we will abstract from all other products of his cultivation, representing them by corn. Let us further assume that he gives as a wage to each of his hands the equivalent of 10 bags of corn; of these 10 bags the worker will consume 3 directly annually; he will use 7 to obtain for himself by trade such other goods, either agricultural or industrial which, after bread, are necessary to life; 20 bags will remain to the cultivator. To simplify the numbers even more, we assume that the owner is the cultivator. Then, he needs 10 bags, 3 directly, and 7 in other necessities of life, to live at the same standard as his workers; 10 other bags will supply him, through exchange, with the pleasures we call luxury goods, those he does not share with the remainder of the working population.

Let us repeat: the estate produces 120 bags of corn, of which 33[7] are eaten directly by those who work on the farm, 77 are exchanged against other necessaries; they are therefore eaten by those who produce the goods the poor buy; 10 are exchanged against luxury goods, they are therefore eaten by those who make the goods the rich buy; since we call someone rich who, after having provided for his needs, can devote a part of his income to his pleasures.

At that time, a mechanical invention, a new machine invented for the cultivation of the soil, or the art of training domestic animals to make them perform human labor, increases by 50 percent the products of human effort. As we have taken as an example a family of owner-cultivators, whose members had more or less equal rights, the invention would inure to the benefit of all equally; eight hours of work would suffice, to the eleven members of this family, to obtain the results they had obtained before with twelve; and if there would not offer itself to them any other final demand equally profitable to them, they would rest four more hours a day.

But, we have postulated society in its actual state; on the one hand, an owner who alone manages all work, who reaps alone its fruits, and who alone profits from inventions; on the other hand, manual workers who have no other possession than their ability to work, and no other income than their wages. Everyone of the workers of our cultivator has produced for him 12 bags of corn; each one will be able, after the invention to produce 18. However, the quantity of corn the cultivator wants to produce is limited, (1) by the extent of his land; (2) by the value of his agricultural capital; (3) by the demand of the market to which he sends the surplus of his harvest. He calculates thus: seven workers, at eighteen bags per man, will produce for him 126 bags; this is 6 more than before; in order to sell them he will, if necessary, discount the price a little bit. He then lays off three of his hands, and he continues to manage his farm with the same amount of acres, the same capital, but with only seven workers, instead of ten, to whom he pays moreover the same wages. Let us also make our calculations for this.

The estate produces 126 bags; we have seven workers and one master to whom we allocated their subsistence of 10 bags per man, for a total of 80 bags. We have in addition 46 bags that belong to the master for his luxuries. As to the first lot, 24 bags will be eaten directly on the estate, instead of the 33 that were consumed before; 56 bags, instead of 77, will be traded for life necessaries, and eaten by those who produce subsistence goods; as to the second lot, 46 bags, instead of 10, must be exchanged against what we have called luxury goods; they will therefore be eaten by those who work in factories that produce luxury goods, but only if the new manufactures that must be created, will be in existence. We have therefore, with a very small increase in production, a noticeable decline in the consumption of two existing industries, agriculture and the manufacture of subsistence goods; we will have on the other hand almost quintupled the demand directed to an industry that before barely existed, the manufacture of luxury goods.

In order to make this change in consumption, resulting from an improvement in industry not induced by a greater demand for work, even more understandable, let us look at this improvement from another point of view. We have assumed that 10 bags of corn represented the appropriate wage of a man; that he eats 3 of them, and that he trades 7, and in that way a major portion of his wages reappear as wages of workers who work for him. The farm, in its primitive state, produced 120 bags of corn, then paid the wages of ten farmhands, their master, and one luxury-goods worker, plus 80 bags that these twelve persons traded with those who supplied them with all other subsistence goods other than corn. This still assumes eight and two-fifths workers working for them. One can see that the latter trade in turn seven-tenths of the corn they do not eat directly, that those who work for them have done the same, up to the entire amount of corn that was distributed between forty persons. Among these forty persons there is only one who consumes luxury goods; and there is only one who produces them.

The industry then takes the first step we have postulated: the product of the cultivators is increased 50 percent by an agricultural invention.[8] The farmer has laid off three of his farmhands, and has brought his production to 126 bags. His farm pays from then on wages of 80 bags, to him and his seven hands. The eight represent a demand of 56 bags for subsistence production, or five and three-fifths workers; these workers, by calling on others, up to the total of 80 bags, which represent the necessary labor to produce the entire harvest, have given bread to twenty-six and two-thirds workers engaged in subsistence production. Comparing this situation to the preceding one, there will be then thirteen and one-third in need, or who will not have yet received their bread. It is true that one expects that they will get it from luxury production. Indeed, the owner offers 46 bags in trade for goods of the luxury industry, or those who can provide for his personal pleasures; and since it did not yet exist, he must encourage it by higher wages; he offers 12, 14, 15 bags of corn, instead of 10, to whoever provides him with the pleasures of his new wealth he wants; all that the worker in luxury goods receives over and above his subsistence wage, he will use in turn for luxury goods; the remainder goes to subsistence production, but this is only after the luxury industry has been called into being, this is only after the 46 bags the owner received in the division will have passed through the hands of the luxury workers, and the surplus will have been traded by them; it is not until then, I say, that bread will be given to all those who offer to work. When this distribution will be completed, of forty-two persons who will henceforth have a share in the harvest, thirty-seven and three-fifths, instead of thirty-nine, will work to produce subsistence goods, four and two-fifths to produce luxury goods, and the population will have increased by two persons.*

Therefore, we come to find, like Mr. Ricardo, that at the end of the cycle, if it is in no way impeded, production will have created a consumption; but this is done by abstracting from time and space, as the German metaphysicians would do; this is by abstracting from all the obstacles which can halt this circulation; and the more we look at them more closely, the more we see that these obstacles are multiplied.

The postulated change has removed three workers from agriculture; and the livelihood of ten in manufacturing, which was before certain, is now more or less questionable; from then on it depends on an uncertain future, the establishment of a new industry.

The reestablishment of equilibrium depends therefore on the swift development of such luxury workers. But as yet they do not exist; they must be born. The owner who only earned ten bags on his farm, was far from dreaming to demand that kind of labor he believes he needs since he earns from it forty-six. The coach builders, the glassmakers, the watchmakers, whose works he wants, are not yet born; if he is compelled to wait for them, from the moment of their conception till the time they will be able to make a livelihood, the process will seem long to men who go hungry, waiting till they know how to produce. The patience of the former will be further put to a cruel test, no matter how short we assume the apprenticeship of the men to be who will agree to learn a new trade.

There exists yet another obstacle; in order to create a new industry, a luxury industry, new capital is needed; machines must be built, raw materials must be procured, giving employment to a distant business, because the wealthy are rarely content with the pleasures that grow in their own garden. Where will we however find this new capital, perhaps very much larger than that needed by agriculture? An impetus has been

*We have assumed that 10 bags represented all the subsistence of the workers, working with that degree of comfort common to their class at that time. The 46 bags will feed then only four and two-fifths workers, in whatever way they are distributed. If their wages rise to 15 bags, the master will employ only three luxury workers; but these three will employ a fourth, and that fourth one a part-time fifth.

given to the entire social system by the invention of the plow, or by the art of yoking animals to it; the invention did not create any new capital. Our luxury workers are still very far from eating the corn of our cultivators, from wearing the clothes of our basic manufactures; they have not yet been created, they are perhaps not yet born, their trades do not exist, the materials on which they ought to work have not yet arrived from the Indies. All those to whom they ought to distribute their bread wait for it in vain.

But let us test another assumption. Our cultivator-owner, at the time he made the discovery that increases the productive powers of labor, instead of discharging three of his workers, keeps all ten. Indeed, these workers, who cannot live except by their labor, will not resign themselves to folding their arms to die of hunger. They know no other trade than that of farming, and as long as there remains a breath in their body, they will continue to offer the strength of their arms at a discount to grow corn, with the increased powers the new inventions have given them. This competition will lower the wage of all farmhands; assuming that it lowers it by only a tenth, and that is surely not much, if we take into consideration, on one hand, the number of hands left without work, and on the other the difficulty the master experiences to increase his production by one-third.*

Under this new assumption, the farm will produce 180 bags, but the ten workers will receive as their share only 90 bags, to which we will add 10 that stand for the share of the master for subsistence goods. From these 100 bags, 33 are consumed directly on the farm, 67 are traded with basic industry.[9] Before the invention that industry consumed 77. The wages there are therefore reduced in a much greater ratio than in agriculture; however everyone lives, everyone works, and everyone can wait for the results that will be produced by the 80 bags that remained in the division to the owner, and are destined to encourage new luxury industries.

If one actually succeeds in creating eight new luxury workers, and they, disposing of 80 bags that came to them in allocation, encourage in their turn the basic industries, then, when the entire circulation is concluded, the population will be found to have increased by a third, and sixty

*Perhaps it will be said that, after having established that ten bags represent the subsistence wage, it is absurd to assume that the workers content themselves with less than subsistence. But we do not know at all what the requisite amount is for maintaining the life of the worker, and we did not intend to discuss that. In every condition of society, more or less prosperous, there exists an ordinary wage, adequate to supply not only the needs, but also the pleasures in keeping with manual labor; this is the wage that, in brief, I have called subsistence; it could not be said to what level it could be reduced, nor to what point the life of the worker can be deprived of any type of happiness.

individuals, instead of forty, must eat the corn of the postulated farm; but it is proper that in this second assumption we have abstracted from time and space.

It is necessary to abstract from space: the new invention has made seven individuals sufficient for the cultivation of an amount of land that before engaged ten. In order not to dismiss these three, not to condemn them to die of hunger, it must be assumed that there is new arable ground, new lands to clear, which would not have been true in an absolute sense of all countries and all times. Moreover, it is not enough that the land to be cultivated exists, it is also necessary that it be in the possession of owners who, as soon as they are offered a profit, will proceed to take it under cultivation. However, it can be seen that the untilled lands of Europe are encumbered so as to remove them from the demands of those who offer to cultivate them by their labor. Here, we have nontransferable parish properties; there, entailed lands of individuals who have neither capital, nor the means to give guarantees to those who would lend to them; besides, vanity seeks to maintain the status quo. The rights of the crown, the church, the nobility, the people, are each opposed to such market behavior, on which economists have counted and whose power appeared to them irresistible. It is actually easier for the English to go and clear the wildernesses of Canada, or those of Kaffirland, than the commons in the neighborhood of London.

It is necessary to abstract from time, if it is assumed that the farmer who has found the means to increase by a third the productive powers of his workers through a mechanical or agricultural invention, will also find an adequate capital to increase his cultivation by a third, to expand by a third his agricultural machinery, his vehicles, his herds, his storage silos, and the circulating capital that must maintain him while he waits for his returns.

Time had to be left out of account when luxury workers, and a ready capital to start luxury industries are assumed, adequate to consume the eighty bags set aside for them this year, instead of the ten that were destined for them the previous year. It was necessary to abstract from time when sixty individuals are postulated, ready to eat the corn the new harvest will produce, while there were only forty to eat the corn of the preceding harvest.

Thus, when an invention in the productive powers of labor is applied to agriculture without being called forth by a preexisting demand, when, moreover, society is arranged in such a manner that there is only one owner, and all others offer their labor at auction for a living, only one profits from the invention the progress of the sciences has inspired;

capitals, resources, men, and factories are lacking to bring the remainder of society into balance with the too rapid pace of agriculture.

Our arguments would be applicable to any other type of industry, just as much as to the one that produces corn; but, if we have reason to fear that, even for this one, our reasoning has seemed at one and the same time too tedious and too hypothetical, we would have had to expect to dishearten our readers even more if we had taken our example from industry, because the consumption the manufacturer makes of his own products is much less than that of the farmer. Still, be it imagined that an invention which saves a third of manual labor is progressively introduced into all the manufactures that produce all the parts of clothing, utensils, and furnishings of the poor; everywhere it will be the factory owner who will profit from it; everywhere, he will dismiss three workers out of ten, he will produce a bit more with a little less people; everywhere he will decrease by three-tenths the consumption his own workers make of his own products, and he will decrease in the same proportion the consumption of those who work for his workers. Under such circumstances, every invention decreases the demand for already existing factories, and creates one, as an offset, that is directed to factories that do not yet exist. Each invention makes the livelihood of a part of the manufactures of subsistence goods dependent on the creation of a luxury industry; however, a luxury industry cannot be created without capital, workers, and a loss of time, which those whose livelihood has been stopped cannot support.*

I hear already complaints that I am opposed to the improvement of agriculture, to advances in the trades, to all progress man is capable of; that without a doubt I prefer barbarism to civilization since the plow is a machine, that the spade is an even older machine; and that, according to my method, it would have inevitably happened that man would cultivate the soil with his hands alone.

I have never said anything of the kind, and I demand leave to protest, once and for all, against any consequences inferred from my method which

*The hatter, with his ten workers, produces at least 1,200 hats a year; he and his workers only consume 11, and his business has not been achieved until he has covered 1,200 heads; still, if we postulate for him the same circumstances as for the farmer, we will see him first destine 1,100 hats to cover 1,100 heads, in order to produce the needed wages for himself and his ten workers, and trading 100 hats against luxury goods for his own use. Whereas after the invention which will increase by a third his productive powers, his manufacture will only consume eight of his hats; the direct trade of his hats with the subsistence sector and agriculture will not use more than 792, but as he will offer 460 to the luxury industries, he will need sixty new heads to wear his hats, and yet he will have three hundred poor who cannot afford his hats till the luxury industry, promoted by the wealthier hatter, is in full production.

I have not deduced myself.[10] I have not been understood by those who attack me, nor by those who defend me, and more than once I have had to be ashamed of my allies as well as my opponents. I have been pictured as being, in political economy, the enemy of society's progress, a supporter of barbarous and oppressive institutions. No, I do not desire any part of what has been, but I want something better of what is. I cannot judge what that is, except by comparing it with the past, and I am far from wanting to restore ancient ruins if I show with their help the eternal needs of a society.

I beg to pay close attention—it is not in any way against machines, against inventions, against civilization that I raise my objections, it is against the new organization of society which, by taking away from the working man all property except his arms, gives him no guarantee against a competition, a mad auction, conducted to his disadvantage, and of which he must necessarily be the victim. Let us assume that all men share equally the product of their labor in which they will have cooperated; then every invention in the trades will, in all possible instances, be a blessing for all of them; because, after every advancement in industry, they will always be able to choose, either to have more leisure with less labor, or to have with the same labor more pleasures. Today, it is not the invention that is the evil; it is the unjust division man makes of its results.[11]

We are, and this has as yet not been sufficiently noticed, in an entirely new state of society, one of which we have as yet no experience whatsoever. We incline to separate completely any type of property from all types of labor, to break all ties between the worker and his employer, to exclude the former from all participation in the profits of the latter. This organization is so new that it is not even halfway instituted, such that only the most industrialized, the richest, the most advanced countries belong to a system we have barely tried out, where agricultural labor, as well as that in the manufactures, will be performed by workers who can be dismissed at the end of every week; this is the road we will follow; this is where I call attention to danger, and not in the inventions of science.

Our senses have become so accustomed to this new organization of society, to that universal competition which degenerates into hostility between the wealthy class and the working class,[12] that we cannot imagine anymore any other type of existence, even of those whose ruins lie about us everywhere. One believes one can answer me with absurdities, by holding up to me the vices of the preceding systems. Two or three systems have actually succeeded, with respect to the status of the lower classes of society; but, because they do not deserve our regret, because after having done first a bit of good, they then imposed frightful calamities on humanity, can it then be concluded that we have today attained to the truth? that we will not discover the fundamental evil of the day labor system, as we have discovered the evils of slavery, of serfdom, of guilds? When these three systems were powerful, nobody imagined, in the same way, what would come afterwards; rectifying the existing order would have seemed similarly either impossible, or absurd. The time will undoubtedly come when our descendants will judge us not any less barbarous for having left the working classes without security, as they will judge, and as we judge ourselves as barbarous, those nations who have reduced the same classes to slavery.

Each of these systems had seemed, in its turn, to be a fortunate invention, to be an advance towards civilization. Slavery itself, however odious its memory may be, followed a savage condition of universal war where man, always under arms, had no spare time to devote to labor, no security for the fruits such labor had produced; slavery, following the slaying of prisoners, constituted progress in society; it permitted the accumulation of wealth, it became, with the Greeks and the Romans, the foundation of a civilization almost equal to our own. As long as the masters remained poor, as long as they worked and ate with their slaves, the condition of the latter was bearable and the population increased. The very progress of the system, the wealth of the masters, their luxury, their ignorance of any work, their disdain for that part of the population that supported their life with their sweat, their cruelty, their greed that incessantly took some portion away from the subsistence of this human cattle, finally spread death among the working classes. They made them vanish at the time of the greatest splendor of the Roman Empire, when the economists, if there were any, perhaps applauded the continuing progress of opulence.

The gnawing canker of antiquity was slavery. The population of the Roman Empire was destroyed by the oppressed condition and the misery to which the slaves had been reduced, and delivered it over to the barbarians; they, at the end of several hundred years, invented a more liberal system; they substituted protective and client relations between the lord and his man for the whip that had been for so long the discipline of the slaves.

Feudalism had its shining and prosperous period, where the armed vassal fought at the side of his lord. When the lord, grown wealthy, dreamed only of acquiring ever more riches, and to display ever greater splendor, he reimposed his yoke anew on the poor, and the feudal system became intolerable.

Then the people gained the system of liberty we have now; but, at the moment when they broke the yoke they had carried for so long, the toilers did not find themselves entirely without property. In the countryside they found themselves joined to land ownership as métayers, as copyholders, and as renting farmers. In the cities they found themselves joined to ownership in their industries as members of guilds and trades they had formed for their mutual protection. It is in our days, at this very time, that the progress of wealth and competition have broken all of these associations.[13] The revolution is not even half completed. But the farmer, grown rich, ceases to work with his hands; he distances himself from the farmhand and treats him niggardly. The head of a workshop, grown rich, instead of working along at the same bench with a journeyman and an apprentice, gives up manual labor, gathers thousands of workers in his factory, and treats them meanly. Certainly, our experience with this social order which sets those who own against those who work is quite recent, for this social order has only begun.

The sort of glut of products of human industry I have sought to explain, could have hardly occurred in earlier periods of society. In a state of barbarism, when every man worked for himself alone, every man knew also his own needs, and there was no fear that he would burden himself with useless weariness to make things for which he had no need. Under the following slave system which permitted the development of a tolerably great civilization, the master in the same way demanded from his slave only those industrial products whose use he had determined in advance. His demand had preceded and nourished labor, his consumption followed immediately; a glut became only possible when the slaveholder turned manufacturer and trader, as is today the planter in Jamaica. In the feudal system, the lord demanded from his vassals rather more services and fighting than profitable labor; industry, far from being animated, was strongly discouraged, and gluts were not the danger. In the guild system, every progress in the arts profited those who plied a trade; hence everyone proportioned his efforts to the market he had to supply; the farmer much preferred to rest than to produce corn he could not sell, and the city guilds have often been accused of never having had another policy than to limit output, to remain in command of the market, and to incline at all times to work less than was demanded in order to sell at a higher price. The situation we will enter on today is entirely new; the working population is free; but no security whatsoever has been given for its subsistence; it must live from its labor; but it cannot see in any way, it has no knowledge whatsoever of whoever will consume the products of its labor; it has no means to gauge its efforts by the remuneration it can expect. When the fate of millions of men rests on a theory no experience has yet validated, it is proper to regard it with some distrust.[14]

Furthermore, one should not believe that the ancients had never thought about the difficulties that engage our attention, that they never sought and found a solution. If the fundamental question of political economy is, as I believe, a balance between consumption and production; if it is a necessary consequence of the progress of the arts, of industry, and of civilization that every working man produce more than the value of what he consumes,[15] and that, as a consequence, the producers alone will not suffice to consume everything, then for every increase in the productive powers of labor, there must be a corresponding increase in the consumption of a class of individuals who produce nothing, or of products that are not in any way common. This is the conclusion Mr. Malthus drew in his latest work in political economy; and he found there a reason to assert that the prodigality of government had sometimes served the public weal by creating a leisure class of consumers without which production would have been stopped soon by glutted markets.

It seems to me that the ancients had come much farther than we in these considerations on the general progress of society. We will not lay the prodigality of the Athenian government to their politics any more than those of the English government to the ultimate principles of Mr. Malthus; but they had recognized that in order to preserve this equilibrium between production and consumption so necessary to societies, three strategies were available: the first, to use the surplus from basic production to feed the workers whose work was unsaleable, and to build public monuments, civil, or religious works; the second, to encourage the luxury of the wealthy, so that they would consume the labor of the poor; the third, to give to the entirety of the citizenry spiritual or patriotic pursuits, to fill the hours the progress of industry allowed them to save from labor.

The first device, which was more or less put into operation by all states in antiquity, can nowhere be seen better developed than in the administration of Egypt. This country was inhabited by an agricultural population whose numbers dazzle the imagination; and since it combined the advantages of a fructifying sun, a fertile soil, and an abundance of water, it drew from the soil an amount of food infinitely superior to what it could consume. The Egyptians had an aversion, either political, or religious, to seafaring. They therefore sought to be self-sufficient; they had little intercourse with foreigners; they did not export their corn nor the products of their manufactures, and the latter never attained to great perfection. Their form of government permitted only a few great lords who consumed, in luxury, what their fellow citizens had produced by their sweat, and indeed, among the ruins of all the temples that cover Egypt, there is no palace left. There existed indeed a numerous class of all-powerful priests; but their religion imposed on them an asceticism that excluded all luxury; their consumption was barely above that of the workers. These priests searched for the means to keep the mass of Egyptians in the habit of constant work, and a frugality equal to their industriousness. They wanted them always ignorant and always submissive; they did not want leisure to permit them to develop in any way their intelligence, instead of their bodies; and they gave them the gigantic task of housing in their temples all the gods of Olympus. Monuments, the likes of which the world will not see again, covered Upper Egypt; their proportions are so colossal, that one almost refuses to believe that human power was enough to erect them; and their execution is so exquisite that it seems that those who lavished their time in this manner had all eternity to finish them by the work of successive generations. The catacombs, the caves of the mountains that adjoin the Nile Valley do not hide any lesser marvels; the immensity of these works overwhelms our senses and our reason. It must have taken the continuous labor of many million workers, for many hundred years, to create this wonder world. Undoubtedly so; but these millions of men were needed to eat the corn from the fields of Egypt. A whole nation of masons and stonecutters was needed to consume what the industrious inhabitants of the Nile Valley produced without end.[16]

Ancient Hindustan also conceals monuments that almost equal those of Egypt in extent and perfection. There also, religion mandated useless, but colossal works, because the social structure had multiplied producers, and had almost eliminated those who consumed without doing anything. The Etruscans, and all those people where priests had great power, adopted more or less the same policy. In Rome monuments antedating the first historical era are rediscovered, whose construction long before the beginning of Roman opulence can hardly be explained, except by the power wielded by the priests over the old inhabitants of the country. Because of such a policy, the entire population could work without glutting the market; morals remained pure, bodies strong, equality was not in any way endangered, everyone participated equally in the enjoyment of the public monuments by the combined labor of the nation. But, on the other hand, the incessant labor of everyone arrested all development of the spirit; also, the nation found itself defenseless in the hands of the ambitious caste of priests who had resolved to govern them.

The second system of antiquity was closest to ours: in Sybaris, Corinth, Tyre, Carthage, and later in Rome, when this capital of the world declined already into its decadence, trade and industry were left to their natural course; the excess of production over the consumption of producers was immense; it sustained first a large foreign trade; but soon after it created a class of debauched rich, whose only occupation was to vary endlessly their pleasures; these rich lived to idle, to consume, to play, in the same way as the remainder of their fellow citizens lived to labor. As the work was done almost entirely by slaves, the strife we see coming into being in our day to lower the wages of artisans did not occur; and assuming that in some trades the market found itself oversupplied, the hardships that could have resulted for the slaves hardly engaged the attention of their contemporaries, and has not left any trace in history.[17]

But the lawgivers of antiquity, who comparatively had a much greater number of free states than we, who had pondered for a long time the idea that government is only instituted for the happiness of its subject people, for the happiness of all, and not for that of a single class, condemned entirely the system of the Sybarites. It appeared to them subversive of republican equality to enact a law that some should work so that the others could have pleasure. They found that an excess of vulgarity and servility always accompanied an excess of opulence; that souls weakened in soft living; that a whirlwind of pleasures was as opposed to the development of the spirit as could be the constant exhaustion of manual labor. They judged that if they had all citizens enjoy a share of leisure gained by the progress of industry, they would improve their character; whereas if they would leave a small minority to complete idleness they would condemn them at the same time to a pursuit of sensuality. Hence, they agreed with all the philosophers and moralists, all religious men, and in particular with the Christian church fathers, in prohibiting luxuries, as necessarily leading to a decay of morals and the decline of the state. It is indeed strange that the unanimous opinion of men whose judgments we respect so much in other matters, do not influence today even slightly our opinions in this regard.

The third system was founded on this principle, adopted by Athens as well as by Sparta, by Rome in its prime, and by all the most renowned republics of antiquity. So that those who had no other income than from their work found a sufficient demand for labor, the republic itself employed almost constantly its citizens, and thus prevented them from offering on their part their labor for sale. The legislator of antiquity, far from encouraging like ours the accumulation of fortunes and luxuries, watched constantly to divide inheritances equally among children in order to maintain a kind of equality in patrimonies, above all to restrain all habits of indolence and ostentation, to remove from the citizens the desire and the opportunity to indulge in too much consumption, to honor sobriety, simplicity, and abstinence. They wanted that, just as everybody had his share in the activities of the body, everybody had also his part in the activities of the mind, and in pleasures. In order to maintain such equal division they dissuaded citizens from handicrafts, and let them devote only a small part of their time to agriculture, or to the exercise of the trades; they called them to the forum to deliberate, to the courts to judge, to the academy, to the portico to hone their mind and lift their soul with noble teachings; to the theater, to educate their taste and inspire them with Attic wit; to the temples, to beguile their imagination, and to join the hopes for the future to the pleasures of life.

The application of machinery to the arts and industry lowered progressively the quantity of labor necessary to support human life, but this was not in any way a reason why the social order should raise an individual dedicated to rest, to consume, to enjoy for two, four, ten, one hundred, a thousand; a person who kept the entirety of his profit, who would even work to reduce the worker's share pari passu as the output increased: the savings made of the labor of all benefited all; the citizen of Athens was content, despite the progress of industry, with a cloak made of the coarsest cloth, with bread and dried figs for food. But surely, the absence of all luxuries had not destroyed the elegance of his mind or the refinement of his taste. By banishing pleasures, as a legislator, he had not lost the activity and resilience of his personality as a private citizen; and because the Athenian had need for wealth, not for himself, but for the nation, the barren soil of Attica was enough for the armaments of the republic which made Asia Minor and Sicily tremble; it was sufficient for the establishment of the colonies that spread to the farthest shores the principles of true civilization. The only luxury of Athens were the men the republic produced; fortunate the country that will be able to raise their likes! Fortunate the whole world if a liberated Greece will soon bring back such equally noble examples!

Perhaps the reader is of the opinion that we have strayed very far from the question discussed between Mr. Ricardo and myself, and it would have been better to show what remained to do, than what was done in antiquity. But what remains to do is a question of infinite difficulty, which we have no intention of dealing with today. We would want permission to convince the economists, as fully as we are ourselves convinced, that their science hereafter follows a false path. But we do not have enough confidence in ourselves to show them what would be the truth; it is one of the greatest efforts to which we can force our mind to visualize the actual structure of society. Who would then be the man enlightened enough to imagine a structure that does not yet exist, to see the future when we have already so much trouble to see the present? Still, if all the enlightened minds finally agree to seek the security society owes to the classes charged with feeding it, perhaps what a single mind cannot accomplish, the joining of the knowledge of all will be able to accomplish.

Let us then conclude the analysis of the system we have taken up, before dreaming of what will have to replace it; let us study its course, let us evaluate it without being distracted by a comparison with an entirely imaginary theory. If I presented here what I consider to be a remedy for the actual ills of society, criticism would abandon the examination or evaluation of such ills, in order to judge my remedy, and to probably condemn it; and the question of the balance of consumption with production would never be decided.

I should only allow myself to declare that, assuming I had imbued minds with such a strong conviction as to be able to gain all the changes I would have desired by legislation, I still would not have had the idea, either to impede the progress of production, or to hold back the application of science to the arts and the invention of machines. I should seek only the means to secure the fruits of labor to those who do the work, to make the machine profitable to the person who puts it to work. If I at last obtained this result, I would turn again to the interest of the producers not to produce an output that would not be demanded of them. As long as a producer can be considered as a single individual, and he is moved by a single interest, he is always led by the proverbial maxim that it is better to rest than to work for nothing. Thus, all the facilities that will be given to him for his work will never lead him to produce more than is demanded of him; he will rest, he will play, when he has done his work, whether it is done in twelve or two hours. It is, to the contrary, the opposition of interest between the producers who cooperate on the same task, between the masters and the workers, that alone causes the glutting of markets; equilibrium between them takes away from the other more important balance between producers and consumers. The masters are persuaded to produce an output, not because the consumer asks them for it, but because the workers offer to them to do it at a lower price.

The task of bringing together anew the interests of those who cooperate in the same production, instead of setting them in opposition, belongs to the legislator; it is without a doubt difficult; but I do not believe for one moment that it is outside the realm of the possible. Much would have been accomplished already if legislation would have been kept from acting in a direction diametrically opposed to the social interest. If all the laws were suppressed that oppose the division of inheritances, and which, by favoring the formation, or the conservation, of great fortunes, prevent capital and ownership in land from being distributed in small parcels to those who do the manual labor; if one suppressed all the laws that protect coalitions of masters against workmen, and all those who take away from workers their natural means of resistance;* the discussion of one or the other, the

*At the very moment this goes to press, in 1824, the newspapers report that in Macclesfield, silkworkers work only eleven hours a day; and when they managed to work twelve hours, the extra hour was paid to them. On Saturday, the 3rd of April, the manufacturers adopted a resolution, as of Monday, to make them work twelve hours a day without paying more than the customary day wage. The workers have resisted, and martial law was proclaimed against them. Yet, what was the motive of the masters? the decline of prices. Because they had already too many goods, they have asked for more at lower prices.

discussion of those which could force the master to guarantee the subsistence of the worker he employs, would be long and difficult, and we will not enter on them in any way today. We are content to have shown in what direction we would look for a remedy to the ills from which society suffers, and to those which threaten it.

While waiting for the time, possibly quite remote, when the combined thoughts of economists will be able to recommend to sovereign authority a change in the system of laws,[18] it seems to us that the discussion we are taking up can have, from today, some practical results. We believe that in human society the rising demand for labor is the constant, regular, and yearly result of the progress of humanity. This demand is in turn the benevolent cause of all industrial development, of all improvements in the arts. When there will be a demand for new labor, that is to say new means to pay workers, and a new need to use it up, all progress the society will make to satisfy such demand will be favorable to everyone. On the one hand, there will be a call for an increase in population; there will be more marriages, more children spared in their tender age, more vigor in their apprenticeships,[19] more useful labor for those who are already grown. Yet, all these results will be secured only by and by, during a fairly long time, in such a way as not to disturb the equilibrium, not to cause any market gluts, so that the new population that will in the course of ten, fifteen, twenty years, enter into active life, come there not to perform the work demanded today, but to serve those today's labor will enrich hereafter.

On the other hand, there will be a call for an increase in the mechanical powers of man. The labor demanded today could only be done by the men existing today; it is therefore necessary, either that they devote more hours every day to their work, or else avail themselves of all the means science gives them to make more than they could produce before: every extension of their productive powers, provided that it does not exceed the ability to pay and consume of those who demanded the labor, every extension I say, will create a new wealth which, in its turn, will call forth a new demand. The wages of these workers, abler and more productive, will be higher, their pleasures will grow with their income; they will ask in turn for a greater number of workers to labor for them, or that the same number turn out a larger output, since they have the means to pay for such an increase. The same sum that has demanded, and served to pay for, new labor, will reappear in a succession of markets, to revive all the old trades.[20] Despite the progress of the mechanical arts, the existing workforce will not be enough to produce all that is demanded of them; the new individuals that have come into the world during that time, will find trades awaiting them when they grow up; the population grows, and agriculture must grow also to feed it.

All movements in society are linked together; one follows from the other, as the various movements of the gears of a watch; but, just as in a watch, it is necessary for the motive force to act where it should so that the gears can connect;[21] if instead of waiting for the impetus that ought to come from the demand for labor, one believes it can be generated by anticipatory production, one would almost do what would be done to a watch if, instead of rewinding the wheel that carries the spring, one would push back another; everything would be broken, the entire machinery would be arrested.

However, society shares in the vital powers belonging to man which will make it overcome partial disorders, and remedy of itself the ill it experiences. When, in whatever branch of industry, output has overtaken demand, and the market is overfull, the workers will strive to change trades, to change the country,[22] to finally accommodate themselves to their new situation, and they will succeed therein almost always in a more or less extended period, provided that major changes which are working themselves out in the mercantile world are not forced. In such a crisis, the prejudices that oppose the adoption of a new invention, the difficulties of communication or imitation, the obstacles of every kind that seem to slow the progress of science applied to the arts, are all advantageous to humanity; they provide time, they permit the vital powers to act, they leave to those who have been stricken the respite to escape from their failures, to heal their wounds. These presumptions which, on numerous occasions, are perhaps the surest guarantee to society, set generally against individual interest a sufficient obstacle for equilibrium to reestablish itself. It happens often, without a doubt, that an industrial entrepreneur, having either invented a useful application of the sciences, or found an advantageous practice abroad, establishes a new industry and produces goods that are not demanded of him. Then he will rely on the hope that he will draw sales from some of the older manufactures, *that he will hurt the trade*, as the technical term goes, but that he will hurt others, and to his profit. There exists usually a kind of balance between individual interests which prevents one of them from entirely overturning all others. This inventor will do everything possible to protect his own secret and to profit alone from it; he will then experience even more the opposition of all his peers whom he tries so hard to hurt, the opposition of all workers who see very well that he tries to lower their wages, and the opposition of all the popular and local prejudices that always lean towards rejection of innovations, the opposition of capitalists who do not willingly lend to undertakings they do not understand and do not know. He will overcome all these obstacles, but slowly, if he causes no shocks, leaving to families he displaces time to readjust, to acquire a new livelihood, or even to the consumers time to create a new demand for labor.[23]

Also, it is not usually the natural progress of industry, as it is brought about by private interest, that has produced the glutting of markets, and which has condemned thousands of workers to unemployment and hunger; it is a motive alien to personal interests that we have seen *destroy* systematically and on a grand scale the *trades,* sometimes by governments that wanted their nation to produce everything they saw others make, and created a hothouse atmosphere for their businesses and made them produce what was not demanded;[24] sometimes by zealous citizens and experts who thought they could not better serve their country than by importing all at once every invention that had made other countries wealthy, by attacking all prejudices, changing all customs, spreading quickly all discoveries as far as they would go, and by demanding from capitalists, in the name of patriotism, the establishment of manufactures they would not have gotten from them as a result of their self-interest.

For now we will leave in peace the governments whose promoter policies have already given rise to many discussions. We will merely address ourselves to those who are led astray by their philanthropy, because it makes them favor with all their power production nobody wants, and in which they themselves can find no interest. If we have succeeded in convincing them that in production there is no assurance of consumption, we will perhaps bring them to give more attention to the principle on which rests their appropriate system of political economy. They ask for absolute liberty for industry because they assume that individual interests, by offsetting each other, will unite in the general interest; they would see then that they themselves disturb this balance of individual interests; that when they create a manufacture out of love for trade and science, and have not heeded the signs of the market, they have often sacrificed men and real interests to an abstract theory. It is the business of learned men to be always ready, by advances in the mechanical arts, of chemistry, the study of nature, to respond to all demands of the market; it is their business to be ready to powerfully help the labor of man, at the very moment when greater labor is demanded of him; but, as long as the present organization persists, as long as the existence of the poor is abandoned to the effects of a free competition, they must not put additional weights into the scale in favor of factory owners, and against workers; they must remember that the fundamental maxim of the economists is *laissez faire et laissez passer*; so that they leave also to generations made superfluous time to *move on.* Otherwise, with the impetus they give, with an imprudent zeal, to the adoption of every invention, they hit constantly first one class, then the other, and they will make all of society experience the sufferings of constant changes, instead of the benefits of improvements.

Translator's Notes to Appendix, Second Article

This article, not at all small, as Sismondi would have it in his note, was published, as the date indicates, between the two editions of *New Principles*. It is mainly a reiteration of the positions taken in the first edition, but it does represent also a development towards some of the changes in the second edition, particularly with respect to conditions in England. One of the notable developments is the reference to Malthus and his *Principles*, as a quasi support for Sismondi's own ideas. Marx had claimed in his *Theorien über den Mehrwert* that Malthus had plagiarized this work from *New Principles*, a claim that appears exaggerated and tendentious and, moreover, designed to hide Marx's own unacknowledged indebtedness to Sismondi. However, it would be probable that Malthus had, in the fashion of the times, taken ideas from Sismondi and used them in his own analysis of English conditions. In a wider context, both Malthus and Sismondi were of course part of an ever increasing literature, mostly socialist, in both countries that was critical of capitalism and the ills of the machine age, such as Owen and the Ricardian Socialists in England, and Saint-Simon and Fourier in France. Malthus and Sismondi are the only major writers who did not seek socialist solutions, but attempted to solve the problem in the context of a property-based capitalistic organization of society. The article is also remarkable, from a present-day perspective, for its many quasi-Keynesian solutions to business-cycle distress. Since the article is shorter than *New Principles,* it brings into better focus the policies Sismondi saw as the remedy for the problems of what he identified correctly as a new and as yet not-well-understood system of production and social organization. In support for government intervention, so abhorrent to classical economists, the article brings in examples from antiquity, Egypt, Athens, and Rome, which reflect the limited knowledge then available about the structures of these societies, and are, even measured against what was known at that time, forced and, to say the least, self-serving. In another way, the article is another example of Sismondi's struggle to free himself from conventional wisdom, and another admission that he does not feel himself capable of presenting a new system that would ensure the greatest happiness to the greatest number, his avowed goal.

1. Keynes, in the *Essays in Biography*, cites Malthus's 1800 pamphlet *An Investigation of the Cause of the Present High Price of Provisions* and remarks that Malthus had developed a method that was "more likely to lead to right conclusions than the alternative approach of Ricardo. But it was Ricardo's more fascinating intellectual construction which was victorious, and Ricardo who, by turning his back so completely on Malthus's ideas, constrained the subject for a full hundred years in an artifical groove." The subject is of course the relation of effective demand to income, and the insight of Sismondi first, and then Malthus, that a rise in national income does not necessarily lead to increased demand, that is, Say's Law. It is an amazing fact that to this day economics has not been able to free itself from the Ricardian system; it revives itself, as the Chicago School demonstrates, in a capitalistic version, and it has of course never died in its Marxist incarnation. The reason may be its apparent ability to provide what seem to be plausible answers to complicated real

questions, even though it is by now clear that the answers may not be answers at all.

2. Ricardo died in 1823. As noted, Sismondi met Ricardo in 1822 at Coppet. Victor de Broglie, the son-in-law of Madame de Staël, had invited Ricardo.
3. This remark is a prescient description of both Japanese export policy and its parallel, Japan bashing. Sismondi's remarks are good international trade theory, although not of the free-trading orthodox variety. As his argument makes clear in the subsequent discussion, a pronounced imbalance in trade because of technological displacement will, in his opinion, be unsustainable and lead to severe distress, as opposed to the conclusions of the unrestricted free-trade doctrine espoused by Ricardo, which is an extension of Say's Law. It has been pointed out, among others by Triffin, that balance-of-payment surpluses are seen as economically advantageous to a nation, therefore putting the burden for adjustment of international imbalances mainly on deficit nations. It was precisely Sismondi's point that surplus nations have also a responsibility for international adjustment, a point which is now, perhaps, becoming part of international practice, if not theory.
4. This is a reference to the Castlereagh cabinet and, among other laws, the Corn Laws. See notes 2 and 14 to the preceding appendix.
5. The allusion to *The Wealth of Nations* should be noted. It is in fact not clear what the *natural* progress of wealth would be. Sismondi and his contemporaries understood it to be a steady increase in the gross product, but, as far as Sismondi was concerned, that was clearly the problem to be discussed. The paragraph raises the additional question whether the relative success of free trade during the nineteenth century was more an artifact of the predominance of Great Britain than the correctness of free-trade doctrine.
6. This quotation was translated from the article. As the second following paragraph makes clear, the quote was made by Ricardo in the course of the conversation on which Sismondi reports. The source is clearly Ricardo's discussion of value in the *Principles,* especially section 4.
7. Three bags each for ten workers and the proprietor.
8. Sismondi uses "découverte" 'discovery,' which in the context could mean an improvement in breeding or new machines.
9. The term used is "manufacture du pauvres", that is, producers of the cheapest necessities used by workers. The term has been translated variously as 'subsistence goods' or as 'basic industry.'
10. This asks what Sismondi would not concede to other writers, for example, McCulloch. Most of his arguments against Ricardianism are based on deducing consequences the authors did not have in view. He also leaves out of account what the Ricardians assumed as a natural consequence of more production, namely automatically lower prices for all commodities, thus stimulating demand. Sismondi contends that such price decreases will not necessarily increase demand, but lead to unemployment because employers, unable to make profits, will reduce their workforce.
11. This short paragraph incorporates in a nutshell Marx's exploitation argument. If the worker had control over his employment conditions, he would choose between more leisure or more work. The state of society does not permit this; hence the worker must produce a surplus for his employer who uses the machine to increase output with the same or less labor. Sismondi differs from Marx in the basic assumption that there is no historical, or any other, necessity

that the system should in fact be the one it is. Where Marx tried to show inevitability to justify revolution, Sismondi calls for reasoned reform based on the insight that man has created his society and can, therefore, alter and improve it. As noted in the annotations to *New Principles,* Sismondi does not need the labor theory of value to underpin his conclusions, as indeed it is not needed in the Marxian system. As the argument shows here even more clearly than in *New Principles*, Sismondi needed to postulate only that owners *possess* machines that increase output that is saleable at the same or slightly lower prices than before, to deduce, from simple business experience, that the owner will receive a larger share of the proceeds because the wages of his employees will not change. And the wages do not change because the owner can hire new employees at the same, or a lower, wage; hence the owner controls the conditions of employment. The argument is, therefore, not really economic at all, but one of power relations in economic guise. The whole Marxian analysis of surplus value based on incorporated labor is a Ricardian irrelevancy designed to give a philosophical justification to a metaphysical argument that can, in fact, be taken out of the Marxian context without invalidating the conclusion. If it is so taken out, the Marxian analysis reduces to the statements given here. Another Marxian idea, worker alienation, is found in the next paragraph.

12. Although this uses the same division Marx used later, Sismondi rejects Marx's postulate of inevitable opposition between the classes, based on his historical studies. These paragraphs make it quite clear that Marx's much advertised *historical materialism* as well as the postulated historical division of societal transformation are Ricardian in the sense that Marx, just as Ricardo, created the necessary examples to buttress his theory, but they had their origin here.
13. This should be compared to Marx's denunciation of the bourgeoisie in the *Communist Manifesto*, where he proclaims that it has broken all idyllic bonds and substituted naked profit in their stead.
14. The historical narrative advanced in justification of this critique is clearly that of Marx in the *Communist Manifesto*. The assumed state of barbarism was a common departing point for social theorizing that appears in Locke, Hobbes, Montesquieu, and Smith. It served as the starting equilibrium point of an assumed simple situation that was made more complex with advancing analysis and had strong affinities with the development of the scientific method derived from physics and mathematics, especially by Descartes and Newton.
15. Sismondi uses value here in the broad sense of real goods and services produced and consumed, rather than with reference to money value. The choice of the term in the context is unfortunate and misleading, but Sismondi may have also thought about incorporated labor, or effort, which goes unremunerated in his system if the goods remain unsold.
16. Clearly, this is the same type of example construction used by Ricardo, even though it builds on a better historical foundation. Aside from the merit of the historical evidence, current at the time and outdated now, it should be noted that Sismondi in effect advanced an idea that is a centerpiece of Keynesian policy prescription; the role of government as the keeper of macroeconomic equilibrium. Despite his protestations of fidelity to Smithian principles, Sismondi reverts at least partially to mercantilistic doctrine. He differs from the mercantilists in his insistence on individual freedom but, judging from the excised portion on marriage restraints on the poor, it is an open question whether he would not have advocated more restrictive policies whenever necessary to achieve the stated goal.

17. Sismondi overlooked historical evidence that was known in his day, namely the record of slave uprisings, and the unruliness of the Roman population dependent on food distribution from public storehouses.
18. This is an ironic and sad statement that must be seen against Sismondi's continuing disagreement with mainstream Ricardian political economy. It has a very contemporary ring now, over 160 years later.
19. It is significant that Sismondi uses "apprentissage" here, instead of "education." The difference suggests that he saw, as everybody else did, the sons and daughters of workers going directly to learn a trade, with just a minimal formal education at some school. He may have had a broader view in using the term, such as a general idea of education, but this is not evident from the context.
20. There are hints of a multiplier concept in other parts of *New Principles*, but this particular statement is unusually direct and clear. Sismondi's unique view of an economic spiral that can expand or contract, based on previous consumption, was obviously also based on a monetary view of circulating purchasing power, although it should be remembered that he was opposed to any form of paper money, or extended credit.
21. As in his examples taken from the hatter's trade, Sismondi always draws on his immediate experience. The watch metaphor is clearly very apt for a son of the city of Geneva.
22. This remark reflects a major difference in perception and practice from today. Sismondi could still assume, with justification, that workers in his day were able to move *between* countries in search of jobs. The intervening developments have turned nations in upon themselves, reserving their workplaces for natives, and economic theory reflects this viewpoint—the labor force is seen in national terms only. Since the end of World War II, some change has occurred because of the widespread use of *foreign workers* in western Europe, and the immigration of *illegal aliens* into the United States. The terms used to characterize these people are themselves indicative of the different viewpoint that governs now. It can be argued that Keynesian analysis, with its emphasis on full employment, is an essentially national approach to cycle theory which reinforces the exclusivity of national labor markets.
23. This last remark opens the possibility that new production in effect can create new demand, but Sismondi, by introducing the time factor, has effectively barred the argument that Say's Law is indeed valid. Moreover, in his analysis, the new demand is tentative and dependent on rearranging existing demand, which may or may not happen, while in Say and Ricardo the connection is causal and almost immediate. The major problem is, however, that the balance sought between consumption and production and, above all, the requirement that new demand *precede* any new production is not a practical prescription for policy; the more complex the economy becomes with economic growth the less a stipulated new demand can be identified. On the other hand, the view that the industrial organization of society is essentially unstable has much in common with the Keynesian analysis, which postulates just *one* equilibrium between aggregate demand and aggregate supply. The solution *both* advance is the call for government to act as a balancing wheel, a solution that revives cameralistic practice. Keynes was conscious of this, as his chapter on mercantilism in the *General Theory* shows; Sismondi was not, since he was still very much occupied with fashioning a substitute for the Smithian system. As the next note shows, he was ambiguous about government as an instrument of

control, particularly as long as such a government was guided by Ricardian ideas.

24. This may refer to the efforts of Colbert to make France an industrialized nation, or, more recently, the efforts of Napoleon to make the Continent independent of England. The *Histoire du Français* surely would have brought that idea to Sismondi's mind.

Third Article

Notes on an Article by M. Say, Entitled "On the Balance of Consumption with Production"

Monsieur Say does not believe at all in letting a doctrine pass without refutation which is opposed to one he has taught. He had asserted "that goods purchase each other, and that their multiplication has no other effect than to multiply the pleasures of humanity and the population of states." He has therefore answered me in July 1824 in the *Revue Encyclopedique*; he did so with all the courtesy I could expect from his character, with all the kindness I expected from his friendship. But what happened to him is what almost always happens to people too much absorbed by their own subject matter to listen patiently to their opponent's; he believed he had read my mind, and he does not understand me at all; at least he replied to a theory I do not recognize in any way as mine.

After having admitted that it is possible to produce, of one good in particular, a quantity exceeding need, he adds, "if it be objected that every human society, by means of man's intelligence, and with the means he can draw from natural agents and from the arts, can produce of all goods suitable to satisfy man's needs and multiply his enjoyments a larger quantity than that same society can consume, I would then ask how it is possible that we know no nation completely provided for, that even in those which are regarded as thriving, seven-eighths of the population lack a multitude of products considered necessary, I will not say in rich families, but in modest households, etc." (p. 20 and following).

Surely, I am most unfortunate if I cannot make understood what I have stated so clearly, (in book 2, ch. 6)[1] "even though society includes a great number of individuals poorly fed, poorly clothed, and poorly housed, it only wants those who can buy; and as we have seen, one can buy only with one's income.'' This I repeated in the article M. Say answers: ''When there will be demand for new labor, meaning new means to pay it, and a new need to consume it, all the progress society will make to satisfy that demand will be advantageous to everyone.'' However, I cannot include, as proof that consumption asks for a larger production, the needs, the wants, the desires of those unfortunates whose numbers, in the wealthiest countries, can be seen to increase without end, who suffer all the pangs of misfortune next to the accumulated goods they possess no means to purchase. If, on the contrary, the things they need are cheaper only because they have been underpaid for making them, I see there another reason why they are unable to satisfy such need.

M. Say says afterwards, it is true: ''It is therefore not the consumers that are lacking in a nation, but the means to purchase. M. Sismondi believes that such means will be more widespread when goods are scarcer, consequently dearer, and their production will give a higher wage to the workers.''[2] I beg your pardon; this is not at all my proposition; I believe that the greatest number of consumers must always be sought among the producers; I believe, in addition, that the producers are the best consumers, that they will have more *means to purchase,* if they have gained from the production in which they have participated, rather than having lost from it. I do not ask at all that goods be scarce, but they be scarce enough, relative to the demand, so that whoever brings them to market may make a legitimate profit from selling them.[3]

M. Say sums up his opinion, on the point in question, as follows: ''if production is more active, the distribution systems more widespread, in a word goods more abundant, nations will be better and more extensively supplied.'' Then he cites to me as a proof: ''the countries where distribution systems are more in evidence and goods in greater abundance, like the most industrious provinces of England, the United States, Belgium, Germany, and of France, are also the wealthiest countries, or if one wishes the least wretched.'' Most certainly, I have never denied that France has been able to double its population, and quadruple its consumption, since the time of Louis XIV, as he holds against me, p. 25; I have only claimed that the multiplication of goods was a great benefit when it was demanded, paid for, and consumed; that to the contrary it was an evil when it was not at all demanded, and the entire hope of the producer rests on taking away a consumer from the products of a rival industry. I have sought to show that the natural course of nations was the progressive growth of their prosperity, a growth caused by a demand for new products, and means to pay for them. But that the consequence of our institutions, of our legislation, has been to strip the working class of all property and security, having pushed it at the same time into excessive labor that has no relation either to demand or purchasing power, and which aggravates as a consequence its misery. For seven years I have pointed to that sickness of the body social, and for seven years it has not ceased to grow. I cannot see in such extended suffering *the frictions that always accompany change,*[4] and, by going back to the source of income, I believe I have shown that the ills we experience are the necessary consequence of the flaws of our system, and they are not yet at an end.

M. Say reproaches me then for asking for the intervention of government because, and I agree with him in this, it has rarely meddled in the management of private wealth without doing damage; but yet it is quite necessary that it intervene to abolish at least the evil it has produced. Also, the legislator who has instituted property, who regulates the division of inheritances, who protects monopolies of all kinds, who resists power but permits cunning, has not remained neutral. I demand that he act again in order to amend what he has created.

I will conclude with M. Say's own words: "These questions are vast, they pertain to all parts of the social economy which has up to now been but little known; but everythings predicts that this type of knowledge is destined to make great advances in the future." It will do this above all if a mind as just and strong as his devotes itself to studying the new phenomenon the rich nations show to us, in which public misery does not cease to grow with material wealth, and in which the class that produces everything is every day brought closer to enjoying nothing.

End of Clarifications

Translator's Notes to Appendix, Third Article

It is likely that Say replied to the previous article, although Sismondi does not make that clear in his answer. However, the title of Say's article refers to Sismondi's title, and the publishing date, July 1824, two months after the article, points in that direction.

1. The translation for this sentence has been taken from the cited chapter in this translation. All other citations have been translated from the text.
2. This remark shows what the difference in viewpoint between Sismondi and the classical school really was: the latter were development economists and saw everything in terms of increasing wealth for poor nations, assuming that such wealth would spread to the population in general by way of ever lower prices, while Sismondi believed that general economic growth was based on increasing general consumption through increasing incomes at all levels. Their difference was the difference between trickle-down economics and bottom-up growth.
3. It would seem reasonable to assume that Say and Sismondi would not have differed on this point.

4. This is clearly another citation from Say's article. As such it is instructive because it points to arguments used in this century, such as Hoover's *Prosperity is just around the corner,* and some of the claims of the modern followers of Say.

Bibliography

Aftalion, Albert. 1970. *L'oeuvre economique de Simonde de Sismondi*. New York: Burt Franklin Reprint.

Bell, John F. 1967. *A History of Economic Thought*. 2d ed. New York: Ronald Press.

d'Andlan, B. 1975. *Madame de Staël*. Coppet.

Defoe, Daniel. 1982. *The Life and Adventures of Robinson Crusoe*. New York: Crown Publishers.

Dickens, Charles. *Hard Times*. London: Library of Classics.

———. *Little Dorritt*. London: Library of Classics.

———. *Martin Chuzzlewitt*. London: Library of Classics.

———. *Nicholas Nickleby*. London: Library of Classics.

———. *Oliver Twist*. London: Library of Classics.

———. *Pickwick Papers*. London: Library of Classics.

Djilas, Milovan. 1957. *The New Class*. New York: Frederick A. Praeger.

Gide, Charles, and Charles Rist. 1948. *History of Economic Doctrines*. New York: Heath.

Heilbroner, Robert L. 1986. *The Worldly Philosophers*. 6th ed. New York: Simon and Schuster.

Keynes, John Maynard. 1950. *A Treatise on Money*. London: Macmillan.

———. 1956. *The General Theory of Employment, Interest and Money*. New York: Harcourt.

———. 1951. *Essays in Biography*. New York: Norton.

Locke, John. 1955. *Of Civil Government Second Treatise*. Gateway ed. Chicago: Regnery.

Maitland, James, Lord Lauderdale. 1804. *An Inquiry into the Nature and Origin of Public Wealth*. Edinburgh.

Marshall, Alfred. 1948. *Principles of Economics*. 8th ed. New York: Macmillan.

Marx, Karl. 1956. *Theorien über den Mehrwert*. 3 vols. Berlin: Dietz Verlag.

———. 1957. *Das Kapital. 3 vols*. Berlin: Dietz Verlag.

———. 1956. "Manifest der kommunistischen Partei." *Marx, Auswahl.* Frankfurt/Main: Fischer Buecher.

Meek, Ronald L. 1963. *The Economics of Physiocracy*. Cambridge, Mass.: Harvard University Press.

Mill, John Stuart. 1920. *Principles of Political Economy with Some of Their Applications to Social Philosophy*. New York: Appleton.

Petty, Sir William. 1963. *A Treatise of Taxes and Contributions*. Reprints of Economic Classics. New York: Kelley.

Ricardo, David. 1895. *Principles of Political Economy and Taxation.* Edited by E. C. K. Gonner. London: George Bell.

Robinson, Joan. 1962. *Economic Philosophy*. Chicago: Aldine.

Rousseau, Jean-Jacques. 1968. *The Social Contract*. New York: Penguin Books.

Salis, Jean R. de. 1973. *Sismondi 1773–1842, La vie et l'oeuvre d'un cosmopolite philosophe*. Geneva: Slatkine.

Say, Jean-Baptiste. 1964. *A Treatise on Political Economy*. Reprints of Economic Classics. New York: Kelley.

Schumpeter, Joseph A. 1954. *History of Economic Analysis*. New York: Oxford University Press.

Sismondi, J. C. L. Simonde de. 1801. *Tableau de l'agriculture Toscane*. Geneve.

———. 1803. *De la richesse commerciale*. 2 vol. Geneve: J. J. Paschoud.

———. 1819. *Nouveaux principes d'economie politique, ou de la richesse dans ses rapports avec la population*. 2 vols. 1st ed. Paris: Delaunay.

———. 1826. *Nouveaux principes d'economie politique, ou de la richesse dans ses rapports avec la population*. 2 vols. 2nd ed. Paris: Delaunay.

———. 1832. *A History of the Italian Republics*. London: Longmans.

Smith, Adam. 1937. *An Inquiry into the Nature and Causes of the Wealth of Nations*. New York: The Modern Library.

Tuan, Mao Lan. 1927. *Simonde de Sismondi as an Economist*. New York: Columbia University Press.

Veblen, Thorstein. 1932. *Theory of Business Enterprise*. New York: Scribner.

Waeber, Paul. 1981. *La Place du "Tableau de l'agriculture Toscane" dans l'oeuvre du jeune Sismondi*. Musées de Geneve, No. 211. 1981.

Young, Arthur. 1801. *An Inquiry into the Propriety of Applying Wastes to the Better Maintenance and Support of the Poor*. London:

Index

The American University
3 1194 006 669 349